TROPICAL RAIN FOREST:
ECOLOGY AND MANAGEMENT

TROPICAL RAIN FOREST: ECOLOGY AND MANAGEMENT

SPECIAL PUBLICATION NUMBER 2 OF THE BRITISH ECOLOGICAL SOCIETY

EDITED BY

S. L. SUTTON*, T. C. WHITMORE†

AND A. C. CHADWICK*

* Department of Pure and Applied Zoology
University of Leeds
Leeds LS2 9JT, U.K.

† Commonwealth Forestry Institute
Oxford University
Oxford OX1 3RB, U.K.

BLACKWELL SCIENTIFIC PUBLICATIONS

OXFORD LONDON EDINBURGH

BOSTON MELBOURNE

1983

Printed in Great Britain
at The Alden Press,
Osney Mead, Oxford

DISTRIBUTORS

U.S.A.
  Blackwell Mosby Book Distributors
  11830 Westline Industrial Drive
  St Louis, Missouri 63141

Canada
  Blackwell Mosby Book Distributors
  120 Melford Drive, Scarborough
  Ontario, M1B 2X4

Australia
  Blackwell Scientific Book Distributors
  31 Advantage Road,
  Highett, Victoria 3190

British Library
Cataloguing in Publication Data

Tropical Rain Forest: Ecology and
  Management—(A Special publication
  of the British Ecological Society; no. 2)
  1. Jungle ecology—Congresses
  I. British Ecological Society. *Tropical Group*
  II. Sutton, S. L.   III. Whitmore, T. C.
  IV. Chadwick, A. C.   V. Series
  574.5'2642'0913   QH541.5.J8

ISBN 0-632-01142-4

EDITORS PREFACE

The reasons for bringing together the papers in this volume are summarized by one of us (TCW) in the Introduction. In this Preface we would like to thank our generous sponsors and others who helped to make the Leeds Symposium on Tropical Rain Forest Ecology and Resource Management such a memorable occasion, and those who helped us produce this volume.

First, our thanks to the anonymous referees who worked with admirable diligence and speed. Dr Edward Broadhead, Editor in Chief of Symposia for the BES, gave us much support and good advice, as did the BES Council generally. The University of Leeds, and in particular the Department of Pure and Applied Zoology, helped considerably both in the production of this volume and in the staging of the Symposium. Sound guidance in the planning of the meeting and the volume was given by the Symposium Committee. Without the munificent support of the Leeds Philosophical and Literary Society the Symposium could not have been contemplated, whilst without the timely recognition and generous help of the British Ecological Society it could not have matured into a full scale international symposium. Financial support from the Royal Society, the World Wildlife Fund, the British Council and UNEP made it possible for the organizers to develop a very full programme. This is reflected in the thirty-four papers in this present volume and the twenty-plus papers in the Supplementary volume, the latter derived from some of the 100+ posters displayed at the meeting. We hope that the written record will prove as stimulating as the spoken presentations in April 1982 at Leeds. Readers might like to know of three further publications.

(i) *Reaching the Rain Forest Roof.* Mitchell, A.W. (1982) A booklet on techniques of access and study in the canopy. 36 pp. £2.50 or £4.50 airmail from B. H. Blackwell Ltd, Broad Street, Oxford.

(ii) *The Preservation of Tropical Moist Forest.* Chadwick, A.C. & Sutton, S.L. (1983) International Relations **7**, 2304–2322.

(iii) Statement of Concern. Drafted by delegates to the Leeds Symposium to voice concern at the continuing degradation of the Tropical Moist Forest (available from the Editors).

We would like to thank Dr Francis Ng for the photograph on which the cover design is based, and Mrs Stephanie Sutton for acting as our secretary.

S. L. SUTTON
T. C. WHITMORE
A. C. CHADWICK

An activity within the
Global Environment Monitoring System
of the
United Nations Environment Programme

CONTENTS

vii

Contents

Contents

INTRODUCTION

T. C. WHITMORE

Commonwealth Forestry Institute, Oxford University

BACKGROUND TO THE LEEDS SYMPOSIUM

At a session of invited contributions held during its Easter meeting of 1961 the British Ecological Society launched a specialist Tropical Group. This was founded at the suggestion of the then President, Professor P. W. Richards, and had the present writer as its first Secretary. The Tropical Group was the first specialist group of the Society. There are now five others.

To celebrate the 21st anniversary of the foundation of the Tropical Group a Symposium was held at Leeds University at Easter 1982, sponsored jointly by the British Ecological and Leeds Philosophical and Literary Societies. This book contains the papers presented at the 1982 Meeting. The ecological subjects discussed were some of those which are currently attracting the attention of tropical rain forest biologists. In some papers new work is described, some of it based on recently developed techniques for working in the upper canopy. The studies range from several years down to only a few months, and from several loci down to a single spot. Other papers review recent work and attempt to arrange the sometimes fragmentary data into a general framework, which is of necessity sometimes speculative. These reviews present hypotheses which provide springboards for further investigations. The overall result of these biological papers is to demonstrate with many novel examples the complexity and great diversity of interactions within rain forests ecosystems.

There is a very widespread concern in the world about the destruction of tropical forests. The last session of the Symposium was devoted to aspects of forest conservation and the maintenance of diversity, although eschewing straight silviculture, a topic which would have needed a complete Meeting to itself. The last part of the book covers biological desiderata for conservation, estimates of the extent of forest remaining, both pantropically and in different regions, and concludes with a trio of papers expressing aspects of global concern for the tropical biome.

Travel around the world has never been easier, and the Symposium was generously sponsored. Despite this there were fewer speakers from the tropics than we had planned, so the balance of papers is not quite what we had hoped to achieve. Each paper is self-contained and as is the usual British practice we have not attempted to rewrite to reflect a single stance or impose a unified terminology. Indeed, we had invited spokesmen of different schools of thought to contribute to the Meeting and feel their different viewpoints show the lively nature of tropical biology. We have, however, aimed for a consistent overall framework. In particular we have used tropical moist forests as a term to embrace both tropical rain forests and tropical seasonal (or monsoon) forests where an author is referring to both these groups of forest Formations.

We hope this volume will appeal to a wide audience interested to discover some of the currently exciting fields of tropical forest science. Attention is drawn to a companion volume, detailed on the cover, which is based mainly on the posters presented at the Meeting. A glance at the titles will indicate their wide scope. They too address a wide spectrum of topical interests.

ARRANGEMENT OF THE PAPERS

In order to help the reader discover the scope of the volume and the inter-relationships between the different papers a brief résumé is given here. The papers are grouped into four sections, of which the first and fourth are sub-divided, as shown in the Contents list (p. vii). Within the sections individual papers are arranged to lead on from one to another.

I   *Aspects of community structure and diversity*

The first four papers (Part IA) discuss aspects of vegetation and floristics and reveal different patterns of diversity in both space and time. Richards examines the three-dimensional structure of the canopy. Benzing reviews much new work on epiphytes and their role in nutrient cycling. Hubbell & Foster give a progress report on a study in Panama of spatial relationships of trees on a 50-ha plot. Sugden analyses the special floristic and structural features of isolated cloud forests in northern South America. The next group of five papers (IB) describe spatial and temporal diversity in the forest canopy of animals, mainly insects, at various scales. Erwin presents data for four different forests near Manaus. Sutton describes similarities in the spatial relationships of canopy insects at seven sites scattered through the tropics. Wolda reviews temporal and spatial variation and finds strong similarities to temperate forest patterns. Broadhead considers Psocoptera. Rees finds differences between wet and dry nights in the Hemiptera flying within a Sulawesi forest canopy. The Section concludes with two papers on the maintenance of diversity (IC), Oldeman on gaps and canopy architecture and Franks & Bossert on predatory army ants on the forest floor.

II   *Plant–animal interactions*

This section considers a subject which many have been vigorously investigating over the past few years. It begins with a paper by Waterman who provides a general review of very scattered data on the role of secondary metabolites in plants. Two themes are then developed. First, a group of papers explores aspects of frugivory and dispersal. Leighton & Leighton present some results of their 2-year comprehensive study on birds, mammals and fruiting trees in lowland forest in Kalimantan. The next two papers examine particular groups: Hopkins & Hopkins on fruits, seeds and dispersers in neotropical *Parkia* and Howe on year-to-year variation in the dispersers of the nutmeg *Virola surinamensis*. Secondly, recent discoveries on leaf predation are examined by Wint, who finds a remarkably similar level in a Panamanian and two New Guinea forests, and Becker who examines seedling survival of two *Shorea* spp. in relation to phytophagy. Finally, Cherrett shows how leaf-cutting ants, *Atta*, appear to have a foraging strategy which does not kill their crop trees.

III   *Decomposition and nutrient cycling*

There has been much recent work and some of the earlier generalizations have become suspect. Proctor reviews tropical litterfall studies, reveals difficulties of non-comparability and makes recommendations. Gong & Ong present data for fine litterfall in a Penang forest. Anderson & Swift give a general review of litter decomposition and expose past misconceptions. Collins analyses the very important, yet varying, role of termites as litter decomposers. Janos attempts an assessment of the role of mycorrhizas which are now believed probably to be nearly ubiquitous in tropical forests. Baillie and Ashton discuss species/soil relationships for Sarawak which suggest that continual addition of mineral nutrients by soil rejuvenation occurs.

IV   *Resource management*

Two papers (IVA) by Ng and by Lovejoy *et al.* discuss biological considerations which must underly successful conservation. Both are concerned with the consequences of fragmentation of remaining virgin forest into tiny areas. These are followed (IVB) by another pair of papers, one by Grainger on attempts to assess how much moist forest remains with a recommendation for refined use of satelite imagery for which Green in the next paper presents some possibilities. The status of moist forest conservation (IVB) for Brazil (Camara), Central America (Hartshorn) and Nigeria (Kio) are then given. The book ends (IVC) with two alternative proposals for fiscal arrangements which could control loss of virgin tropical forest (Guppy, Rubinoff), and, appropriately for a Symposium held in England, concludes with an assessment of Britain's policy towards tropical moist forests and how this could be revitalized (Johnson).

PART I
ASPECTS OF COMMUNITY STRUCTURE AND DIVERSITY

A · VEGETATION AND FLORISTICS

The three-dimensional structure of tropical rain forest

P. W. RICHARDS

14 Wootton Way, Cambridge CB3 9LX, England

SUMMARY

1   The three-dimensional structure of forests determines their internal microclimates and the distribution of animal food resources within them.

2   Profile diagrams are a useful method of portraying this structure, but their value is illustrative rather than quantifiable.

3   Single-dominant tropical rain forests show clearly-defined strata, but Mixed forests usually do not.

4   More important than the stratification of the trees is the boundary between the euphotic zone in which the crowns are more or less fully exposed to sunlight (the 'canopy'), and the shaded oligophotic zone (the 'undergrowth') beneath. This boundary corresponds approximately with Oldeman's 'morphological inversion surface'.

It is important to understand the three-dimensional structure of tropical rain forest (or indeed any other kind of forest) because the amount of space occupied by the trunks, branches, twigs and leaves of the trees at different levels determines the internal microclimates and the energy available for the other organisms. The structure of the forest, therefore, to a large extent controls the distribution of smaller plants such as epiphytes. More importantly, by controlling the availability of their food resources and possible methods of locomotion and communication, it determines the activities and distribution of the animals. The pattern of large and small tree trunks on the ground is also, of course, ecologically important, as well as their arrangement in the vertical plane. Microclimatic and soil conditions differ greatly from place to place within short distances and, because of that, conditions for seed germination, for seedling establishment and for animals. For example, the environment of small invertebrates is very different close to the base of a large buttressed tree and at points midway between two trees.

To describe the structure of a tropical forest accurately, either in words or in quantitative terms presents considerable problems. During this symposium words such as 'canopy', 'undergrowth' and 'stratum' (or 'storey') will no doubt be used, but in fact these terms are given different, sometimes contradictory, meanings. I think it may save a certain amount of discussion at cross purposes if I make a few general points about the structure of rain forests. What I have to say is rather elementary but at least I shall be brief.

The first point is the rather obvious one that rain forests are always very heterogeneous structurally, and in several different ways. Even primary rain forest

(a)

(b)

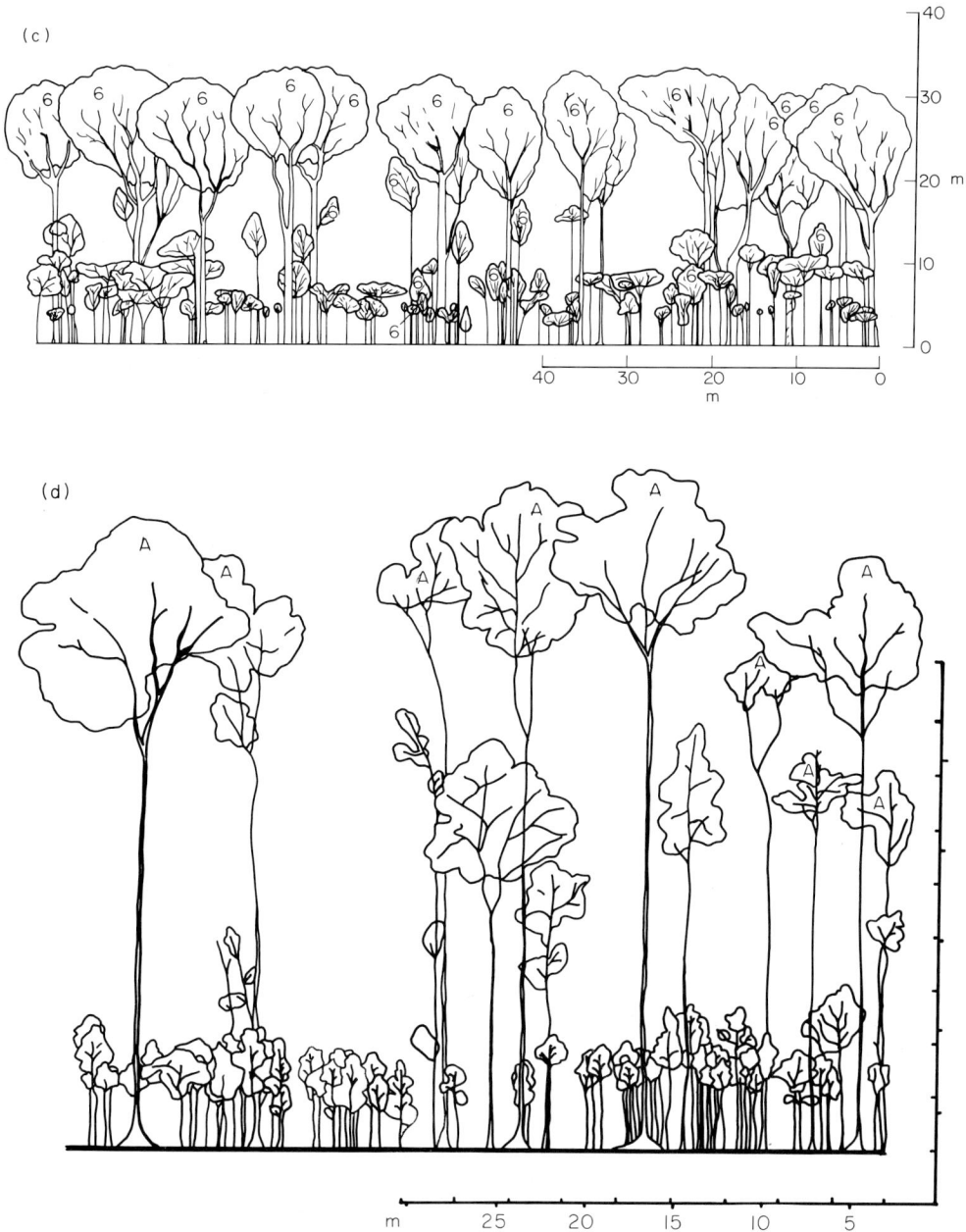

FIG. 1. Profile diagrams of tropical rain forests. (a) Mixed forest, Moraballi Creek, Guyana. (b) Mixed Dipterocarp forest, Gunong Dulit, Sarawak. (c) Forest of *Gilbertiodendron dewevrei* (De Wild.) J. Léonard, Ngula, Zaire. (d) *Shorea albida* Sym. ('meranti bunga') peat swamp forest, near Badas, Brunei. The diagrams represent strips of forest 25 ft (7·6 m) wide: trees under 15 ft (4·6 m) are omitted. In (c) trees marked '6' are the dominant species: in (d) trees marked 'A' are *Shorea albida* Sym.

(a) from Davis & Richards (1933–34, Fig. 6), (b) from Richards (1936, Fig. 2), (c) from Louis (1947, p. 9;13).

which has not been logged, farmed or otherwise disturbed by man has numerous gaps due to the death of large old trees, and often also gaps caused by lightning strikes, windfalls, landslips and other natural causes. There are also areas where old gaps are being filled by the growth of young trees. Whitmore (1975) took a valuable step forward by recognizing that all primary rain forest consists of 'mature', 'gap' and 'building' phases, using the terms originally applied to British beechwoods by A. S. Watt (1947). Until recently, descriptions of rain-forest structure have usually dealt only with the mature phase and have largely ignored the gap and building phases.

The second point concerns profile diagrams. The profile diagram technique, in the sense of profiles of narrow strips of forest based on exact measurements of the position, height and width and depth of crown of all trees over an arbitrary lower height limit, was first introduced in the paper by the late Mr T. A. W. Davis and myself on the rain forest of Moraballi Creek, Guyana (1933) (Fig. 1a). Since then it has been very widely used and innumerable profiles of many sizes and descriptions have been published, not all of them based on adequate measurements. Various improvements on the original method have been suggested; one of the most useful is Oldeman's (1974) method of distinguishing between immature, mature and overmature trees (or, as he calls them, trees of the future, the present and the past) (Fig. 2). Lianes ('vines') though not as abundant in mature primary forest as in secondary forest and gaps, form an important part of the structure. They contribute a considerable proportion of the foliage—about one third in a sample of Mixed Dipterocarp forest at Pasoh, Malaysia (Kira 1978), but it is difficult to show them accurately in profile diagrams and they are usually omitted.

Profile diagrams are of course an attempt to give a two-dimensional representation of a three-dimensional structure. They should be, but often are not, accompanied by a ground plan of the profile strip. Some people, e.g. Aubréville (1965), have tried to delineate forest structure by means of three-dimensional block diagrams. This method is useful for savanna woodlands and similar open types of vegetation, but to apply it accurately to rain forests would be even more laborious than drawing conventional two-dimensional profiles.

I believe that profile diagrams still have a considerable value, but it is mainly illustrative; their limitations are not always realized. One such limitation is that they are not random samples and are made at subjectively selected sites. This is almost inevitable because whether the trees are felled and then measured with tapes, as in my original Guyana profile, or whether their heights are estimated by means of a Haga altimeter or some similar instrument, drawing a profile diagram is time-consuming. But profiles at closely adjacent sites may show considerable differences of structure, as Pires & Moraes (1966) showed at Mocambo in Amazonia. Profiles are nevertheless useful for portraying features of forest structure that are not easily appreciated from photographs or quantitative data. They are valuable for comparing types of forest of widely different structure, such as the *Gilbertiodendron dewevrei* (De Wild.) J. Léonard forest of eastern Zaire (Fig. 1c) and the Mixed forest of the same region or different stages in a succession.

The view that there are recognizable strata in tropical rain forests is often discussed. Some people regard strata as objectively demonstrable, others consider that they are purely arbitrary divisions cf what is in fact a continuum. Both views are in my opinion something of an oversimplification. Primary tropical rain forests most often consist of trees of very numerous species, varying in their size at maturity from treelets 1–2 m high to giant emergents of 60 m or more. Such forests are Mixed (or Multi-dominant) rain forests, but there are also other types which I call 'Single-dominant forests'; these are widespread in some parts of the tropics. In them a large proportion, in some cases 90% or more, of the large trees in the stand belong to one (or occasionally two) species. In the Mixed types of rain forest, strata are not usually evident (Figs 1a and b), though when numbers of trees are plotted against height-classes there are sometimes rather indistinct peaks at certain height classes (see Richards 1952, Fig. 3, p. 24). On the other hand, in Single-dominant forests such as the *Gilbertiodendron* forest mentioned above, the *Mora excelsa* and *Prioria copaifera* forests of northern tropical America and the *Shorea albida* peat-swamp forest of Sarawak (Fig. 1d), the strata are very obvious when the forest is seen in profile. There are also forests with intermediate types of structure in which strata seem to be present but are not so clear.

In my *Tropical Rain Forest* (1952) it was stated that there are five strata of erect plants (referred to from above downwards as A, B, C, D and E) in most types of Mixed and Single-dominant rain forests. For purposes of description this terminology is, I think, still valid, but I now recognize that in most types of Mixed rain forest the boundaries between the strata are more or less arbitrary and cannot be objectively defined.

When the tropical rain forest is considered as a functioning ecosystem rather than from a purely structural point of view it seems to me that what matters is not whether the total heights of the trees are stratified or not, but how the density of foliage, including the leaves of the lianes, varies at different levels. On this, unfortunately, profile diagrams give only very inexact information. Accurate data on foliage density can be obtained only by destructive sampling and are at present available only for small areas in very few places.

In Mixed rain forest near Manaus in Amazonia, Klinge, Rodrigues, Brünig & Fittkau (1975) measured the above-ground phytomass of the vegetation on a 0·2-ha sample plot and divided it arbitrarily into six strata, A, B, C 1, C 2, D and E. They found that 58% of the total phytomass and nearly 40% of the leaf phytomass was in the B stratum (16·7–25·9 m above ground level), corresponding more or less to my B stratum in the Guyana Mixed forest.

Kira, Shinozaki & Hozumi (1969) investigated the vertical distribution of the foliage in rain forests in south-east Asia. In Mixed forest at Khao Chong in Peninsular Thailand they found that the leaf area index was highest in the B stratum (20–25 m). In the Mixed Dipterocarp forest at Pasoh in Malaya (Kira 1978) they determined the leaf area density (ha ha^{-1}m^{-1}) and the leaf biomass density (t ha^{-1}m^{-1}) of the trees and lianes at different levels on a clear-felled plot 100×20 m. They found that there were two maxima of leaf area and biomass density: one at 20–35 m above ground, corresponding to the B story, and another below 5 m where, in the area sampled, treelets, saplings and small palms were (perhaps unusually) abundant.

If the data quoted are typical it seems clear that in the Mixed rain forest it is the

(a)

ᴹᴹᴹᵂ = Epiphytes or foliage of lianes

Height (m)

(b)

metres —

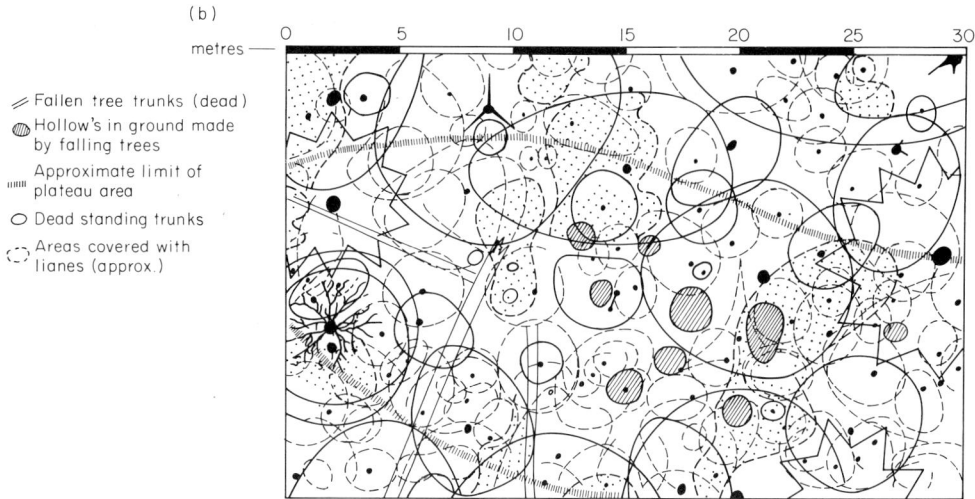

Fallen tree trunks (dead)

Hollow's in ground made by falling trees

Approximate limit of plateau area

○ Dead standing trunks

Areas covered with lianes (approx.)

Fig. 2. Forest at Rivière Sinnamary, French Guyana. After Oldeman (1974) Figs 49, 50. (a) Profile diagram of Mixed forest. The dotted line represents the inversion surface. Conventions: thick outline, mature trees; thin outlines, over-mature trees; stippled crowns with fine dotted outlines, immature trees. Thick dashed outlines are crowns of trees the bases of which are outside plot. (b) Plan of profiles strip (20 m wide). Conventions as in (a) except that immature trees are not stippled.

crowns of the B storey trees at about 20–30 m which are usually the densest layer. This applies to the mature phase of primary forest but is not necessarily true of the building phase or of secondary forest. So if any precise meaning is to be given to the word 'canopy', it should refer to the B storey, together with the crowns of the emergent A storey trees which rise above it.

The lower boundary of the canopy, so defined, corresponds quite closely with the 'morphological inversion surface' of Oldeman (1974) and Hallé, Oldeman & Tomlinson (1978) (Fig. 2). This is an imaginary plane joining the bases of the lowest branches of the B storey trees. It varies in height from place to place within a forest, and is undulating rather than flat. The importance of the inversion surface is that it separates the tree crowns which are more or less fully exposed to sunlight from those which, apart from moving sunflecks, receive mainly light transmitted through, or reflected from, leaves. Above this surface there is a considerable amount of air movement and both temperature and humidity are relatively variable; below it the air is normally still and conditions are much more constant.

I would like to call the region of the forest above the inversion surface the *euphotic zone* and the shaded region below it the *oligophotic zone*. The former is much the most productive part of the ecosystem because it receives most energy. Kira, Shinozaki & Hozumi (1969) estimated that at Khao Chong the emergent (A storey) trees were responsible for more than half the total productivity of the whole stand; the A and B strata together must account for a much greater proportion than that. The leaves, flowers and fruits of the euphotic zone provide food for an abundant and diverse population of herbivorous animals which have plenty of free space in which to fly, glide or move in other ways. In the oligophotic zone flowers and fruits are comparatively scarce and the most abundant animal foods are wood and decaying plant materials. The litter of dead leaves and other plant fragments falling from above forms an important part of the diet of some animals living at or near ground level. Is it perhaps fanciful to liken the euphotic zone of the forest to the well illuminated plankton-inhabited photic zone of the ocean, which supplies food and energy to the dark or poorly-illuminated water below it?

REFERENCES

Aubréville, A. (1965). Principes d'une systématique des formations végétales tropicales. *Adansonia*, **5**, 153–196.

Davis, T.A.W. & Richards, P.W. (1933). The vegetation of Moraballi Creek, British Guiana: an ecological study of a limited area of tropical rain forest. Part I. *Journal of Ecology*, **21**, 350–384.

Hallé, F., Oldeman, R.A.A. & Tomlinson, P.B. (1978). *Tropical Trees and Forests*. Springer-Verlag, Berlin.

Kira, T., Shinozaki, K. & Hosumi, K. (1969). Structure of forest canopies as related to their primary productivity. *Plant & Cell Physiology*, **10**, 129–142.

Kira, T. (1978) Community architecture and organic matter dynamics in tropical lowland rain forests of Southeast Asia with special reference to Pasoh Forest, West Malaysia. *Tropical Trees as Living Systems* (Ed. by P. B. Tomlinson & M. H. Zimmermann), Ch. 24, pp. 561–590. Cambridge University Press, Cambridge.

Klinge, H., Rodrigues, W.A., Brünig, E. & Fittkau, E.J. (1975). Biomass and stucture in a Central Amazonian forest. Ch. 9 *Ecological Studies, Vol. II, Tropical Ecological Systems. Trends in Terrestrial and Aquatic Research* (Ed. by F. B. Golley & E. Medina), Ch. 9, pp. 115–122. Springer-Verlag, Berlin.

Louis, J. (1974). *Contribution à l'étude des forêts équatoriales congolaises*. Comptes Rendus de la Semaine Agricole de Yangambi (26 Fév.–5 Mars 1947), Deuxieme Partie. I.N.É.A.C. Publications (Hors Série), Bruxelles.

Oldeman, R.A.A. (1974). L'architecture de la forêt guyanaise. *Mémoires ORSTOM*, no. 73. O.R.S.T.O.M., Paris.

Pires, J.M. & Moraes, V.H. (1966). Programa de botânica. a. Composicão da mata de terra firme de Reserva Mocambo. *Relatorio Anual*. Instituto de Pesquisas e Experimentacão Agropecuarias do Norte, Belém, Pará, Brazil (duplicated).

Richards, P.W. (1936). Ecological observations on the rain forest of Mount Dulit, Sarawak, Part I. *Journal of Ecology*, **24**, 1–37.

Richards, P.W. (1952). *The Tropical Rain Forest*. Reprinted with corrections 1979. Cambridge University Press, Cambridge.

Watt, A.S. (1947). Pattern and process in the plant community. *Journal of Ecology*, **35**, 1–22.

Whitmore, T.C. (1975). *Tropical Rain Forests of the Far East*. Clarendon Press, Oxford.

Vascular epiphytes: a survey with special reference to their interactions with other organisms

DAVID H. BENZING

Department of Biology, Oberlin College, Oberlin, Ohio 44074, U.S.A.

SUMMARY

1 Attempts to analyse the structure and function of tropical forest ecosystems cannot be wholly successful until epiphytes are given due consideration.

2 Although poorly understood and often overlooked, epiphytes are numerous, diverse and often very abundant in situations where tree crowns are humid most of the year.

3 By virtue of the nutritional profile and because they live along primary flux routes, epiphytes are major participants in the movements of mineral nutrients within tropical forests. Their low productivity and substantial powers of nutrient accretion increase their impact on biogeochemical cycling and the structure and performance of the ecosystem as a whole. The nature of their impact will be determined by many factors, including the kinds of epiphytes involved and the fertility and moisture status of the ecosystem.

4 Epiphytes may also be more important to forest fauna than their simple numbers and biomass would suggest.

INTRODUCTION

Vascular epiphytes, excluding those such as Loranthaceae which bear haustoria, are generally viewed as commensals; their influence on individual supporting plants (phorophytes) is considered minor in most instances and of little consequence among factors that shape the structure and interactions of the ecosystem as a whole. Undeniably, establishment within a tree's canopy offers an autotroph cost-efficient access to sunlight by obviating investment in massive stems. For a small plant capable of procuring all the resources it requires without contact with soil, epiphytism is a very effective strategy indeed in communities dominated by much taller vegetation. In many mature forests epiphyte loads probably outweigh understory herbs, especially in the moist neotropics and wetter regions in Australasia. Not infrequently, the collective leaf surface areas of epiphytes appear to exceed those of hosting trees.

Epiphytic aroids, bromeliads, ferns and the like are much more than innocuous hitch-hikers whose fortunes are unaffected by their choice of support or its condition. Were this not so, the host ranges of these organisms would be far wider than they are. Phorophytes can be adversely affected in several ways by their crown residents, quite possibly with substantial consequences for the diversity and productivity of the whole community. Relationships between numerous epiphytes and many animals, on the

11

other hand, are clearly mutualistic. At the very least, there are considerably more interactions between an epiphyte and its varied associates than is outwardly apparent. These interactions, plus the diversity and pervasiveness of epiphytism, provide a focus for the discussions that follow. Note must also be made of the means whereby plants exploit aerial habitats; those concerned with procuring mineral nutrients and moisture are particularly crucial to the epiphyte's impact on other organisms situated within its sphere of influence.

EPIPHYTE DIVERSITY, ABUNDANCE AND DISTRIBUTION

Vascular epiphytes are both numerous and diverse. If a tally is made of every plant capable of growing on a tree without either tapping host vasculature or using the soil below, the total approaches 30 000 species or about 10% of all tracheophytes. Excluded from this list are those normally terrestrial plants that occasionally colonize a knothole or root in a debris-filled crevice as accidental epiphytes. A recent survey (Madison 1977) indicates that about 850 genera in sixty-eight families (Table 1) have at least one nonparasitic, canopy-dwelling species. Most families with more than occasional epiphytic members are predominantly tropical and herbaceous, but exceptions occur on both counts, e.g. Ericaceae. Distribution through the taxonomic system, although broad, is puzzling in its inconsistency. Orchidaceae, a giant assemblage encompassing at least 25 000 species, has achieved unequalled success in canopy habitats and alone accounts for more than half of all vascular epiphytes. Araceae and Bromeliaceae make the preponderance of liliopsids even more disproportionate. Most dicotyledonous representatives also belong to a few families; more than two-thirds of them are in Ericaceae, Gesneriaceae, Melastomataceae, Moraceae (if its stranglers are included) and Piperaceae.

Equally striking is the low incidence of epiphytism among many other large angiosperm taxa. Although including numerous small-bodied species, many with tropical affinities, and, in some cases, bird- or wind-dispersed seeds, such families as Compositae, Euphorbiaceae, Leguminosae and grasses are absent in most canopy habitats. Gymnosperms are rarely epiphytic, but this is consistent with their very slow maturation, massive axes, anemophily, and heavy seeds. In contrast, pteridophytes seem well qualified to exploit tree crowns and, in fact, at least 20% of them do. Epiphytism has evolved many times, often more than once in the same family, but only occasionally has its great potential been realized. Clearly, an arboreal existence entails much more than just being able to resist the pull of gravity.

Epiphytism is unevenly developed geographically as well as systematically. While less in aggregate land area, neotropical habitats harbour many more kinds of epiphytes than do palaeotropical forests. Africa's epiphyte flora is particularly impoverished, presumably reflecting repeated bouts of aridity and a lack of moist refugia during the late Pleistocene (Simpson & Haffer 1978; Brown & Ab'Saber 1979). Australian vascular epiphytes number fewer than 400 species (Wallace 1983). Chance may account for some of these discrepancies. Orchidaceae are especially well developed in

Table 1. Numbers of epiphytic species within families of vascular plants, after Madison (1977) with some modifications

PTERIDOPHYTA

Aspidiaceae	159
Aspleniaceae	400
Davalliaceae	185
Hymenophyllaceae	500
Lycopodiaceae	many
Ophioglossaceae	2
Polypodiaceae	970
Psilotaceae	8
Schizeaceae	2
Selaginellaceae	many
Vittariaceae	142

GYMNOSPERMAE

Gnetaceae	3
Podocarpaceae	1
Zamiaceae	2

MONOCOTYLEDONAE

Agavaceae	1
Amaryllidaceae	1
Apostasiaceae	1
Araceae	850
Bromeliaceae	919
Burmanniaceae	2
Commelinaceae	3
Costaceae	4
Cyclanthaceae	31
Gramineae	2
Liliaceae	17
Orchidaceae	20 000
Pandanaceae	4
Philesiaceae	2
Rapateaceae	6
Zingiberaceae	14

DICOTYLEDONAE

Aquifoliaceae	1
Araliaceae	73
Asclepiadaceae	135
Balsaminaceae	5
Begoniaceae	10
Bignoniaceae	3
Cactaceae	133
Campanulaceae	18
Celastraceae	2
Clusiaceae	92
Compositae	3
Crassulaceae	4
Cunoniaceae	3
Dulongiaceae	1
Elaeocarpaceae	1
Ericaceae	483
Gentianaceae	1
Gesneriaceae	549
Griseliniaceae	3
Lentibulariaceae	12
Marcgraviaceae	94
Melastomataceae	483
Moraceae	521
Myrsinaceae	28
Myrtaceae	7
Nepenthaceae	6
Onagraceae	3
Piperaceae	710
Pittosporaceae	5
Potaliaceae	20
Ranunculaceae	1
Rosaceae	3
Rubiaceae	217
Scrophylariaceae	6
Solanaceae	33
Urticaceae	41
Vitaceae	4
Winteraceae	1

the New World, as are epiphytic Araceae and Gesneriaceae. Bromeliaceae and Cactaceae are almost entirely American. No comparable asymmetries favour other tropical regions. Several families with epiphytic members are largely or wholly Old World, e.g. Asclepiadaceae, Myrtaceae, Nepenthaceae, Pittosporaceae, but none of these has been very successful in generating canopy-adapted populations. On balance, ferns and monocotyledons other than orchids constitute a greater proportion of the Old World epiphytic flora (Madison 1977).

Epiphytic diversity is greatest in wet midmontane forests. Moisture seems to be the most important ecoclimatic variable needed for epiphytic success. Year-round, high atmospheric humidity rather than a high total rainfall is most conducive to epiphyte abundance in some South American locations (Sugden & Robins 1979). Diversity diminishes with increasing latitude, elevation above about 2000 m, and severity of dry seasons. Cool montane cloud forests support some of the most luxuriant epiphyte growths, but a few species often account for much of the total biomass. Canopies of drought-deciduous and even cactus forests may harbour vascular epiphytes (for example in Mexico and Peru); here, both biomass and diversity are low, but those epiphytes present possess remarkable tolerances for a variety of abiotic stresses (see below). Secure attachment to bark or bare rock is often obligatory for these species, since prolonged contact with moist substrata during wet months can be lethal (Benzing & Renfrow 1971a; Benzing, Seemann & Renfrow 1978). Inexplicably, tree crowns in some lowland wet forests, seemingly quite suitable for the much more common and productive mesic epiphytes, remain largely unoccupied.

Compared to parasites, most true epiphytes enjoy relatively broad phorophyte preferences. Moreover, a given tree type is often either epiphyte-free or serviceable to most, if not all, canopy dwellers whose seeds lodge in its crown. Bark texture, stability and wettability are the most important physical determinants of seedling success (Benzing 1978a). The leaf area index of the phorophyte is critical to all life stages since it influences microclimate and energy inputs, except at exposed canopy margins. Open-crowned, slow-growing trees with absorbent, coarse but stable, bark make the best supports. Allelopathic agents may affect host quality in some instances (Frei & Dodson 1972). A tree's susceptibility to leaching and hence the nutritional quality of its canopy fluids could also be important. Many factors influence nutrient leakiness, including leaf age, wettability and nutritional status (Tukey 1970). Certain orchids may be confined to only those supports capable of hosting their mycorrhizal fungi (Sanford 1974; Jonsson & Nylund 1979).

Some information is available on species packing and resource partitioning among epiphytes. Bromeliads and orchids have attracted most of the attention (Pittendrigh 1948; Sanford 1968; Went 1940; Johansson 1974). Species inhabiting the same area of forest and even the same tree crowns may differ in their light and humidity requirements. Pittendrigh (1948) recorded specific patterns of shoot and root form and function associated with bromeliads occupying various levels along vertical canopy gradients in Trinidad. Sanford's (1968, 1969) and Johansson's (1974) data on some West African orchid floras rank among the most extensive and refined so far assembled, but higher densities (forty-seven species on a single tree) have been recorded elsewhere (Dunsterville 1961). Tree crowns are probably not as hetero-geneous as these high species counts suggest. Many epiphytes, including closely-related species, form guild-like assemblages on the same hosts, apparently preferring similar bark qualities and degrees of exposure and humidity. Benzing (1981) has offered an explanation for this phenomenon which draws on lessons learned from other communities, where high diversity is maintained by habitat disturbance and associated patchiness.

ADAPTATIONS OF EPIPHYTES

Epiphytism is based on several capacities: (a) economic use of scarce resources with emphasis on reproduction; (b) high vagility; (c) an effective means of attachment; (d) deployment of unusual methods of procuring and conserving moisture and minerals. Obvious as these general requisites may be, they offer little insight into the identities and workings of those specific adaptations evolved by various lineages as they radiated into canopy habitats. Although logically more rigorous, an *a priori* approach founded on optimality theory is less likely to be fruitful here than a deductive one based on assessments of cause and effect. Features that allow an epiphyte to forgo dependence on soil are most easily determined by identifying the selective forces responsible for their origin and seeking conformities among diverse taxa with similar ecologies. Comparisons with related plants in other kinds of habitats are also revealing. No simple answers can be expected; different design constraints had to be overcome each time a major lineage generated epiphytic genotypes. Non-homologous organs and tissues were modified to counter similar environmental challenges.

For our purposes, forest canopies should be visualized as unusually hostile to epiphytes. There are four primary constraints: patchiness and disturbance require high vagility and fecundity on the part of the epiphyte; drought and infertility impair or suppress its productivity. Patchiness is imposed by dispersions of serviceable among unserviceable trees and, on a finer scale, within each accommodating crown by separation of appropriately exposed branches. Disturbance (bark exfoliation, falling twigs, and eventually death of whole tree) renders the epiphytic biotope unstable, especially for sparsely-provisioned, slow-maturing organisms—a profile that fits many epiphytes, including all inhabitants of relatively arid tree crowns.

For epiphytes, the physical stresses, drought and infertility, tend to go hand in hand. Mineral nutrients and moisture are intermittently rather than continuously available in all but the wettest climates. Although nutrient-charged water passes through a forest with some regularity, its movements are rapid and leave little residue. Occasional fluxes can be sufficiently charged to permit luxury consumption but both stemflow and throughfall are usually dilute (Benzing & Renfrow 1980). Furthermore, atmospheric inputs may be very uneven. For instance, Kellman, Hudson & Sanmugadas (1982) discovered that 50% or more of the annual inputs of Ca, K, Mg, P and N entering a Honduran forest were received in just 1–8 rain days. Rainfall may, of course, be supplemented with leached substances before reaching the ground, but whatever the period and periodicity of supply, almost every canopy surface is characterized by frequent and/or prolonged intervals of extreme deprivation, and these temporal constraints must be considered in any attempt to understand the adaptive biology of epiphytism.

Epiphytes ameliorate stress by several strategies. CAM and succulence are common among epiphytic taxa and, in some species at least, promote high water-use efficiency (Benzing *et al.*, 1982; C. Martin, pers. comm.). Compared to the C_3 mode, C_4 photosynthesis could also provide water (and nitrogen) economy; it has not yet been detected among epiphytes, but we should continue to search for its presence. Choice of substratum can be all-important, thus humus epiphytes root on bark moist enough to support layers of lichens, algae and bryophytes which protect their drought-sensitive roots, while tank bromeliads, 'trash-basket' ferns, aroids and orchids collect soil substitutes. Some bromeliads and orchids that grow on unmodified bark, free of associated debris, prolong contact with ambient fluids by employing unconventional absorptive tissues comprised of dead cells: foliar indumenta in the former and root velamina in the latter (Benzing & Ott 1981). Engorged on first contact with precipitation, these organs retain fluids after bulk movements of water have ceased, allowing the organism additional time to absorb immobilized mineral and moisture into adjacent living shoot and root tissues. The search for similar moderation of temporal constraints on moisture and salt procurement in other epiphytes should continue. Assessments of bark chemistry, especially measurements of ion exchange capacity and the concentrations of nutrients, are also needed, since most epiphytes maintain close contact with stem surfaces. Preliminary studies show that different amounts of N and P can be extracted from the same kind of bark depending on the nutritional status of the phorophyte (Benzing & Renfrow 1974b).

Epiphytes counter infertility by deploying a wide variety of oligotrophic features. In the first place, tissue concentrations of N, P and K may be unusually low (see Benzing & Renfrow 1974a; Benzing & Davidson 1979). Secondly, juvenile stages tend to be prolonged, although maturation may be structurally precocious, requiring no more than the production of a small shoot bearing few leaves and supporting roots. A third feature, vegetative reduction, is especially pronounced among some of the more stress-tolerant bromeliads and orchids (Benzing & Ott 1981) and may be associated with a need for high fecundity. Drawing on unconventional nutrient sources constitutes a fourth tactic; for example, tank bromeliads are more productive and better provisioned with N, P and K than are some non-impounding relatives, probably because tank leaves provide access to abundant moisture and minerals derived from intercepted litter and animal activity (Benzing & Renfrow 1974a). Additional strategems include myrmecophytism (Huxley 1980), perennation via serial, determinate offshoots or telescoped, indeterminate axes (the latter may promote nutrient-use efficiency in oligotrophs), and evergreenness, a feature used by virtually all epiphytes to retain hard-won N and P for extended intervals. Most species are also iteroparous and produce wind-dispersed seeds lacking appendages. In some cases at least, the seeds are smaller than those of terrestrial relatives (Madison 1977). Pollination is almost always zoophilous, perhaps because anemophily would be too expensive for small, oligotrophic, thinly-dispersed plants.

Despite great proficiency in nutrient scavenging and exploiting achieved by these several adaptations, the growth of even the most specialized atmospheric bromeliads can be limited, often severely, by inadequate supplies of N, P and K (Benzing & Renfrow 1971b; Benzing 1978b; Benzing & Davidson 1979). Individuals on phorophytes which are nutrient-stressed are less vigorous than on those which are better nourished. Although more mesic epiphytic taxa may be numerous and productive enough to compete on wet sites (but see Hazen 1966), those adapted to arid regions emphasize stress tolerance and occupy little of what appear to be accessible bark surfaces. These extreme epiphytes approach Grime's (1977) fourth and most demanding strategy which obliges an organism to counter high levels of both disturbance and stress. Only some orchid lines, the tillandsioid bromeliads and a few other scattered lineages have evolved genotypes with sufficient regenerative power to endure the most stressful habitats and still cope with heavy mortality (Benzing 1978c). Species of this unique type deserve special attention since their adaptive features are likely to be exaggerations of those present in the far more numerous mesic forms, and thereby particularly amenable to functional analysis.

INTERACTIONS BETWEEN EPIPHYTES AND ASSOCIATED ANIMALS

Many animals associate with epiphytes for non-trophic rewards. Neotropical forests often contain more bromeliad hiding and breeding sites than are provided by all the water-impounding terrestrial plants, including heliconias, combined. Knowledge of bromeliad microcosms remains superficial, however, consisting of little more than lists of arthropods and amphibians collected from tanks. Information on community structure and dynamics falls well short of that available for *Heliconia* floral-bract microcosms (Seifert 1982). Since bromeliad shoots are much longer-lived, their biota may be more complex and better integrated. Some insect larvae at least are so tank-dependent that the diseases the adult insects transmit have on occasion been abated simply by eliminating the offending epiphytes (Pittendrigh 1946).

Bromeliad tanks appear to be little more than vessels that could just as well be fashioned of inert materials (Laessle 1961; Benzing, Derr & Titus 1971). Unlike the fluids in *Heliconia* bracts, those impounded by bromeliads do not receive supplements from plant secretions. Food chains are based on detritus or algae, depending on the epiphyte's location in the forest profile. Dissolved carbon dioxide and oxygen levels are affected more by exposure and microcosm inhabitants than by the epiphyte's leaves. The latter, however, by virtue of their shape and pigmentation, appear to be designed to recruit organisms by rendering the tank microcosm more equable (Benzing & Friedman, 1981). Without well-developed, hospitable tanks, the impounding bromeliad would be deprived of its primary nutrient source.

Mutualisms involving ants and ant-fed epiphytes have been demonstrated in five angiosperm families and two fern genera (Huxley 1980; Thompson 1981). Orchids should probably be added to this list, e.g. *Caularthron bilamellatum* and *Schomburgkia* spp. (Dressler 1981). Nutrition rather than defence seems to be the primary benefit gained by each of these epiphytes; the ants can be very timid. Field studies comparing inhabited individuals with others where ants have been excluded would be instructive. Depending on the plant, individual leaves, stems or interfoliar chambers are used as nesting sites. Entrances sometimes develop spontaneously, e.g. *Hydnophytum, Schomburgkia,* but others must be excavated by colonizers (*Tillandsia caput-medusae*; Benzing 1970). Non-specificity is the rule. Several ant taxa may inhabit a single epiphyte, sometimes simultaneously, but they also nest elsewhere in knotholes and

can still vie with those of competitors on the forest floor, but unless the shoot surfaces of the tree are sufficiently absorbent, epiphytes in their crowns will have unchallenged access to canopy nutrients moving between the foliage and the soil below. Moreover, impounding species can intercept nutrient resources in litter as well as in stemflow and throughfall.

Nutritional piracy, though operational to some degree wherever epiphytes occur, will be important in an ecosystem only where these organisms immobilize significant proportions of the scarcest nutrient resources (Fig. 2a). Here, epiphytes in the canopy yielding little litter—in essence, a compartment with considerable powers of nutrient accretion but a slow turnover—could impose substantial nutrient deprivation on phorophytes which rely on tight external recycling to maintain adequate nutrition. Should piracy be substantial, phorophytes might even exhibit reduced vigour. Such may be the case in a sterile South Florida strand community dominated by dwarf *Quercus virginiana* whose crowns harbour the oligotrophic bromeliads *Tillandsia recurvata* and *T. usneoides* (Benzing & Seemann 1978). Much of the N, P and K present there is contained in the abundant bodies of these two very effective nutrient scavengers. Moreover, the soils on which the trees grow are nutrient-poor and the oak foliage contains less N than do leaves borne by more robust individuals on more fertile sites nearby. Were the scarce macronutrients accumulated by low-performance (CAM) tillandsias captured and held with the oak's tissue instead, the structure and productivity of this ecosystem might be considerably greater. Endowed as they are with moisture continuously supplied through roots deep in the soil, and adapted for C_3 photosynthesis, oak trees probably yield far greater energy-carbon returns from equal mineral nutrient investments. Incidentally, mesic epiphytes of C_3-type would more closely compensate for the diminished productivity they might impose on a host (Fig. 2b).

There are other aspects of piracy, including one that clearly benefits a heliophilic perpetrator capable of reducing the vigour of its host. Dense crowns produced by well-nourished trees are poor sites for this kind of organism. Sparsely leafy canopies of nutrient-stressed trees may produce weaker leachates (Benzing & Renfrow 1974b), but many epiphytes appear to be more tolerant of low-quality nutrient sources than of heavy shade. The ability of exposure-tolerant epiphytes to impose nutritional stress on their supports, thus rendering the crowns of these trees less opaque, must be considered as both beneficial to the epiphyte and deleterious to its phorophyte. But what about the broader effects of epiphytes on the ecosystem as a whole?

If the stability of the system is great enough, epiphyte loads might approach saturation and so achieve a kind of nutritional equilibrium with associated vegetation (Fig. 2c). Thereafter, intercepted nutrients would approximately equal those lost to the soil, and adjacent plant life would no longer be denied nutrients through the pirating activities of canopy occupants. It is under these conditions that the influence of epiphyte biomass as a means of increasing the ecosystem's capacity to intercept and store nutrients would be paramount (Fig. 2d). Nadkarni (1981) has suggested that extensive colonies of bark-dwelling bryophytes and ferns swell the nutrient resources of a temperate rain forest ecosystem. Canopy roots are also present there, allowing

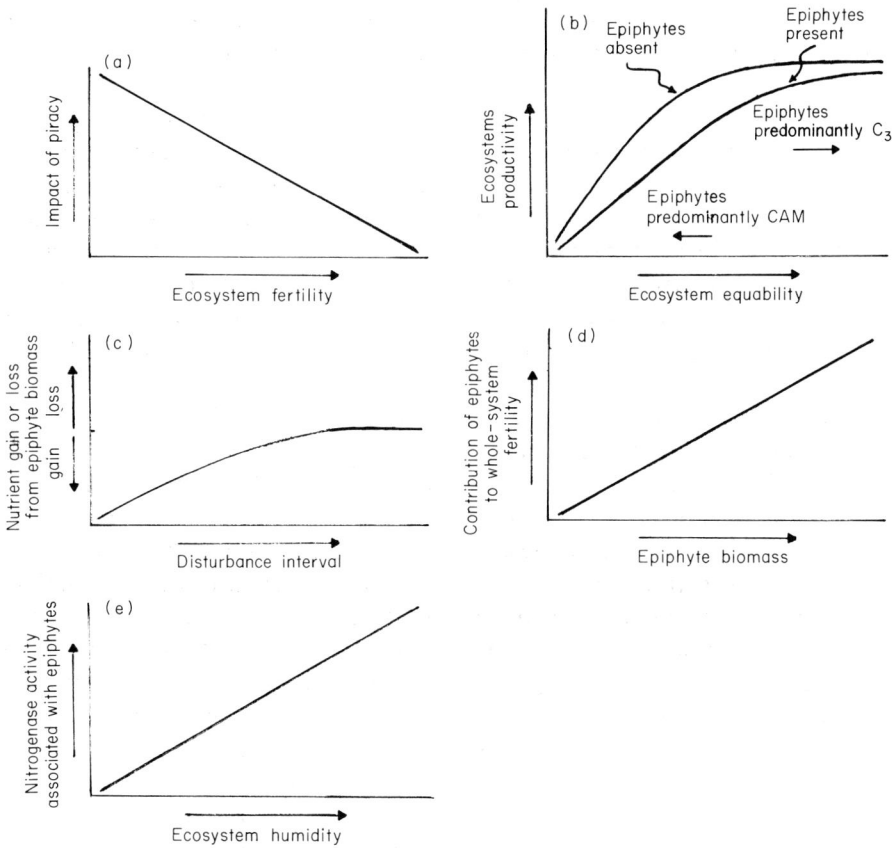

Fig. 2. Simple models depicting the impact vascular epiphytes may have on forest-ecosystem productivity and nutritional dynamics. In natural associations, the relationship between each pair of parameters will undoubtedly be affected by all the other factors as well. (a) Impact of nutritional piracy as a function of ecosystem fertility. Epiphytes will be able to stress associated vegetation to the greatest degree where essential mineral nutrients are least abundant. On fertile sites, trees grow too fast and their canopies become dense—too dense to accommodate large numbers of epiphytes. (b) Whole-system productivity as a function of ecosystem equability. On dry, relatively sterile sites, well-developed colonies of CAM epiphytes will employ mineral nutrient capital rather inefficiently for carbon gain. Where C_3-type epiphytes prevail, the mineral nutrients they deploy will yield greater carbon-energy returns more closely approximating the output of displaced host foliage. (c) Mineral nutrient gain and loss from epiphyte biomass as a function of disturbance interval or, in effect, the maturity of the compartment represented by these organisms. Epiphytes will continue to build nutrient stores until their populations become mature. At that point, mineral nutrients will leave the epiphyte biomass at about the same rate they are absorbed. (d) Enhancement of a forest ecosystem's mineral nutrient retention powers as a function of epiphyte biomass. As canopies become saturated with epiphytes, nutrient capture and storage capacity increase. (e) Nitrogenase activity associated with epiphytes as a function of canopy humidity. Greatest N_2 inputs should occur when epiphyte loads are maximal and the phyllosphere is moist much of the year.

hosts to exploit this largess more directly. Epiphytes will exert very different effects on sites where severe disturbances dissipate nutrient capital often enough to preclude the steady state proposed above. Under these circumstances, epiphyte colonies will be constantly regenerating, all the while depriving their hosts of mineral nutrients (Fig. 2c). When disturbances are frequent enough to prevent the establishment of epiphytes, their adverse effects will, of course, be eliminated. To what extent these nutrient scavengers affect the productivity of the whole system is unclear. Another phenomenon confuses the issue still further. Any epiphyte, but particularly an impounding one, increases humidity in the canopy, thereby creating more favourable conditions for nitrogen fixation (Fig. 2e). Below ground, biological nitrogen reduction is principally energy-limited, but moisture may well be a greater constraint higher up the forest profile. At least some epiphytes are quite accommodating to epiphyllous microbes; a recent survey of diverse phyllospheres ranked those of forty-one epiphytic plants, mostly orchids, as extensively populated by nitrogen fixers (Sengupta *et al.*, 1981). Should these findings prove to be representative, vascular epiphytes (as well as lichens with blue-green symbionts) may emerge as major sources of nitrogen in some tropical forests.

Many factors inherent to individual ecosystems and their resident epiphytes determine the influences the latter have on a particular forest community's structure and dynamics. Attempts are now under way to explore some of these interactions using computer simulations and mathematical models. The success of these efforts, of course, will ultimately hinge on the quality of the information available on a variety of diverse topics. These range from nutrient turnover by C_3 and CAM epiphytes and their hosts to aspects of soil chemistry and disturbance patterns within the hosting ecosystems. It may be hoped that some of the more serious gaps in our knowledge of these subjects will be remedied in the near future.

ACKNOWLEDGMENTS

Much of the experience I gained during the course of these studies on vascular epiphytes was made possible by grants from the National Science Foundation. My appreciation extends to Michael Zimmerman and T.C. Whitmore, who read the manuscript and provided helpful comments.

REFERENCES

Benzing, D.H. (1970). An investigation of two bromeliad myrmecophytes: *Tillandsia butzii* Mez, *T. caput-medusae* E. Morren and their ants. *Bulletin of the Torrey Botanical Club*, **97**, 109–115.

Benzing, D.H. (1978a). Germination and early establishment of *Tillandsia circinnata* Schlecht. (Bromeliaceae) on some of its hosts and other supports in southern Florida. *Selbyana*, **5**, 95–106.

Benzing, D.H. (1978b). The nutritional status of three *Encyclia tampensis* (Orchidaceae) populations in southern Florida as compared with that of *Tillandsia circinnata* (Bromeliaceae). *Selbyana*, **2**, 224–229.

Benzing, D.H. (1978c). The life history profile of *Tillandsia circinnata* (Bromeliaceae) and the rarity of extreme epiphytism among the angiosperms. *Selbyana*, **2**, 325–337.

Benzing, D.H. (1979). Alternative interpretations for the evidence that certain orchids and bromeliads act as shoot parasites. *Selbyana*, **5**, 135–144.

Benzing, D.H. (1981). Bark surfaces and the origin and maintenance of diversity among angiosperm epiphytes: a hypothesis. *Selbyana*, **5**, 248–255.

Benzing, D.H., Bent, A., Moscow, D., Peterson, G. & Renfrow, A. (1982). Functional correlates of deciduousness in *Catasetum integerrimum* (Orchidaceae). *Selbyana*, **7**, 1–9.

Benzing, D.H. & Davidson, E. (1979). Oligotrophic *Tillandsia circinnata* Schlecht. (Bromeliaceae): an assessment of its patterns of mineral allocation and reproduction. *American Journal of Botany*, **66**, 386–397.

Benzing, D.H., Derr, J. & Titus, J. (1971). Factors affecting the water chemistry of microcosms associated with the epiphytic bromeliad *Aechmea bracteata*. *American Midlands Naturalist*, **87**, 60–70.

Benzing, D.H. & Friedman, W.E. (1981). Patterns of foliar pigmentation in Bromeliaceae and their adaptive significance. *Selbyana*, **5**, 224–240.

Benzing, D.H. & Ott, D.W. (1981). Vegetative reduction in epiphytic Bromeliaceae and Orchidaceae: its origin and significance. *Biotropica*, **13**, 131–140.

Benzing, D.H. & Renfrow, A. (1971a). Significance of the patterns of CO_2 exchange to the ecology and phylogeny of the Tillandsioideae (Bromeliaceae). *Bulletin of the Torrey Botanical Club*, **98**, 322–327.

Benzing, D.H. & Renfrow, A. (1971b). The biology of the atmospheric bromeliad *Tillandsia circinnata* Schlecht. I. The nutrient status of populations in South Florida. *American Journal of Botany*, **58**, 867–873.

Benzing, D.H. & Renfrow, A. (1974a). The mineral nutrition of Bromeliaceae. *Botanical Gazette*, **135**, 281–288.

Benzing, D.H. & Renfrow, A. (1974b). The nutritional status of *Encyclia tampense* and *Tillandsia circinnata* on *Taxodium ascendens* and the availability of nutrients to epiphytes on this host in South Florida. *Bulletin of the Torrey Botanical Club*, **101**, 191–197.

Benzing, D.H. & Renfrow, A. (1980). The nutritional dynamics of *Tillandsia circinnata* in southern Florida and the origin of the 'air plant' strategy. *Botanical Gazette*, **141**, 165–172.

Benzing, D.H. & Seemann, J. (1978). Nutritional piracy and host decline: a new perspective on the epiphyte-host relationship. *Selbyana*, **2**, 133–148.

Benzing, D.H., Seemann, J. & Renfrow, A. (1978). The foliar epidermis in Tillandsioideae (Bromeliaceae) and its role in habitat selection. *American Journal of Botany*, **65**, 359–365.

Brown, K.S. Jr. & Ab'Saber, A.N. (1979). Ice-age forest refugia and evolution in the neotropics; correlation of paleoclimatological, geomorphological and paleoecological data with modern biological endemism. *Paleoclimas (Sao Paulo)*, **5**, 1–30.

Cook, M.T. (1926). Epiphytic orchids, a serious pest on citrus trees. *Journal of the Department of Agriculture, Puerto Rico*, **10**, 5–9.

Dressler, R.L. (1981). *The Orchids*. Harvard University Press, London.

Dunsterville, G.C.K. (1961). How many orchids on a tree? *American Orchid Society Bulletin*, **30**, 362–363.

Frei, Sister John Karen & Dodson, C.H. (1972). The chemical effect of certain bark substrates on the germination and early growth of epiphytic orchids. *Bulletin of the Torrey Botanical Club*, **99**, 301–307.

Furman, T.E. & Trappe, J.M. (1971). Phylogeny and ecology of mycotrophic achlorophyllous angiosperms. *Quarterly Review of Biology*, **46**, 219–225.

Grime, J.P. (1977). Evidence for the existence of three primary strategies in plants and its relevance to ecological and evolutionary theory. *American Naturalist*, **111**, 1169–1194.

Hazen, W.E. (1966). Analysis of spatial pattern in epiphytes. *Ecology*, **47**, 634–635.

Huxley, C. (1980). Symbiosis between ants and epiphytes. *Biological Review*, **55**, 321–340.

Johansson, D. (1974). Ecology of vascular epiphytes in West African rain forest. *Acta Phytogeographica Suecica*, **59**, 1–136.

Johansson, D. (1977). Epiphytic orchids as parasites of their host trees. *American Orchid Society Bulletin*, **46**, 703–707.

Jonsson, L. & Nylund, J.E. (1979). *Favolaschia dybowskyana* (Singer) Singer (Aphyllophorales), a new orchid mycorrhizal fungus from tropical Africa. *New Phytologist*, **83**, 121–128.

Kellman, M., Hudson, J. & Sanmugadas, K. (1982). Temporal variability in atmospheric nutrient influx to a tropical ecosystem. *Biotropica*, **14**, 1–9.

Laessle, A.M. (1961). A micro-limnological study of Jamaican bromeliads. *Ecology*, **42**, 499–517.

Madison, M. (1977). Vascular epiphytes: their systematic occurrence and salient features. *Selbyana*, **2**, 1–13.

Madison M. (1979). Additional observations on ant-gardens in Amazonas. *Selbyana*, **5**, 107–115.

Nadkarni, N. (1981). Canopy roots: convergent evolution in rainforest nutrient cycles. *Science*, **214,** 1023–1024.

Orús, M.I., Estévez, M.P. & Vicente, C. (1981). Manganese depletion in chloroplasts of *Quercus rotundifolia* during chemical simulation of lichen epiphytic states. *Physiologia Plantarum*, **52,** 263–266.

Pittendrigh, C.S. (1946). Bromeliad malaria in Trinidad, W.W.I. *American Journal of Tropical Medicine and Hygiene*, **26,** 47–66.

Pittendrigh, C.S. (1948). The bromeliad–Anopheles–malaria complex in Trinidad. I. The bromeliad flora. *Evolution*, **2,** 58–89.

Rolfe, R.A. (1914). Leafless orchids. *The Orchid Revue*, **22,** 73–75.

Ruinen, J. (1953). Epiphytosis. A second view on epiphytism. *Annales. Bogorienses*, **1,** 101–157.

Sanford, W.W. (1968). Distribution of epiphytic orchids in semi-deciduous tropical forest in southern Nigeria. *Journal of Ecology*, **56,** 697–705.

Sanford, W.W. (1969). The distribution of epiphytic orchids in Nigeria in relation to each other and to geographic location and climate, type of vegetation and tree species. *Biological Journal of the Linnaean Society*, **1,** 247–285.

Sanford, W.W. (1974). The ecology of orchids. *The Orchids* (Ed. by C. L. Withner), Scientific Studies, pp. 1–100. John Wiley & Sons, New York.

Seifert, R. (1982). Neotropical *Heliconia* insect communities. *Quarterly Review of Biology*, **57,** 1–28.

Sengupta, B., Nandi, A.S., Samanta, R.K., Pal, D., Sengupta, D.N. & Sen, S.P. (1981). Nitrogen fixation in the phyllosphere of tropical plants: occurrence of phyllosphere nitrogen-fixing microorganisms in eastern India and their utility for the growth and nitrogen nutrition of host plants. *Annals of Botany*, **48,** 705–716.

Simpson, B.B. & Haffer, J. (1978). Speciation patterns in the Amazonian forest biota. *Annual Review of Ecology and Systematics*, **9,** 497–518.

Strong, D.R. Jr. (1977). Epiphyte loads, tree falls, and perennial forest disruption: a mechanism for maintaining higher tree species richness in the tropics without animals. *Journal of Biogeography*, **4,** 215–218.

Sugden, A.M. & Robins, R.J. (1979). Aspects of the ecology of vascular epiphytes in Colombian cloud forests. I. The distribution of the epiphytic flora. *Biotropica*, **11,** 173–188.

Thompson, J.N. (1981). Reversed animal-plant interactions: the evolution of insectivorous and ant-fed plants. *Biological Journal of the Linnaean Society*, **16,** 147–155.

Tukey, H.B. Jr. (1970) The leaching of substances from plants. *Annual Review of Plant Physiology*, **21,** 305–324.

Ule, E. (1901). Ameisengärten in Amazonasgebiet. *Botanische Jahrbücher für Systematik—Leipzig*, **30,** Beibl. 68, 45–52.

Wallace, B.J. (1983). *The Australian vascular epiphytes: flora and ecology.* Ph.D. Thesis, University of New England, New South Wales, Australia.

Weber, N.A. (1943). Parabiosis in neotropical 'ant gardens'. *Ecology*, **24,** 400–404.

Went, F.W. (1940). Soziologie der Epiphyten eines tropischen Urwaldes. *Annales du Jardin botanique de Buitenzorg*, **50,** 1–98.

Wheeler, W.M. (1921). A new case of parabiosis and the 'ant gardens' of British Guiana. *Ecology*, **2,** 89–103.

Diversity of canopy trees in a neotropical forest and implications for conservation

STEPHEN P. HUBBELL

*Program in Evolutionary Ecology and Behavior, Department of Zoology,
University of Iowa, Iowa City, Iowa 52242 U.S.A.*

ROBIN B. FOSTER

*Department of Botany, Field Museum of Natural History,
Chicago, Illinois 60605, U.S.A.*

SUMMARY

1 A complete map of all trees over 20 cm in diameter at breast height (dbh) in a 50-ha plot of tropical rain forest in Panama has revealed patterns of tropical tree distribution and abundance over a large area in unprecedented detail. Most species are patchily distributed, many are random, and few if any are uniformly spaced. Among the patchily-distributed species are several which closely follow topographic features of the plot. This patchiness has a major effect on the species composition of local stands. In particular, clumping results in an average increase of 3·2-fold in the probability that a tree will be next to one or more conspecifics among its five nearest neighbours.

2 Species–area relationships were explored in detail to evaluate the effect of non-random dispersion patterns on the rate of species addition with increased plot size. Patchy tree distributions, especially of rare species, caused a 10–20% underestimation of the true species richness in extrapolation to larger plot sizes, a fact of potential importance in rain forest conservation. This underestimation is reflected in the fact that the modal abundance octave of lognormal distributions fitted to the species abundance data does not increase proportionally with increases in sample (plot) size. The implication of this result is that rare species become ever rarer, relative to common species, as plot size increases.

3 A community analysis of species composition by hectare revealed considerable local differentiation of stands within the 50 ha. A spatial autocorrelation study found that mean similarity declines nearly exponentially with distance, and that measurable stand-differentiation effects persist to a distance of approximately 500 m. Distance explained much more of the variance in similarity between stands than topography. A 'space constant', in analogy with the time constant of first-order decay processes, is proposed to describe the 'spatial decay' of similarity in forest stands with increasing distance of separation between stands.

INTRODUCTION

Tropical rain forests are acknowledged to harbour the greatest wealth of biological and genetic diversity of any terrestrial community. It is a tribute to our ignorance about these forests that the most obvious question: Why are they so rich in tree species? continues to pose a difficult challenge to community theory (Hubbell 1980) and evolutionary biology (Ashton 1969). The mystery is even deeper than is commonly supposed, because not all tropical forests are rich in tree species; indeed, some are very species-poor (Whitmore 1975; Connell 1978).

The massive destruction of tropical forests worldwide comes at a tragic time when our knowledge of the organization, functional dynamics, and even the alpha taxomony of many threatened forests is still rudimentary. Urgently needed conservation and management efforts are made considerably more difficult by this lack of basic knowledge. One can debate how the scientific community ought best to respond to this situation; but it seems certain that only by significantly increasing the amount of research done on tropical forests is there hope of obtaining the knowledge required for making intelligent planning decisions.

Recently, a long-term, large-scale study was initiated on Barro Colorado Island (BCI), Panama, a $15 \cdot 6$ km^2 biological reserve in Gatún Lake. In 1980, a $0 \cdot 5$ km^2 plot of forest was surveyed and permanently divided into 1250 quadrats of 20×20 m; and a detailed census and map of all woody plants with stem diameters at breast height (dbh) $\geqslant 1$ cm is now in preparation. In the 50-ha plot, there are approximately 238 000 self-supporting woody plants, and an estimated 28 500 lianas and woody hemiepiphytes, with stem diameters > 1 cm dbh, representing over 300 species of trees and climbers. All of these plants are being individually tagged, identified to species, measured by dbh, and mapped to the nearest square meter. The long-term objectives of the study are: (i) to describe the life histories of many of the tree species in the BCI plot by following the fate (survival, growth, and reproduction) of large populations of individually tagged trees; (ii) to record tree population dynamics in space and time, with the goal of discriminating among competing equilibrium and non-equilibrium hypotheses of tropical forest organization (Connell 1978; Huston 1979; Hubbell 1979, 1980); and (iii) to provide a very large demographic data base for other research scientists working on diverse aspects of the biology of tropical tree species.

The large plot offers an unparalleled opportunity to examine the population structure of rare tropical tree species. At present, only the data for trees > 20 cm dbh have been analysed (7614 individuals of 186 species in 50 ha). The first part of the paper addresses the following questions about the spatial dispersion of individual tree populations and local stand composition: (1) In what manner are tree populations distributed in space? (ii) Are there recognizable general categories of dispersion pattern? (iii) In small areas, to what extent are tree species well-mixed, and what is the probability that neighbouring trees will be conspecific? The remainder of the paper addresses questions concerning species–area relationships, dominance–diversity patterns, and regional stand differentiation within the plot: (iv) How rapidly do tree species accumulate with increasing area? (v) How do non-random dispersion patterns affect this species–area curve? (vi) Are there systematic changes in dominance–diversity patterns with increasing sample size? (vii) How accurately can the total number of species in the known community be estimated from subsamples? Finally, (viii) to what extent do local stands on small areas differ from one another, and how does this differentiation depend on the distance and difference in physiography between the stands?

STUDY SITE AND METHODS

Barro Colorado Island (BCI) is located in an artificial lake (Gatún Lake) in the zone of the Panama Canal. BCI was chosen as the site for this study because of the extremely well known flora of the island (Croat 1978), the extensive earlier vegetation studies of Knight (1975), and the excellent long-term reserve prospects for the island. An area of 50 ha assured a sampling adequacy for rare tree species at least equal to that obtained in a 13-ha study of dry forest in Costa Rica (Hubbell 1979), a forest with less than half as many species per hectare as BCI. The 50-ha tract of forest lies on the central plateau of the island at elevations ranging from 120 to 155 m above mean sea level (Fig. 1). All but 2 ha of the plot lies in what has been called 'old forest' viz. forest mostly 300 years old, and perhaps older (Foster & Brokaw 1982). Half of the island was cut at the time of Canal construction, 70–100 years ago, and this area is now in late secondary succession. No part of the island is likely to have escaped shifting agriculture at some time during the past, especially during pre-Columbian times, when the region was fairly densely populated (Bennett 1968). The site has moderate relief, with 0–21% slopes; but almost half (48%) is flat (< 3% slopes). There are three easily recognized habitat types (Fig. 1): (i) moderate to steep slopes (10–21%) with shallow (< 50 cm) soil depths and good drainage; (ii) flat to gently sloping upland areas (0–10%) with intermediates (0·5–1 m) soil depths; and (iii) flat (0–3%) lowland areas with deeper soils (> 1 m) and subject to relatively long periods of flooding or soil saturation. The soils are derived from a thin basaltic cap over thick deposits of Cretaceous marine sediments, and are probably relatively fertile for tropical soils (Jordan & Herrera 1981).

A total of 7614 trees over 20 cm dbh, representing 186 species, were recorded in the BCI plot in the 1980 census. Of these species, only thirty-three had an average density of one or more trees > 20 cm dbh per hectare (Table 1). However, it is incorrect to infer from these data that all remaining tree species in the plot are rare. Many species are quite common but seldom or never achieve an adult size over 20 cm dbh. This lower cutoff is sufficiently small for all trees in the 'canopy' to have been counted, at the risk of including some individuals of primarily subcanopy species. As is often the case, the canopy of the BCI forest is difficult to define rigorously. The larger trees in the BCI forest mostly reach mature heights in the 25–35 m range, with a few emergents over 40 m; therefore, we operationally defined the 'canopy' as the vegetation layer above 25 m.

RESULTS

Individual species patterns

Formal quantitative analysis of the dispersion patterns of all species will be undertaken only after the data for the smaller size-class stems have been fully assembled. However,

(a)

(b)

Contour Interval: 1 m   Scale: ⊢——100m——⊣   Elevation: m. above s.l.   S. P. Hubbell 1980

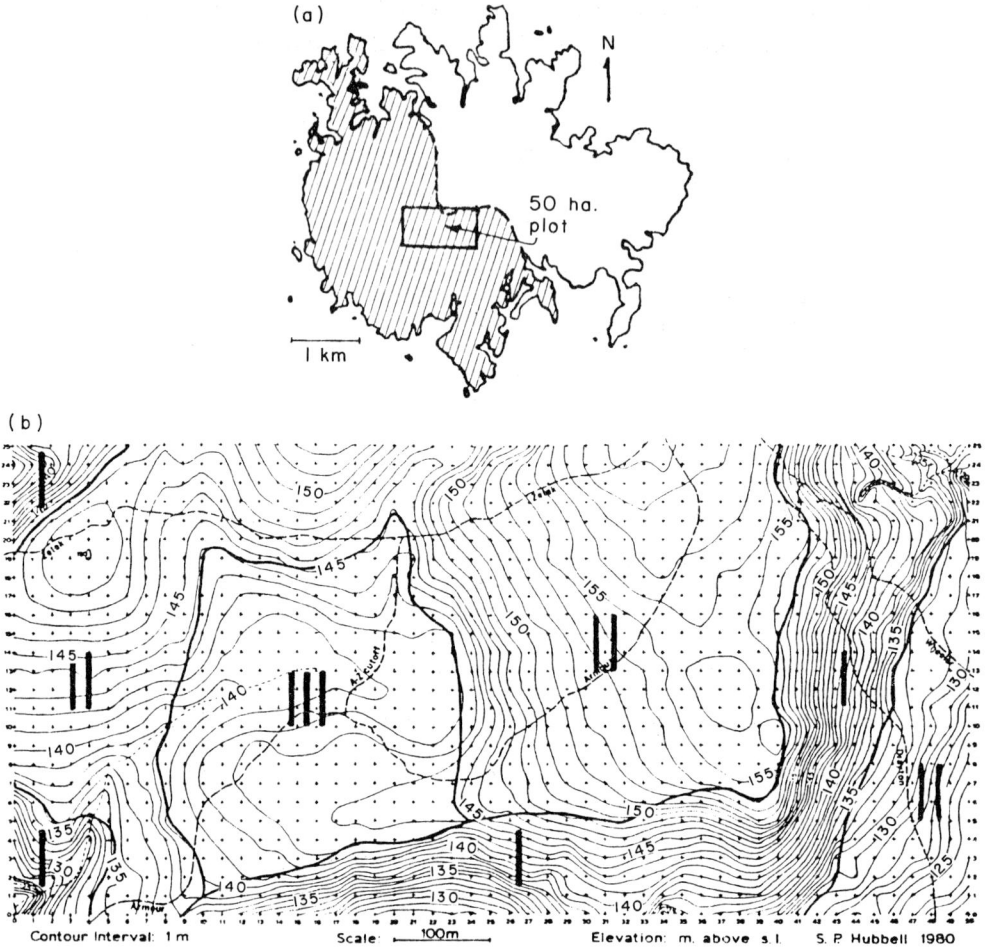

FIG. 1. (a) Barro Colorado Island, showing the location of the 50-ha plot. The hatched area represents old forest, and the open area represents 70-year old second-growth forest. (b) Detail of the 50-ha site, showing boundaries between the three major habitat types. I: steep slopes; shallow soils. II: gently sloping uplands of the plateau; soils of intermediate depth. III: flats subject to frequent and prolonged flooding; deep soils. Contour lines are drawn at 1-m intervals.

a number of important qualitative conclusions about these patterns can already be drawn from the information presently available. There are at least three recognizable categories of dispersion pattern. These are: (i) species which appear to be randomly or near-randomly distributed over the plot; (ii) species which are clumped and whose patches follow easily recognized topographic features of the plot; and (iii) species which are clumped, but whose patches are spatially uncorrelated with topography.

A typical example of a species in the first category is *Trichilia tuberculata* (*T. cipo* in Croat 1978) in the Meliaceae, the commonest canopy tree in the plot (Fig. 2). On a very local basis, trees of *T. tuberculata* may exhibit slight contagion; but the patches are 'fine-grained' and bear no obvious relationship to slopes or flat areas. Species in this category run the gamut in abundance from extremely common to quite rare.

TABLE 1. Common tree species and their abundances in the 50-ha permanent plot on Barro Colorado Island, Panama. Trees over 20 cm dbh only. Species nomenclature follows Croat (1978)

Species	Family	No. of trees
Alchornea costaricensis	Euphorbiaceae	107
Alseis blackiana	Rubiaceae	430
Apeiba membranacea	Tiliaceae	150
Beilschmiedia pendula	Lauraceae	166
Brosimum alicastrum	Moraceae	85
Casearia arborea	Flacourtiaceae	102
Cecropia insignis	Moraceae	166
Cordia bicolor	Boraginaceae	139
Dendropanax stenodontus	Araliaceae	51
Guapira costaricana	Nytaginaceae	57
Guarea guidonia	Meliaceae	170
Guatteria dumetorum	Annonaceae	133
Gustavia superba	Lecythidaceae	208
Heisteria concinna	Olacaceae	88
Hirtella triandra	Chrysobalanaceae	163
Hura crepitans	Euphorbiaceae	81
Jacaranda copaia	Bignoniaceae	153
Lonchocarpus velutinus	Fabaceae: Papilionoideae	70
Luehea seemannii	Tiliaceae	62
Ocotea skutchii	Lauraceae	85
Poulsenia armata	Moraceae	213
Pouteria unilocularis	Sapotaceae	86
Prioria copaifera	Fabaceae: Caesalpinioideae	151
Protium tenuifolium	Burseraceae	179
Pterocarpus rohrii	Fabaceae: Papilionoideae	50
Quararibea asterolepis	Bombacaceae	472
Simarouba amara	Simaroubaceae	114
Tabernaemontana arborea	Apocynaceae	188
Tetragastris panamensis	Burseraceae	176
Trichilia tuberculata†	Meliaceae	1024
Virola sebifera	Myristicaceae	204
Virola surinamensis	Myristicaceae	106
Zanthoxylum belizense	Rutaceae	68
Total individuals of all species		5697

† *T. cipo* in Croat (1978).

The second group of species are those which are distinctly patchy in dispersion and are correlated with easily recognized topographic or edaphic features of the plot. *Poulsenia armata* (Moraceae) occurs predominantly on steeper slopes (Fig. 3), where it is the third most abundant species among the trees over 20 cm dbh. Note, however, that *Poulsenia* also occurs over much of the upland plateau but in this flatter terrain it is

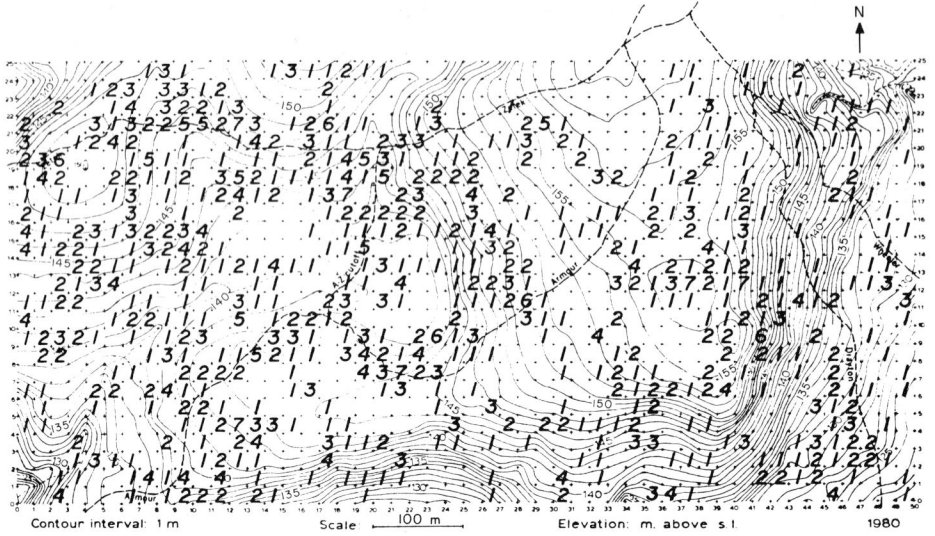

Trichilia tuberculata

Fig. 2. Map of all individuals of *Trichilia tuberculata* ⩾ 20 cm dbh in the 50-ha plot. The numbers on the map represent the number of *T. tuberculata* trees in the designated 20 × 20 m quadrat.

rare. In fact, virtually all of the species which show correlations with topography or soil also exist at much lower density throughout the remainder of the plot.

The third category of species are those that occur in patches, which do not correspond either to obvious topographic features, or to edaphic features (so far as is

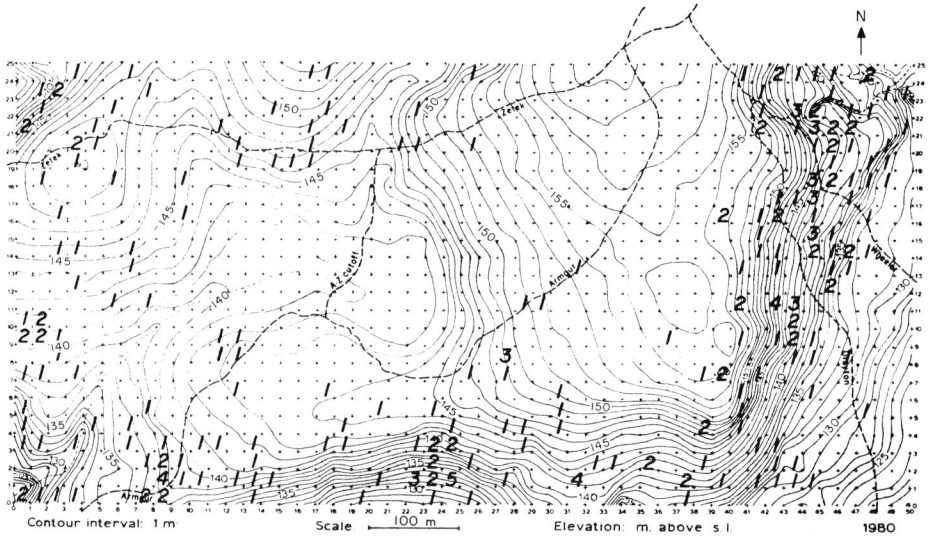

Poulsenia armata

Fig. 3. Map of all individuals of *Poulsenia armata* ⩾ 20 cm dbh in the 50-ha plot.

known at present). *Beilschmiedia pendula* (Lauraceae) is an example; one of the two large clumps of this species occurs on a steep slope, whereas the other is located on the upland plateau (Fig. 4). Another example is *Cecropia insignis* (Moraceae) (Fig. 5).

Most of the tree species exhibit clumped dispersion patterns, especially at very local distance scales. Consequently, species are not randomly intermingled in space, and trees are likely to have more conspecific trees as immediate neighbours than predicted by chance. If there is random mixing, the probability that the first nearest neighbour is a conspecific is simply the proportion of the given species in the entire plot. Because this proportion is fairly small for most species, it is expedient to consider more neighbours

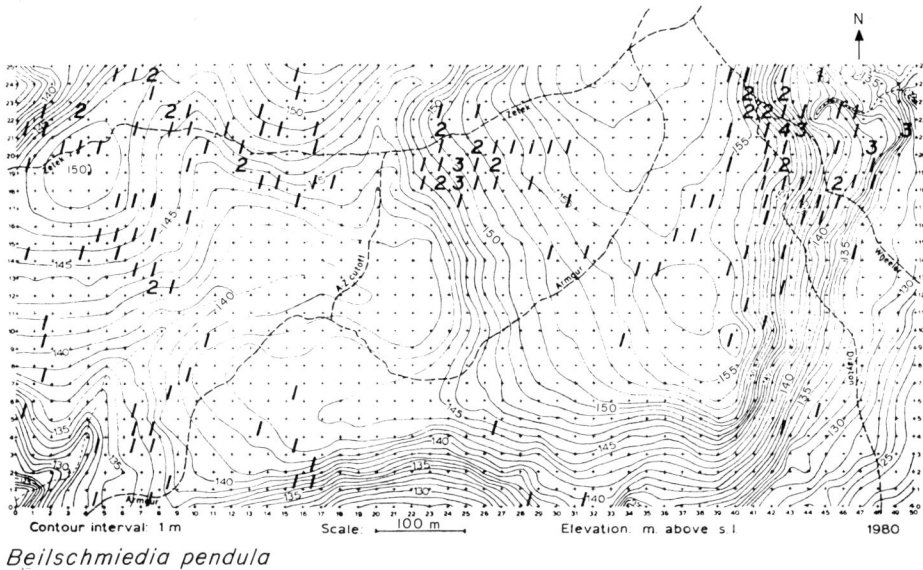

Beilschmiedia pendula

Fig. 4. Map of all individuals of *Beilschmiedia pendula* ≥ 20 cm dbh in the 50-ha plot.

than the first. It is a straightforward calculation using the binomial distribution to obtain the probability of x conspecific trees in a set of n neighbouring trees assuming random intermingling. This was investigated for the eastern 20 ha of the plot. In the BCI forest, each tree crown is surrounded by the crowns of approximately five other trees (six trees would represent perfect hexagonal packing). Accordingly, the observed and expected probabilities were calculated for obtaining at least one conspecific tree in the five immediate neighbours of a randomly chosen individual of twenty of the commonest species.

Of these twenty species, fourteen show significantly greater probabilities of one or more conspecifics among their five nearest neighbours than expected (Fig. 6). The probabilities of drawing a conspecific were adjusted appropriately to the 20-ha area sampled. More of these species may show significant departures from randomness when sample sizes are increased to the full 50 ha. For these fourteen species, a randomly chosen tree in the canopy has at least one chance in four, and sometimes better than a 50/50 chance, of being next to, or very close to, another tree of the same species. Although these probabilities are high in part because these are the commonest species in the canopy, it should be emphasized that clumping is responsible for raising these probabilities an average of 3·2-fold ± 1·8 (1 S.D.) over expected values in the fourteen significantly clumped species. Thus, clumping has a major effect on the demographic neighbourhood of individual trees.

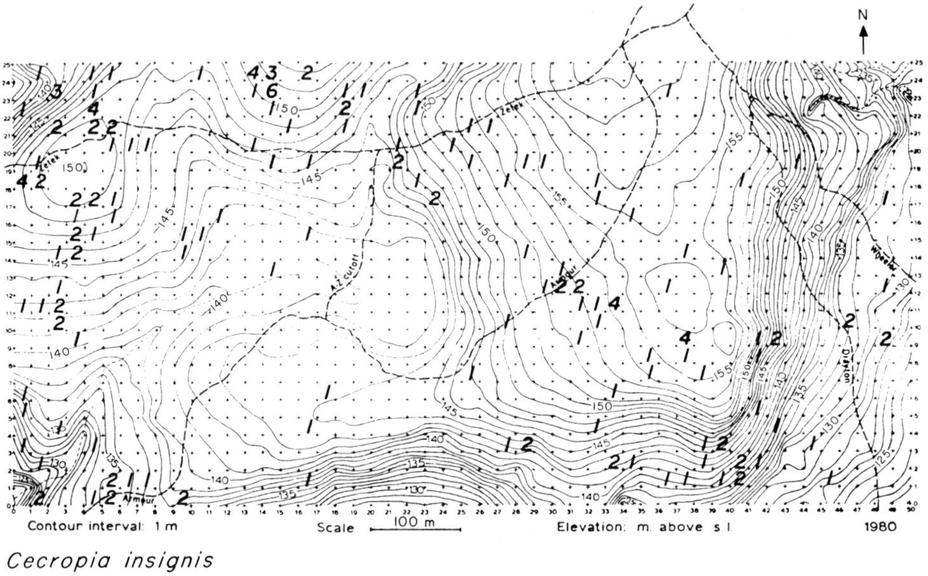

Cecropia insignis

FIG. 5. Map of all individuals of *Cecropia insignis* ⩾ 20 cm dbh in the 50-ha plot.

Species–area relationships

The non-random dispersion patterns of tree species in the canopy of the BCI forest also affect the rate at which species are accumulated with increasing plot size. Because the abundances of all species are known exactly for the entire 50-ha plot, it is possible to compute an expected species–area curve for the plot under the assumption of random dispersion of all species. The observed species–area curve can then be tested against the expected curve.

The mean and variance of the expected number of species in a given fraction, a, of the total area, given known abundances of the species in the total area, can be derived by simple statistical argument, as Coleman (1979) has shown. Let S be the total number of species in the entire area, in which there are $n(i)$ individuals of the ith species. Then the probability that the species i is absent from fractional subarea, a, is given by: $(1-a)^{n(i)}$. Since the species are assumed to be independently distributed under the null hypothesis, the mean (s) and variance (v) of the number of species expected in fractional area, a, are given by:

$$s(a) = S - \sum_{i=1}^{S}(1-a)^{n(i)}$$

$$v(a) = \sum_{i=1}^{S}(1-a)^{n(i)} - \sum_{i=1}^{S}(1-a)^{2n(i)}$$

As might be anticipated, the observed and expected species–area curves are significantly different for the canopy of the BCI forest. The observed curve rises more slowly than the expected species–area curve (Fig. 7). The differences appear small on the log–log plot, but the observed curve lags behind the expected curve by six to ten species for sample sizes in the range of 1–15 ha. The curves must converge, of course, as the sample area approaches the total area ($a = 1$). Thus, by 25 ha the observed and expected curves are only 3·7 species apart.

Patchiness affects the variance even more strongly. There are big differences between the observed and expected variances of the number of species per subsampled area. Because of clumping, observed variances are consistently and considerably greater than expected variances. At a sample size of 1 ha, the ratio of observed to

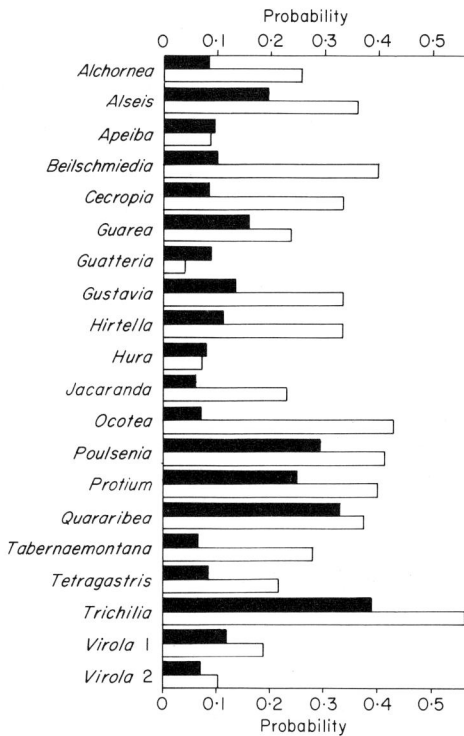

FIG. 6. Observed (□) and expected (■) probability of having at least one conspecific tree among the five nearest neighbour trees, for the twenty most common tree species in the canopy. The observed probabilities are significantly greater than expected probabilites based on random mingling of tree species in fourteen of the twenty species. The six species not displaying differences are *Apeiba*, *Guarea*, *Guatteria*, *Hura*, *Virola sebifera* (1) and *V. surinamensis* (2).

expected variance is 41·4/22·5, a 1·8-fold difference. When the sample increases to 5 ha, however, this ratio grows to 111·0/22·9, a 4·8-fold difference. As with the means, the difference in variances must also decline as the sample area approaches the total area. Thus, when 25 ha have been enumerated, the ratio of variances has dropped to 18·0/10·1, again a 1·8-fold difference.

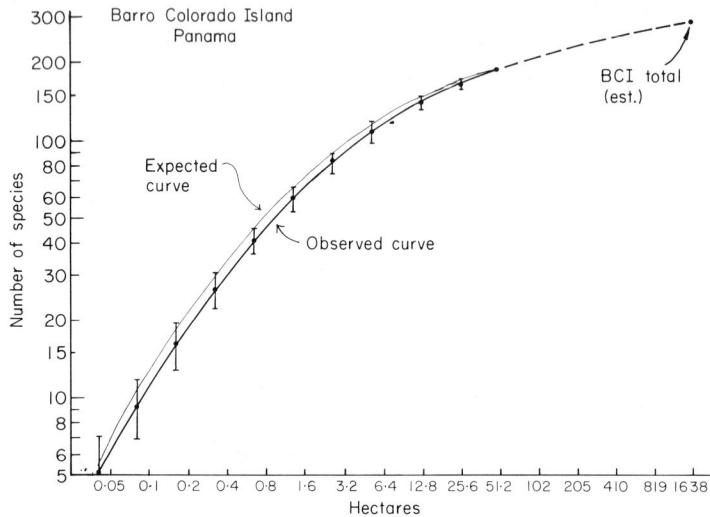

FIG. 7. Species–area curve for the 50-ha plot, trees ⩾ 20 cm dbh only. The lower line is the observed curve, and its 95% confidence limits. The upper curve is the expected species–area curve for the 50–ha plot, given known abundances of all species in the entire plot. The estimated number of species for the entire island is based on Croat (1978).

Patterns of dominance and diversity

The relative abundances of tree species in the canopy layer of the entire 50 ha plot are lognormally distributed. A fit of a truncated lognormal with a mode in the octave of four to eight individuals per species gave the best least-squares fit (Fig. 8) and an equation of:

$$s(R) = 33·67 \ e^{-0·068R^2},$$

where $s(R)$ is the expected number of species in the Rth octave to the right or left of the modal octave, and $s(0) = 33.67$. One of the elegant features of this model is that the total number of species in the sample universe can be estimated from a subsample (Preston 1948), provided the assumptions of the model are met. If the sample size is large enough to detect the mode, then in principle the total number of species can be estimated by doubling the number of species in octaves to the right of the modal octave, and adding this figure to the number in the modal octave. Using the fitted distribution in Fig. 8, we can estimate the total number of canopy species that should ultimately be found on BCI. This procedure yields an estimate of 228 species. It is possible to check this estimate with reasonable precision by estimating the number of tree species which can attain $\geqslant 20$ cm dbh in Croat's (1978) flora of the island. This check reveals that the figure obtained from the lognormal for the 50-ha plot underestimates the expected total for the island (approximately 288 species) by about 20%.

This underestimation is probably caused by large-scale patchiness of species distributions on the island. Hairston (1959) noted that the lognormal estimation procedure makes the implicit assumption that the species are randomly distributed and randomly sampled. If species are clumped, and especially if rare species are systematically more clumped than common species, then rare species will be

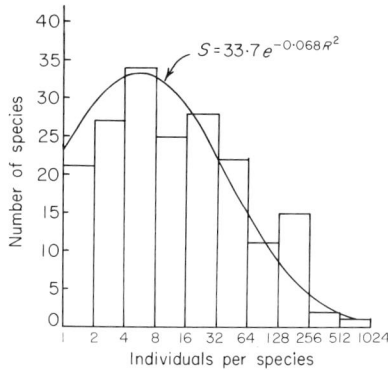

Fig. 8. Lognormal distribution fitted to the relative species abundance data for all trees $\geqslant 20$ cm dbh in the entire 50-ha plot. Species have been grouped into octaves of abundance.

under-represented in samples. The result is that the mode of the lognormal distribution will not increase by a factor of 2 with a doubling of number of individuals in the sample, but will increase by some lesser factor.

Because considerable patchiness in tree dispersion patterns was already detected at scales of one to several hectares within the plot, it was of interest to check whether the behaviour of the mode was indeed to increase more slowly than by a factor of two with each doubling of sample size. What we found was somewhat surprising (Fig. 9). Through three doublings of area, from 1·28 ha (32 20 × 20 m quadrats) to 10·24 ha (256 20 × 20 m quadrats), the mode kept pace with the sample size. However, in going from 10·24 ha to 50 ha (Fig. 8), a 4·9-fold increase in area, the mode not only did not increase on the order of 4-fold, but in fact actually *decreased* 2-fold. This provides strong evidence that the spatial scale of clumping on which the lognormal sampling assumption fails to hold is in the range of 10–50 ha.

A second curious feature of the distributions in Fig. 9 is the extraordinary abundance of species represented by single individuals, a pattern absent from the lognormal for the total plot (Fig. 8). There are several biologically interesting possibilities to explain this phenomenon, and one uninteresting possibility. We suspect that the uninteresting possibility is the most likely, namely that in every few hectares, there is one exceptionally large individual of each of several common understory species which happens to exceed our minimum census diameter. A cursory check of the species which tend to occur as singletons suggests that half to two-thirds of the species are indeed common understory species. If these species are removed, however, there is still a slight excess of singleton species, especially in the 10·24 ha samples. One biologically interesting explanation for this pattern in small but not large samples would be local regular spacing of the individuals of rare species, but randomness on

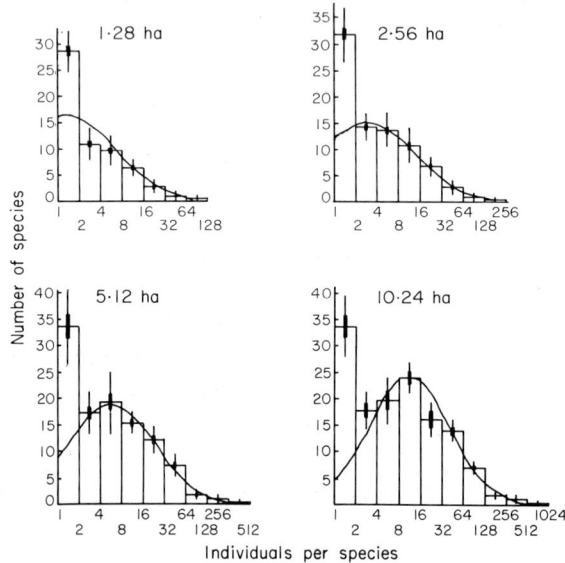

FIG. 9. Progressive shift in the mode of the lognormal to the right one octave for each doubling of sample size, in the range of 1·28 ha (32 20 × 20 m quadrats) to 10·24 ha (256 20 × 20 m quadrats). Number of species in the ones category was not used in fitting the lognormal distribution. Thin vertical lines are one S.D.; heavier vertical bars are one S.E.

larger spatial scales, leading to an over-representation of rare species in small samples. However, as noted earlier, there are few if any uniformly spaced tree species in the BCI forest. A second possibility is that the dispersion patterns of several rare species are positively correlated spatially. This pattern was found in a number of rare dry-forest species in Costa Rica (S. P. Hubbell, unpubl.), but this possibility remains to be investigated on BCI. A third possibility is that the lognormal distribution is simply an inadequate model for the relative abundance data of canopy trees in this forest. After all, the lognormal was proposed as an inductive model of relative species abundance, not a model deduced from community theory.

Regional differentiation of stand composition

Thus far, discussion has focused on how patchy tree distributions can affect the species composition of very local stands in the immediate neighbourhood of individual trees, but not the extent to which such patchiness can influence community composition on a larger scale. The patterns of dominance and diversity on different spatial scales do lead one to expect large-scale patchiness, particularly in the range of 10–50 ha. One can examine this possibility in greater detail by performing a simple spatial autocorrelation analysis of the similarity in canopy species composition among the fifty 1-ha stands in the plot. This is done by computing the correlation between the relative abundances of species in hectare i and in hectare j, and grouping and averaging the coefficients according to the distance separating the ith and jth hectares. For analytical simplicity in obtaining a first-order estimate of the effect of distance on similarity, we lumped hectares in the primary frame (those hectares immediately surrounding the focal hectare) as being at 100 m from the focal hectare, lumped those in the second frame as being at 200 m, and so on.

The results of this analysis reveal a dramatic effect of distance on average stand similarity (Fig. 10). Average stand correlations drop precipitously and nearly exponentially with increasing distance, levelling out at about 500 m to a background level of similarity. In the figure, two curves are drawn, one for all species, and the other for common species, defined for present purposes as species having an average census density of at least one tree $\geqslant 20$ cm dbh per hectare. The background level of similarity is higher when all species are considered because many of the rare species will be absent from both hectares being compared. This puts many points of the correlation plot on (0,0), which tends to force the regression to pass more nearly through the origin, thereby elevating the apparent similarity of the hectares. Thus, in the curve for all species, similarities between hectares are considered greater if species are absent from both as well as present in both. However, absence of a species is more likely to be

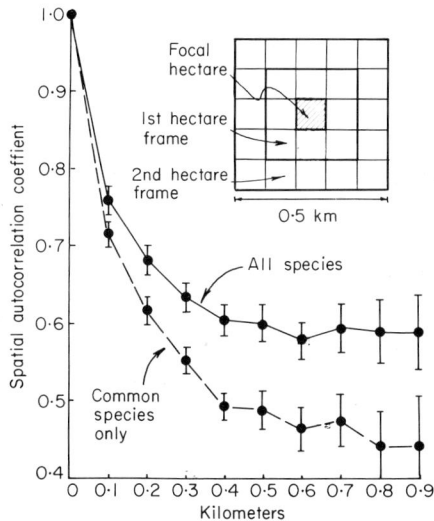

FIG. 10. Spatial autocorrelation coefficients as a function of distance from focal hectare. See text for explanation.

biologically interesting when a species is common; consequently, the curve which is restricted to the common species is perhaps more useful biologically in defining overall community patchiness.

These results indicate that simple distance between stands is able to explain a significant fraction of the variation in correlations between canopy species composition between hectares. An important question remains, however, concerning the degree to which topographic and edaphic site factors also explain variation in these correlations. Are two hectares of forest more dissimilar if they differ more in slope or soils? How important are these effects relative to the distance between stands in the BCI plot? The soil data to answer these questions fully have yet to be obtained, but a tentative answer regarding the relative importance of topography and distance is possible. Partial regression analysis was used on a model of three main effects: distance, difference in slope, and difference in degree of relief (slope variance across quadrats) within hectares. Because of the exponential relationship between mean correlation and distance, the correlations were log-transformed after addition by unity; this transformation resulted in a substantial increase in total explained variance ($r^2 = 0.71$). All three effects were significant ($P < 0.0001$); but of these variables, distance accounted for 85% of the explained variance. Thus, while there is an effect of topographic similarity, it is weak in comparison with the effect of distance separating the stands.

These results are presented with the caveat that the relative importance of distance and topography could be different or even reversed in other sites. A site as uniform as possible on BCI was chosen for the 50-ha plot. Thus, it might well be that in a topographically much more heterogeneous site, the relative effects of topographic differences would be magnified considerably. Moreover, the effects of differences in soils and history cannot yet be evaluated, and these factors are expected to explain additional variance in the spatial correlations.

DISCUSSION

We are still in a stage of preliminary data analysis of the first (1980–82) census of the BCI plot, so the conclusions reached here are tentative. For canopy trees, however, some qualitative and quantitative results seem unlikely to change. First, most of the tree species appear to have their own individualistic dispersion patterns, with only weakly developed associations by habitat in some species. Secondly, most of the species in the plot are unevenly distributed and many are highly clumped. Sometimes these clumps are easily associated with topographic features of the plot; but in most cases, they are not. Thirdly, even though most species are clumped, they are almost always present in low numbers as rare species elsewhere in the plot.

Several hypotheses warranting further study can be suggested to account for these differences in tree distribution pattern. For species exhibiting essentially random dispersion over the entire plot, it is reasonable to conclude that all sites are equally good (or bad) for successful establishment and maturation, and that the ecological physiology of the species is broadly adapted to cope with the range of site differences expressed in the 50-ha plot.

For species which are clumped, and whose patches clearly correspond to topography or soils, it is reasonable to look for special site requirements and adaptations. An interesting question is whether these species are better competitors than the randomly distributed species in these sites, or whether it is more the case that they are at a competitive disadvantage everywhere else. Equilibrium models of tropical forest organization would not predict the continuing persistence of a tree species which does not enjoy a competitive advantage at some site in the forest (Connell 1978). However, non-equilibrium models reveal that, even a species which is no more than a competitive equal in some areas, and at a distinct disadvantage elsewhere, can persist in the forest for very long periods of time before going locally extinct (Hubbell 1979; Wright & Hubbell 1983).

For species which are distributed in patches which bear no discernible relationship to topography or soils, it is tempting to conclude that these are species whose success is more strongly influenced by transient historical factors, such as tree-fall disturbances, or recent spread from a few colonizing ancestors, than by microsite conditions which are fixed in space or very slowly changing, such as factors related to topography. Of course, the possibility always exists that there are fixed site factors about which we know nothing; but the real test will come by following the spatial movement of the tree populations through time. For at least one of the species used to illustrate this pattern (*Cecropia insignis*), there is clear evidence that there can be no fixed spatial pattern because this is a pioneer species which successfully establishes only in large tree-fall gaps.

It is of some interest that species which are highly aggregated nevertheless are still present in low numbers as rare species elsewhere in the plot. The question arises whether the sparse subpopulations are self-maintaining, or simply represent accidental establishments of rare individuals, through good fortune, outside the normal habitat for the species. Our suspicion is that these sparse populations are largely if not entirely maintained by continual immigration from the dense populations, and would disappear relatively rapidly without such immigration. With repeated censuses of the plot, it should be possible to determine the relative reproductive performance of isolated and aggregated trees to address this question.

As a direct consequence of the clumping of most species, there is non-random mixing of tree species in the canopy. Individual trees are much more likely to be near conspecific trees than if neighbours were dictated by random chance. The effect of clumping on the probability of neighbouring conspecifics is surprisingly great: in fourteen clumped species, the average increase due to clumping in the probability of at least one conspecific tree in the five nearest neighbours is over 3-fold.

Of some relevance to rain forest conservation efforts is the effect of such patchiness on the rate at which species richness and population sizes of individual tree species increase with area. These results clearly show that the effect of clumping is to increase considerably the variance in rate of species addition with area; and it follows that the same effect occurs on rates of population increase with area as well. Thus, if a plot happens to be placed in a patch of a particular species, the population size of this species will increase rapidly with area; whereas, if it is in an area sparsely populated by the species, its numbers will obviously increase much more slowly with increased area. Reserve placement may be difficult to optimize for more than a few species at the same time if, as seems the case for the BCI plot, the patches of tree species are positively associated in space only rarely. Clearly, both the intensity of clumping and the covariation of population patches among species can be a factor in deciding on the relative merits of the 'stratified sample' strategy of a system of many small reserves vs. the 'aggregate' strategy of a few large reserves. Problems of small population size and stochastic extinction in small vs. large reserves have been treated theoretically in the context of the theory of island biogeography elsewhere (Richter-Dyn & Goel 1972; Wright & Hubbell 1983).

The question of scale is of course critical in all such discussions. How big are the patches in tropical rain forest? If the patches are small, on the order of several hectares, whereas on larger scales the species are well mixed, then there may be no special advantage to a stratified reserve strategy. If, on the other hand, patchiness is much more pronounced on much larger scales (Foster 1980), there may be little alternative to a stratified reserve strategy. It is thus of some importance to establish the degree to which species aggregate and associate in the 50-ha plot on BCI, and to measure the local and 'regional' differentiation of stands within the plot.

If the BCI forest turns out to be relatively typical of lowland tropical rain forest, then the results of the spatial autocorrelation analysis (Fig. 10) suggest that patch sizes in rain forest measure on the order of 0·5 km across. Beyond a distance of 500 m between stands in the BCI plot, stand similarities are reduced to a relatively constant low background level. It should be cautioned that the individualistic nature of the dispersion patterns of most of the tree species, especially in forests as floristically rich as that of BCI, will frustrate attempts to define forest patches too rigorously. The fact that community similarities decline smoothly and nearly exponentially with distance is fair warning that rain forest patches are indeed very 'fuzzy' floristic sets.

This indistinctness, however, may possibly be turned to an advantage in generating a useful comparative scale of patchiness in different forests. We might wish to ask, for example: Do community similarities decay at similar rates with distance in Malesian dipterocarp forests as in Panamanian forests? In temperate vs. tropical forest in general? We speculate that the decline in similarity will often be nearly exponential with distance in most forests, suggesting that a relatively simple lumped diffusion process can be used to describe the intergradation between neighbouring forest communities. If this is true, then it should be possible to define a useful 'space constant', in analogy to the time constant of first-order temporal decay processes. This space constant would describe the spatial rate of decay of forest community similarity. The time constant of a first-order decay process is defined as that amount of time it takes for the fraction, $1 - 1/e$, of the initial value to decay, which amounts to a 63·2% loss. For the canopy tree community of the BCI forest, considering common species only (Fig. 10), the estimate of the space constant is approximately 200 m, by which distance there has been a loss of about 63% in community similarity.

Until there is more information on minimum critical population sizes for tropical tree species, it will remain difficult to convert information on tree abundance and diversity into concrete recommendations for reserve sizes. In the BCI plot, only thirty-three out of 186 tree species > 20 cm dbh were represented by more than fifty individuals (1 tree ha^{-1} in crude density). Even taking into account the fact that many of the remaining species will be shown to be much more abundant when smaller size classes are enumerated, it is still expected that a relatively large number of species will remain very rare. The results of fitting lognormal distributions to the relative species abundance data for increasing plot sizes support this expectation: rare tree species become increasingly rare, relative to common species, as plot size increases. The maintenance of these very rare species in tropical rain forests remains a grand mystery.

ACKNOWLEDGMENTS

This research was supported by a grant from the U.S. National Science Foundation. We also thank the Smithsonian Tropical Research Institute for its encouragement and support, and Diane Gutenkauf, Jorge Hernandez, Allen Herre and Emily Whitney for their assistance in the field.

REFERENCES

Ashton, P.S. (1969). Speciation among tropical forest trees: some deductions in light of recent evidence. *Biological Journal of the Linnaean Society, London,* **1**, 155–196.

Bennett, C.F. (1968). *Human Influences on the Zoogeography of Panama.* 124 pp. University of California Press, Berkeley, California, U.S.A.

Coleman, B.D. (1979). *On random placement and species–area relations.* Research Report 79–18, Department of Mathematics, Carnegie-Mellon University, Pittsburgh, Pa., U.S.A.

Connell J.H. (1978). Diversity in tropical rain forests and coral reefs. *Science,* **199**, 1302–1310.

Croat, T.B. (1978). *The Flora of Barro Colorado Island.* 934 pp. Stanford University Press, Stanford, California, U.S.A.

Foster, R.B. (1980). Heterogeneity and disturbance in tropical vegetation. *Conservation Biology: An Evolutionary–Ecological Perspective* (Ed. by M. E. Soulé & B. A. Wilcox), pp. 75–92. Sinauer, Sunderland, Mass., U.S.A.

Foster, R.B. & Brokaw, N.V. (1982). Structure and history of the vegetation of Barro Colorado Island. *The Ecology of a Tropical Forest* (Ed. by E. G. Leigh *et al.*), pp. 67–81. Smithsonian Institution Press, Washington, D.C., U.S.A.

Hairston, N.G. (1959). Species abundance and community organization. *Ecology,* **40**, 404–416.

Hubbell, S.P. (1979). Tree dispersion, abundance, and diversity in a tropical dry forest. *Science,* **213**, 1299–1309.

Hubbell, S.P. (1980). Seed predation and the coexistence of tree species in tropical forests. *Oikos,* **35**, 214–299.

Huston, M. (1979). A general hypothesis of species diversity. *American Naturalist,* **113**, 81–101.

Jordan, C.F. & Herrera, R. (1981). Tropical rain forests: are nutrients really critical? *American Naturalist,* **117**, 167–180.

Knight, D.H. (1975). A phytosociological analysis of species-rich tropical forest on Barro Colorado Island, Panama. *Ecological Monographs,* **45**, 259–284.

Preston, F.W. (1948). The commonness, and rarity, of species. *Ecology,* **29**, 254–283.

Richter-Dyn, N. & Goel, N.S. (1972). On the extinction of a colonizing species. *Theoretical Population Biology,* **3**, 406–433.

Whitmore, T.C. (1975). *Tropical Rain Forests of The Far East.* Clarendon Press, Oxford.

Wright, S.J. & Hubbell, S.P. (1983). Stochastic extinction and reserve size: a focal-species approach. *Oikos* (in press).

Determinants of species composition in some isolated neotropical cloud forests

ANDREW M. SUGDEN

Botany School, Downing Street, Cambridge, CB2 3EA, England

SUMMARY

1 The distributional, autecological and reproductive characteristics of species in insular floras are important to the understanding of determinants of species composition on islands. To illustrate this fact, a comparison is made of the characteristics of the trees and shrubs of three isolated low-altitude cloud forests surrounded by arid lowlands on the Caribbean coast of Colombia and Venezuela. The cloud forests, on the summits of mountains less than 1000 m high, have the physiognomy of upper montane rain forest, and may be of recent origin.

2 The composition of the three forests is very different, but the species in each case have similar characteristics, including wide geographical distribution and habitat range, a tendency to occur in early successional habitats, and adaptation for endozoic bird dispersal. Few of the species are montane forest specialists and endemism is low. Proportions of dioecious species range from 15% to 29%.

3 Most of these characteristics, except for the relatively high levels of dioecy, are features of young isolated habitats. Other upper montane rain forests have higher endemism and more specialist species.

4 These facts suggest that random colonization has played an important part in determining the species composition of the cloud forests. The paucity of montane forest specialists may be due to relatively infrequent dispersal, while the predominance of widespread species of successional habitats may reflect their higher rate of dispersal.

INTRODUCTION

Recent publications dealing with aspects of the equilibrium theory of island biogeography have lamented the lack of information and understanding of the biology of species comprising insular biota (Connor & Simberloff 1978; Gilbert 1980; Wilcox 1980; Williamson 1981). Attempts to account for species composition on islands using mathematical models and statistical techniques remain controversial even for organisms, such as birds, where niches or guilds are more readily distinguished than in plants; see, for instance, the current debate on the degree to which random events of colonization influence species composition (Connor & Simberloff 1979; Abbott 1980; Diamond & Gilpin 1982; Wright & Biehl 1982). Much has been made of the potential applications of island biogeographical theory to conservation (Frankel & Soulé 1981, and references therein; Myers 1981) and it is important that these be viewed in realistic perspective, i.e. alongside the biological facts of the effects of isolation on species

43

altitudinal zonation of common tree species. The zone above the ecotone with dry vegetation (*c.* 450 m) is dominated by *Clusia rosea*, with individuals up to 30 m tall. Above this zone (*c.* 550 m), canopy height decreases to 12–15 m, and *Croton xanthochloros* and *Terminalia amazonia* become prominent. *Myrcianthes cf. compressa* and *Euterpe karsteniana* are most frequent in the next zone (*c.* 700–850 m), where canopy height decreases to 5–10 m. Finally, on the windswept slopes near the summit (930 m), there is a low thicket of *Clusia cf. alata* and *Blakea monticola* with intermittent herbaceous patches. Many of the woody species, nevertheless, occur in varying quantities in most of the zones. On Santa Ana, the vegetation is distinctly patchy: *Clusia rosea, C. multiflora, Geonoma paraguanensis, Euterpe karsteniana, Rapanea coriacea, Weinmannia pinnata*, and even *Sporobolus* sp. can all be found forming almost pure stands, while in other parts more mixing occurs. Canopy heights range from 0·5 m to 20 m. This patchiness is partly related to altitude and aspect (exposure), and may also reflect vegetative reproduction and the occurrence of landslides on the very steep slopes of this rugged mountain.

COMPARISONS OF SPECIES COMPOSITION AND SPECIES CHARACTERISTICS

Methods

The following sections compare species composition and characteristics of each flora. The comparisons are based on data summarized in the Appendix, and concern trees and shrubs only. The species lists derive from my own collections made in 1975, 1977 (Sugden 1982a), 1981 and 1982, from specimens in the national herbaria in Bogotá and Caracas and the herbaria of the Sociedad de Ciencias Naturales La Salle (Caracas) and the Proyecto Flora Falcón (Coro, Falcón), and from Johnston's (1909) flora of Margarita. Data on distribution and autecology are from specimens at the above herbaria and at Kew, and from local floras and monographs. Information on dispersal mechanisms are from published observations and considerations of fruit and seed morphology. The incidence of dioecy is estimated on the basis of existing knowledge of the taxa concerned.

Where appropriate, further comparisons are made with other wet tropical montane forests and insular floras.

Species composition

Of the ninety-eight species listed in the Appendix, forty occur on Macuira, twenty-four on Santa Ana, and fifty-six on Margarita. Six species (*Actinostemon concolor, Clusia rosea, Croton hircinus, Guapira fragrans, Miconia laevigata* and *Rapanea guianensis*) occur in all three localities; inclusive of these species, Santa Ana shares nine species with Margarita and nine with Macuira, and Macuira shares eleven species with Margarita. There are only seventeen species that occur on more than one of the mountains, and the floras may thus be considered as distinct assemblages (Sugden 1982b).

Geographical distribution

The flora of each mountain consists mainly of widely-distributed species, i.e. species whose distributions extend around all three mountains. Less than 30% of the species in each flora have distributions extending around only one or two of the mountains. The Margarita flora contains species known only from the Lesser Antilles, e.g. *Styrax glaber*, or from the Venezuelan Cordillera de la Costa, e.g. *Maytenus karstenii*. Santa Ana has two species, *Ilex truxillensis* and *Psychotria calciphila*, known only from the Cordillera de la Costa, as well as the miniature palm, *Geonoma paraguanensis*, that also occurs on the Sierra de San Luis, 80 km to the south. Narrowly-distributed species on Macuira include the shrub *Rudgea marginata*, known only from Colombia, and the tree *Stemmadenia minima*, otherwise known from Panama. Thus, no single source of derivation can be invoked for any of the floras.

Endemism

The three mountains support very few endemic species and no endemic genera. Endemic species on Margarita are *Blakea monticola* (Melastomataceae) *Inga macrantha* (Leguminosae) and *Bactris falcata* (Palmae); on Santa Ana, *Ardisia cuneata* (Myrsinaceae); on Macuira, *Cordia macuirensis* (Boraginaceae). The status of at least two of these species (*Cordia macuirensis* and *Bactris falcata*) as distinct taxa is in doubt (Sugden 1982b; J. Dransfield, pers. comm.).

Neotropical upper montane rain forests typically have higher levels of endemism. Specific endemism in vascular plants on Cerro Turumiquire (2600 m) and the mountains of the Paria Peninsula (1370 m), respectively south and southeast of Margarita, exceeds 10% of the total floras (Steyermark 1966, 1973, 1977); on the Sierra de San Luis (1500 m) the level is *c.* 6% (Steyermark 1975). On the Sierra Nevada de Santa Marta (5775 m), the underexplored, isolated massif 250 km southwest of Macuira, the level of specific endemism may be at least as high (e.g. Wurdack 1976). Of the sixty-seven trees and shrubs occurring in upper montane rain forest in Jamaica (Grubb & Tanner 1976), 54% are endemic to Jamaica (Adams 1972).

The low endemism on Macuira, Santa Ana and Margarita is more comparable to that of the moist uplands of the Galápagos islands, where the flora has apparently been recruited by long-distance dispersal (Porter 1976) over the last 10 000 years (Johnson & Raven 1973).

Ecological distribution

The floras contain large elements of species not noted for their restriction to moist montane forests. Most species on each mountain occur from near sea-level to at least 1000 m elsewhere in their geographical range, and some, e.g. *Rapanea guianensis*, extend from near sea-level to more than 2500 m. A few species, e.g. *Erythroxylon* spp, are exclusively lowland in their distribution, not normally occurring above 500 m.

Species confined to moist montane habitats are correspondingly few, accounting for 9%, 35% and 15% of the floras of Macuira, Santa Ana, and Margarita respectively.

The flora of Santa Ana thus appears to be the most specialized of the three, although it actually contains fewer montane forest 'specialists' than Margarita. Notable montane forest species are *Clusia cf. alata, C. multiflora, Ilex glaucophylla, I. truxillensis, Rapanea coriacea* and *Persea caerulea.*

More than 50% of the species in each flora (elsewhere in their range) occur in habitats subject to frequent or recent disturbance (forest gaps and edges, riverbanks, roadsides, cultivated land, etc.). A similar proportion occurs in relatively dry, seasonal habitats (deciduous woodlands, savanna, cerrado, etc.), though not in the very dry lowlands surrounding the isolated cloud forests. Species occuring in both wet disturbed and dry seasonal habitats include *Rapanea guianensis, Margaritaria nobilis, Casearia sylvestris, Chiococca alba, Oreopanax capitatum* and *Conostegia icosandra.* These habitats are unlike upper montane rain forest, where the frequency of natural disturbances and the light flux at the forest floor are low.

Lack of specialization, like low endemism, is uncharacteristic both of neotropical montane forests and older isolated habitats. Plants in the elfin forest on the summit of Pico del Este (1051 m), Puerto Rico, are 'clearly selected', and plants introduced to the forest from other habitats 'barely survive' (Howard 1970). The high levels of regional endemism in the low cloud forests of Panama (Lewis 1971), the montane forests of the Lesser Antilles (Beard 1949), and the coastal mountains of Venezuela (Steyermark 1979a) indicate greater ecological specialization. Lower levels of regional endemism and specialization have been observed in younger montane floras, for instance, in New Guinea (Johns 1976; Smith 1977). Endemism to particular vegetation types is pronounced in other isolated archipelago-like neotropical habitats, for instance on the Venezuelan *tepuis* (Steyermark 1979b), the *páramos* of the Andes (Cleef 1979), the *campinas* of lowland Amazonia (Macedo & Prance 1978; Anderson 1981), or the present-day forest refuges (the *brejos*) in northeastern Brasil (Andrade-Lima 1982).

A high frequency of species characteristic of successional habitats is a feature of young insular habitats. On Krakatau the vegetation appears to be in a state of arrested succession because climax species have not yet arrived on the island (Flenley & Richards 1982). The same may be true of the 'tropicalpine' vegetation of Mt Wilhelm, New Guinea (Smith 1977).

Dioecy

Species known to be dioecious account for 15%, 29% and 25% of the floras of Macuira, Santa Ana and Margarita respectively. If weighted by basal area contributions (see Tanner, 1982) these levels would be somewhat different; in particular, the level for Macuira would be increased because of the dominance of *Guapira fragrans* and *Rapanea guianensis* (Sugden 1982a), both of which are dioecious. The levels are similar to those in other neotropical montane forests; 21–36% of trees in Jamaican upper montane rain forest, and 31% of trees in a Venezuelan lower montane rain forest, are dioecious (Tanner 1982; Sobrevila & Kalin Arroyo 1982). Though such levels are perhaps high for young isolated habitats, in which obligate outbreeding systems are said to be disadvantageous (Ehrendorfer 1979), it is worth noting that dioecy is sometimes prevalent in species of successional habitats (e.g. Falinski 1980).

Dispersal

More than 80% of the species on each mountain show adaptations for endozoic bird dispersal (small-seeded berries, edible fleshy 'capsules', small arillate seeds, etc.). Four species on Macuira show no obvious adaptation, although they have small seeds, and two others may be dispersed externally by birds (Sugden 1982c). On Santa Ana, only *Weinmannia pinnata* and *Actinostemon concolor* show no obvious adaptation, while on Margarita there are several species with winged diaspores (*Tabebuia* spp, *Terminalia amazonia*, *Roupala montana*, *Melochia caracasana*) and three legumes for which bird dispersal is unlikely.

Unspecialized mechanisms for endozoic bird dispersal are prevalent in other wet tropical montane forests for which data are available (see Tanner, 1982, and references therein). In Jamaican upper montane rain forest, 82% of the tree species show adaptations for endozoochory (Tanner 1982); this mechanism also predominates in the moist uplands of Polynesia (Carlquist 1967) and the Galápagos islands (Porter 1976).

Migrant birds, both local and North American, may have been responsible for the introduction of most of the woody species of the Macuira cloud forest (Sugden 1982c). The same may be true for the woody floras of Santa Ana and Margarita. Yepez-Tamayo (1963) recorded more than thirty migrant taxa on Margarita, many of which are at least partially frugivorous. Migrants in the neotropics have a greater proportional impact, compared to residents, at fruiting trees on small islands and in montane forests than on large islands and in lowland forests (Orejuela, Raitt & Alvarez 1980; Leck 1972a,b). Also, there may be a tendency for fruits of a given species to be consumed by a greater proportion of the total bird species than in mainland habitats (Cruz 1981), thus providing more varied, if not greater, opportunities for dispersal.

DISCUSSION AND CONCLUSIONS

The foregoing shows that the cloud forests of Macuira, Santa Ana and Margarita are dissimilar in species number and composition but similar in species characteristics. They resemble other tropical upper montane rain forests in physiognomy, dispersal mechanisms and (at least superficially) in levels of dioecy, but differ markedly from these in the geographical and ecological distribution of their floristic elements. In endemism and autecology they are more similar to isolated habitats of recent origin than to older isolated habitats. Thus, while the species assemblages on each mountain are idiosyncratic, the biological characteristics of those species conform to similar patterns.

The differences in species number can be related at an intuitive level to the differences between the mountains summarized in Table 1. The low species number on Santa Ana, compared to Margarita, is probably due to its smaller area (1/20 of Margarita). Margarita has a higher species number than Macuira, although its forests cover just over half the area, and this may reflect greater edaphic variety and habitat diversity, and greater proximity to potential sources of colonizers. Nevertheless, it is impossible satisfactorily to separate the effects of these factors.

The differences in composition, on the other hand, cannot be explained in terms of the differences between the mountains, since the distribution and ecology of the majority of the species suggest a capacity for survival in any of the cloud forests. Where the few narrowly-distributed species are concerned, the floristic differences simply reflect geographical accident.

These findings lend weight to the earlier contention (Sugden 1982b) that random events of colonization have been important in determining species composition on the three mountains. A convincing explanation is nevertheless required for the relative paucity of montane forest 'specialists' in the cloud forests, given that such species tend to have propagules suitable for long-distance dispersal. The hypothesis of competitive exclusion on a priority basis (see Introduction) is unsatisfactory as it stands, but becomes more reasonable given the following considerations: (a) the chance of dispersal to a particular locality may be greater for successional species with wide natural distribution and ecological tolerance, since these species will be encountered more often by more dispersal agents than specialist species with restricted distribution; (b) removal rates of seeds may be higher in disturbed sites than in climax vegetation (Thompson & Willson 1978), and species richness of dispersal agents (birds) may be higher in forest gaps than in climax forest (Schemske & Brokaw 1981); (c) the fruiting seasons of successional and generalist species in the neotropics tend to be longer than those of specialist species of climax forest (Gómez-Pompa & Vasquez-Yanes 1976) and the seeds of pioneer species tend to be long-lived compared to those of mature forest species (Guevara-Sada & Gómez-Pompa 1976; Cheke, Nanakorn & Yankoses 1979; Bazzaz & Pickett 1980; Holthuijzen & Boerboom 1982); the long-lived seeds of gap colonists may be particularly suited to colonization of islands (Mabberley 1979). All of these factors would be expected to reduce the chances of successful colonization and establishment of specialist, climax forest species in new areas. Very little is known, however, about the ecology of establishment and regeneration in upper montane rain forests, and this area is ripe for further field investigations.

Finally, the importance must be stressed of considering suites of species characteristics in studies of the composition of insular floras. For instance, dioecy may be less disadvantageous for colonization of islands if it is associated with efficient dispersal mechanisms and unspecialized flowers suited to generalist pollinators (e.g. *Guapira fragrans*, *Rapanea guianensis*). Efficient dispersal mechanisms will not lead to wide distribution if ecological requirements are very precise. Had this been a survey of dispersal mechanisms and levels of dioecy alone, it might not have demonstrated any important differences between the isolated cloud forests of coastal Venezuela and Colombia and other upper montane rain forests.

ACKNOWLEDGMENTS

I repeat my thanks to all those acknowledged in Sugden (1982a) for assistance in Colombia. Fieldwork in Venezuela was financed under the Royal Society–CONICIT exchange agreement, and by grants from the Percy Sladen Memorial Fund and the Cory Fund. For valuable logistic and other help in Venezuela I am grateful to S.

Barreto, L. Castro, A. Colma, B. Garófalo, O. Huber, P. Henley, S. Matteucci, A. Rincon, E. Sosa, O. Walker and R. Wingfield, to the directors of the Herbario Nacional de Venezuela and the Sociedad de Ciencias Naturales La Salle, and to the Ministerio del Ambiente y de los Recursos Naturales Renovables (MARNR) and the Instituto Nacional de Parques (INPARQUES). D. Philcox, R. Harley and others at the Royal Botanic Gardens, Kew, assisted with the identification of plant material. Helpful comments on earlier drafts were provided by R. T. T. Forman, P. J. Grubb, D. J. Mabberley, P. W. Richards, E. V. J. Tanner, and F. White.

REFERENCES

Abbott, I. (1980). Theories dealing with the ecology of landbirds on islands. *Advances in Ecological Research*, **11**, 329–371.

Adams, C.D. (1972). *Flowering Plants of Jamaica*. University of the West Indies, Mona, Jamaica.

Anderson, A.B. (1981). White-sand vegetation of Brazilian Amazonia. *Biotropica*, **13**, 199–210.

Andrade-Lima, D. (1982). Present-day forest refuges in northeastern Brazil. *Biological Diversification in the Tropics* (Ed. by G. T. Prance), pp. 245–51. Columbia University Press, New York.

Bazzaz, F.A. & Pickett, S.T.A. (1980). Physiological ecology of tropical succession: a comparative review. *Annual Review of Ecology and Systematics*, **11**, 287–310.

Beard, J.S. (1949). *The Natural Vegetation of the Windward and Leeward Islands*. Oxford Forestry Memoirs, 21.

Bonatti, E. & Gartner, S. (1973). Caribbean climate during Pleistocene Ice Ages. *Nature*, **244**, 563–565.

Carlquist, S. (1967). The biota of long-distance dispersal. V. Plant dispersal to Pacific islands. *Bulletin of the Torrey Botanical Club*, **94**, 129–162.

Cheke, A.S., Nanakorn, W. & Yankoses, C. (1979). Dormancy and dispersal of seeds of secondary forest species under the canopy of a primary tropical rain forest in northern Thailand. *Biotropica*, **11**, 88–95.

Cleef, A.M. (1979). The phytogeographical position of the neotropical vascular páramo flora with special reference to the Colombian Cordillera Oriental. *Tropical Botany* (Ed. by K. Larsen & C. B. Holm-Nielsen), pp. 175–84. Academic Press, London.

Connor, E.F. & Simberloff, D.S. (1978). Species number and compositional similarity of the Galápagos flora and avifauna. *Ecological Monographs*, **48**, 219–248.

Connor, E.F. & Simberloff, D.S. (1979). The assembly of species communities: chance or competition? *Ecology*, **60**, 1132–1140.

Cruz, A. (1981). Bird activity and seed dispersal of a montane forest tree (*Dunalia arborescens*) in Jamaica. *Biotropica*, **13** (suppl.), 34–44.

Diamond, J.M., & Gilpin, M.E. (1982). Examination of the 'null' model of Connor and Simberloff for species co-occurrences on islands. *Oecologia*, **52**, 64–74.

Ehrendorfer, F. (1979). Reproductive biology in island plants. *Plants and Islands* (Ed. by D. Bramwell), pp. 293–306. Academic Press, London.

Falinski, J.B. (1980). Vegetation dynamics and sex structure of the population of pioneer dioecious woody plants. *Vegetatio*, **43**, 23–38.

Flenley, J.R. & Richards, K. (Eds) **(1982).** The Krakatoa Centenary Expedition. Final Report. *University of Hull Department of Geography Miscellaneous Series*, **25**, 1–196.

Frankel, O.H. & Soulé, M.E. (1981). *Conservation and Evolution*. Cambridge University Press, Cambridge.

Gilbert, F.S. (1980). The equilibrium theory of island biogeography: fact or fiction? *Journal of Biogeography*, **7**, 209–235.

Gómez-Pompa, A. & Vasquez-Yanes, C. (1976). Estudios sobre sucesión secundaria en los trópicos calidohumedos: el ciclo de vida de las especies secundarias. *Regeneración de Selvas* (Ed. by A. Gómez-Pompa, C. Vasquez-Yanes, S. del Amo & A. Butanda), pp. 579–93. Compañia Editorial Continental, Mexico.

Grant, P.R. & Abbott, I. (1980). Interspecific competition, island biogeography and null hypotheses. *Evolution*, **34**, 332–341.

Grubb, P.J. & Tanner, E.V.J. (1976). The montane forests and soils of Jamaica: a reassessment. *Journal of the Arnold Arboretum*, **57**, 313–368.

Guevara-Sada, S. & Gómez-Pompa, A. (1976). Determinación del contenido de semillas de suelo superficial de una selva tropical de Veracruz, Mexico. *Regeneración de Selvas* (Ed by A. Gómez-Pompa, C. Vasquez-Yanes, S. del Amo & A. Butanda), pp. 203–32. Compañia Editorial Continental Mexico.

Holthuijzen, A.M.A. & Boerboom, J.H.A. (1982). The *Cecropia* seedbank in the Surinam lowland rain forest. *Biotropica*, **14**, 62–68.

Howard, R.A. (1970). The 'Alpine' plants of the Antilles. *Biotropica*, **2**, 24–28.

Johns, R.J. (1976). A classification of the montane forests of Papua New Guinea. *Science in New Guinea*, **4**, 105–127.

Johnson, M.P. & Raven, P.H. (1973). Species number and endemism: the Galápagos archipelago revisited. *Science*, **179**, 893–895.

Johnston, J.R. (1909). *Flora of the Islands of Margarita and Coche, Venezuela.* Contributions of the Gray Herbarium, 37.

Koopman, K.F. (1958). Land bridges and ecology of bat distribution on islands off the northern coast of South America. *Evolution*, **12**, 429–439.

Lack, D. (1976). *Island Biology, Illustrated by the Land Birds of Jamaica.* Blackwell Scientific Publications, Oxford.

Leck, C.F. (1972a) Observations of birds at *Cecropia* trees in Puerto Rico. *Wilson Bulletin*, **84**, 498–500.

Leck, C.F. (1972b). The impact of some North American migrants at fruiting trees in Panama. *Auk*, **89**, 842–850.

Lewis, W.H. (1971). High floristic endemism in low cloud forests of Panama. *Biotropica*, **3**, 78–80.

Mabberley, D.J. (1979). Pachycaul plants and islands. *Plants and Islands* (Ed. by D. Bramwell), pp. 259–77. Academic Press, London.

Macedo, M. & Prance, G.T. (1978). Notes on the vegetation of Amazonia. II. The dispersal of plants in Amazonian white sand campinas: the campinas as functional islands. *Brittonia*, **30**, 203–215.

Morley, T. (1975). The South American distribution of the Memecyleae (Melastomataceae) in relation to the Guiana area and to the question of forest refuges in Amazonia. *Phytologia*, **31**, 279–296.

Myers, N. (1981). Conservation needs and opportunities in tropical moist forests. *The Biological Aspects of Rare Plant Conservation* (Ed. by H. Synge), pp. 141–52. John Wiley & Sons, Ltd, Chichester.

Orejuela, J.E., Raitt, R.J. & Alvarez, H. (1980). Differential use by North American migrants of three types of Colombian forests. *Migrant Birds in the Neotropics* (Ed. by A. Keast & E. S. Morton), pp. 253–64. Smithsonian Institution Press, Washington, D.C.

Porter, D.M. (1976). Geography and dispersal of Galápagos vascular plants. *Nature*, **264**, 745–746.

Pregill, G.K. & Olson, S.L. (1981). Zoogeography of West Indian vertebrates in relation to Pleistocene climatic cycles. *Annual Review of Ecology and Systematics*, **12**, 75–98.

Rieger, W. (1976). *Vegetationskundliche Untersuchungen der Guajira-Halbinsel (Nordost-Kolumbien).* Giessener Geographische Schriften, Heft 40.

Salgado-Labouriau, M.L. (1982). Climatic change at the Pleistocene–Holocene boundary. *Biological Diversification in the Tropics* (Ed. by G. T. Prance), pp. 74–77. Colombia University Press, New York.

Schemske, D.W. & Brokaw, N. (1981). Treefalls and the distribution of understory birds in a tropical forest. *Ecology*, **62**, 938–945.

Smith, J.M.B. (1977). Origins and ecology of the tropicalpine flora of Mt. Wilhelm, New Guinea. *Biological Journal of the Linnean Society*, **9**, 87–132.

Snow, D.W. (1965). A possible selective factor in the evolution of fruiting seasons in tropical forest. *Oikos*, **15**, 274–281.

Snow, D.W. (1981). Tropical frugivorous birds and their food plants: a world survey. *Biotropica*, **13**, 1–14.

Sobrevila, C. & Kalin Arroyo, M.T. (1982). Breeding systems in a montane tropical cloud forest in Venezuela. *Plant Systematics and Evolution*, **140**, 19–37.

Steyermark, J.A. (1966). El Cerro Turumiquire y la región oriental adyacente. *Acta Botanica Venezuelica*, **1** (3–4), 104–168.

Steyermark, J.A. (1973). Preservemos las cumbres de la Península de Paria. *Defensa de la Naturaleza*, **Año 2**, 33–35.

Steyermark, J.A. (1975). Flora de la Sierra de San Luis (Estado Falcón, Venezuela) y sus afinidades fitogeográficas. *Acta Botanica Venezuelica*, **10**, 131–218.

Steyermark, J.A. (1977). Future outlook for threatened and endangered species in Venezuela. *Extinction is Forever* (Ed. by G. T. Prance), pp. 128–35. New York Botanical Garden, New York.

Steyermark, J.A. (1979a). Plant refuge and dispersal centres in Venezuela: their relict and endemic element. *Tropical Botany* (Ed. by K. Larsen & C. B. Holm-Nielsen), pp. 185–221. Academic Press, London.

Steyermark, J.A. (1979b). Flora of the Guayana highland: endemicity of the generic flora of the summits of the Venezuelan tepuis. *Taxon*, **28**, 45–54.

Sugden, A.M. (1982a). The vegetation of the Serranía de Macuira, Guajira, Colombia: a contrast of arid lowlands and an isolated cloud forest. *Journal of the Arnold Arboretum*, **63**, 1–30.

Sugden, A.M. (1982b). The ecological, geographical and taxonomic relationships of an isolated Colombian cloud forest, with some implications for island biogeography. *Journal of the Arnold Arboretum*, **63**, 31–61.

Sugden, A.M. (1982c). Long-distance dispersal and the cloud forest flora of the Serranía de Macuira, Guajira, Colombia. *Biotropica*, **14**, 208–219.

Tamayo, F. (1941). Exploraciones botánicas en la Península de Paraguaná, Estado Falcón. *Boletin de la Sociedad Venezolana de Ciencias Naturales*, **7**, 1–90.

Tanner, E.V.J. (1982). Species diversity and reproductive mechanisms in Jamaican trees. *Biological Journal of the Linnean Society*, **18**, 263–278.

Taylor, G.C. (1960). *Geology of the island of Margarita, Venezuela*. Ph.D. thesis, Princeton University, Princeton.

Terborgh, J. (1975). Faunal equilibria and the design of wildlife preserves. *Tropical Ecological Systems: Trends in Terrestrial and Aquatic Research* (Ed. by F. Golley & E. Medina), pp. 369–80. Springer-Verlag, New York.

Thompson, J.N. & Willson, M.F. (1978). Disturbance and the dispersal of fleshy fruits. *Science*, **200**, 1161–1163.

Whitmore, T.C. (1975). *Tropical Rain Forests of the Far East*. Clarendon Press, Oxford.

Wilcox, B.A. (1980). Insular ecology and conservation. *Conservation Biology—an Evolutionary-Ecological Perspective* (Ed. by M. E. Soulé & B. A. Wilcox), pp. 95–118. Sinauer Associates, Sunderland, Massachusetts.

Williamson, M. (1981). *Island Populations*. Oxford University Press, Oxford.

Willis, E.O. (1966). Competitive exclusion and birds at fruiting trees in western Colombia. *Auk*, **83**, 479–480.

Wright, S.J. & Biehl, C.C. (1982). Island biogeographic distributions: testing for random, regular, and aggregated patterns of species occurrence. *American Naturalist*, **119**, 345–357.

Wurdack, J.J. (1976). Endemic Melastomataceae of the Sierra Nevada de Santa Marta, Colombia. *Brittonia*, **28**, 138–143.

Yepez Tamayo, G. (1963). Ornitología de las Islas Margarita, Coche, y Cubagua (Venezuela). Primera parte. *Memorias de la Sociedad de Ciencias Naturales La Salle*, **23** (65), 75–112.

APPENDIX

Trees and shrubs of the cloud forests of the Serranía de Macuira, Cerro Santa Ana, and the western mountains of Margarita Island.

Column 1: Occurrence of each species on the three mountains. 1 = Macuira; 2 = Santa Ana; 3 = Margarita.

Column 2: Geographical distribution. C = Pan-Caribbean; CC = Cordillera de la Costa, Venezuela; Col = Colombia; E = Endemic; GA = Greater Antilles; Gal = Galapagos; LA = Lesser Antilles; M = Mainland neotropics; N = Neotropical; NSA = Northern South America; P = Pantropical; Pan = Panama; SA = Tropical South America; SSL = Sierra de San Luis, Venezuela; TT = Trinidad & Tobago; U = Uncertain; Ven = Venezuela; WI = West Indies.

Column 3: Altitudinal range (m).

Column 4: Occurrence in disturbed and early successional habitats (only for species where data are sufficient and reliable).

Column 5: Incidence of dioecy.

Column 6: Likely mode of long-distance dispersal. 1 = birds, endozoic; 2 = birds, ectozoic; 3 = wind; U = uncertain.

	1	2	3	4	5	6
Acanthaceae						
Aphelandra pulcherrima (Jacq.) H.B.K.	1	M	0–1800			2 (Sugden 1982c)
Ruellia macrophylla Vahl	1	SA, GA	100–1400			2 (Sugden 1982c)
Amaranthaceae						
Alternanthera pubiflora (Benth.) Kuntze	1	M	0–3000	+		1 (Sugden 1982c
Chamissoa altissima H.B.K.	1	N	0–2000	+		1 (Sugden 1982c
Aquifoliaceae						
Ilex glaucophylla Steyermark	3	CC	1100–1500		+	1 (Snow 1981)
I. sideroxyloides (Sw.) Griseb.	3	WI	100–1400		+	1 (Snow 1981)
I. truxillensis Turcz. (sp. aff.)	2	CC	600–1400		+	1 (Snow 1981)
Apocynaceae						
Stemmadenia minima A. Gentry	1	Pan.	800–1000			1 (Snow 1981)
Araliaceae						
Dendropanax arboreum (L.) Dec. & Planch.	1,3	C	0–2100		+	1 (Lack 1976)
Oreopanax capitatum (Jacq.) Dec. & Planch.	2,3	N	100–2400		+	1 (Snow 1981)
Bignoniaceae						
Tabebuia chrysantha Nichols.	3	M	100–1600		+	3
T. serratifolia (Vahl) Nichols.	3	SA	0–1000		+	U
Boraginaceae						
Cordia macuirensis Dugand & I. M. Johnst.	1	E	600–900			1 (Snow 1981)
C. polycephala (Lam.) I. M. Johnst.	3	N	100–1300		+	1 (Snow 1981)
Tournefortia hirsutissima L.	3	N	0–2300		+	1 (Snow 1981)
T. volubilis L.	3	N	0–1500		+	1 (Snow 1981)
Celastraceae						
Maytenus karstenii (Kl.) Reiss.	3	CC	0–2300		+	1
Chrysobalanaceae						
Licania membranacea Sagot	3	NSA, TT	0–900			U
Clusiaceae						
Clusia cf. *alata* Planch. & Triana	3	SA	1300–2500		+	1 (Snow 1981)
C. cf. *flava* Jacq.	3	WI	0–1500		+	1 (Snow 1981)
C. multiflora H.B.K.	2	SA	1800–3300		+	1 (Snow 1981)
C. rosea Jacq.	1,2,3	C	0–2000		+	1 (Lack 1976)
Combretaceae						
Terminalia amazonia (Gmel.) Exell	3	M	0–1100		+	U
Compositae						
sp. indet.	1					3
Cunoniaceae						
Weinmannia pinnata L.	2	C	800–3000			U
Ericaceae						
Vaccinium latifolium Benth. & Hook. f.	3	LA	600–1200			1
Erythroxylaceae						
Erythroxylon cumanense H.B.K.	3	NSA	0–200	+		1
E. havanense Jacq.	3	C	100–400	+		1

Euphorbiaceae						
Acalypha diversifolia Jacq.	1	M	0–2100	+		U
Actinostemon concolor (Spreng.) Muell.-Arg.	1,2,3	CC, LA	0–700	+		U
Croton hircinus Vent.	1,2,3	LA, NSA, Pan.	100–1300	+		1
C. xanthochloros Croizat	3	Ven.	0–1500	+		U
Euphorbia cotinifolia L.	1	SA	U	+		U
Margaritaria nobilis L.f.	1,3	N	0–1300	+	+	1 (Snow 1981)
Flacourtiaceae						
Casearia sylvestris Sw.	3	N	0–2300	+		1 (Snow 1981)
Lauraceae						
Nectandra coriacea (Sw.) Griseb.	3	WI	0–1000	+		1 (Snow 1981)
Persea caerulea (Ruiz & Pav.) Mez	1,2	M	500–2000	+		1 (Snow 1981)
Phoebe cinnamomifolia (H.B.K.) Nees	3	SA	1000–2000	+		1
Leguminosae						
Calliandra surinamensis Benth. (sp. aff.)	3	SA	0–500	+		U
Cassia fruticosa Mill.	3	SA	0–1700	+		U
Inga macrantha J. R. Johnst.	3	E	600–800			U
Malvaceae						
Malvaviscus arboreus Cav.	1	N	0–3000	+		U
Melastomataceae						
Blakea monticola J. R. Johnst.	3	E	600–900			1
Conostegia icosandra (Sw.) Urban	1,2	C	0–1900	+		1 (Willis 1966)
Miconia acinodendron (L.) Sweet	1	SA	0–1700	+		1 (Snow 1965)
M. laevigata (L.) DC.	1,2,3	C	0–2400	+		1 (Snow 1981)
M. mirabilis (Aubl.) L. O. Wms.	2	SA, LA	0–1900	+		1 (Snow 1981)
M. prasina DC.	3	N	0–900	+		1 (Snow 1981)
Mouriri rhizophoraefolia (DC.) Triana	1	CC, TT	100–700			1 (Morley 1975)
Moraceae						
Cecropia peltata L.	1,3	C	0–1500	+	+	1 (Snow 1981)
Ficus nymphaeifolia P. Miller	3	N	0–2300	+		1
F. yoponensis Desv	3	M	0–1500	+		1
F. perforata L.	1	N	0–1200	+		1 (Lack 1976)
Myrsinaceae						
Ardisia cuneata Lundell	2	E	600–800			1 (Snow 1981)
Rapanea coriacea Sw.	2	N	800–3300	+	+	1
R. guianensis Aubl.	1,2,3	N	0–3500	+	+	1 (Sugden 1982c)
Myrtaceae						
Myrcia coriacea DC.	3	U	U			1 (Snow 1981)
M. fallax (Rich.) DC.	1	N	100–2200	+		1 (Snow 1981)
M. splendens (Sw.) DC.	1	N	U			1 (Snow 1981)
Myrcianthes cf. *compressa* (H.B.K.) McV	3	CC	1500–2000			1
M. fragrans (Sw.) McV.	1,2	C	0–2500			1 (Sugden 1982c)
Siphoneugena densiflora Berg	2	U	600–2400	+		1
Nyctaginaceae						
Guapira fragrans (Dum.-Cours.) Little	1,2,3	C	0–900		+	1 (Lack 1976)
G. olfersiana (L., K. & O.) Lundell	3	NSA	U		+	1
Pisonia aculeata L.	3	P	0–700	+	+	1 (Snow 1981)
Ochnaceae						
Ouratea guildingii (Planch.) Urban	3	CC, LA	0–250			1
O. nitida (Sw.) Engler	1	C	0–300			1 (Sugden 1982c)
Oleaceae						
Linociera caribaea (Jacq.) Knobl.	3	C	0–900			1

Palmae
Acrocomia sclerocarpa Mart.	3	U	U			U
Bactris falcata J. R. Johnst.	3	E	600–900			1 (Snow 1981)
Euterpe karsteniana Engel	2,3	Col., Ven.	700–1400			1 (Snow 1981)
Geonoma paraguanensis Karst.	2	SSL	700–1400			1 (Snow 1981)
G. pinnatifrons Willd.	3	CC, LA	500–2200			1 (Snow 1981)

Piperaceae
Piper sp.	1					U

Polygonaceae
Coccoloba coronata Jacq.	1	LA, NSA, Pan.	0–800	+	+	1 (Sugden 1982c)

Portulacaceae
Talinum paniculatum (Jacq.) Gaertn.	1	N	400–3000			1 (Sugden 1982c)

Proteaceae
Roupala montana Aubl.	3	N	300–2300	+		U

Rubiaceae
Chiococca alba (L.) Hitch.	1,3	N	0–2000	+		1 (Snow 1981)
Genipa spruceana Steyermark	1	SA	0–600	+		1 (Snow 1981)
Gonzalagunia spicata (Lam.) Gómez	3	SA, WI	100–400			1 (Snow 1981)
Guettarda divaricata (H. & B.) Standl.	1	Col, Ven.	U			1 (Sugden 1982c)
G. scabra (L.) Vent.	3	WI	U			1
Psychotia alba Ruiz & Pav.	1,3	M	0–2300			1 (Snow 1981)
P. barbiflora A. DC.	1	SA, Gal.	0–1500	+		1 (Snow 1981)
P. calciphila Steyermark	2	CC	1000–1400			1 (Snow 1981)
P. deflexa DC.	2	N	0–1400			1 (Snow 1981)
P. horizontalis Sw.	2	N	400–1300	+		1 (Snow 1981)
P. muscosa (Jacq.) Steyermark	3	SA	500–1100			1 (Snow 1981)
P. nervosa Sw.	1	C	0–1500			1 (Snow 1981)
Randia formosa (Jacq.) Schum.	1	SA, LA	0–900	+		1 (Sugden 1982c)
Rudgea marginata Standl.	1	Col.	100–800			1 (Snow 1981)

Rutaceae
Esenbeckia grandiflora Mart.	3	SA	0–1600			U

Solanaceae
Cestrum alternifolium (Jacq.) O. E. Schulz	1	CA, LA, NSA	0–1800	+		1 (Sugden 1982c)

Sterculiaceae
Melochia caracasana Jacq.	3	CC	0–1000			U

Styracaceae
Styrax glaber Sw.	3	LA	100–800			1

Thymeleaceae
Daphnopsis americana (Mill.) J. R. Johnst.	2,3	C	400–1800	+	+	1

Verbenaceae
Citharexylum fruticosum L.	2	WI, SA	100–400			1 (Snow 1981)

Violaceae
Rinorea lindeniana (Tul.) Kuntze	3	SA	100–1400	+		U

PART I

B · ANIMALS, MAINLY INSECTS

Beetles and other insects of tropical forest canopies at Manaus, Brazil, sampled by insecticidal fogging

TERRY L. ERWIN

Department of Entomology, National Museum of Natural History,
Smithsonian Institution, Washington, D.C. 20560

SUMMARY

Data gathered from canopy insect samples taken by a fogging technique indicate that a high percentage of species are confined to one type of forest. Of the forest types in the Manaus, Brazil area, the Mixed-water inundation forest is richest in species, the White-water inundation forest is richest in numbers of individuals. The Terra firme, or non-flooded forest, contains the highest number of restricted species. The White-water forest species are on average larger than species of the other three forest types studied; the species of the Terra firme forest are the smallest. In all forests, 97% of the beetle species are less than 8 mm total length. Herbivores are the largest species, fungivores the smallest. Weevils and leaf-beetles (Curculionidae and Chrysomelidae) are by far the dominant forms of beetle life in the canopy. However, in all samples in all forests thus far fogged, Formicidae (ants) are dominant in number of individuals and biomass.

INTRODUCTION

Results and conclusions drawn from any field study must be considered in the light of the adequacy of methods utilized. Large scale and/or complicated studies often suffer from becoming more an experiment with tools than data gathering on the biota. Misleading data from sloppy (but at first glance sophisticated) field work results first in errors in the original paper, which then, by citation, ripple through subsequent works for years. Not only must we guard against accepting such data from others, we must strive to make our own experiments in the field conform to sound ecological principles, despite the difficulty of doing so under often adverse conditions. The purpose of the present paper is to document the history of the canopy fogging technique as used in the neotropics by certain workers and how that technique has evolved into a reliable tool for canopy arthropod studies. The second purpose is to draw attention to data and analyses previously published concerning canopy beetles of Panama and contrast them with new data from the Amazon Basin. Both geographic areas were studied with a primitive fogging technique, nonetheless certain aspects are scientifically interesting. Data concerning canopy arthropods of south-eastern Peru gathered with a much improved fogging technique are presently under analysis and will be reported in a separate paper.

This later study is designed to gather materials in such a way that current and future studies are enhanced to a maximum degree satisfying what Raven, in a public address to the International Council of Museums (Mexico City, 1980), called a need to 'record coexistence and to be able to retrieve, for study, whole groups of organisms that occurred together for further analysis.'

MATERIAL AND METHODS

Processing of insect samples

Acquisition of material is described below. All Coleoptera and other insects discussed herein were prepared by the Smithsonian Institution Insect Sorting Center at San Jose State University in California, under the supervision of J. Gordon Edwards. Subsequent to preparation, Janice Scott labelled and alpha-sorted all material to morphospecies; final checking was done by me, my colleague Warren Steiner, and the USDA Coleopterists of the Systematic Entomology Laboratory in Washington (Anderson, Gordon, Kingsolver, Spilman, White and Whitehead). Scott, Gloria House, and Linda Sims measured all species by selecting the largest and smallest individuals in a morphospecies series to provide a range and then assigned each to a size class. Trophic levels were determined through consultation with many coleopterists. For further details, see Erwin & Scott (1980).

Methods of canopy fogging

The first attempt at true fogging of forest canopies seems to have been that of Roberts (1973). Others (Martin 1966; Gagné & Martin 1968) had earlier obtained canopy samples with hydraulic sprayers, but later Gagné (1979; based on work done in 1973) switched to the use of the resonant pulse fogger. Roberts' (1973) discussion of field methods describes almost exactly the techniques of Montgomery and Lubin in the first fogging of lowland seasonal forest in Panama and subsequent studies in Venezuela and Brazil. The only difference was the adaptation by them of Gagné's (1979) use of a Dyna-fog machine and suspended cloth sheets for the collection of insect-rain. For later studies, Montgomery ran the suspended sheets along a 50-m transect with sheets paired and the fogger hoisted four or five times along and over the transect. For the last study of Manaus operated by Montgomery (August, 1979), I introduced moulded plastic funnel trays (Fig. 1) with 4 oz Nalgene collecting bottles in place of the cloth sheets, in order to protect the more delicate species which were previously damaged using the suspended sheet technique. These plastic trays also served for better assessment of which insect species fell from which tree because they were more easily positioned. However, these trays were very heavy and difficult to transport far from roads or boat moorings; they also were too shallow and brushing was required to get specimens into the bottles, thus some damage and loss still occurred. Numerous problems with the modified Roberts' technique resulted in samples that could only be analysed in a general way (Erwin & Scott 1980; Erwin 1981). These problems were: (i) wind drift of the insecticide fog away from the transect so that some trays or sheets had

surveyed and marked; perpendicularly, at the middle of each side, a 15-m line is marked off. With the aid of a line-throwing gun (Fig. 3), pulleys are placed as high as possible in the four trees and to the outside of the plot (not directly over it). Over these pulleys, 'pull-up' ropes are set and tied off for hoisting the fogger during fogging

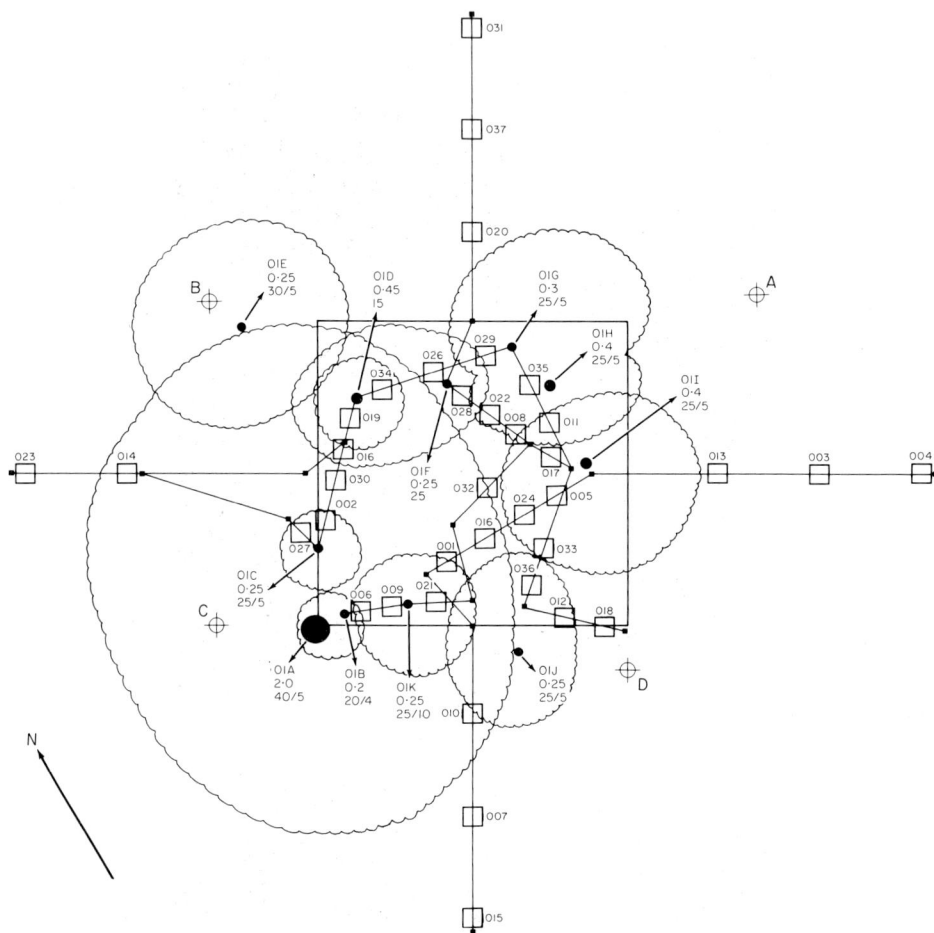

FIG. 2. Configuration of plot for canopy sampling at Tambopata Reserve, Peru, showing assigned tree numbers/letters, tray numbers, tree dbh and canopy height/depth, and fogger pull-up sites (letters A–D). Plot size equals 12 × 12 m, tray size equals 1 m².

operations. Within the plot area of 144 m² lines are tied horizontally between trees in a non-arbitrary way at about 2 m height. Arrangement of trays (Fig. 2) is scattered depending upon availability and position of trees on which to tie the support lines. On these 'clothes-lines' are suspended twenty-five trays (Fig. 4), each 1 m² in surface area relative to the ground, as sampling surfaces to catch the 'rain' of dead insects after fogging the canopy. The trays are collapsible plastic with square aluminium frames and are funnel-form; at the bottom of the funnel is screwed a 4 oz Nalgene bottle with 70% alcohol preservative. Outside the plot area, perpendicular to each side, are strung three additional trays at 5-m intervals (Fig. 2) to catch individuals which leave the fogged area before dying and dropping. In addition, these outlier trays collect wind drift should there be any, thus providing a measure of the success rate of capture within the

FIG. 3. Line-throwing gun used to establish rope and pulley system in canopy. Adapted fishing reel aids in line retrieval.

plot area, and also telling something of the kind of species with higher escape capabilities. Other tests of internal consistency are run at selected sites; e.g. sites are refogged a few days later to determine recolonization and recruitment, drop times are duplicated sequentially, and branches are shaken after initial samples are bottled to see how much of the biota is left lying on leaf surfaces or on branch tops. Special collecting trays for rainy season samples are now under design; during a fogging operation a sudden downpour will instantly fill the plastic tray with water and wash away specimens, thus ruining several days work.

Once the set-up is in order for fogging, preparations are made to return to the site early the next day when there is little or no wind blowing and warm air is rising from the forest floor. Although the commercial Dyna-fog machine is normally hand-operated, I attach a small radio-controlled servo unit to the on/off lever so that the machine can be automatically turned on while up in the canopy. The radio-controlled fogging machine is started and hoisted into the canopy; at 15 m above the forest floor the fog is turned on by the radio and it is run for 1 min at a dial setting of '5' (density of fog). The process is

Fig. 4. Plot fogging technique used in Tambopata, Peru, showing foldable plastic sampling trays suspended in Terra firme forest.

repeated at each of the four corners. Formulation of the insecticide is set to provide 40 000 cubic metres of fog during this 4-min period, thus completely over-fogging the amount of canopy available in the plot (about 3–4000 m³). The fogger is moved vertically above 15 m and rotated 90° at each of the four pull-ups (Fig. 5). In this way, the entire 4000 m³ of canopy receives an even amount of insecticide fog and is overfogged enough to make up for any special circumstances, e.g. deeper canopy, denser foliage, wind, or pull-up lines being slightly away from corners, etc. It is the 'over-fog' capability which allows comparisons between samples; replicate series are a back-up to confirm that samples are comparable. Drop-time is 3 hours from the end of fogging at each plot. Material is then collected from the trays and subsequently transferred from 4 oz bottles to 4 dram vials for return to the processing laboratory in Washington. Measures are made electronically (Erwin 1978) and all data (including species numbers, counts, and measures, and all information about tree sizes and positions, species, and ages) are stored as computer readable and accessible. The number of plots needed per forest type to assure adequate coverage of tree species present is determined using a planned transect method (Scott Mori, pers. comm.) and a survey system like that of Hubbell & Foster (1983). Concurrent recolonization studies to assess faunal recovery in previously fogged canopy are under way and will be presented separately.

FIG. 5. Radio-controlled Dyna-fog machine in canopy being rotated through 90° angle.

Protocol for sampling regime

Forests for sampling are selected at reserves or near research stations where logistics are not overwhelmingly complicated. The amount of field gear and personnel needed for this kind of project are considerable and certain transportation requirements can be found only in areas accustomed to large scientific expeditions. Sites at each forest are selected by visual observation of canopy and understorey conditions with regard again to logistics of operating machinery and also maturity or type of forests, remoteness from homes or settlements and remoteness to other long-term study sites where living insects are being studied.

FAUNA OF EARLY DRY SEASON (WITH INUNDATION) OF FOUR TYPES OF FOREST AT MANAUS, BRAZIL

Erwin & Scott (1980) provided an analysis of the Coleoptera fauna of a single species of canopy tree in lowland seasonal forest of Panama. Although the fogging technique was in a primitive state of development, certain aspects of the fauna could be ascertained. Similarly, samples from the second large study at Manaus (August–September, 1979) could be analysed in a general way. Results and data from this second study are here presented for the first time.

All histograms and tables herein are based on analyses of 49% of the trays in ten 50-m transects, three in each of the Black-water inundation forest, Mixed-water inundation forest, Terra firme forest, and one in the White-water inundation forest. Replicate transects within each forest type were proximate to each other, not more than 1000 m distance. All sites are within 70 km of Manaus (Fig. 6) and were fogged in the early dry season when the rivers were beginning to subside, but the forests were still completely inundated. The inundation forest types are fully described by Adis (1981); Beck (1969, 1971); Irmler (1975, 1977); and Prance (1979). Ranzani (1980) described the soils of the Terra firme fogging site. Beck (1971) described the Terra firme forest at Reserva Ducke near Manaus, similar visually to that fogged some 40 km north, but no description of the fogged forest as such exists. Figure 7 shows the total number of adult and immature insects (usually prepared by pinning, the alcohol specimens are not yet counted) in ascending order of quantity. Hymenoptera, excluding ants, rank only third behind Coleoptera and Homoptera; however, as in all samples since those in Panama taken in 1974, ants are dominant in the canopy, both in numbers and in biomass. Ants are certainly the force to be reckoned with in the tropics. Field observations and preliminary counts of Peruvian samples recently obtained uphold these figures, with the exception that Diptera (ranked fourth in Manaus) seems to be most dominant, at least in the rainy season samples. Ants constitute one-sixth of the arthropods in rainy season samples of the young Terra firme forest at Tambopata, Peru.

Figure 8 shows the number and percentage of adult and immature insects per forest type. Based on extrapolation to 100% of the samples, the single sample from the White-water system is lower than any other forest, but only slightly lower than the Black-water; Mixed-water is considerably higher than all other samples; and the Terra firme forest is intermediate. Figure 9, also based on extrapolation to 100% of the samples, shows nearly the same for adult Coleoptera, except Black-water is slightly lower than White-water and Mixed-water is by far higher than any other forest type. Figure 6 shows the geographical location of the fogging sites with respect to Manaus and each other. In addition, Fig. 6 presents graphically data given in Tables 1 and 2. Species restriction to each forest is marked and very few species are shared among combined samples of transects in more than two types of forest. Table 1 shows that fully 83% of the beetle species are restricted to one type of forest in the dry season; only 14% are shared between two forest types and 3% among three or more forest types. Table 2 shows that of the 83% restricted species of beetles, most are found in the Terra firme forest, least in the White-water forest.

With regard to sizes of individuals of beetle species in the different forest types see Fig. 10 and Tables 3 and 4. Terra firme forest appears to have more species of smaller size, peaking at 1 mm, and it also contains the largest species; the larger size classes appear to be rather regular, thus the 'curve' is more or less a regular sigmoid one. All other forest types have a peak at 2 mm with many fewer species in the 1 mm class, the

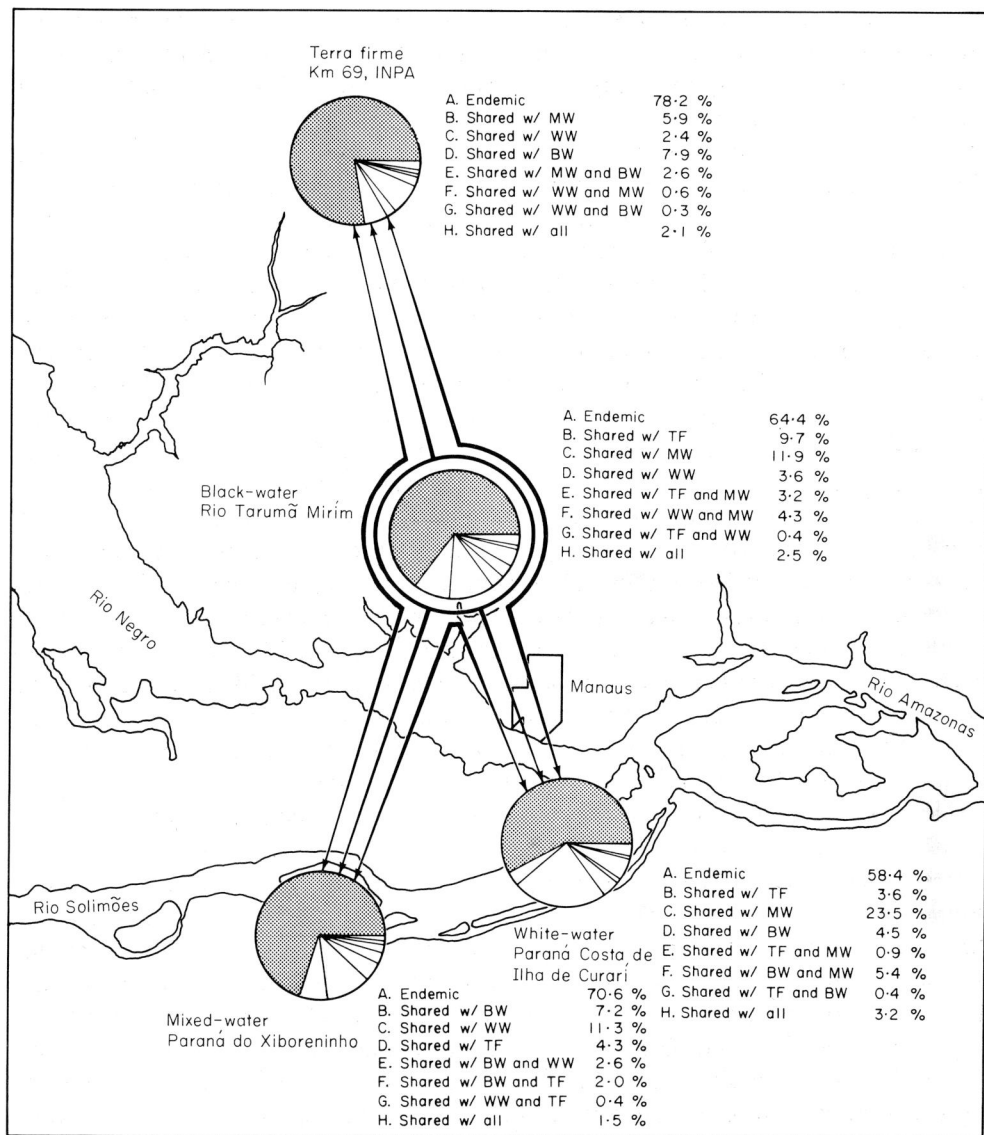

FIG. 6. Coleoptera species shared between and among forest types at Manaus, Brazil, overlain on generalized map of area showing location of fogging transects. Percentage of total fauna shared among forest types is represented by pie diagrams which are to be read counterclockwise beginning with larger shaded area as 'A'.

Mixed-water having the most, and White-water the least. Both the Mixed and Black-water forests have a very irregular occurrence of larger size classes; but the White-water is not too irregular. The Mixed-water forest has a higher proportion of 3 mm size class; the White-water has a paucity of species in the 5 mm size class; the Black-water 'curve' flattens out between 5 and 7 mm, unlike that of any other forest.

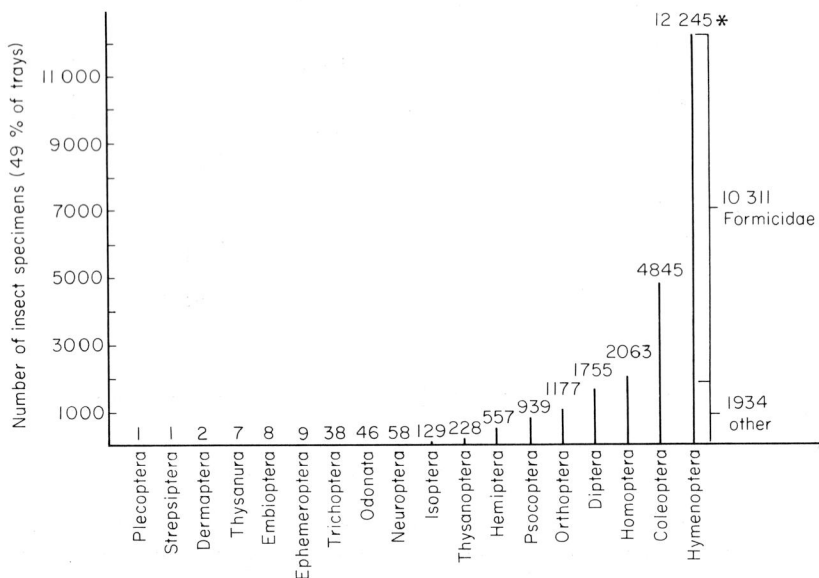

FIG. 7. Insect specimens fogged from four types of forest at Manaus, Brazil, arranged by Order with numbers of each*. Hymenoptera was highest due to a great number of ants.

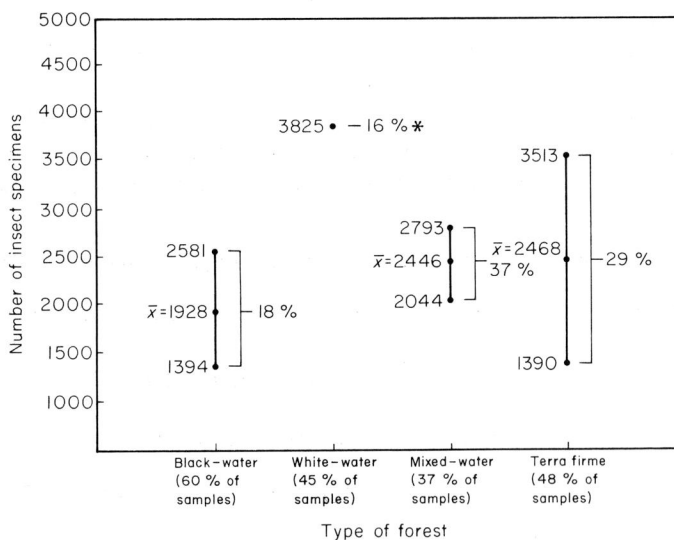

FIG. 8. Insect specimens fogged from four types of forest at Manaus, Brazil, with range, mean, and percentage of total catch*. White-water forest was sampled only along one transect.

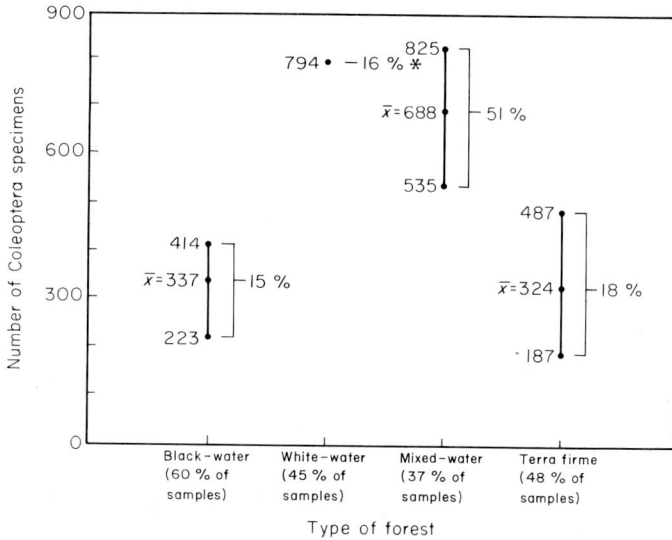

FIG. 9. Adult Coleoptera specimens fogged from four types of forest at Manaus, Brazil, with range, mean, and percentage of total catch*. White-water forest was sampled only along one transect.

Table 3 shows that smallest beetles occur in the Terra firme, the largest in the White-water forests. Table 4 indicates that 54% of all species in all forests are 2 mm or less, and 97% of all species sampled are 8 mm or less. Further testing of the methods in Peru will need to be done to see if large species so notable in tropical forest are non-canopy species or whether the scarcity of larger size classes in our samples is simply because fogging does not bring them down.

Tables 5 and 6 provide information on the trophic levels of adult Coleoptera species of the canopy. Table 6 lists all families in four general trophic classes; within each class families are listed in descending order of mean length, except the subfamilies

TABLE 1. Distribution of adult Coleoptera species among four forest types at Manaus

Restricted, one forest	Shared, two forests	Shared, three forests	Shared, four forests
83%	14%	2%	1%

Total species: 1080; total specimens: 24 350.

TABLE 2. Distribution (%) of restricted Coleoptera from Table 1

Forest type	Restricted species	Percentage of total
Black-water forest	179	20
White-water forest	129	14
Mixed-water forest	325	30
Terra firme forest	266	36
Total	899	

TABLE 6. (*cont.*)

Tropic group (family:subfamily)	Mean length (mm)	No. of species
Scolytidae	1·67	12
Languriidae	1·33	3
Anobiidae	1·25	36
Phalacridae	1·17	12
Scavengers		
Tenebrionidae	4·17	57
Ptinidae	2·00	1
Nitidulidae	1·94	16
Anthicidae	1·69	13
Dermestidae	1·00	6
Euglenidae	1·00	6
Hydrophilidae	1·00	1
Fungivores		
Anthribidae	3·50	6
Platypodidae	2·50	4
Endomychidae	2·17	6
Erotylidae	1·67	3
Lathridiidae	1·00	3
Pselaphidae	1·00	3
Scaphidiidae	1·00	1
Biphyllidae	1·00	1
Ciidae	1·00	1
Eucinetidae	1·00	1
Predators		
Lampyridae	9·57	7
Lycidae	6·38	4
Cleridae	5·30	5
Eucnemidae	3·33	3
Carabidae	3·23	13
Ostomatidae	3·00	1
Trogossitidae	3·00	4
Staphylinidae	2·67	35
Melyridae	2·00	2
Rhizophagidae	2·00	1
Coccinellidae	1·66	50
Colydiidae	1·60	5
Cucujidae	1·60	5
Histeridae	1·50	2
Corylophidae	1·00	7
Scydmaenidae	1·00	1
Unknown food requirements		
Chelonariidae	1·00	1
Clambidae	1·00	4
Discolomidae	1·00	1
Nonidentifiable families		5

of Curculionidae and Chrysomelidae which are listed in alphabetical order. In addition the number of species is given for each family. Table 5 shows that herbivores are the largest and fungivores the smallest in terms of mean size of individuals. It should be noted however, that family trophic assignments are based on best-estimates of material collected with full recognition that some families have diverse food preferences among species.

CONCLUSIONS

The most important conclusion to be drawn from the data presented above is a substantiation of the prediction (Erwin 1981; Erwin & Adis 1982) that tropical canopy species have low powers of vagility, thus are found restricted to forest types. Of the 1080 species of adult Coleoptera here analysed, 83% are restricted to one kind of forest ('endemics' of Fig. 6), 14% are restricted to two forest types. This clearly supports the prediction that there may be as many as 30 000 000 species of insects in the world (Erwin 1982), given the number of forest types in the Amazon Basin alone. It is also of importance when setting aside tracts of land for conservation to know that in terms of insects, at least, geographically small biotypes are unique to thousands of species.

Another major finding is that the Mixed-water forest is the richest by far in species of insects indicating its general richness in other biota and its probable higher nutritional state in comparison with other forest types. However, the Terra firme is the richest in terms of restricted species and second richest in numbers of species, and the White-water (based on one transect) is the richest in terms of individuals. The richness of restricted species in the Terra firme forest is perhaps explained partly by the fact that this type of forest seems to carry a higher load of smaller species (1 mm class, see Fig. 10); another possible explanation is the susceptibility of Terra firme forests to refugial-breakup during the Tertiary (Prance 1982a). The richness of individuals in the White-water is possibly due to the disturbed nature of the habitat and its continuous distribution over large distances (rivers of the Amazon Basin). The White-water system is in a constant state of flux during flooding and probably acts like a pioneer community, thus a few species produce high numbers of dispersants; note also that small beetles, those with potentially greater dispersal problems, are relatively few in this habitat, whereas the Terra firme has the highest number of small species. The White-water forest is lowest among the four in terms of species, although the numbers recorded here are based on a single transect and must be regarded as tentative. The plants in this transect however, are more continuously distributed over wide areas (i.e. along White-water riverine systems and gallery forests away from Amazonia proper) than are plants of the other types of forest (Prance 1982b); thus, it is likely that insect species of this habitat too are more widespread.

Among adult Coleoptera, first the Curculionidae and then Chrysomelidae are the dominant forms of canopy life. No other groups in any trophic level approach the richness of species of these two families. Tenebrionidae are the dominant scavengers, Anthribidae and Endomychidae the dominant fungivores, and Coccinellidae and Staphylinidae the dominant predators. In terms of size (mean length), Scarabaeidae

The spatial distribution of flying insects in tropical rain forests

S. L. SUTTON

Department of Pure and Applied Zoology, Baines Wing, Leeds University,
Leeds, LS2 9JT, U.K.

SUMMARY

1 Low power u.v. light traps were used to study the spatial distribution of flying insects in rain forests in Sulawesi, Brunei, Papua New Guinea and Panama.

2 A vertical series of traps at four levels between floor and upper canopy indicated marked concentrations in the upper canopy in Homoptera, Heteroptera, Lepidoptera, Diptera, Hymenoptera and Coleoptera. Ephemeroptera were concentrated at mid-levels.

3 On the basis of previous work, the Sulawesi vertical gradients can be interpreted as due to the flatness of the site.

4 Homopteran diversity (number of Recognizable Taxonomic Units) in Panama, Brunei and Sulawesi was highest in the upper canopy, but log series α varied little between levels. Morishita–Horn's similarity index indicated no abrupt interface between levels.

5 Overall α values for Homoptera from the vertical series were 58, 88 and 33 for Panama, Brunei and Sulawesi, respectively.

6 Horizontal series of traps in tree crowns in Sulawesi, Papua New Guinea and Panama showed that some crowns produced relatively low numbers for all major taxa. Differences in numbers were as great between crowns of the same species as between crowns of different species.

7 Homoptera diversity (log series α) varied little between tree crowns, while Morishita–Horn similarity values were high, but no greater for the same tree species than for different tree species.

8 These data do not suggest that each tree crown contributes to high insect diversity by acting as a distinctive sub-habitat, at least so far as flying Homoptera are concerned.

INTRODUCTION

Two aspects of small-scale spatial distribution of flying insects in tropical rain forest have been examined: (i) vertical stratification between forest floor and upper canopy (= canopy or euphotic zone *sensu* Richards 1983); (ii) horizontal distribution between tree crowns in the upper canopy. (i) was an extension of previous work carried out in Zaire (Sutton & Hudson 1980) and in Panama, Papua New Guinea and Brunei (Sutton, Ash & Grundy 1983). The work reported here under (i) concludes this survey of the vertical distribution of flying insects at seven sites in Africa, S.E. Asia and

Central America, using standardized equipment and techniques. (ii) was a first attempt to look at the extent to which each tree crown represents a separate faunal association rather than one point in a large pool of freely dispersing flying insects. It needs to be emphasized that the trapping method samples only flying insects. It tells us nothing directly of the distribution of the immature stages of these insects and therefore cannot tell us whether tree crowns have immature insect faunas restricted to each one. Nevertheless, knowledge of the distribution of adult insects is useful in its own right.

The aim was to combine the two approaches to gain understanding of the small-scale spatial distribution of flying insects in tropical rain forest. Hitherto no such analysis has been attempted. Studies so far have concentrated on larger units, e.g. differences in flying insect composition in different types of rain forest in Sarawak (Holloway 1983a, b) and in South America, Erwin (1983). Also reported here is a first attempt at the comparison of diversity of Homoptera in three of the seven sites.

Site description

Morowali Walkway Camp, Sulawesi

This site was 25 km NE of Kolonodale (1°51'S, 121°30'E) in east central Sulawesi (Sulawesi Tengah), 5 km upriver from the bay of Teluk Tomori. Traps were run from 14 February to 16 March 1980 (vertical series) and 20–26 March (horizontal series). Full moon was on 2 March, halfway through the vertical series.

Rainfall was *c.* 4000 mm year^{-1} (Laurie 1980). The area has a tropical monsoon climate with a relatively dry season from September to March. During the trapping period there was one long period of dry weather and several with heavy storms, with up to 42 mm during the 3 hour trapping period. Temperature varied between 24 and 28°C during trapping and humidity was always close to saturation. Full details are given in Rees (1983). The forest showed a number of similarities with the site at Buso, Papua New Guinea (Sutton *et al.* 1983) being an evergreen lowland alluvial rain forest tending towards swamp forest. Cutting of a small proportion of upper canopy trees by rotan gatherers has resulted in some disturbance, but there were no logging operations in the area.

The site was flat and low lying, 5 m above sea level. It was poorly drained with frequent standing water after rain. For the vertical trapping series, traps were hung from a 40 m *Syzygium syzygioides* (Miq.) Merrill and Perry (= *Eugenia cymosa* Lamarck), which was in flower, and was very common in the area. There was a semi-continuous leaf layer between 20 and 30 m with emergents to 40 m. The understorey was well developed, rich in species of *Daemonorops* and *Calamus* (Palmae-rotans). The vertical trapping tree overlooked a clear-flowing creek called the Soluwo, lined by *Pandanus* spp. (screw pines). Epiphytes were only moderately well developed and woody climbers other than rotans were not common. A full description of the area is given in Laurie (1980).

For the horizontal trapping series in Sulawesi, use was made of a 110-m long aerial walkway, suspended at 30 m. Traps were hung in five tree crowns along its length.

Crown trap 1 was the top trap of the vertical series 300 m from the walkway. Crowns II and III were the same species as Crown I, *S. syzygioides*. Crown IV was *Sarcotheca celebica* Veldk. Averrhoaceae (= Oxalidaceae), Crown V is as yet unidentified and Crown VI was *Gonostylus macrophyllus* Airy Shaw Thymelaeaceae. This was host to a strangling fig (*Ficus* sp.) and was adjacent to Crowns V and VI. *S. syzygioides* was in full flower over the trapping period, which may have influenced the nature and abundance of insects trapped by acting as a 'honey-pot', but see Discussion.

In Papua New Guinea there were again three crowns of one species and three of different species, traps positioned along two aerial walkways 30 m up. Crowns I–III were *Anisoptera thurifera* (Blanco) Bl. (Dipterocarpaceae), 20 m apart. Crowns IV–VI were 2 km distant. Crown VI was *Pometia pinnata* J.R. & G. Forst. Crown V is a species yet to be identified, and Crown VI was another *A. thurifera*.

The Panama horizontal series consisted of four crowns, all of different species of the family Leguminosae. Crown I was a *Dussia* sp., Crown II was *Dialium guianense* (Aublet), Sandwith, Crown III was *Pterocarpus officinalis* Jacquin and Crown IV was the same species as I. The crown of this last tree was almost entirely overlapped by that of *Couratari scott-mori* Prance (Lecythidaceae) growing 2 m away. Full descriptions of the Panama and Papua New Guinea sites are given in Sutton *et al.* (1983).

MATERIALS AND METHODS

The type of light trap and techniques used were described in Sutton (1979) and Sutton & Hudson (1980). Traps were run at *c.* 30 m, 20 m, 10 m and 1 m above ground level. The insects in each trap were killed with ethyl acetate and stored in alcohol (stored dry in the case of Lepidoptera). In Sulawesi the trapping period was from 19.00 to 22.00 hours each night. For the vertical series the traps were run for a whole lunar cycle but catches were very poor during the full moon period. Altogether there were twenty-seven nights of trapping. In Sulawesi the horizontal series (between crowns) study was run for six nights. Failure of two traps on the first night resulted in five sets of usable data, for 22–26 March, for 3 hours a night.

Trapping in Papua New Guinea for the horizontal series was over two periods: Crowns I–III were trapped for six nights between 24 and 31 October 1979, Crowns IV–VI after completion of the second walkway, for seven nights between 6 and 13 November, for 10 hours a night in both cases. At San Blas in Panama the four crowns were trapped for nine nights between 13 February and 5 March, 1980 for 10 hours nightly.

Sorting of Homoptera to Recognizable Taxonomic Units (RTU) was carried out to allow analysis of diversity. Sorting of the Panamanian material to RTU was carried out by Dr Henk Wolda and his staff, who identified to named genera. Sorting of the Sulawesi and Brunei material was done by Dr C. J. C. Rees and Joe Cole respectively and was checked by Dr W. J. Knight and his staff of the British Museum (Natural History). The relationship of RTU to museum recognized morphospecies was good with disagreement in only 10% of cases. Errors were either colour morphs being allocated to separate RTU, or conversely, the lumping of a number of morphospecies in one RTU as, e.g. in the genus *Batracomorphus*, which is very critical with many species not yet fully differentiated from each other by museum taxonomists. There was no indication that the RTU exercise, over the whole range of material, seriously over or underestimated the number of morphospecies. The extent to which RTU and morphospecies represent 'real' species in tropical forests remains a matter of much needed investigation. The effect of errors in the RTU separation will be partly self-cancelling in terms of the calculation of indices, but on balance there will probably be an underestimation of diversity between sites. Holloway (1984) states that, in the Lepidoptera, the splitting of critical groups reveals a series of species restricted to different foodplants. This is probably true of the Homoptera also. If feeding specificity of the stages is reflected to any degree in the restriction of adult distribution then resolution of critical genera will lead to an increase in recorded diversity of adult Homoptera between sites (in this study between vertical levels or tree crowns).

RESULTS

Vertical series: distribution numbers in Sulawesi

Except for the Ephemeroptera, all the major taxa caught in any number (>100 specimens) were heavily concentrated in the upper canopy (Levels 1 and 2) (Table 1 and Fig. 1). In the Homoptera, Lepidoptera, Diptera and Hymenoptera more than half the total catch was taken in the top trap, at 30 m. Ninety per cent of Homoptera and 80% of Diptera were taken at 20 m and 30 m (Levels 1 and 2), when the samples are combined. The Ephemeroptera showed a heavy concentration at Level 3.

The numbers are compared (Fig. 2) with the results from the two Zaire sites (Sutton & Hudson 1980) and from Panama, Papua New Guinea and two sites in Brunei (Sutton *et al.* 1983). With regard to the distribution of the Lepidoptera, Diptera and Coleoptera between levels, the seven sites can be divided into those with and those without steep gradients in numbers caught at the different levels. Figure 2a–c shows the results for these three major taxa. Only two other major taxa occur at all seven sites in

TABLE 1. Total numbers of major taxa trapped during twenty-seven trapping periods (14 Feb–16 March 1980): Morowali, Sulawesi (Celebes)

	Levels				
	1	2	3	4	
		Height (m)			
	26	18	9	1	Total
Ephemeroptera	34	179	1543	331	2087
Homoptera	2479	376	164	141	3160
Heteroptera	427	197	131	97	852
Lepidoptera	2253	996	509	288	4046
Diptera	9105	2773	1392	1613	14883
Hymenoptera	7196	2916	1750	1944	13806
Coleoptera	5467	3378	2277	1842	12964

numbers greater than 100). These are the Homoptera and the Hymenoptera. The former (Fig. 2d) show steep gradients at all sites, although the steepness is greater at the four sites which also showed steep gradients for the other taxa. The Hymenoptera (Fig. 2e) show a less uniform picture. The super-abundance of species of agaonids in the upper canopy at the sites indicated, and of winged stages of ants at low levels in Papua New Guinea heavily influenced this picture. The possible significance of the topography of the sites in relation to the gradients in numbers shown by the taxa is considered in the Discussion.

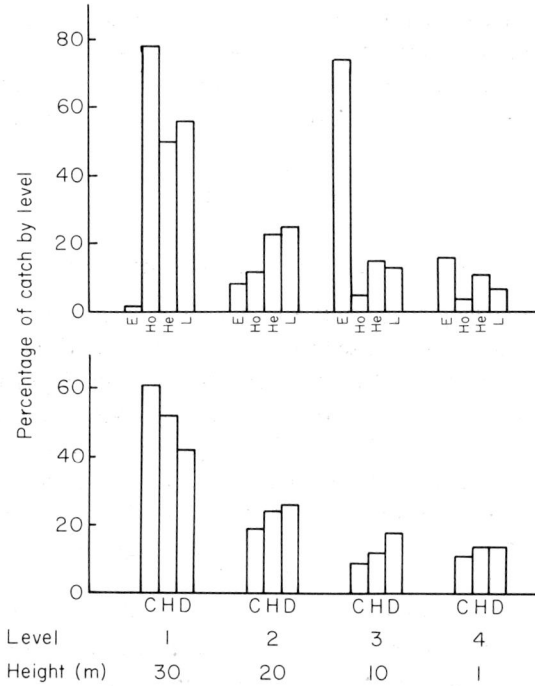

FIG. 1. Percentage of catch by level at Morowali, Sulawesi (Celebes) for major insect taxa. E, Ephemeroptera; Ho, Homoptera; He, Heteroptera; L, Lepidoptera; D, Diptera; H, Hymenoptera; C, Coleoptera.

Vertical series: Homoptera diversity

At three sites data are available on the distribution of individuals of Homoptera between taxa, as RTU, for the four vertical levels (Table 2). Total numbers are not directly comparable because of differences in trapping effort, which are themselves a reflection of the relative abundance of insects between sites, probably due largely to seasonality. On a trap-hour basis, numbers are much greater in Brunei than elsewhere. Trapping in Panama coincided with the driest dry season for many years (H. Wolda, pers. comm.) which very probably depressed the catch there. Total RTU diversity is also greatest in Brunei. The highest RTU numbers are found at Level 1 in the upper

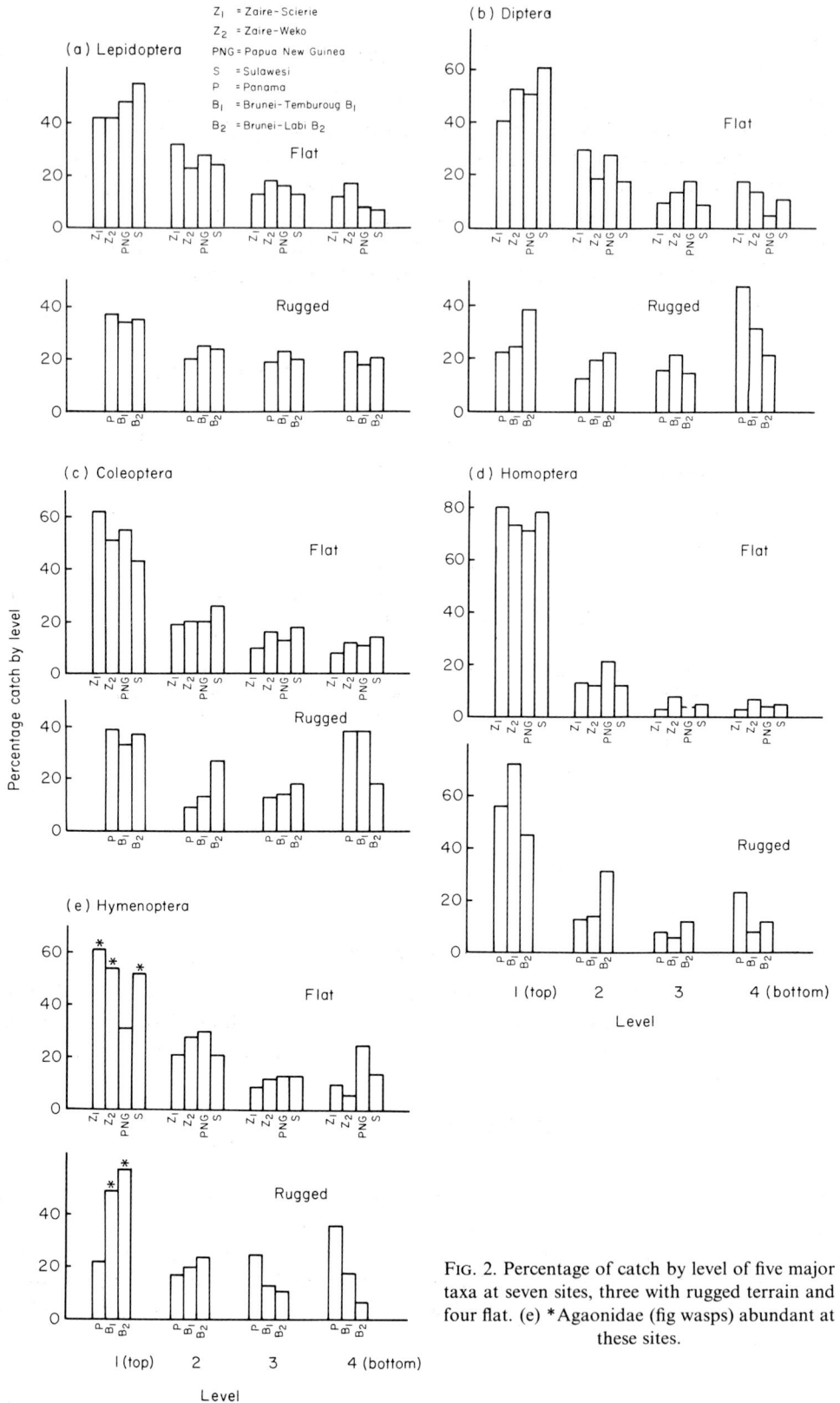

FIG. 2. Percentage of catch by level of five major taxa at seven sites, three with rugged terrain and four flat. (e) *Agaonidae (fig wasps) abundant at these sites.

canopy, but diversity, in the sense of the number of RTU in relation to the number of individuals, does not drop greatly below the upper canopy in Panama and Brunei. These features are reflected in the log series α values, which appear to show a difference in pattern between Sulawesi and the other sites, although values in many cases are uncertain because of limited sample size. Broadhead (1983) has shown that for Psocoptera from rain forest in Panama α values for samples of < 500 individuals are very approximate. The total α values can be more safely compared, being based on samples of large size.

TABLE 2. Homoptera diversity: vertical series

Individuals	Level				
	1	2	3	4	Total
San Blas, Panama	474	93	54	120	741
Labi, Brunei	399	288	112	119	918
Morowali, Sulawesi	1425	410	116	82	2033
RTU					
San Blas, Panama	107	47	36	55	152
Labi, Brunei	109	96	60	60	214
Morowali, Sulawesi	120	49	32	28	135
Log Series α					
San Blas, Panama	43·1	—*	—*	39·3	58·0
Labi, Brunei	49·5	50·4	52·6	48·3	87·8
Morowali, Sulawesi	31·4	20·5	21·0	—*	32·7

Trapping effort:
Panama   100 h over 10 nights
Brunei   15 h over 5 nights
Sulawesi   30 h over 10 nights

* n too small to estimate α.
RTU, Recognizable Taxonomic Units.

Vertical series: overlap between levels

The Homoptera data can also give some indication of the extent to which each level represents a different set of species. RTU overlap between levels has been analysed using the Morishita–Horn similarity index (Wolda, 1981), with logarithmic transformation of the data.

$$C_\lambda = \frac{2\sum(n_{1i} \cdot n_{2i})}{(\lambda_1 + \lambda_2) \cdot N_1 N_2} \qquad \text{where } \lambda_j = \frac{\sum n_{ji}^2}{N_j^2}$$

where n_{ji} = the number of individuals of species i in sample j and N_j = the number of individuals in sample j. Log transformation, $l_n (n_{ji} + 1)$.

Table 3 suggests that there is no sharp boundary between the upper canopy taxa and those below, similarity falling off in a steady and gradual manner, with a minimum of 0·68 between top and bottom in Sulawesi, and a lower degree of similarity (0·31) in Panama.

TABLE 3. Morishita–Horn similarity index, vertical trap
series: Homoptera, Recognisable Taxonomic Units

		LEVEL		
	1 (top)	2	3	4 (bottom)
L 1		0·92	0·73	0·68 S
E				U
V 2	0·64		0·83	0·76 L
E				A
L				W
3	0·48	0·51		0·81 E
				S
4	0·31	0·42	0·70	

PANAMA

Horizontal series: number of major taxa

Results of the study of abundance horizontally from tree crown to tree crown are shown in Table 4 and Fig. 3. For each taxon there is a marked departure from equality in the number caught in the different tree crowns in most cases, whether the crowns are of the same species or not.

In both Papua New Guinea and Panama one of the crowns of the 'different' tree species was notably less productive than the others, for all major taxa. Crown III in Papua New Guinea was also consistently poor, Crown I in Sulawesi consistently prolific.

Horizontal series: Homoptera diversity

Data are available for differences in Homoptera diversity, in terms of RTU from crown to crown in Panama and Sulawesi (Table 5). Although based on limited data these suggest no very great contrast in the diversity of each crown. With regard to the overlap of taxa between one crown and another in Sulawesi, Table 6 shows Morishita–Horn similarity values (Wolda 1981) for the complete data set, and the values on removal of delphacid H60, the dominant homopteran in the upper canopy during this horizontal trapping series. The high overall values are thereby cut considerably, but values remain generally similar, except for a high figure of 0·8 between Crowns I and VI. This is unexpected, as these crowns are of different species and 300 m apart. There is no suggestion in Table 6 of greater similarity between crowns of the same species and crowns of different species, although the small numbers available limit the reliability of the data.

DISCUSSION

Vertical distribution

The concentration of major taxa in the upper canopy is more marked, both in the range of taxa and the steepness of the numbers gradient, in Sulawesi than in any other of the seven sites sampled in this study, which used standardized equipment and techniques on a pan-tropical basis. Of the major taxa at Sulawesi, only the Ephemeroptera, with a strong peak 10 m up, show any departure from the general pattern. Similar peaks at between 10 and 20 m are shown by Ephemeroptera at the two other sites where they occurred in numbers—at San Blas in Panama and Ulu Temburong in Brunei.

TABLE 4. Numbers trapped in each tree crown

	Tree crowns						
	Same tree sp.				Different tree spp.		
	I	II	III		IV	V	VI
Buso, Papua New Guinea							
Orthoptera	58	23	15		16	58	0
Homoptera	137	96	22		73	79	21
Heteroptera	37	27	17		63	49	9
Lepidoptera	500	617	341		1132	865	184
Diptera	168	104	83		399	207	42
Hymenoptera	274	388	242		476	2030	544
Coleoptera	335	356	273		793	1006	204

Crowns I–III, six trapping period 24–31 Oct 1979; 60 trap hours.

Crowns IV–VI, seven trapping periods 6–13 Nov. 1979; 70 trap hours.

	I	II	III		IV	V	VI
Morowali, Sulawesi							
Homoptera	333	144	75		146	40	141
Heteroptera	77	21	37		31	9	46
Lepidoptera	234	157	109		148	82	165
Diptera	1376	675	595		673	543	564
Hymenoptera	440	98	108		117	115	200
Coleoptera	460	240	297		208	226	494

Five trapping periods 22–26 March 1980; 15 trap hours.

	Different tree spp.			
	I	II	III	IV
San Blas, Panama				
Homoptera	188	183	213	63
Lepidoptera	1102	996	685	464
Diptera	661	559	474	122
Coleoptera	1178	908	423	241

Nine trapping periods 13 Feb–5 March 1979; 90 trap hours.

Consideration of the distribution of major taxa at all the seven sites shows that in three out of five of the major taxa considered, the distribution patterns fall into two groups, one with steep gradients and the other without (Fig. 2a–e). These two groupings are consistent in all three taxa, and are also evident in the Homoptera, as a difference in the steepness of the gradient. It was suggested previously (Sutton *et al* 1983) that the explanation of this dichotomy might lie in the topography of the site, since steep numbers' gradients were associated with the three flat sites then analysed,

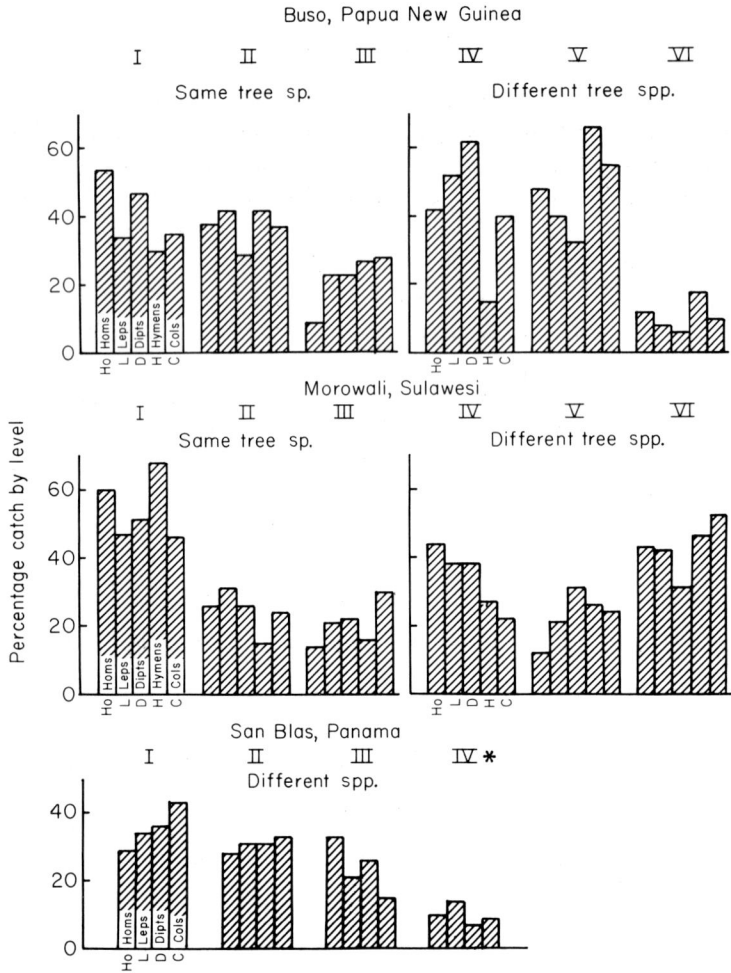

FIG. 3. Percentage catch by level of five major taxa between tree crowns in Papua New Guinea, Sulawesi and Panama. Ho, Homoptera; L, Lepidoptera; D, Diptera; H, Hymenoptera; C, Coleoptera; ∗ mixed crown at Panama site, one species same as I (see text).

TABLE 5. Homoptera diversity: horizontal series

	Tree crowns				
San Blas, Panama	I	II	III	IV	Total
Individuals	188	183	213	63	647
RTU	64	62	70	34	129
Log Series α	32·0	37·2	36·3	∗	50·0

	Same tree sp.			Different tree spp.			
Morowali, Sulawesi	I	II	III	IV	V	VI	Total
Individuals	302	130	73	142	30	118	795
RTU	57	32	21	35	14	37	90
Log Series α	20·8	13·6	∗	15·0	∗	18·5	26·2

∗ n too small to estimate α.
RU, Recognizable Taxonomic units.

and lack of gradients with three rugged sites. Sulawesi would be predicted on this basis, as a flat site, to have very marked gradients. This is indeed the case. Why flat terrain might have strong gradients is not known, but consideration of Oldeman's 'morphological inversion surface' concept (Richards 1983) leads to some intriguing ideas. The morphological inversion surface corresponds to the 'level of insertion of major trunk forks' (Hallé, Oldeman & Tomlinson 1978 p. 356) and is the undulating surface caused by linking up these points in Oldeman's 'trees of the present'. Richards suggests that it should define the interface between the euphotic and oligophotic zones of the forest. It

TABLE 6. Morishita–Horn similarity index, Sulawesi. Horizontal series (tree crown to crown), Homoptera Recognizable Taxonomic Units

CROWN	CROWN I (Same tree sp.)	II (Same tree sp.)	III (Same tree sp.)	IV (Different tree spp.)	V (Different tree spp.)	VI (Different tree spp.)	TOTAL SAMPLE
I		0·92	0·87	0·91	0·87	0·97	
II	0·58		0·85	0·89	0·87	0·92	
III	0·44	0·41		0·88	0·89	0·92	
IV	0·53	0·48	0·54		0·87	0·92	
V	0·50	0·51	0·66	0·50		0·91	
VI	0·80	0·57	0·66	0·57	0·67		

WITHOUT TAXON H60 (A DELPHACID)

	I	II	III	IV	V	VI
Total n	302	130	142	30	73	118
n−taxon H60	177	85	93	21	49	75

seems reasonable to suppose that most insects, other than dead wood and litter specialists, will be found in the euphotic zone (the upper canopy of many authors). If we further postulate that flying insects are very responsive to tree crowns rather than to the gaps between them, because of microclimatic or trophic preferences, we can think of the distribution of flying insects in the euphotic zone as a series of clusters each corresponding to a tree crown. There is every reason to suppose that there is much interchange between these clusters, but that does not invalidate their existence. In a forest of fairly uniform tree crown height (the Morowali walkway site is of this type and the *Shorea albida* Sym. peat swamp forest of northern Borneo would be an extreme example) the clusters will all be on the same level and flying insects will be strongly layered. On rugged ground, if the unevenness of the terrain is reflected in unevenness of crown and hence cluster height, the effect of interchange between crowns will be to blur the layering. Further, in a forest (e.g. mixed dipterocarp), with a great variety of crown height, poor definition of layering will also be found. Mixed dipterocarp forest on rough terrain, as at Labi in Brunei, can be expected to have particularly poor definition of layers of flying insects as was indeed found in this study. This cluster hypothesis can readily be tested and modelled. The prediction is that the more uneven the morphological inversion surface the less marked will be the vertical gradients of flying insects. This could quite possibly apply to temperate as well as to tropical forests. The extent to which the base of these hypothetical clusters is linked to the morphological inversion surface rather than to the related ecological inversion surface (Hallé *et al.* 1978) will depend on the relative importance of foliage density, flower presence and the like, versus light intensity, humidity and other physical variables as effective cues for 'station-keeping' by flying insects.

Homopteran diversity

The figures for Homoptera diversity from Panama, Papua New Guinea and Sulawesi (Table 2) are the first to be gathered by a standardized method. It is therefore of interest to note that the overall α values conform with predictions of relative diversity so far as Brunei and Sulawesi are concerned. The latter is considered to have an impoverished fauna due to its long isolation from other land masses (George 1981). The Panama α value of 58 is a dry season figure, and a severe dry season at that. Wolda (1979) gives data for Panama from which it is possible to calculate α values ranging from 35 for dry season to 55 for wet season, using a comparable trapping system. The figure in our study is relatively high, since it refers to the dry season. The Panama values seem unexpectedly low relative to the Brunei value of 88. The severity of the dry season is likely to be a factor but the difference may also reflect the richness of the mixed dipterocarp rain forest.

Table 2 shows that both in terms of the number of individuals and numbers of species (indicated by RTU) Homoptera are concentrated in the upper canopy, but that α values remain relatively constant from floor to upper canopy. This implies that diversity in terms of the number of species is greater in the upper canopy simply because of higher density and hence greater sample size in these upper levels, rather than because of a greater concentration of species relative to the number of individuals.

Table 3, bearing in mind the small samples involved, gives some indication of the overlap between vertical levels in species composition and provides no support for the idea of the existence of a distinct upper canopy fauna, rigidly separate from a ground fauna. Different preferences do exist, but the common species tend to have some representation at all levels. This was especially true in Sulawesi. At Labi in Brunei, of 222 RTU, only eighteen (8%) were found at ground level and not above, and only in ones and twos, and no species were more common at ground level than above. This indicates that there is no distinctive floor-based homopteran fauna. The commonest species, e.g. *Eoscarta seimundii* Lall. occurred in steadily decreasing numbers towards the ground, only the most common occurring in any numbers at ground level.

Horizontal distribution

The aim of the horizontal trap series was to assess the variation in numbers of individuals and species diversity between tree crowns in close proximity. Table 4 and

Fig. 3 demonstrate the relatively poor performance of some tree crowns, but it is not possible to say how much of this is due to properties of the crown itself and how much to the location (aspect) of the trap affecting its efficiency. This will be influenced by the extent to which the trap lamp is directly visible and this will be determined by the density of the surrounding foliage, which will vary from crown to crown. The obscuring effect of the foliage will perhaps be offset by the extra glow of reflected light from the leaves, but as we have no knowledge of how insects respond to direct or reflected light from low power u.v. lamps we cannot predict the effect of foliage density on trap efficiency. Unfortunately, this variable can never be fully standardized, although careful siting within crowns does minimize the problem. As regards the suitability of low power u.v. traps for studying the localization of flying insects, the general view is that they attract insects only from the immediate vicinity and are therefore much better than the more powerful m.v. traps, although still subject to all the bias from which light traps suffer. For suitable groups of insects they offer a highly practical means of study. Whilst this technique is appropriate for localizing the distribution of flying insects, it does not, of course, tell us anything about the localization of the immature stages. Here integration of light trapping techniques with insecticidal fogging (Erwin 1983) may prove to be the way forward (C. J. C. Rees, N. E. Stork & S. L. Sutton, unpublished).

Factors other than foliage density which might affect trap efficiency were discussed at length in Sutton & Hudson 1980. In the present work it is unlikely that wind affected trap efficiency because the trapping periods were, for the most part, calm. The possibility that some trees were more successful as trapping sites than others because they were in flower and attracting numerous insects, or were close by such trees, would appear to be of little consequence because, although in Sulawesi the mean number of insects in the three crowns of *S. syzygioides* was higher than in the crowns of the other three species, this was largely due to Crown I, suggesting that the high density of insects in that crown was due to something other than flowering *per se*. The variation between the *S. syzygioides* crowns was greater than between the crowns of the three different tree species (Table 4).

The load of epiphylls, epiphytes and climbers must influence the catch in any particular tree crown, but we have no analysis of the associated flora and no indication of what this influence might be.

Table 5 suggests that diversity in terms of log series α for Homoptera is fairly uniform from crown to crown, with numbers of RTU differing considerably, but in line with the number of individuals. Crown I in Sulawesi contains a high proportion of the total RTU recorded, but in general each crown has less than 50% of the total RTU found. The overall α values of 50 and 26 for Panama and Sulawesi (Table 5) agree quite well with values of 58 and 33 from the vertical series at each site (Table 2).

The degree of uniformity between tree crowns is explored further in Table 6, which assesses the overlap in Homoptera RTU between tree crowns. Including the ubiquitous and abundant delphacid H60, there is very high similarity using the Morisita–Horn index, with no greater overlap between crowns of the same species than between those that were different. Removal of H60 lowered similarity values greatly without changing the overall picture except that Crown I and VI now show a remarkably high affinity. Crown I was *Syzygium syzygioides*, Crown VI was *Gonostylus macrophyllus* and they were 300 m apart, so the high similarity is due neither to affinity or proximity.

Each tree crown, because of its attendant flora, must be considered as a plant complex rather than a single species. The data presented suggest that flying insects circulate generally between the tree crowns, as in a large pool, and that each crown cannot be considered as an animal association with distinct boundaries. On this evidence tree crowns cannot be seen as separate entities with specialist insect faunas, contributing to the high diversity of insects by providing a whole range of sub-habitats. However, these present data are only concerned with flying homopterans. What the young stages of these insects do is crucial and very probably different, and there is as yet no comparable crown-to-crown data for other insect groups, although much work is in progress (Erwin 1983).Taken together the results of the vertical and horizontal series present a picture of a free-flying fauna without clear cut vertical zonation but concentrated in the upper canopy, dispersing readily between tree crowns while at the same time varying much in density from one crown to another.

ACKNOWLEDGMENTS

I gratefully acknowledge the help of many members of Operation Drake and the Muzium Brunei, including John Blashford-Snell, Ben Gaskell, Derek Jackson, Md. Jaya, Lim Jock Seng, Bob Powell, John Prasanto, Dato' Shariffudin, Mike Swaine, Wandy Swales and Andrew Sugden. Walkway constructors were led by Mike Christie, Louis Gallagher, Mike Prior and John Rimmer. Field data were collected by Caroline Ash, Angela Grundy, Jan Morton and Willy Wint, and processed by John Biglin, Joe Cole, Puspah and Gillian Richardson. Bill Knight, Andrew Lack and Henk Wolda gave much help with identifications. Finally, many thanks are due to Leeds University and to the governments of Brunei, Indonesia, Panama and Papua New Guinea. This work was carried out as a joint project with Chris Rees of York University, U.K.

REFERENCES

Broadhead, E. (1983). The assessment of faunal diversity and guild size in tropical forests with particular reference to the Pscoptera. *Tropical Rain Forest: Ecology and Management* (Ed. by S. L. Sutton, T. C. Whitmore & A. C. Chadwick), pp. 107–119. Blackwell Scientific Publications, Oxford.

Erwin, T.L. (1983). Beetles and other insects of tropical forest canopies at Manaus, Brazil, sampled by insecticidal fogging techniques. *Tropical Rain Forest: Ecology and Management* (Ed. by S. L. Sutton, T. C. Whitmore & A. C. Chadwick), pp. 59–75. Blackwell Scientific Publications, Oxford.

George, W. (1981). Wallace and his line. *Wallace's Line and Plate Tectonics* (Ed. by T. C. Whitmore), pp. 3–8. Clarendon Press, Oxford.

Hallé, F., Oldeman, R. A. A. & Tomlinson, P. B. (1978). *Tropical Trees and Forests, An Architectural Analysis.* Springer-Verlag, Berlin.

Holloway, J. D. (1983a). *Insect surveys: an approach to environmental monitoring.* Proceedings 12th National Italian Entomological Congress, Rome, 1980.

Holloway, J.D. (1983b). The larger moths of the park: a preliminary assessment. *Gunung Mulu National Park, Sarawak* (Ed. by A. C. Jermy & K. Kavanagh), Sarawak Museum Journal, Supplement 2. (in press).

Holloway, J. D. (1984). Moths as indicator organisms for categorising rain forest and monitoring changes and regeneration processes. *Tropical Rain Forest: Ecology and Management, Supplementary Volume* (Ed. by A. C. Chadwick & S. L. Sutton), Proceedings of the Leeds Philosophical and Literary Society. (Scientific Section). (in press).

Laurie, A. (1980). *Morowali Nature Reserve, a plan for conservation.* World Wildlife Fund Report.

Rees, C.J.C. (1983). Microclimate and flying Hemiptera fauna of a primary lowland rain forest in Sulawesi. *Tropical Rain Forest: Ecology and Management* (Ed. by S. L. Sutton, T. C. Whitmore & A. C. Chadwick), pp. 121–136. Blackwell Scientific Publications, Oxford.

Richards, P.W. (1983). The three-dimensional structure of tropical rain forest. *Tropical Rain Forest: Ecology and Management* (Ed. by S. L. Sutton, T. C. Whitmore & A. C. Chadwick), pp. 3–10. Blackwell Scientific Publications, Oxford.

Sutton, S. L. (1979). A portable light trap for studying insects of the upper canopy. *The Brunei Museum Journal*, 4(3), 156–160.

Sutton, S. L. & Hudson, P. J. (1980). The vertical distribution of small flying insects in the lowland rain forest Zaire. *Zoological Journal of the Linnean Society*, **68**, 111–123.

Sutton, S.L., Ash, C.P. & Grundy, A. (1983). The vertical distribution of flying insects in the lowland rain forest of Panama, Papua New Guinea and Brunei. *Zoological Journal of the Linnean Society*, **78**, (in press).

Wolda, H. (1979). Abundance and diversity of Homoptera in the canopy of a tropical forest. *Ecological Entomology*, **4**(2), 181–190.

Wolda, H. (1981). Similarity indices, sample size and diversity. *Oecologia (Berl)*, **50**, 296–302.

Spatial and temporal variation in abundance in tropical animals

HENK WOLDA

Smithsonian Tropical Research Institute, P.O. Box 2072
Balboa, Republic of Panama

SUMMARY

Data which are sufficiently extensive and detailed on spatial and temporal dynamics of abundances of tropical animals are largely lacking, but some points begin to emerge. Seasonal variation is the rule rather than the exception in tropical animals even in areas where seasonal changes in the weather are minimal. In the tropics too, then, stability is best studied using data covering an entire year. Data on spatial variation are minimal, but movements of individuals are important and, because of a large beta-diversity, cause an impressive inflow of species into habitats where they 'do not belong'. The few existing data on vertebrates do not suggest that tropical species fluctuate less than their temperate counterparts. In insects, variance in abundance at a given mean is, on the average, identical to that of temperate insects and trends in relative abundances of tropical insects also are not significant. All available information suggests that tropical animals do not differ from temperate zone species in terms of temporal stability.

INTRODUCTION

A discussion of spatial and temporal variations in abundance of tropical animals should, ideally, be based on a number of good data sets. There are some data, but it seems advisable to point out their limitations immediately. An excellent example of what spatial and temporal fluctuations in abundance mean and how they should be studied together is given by the Rothamsted Insect Survey (Taylor 1978, 1981; Taylor & Taylor, 1979). With a large network of light traps and suction traps over the British Isles and part of the continent of Europe, many of which have been operated over several years, a fair picture can be obtained of the temporal fluctuations and how they vary over a large area. This work demonstrates that any study which concentrates on only one or at best a few points in space, misses a large and important part of the story. There are only a few areas in the world for which such data exist and none of them is in the tropics, neither for insects nor for other animals. We will have to be content with what data there are. A few examples of studies on spatial variation are: for birds, Orians (1969) in Costa Rica and Terborgh (1970) in Peru; Inger (1980) compared frogs and lizards from three sites in southeast Asia and Heatwole & Sexton (1966) in two sites in Panama; Mellow (1980) investigated the rodents in three localities in Brazil; Janzen (1973a,b), Janzen & Schoener (1968) and Janzen *et al.* (1976) compared the insect faunas in a number of sites in Costa Rica, in the Caribbean and along an altitudinal gradient in Venezuela, and I have done so in Panama (Wolda 1980b; Wolda & Fisk 1981). Many of these and other studies cover only a short period of time, which makes interpretation of the results difficult. Few studies cover two or more years, e.g. Happold (1977) and Mello (1980) for mammals, Wolda (1978a,b, 1980a,b, 1982, 1983a) McElravy *et al.* (1981) and McElravy, Wolda & Resh (1982) for Panamanian insects. Long-term studies, here defined as studies which cover 10 years or more, are very rare indeed. The few in existence include Bigger (1976) for some Ghanaian insects on cocoa, Karr, Schemske & Brokaw (1982) for Panamanian birds and Andrews & Rand (1982) for a Panamanian lizard. The word 'long-term' is, of course, mostly wishful thinking as 10, or even 20 years is a short time span in the life of most populations. As a terrestrial ecologist in a tropical forest I envy some limnologists who, with their sediment cores, have been able to study the history of the local populations of some aquatic organisms, such as chironomids, over a very long period indeed. Warwick (1980) covered 2800 years of the history of chironomid populations in Canada in great detail. Several others have covered even longer time spans, but usually with a small resolution in time. Nevertheless, such studies, e.g. Bradbury *et al.* (1981) make one realize the limitations of these terrestrial studies, such as my own insect studies on Barro Colorado Island in Panama, where I now am the proud owner of all of 8 years of data on Homoptera and 7 on cockroaches.

SEASONALITY

Correlated with seasonal changes in the weather, especially temperature, temperate zone organisms undergo dramatic changes in abundance and activity. For this, and other, reasons, it is advisable to use data which cover an entire year when comparing different sites and/or different years (e.g. den Boer 1963; Taylor & Woiwod 1980). This is also true for the tropics, with rainfall rather than temperature being the conspicuous seasonal component in the weather. Not all animals in a tropical forest show clear seasonal changes in abundance, breeding activity etc., even in areas with a pronounced dry season, but most do. A few examples may exemplify this point. There is a seasonal component in breeding in bats in Malaysia (Gould 1978) and Panama (C. O. Handley, pers. comm.). Squirrels breed seasonally in Gabon (Emmons 1979). There is a seasonal variation in abundance in frogs in Panama (Toft 1980) and some toads are highly seasonal in their breeding (Wells 1979). Iguanas in Panama have a very short egg-laying season (A. S. Rand, pers. comm.) in February in Panama, even in areas where February is not in the middle of the dry season. Birds are seasonal (Karr 1976; Karr *et al.* 1982; Greenberg 1981; Crome 1975) even in areas with relatively little seasonal variation in rainfall such as Sarawak (Fogden 1972). Seasonal variation in insects has been documented for many species ever since the pioneering studies by Davis (1945) and Dobzhansky & Pavan (1950). For a brief literature survey see Wolda (1978a). It has become clear that one should not make general statements about seasonality of tropical animals. Some species of birds are very different from others at one and the same site (Karr 1976). The cicadellid *Polana scinna* DeL. & Fr. showed no detectable seasonal variation in abundance in a site where virtually all other cicadellids, including some congenerics, are highly seasonal (Wolda, 1980a). Scarab beetles tend to have, on average, much shorter seasons of presence as adults than cerambycids, Homoptera or cockroaches, while termites are among the most seasonal of tropical insects (H. Wolda, unpubl.). Seasonality also depends a great deal on the climate and other features of the site in question. Mosquitoes in some areas in Panama are highly seasonal (Galindo *et al.* 1956) but are much less variable in abundance in areas with enough water (breeding sites) throughout the year (Boreham, pers. comm.). In other areas still they fluctuate violently and aseasonally (Wolda & Galindo 1981). One of the parameters useful in describing seasonal variation in abundance is the Seasonal Range (SR), which is the length of the season of presence of the adults measured in weeks. For Homoptera from light traps in five Panamanian localities the values for SR for all species are plotted in Fig. 1. Las Cumbres and BCI are lowland sites and Boquete a mountain site, with a pronounced dry season of some 4 months. Fortuna shows no seasonal variation in the amount of rainfall per month and is as non-seasonal a site as occurs anywhere in the tropics. Miramar has no real dry season, but a tendency for less rain in the months of September and March. The values for SR tend to be larger in areas with less seasonality in the rainfall, although species with very short seasons occur in all sites. Data on Homoptera from three temperate sites are included in Fig. 1 for comparison.

Variations in the seasonal weather pattern affect, sometimes severely, the seasonality of animals. For Barro Colorado Island (BCI) Fig. 2 gives the rainfall per day for the months November to May, which includes the dry season. In some years the rainy season started as early as 1 April (1978), in others as late as 21 May (1977). Sometimes there are a few successive days of rain in the middle of the dry season (1974, 1975) which can have a strong effect of the seasonal pattern and abundance of some species (Wolda 1978a). The 'dry' season 1980/81 was the wettest on record and the 1976/77 dry season the longest on record (information available since the beginning of this century). The beginning of the rains to a large extent affects the timing of the occurrence, or of the seasonal peak, of many species. Figure 3 exemplifies this for *Muirolonia metallica* Fowler (Cixiidae, Homoptera). The beginning of the dry season also can have an effect on the timing of species. Figure 4 illustrates this for the cicada *Dorisiana viridis* Olivier. These effects are clearly visible, but are not necessarily of a dramatic or catastrophic nature. However, they can be. Brown pelicans (*Pelecanus occidentalis* L.) breed in the large colony in the trees on the shores of Taboga Island, in the bay of Panama. Normally in the dry season the prevailing offshore winds cause an upwelling in the Bay, with an associated lower surface temperature and an increased availability of fish for the pelicans. G. G. Montgomery (pers. comm.) found that pelicans start breeding as soon as the water temperature drops. However, they also stop when the temperature increases again. In 1981 the temperature fluctuated and many nests were abandoned, while others successfully fledged young. In 1982 the temperature did not drop until very late, rose again after less than 2 weeks with the result that the nests were abandoned. As late as late March temperatures went down again and several pelicans started breeding again, but probably too late. In other words, changes in the wind pattern determine the success or failure of many hundreds

or even thousands of pelican nests. In front of BCI is the small island of Slothia where many iguanas breed. In 1981 the dry season was very wet, especially January, and the egg-laying season was delayed by some 2 weeks. These eggs normally hatch in late April. However, the rains started in mid-April and fell in large quantities day after day,

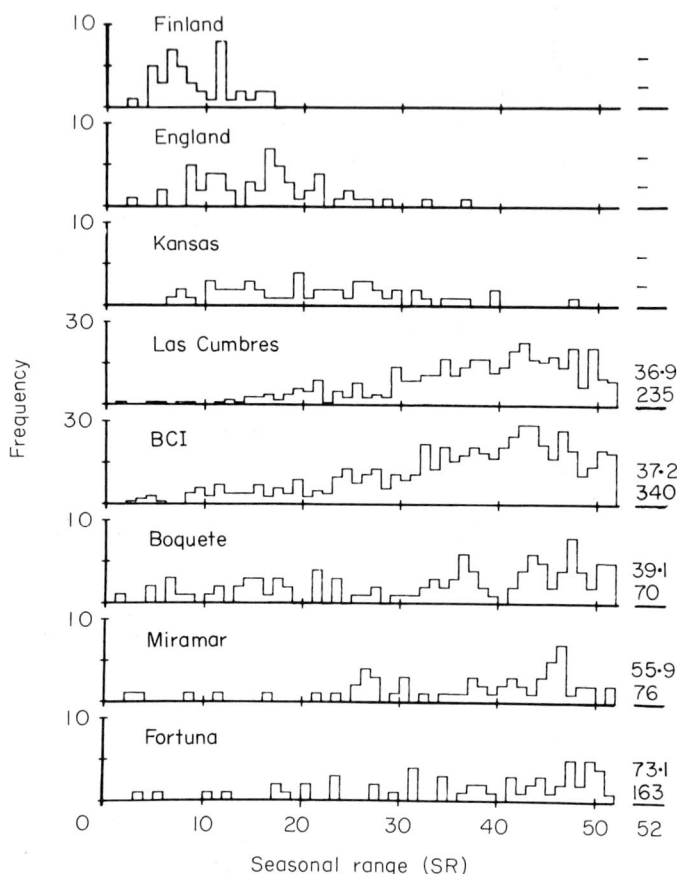

FIG. 1. Seasonal Range, in weeks (=length of the active season of adults corrected for sample size), for species of Homoptera found in five sites in Panama and three in the temperate zone. The number of species present around the year (SR = 52) is listed on the right together with the percentage this is of all species at that site. Las Cumbres, Barro Colorado Island (BCI) and Miramar are in the lowlands, Boquete and Fortuna in the mountains. Miramar has no dry season but diminished precipitation in March and September, Fortuna has no seasonal variation in rainfall and the other Panamanian sites have a pronounced dry season of 4 months.

so that the soil was saturated with water with unusual rapidity. Only a few iguanas hatched, probably all from one nest. All the others died, probably drowned in the eggs (A. S. Rand, pers. comm.). The dry season is the adverse season for many tropical animals, but these two examples show that some animals take special advantage of the dry season for breeding, just as many trees flower during the dry weather.

SPATIAL VARIATION

There are no suitable data to study spatial dynamics in the tropics such as Taylor has done for British moths and aphids. There are some lines of evidence, however, which suggest that the ingredients for an important spatially dynamic system are present.

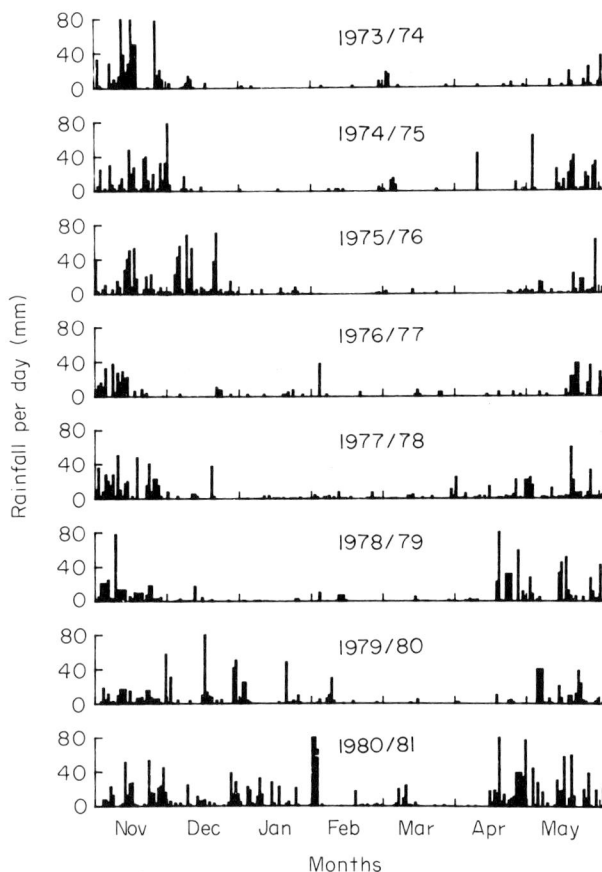

FIG. 2. Rainfall per day on Barro Colorado Island from November through May, which includes the dry season. Rainfall in excess of 80 mm per day is plotted as 80 mm.

First of all, not only the intra-site diversity is very high, but also the between site (beta-) diversity is much larger than in most temperate systems. A suitable way to look at between site diversity is by employing similarity indices. To the best of my knowledge the only similarity index which is unbiased (Wolda 1981), unaffected by sample size and diversity and which has an unbiased estimate of the variance of the index is Grassle & Smith's (1976) index which they call NESS (m) and which I prefer to refer to as C_m. The variance is given by Smith, Kravitz & Grassle (1979). I have arbitrarily chosen 20 as the value of m. This value is considered high enough to overcome the strong influence of the more common species and at the same time small enough to be able to use it for rather small samples. It is fixed at this level in order to make the results of the calculations comparable. This index is a generalization of the Morisita index, and has the advantage over that index that it is not so sensitive to just the common species, if the

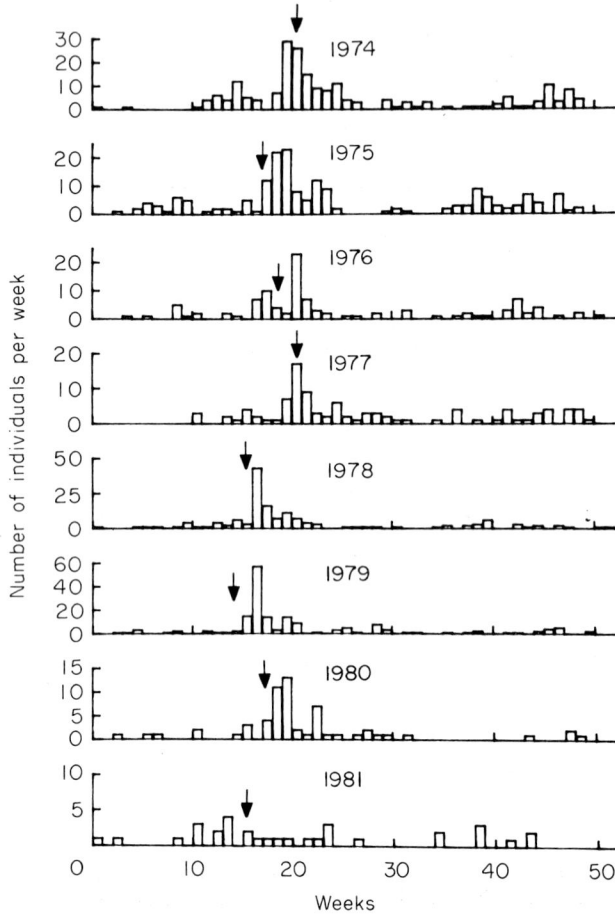

FIG. 3. Number of individuals per week of *Muirolonia metallica* Fowler during 8 years on Barro Colorado Island. Arrows indicate the onset of the rainy season.

value of the parameter *m* chosen is high enough. At $m = 1$ the C_m index is identical to the Morisita index.

For cockroaches, for the six sites with information on species composition and relative abundances (obtained with light-traps), there are fifteen similarly indices. Of these, five (33%) have values less than 0·1 and only two (13%) have values over 0·4 (Wolda 1983b). For Homoptera I have light-trap samples from nine sites which give thirty-six similarity indices. Of these fifteen (42%) have values smaller than 0·1 and only two (6%) have values over 0·4. These are very low values compared with similar data from temperate areas. There is a considerable dispersion, an exchange of individuals between sites (Wolda 1977; Robbins & Small 1981) and with the high beta-diversity in spite of this, the chances are that many of these vagrants are of species which 'do not belong' in the sites where they end up. This explains the extraordinarily high frequency

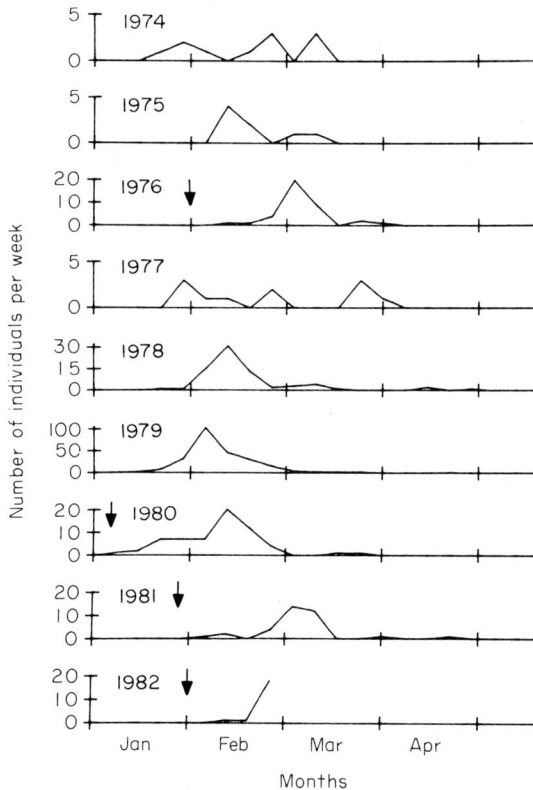

FIG. 4. Number of individuals per week of the cicada *Dorisiana viridis* Olivier on Barro Colorado Island. The end of the rainy season, if occurring after 1 January, is indicated by an arrow. In the other years the rainy season ended some time in December, except in 1976 (mid-November).

of rare species in samples of cockroaches and Homoptera. For instance, even after 7 years of collecting and after more than 160 000 individuals and over 900 species, the class of species of Homoptera with only one individual is still unusually abundant. Many of these could be vagrants from elsewhere (H. Wolda, unpubl.). These insect movements may mostly be directed by the prevailing winds, but some more 'deliberate' movements should not be ruled out. In birds individuals of several species have been shown to move along vegetation or moisture gradients, depending on the circum-stances (J. R. Karr, pers. comm.). This dispersal occurs on the scale of a few kilometers, but also on a larger scale. Birds from the Pacific side of Panama move to moist sites towards the Atlantic if the dry season is very dry, but not if during the dry season there is some rain. J. R. Karr (pers. comm.) has shown that, not unlike the moths in Britain, one obtains a very distorted picture if one relies on the data from one site only. In birds there is, of course, also the large-scale seasonal migration both within the tropics (Morton 1977) and between the tropics and the temperate zone.

TEMPORAL VARIATION

In the present paper the word stability will be used in two related but different ways. It either means absence of a gradual change, i.e. absence of a trend, or a small variance. Only point samples, data from one, or at best a few, sites are available for discussion. In order to evaluate stability in a tropical forest it is useful to use temperate data for comparison. Happold (1977) compares a few years of data on rodents in a Nigerian forest with data from Wytham Wood and concludes that tropical rodents have a smaller variance, and are more stable than their temperate counterparts, at least in forests. In savannah areas the fluctuations are larger and Mello's data from Brazil (Mello 1980) fit this idea. Leigh (1975) discusses data on various mammals and concludes that howler monkeys from Barro Colorado do not have a smaller variance than temperate herbivores. Karr *et al.* (1982) present data on samples of birds taken by mistnets in exactly the same sites in 1968/69 and 1977/78 and report considerable changes in these 10 years in their study site in Panama. Andrews & Rand (1982), in a 10-year study of *Anolis limifrons* on BCI, find a six-fold variation in abundance 'which is considerably greater than has been observed for lizards from temperate regions'. This evidence on vertebrates is rather limited, but it does not tend to support Happold's contention that vertebrates in tropical forests fluctuate less, are more stable, than their temperature counterparts.

Bigger (1976), with 10 years of data on cocoa insects in Ghana, concludes that in the cocoa ecosystem population cycles are observed in many species and that the amplitude of the cycles is comparable to that of temperate insects. Wolda (1978b) compared a large number of data from both the tropics and the temperate zone and concluded that in terms of variation in abundance from one year to the next, insects from the humid tropics fluctuate just as much as insects from the humid temperate zone. Even large-scale changes, changes which often are called 'outbreaks' occur in tropical forests. Gray (1982) gives several examples for insects. Wolda & Foster (1978) added to these examples. A. S. Rand, M. J. Ryan & K. E. Troyer (unpubl.) report a population explosion in a frog *Hyla rufitela* on BCI in Panama.

On a longer time scale the available data are scarce. Moreover, these data become more and more difficult to interpret because all habitats change. In order to test whether the relative abundances of the species in a particular site just fluctuate in time or whether they show a trend, I compared the first year of a data set with each of the later years, using the similarity index C_{20}. Figure 5 shows the values for underwing moths (Catocala) in Connecticut (Sargent 1976) with the standard deviations. There obviously is a highly significant trend in the data, which means that the relative abundances of the species of *Catocala* involved change gradually. In some other data

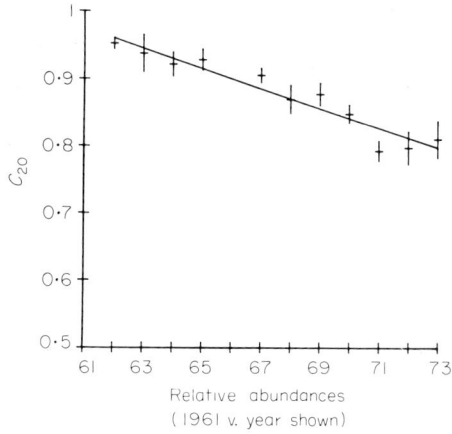

FIG. 5. Underwing moths (*Catocala*) in Connecticut (Sargent 1976). Using the similarity index $C_{20}(=$ NESS) the relative abundances of the species in each year is compared with those in the first year. Standard deviations for each C_{20} value are given. The highly significant trend points to a gradual change in the species abundances.

sets the variation around the trend line is much larger and in others again there is no significant trend at all. Figure 6 summarizes a number of data with just the regression lines. The two BCI data sets are indicated by dashed lines. The Homoptera showed a highly significant trend, the cockroaches did not. It is difficult to draw definite conclusions from this rather messy figure, but it should be clear that the tropical data are not conspicuously different from the temperate ones.

Another way to look at stability is to relate the amplitude, or rather the variance, of the fluctuations to mean abundance. A species with relatively small variance fluctuates

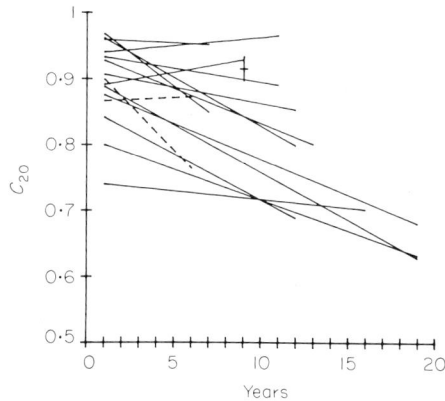

FIG. 6. Trends in relative species abundances in a series of data sets is summarized giving only the regression lines (cf. Fig. 5). Continuous lines are for temperate data, dashed for data from Barro Colorado. The Homoptera show a clear trend, the cockroaches do not. A data point for birds in Panama (Karr *et al.* 1982) is also included.

less, is more stable, than a species with the same mean but a larger variance. Figure 7 plots, on a double log scale, variance against mean for the cockroach species on BCI. The data cover 6 years. The relationship is significantly non-linear. However, leaving out the data with a log mean smaller than one, a straight line fits the data well. This curvilinear relationship is generally found in such data, including the moths from Rothamsted which Williams (1939) studied from 1933 to 1936 and later from 1946 to 1949. The data for the latter years were kindly given to me by Prof. L. R. Taylor of Rothamsted Experimental station. Taking only the data with log mean larger than one, the regression lines (principal axis rather than ordinary regressions) are plotted in Fig. 8 for three major groups of Homoptera on BCI (continuous lines), cockroaches on

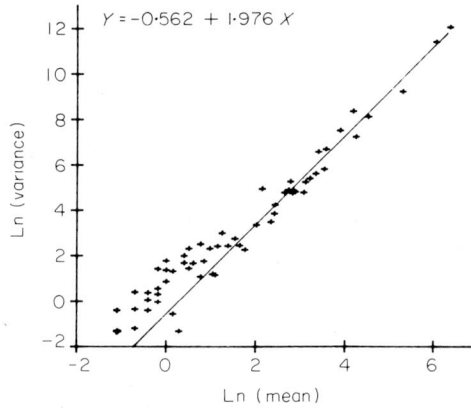

FIG. 7. For each species of cockroach on Barro Colorado Island the variance of the abundances per year over 6 years is plotted against the mean over that period on a double (natural) log scale. The relationship is significantly non-linear, but taking only data with log mean at least one, it is linear and this line is plotted.

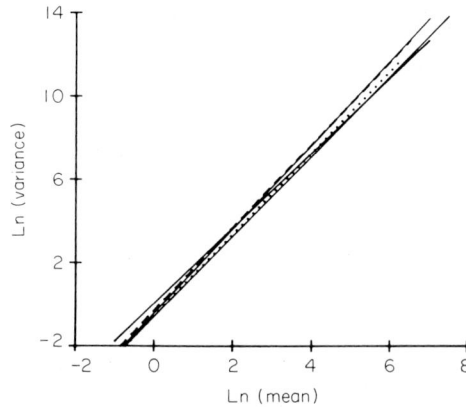

FIG. 8. Regression lines, such as the one in Fig. 7, are plotted for three groups of Homoptera (Fulgoroidea, Cicadellidae and the rest) on Barro Colorado Island (continuous lines), for cockroaches on BCI (dotted line) and for British moths (dashed line). The lines are so similar that they are difficult to distinguish: tropical insects fluctuate just as much as do temperate ones.

BCI (dotted line) and British moths (dashed line). The lines are incredibly close and there is no indication at all that tropical insects are less variable, or more stable, than temperate insects, not even in a complex and very diverse tropical rainforest subject to the minimal human interference.

This brief survey of temporal and spatial variation in tropical animals is biased. It is biased towards the organisms I know best, the insects, and the sites I am most familiar with, the Neotropics and more specifically Panama. However, the data generally tend to support the hypothesis that temporal variations of abundance of species at any one site, apart from seasonal variations, tend to be very similar to those in temperate areas. It seems highly likely that spatial dynamics are at least as large as they are in temperate areas and because of the high beta-diversity may be more spectacular.

ACKNOWLEDGMENTS

Help received from various people is gratefully acknowledged: M. Estribí, Ing. C. Estribí, S. Martínez, B. de León, A. Sandberg and N. Yishui. The study on BCI was partly supported by the Smithsonian Environmental Sciences Program, the one in Miramar by a Research Award of the Smithsonian Institution and that in Fortuna by the Instituto de Recursos Hidráulicos y Electrificación.

REFERENCES

Andrews, R.M. & Rand, A.S. (1982). Seasonal breeding and long-term population fluctuations in the lizard *Anolis limifrons*. *Ecology of a Tropical Forest: Seasonal Rhythms and Long-term Changes*. Ed. by E. G. Leigh, A. S. Rand & D. M. Windsor), pp. 405–412. Smithsonian Press, Washington, DC, U.S.A.

Bigger, M. (1976). Oscillations of tropical insect populations. *Nature*, **259**, 207–209.

Boer, P.J. den (1963). *Lebeort (Habitat)-bindung einiger Wald-Carabidenarten in Drente (Holland) in Zusammenhang mit Waldtypus, Boden und Strukturelementen des Waldes*. Coenological Colloquium Zagreb, 1963, 1–16.

Bradbury, J. Platt, Leyden, B., Salgado-Labouriau, M., Lewis, W.M., Schubert, C., Binford, M.W., Frey, D.G., Whitehead, D.R. & Weibezahn, F.H. (1981). Late Quaternary environmental history of Lake Valencia, Venezuela. *Science*, **214**, 1299–1305.

Crome, F.H.J. (1975). The ecology of fruit pigeons in tropical Northern Queensland. *Australian Wildlife Research*, **2**, 155–185.

Davis, D.E. (1945). The annual cycle of plants, mosquitos, birds and mammals in two Brazilian forests. *Ecological Monographs*, **15**, 243–295.

Dobzhansky, T. & Pavan, C. (1950). Local and seasonal variations in relative frequencies of species of Drosophila in Brazil. *Journal of Animal Ecology*, **19**, 1–14.

Emmons, L.H. (1979). Observations on litter size and development of some African rainforest squirrels. *Biotropica*, **11**, 207–213.

Fogden, M.P.L. (1972). The seasonality and population dynamics of equatorial forest birds in Sarawak. *The Ibis*, **114**, 307–343.

Galindo, P., Trapido, H., Carpenter, S.J. & Blanton, F.S. (1956). The abundance cycles of arboreal mosquitos during six years at a yellow fever locality in Panama. *Annals of the Entomological Society of America*, **49**, 543–547.

Gould, E. (1978). Rediscovery of *Hipposideros ridleyi* and seasonal reproduction in Malaysian bats. *Biotropica*, **10**, 30–32.

Grassle, J.F. & Smith, W. (1976). A similarity measure sensitive to the contribution of rare species and its use in investigation of variation in marine benthic communities. *Oecologia (Berl.)*, **25**, 13–22.

Gray, B. (1972). Economic tropical entomology. *Annual Review of Entomology*, **15**, 273–294.

Greenberg, R. (1981). The abundance and seasonality of forest canopy birds on Barro Colorado Island, Panama. *Biotropica*, **13**, 241–251.

Happold, D.C.D. (1977). A population study on small rodents in the tropical rainforest of Nigeria. *La Terre et al Vie*, **31**, 385–457.

Heatwole, H. & Sexton, O.J. (1966). Herpetofauna comparisons between two climatic zones in Panama. *American Midland Naturalist*, **75**, 45–60.

Inger, R.F. (1980). Relative abundances of frogs and lizards in forests of Southeast Asia. *Biotropica*, **12**, 14–22.

Janzen, D.H. (1973a). Sweep samples of tropical foliage insects: Description of study sites, with data on species abundances and size distributions. *Ecology*, **54**, 659–686.

Janzen, D.H. (1973b). Sweep samples of tropical foliage insects: effects of seasons, vegetation types, elevation, time of day, and insularity. *Ecology*, **54**, 687–708.

Janzen, D.H. & Schoener, Th. W. (1968). Differences in insect abundance and diversity between wetter and drier sites during a tropical dry season. *Ecology*, **49**, 96–110.

Janzen, D.H., Ataroff, M., Fariñas, M., Reyes, S., Rincón, N., Soler, A., Soriano, P. & Vera, M. (1976). Changes in the arthropod community along an elevational gradient in the Venezuelan Andes. *Biotropica*, **8**, 193–203.

Karr, J.R. (1976). Seasonality, resource availability, and community diversity in tropical bird communities. *The American Naturalist*, **110**, 973–994.

Karr, J.R., Schemske, D.W. & Brokaw, N. (1982). Temporal variation in the undergrowth bird community in a tropical forest. *Ecology of a Tropical Forest: Seasonal Rhythms and Long-term Changes* (Ed. by E. G. Leigh, A. S. Rand & D. H. Windsor), pp. 441–453. Smithsonian Press, Washington, DC, U.S.A.

Leigh, E.G. (1975). Population fluctuations, community stability and environmental variability. *Ecology and Evolution of Communities* (Ed. by M. L. Cody & J. M. Diamond), pp. 51–73. Harvard University Press, Cambridge, Mass., U.S.A.

McElravy, E., Resh, V.H., Wolda, H. & Flint, O.S. (1981). Diversity of Trichoptera in a 'non-seasonal' tropical environment. *Proceedings Third International Symposium on Trichoptera* (Ed. by G. Moretti), pp. 149–156. W. Junk, The Hague, Netherlands.

McElravy, E., Wolda, H. & Resh, V.H. (1982). Seasonality and annual variability of caddisflies adults (Trichoptera) in a 'non-seasonal' tropical environment. *Archiv für Hydrobiologie*, **94**, 302–317.

Mello, D.A. (1980). Estudo populacional de algumas espécies de roedores do Cerrado (Norte do município de Formosa, Goiás). *Revista Brasileira de Biologia*, **40**, 843–860.

Morton, E.S. (1977). Intratropical migration in the yellow-green vireo and piratic flycatcher. *The Auk*, **94**, 97–106.

Orians, G.H. (1969). The number of bird species in some tropical forests. *Ecology*, **50**, 783–801.

Robbins, R.K. & Small, G.B. Jr. (1981). Wind dispersal of Panamanian hairstreak butterflies (Lepidoptera: Lycaenidae) and its evolutionary significance. *Biotropica*, **13**, 308–315.

Sargent, T.D. (1976). *Legion of the Night: The Underwing Moths*. University of Massachusetts Press, Amherst, Mass., U.S.A.

Smith, W., Kravitz, D. & Grassle, F.J. (1979). Confidence intervals for similarity measures using the two-sample jackknife. *Multivariate Methods in Ecological Work* (Ed. by L.Orlocci, R. Rao & W. M. Stiteler), pp. 253–262. International Cooperative Publishing House, Fairland, Maryland, U.S.A.

Taylor, L.R. (1978). Bates, Williams, Hutchinson—a variety of diversities. *Diversity of Insect Faunas* (Ed. by L.A. Mound & N. Waloff), pp. 1–18. Blackwell Scientific Publications, Oxford.

Taylor, L.R. (1981). The Rothamsted Insect Survey—an approach to the theory and practice of synoptic pest forecasting in agriculture. *Movements of Highly Mobile Insects: Concepts and Methodology in Research* (Ed. by R. L. Rabb & G. G. Kennedy), pp. 147–185. North Carolina State University Press.

Taylor, R.A.J. & Taylor, L.R. (1979). A behavioural model for the evolution of spatial dynamics. *Population Dynamics* (Ed. by R. M. Anderson, B. D. Turner & L. R. Taylor), pp. 1–27. Blackwell Scientific Publications, Oxford.

Taylor, L.R. & Woiwod, I.P. (1980). Temporal stability as a density-dependent species characteristic. *Journal of Animal Ecology*, **49**, 209–224.

Terborgh, J. (1970). Distribution of environmental gradients: theory and a preliminary interpretation of distributional patterns in the avifauna of the Cordillera Vilcabamba, Peru. *Ecology*, **52**, 23–40.

Toft, C.A. (1980). Seasonal variation in populations of Panamanian litter frogs and their prey: a comparison of wetter and drier sites. *Oecologia (Berl.)*. **47**, 34–38.

Warwick, W.F. (1980). Chironomidae (Diptera) responses to 2800 years of cultural influence: a palaeolimnological study with special reference to sedimentation, eutrophication, and contamination processes. *The Canadian Entomologist*, **112**, 1193–1239.

Wells, K. (1979). Reproductive behavior and male mating success in a neotropical toad, *Bufo typhonius*. *Biotropica*, **11**, 301–307.

Williams, C.B. (1939). An analysis of four years captures of insects in a lighttrap. I. General survey; sex proportion, phenology, and time of flight. *Transactions Royal Entomological Society London*, **89**, 79–131.

Wolda, H. (1977). Fluctuations in abundance of some Homoptera in a neotropical forest. *Geo-Eco-Trop*, **1**, 229–257.

Wolda, H. (1978a) Seasonal fluctuations in rainfall, food and abundance of tropical insects. *Journal of Animal Ecology*, **47**, 369–381.

Wolda, H. (1978b). Fluctuations in abundance of tropical insects. *The American Naturalist*, **112**, 1017–1045.

Wolda, H. (1980a). Seasonality of tropical insects. I. Leafhoppers (Homoptera) in Las Cumbres, Panama. *Journal of Animal Ecology*, **49**, 277–290.

Wolda, H. (1980b). *Fluctuaciones estacionales de insectos el el tropico: Sphingidae*. Memorias del VI Congreso de la Sociedad Colombiana de Entomologia "SOCOLEN" (July 1979) pp. 10–58. Socolen, Cali, Colombia.

Wolda, H. (1981). Similarity indices, sample size and diversity. *Oecologia (Berl.)*, **50**, 296–302.

Wolda, H. (1982). Seasonality of leafhoppers (Homoptera) on Barro Colorado Island, Panama. *Ecology of a Tropical Forest: Seasonal Rhythms and Long-term Changes* (Ed. by E. G. Leigh, A. S. Rand & D. M. Windsor), pp. 319–330. Smithsonian Press, Washington, DC, U.S.A.

Wolda, H. (1983a). Seasonal distribution of sloth moths (*Cryptoses choloepi* Dyar) (Pyralidae: Chrysauginae). *The Evolution and Ecology of Armadillas, sloths and vermilinguas (Mammalia, Xenarthra: Edentata)* (Ed. by G. G. Montgomery). Smithsonian Press, Washington D.C., USA. (in press).

Wolda, H. (1983b). Diversity: diversity indices and tropical cockroaches. *Oecologia (Berlin)*, (in press).

Wolda, H. & Fisk, F.W. (1981). Seasonality of tropical insects. II. Blattaria in Panama. *Journal of Animal Ecology*, **50**, 827–838.

Wolda, H. & Foster, R. (1978). *Zunacetha annulata* (Lep: Dioptidae), an outbreak insect in a neotropical forest. *Geo-Eco-Trop*, **2**, 443–454.

Wolda, H. & Galindo, P. (1981). Population fluctuations of mosquitos in the nonseasonal tropics. *Ecological Entomology*, **6**, 251–280.

The assessment of faunal diversity and guild size in tropical forests with particular reference to the Psocoptera

EDWARD BROADHEAD

Department of Zoology, Leeds University
Leeds LS2 9JT, U.K.

SUMMARY

1 The diversity of the psocid fauna is compared at different sites within a lowland tropical forest and in various forest types in different parts of the world. Sampling methods and their biases and the size of sample and the representation of diversity are discussed.

2 The relative abundances of the 148 psocid species in two light traps run continuously over 1 year on Barro Colorado Island, Panama, (BCI) show a satisfactory fit to the log-series. Collections of 1000 individuals or more give α values close to the final value based on 10 092 individuals but little reliance can be placed on collections of < 500 individuals from this particular habitat.

3 On BCI, psocid abundance over the entire year is very similar in the upper canopy and at near-ground level. It varies from the wet to the dry season more in the upper canopy than near the ground. There are modal differences in species composition between these two strata but there are no exclusively upper canopy or near-ground species.

4 There is a progressive increase in psocid diversity from temperate to tropical forest, from the lowest diversity in England ($\alpha = 1 \cdot 34$) through S. Australia, Jamaica and montane East Africa, to Trinidad and montane Panama, to the highest diversity in the lowland forest of BCI ($\alpha = 24 \cdot 38$).

5 The biases of five collecting techniques, direct count, beating branches, suction trap, light trap and insecticidal fogging, are discussed.

6 Guild size in England and on BCI is assessed with reference to the two major niche differentiations of the Psocoptera; namely, the bark- and the foliage-frequenters, and the alga-fungal spore and the lichen eaters.

INTRODUCTION

There has, in recent years, been much theorizing about the factors which have produced the high diversity of plant and animal life in the tropics, particularly in tropical forests, and about the relative importance of historical, environmental and biotic explanations of this high diversity. Rosen (1981) has summarized the arguments. Studies of tropical biotas have centred on many aspects among which may be instanced: the relation between climate and forest structure (Leigh 1975), stratification in tropical forests (Smith 1973), insect size patterns (Schoener & Janzen 1968),

107

immigration and extinction rates and equilibria in small units (Simberloff & Wilson 1969), community diversity and resource availability (Karr 1976) and patterns of population fluctuation and of seasonality (Wolda 1978, 1980; Wolda & Foster 1978).

The upper canopy of the tropical forest, the most inaccessible of all the tropical habitats, is only now being subjected to sustained and organized studies. As far as invertebrate animals are concerned these studies are being carried out, of necessity, by the use of trapping methods, e.g. the long-term light trapping by Wolda on Barro Colorado Island, or by insecticidal fogging of the canopy, e.g. the fogging of fifteen trees of *Luehea seemannii* Triana & Planch carried out by Montgomery and Lubin in 1975–76 in the Panama Canal area from which reports of the Homoptera (Wolda 1979) and of the Coleoptera (Erwin & Scott 1980) have so far been published. Erwin in this volume describes fogging techniques recently in use in Manaus, Amazonia. Studies of faunal diversity for a long period have been confused rather than clarified by the great proliferation of diversity indices. This phase of confusion seems now to be coming to an end with the demonstration by Taylor, Kempton & Woiwod (1976) of the superiority of α, the diversity parameter of the log-series model. There has, however, been no critical assessment of the biases of the various sampling methods on which these studies of diversity are based. There has also, as yet, been very little concern with the identity of the species themselves or with their biology. Indeed, in most taxa we have little or no information on the precise resources required by the various species and in some taxa the majority of the species are unknown, e.g. of the 295 species of Psocoptera from Panamanian forests which I have recognized, 89·5% are undescribed.

MATERIALS

The aim of the present paper is to bring together the results of several surveys of Psocoptera in tropical forests and in other kinds of forests and to interpret these results in the light of what we know about psocid ecology. I draw upon the results of the following, as yet unpublished, surveys of psocid populations in Panama. The psocid collection, representing weekly sampling by Dr Wolda's two light traps, one 3 m from the ground, the other directly above it in the canopy 27 m from ground level, run continuously for 1 year in the lowland monsoon forest (121 m altitude) on BCI, is the largest and the most informative one. I have also analysed the collection from Dr Wolda's single light trap, run daily in the canopy for 6 months and near ground level for 2 years in a montane forest (1050 m altitude) at Fortuna, Chiriquí Province. My own collections are: from fogging the crowns of three trees of *Luehea seemannii* on the Pipeline Road, 1978; from fogging the canopy of eight trees in the humid forest at the Atlantic end of the Canal near Gatun and of eight trees in the monsoon forest at the Pacific end of the Canal 8 km SW of Balboa, 1979; by beating branches of the natural shrub understorey along the Zetek Trail and of mango (*Mangifera indica* L.) in clearings near the Laboratory, BCI. I have also used the original data from my psocid survey in East Africa (Broadhead & Richards 1980, 1982) and from the Ph.D. theses of Turner (1972) and of Evans (1977); I have also briefly examined the psocids obtained by Montgomery & Lubin by fogging *Luehea seemannii* on the Pipeline Road, Canal area, in 1976.

RESULTS

Niche differentiations in Psocoptera

The Psocoptera, the major group of animals adapted as micro-epiphyte feeders, number about 2500 species, nearly all of them arboreal. The arboreal species in Britain fall into two groups, the bark-, and the foliage-frequenters, feeding from and ovipositing on the bark and on the leaves, respectively. Of the nine commonest bark-frequenting species on larch (*Larix decidua* Mill.) in northern England (Broadhead 1958), seven species feed primarily on *Pleurococcus* and fungal spores. When these preferred foods are scarce, they will take lichen but this results in higher mortality and lower natality rates. The other two species are primarily lichen feeders. When their preferred food, lichen, is scarce, *Pleurococcus* and fungal spores are readily accepted with no deleterious effect, in laboratory tests, on oviposition and mortality rates. Nevertheless, they do not maintain populations on the less preferred foods in nature in places where lichen is scarce. All the British foliage-frequenting species studied by New (1970) are *Pleurococcus* and fungal spore feeders. In Britain and western Europe, then, the two major niche differentiations concern the place to feed and oviposit (bark or leaf), and the food preferred (alga-fungal spore mixture or lichen). Elsewhere, what little is known rests entirely on examination of gut contents (Turner 1974 for Jamaican psocids, and Broadhead & Richards 1980, 1982 for East African psocids). Species richness increases from temperate to tropical regions. Britain has fifty-one indigenous species (Broadhead 1964) with twenty-three species recorded from larch. Turner (1972) in a 2-year study recorded eighty-six species from Jamaica with fifty-three species from mango. Evans (1977), in a 2-year study, recorded 150 species from Trinidad with 116 species from mango. In the period 1977–81 I have recognized 295 species from Panama, 219 of these from the Canal area. Psocid densities have been recorded only from England and Trinidad. In northern England, densities on larch trees reach 594 – 4317 individuals m^{-2} of the bark of the branches whereas in Trinidad densities of only thirty-five and fifty-three individuals m^{-2} of bark surface have been reported for mango and citrus respectively (Broadhead & Evans 1977). Densities, although not measured, are certainly very much lower in the shrub stratum of the forest on BCI than they are in Trinidad.

Patterns of abundance on Barro Colorado Island

Comparison will first be made of species discovery curves for Jamaica (Fig. 1) and BCI (Fig. 2). Figure 1 summarizes the progressive discovery of species in monthly samples taken by beating branches of mango at four altitudes in the Blue Mountains, Jamaica, over a period of 20 months. The upper asymptote is reached within 1 year's sampling when only 300–600 individuals have been taken at any one site. By contrast, in the far richer and more complex lowland forest of BCI, the combined captures in the two light traps (Fig. 2) show a continuous increase during the year to 148 species, with more species still appearing when 10 000 individuals have been taken. Bayesian analysis,

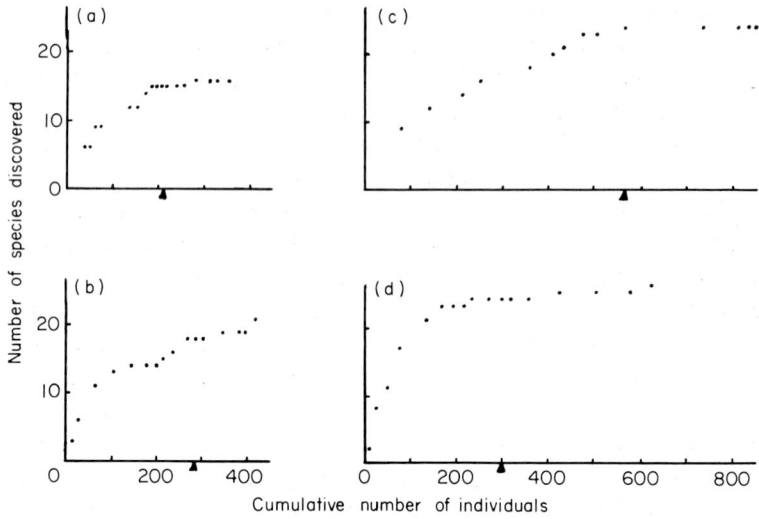

FIG. 1. The cumulative discovery of psocid species with increasing sampling effort over a 20-month period from mango, *Mangifera indica*, at four altitudes in the Blue Mountains, Jamaica. Arrowhead indicates 1 year's sampling: (a) 305 m, (b) 610 m, (c) 915 m, (d) 1220 m altitude (drawn from data of Turner 1972)

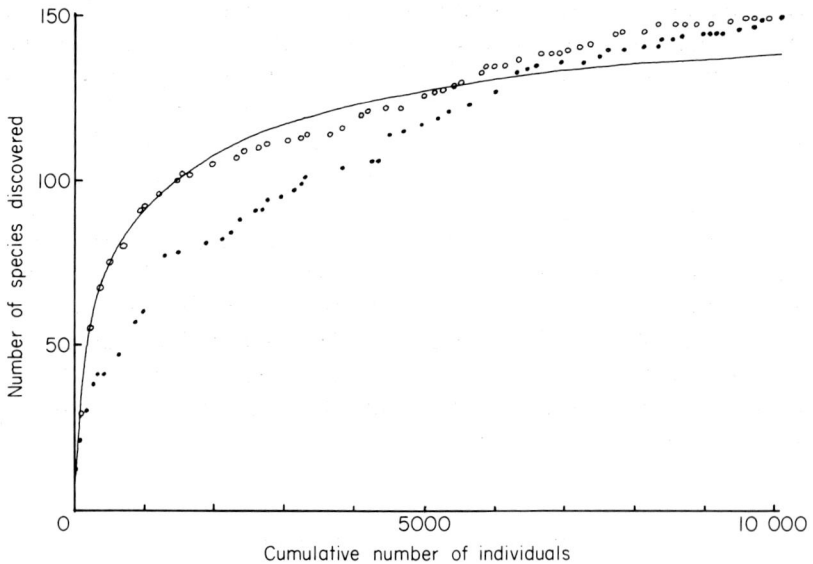

FIG. 2. The cumulative discovery of psocid species with increasing sampling effort over 1 year, BCI, Panama. Captures from upper canopy and near-ground light traps combined: (●) with weeks in temporal order; (○) with weeks in random order; (——) Poisson expectation (after E. Broadhead & H. Wolda, unpublished)

which is based on a prior assumption about the distribution of the number of the unobserved species, suggests that another fifteen to thirty-five species are yet to be discovered at this particular site. The continuous line of Fig. 2 is based on the Poisson expectation, assuming a random distribution of all individuals in time. The discrepancy between observed and expected curves is due almost entirely to phenological patterns of the various species since the species discovery curve constructed by taking weeks at random accords closely with the Poisson.

The BCI light trap data can also be expressed as a species abundance distribution (Fig. 5a). The total collecton of 10 092 individuals over 148 species has a long tail of rare species. One third of all the species are represented each by only one to four individuals over the entire year's trapping. This curve shows a satisfactory fit to the log series ($\chi^2 = 20\cdot36$, d.f. 20, $P = 0\cdot45$) so that the α diversity index can be used as a valid summary. Taylor, et al. (1976) have demonstrated the superiority of α, the diversity parameter of the log-series model, over other diversity indices in discriminating between species structures at different sites, at least when applied to large samples of nocturnal Lepidoptera taken in light traps. They pointed to the desirability of testing the fit of large samples of other taxa to the log-series before this diversity statistic is used extensively. The practical difficulties in assessing satisfactoriness of fit to the log-series originate partly from the fact that establishment of a fit derives only from failure to demonstrate a significant difference, a failure more likely to occur when only small collections are available, and partly from the necessity of collating categories in order to use the χ^2 test which results in loss of information. We can obtain some guidance as to the size of collection necessary in order to have reasonable confidence in the use of the α index in the following way. Figure 3 shows the cumulative values of α as the size of the light trap collection of psocids on BCI increases progressively week by week over the 1-year period. There is a wide fluctuation from 15·7 to 9·4 over the first 2 weeks with a collection of < 100 individuals. The index then steadily rises until, with a collection of 6500 individuals after 33 weeks of trapping, the value of α at 23·92 almost attains its final level of 24·59. This steady rise in α results from the phenological patterns of appearance of adults of the various species, since the light traps capture adults only. In order to examine the relation of α to sample size alone, we can remove this phenological component by drawing weeks out at random and calculating cumulative values of α. Eight such sets of data obtained by taking a random permutation of the weeks are set out in Fig. 3. Collections of 1000 individuals or more give α values reasonably close to its final value. Collections of < 500 individuals are clearly likely to give very variable results.

Stratification and seasonal patterns

The stratification of psocid populations and its response to seasonal changes are indicated by comparison of the captures in the upper canopy and in the near-ground light traps on BCI. In 1977–78 when the trapping was carried out, the island had a well marked dry season of 21 weeks from mid-December to mid-May and a well marked wet season of 31 weeks. The stratification of these psocid populations in terms of density, of diversity and of species identity is very small.

Psocid abundance over the entire year is very similar in the canopy and at near-ground level. There is very little difference in size of total catch in the two traps (Table 1). Psocid density, as judged by the mean numbers of individuals captured per week (Table 1), is greater in the wet season than in the dry season, but this is due largely

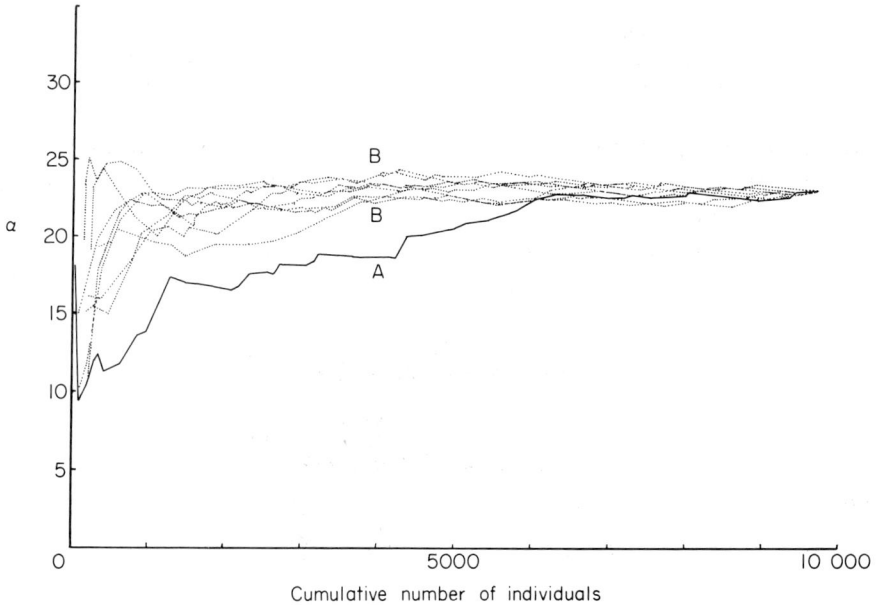

FIG. 3. Cumulative values of α with increasing sampling effort for light trap captures of Psocoptera over 1 year, BCI, Panama. Captures from canopy and near-ground light traps combined: A, data obtained by taking the weeks in chronological order; B–B, eight sets of data obtained by taking a random permutation of the weeks.

to changes in density in the canopy. In fact, in the lower stratum of the forest, buffered as it is from major climatic changes, psocid densities show little change from season to season.

In terms of diversity, the near-ground psocid population is slightly but significantly more diverse than the canopy population (Table 1). This diversity is greatest in the late wet season.

With regard to species composition of the canopy and near-ground psocid populations, there are no exclusively canopy or understorey species. The seventy-seven species represented in the year's light trap captures by $\geqslant$ ten individuals occur in both the canopy and in the lower trap. There are, however, modal differences in species composition. Nineteen species are significantly more numerous, and twenty-three species are significantly less numerous, in the canopy trap than in the near-ground trap. Many of the other species show non-significant differences because of the small number of individuals captured, but it is noteworthy that three of the nine commonest

TABLE 1. Psocid density and diversity in monsoon forest, Barro Colorado Island, Panama, from 1 year's light trap captures. Mean numbers of individuals captured per week, total captures and the log-series parameter α for captures in the upper canopy and near the ground

	Mean no. of individuals per week		Total capture	α with 95% confidence limits
	Wet season	Dry season		
Canopy trap	125·6	62·5	5250	22·77 ± 1·79
Lower trap	94·9	85·6	4842	25·75 ± 1·98
Both traps	220·5	148·1	10092	24·59 ± 1·64

species are equally represented in both canopy and lower traps. The variation of species composition of the psocid populations with the season can be illustrated by the relative abundance of adults of six of the fourteen commonest species taken in the light traps (Fig. 4). The six have been chosen to show the complete range of phenologies from

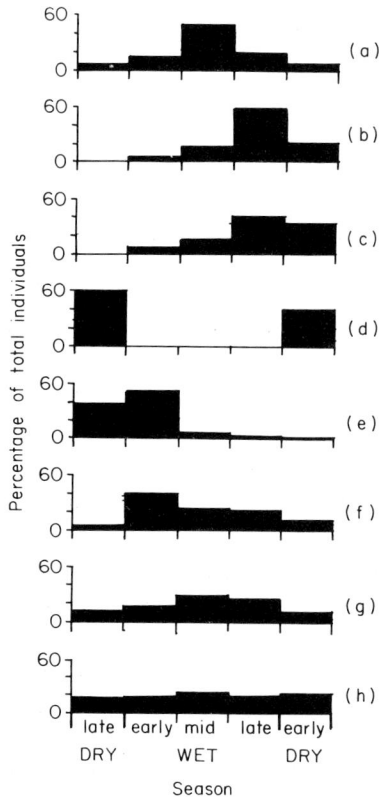

FIG. 4. Seasonal abundance of adults of six common psocid species (near-ground and upper canopy traps combined) and of total psocids in canopy and near ground in the monsoon forest, BCI, Panama over 1 year. (a) *Blaste* sp. C., (b) Caeciliid genus III sp. C-2., (c) *Ptiloneura* sp. C., (d) *Ptycta* sp. E., (e) *Isthmopsocus* sp. B., (f) *Triplocania* sp. F., (g) total psocids, canopy, (h) total psocids, near-ground trap.

exclusively dry season species, e.g. *Ptycta* sp. E, to almost exclusively wet season
species, e.g. *Blaste* sp. C and *Triplocania* sp.F. The climate here is sufficiently seasonal
to impose a seasonal pattern on most species, but the seasons are not so rigorous as to
impose the same pattern on all of them. Moreover, all these varied patterns combine
to give a distribution of total psocids, which indicates that the psocid population as a
whole is grazing on the micro-epiphytes in this forest to a remarkably uniform degree
throughout the year—especially so in the lower stratum of the forest.

Diversities in different forest types and climates

From surveys such as these, there follow two broad lines of enquiry: on the one hand,
comparison of faunal diversities in forests of different types and in different climates,
and so to a consideration of the limitations set by time and place; on the other hand,

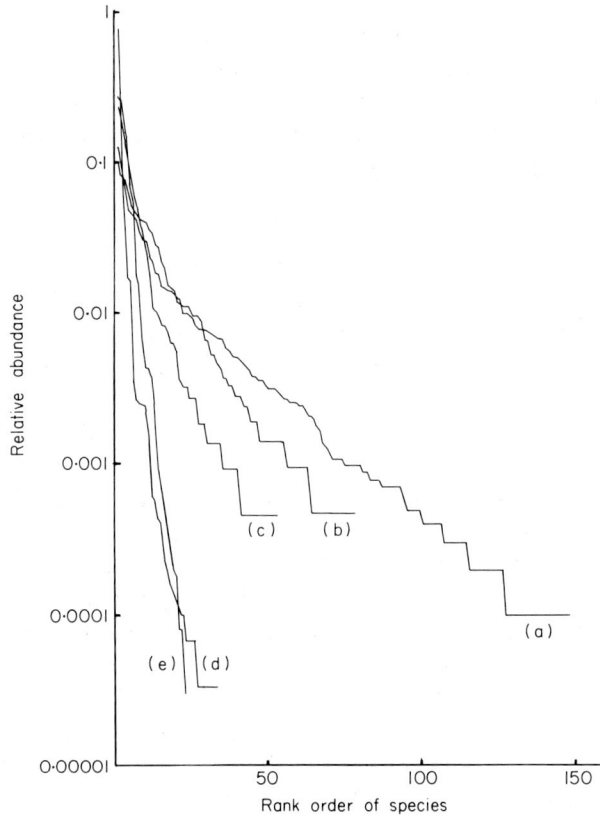

FIG. 5. Species abundance distributions of five collections of Psocoptera. Log proportional abundance
against ranked species: (a) Panama, BCI, light traps, canopy and near-ground combined, $\alpha = 24\cdot59$; (b)
Panama, Fortuna, montane forest, light trap near ground, $\alpha = 15\cdot94$; (c) Panama, Fortuna, montane forest,
light trap, canopy, $\alpha = 9\cdot79$; (d) Jamaica montane forest, *Juniperus lucayana* Britton, beating branches,
$\alpha = 3\cdot66$; (e) England, larch *Larix decidua* Mill., beating branches, $\alpha = 2\cdot36$.

intensive studies directed to the ecological processes maintaining this diversity at any one place. Let us take each of these in turn.

Species abundance distributions are given in Fig. 5 for five of the large collections available. The Panamanian collections are: the total collection from Wolda's two light traps in the lowland forest, BCI ($n = 10\,092$ individuals), the light trap collections from the montane forest at Fortuna, with the trap in the near-ground position ($n = 2110$) and then with the trap in the upper canopy ($n = 2191$). The Jamaican data obtained by beating *Juniperus lucayana* Britton weekly over 1 year at an altitude of 1220 m in the Blue Mountains ($n = 29\,838$) are taken from Turner (1972). The data for northern England, obtained by beating branches of larch at many localities in Yorkshire in the late summer ($n = 39\,699$), are taken from Broadhead (1958, Table 6). To all these a satisfactory fit to the log-series obtains. Table 2 records the values of α for twenty-five collections of psocids, eighteen of which each comprise > 1000 individuals. The α diversity index steadily increases from the temperate climate of northern England, where psocids overwinter in the egg stage, through the Mediterranean climate of Melbourne, South Australia, where adult psocids are present throughout the year, to the tropical montane climates of East Africa at altitudes of 2438–3200 m and of Jamaica at altitudes up to 1220 m. Trinidad, only 11 km from the continental land mass and less isolated than Jamaica, has a higher diversity and the highest diversities occur in the lowland tropical forests of Panama.

Sampling bias

These indices in Table 2 are obtained by five collecting techniques. The first—direct count on twigs—gives a virtually unbiased collection. The straight larch twigs were quickly enclosed in 25-cm long test tubes, the contents being then examined in the laboratory so that all developmental stages from first instar to adult were accurately recorded. Beating branches of larch trees in Britain gives little bias of adults since few adults fly away. These, as well as the Jamaican, data include nymphs identified to species as well as adults, but the early instars tend not to be dislodged by beating. Moreover, beating underestimates those few psocid species which habitually live under silken tents. The remaining data of Table 2 refer to adults only. Suction trapping clearly takes those species which fly most but the extent of this bias is not known. The relative biases of light trapping, fogging and beating in Panama can be judged by comparing the proportional distribution of individuals over the various families (Fig. 6). The histograms of the near-ground light trapping on BCI and of beating shrubs along the Zetek Trail on BCI are directly comparable. The two most outstanding biases are: the Archipsocidae (twenty-one spp.), which for the most part live under silken webs on the bark, are obtained by beating but are excluded by the other techniques; the Lepidopsocidae (ten spp.), which are obtained in large numbers by fogging and beating, are almost absent in the light traps.

The number and size of psocid guilds in tropical forest

Finally, how many guilds exist among these psocids in the tropical forest and what are their sizes compared with those in temperate forests? Of the 148 species present in the

TABLE 2. The diversities of Psocoptera in various climates and forest types

	Source of data	Collecting method	No. of collections	Size range of collections (no. of individuals)	Mean α	Range of α
ENGLAND	Broadhead (1958)	direct count & beating	4	1016–39 699	1·34	0·68–2·36
SOUTH AUSTRALIA	New (1975)	suction trap	4	1203–1829	3·22	3·01–3·58
EAST AFRICA	Broadhead & Richards (1980, 1982)	beating	1	746	5·74	5·74
JAMAICA	Turner (1972)	beating	4	2090–29 838	4·95	3·66–6·52
TRINIDAD	Evans (1977)	beating	3	959–2653	12·84	11·81–14·81
PANAMA						
MONTANE (Fortuna)	Broadhead & Wolda (unpubl.)	light trap	2	2110–2191	12·87	9·79–15·94
LOWLAND (Canal area)	Broadhead & Wolda (unpubl.)	light trap	2	4842–5250	24·38	22·77–25·75
LOWLAND	Broadhead (unpubl.)	fogging	4	317–787	20·79	17·50–24·18
LOWLAND	Broadhead (unpubl.)	beating	1	259	19·59	19·59

light traps on BCI, sixty-one species—all those represented by ≥ twenty-five individuals—made up 95% of the total psocid population. It is possible to give only rough estimates of the two main niche differentiations among these sixty-one species. Regarding the Psocidae, Myopsocidae, Philotarsidae, Peripsocidae and Pseudocaeciliidae as bark-frequenters and the Caeciliidae, Lachesillidae and Ectopsocidae as foliage-frequenters there are at least thirty-two species of the former and fourteen species of the latter. The foods taken by the thirty commonest species comprise fungal

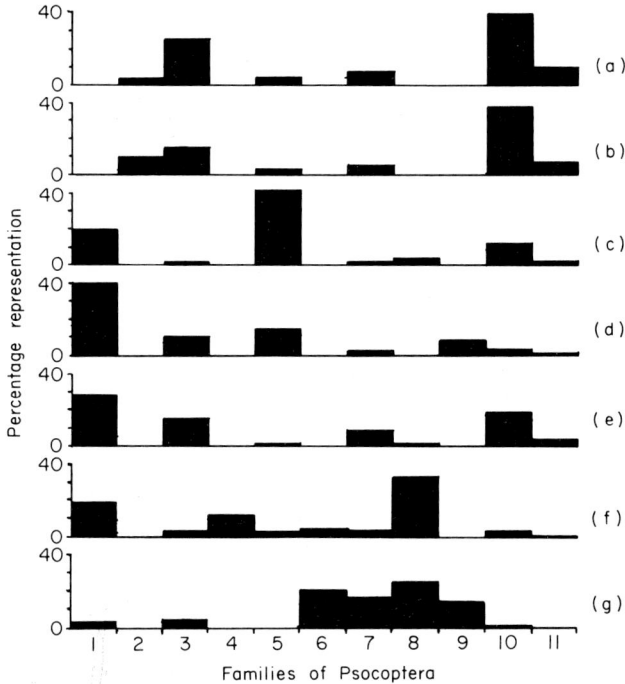

FIG. 6. Proportional distribution of individuals over eleven families of Psocoptera at seven forest sites, Panama Canal area (families represented by < 5% at any one site excluded): (a) BCI canopy light trap; (b) BCI near-ground light trap; (c) Pipeline Road, canopy fogging of *Luehea seemannii*, 1978; (d) near Gatun, humid forest canopy, fogging eight trees; (e) near Balboa, monsoon forest canopy, fogging eight trees; (f) BCI beating branches of shrub understorey, Zetek Trail; (g), BCI beating branches of *Mangifera indica* near laboratory. Key to families: 1, Lepidopsocidae; 2, Ptiloneuridae; 3, Caeciliidae; 4, Asiopsocidae; 5, Lachesillidae; 6, Ectopsocidae; 7, Pseudocaeciliidae; 8, Archipsocidae; 9, Hemipsocidae; 10, Psocidae; 11, Myopsocidae.

spores of various kinds, free-living algal cells and, in some species, some lichen. Table 3 indicates the patterns in five of these species. The presence of lichen in the gut up to a proportion of 25% does not, however, indicate a lichen-feeder (Broadhead 1958) and indeed the lichenophilous habit can be demonstrated only by laboratory experiment. In only two of the thirty species was lichen found abundantly in the gut, so that the great majority of these species appear to be alga-fungal spore feeders, and among these are about sixteen species of bark-frequenters. Assuming these thirty species to be representative of the sixty-one species, it is likely that on BCI, among those species which make up 95% of the total psocid population, there is a guild of at least thirty-two species of bark-frequenting psocids exploiting the alga-fungal spore mixture, as compared with seven species in northern England. The size of the ecological problem of the maintenance of this coexistence is greater in the tropics, and there have been many suggested explanations, of which spatial hererogeneity plus migration on the one hand, and predation pressure on the other, are two important ones. I would, however, suggest another possibility derived from the findings of a detailed population dynamics study of two *Mesopsocus* species, which I carried out some years ago (Broadhead &

TABLE 3. Gut contents of five of the common psocid species in light traps, Barro Colorado Island, Panama. +, infrequent; + +, common; + + +, abundant

	Lichen	Thick-walled fungal hyphae & spores	Thin-walled fungal hyphae & spores	Algal cells
Blaste sp. C		+ +	+ +	+
Caecilius sp. X-1		+ + +	+ + +	
Caecilius sp. R	+	+	+ + +	
Myopsocus sp. D	+ + +	+ +		+
Thyrsopsocus sp. E	+ +	+ +	+ +	+ +

Wapshere 1966). In larch woodlands in northern England, two *Mesopsocus* species are very abundant and feed on the same food at the same time at the same place. It was found that each *Mesopsocus* species was limited in density by intraspecific competition for oviposition sites which differed modally in the two species, and evidently this limitation of density effectively prevented a food shortage developing as a result of psocid grazing. Yet, there appeared to be many suitable but unused oviposition sites on the bark. The real universe for oviposition was clearly much more tenuous than the apparent one. A larch twig is, in fact, a very busy place. Not only was one oviposition site every 13 cm length of twig taken up by a previous year's egg batch not yet eroded away, but there was one individual every 6·7 cm length of twig of another kind of animal (lachnids, psyllids, spiders, anthocorids, syrphid larvae etc.), which would interfere with the oviposition of a *Mesopsocus* female. Perhaps we should pay attention to the animals of other species operating not necessarily as predators or competitors but merely as interferers which, by their mere presence as well as by their movements, will reduce both the time and the space available to any particular species.

ACKNOWLEDGMENTS

I wish to thank Dr Henk Wolda for putting his light trap collections of Psocoptera at my disposal and Dr E. L. Mockford, who has given so freely of his time and expertise in helping me with problems of psocid taxonomy. The Royal Society, the Natural Environment Research Council and the Smithsonian Scholarly Studies Program have given me financial support for my work in Panama.

REFERENCES

Broadhead, E. (1958). The psocid fauna of larch trees in northern England—an ecological study of mixed species populations exploiting a common resource. *Journal of Animal Ecology*, **27**, 217–263.

Broadhead, E. (1964) Psocoptera. *A Check List of British Insects* (Ed. by G. S. Kloet & W. D. Hincks), pp. 23–25. Handbooks for the Identification of British Insects XI(1). Royal Entomological Society, London.

Broadhead, E. & Evans, H.A. (1977). The diversity and ecology of the Psocoptera in tropical forests. *Actas del IV Simposium internacional de Ecologia tropical.* **1**, 183–196.

Broadhead, E. & Richards, A.M. (1980). The Peripsocidae and Psocidae (Psocoptera) of East Africa. *Systematic Entomology*, **5**, 357–397.

Broadhead, E. & Richards, A.M. (1982). Psocoptera of East Africa—a taxonomic and ecological survey. *Biological Journal of the Linnaean Society*, **17**, 137–216.

Broadhead, E. & Wapshere, A.J. (1966). *Mesopsocus* populations on larch in England—the distribution and dynamics of two closely-related coexisting species of Psocoptera sharing the same food resource. *Ecological Monographs*, **36**, 327–388.

Erwin, T.L. (1983). Beetles and other insects of tropical forest canopies at Manaus, Brazil sampled by insecticidal fogging. *Tropical Rain Forest: Ecology and Management* (Ed. by S. L. Sutton, T. C. Whitmore & A. C. Chadwick), pp. 59–75. Blackwell Scientific Publications, Oxford.

Erwin, T.L. & Scott, J.C. (1980). Seasonal and size patterns, trophic structure and richness of Coleoptera in the tropical arboreal ecosystem: the fauna of the tree *Luehea seemannii* Triana & Planch in the Canal zone of Panama. *The Coleopterists Bulletin*, **34**, 305–322.

Evans, H.A.V. (1977). *Ecological and taxonomic studies of the Psocoptera of Trinidad.* Ph.D. thesis, University of Leeds.

Karr, J.R. (1976). Seasonality, resource availability and community diversity in tropical bird communities. *The American Naturalist*, **110**, 973–994.

Leigh, E.G. (1975). Structure and climate in tropical rain forest. *Annual Review of Ecology and Systematics*, **6**, 67–86.

New, T.R. (1970). The relative abundance of some British Psocoptera on different species of trees. *Journal of Animal Ecology*, **39**, 521–540.

New, T.R. (1975). Aerial dispersal of some Victorian Psocoptera as indicated by suction trap captures. *Journal of the Australian Entomological Society*, **14**, 179–184.

Rosen, B.R. (1981). The tropical high diversity enigma—the corals'-eye view. *The Evolving Biosphere* (Ed. by P. L. Forey), pp. 103–129. British Museum (Natural History), Cambridge University Press, Cambridge.

Schoener, T.W. & Janzen, D.H. (1968). Notes on environmental determinants of tropical versus temperate insect size patterns. *The American Naturalist*, **102**, 207–224.

Simberloff, D.S. & Wilson, E.O. (1969). Experimental zoogeography of islands: the colonisation of empty islands. *Ecology*, **50**, 278–296.

Smith, A.P. (1973). Stratification of temperate and tropical forests. *The American Naturalist*, **107**, 671–683.

Taylor, L.R., Kempton, R.A. & Woiwod, I.P. (1976) Diversity statistics and the log-series model. *Journal of Animal Ecology*, **45**, 255–272.

Turner, B.D. (1972). *Taxonomic and ecological studies of the Psocoptera of Jamaica.* Ph.D. thesis, University of Leeds.

Turner, B.D. (1974). The population dynamics of tropical arboreal Psocoptera (Insecta) on two species of conifers in the Blue Mountains, Jamaica. *Journal of Animal Ecology*, **43**, 323–337.

Wolda, H. (1978). Fluctuations in abundance of tropical insects. *The American Naturalist*, **112**, 1017–1045.

Wolda, H. (1979). Abundance and diversity of Homoptera in the canopy of a tropical forest. *Ecological Entomology*, **4**, 181–190.

Wolda, H. (1980). Seasonality of tropical insects. 1. Leafhoppers (Homoptera) in Las Cumbres, Panama. *Journal of Animal Ecology*, **49**, 277–290.

Wolda, H. & Foster, R. (1978). *Zunacetha annulata* (Lepidoptera: Dioptidae), an outbreak insect in a neotropical forest. *Geo-Eco-Trop*, **2**, 443–454.

Microclimate and the flying Hemiptera fauna of a primary lowland rain forest in Sulawesi

CHRISTOPHER J. C. REES

Department of Biology, University of York, Heslington, York. YO1 5DD, U.K.

SUMMARY

1 Flying Homoptera and Heteroptera have been sampled with light and suction traps set at different heights between forest floor and canopy leaf layer in primary lowland rain forest in eastern Sulawesi. Correlated microclimatic measurements were made.

2 Bugs are caught in far greater numbers in the canopy than below it and the catches of most families of bugs increase steadily with increasing rainfall during the trapping period. Relatively more bugs fly in the canopy compared with the subcanopy on wet nights than do under rainless conditions.

3 The more rain falling during the trapping period, the higher is the modal weight among both flying Homoptera and Heteroptera.

4 Increased flight activity in cicadellids is not correlated with saturation deficit over the range 0–3·5 mbar, nor with the amount of rain falling in the 21 hours prior to trapping.

5 Bug faunas flying in dry spells are dissimilar in species composition to those of wet spells, but for similarly sized samples the log-series α diversity is independent of amount of rainfall.

6 On dry nights, a moon above the horizon during the trapping period significantly depresses catches of bugs in the tree canopy, but not below it.

7 It is suggested that rain may screen the bugs against echolocative predation by bats; the sizes of those that fly when there is no rain are mostly below the size at which 100 kHz ultrasound is efficiently scattered. These are mostly delphacids, in which flight activity is not significantly correlated with rainfall occurring at the time of flight.

INTRODUCTION

This paper examines some ways in which the vertical spatial distribution, catch sizes and species diversity of flying Homoptera and Heteroptera appear to be related to microclimatic factors in a lowland rain forest in eastern Sulawesi, Indonesia. The work was carried out during the limited period of a few weeks in February and March 1980 which was available for the Sulawesi phase of the expedition series 'Operation Drake', and has less of both the complication and interest that longer term observation of phenological effects might have provided. Little is known about the regulation of flight activity in rain forest insects and it will be shown here that, at least for Hemiptera, the amount of rain falling during the period of trapping affects very strongly the numbers and species composition of the flying bug population, and also the distribution of body size amongst them.

MATERIALS AND METHODS

Study site

The insect traps and microclimate recording equipment were set up in lowland evergreen rain forest beside the Soluwo River, in the Morowali district of eastern central Sulawesi, Indonesia (Lat. 1°51′ S, Long. 121°30′ E) at a site about 12 km inland, and a ground altitude of 5 m. The forest here has a rather uneven main canopy leaf layer between 20 and 30 m above ground level and quite numerous canopy gaps due to tree falls. Palms, especially climbing genera such as *Daemonorops*, *Calamus* and *Korthalsia* were abundant, and the forest showed signs of seasonal waterlogging. It corresponded closely with type A4c, according to the classification of Longman & Jenik (1974). *Syzygium syzygoides* (Miq.) Merrill and Perry was a common main canopy tree.

Traps and trap deployment

A pulley was slung from a major branch of a semi-emergent *Syzygium* at a height of 32 m above the ground. Two further pulleys were attached, one at the base of the same tree, and another to the base of a second tree, a *Garcinia* species 14 m distant. An endless triangular trap hoisting rope loop was then threaded through these pulleys. The hypotenuse of the loop made an angle of about 65° with the ground, and carried the four light traps, hung from it so that they would operate 30 m, 20 m, 10 m and 1 m above the ground. The trap line could be locked in any position during hoisting with a Jumar rope jamming clamp, which was itself anchored to the ground. This deployment resembled that used by Sutton & Hudson (1980) in Zaire. The four suction traps were hung from an identical roping system, from the crown of the same *Syzygium* tree to another ground anchor tree. The angle included between the lines of light and suction traps was about 5°.

Light traps. These were substantially the same 8 watt ultraviolet-rich fluorescent tube traps as those designed by Sutton (1980), each modified to carry an anemometer and photometer. Their electrical outputs were transmitted to recording equipment on the ground along the same multiple core cable as took power to the trap lights.

Suction traps. These were 9 inch diameter enclosed nylon mesh cone traps, powered by 9 inch coaxial 75 watt 240 volt 'Vent-Axia' fans, similar to the 46 cm propeller traps developed by Johnson & Taylor (1955).

Proximity of the traps to vegetation. The 30 m traps were within the crown of a *Syzygium* (Myrtaceae.) The 20 m traps were about 2 m clear of the crown of a *Garcinia* sp. (Guttiferae). The 10 m traps were at least 5 m clear of any foliage. The 1 m traps were about 2 m from the trunk of another *Garcinia* sp. close to young *Daemonorops* (Palmae) and *Freycinetia* Pandanaceae).

Trapping period and times. Continuously from 19.00 until 22.00 hours (local time) on most nights between 14 February and 16 March 1980, and on a few nights during the following fortnight.

Microclimate recording equipment. Anemometers and light meters were carried on all four light traps. An electrically aspirated thermistor psychrometer was suspended from the *Syzygium* so that it could be hoisted to any of the trap heights. Rainfall was measured with a 5 inch diameter funnel raingauge attached to a bridge across the Soluwo River about 30 m distant horizontally from the light trap line. No tree canopy interrupted the fall of rain into this gauge, so that it probably gave accurate estimates of what would have been falling onto the upper surface of the tree canopy nearby. Measurements of ambient light intensity during trapping periods were frustrated by the failure of the photometers. An index of potential lunar exposure has been calculated. The British Admiralty tables of Astronomical Ephemeris (1980) permit the determination of the fraction of any 3-hour trapping period for which the moon would have been above the horizon on a given date: (call this $0 < = V < = 1$). It is also possible to calculate the fraction of the lunar projected surface, as seen from earth, that would then have been illuminated (call this $0 < = S < = 1$). The lunar index (M) is then defined as $0 < = M = V \cdot S < = 1$. Clearly this makes no allowance for cloud cover.

RESULTS

Overall pattern of vertical distribution of Hemiptera

The highest light trap, and the upper two suction traps caught the largest numbers of individual Homoptera and Heteroptera. Figure 1 compares numbers of individuals

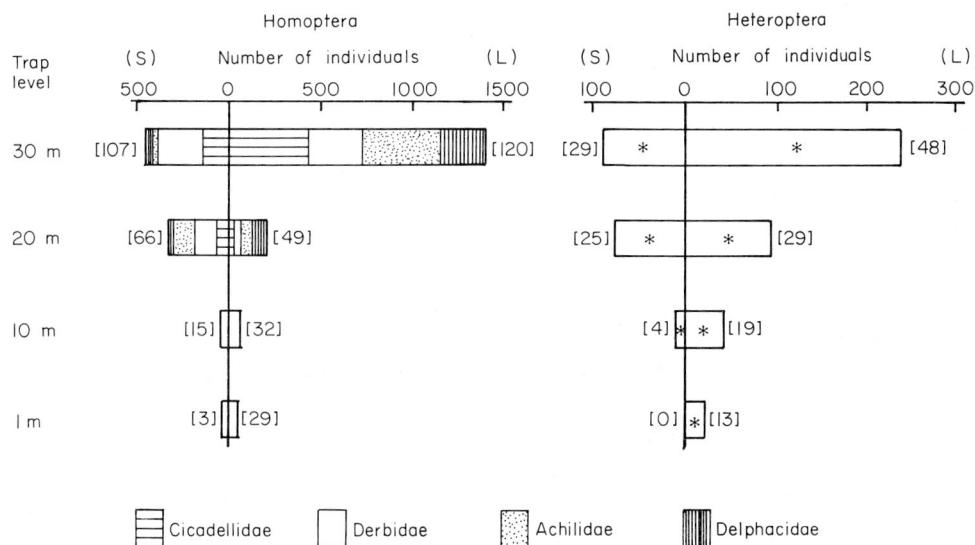

FIG. 1. Vertical distribution of individual Homoptera and Heteroptera. Bar lengths represent cumulative totals caught between 19.00 and 22.00 hours on 5 February 1980 and 8–16 February 1980 in light (L) or suction (S) traps respectively to the right and left of the vertical base line. Proportions represented by the more commonly occurring families of Homoptera are shown for the 30 m and 20 m traps. Figures in square brackets are numbers of RTUs present. (*RTU: species which differ from each other clearly; literally, Recognizable Taxonomic Unit).

and of recognizable taxonomic units (RTU) caught at the four trap levels in suction or
light traps, accumulated over the ten nights on which both types of trap were
simultaneously deployed. The canopy-concentrated distribution pattern was broadly
similar for the four more frequently encountered Homopteran families: Cicadellidae,
Derbidae, Achilidae and Delphacidae.

Although the samples from the 30 m light trap are far larger than from any of the
other light traps, a substantial proportion of the ten commonest species of Homoptera
caught by it remain among the ten commonest species caught by all three lower traps.
In Figure 2, light trap catches have been pooled for (a) four nights when the rainfall
averaged 36 mm during the trapping period and (b) eighteen nights when there was no
rain. The assemblages of RTUs and their relative abundances differ between (a) and
(b), but under both conditions, the lower samples appear to be made up substantially

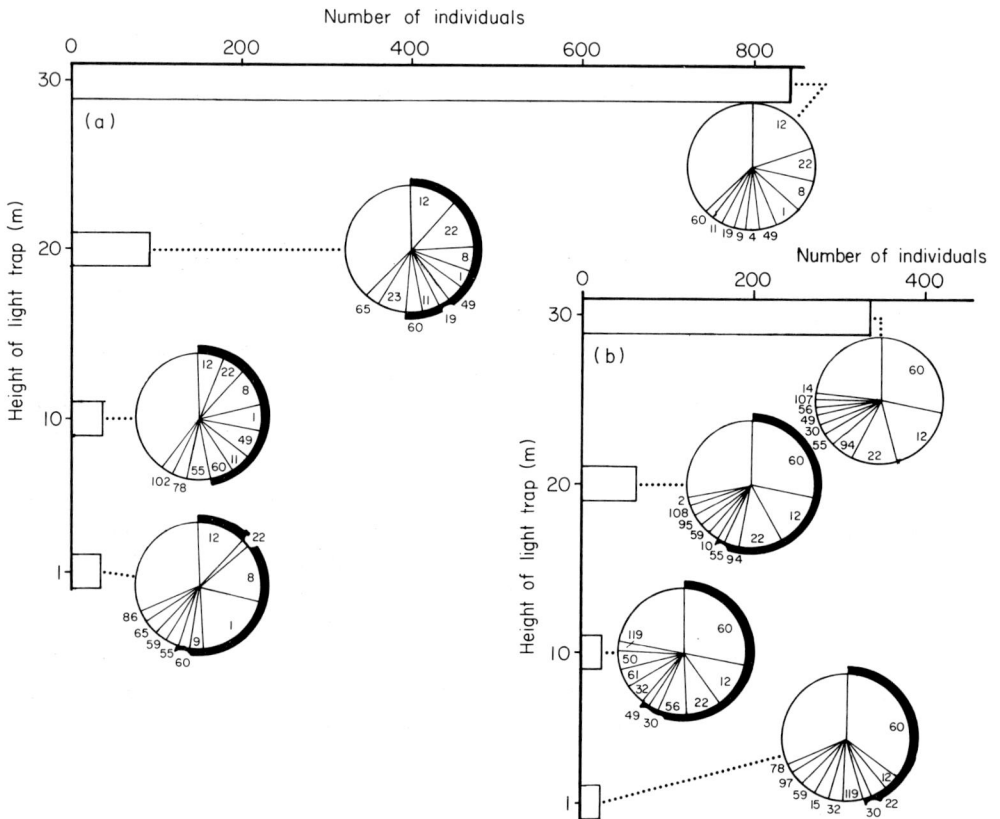

FIG. 2. Vertical distribution of Homoptera caught in light traps between 19.00 and 22.00 hours: (a)
cumulative catches over four nights (19.2.80, 12, 14 and 15.3.80) when the average rainfall during trapping
was 36 mm; (b) cumulative catches over eighteen nights (15, 16, 18, 23–29.2.80, 4–11.3.80) when there was no
rain during trapping. The pie diagrams show the proportions of each total cumulative catch represented by
the ten commonest RTUs (numbered) and those that the subcanopy samples had in common with the 30 m
(canopy) sample, enclosed within thick circumferences.

of insects which are most abundantly caught by the 30 m trap in the canopy on that
night.

Marches of microclimatic variables and the lunar index during the study period

These data are summarized graphically in Figs 3 and 4. Mean dry bulb air
temperatures, water vapour pressure saturation deficits and wind runs are shown for
the 30 m trap level for the trapping periods on each observation night between 19.00

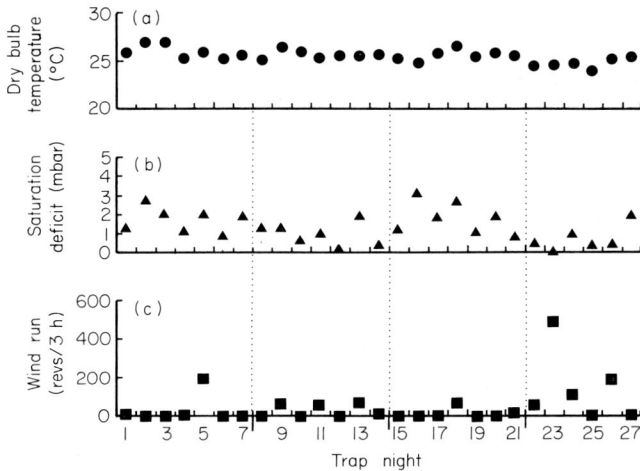

FIG. 3. Marches of (a) average dry bulb air temperature (°C), (b) water vapour saturation deficit (mbar) and
(c) wind run (anemometer revolutions/3 h) for successive trapping periods (19.00–22.00 hours) on the
twenty-seven nights for which dates are given in Fig. 4. These data are for the canopy (30 m) trap. Dotted
lines are to aid registration. 100 revs/3 h is approximately equivalent to an average wind speed of 0·2 m.s^{-1}.

and 22.00 hours in Fig. 3. Marches of rainfall and lunar index (see above) appear in
Fig. 4, which also shows the total numbers of Homoptera (excluding Delphacidae, for
reasons which will be explained later) caught in the 30 m light trap on corresponding
nights. The period of study included two wetter spells (14–19 February and 11–16
March 1980) separated by a much drier spell (21 February–10 March 1980).
Cumulative 24-hour rainfall totals for these three periods were 159·3 mm, 186·9 mm
and 20·7 mm, respectively. It will be apparent from Fig. 4 that the main period when
there was much potential lunar exposure coincided with the spell of almost rainless
trapping nights.

Relationships between the numbers of Hemiptera and microclimate

The only really obvious correlations were those between total numbers of Hemiptera
caught and the rainfall measured during the trapping period. This is crudely apparent
from Fig. 4, and in more detail for Homoptera and Heteroptera separately in Fig. 5,
which relates to 30 m light trap samples. Similar increases in numbers with increasing

rainfall are found for the combined catches of the three lower light traps. Regression equations and correlation coefficients for these samples (corresponding to the others given in Fig. 5) were:

$$N = 14 \cdot 8 + 1 \cdot 87 \ R \ (r = 0 \cdot 87, \ t = 5 \cdot 03, \ P < 0 \cdot 001) \text{ for subcanopy Homoptera and}$$
$$N = 12 \cdot 4 + 0 \cdot 63 \ R \ (r = 0 \cdot 73, \ t = 3 \cdot 21, \ P < 0 \cdot 02) \text{ for subcanopy Heteroptera,}$$

where N is the catch size, R is the rainfall (mm/3 h), r is the correlation coefficient and t

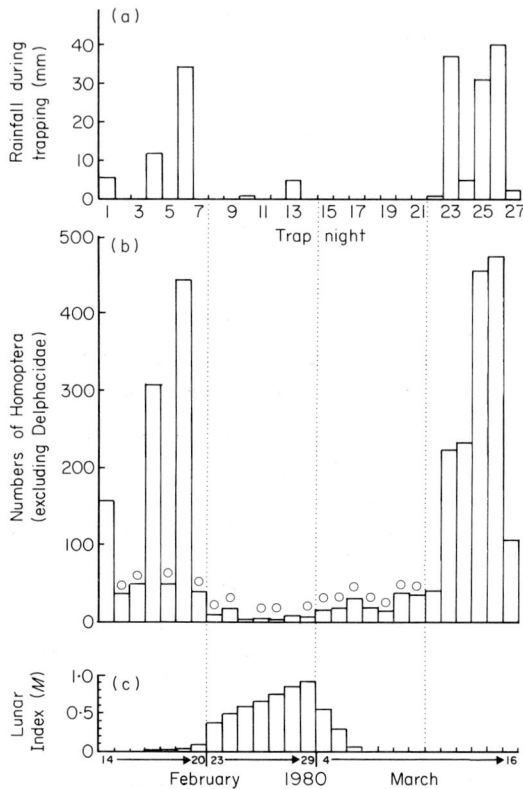

FIG. 4. Marches of (a) rainfall (mm), (b) numbers of Homoptera caught (excluding Delphacidae) and (c) lunar index, M (see text) for successive trapping periods on the twenty-seven nights shown. Data are for the 30 m light trap. There are breaks in the sequence between 20 and 23 February and between 29 February and 4 March 1980, when no trapping could be done. Open circles emphasize rainless trapping periods. Dotted lines are to aid registration. Delphacidae have been excluded because their numbers are independent of rainfall (see Fig. 5d).

is Student's t, relating to the probability P that the slope of the regression does not significantly differ from zero. The majority of the Homoptera were Cicadellidae, Derbidae, Achilidae, Cixiidae or Delphacidae. Delphacidae alone among these families showed no significant tendency to be caught more often when there was more rain during the trapping period. This is shown in Fig 5d. The numbers of cicadellids caught seem to be especially enhanced by increased rainfall (Fig. 5c).

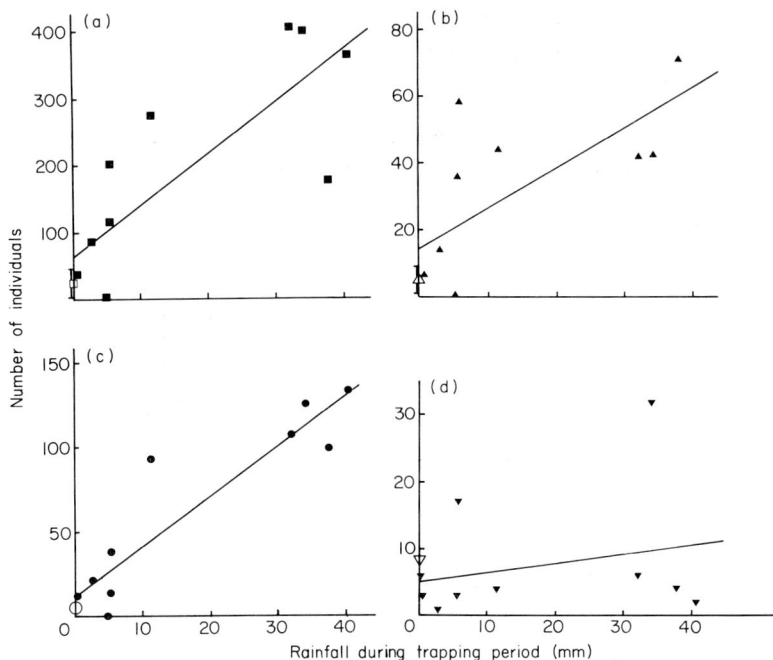

Fig. 5. Canopy light trap (30 m) catch sizes for all (a) Homoptera, (b) Heteroptera, (c) Cicadellidae and (d) Delphacidae in relation to rainfall during the trapping period. The regression lines are:

in (a)	$N = 61\cdot0 + 7\cdot83\ R$	$r = 0\cdot82$	$t = 4\cdot49$	$P < 0\cdot01$
(b)	$N = 14\cdot6 + 1\cdot20\ R$	$r = 0\cdot71$	$t = 2\cdot94$	$P < 0\cdot05$
(c)	$N = 11\cdot0 + 3\cdot01\ R$	$r = 0\cdot92$	$t = 7\cdot52$	$P < 0\cdot001$
(d)	$N = 5\cdot1 + 0\cdot14\ R$	$r = 0\cdot26$	$t = 0\cdot84$	NS

where N is the catch size, R is rainfall (mm/3 h), r is the correlation coefficient. Values of Student's t are given and the probability that the slope does not differ significantly from zero. Large open symbols are mean catch sizes for all rainless trapping periods (eighteen nights). These have been entered as single data points in calculating the regressions.

Rainfall and the size of Hemiptera which fly

Specimens of all RTUs were weighed, using a Cahn electrobalance (sensitivity 1 μg). Fresh wet weights could not practicably be measured at the site of collection, and the values are derived from specimens which were externally dried, but still contained 70% alcohol preservative. The body length of each RTU was also measured.

The stereogram shown in Fig. 6 suggests that the greater the amount of rain which falls during a trapping period, the larger is the modal weight of Homoptera among those that fly, and are caught. Heteroptera show a similar response: equivalent data are given for these insects in Table 1. The relationships between body weight and body length for all RTUs are well fitted by the following regression lines:

Homoptera (221 RTUs) $\log_e W = -3\cdot37 + 2\cdot65 \log_e L$ $(r = 0\cdot904)$
Heteroptera (117 RTUs) $\log_e W = -3\cdot15 + 2\cdot79 \log_e L$ $(r = 0\cdot956)$

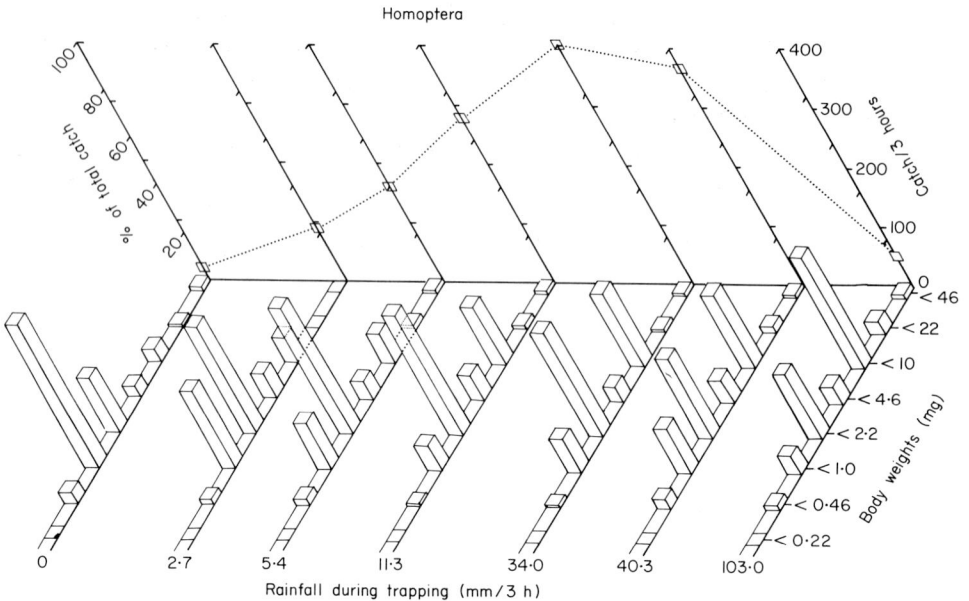

Fig. 6. Total canopy (30 m) light trap catches of Homoptera in relation to rainfall during the trapping period and to the distribution of body weight among those caught. The samples for zero rainfall represented eighteen nights' accumulated catches. All others represent one trapping period. The axis for rainfall is approximately logarithmic. The sample during 103 mm rainfall was taken on 21 March 1980 after the main part of the study, but using the same light trap and tree.

TABLE 1. Percentage distribution of body weights among Heteroptera caught in the 30 m light trap under various conditions of rainfall during trapping

Rainfall during trapping (mm)	Body weight classes (mg)								
	0·1–0·21	0·22–0·45	0·46–0·99	1·0–2·1	2·2–4·5	4·6–9·9	10–21	22–45	>45
0·0	3·2	41·9	16·1	29·0	3·2	4·8	1·6	0·0	0·0
4·5	3·8	16·6	14·3	14·3	19·0	5·7	14·3	7·6	2·9
11·3	0·0	4·5	2·3	47·7	20·5	9·1	4·5	2·3	9·1
33·0	1·2	8·2	3·5	31·8	30·6	5·9	11·8	3·5	3·5
39·0	0·0	0·0	4·5	15·7	23·6	22·5	24·7	7·9	1·1

A body weight of 1 mg corresponds to a body length of approximately 3·1 mm, and a weight of 10 mg corresponds to a length of approximately 7·1 mm.

where W is body weight (mg) and L is body length (mm). During dry trapping periods, therefore, more than 60% of the Homoptera would be expected to be less than 3·6 mm in body length, but on the wettest nights more than 50% of them would be over 6·4 mm long.

Cicadellid catches, atmospheric water vapour saturation deficit and the amount of rain falling during the 21 hours prior to each trapping period

The catch sizes of Cicadellidae, and hence their flight activity proved to be more closely correlated with rainfall during trapping than those of any other homopteran family, or of Heteroptera. Two other aspects of the water status of their environment have been examined in relation to cicadellid catches by the canopy (30 m) light trap. Their numbers are plotted against the average water vapour pressure deficit at 30 m during trapping, in Fig. 7. There is no consistent relationship between the total cicadellid catch and the amount of rain which fell in the 21 hours prior to each trapping period; this conclusion is drawn from the regression fitted to these data: $N_c = 29 \cdot 7 + 1 \cdot 32\, R_p$ where N_c is the catch of individual cicadellids on a given night (19.00–22.00 hours) and R_p is

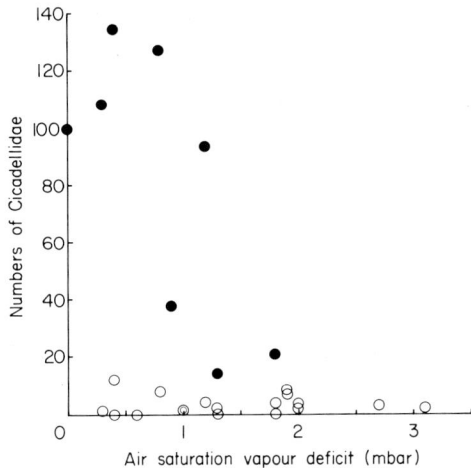

FIG. 7. Numbers of individual Cicadellidae caught by the 30 m light trap under various conditions of atmospheric water vapour saturation deficit. Filled circles represent trapping periods when there was at least 1 mm of rainfall. Open circles represent rainless trapping periods.

the total rainfall during the preceding 21 hours (mm). The correlation coefficient $r = 0 \cdot 36$ and the slope does not differ significantly from zero ($t = 1 \cdot 57$, 19 data points).

Few, or no cicadellids are caught, even when the saturation deficit is less than 1 mbar, if there is no actual rainfall during trapping. Catches remain independent of saturation deficit, at any rate within the range 0–3·5 mbar, and very small. During trapping periods with rain, the saturation deficit tends to be smaller, and the catches much bigger, even when little or no rain has fallen in the 21 hours prior to trapping. Greater humidity, by itself, does not seem to be associated with larger cicadellid catches. During daylight hours, when saturation deficit can rise to over 16 mbar in the canopy, desiccating effects may become important in reducing the numbers of Hemiptera which fly; certainly, very few indeed were caught by suction traps at such times.

Similarity of the homopteran faunas which are active during wet and dry trapping spells

Figure 4 shows that there were two wetter spells separated by a dry spell during the

5-week study period. The dry spell lasted for about 15 days, and very little rain fell during any of the trapping periods then. Canopy light trap catches taken on trap nights 4 and 6 (17.2.80 and 19.2.80) were compared with catches made on nights 25 and 26 (14.3.80 and 15.3.80) and with catches made cumulatively between nights 7 and 22 (dry spell: 20.2, 23–29.2 and 4–11.3.80). The Morishita (1959) index of similarity C_λ, as modified by Horn (1966) was used to compare the five samples each with another. Wolda (1981) has found this index to be little affected by sample size.

The index of similarity

$$C_\lambda = \frac{2 \sum (n_{1i} \cdot n_{2i})}{(\lambda_1 + \lambda_2) \cdot N_1 N_2}, \quad 0 < \; = C_\lambda < \; = 1$$

where

$$\lambda_j = \frac{\sum n_{ji}^2}{N_j^2},$$

N_j is the number of individuals in sample j and n_{ji} is the number of individuals of species i in sample j. The results are given in Table 2. Catches on nights 4, 6, 25 and 26 (all during wet spells) are all far more similar to one another (C_λ range 0·75–0·91) than to catches accumulated on nights 7 to 22 (dry spell) (C_λ range 0·33–0·46).

TABLE 2. Indices of similarity for catches of Homoptera made in the canopy during wet or dry conditions

Trapping night no.	Rainfall during trapping (mm)	No. of RTU	Number of individuals	Comparison night number and similarity indices, C_λ			
				6	7–22	25	26
4	11·3	57	278	0·91	0·34	0·80	0·79
6	34·0	66	401	.	0·46	0·81	0·75
7–22 pooled	av. 0·3	55	318	.	.	0·33	0·36
25	32·0	70	406	.	.	.	0·79
26	40·3	55	368	.	.	.	.

Nights 4 and 6 were during the first wet spell (17.2.80 and 19.2.80), nights 7–22 were the dry spell (20.2.80, 23–29.2.80 and 4–11.3.80) and nights 25–26 were during the second wet spell (14–15.3.80). The similarity indices were calculated using the Morishita–Horn index, which is given in the text.

Diversity of Hemiptera samples on nights with differing amounts of rainfall

Homoptera and Heteroptera RTU abundance distributions differ somewhat from log-series distributions mainly because there are more rare species than this model predicts. Log series α diversity indices have been calculated for the samples of Homoptera and Heteroptera which were caught by the four light traps cumulatively on nights when various different rainfalls were recorded during trapping. These data are shown in Fig. 8. Log series α diversity appears to be little affected by the amount of rain falling, even though nightly catches are greatly reduced when none is recorded. The sample used to calculate the diversity index on dry nights represents the cumulative catches of eighteen trapping periods. On any one dry night there are too few insects in

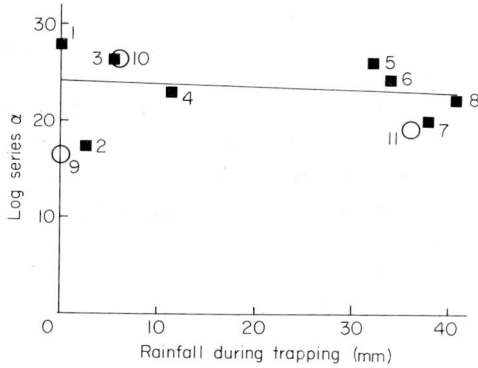

FIG. 8. Log series α diversity indices estimated for catches of Homoptera (■) and Heteroptera (○) made collectively at all four light traps during various extents of rainfall whilst trapping (mm)/3 h). Numbers, *n* on points refer to the following list of individual (I) and RTU (S) totals in the format *n*:(I,S).

1:(575,86) 2:(110,35) 3:(413,75) 4:(317,62) 5:(466,77) 6:(525,77)
7:(234,51) 8:(482,70) 9:(281,48) 10:(260,63) 11:(310,55).

The fitted regression line is: $\alpha = 24\cdot3-0\cdot03\,R$, $r = -0\cdot15$, $t=0\cdot36$ and does not differ significantly in slope from zero. It applies to the data points for Homoptera only.

the sample to calculate a value for α. The pooling requires the assumption that each nightly catch is a random subset of a total flying bug fauna which is homogeneous over the entire dry spell.

Is the flight activity of Hemiptera in any way related to the potential visibility of the moon?

Table 3 shows the numbers of Homoptera and Heteroptera which were collected at different trapping heights under two conditions of potential lunar exposure. All the

TABLE 3. Numbers of Homoptera or Heteroptera which were collected at different trap sites under conditions of differing lunar exposure

		Mean numbers of insects caught when			
Insect group	Sampling site	Moon, $M>0\cdot3$ ($n=7$)	No moon, $M<0\cdot07$ ($n=8$)	Comparison t	P
Homoptera	30 m canopy trap	$10\cdot0\pm8\cdot0$	$36\cdot1\pm14\cdot2$	4·45	$<0\cdot002$
	Lower traps, at 1, 10 and 20 m; pooled.	$9\cdot3\pm5\cdot2$	$13\cdot4\pm8\cdot6$	1·13	NS
Heteroptera	30 m canopy trap	$1\cdot7\pm1\cdot4$	$9\cdot1\pm6\cdot4$	3·19	$<0\cdot02$
	Lower traps at 1, 10 and 20 m; pooled	$7\cdot3\pm3\cdot6$	$13\cdot8\pm11\cdot0$	1·57	NS

The index M is the product of the fraction of the moon's surface which was illuminated (as seen from Earth in flat disc projection) and the fraction of the 3-hour trapping period for which it would have been above the horizon; *n* is the number of separate trapping periods; mean catches, standard deviations and comparison Student's *t* values are given.

nights for which data are given were rainless. The spell during which potential lunar exposure coincided with trapping hours was almost totally rainless. The results suggest that both Homoptera and Heteroptera were more often caught in the canopy on moonless nights (Lunar index $M < 0.07$) than on those when the index (see above) was greater than 0.3, i.e. well illuminated, even if often through cloud. This difference was not apparent between the catches of traps positioned below the canopy taken under the two classes of lunar exposure conditions. Sample sizes are small because few bugs fly on rainless nights, but there were too few nights when rain during trapping coincided with an illuminated moon potentially visible above the horizon for a comparison to be made with wet, moonless nights, of which there were many.

General effects of wet or dry conditions upon the vertical distribution of Hemiptera

Table 4 shows the accumulated total catches of Homoptera and Heteroptera at the four light trap levels for two sets of trapping conditions: 'wet' periods when at least 2.7 mm of rain fell in the 3 hours (nine nights numbers 1, 4, 6, 13, 23–27) and 'dry' periods when no rain fell (sixteen nights numbers 2, 3, 5, 7–9, 11, 12, 14–21).

TABLE 4. Vertical distribution of Homoptera and Heteroptera individuals between light traps under wet or dry conditions

Order	Conditions	Height of light trap above ground (m)				
		30	20	10	1	
Homoptera	Wet	2040	273	123	88	
		(1980)	(301)	(132)	(111)	$\chi^2 = 51.7$
	Dry	402	98	40	49	P(3 d.f.) < 0.001
		(462)	(70)	(31)	(26)	
Heteroptera	Wet	328	137	71	34	
		(286)	(133)	(87)	(64)	$\chi^2 = 73.1$
	Dry	92	58	56	60	P (3 d.f.) < 0.001
		(134)	(62)	(40)	(30)	

'Wet' conditions are represented by the cumulative catches on nights numbers 1, 4, 6, 13 and 23–27 (average rainfall 19·3 mm/3 hours) and 'dry' conditions by nights numbers 2, 3, 5, 7–9, 11, 12 and 14–21 (average rainfall zero). Expected values for homogeneous distributions are shown in brackets.

Calculation of χ^2 for the two contingency tables gives values which imply that the vertical distributions of both Homoptera and Heteroptera differ significantly ($P < 0.001$) between 'wet' and 'dry' nights. Although more insects are still captured on dry nights by the 30 m canopy trap than by any of the lower ones, the topheaviness of distribution is much reduced especially for Heteroptera. It is as if the flying bug population shrinks further back below the canopy surface into the forest on dry nights.

DISCUSSION

By far the largest catches of Homoptera during any given trapping period are always made in the main canopy leaf layer, here represented by the lower part of a *Syzgium*

Tropical rain forest, architecture, silvigenesis and diversity

ROELOF A. A. OLDEMAN

Wageningen Agricultural University, 'Hinkeloord', P.O. Box 342, 6700 AH Wageningen,
The Netherlands

SUMMARY

1 Tropical rain forest architecture and dynamics may be analysed into three integration levels (Fig. 1): (i) the eco-unit or regeneration unit, (ii) the chrono-unit or developmental mosaic and (iii) the silvatic unit or successional mosaic. Architecture is the complex of forms relevant to one integration level. Measured profile diagrams provide base data.

2 An *eco-unit* is a vegetation unit which has started to grow on one surface at one moment (Fig. 2).

3 *A chrono-unit* is the minimal surface to include all phases (aggrading, steady-state and degrading) of one specific eco-unit (Fig. 3).

4 A *silvatic unit* includes chrono-units of all eco-unit types on one site. Silvigenesis is the preferred term for the complex of forest-shaping processes, only some of which are clearly successional (Fig. 4).

5 Eco-unit diversity and environmental gradients between eco-units co-determine the range of spatial niches, and hence the potential species diversity. New eco-units which appear during the degrading phases of one eco-unit are either smaller because all trees do not fall at the same time, or larger if a catastrophe interferes. The ultimate and smallest eco-unit is the 'chablis' or one-tree gap of the old rain forest. The inverse relationship suggested between eco-unit size and diversity appears to hold true when moving away from lowland tropical rain forest to less hospitable environments: eco-unit size increases while diversity decreases.

INTRODUCTION

Because the present analysis of the rain forest is entirely based on *form* and its modificatons, this article should first be studied from the illustrations. Definitions, literature and derived niche structure as an indication for species diversity can be found in the text afterwards. The following principles are consistently applied:

(i) As illustrated on Fig. 1, form elements are only used as far as relevant to their own integration level. Form at one level, without details from lower levels or contexts from higher ones is *architecture*.

(ii) *Architecture* at each level is *explained* in terms of the next lower one. Descriptive models are limited to one level, explicative ones use several (cf. de Wit, e.g. 1975; Oldeman 1974).

(iii) Architecture is observed at one moment in time, represented as a scale-drawing

139

(e.g. a profile diagram and map for an ecosystem), and diagrammatically abstracted in Figs 1–5.

(iv) Growth dynamics are considered as a sequence of architectural growth phases (Hallé & Oldeman 1970; Oldeman 1974, 1978, 1979, 1980; Edelin 1977; Hallé, Oldeman & Tomlinson 1978; Torquebiau 1979, 1981; Koop 1981; and others).

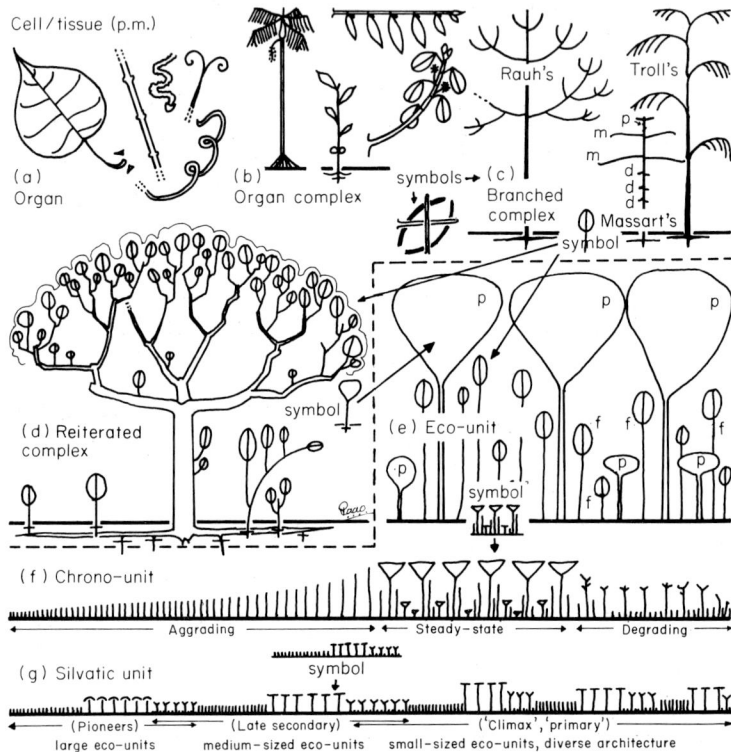

FIG. 1. Architectural integration levels from cell/tissue (p.m.), through organ (a), organ complex (b), branched complex exemplified by Rauh's, Massart's and Troll's models (c) and reiterated complex (d), to the collective levels (e) to (g). Note organ complex as subsystem of either eco-unit (palm, seedling) or branched complex (branches, trunk). In the eco-unit (e) p = trees of the present; f = trees of the future. In the chrono-unit (f) an aggrading phase is organizing itself under the degrading one; this links chrono-units of different kinds in the silvatic unit (g). Systems at each level figure in higher-level systems as symbols. Broken line separates individual from collective systems.

(v) The diagnosis of the architectural growth phase of a system at one level is made by the diagnosis of the architectural 'state' of its component systems one level lower. For instance, a tree can be understood in terms of developing, developed and decaying branches (Fig. 1c in terms of *symbols* from Fig. 1b); or an eco-unit growth phase (Figs 1e, 2) in terms of tree architecture (Fig. 1c, d). To be clear for each level, the following terms have been used per level:

State:	Developing (potential)	Developed (mature)	Decaying (deteriorating)
Tree (plant) (Fig. 1e)	of the future	of the present	of the past
Eco-unit (Fig. 3)	aggrading	steady-state	degrading
		(cf. Bormann & Likens 1979)	
Chrono-unit (Fig. 4)	appearing	dominating	surrendering

(vi) Because *scale*-drawings are the basis of this method, it is quantitative and can be transcribed in numerical terms and be treated by computer (De Reffye 1979; Hofman 1981). The observations can be repeated and hence are objective.

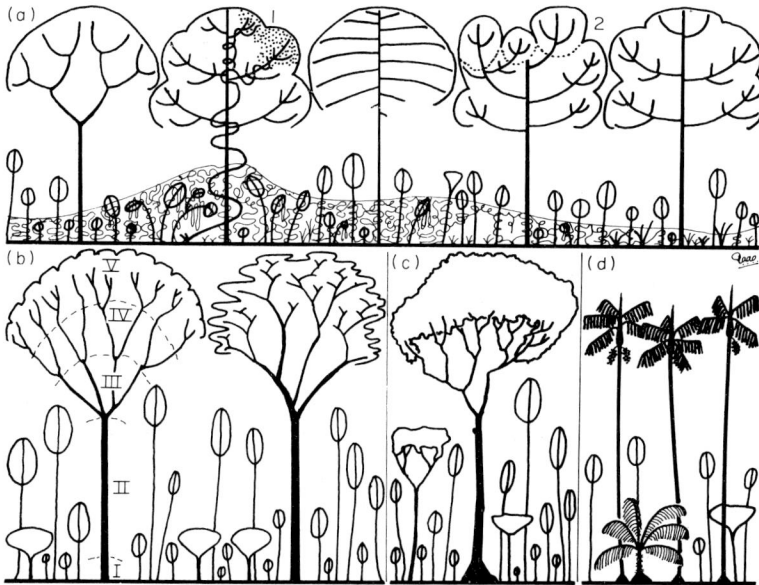

FIG. 2. Eco-units differing in size and architecture, all steady-state (cf. Figs 1f and 3). (a) Large-sized 'pioneer' eco-unit, note model-conform trees with little reiteration if any (tree 2) and lianes (on tree 1); undergrowth diversification in set of the future announces future breaking-up into smaller eco-units (for data see, e.g. Kahn 1982). (b) Medium-sized 'late secondary' eco-unit, note reiterated trees of the present, to the left zones I–V are distinct epiphyte biotopes; two structural sets of the present. (c) Small eco-unit, as grown on a chablis (Fig. 4f); note complex architecture with three structural sets (after South American data). (d) Small-sized palm eco-unit as currently found in Amazonia, also see de Granville (1978); lower structural set with both a dicot and a palm. All diagrams abstracted from field data and scale drawings.

We will be mainly concerned here with the integration levels from the eco-unit upwards (Fig. 1e–g), their relevance to niche diversification, and their manifestation on different sites.

ECO-UNITS OR REGENERATION UNITS

An eco-unit (Fig. 2) is a vegetation unit which has started to grow at one well-defined moment on one well-defined surface (Oldeman 1981). The *surface* is determined by the

Architecture, silvigenesis and diversity

origin: large by storms, earthquakes, machines; intermediate or small by falling trees or trees dying upright. The *moment* is determined by the frequency of the originating factors: forest fires are rare but tree-falls are frequent in many rain forests.

The smallest eco-unit origin is here called *chablis*. The ancient French word chablis denotes the uprooting of a tree, the fallen tree itself, the resulting opening in the forest and the debris on the forest floor (Fig. 4f, g). Many tropical forest peoples have words for this concept, lost in English, and which implies much more than a mere 'gap' or 'windthrow'.

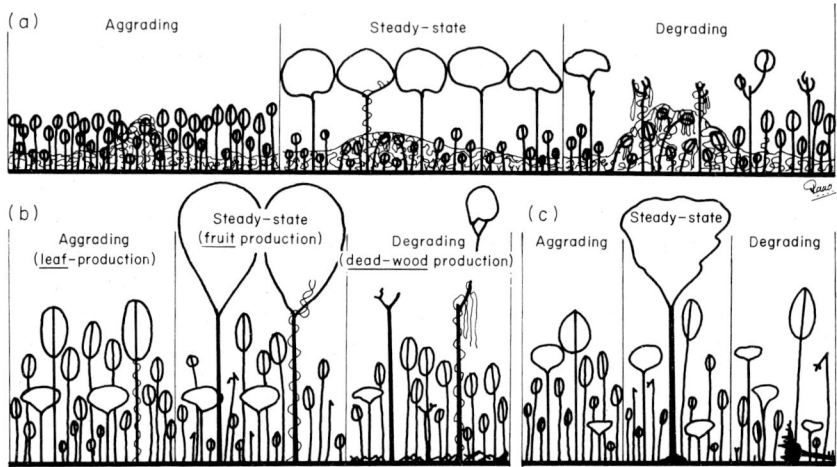

FIG. 3. Chrono-units differing in size, architecture and development pattern; note lower structural sets being formed first and higher ones later (cf. Kahn, 1982; R. van de Winckel, unpubl.). (a) 'Pioneer' chrono-unit, breaking up into smaller eco-units in the degrading phase; architecture monotonous, hence species diversity low (data: cf. Lescure 1978). (b) 'Late secondary' chrono-unit, exemplifying different food niches in each phase: emphasis on leaves, fruits and dead wood, respectively. (c) One-tree 'climax' or 'primary' chrono-unit, the degrading phase being a chablis (cf. Fig. 4f).

The general architecture at the level of an eco-unit depends on its origin and on the architecture of its trees, at lower levels. Figures 2 and 3 show this for eco-units of different sizes having developed from architecturally different situations, and bearing different kinds of forest. The comparative characteristics of trees which build such 'pioneer', 'late-secondary' or 'climax' forest patches have been listed by Budowski (1965) for Costa Rica.

The trees, by means of their architecture, divide the volume occupied by their eco-unit into small volumes, each with its micro-climatological and nutrient conditions. These smaller volumes contain organisms of smaller sizes, according to their specific autecological requirements (Fig. 2b; I–V, after Johansson 1974). In their turn, they create still smaller volumes with their own properties, apt to accommodate still smaller organisms, such as the insect niches in and around epiphytes (Benzing 1983), or trophic niches for monkeys (van Roosmalen 1980).

The more varied the architecture of the trees constituting an eco-unit, the more diverse are its niches, and the richer in species are its flora and fauna. Figure 2 shows that pioneer forest is architecturally homogeneous and its floristic poverty is well-known (Lescure 1978). Late secondary forest has a more diverse architecture and a richer flora and fauna (Charles-Dominique *et al.* 1981). Very small 'primary forest' eco-units are most diverse of all (Oldeman 1974).

Niches within a growing eco-unit are co-determined by its 'ecological inheritance'. This consists of soil components of its original surface, influenced by the agency having cleared the preceding forest (e.g. earthquake v. fire or machines), and of the 'survivors' from the preceding forest. These last include coppice shoots or suckers (Fig. 1d), frequent in some forests and rare in others, and the 'seed-bank' in the soil (cf. Vazquez Yanes 1976; Holthuijzen & Boerboom 1982; bibliography in Whitmore 1982, 1983).

CHRONO-UNITS OR DEVELOPMENTAL MOSAICS

A chrono-unit (Figs 1f and 3) is the mininum surface at any one site needed for all architectural growth phases (aggrading, steady-state, degrading) of an otherwise identical eco-unit 'type' ('age-mosaic', see Oldeman 1980). The growth phases of artificial eco-units, i.e. the forester's stands, have long-standing names (e.g. Mayer 1980). A chrono-unit is different from another if its constituting eco-units (one level lower) are different. The concept is abstract, because eco-units in different growth phases are scattered in the forest, but it is a useful tool in the diagnosis of silvatic units, and corresponds to 'age-class structures of stands in a forest' used in forestry (see Edlin 1976, p. 226).

A still more abstract concept is that of the 'state' of a chrono-unit, needed to explain the architecture at the next higher level, i.e. the silvatic unit (Fig. 4a–e). When, in a forest, some type of eco-unit is only present in young, developing growth phases (cf. Fig. 3 'aggrading'), e.g. pioneer patches in an old forest just after a hurricane, this chrono-unit is called 'appearing' (see Introduction). If such a chrono-unit contains near-equal proportions of aggrading, steady-state and degrading eco-units, it holds its own in the forest and is called 'dominating'. If the chrono-unit mostly contains decaying eco-units (cf. Fig. 3, 'degrading'), it soon will yield most or all of its surface to other kinds of eco-units; in this state it is 'surrendering'.

In the chrono-unit only steady-state eco-units show a layered architecture (Fig. 3). In the other growth phases the architecture is not yet layered (aggrading) or has ceased to be so (degrading). Layering during steady-state phases is defined exclusively by sets of trees of the present (Fig. 1e:p). Hence, there are no conventional 'strata', because the architecture of the other trees, of the future (developing; Fig. 1e:f) and of the past (decaying), does not determine the set of the present but is determined by it. Their niches are shaped by the trees of the present, as described before for other organisms. Steady-state eco-units cover only part of the forested surface: cf. 'mature phase' on Fig. 2.3 in Whitmore (1975). Layering, although occurring in certain forest parts, therefore is not a general, omnipresent feature of tropical rain forests (cf. Rollet 1974).

The architecture of the eco-unit determines the available niches for organisms other than trees. Eco-unit architecture changes with growth so that niches appear and

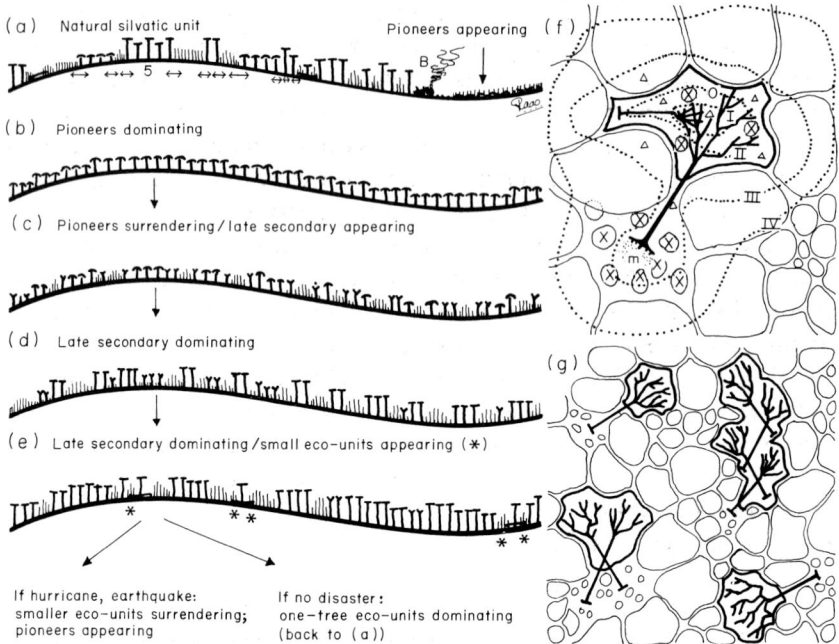

FIG. 4. Silvatic unit and its dynamics after large-scale destruction. (a) Natural tropical rain forest silvatic unit with balanced proportions of large, medium and small eco-units (5 = five small ones; double arrows = gradients, cf. Fig. 4f); destruction by bull-dozer (B), pioneers appearing afterwards. (b) to (e). Dynamics of silvatic unit explained in terms of chrono-unit subsystems which may be potential (appearing), mature (dominating) or deteriorating (surrendering), finally as chablis eco-units (stars under (e)). Alternatives after (e): also see Fig. 5A. (f) Chablis, schematic drawing after data from Florence (1981); thick line = chablis as defined by crown projections; stippled lines = 'isoluxes' from 80% (I) to 10% of macroclimatic illumination (IV), defining horizontal gradients from the chablis centre outwards; m = mineral soil, o = organic soil; Δ = pioneer tree, X = survivor. (g) Some of the chablis types after Mutoji-A-Kazadi (1977) and Florence (1981); note diversity of horizontal gradient-forming architecture and mark aggrading phases (small crowns) among steady-state phases (large crowns); the aggrading phases may sometimes be considered as a 'network' between steady-state ones (R. van de Winckel, unpubl.).

disappear, e.g. monocot niches (de Granville 1978) or trophic niches for animals (Fig. 3b). A chrono-unit hence has a higher niche diversity than each of its eco-units (compare Figs 2b and 3b). Therefore, its species diversity also is higher.

SILVATIC UNITS OR SUCCESSIONAL MOSAICS

A silvatic unit (Figs 1g, 4a and 5B) is the minimum surface at any one site needed for all architectural growth phases of all locally possible chrono-units ('succession mosaic', see Oldeman 1980). It is more than the sum of the scattered eco-units of different kinds (Figs 2 and 3), which are its constituents. This is so because eco-units are not separated from each other by linear limits, but by zones of interaction. Ecological factors in these zones change gradually, e.g. illumination (Fig. 4f,g), around the young, small aggrading eco-unit which is a chablis.

At first sight, architectural diversity within the silvatic unit, supplemented by the diversifying effect of interaction zones, makes for an enormous increase in niche diversity, i.e. in species diversity. This effect seems to be counter-balanced, at least in some cases, by a wide ecological range of organisms. For instance, experiments in Surinam (Holthuijzen & Boerboom, 1982) and architectural studies in Gabon (Florence 1981) show that common pioneer species germinate at between 20% and 100% of full macroclimatic illumination. Such behaviour of pioneer trees along gradients may explain some of the observations of Sugden (1983).

The larger the eco-units, the less extensive are the zones of interaction in a silvatic unit (Fig. 5B, top to bottom), and the simpler the architecture of each eco-unit. Dominance of small eco-units makes for more interaction zones and more complex architecture per eco-unit, i.e. for greater species richness. Patches of rare trees (Hubbell & Foster, 1983) may well correspond to unusual eco-units with a rare architecture.

For a silvatic unit occupying an extended homogeneous site the proportions of its surface covered by different chrono-units should be statistically predictable using the average frequency and destructive effect of agencies creating new eco-units at the expense of old ones: wind, fire, inundation, squalls, etc. and the development rate of different eco-unit 'types' (see Fig. 5B).

SILVIGENESIS OR SUCCESSION

Silvigenesis (Fig. 5A, all arrows) is the complex of all processes occurring in silvatic unit development (Oldeman 1974). It includes secondary succession (Fig. 5A, left-to-right arrows) but also accounts for instability factors (right-to-left). Primary succession on large areas in principle follows the same rules but is much slower if seed sources are far away; in extreme cases it may be accompanied by speciation. For primary succession, a bottom-to-top model (Fig. 5B) might apply, because site modification plays a role.

Factors favouring development from large to smaller eco-units, i.e. from pioneer to 'primary' forest, are tree mortality spread over many years in a large eco-unit so that it becomes 'fragmented' into smaller ones (Oldeman 1981), and differential development in the undergrowth of large eco-units, preparing future fragmentation (Figs 2a and 3a; Kahn 1982). Factors favouring the birth of larger eco-units at the expense of smaller ones often are abiotic, such as fire, wind, inundation, earthquake, but sometimes also biotic (e.g. pests).

Figure 4a–e shows silvigenesis after forest-clearing by man. The tendencies are for eco-units to become progressively smaller, until they are balanced again against local large-scale natural agencies creating large eco-units. Silvatic unit architecture and development (in terms of eco-units and chrono-units) become more complex and more niches are created. Potential species richness hence also increases. How far this tendency becomes reality, i.e. how many of these niches become effectively occupied, depends on a number of factors outside the strict scope of this paper. Important among these are pollination, seed dispersal and animal migration, if all species are still available near the pioneer zone here considered (Fig. 4a–e).

It should be stressed that the image of the silvatic unit, a kaleidoscopic shifting mosaic of large and small eco-units, in more or less predictable proportions if the

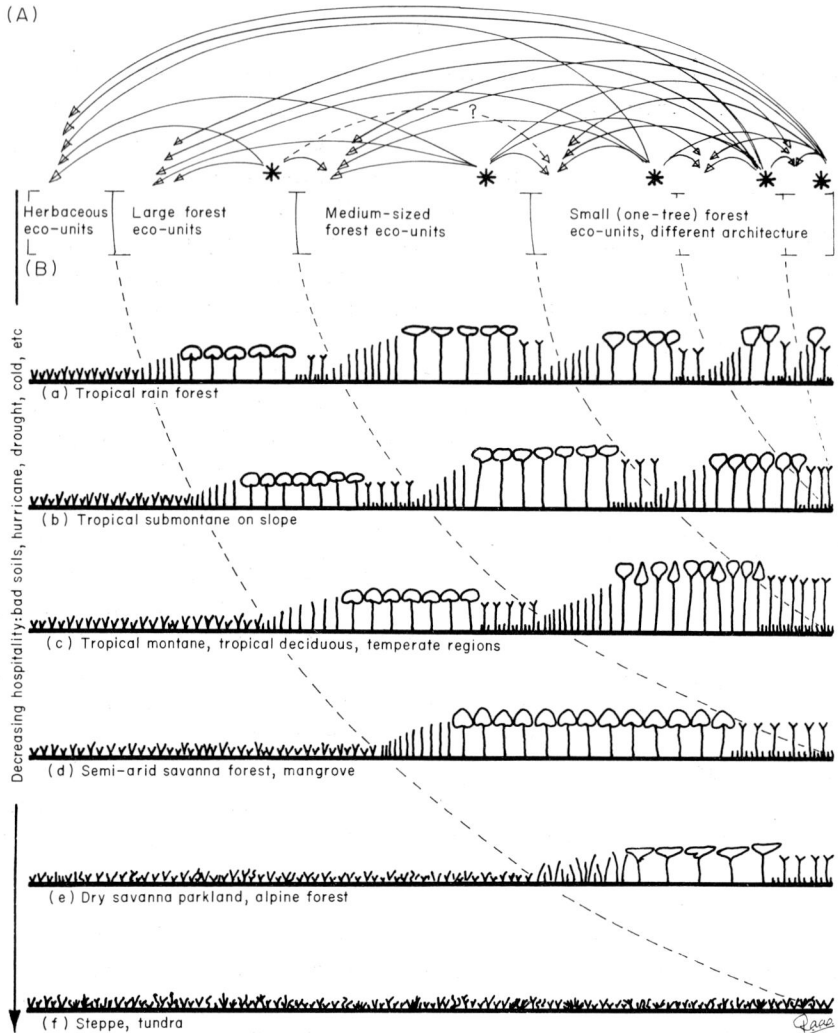

FIG. 5. Silvigenesis and silvatic units in environments with decreasing 'hospitality'. (A) Silvigenesis: depending on the kind of destruction (star), the next local eco-unit may be any of the represented ones, but a direct 'jump' from pioneer to smallest eco-unit (?) is improbable. In principle, every eco-unit may succeed to every other one; there is no clear-cut 'succession' except in cases of wholesale destruction (Fig. 4a–e). (B) Decreasing 'hospitality' implies more frequent wholesale destruction, hence small-scale eco-units have less time to develop and become improbable. Proportions hypothetical, principle checked for (a) and (b) by R. A. A. Oldeman (unpubl.) and (c) by Koop (1981). Note suggestion of higher diversification in herbaceous eco-units with decreasing hospitality: to be studied.

arrow-factors (Fig. 5A) are known, differs from the 'tropical rain forest ecosystems' in terms of species numbers and frequencies. Eco-units, chrono-units and silvatic units have their proper dimensions and structure in space, and their proper life span. Species, populations, and the ecosystem they define have either arbitrary or no spatial dimensions. Combination of the two images will be extremely useful.

DIVERSITY AND THE SILVATIC UNIT

The tropical rain forest provides 'home and table for wild-life' (Jacobs 1981). The analogy might be more appropriate with a town (silvatic unit) in which there are quarters (chrono-units) with streets (eco-units) each providing shops, homes, etc. (niche-volumes). Architectural analysis should complement 'average structure analysis' over large surfaces. Holdridge *et al.* (1971) visualized averaged structures as 'idealised profile diagrams': heliophilous *Scheelea* palms require chablis (Fig. 96), but are shown as growing beneath a dense, closed canopy in the 'idealised' profile (Fig. 97). However, architectural diversity, not average structure, creates the niches for *Scheelea* and other forest organisms.

As long as only average structures are known, niches of tropical rain forest plants and animals will continue to be represented as lists or matrices of ecological requirements. As stated before, niches are real spaces with real life spans inside the eco-unit, the chrono-unit and the silvatic unit. If van Roosmalen (1980) left out some integration levels from his otherwise splendid analysis of black spider monkey ecology in Surinam, Charles-Dominique *et al.* (1980, French Guiana), Hladik & Hladik (1980, Gabon) and Hladik (1978) started to include architectural elements in animal ecology. Herbivore niches (cf. Fig. 3b) have rapid dynamics, related to leaf phenology; insects also follow rapidly appearing and disappearing niches (Stocki 1981). Such minutely sized, short-living niche-volumes are all derived from overall eco-unit architecture; their properties can, however, easily be disturbed, for instance by light traps.

The frequency or rarity of precise niche-volumes in the rain forest pre-conditions the abundance or rarity of species adapted to live in such volumes. 'Freak' niches either remain empty or house ubiquitous organisms. The species richness of the tropical rain forest, however, suggests a high proportion of specialists, dependent on particular niche spaces provided with sufficient frequency by the developing forest architecture (e.g. see Chan & Appanah 1981).

Can the analysis of silvatic unit architecture be a measure for derived niche diversity and so for species diversity of the rain forest? Mutojii-A-Kazadi (1977) tried to use aerial photographs at the usual 1:40 000 or 1:50 000 scale, but encountered problems of resolution and contrast. A scale between profile diagram (*c.* 1:200) and 'normal' aerial photographs would be needed. This is being developed by Hladik & Hladik (1980) using a tethered balloon in Gabon, A. P. Vooren (using a powered glider in Ivory Coast) and in Kalimantan by the Bukit Raya Expedition using a helicopter. Aerial photographs at scales between 1:2 000 and 1:5 000 are to be used for this intermediate step.

SILVATIC UNITS AND ENVIRONMENTAL HOSPITALITY

Site factors render an environment more or less hospitable to forest (Fig. 5B; Oldeman, 1981). Hospitality decreases if, alone or in combination, the impact and frequency of the following factors increase: earthquakes (Garwood, Janos & Brokaw 1979), storms

(Whitmore 1974), fire (e.g. Central Kalimantan, 1982, French Guiana, 1977), epidemics and pests, thunderstorms (see map with tropical thunderstorm frequency in Nieuwolt, 1977), soil factors favouring loosening of roots, e.g. by waterlogging or in marshes (North German soils: Koop, 1981), or steep slopes ('toposéquence', see Beaudou *et al.* 1978).

When hospitality decreases, the local silvatic unit contains more large and less small eco-units. As explained above, this makes for less niches and so for fewer species. The role of slope as a hospitality factor may for instance explain the different insect distributions in the Brunei rain forest on flat and 'rugged' terrain (Sutton 1983). The less hospitable the site, the higher becomes the proportion of herbaceous vegetation against forest (Fig. 5B, a–f). In herbaceous vegetation, other architectural rules apply (N'Diaye 1977).

Hospitality decreases with increasing altitude, latitude, and between the tropics from humid to arid zones, from deep to shallow soils, from gradual to steep slopes. This agrees with the decreasing species diversity recorded from tropical lowland to tropical semi-arid forests, to mangroves and towards the temperate and tropical montane forests. Human influence is an important unfavourable factor to forests in the whole world.

Koop (1981) defined a 'minimal structure area' as 'the minimal area in which all representative stages and phases of the forest development continue to be present by self-regulation of the forest.' This corresponds roughly to the silvatic unit presented here. A realistic minimal area, however, would need to be larger to allow for destruction risks to the rarest eco-unit and for the area needed by all local rain forest species to maintain a viable population (Whitmore 1975). The correction factors to be used, however, are not even approximately known as yet.

CONCLUSION

The tropical rain forest is so complex that it probably will never be completely understood by man. It is hoped that the present approach may be a useful complement to other existing methods, and may contribute to both proper treatment and correct management of the rain forest, which deserves to be considered with awe and handled with respect and patience.

REFERENCES

Beaudou, A.G., Blic, P. de, Chatelin, Y., Collinet, J., Filleron, J.C., Guillaumet, J.-L., Kahn, F., Zueli, K.B. & Richard, J.F. (1978). Recherche d'un langage transdisciplinaire pour l'étude du milieu naturel. Paris, *Travaux et Documents ORSTOM* 91.

Benzing, D.H. (1983). Vascular epiphytes: a survey with special reference to their interactions with other organisms. *Tropical Rain Forest: Ecology and Management* (Ed. by S. L. Sutton, T. C. Whitmore & A. C. Chadwick), pp. 11–24. Blackwell Scientific Publications, Oxford.

Bormann, F.H. & Likens, G.E. (1979). *Patterns and Process in a Forested Ecosystem.* Springer, Berlin.

Budowski, G. (1965). Forest species in successional process. *Turrialba*, **15**(1), 40–42.

Chan, H.T. & Appanah, S. (1981). Reproductive biology of some Malaysian dipterocarps, flowering biology. *Malaysian Forester*, **43**, 132–143.

Charles-Dominique, P., Atramentowicz, M., Charles-Dominique, M., Gérard, H., Hladik, A., Hladik, C.M. & Prévost, M.F. (1981). Les mammifères frugivores arboricoles nocturnes d'une forêt guyanaise: interrelations plantes-animaux. *Revue d'Ecologie (La Terre et la Vie)* **35**, 341–435.

Edlin, D. (1976). *The Natural History of Trees.* Weidenfeld & Nicholson, London.

Edelin, C. (1977). *Images de l'architecture des Conifères.* Thèse de Spécialité, Université Montpellier.

Florence, J. (1981). *Chablis et sylvigénèse dans une forêt dense humide sempervirente du Gabon.* Thèse de Spécialité, Université Strasbourg.

Garwood, N.C., Janos, D.P. & Brokaw, N. (1979). Earthquake-caused landslides: a major disturbance to tropical forests. *Science*, **205**, 997–998.

Granville, J.-J. de (1978). *Recherches sur la flore et la végétation guyanaises.* Thèse ès Sciences, Université Montpellier.

Hallé, F. & Oldeman, R.A.A. (1970). *Essai sur l'architecture et la dynamique de croissance des arbres tropicaux.* Paris, Masson & Cie, (English translation 1975, Kuala Lumpur, Penerbit Universiti Malaya).

Hallé, F., Oldeman, R.A.A. & Tomlinson, P.B. (1978). *Tropical trees and forests: an architectural analysis.* Springer, Berlin.

Hladik, A. (1978). Phenology of leaf production in Gabon: distribution and composition of food for folivores. *The Ecology of Arboreal Folivores* (Ed. by G. G. Montgomery), pp. 51–71. Smithsonian Institution, Washington.

Hladik, A. & Hladik, C.M. (1980). Utilisation d'un ballon captif pour l'étude du couvert végétal en forêt dense humide. *Adansonia, n.s.*, **19**, 325–336.

Hofmann, J.-P. (1981). *Recherche de critères de sélection pour la résistance à la casse au vent chez* Hevea brasiliensis. Thèse ès Sciences, Université de Paris-Sud, Centre d'Orsay.

Holdridge, L.R., Grenke, W.C., Hatheway, W.H., Liang, T. & Tosi, T. (1971). *Forest Environments in Tropical Life Zones.* Pergamon, Oxford.

Holthuijzen, A.M.A. & Boerboom, J.H.A. (1982). The *Cecropia* seedbank in the Surinam lowland rain-forest. *Biotropica*, **14**, 62–68.

Hubbell, S.P. & Foster, R.B. (1983). Diversity of canopy trees in a neotropical forest and implications for conservation. *Tropical Rain Forest Ecology and Management* (Ed. by S. L. Sutton, T. C. Whitmore & A. C. Chadwick), pp. 25–41. Blackwell Scientific Publications. Oxford.

Jacobs, M. (1981). *Het tropisch regenwoud: een eerste kennismaking.* Coutinho, Muiderberg.

Johansson, D. (1974). Ecology of vascular epiphytes in West African rain-forest. *Acta Phytogeographica Suecica*, **59**, 69.

Kahn, F. (1982). La reconstitution de la forêt tropicale humide: Sud-Ouest de la Côte-d'Ivoire. *Mémoires ORSTOM*, 97.

Koop, H. (1981). *Vegetatiestructuur en dynamiek van twee natuurlijke bossen: het Neuenburger en Hasbrucher Urwald.* (with English summary). PUDOC, Wageningen.

Lescure, J.-P. (1978). An architectural study of the vegetation's regeneration in French Guiana. *Vegetatio*, **37**, 53–60.

Mayer, H. (1980). *Waldbau auf soziologisch-ökologischer Grundlage.* 2nd edn. Fischer, Stuttgart.

Mutoji-A-Kazadi (1977). *Notes de sylvigénèse pour la Guyane: transect et photographies aériennes.* Rapport D.E.A., Université Montpellier.

N'Diaye, P. (1977). *Préliminaire à l'étude architecturale des végétations herbacées.* Rapport D.E.A., Université Montpellier.

Nieuwolt, S. (1977). *Tropical Climatology: An Introduction to the Climates of the Low Latitudes.* Wiley, Chichester, New York.

Oldeman, R.A.A. (1974). L'architecture de la forêt guyanaise. *Mémoires ORSTOM* 73.

Oldeman, R.A.A. (1978). Architecture and energy exchange of dicotyledonous trees in the forest. *Tropical Trees as Living Systems* (Ed. by P. B. Tomlinson & M. H. Zimmerman), Chapter 23. Cambridge University Press, Cambridge.

Oldeman, R.A.A. (1979) Quelques aspects quantifiables de l'arborigénèse et de la sylvigénèse. *Oecologia Plantarum*, **14**, 1–24.

Oldeman, R.A.A. (1980). *Grondslagen van de bosteelt.* LH-Bosteelt, Agricultural University Wageningen.

Oldeman, R.A.A. (1981). *The design of ecologically sound agroforests.* ICRAF, Nairobi (in press).

Reffye, Ph. de (1979). *Modelisation de l'architecture des arbres par des processus stochastiques.* Thèse ès Sciences, Université Paris-Sud, Centre d'Orsay.

Rollet, B. (1974). *L'architecture des forêts denses humides sempervirentes de plaine.* C.T.F.T. Nogent sur Marne.

Roosmalen, M.G.M. van (1980). *Habitat preferences, diet, feeding strategy and social organization of the black spider monkey* (Ateles paniscus paniscus *Linnaeus 1758) in Surinam.* D.Sc. thesis, Agricultural University Wageningen (Netherlands).

Stocki, J. (1981). *Preliminary study on insect life-spaces in Oostereng forest.* Rapport LH-Bosteelt, Agricultural University, Wageningen.

Sutton, S.L. (1983). The spatial distribution of flying insects in tropical rain forest. *Tropical Rain Forest: Ecology and Management* (Ed. by S. L. Sutton, T. C. Whitmore & A. C. Chadwick), pp. 77–91. Blackwell Scientific Publications, Oxford.

Sugden, A.M. (1983). Determinants of species composition in some isolated neotropical cloud forests. *Tropical rain forest ecology and management* (Ed. by S. L. Sutton, T. C. Whitmore & A. C. Chadwick), pp. 43–56. Blackwell Scientific Publications, Oxford.

Torquebiau, E. (1979). *The reiteration of the architectural model: a demographic approach.* Rapport D.E.A., Université Montpellier.

Torquebiau, E. (1981). *Analyse architecturale de la forêt de Los Tuxtlas (Veracruz, Mexique).* Thèse 3me Cycle, Université Montpellier.

Vazquez-Yanes, C. (1976). Estudios sobre la ecofiysiología de la germinación en una zona cálido-húmeda de México. C. *Regeneración de Selvas* (Ed by A. Gomez Pompa & C. Vazquez-Yanes), pp. 279–387. Compania Editorial Continental, México.

Whitmore, T.C. (1974). *Change with time and the role of cyclones in tropical rain-forest on Kolombangara, Solomon Islands.* Institute Paper, 46. Commonweath Forestry Institute, Oxford.

Whitmore, T.C. (1975). *Tropical Rain Forests of the Far East.* Clarendon Press, Oxford.

Whitmore, T.C. (1982). On pattern and process in forests. *The Plant Community as a Working Mechanism* (Ed. by E. I. Newman), pp. 45–59. Blackwell Scientific Publications, Oxford.

Whitmore, T.C. (1983). Secondary succession from seed in tropical rain forests. *Forestry Abstracts*, **44,** (in press).

Wit, C.T. de (1975). Modellen als brug tussen proces en systeem. *Productiviteit in Biologische Systemen* (Ed. by G. J. Vervelde), pp. 157–170. PUDOC, Wageningen.

The influence of swarm raiding army ants on the patchiness and diversity of a tropical leaf litter ant community

NIGEL R. FRANKS*

Museum of Comparative Zoology, Harvard University, Cambridge, MA 02138, U.S.A.

WILLIAM H. BOSSERT

Biological Laboratories, Harvard University, Cambridge, MA 02138, U.S.A.

SUMMARY

1 The swarm raids of *Eciton burchelli* selectively remove ant colonies of certain species that nest on the floor of the tropical rain forest, thereby creating space in which other ants can prosper. In this way the foraging army ants initiate a process of succession in the ant community.

2 A computer simulation model that incorporates the foraging patterns of individual army ant colonies has been developed to estimate the frequency at which areas of the forest floor are raided and re-raided.

3 Data from sampling ants in the aftermath of swarm raids coupled with the findings of the simulation model suggest that approximately half of the area of Barro Colorado Island is undergoing the process of ant succession.

4 The analyses suggest that the army ants not only preserve the species diversity of the leaf litter ants, but maintain a fairly constant fraction of the forest floor in each stage of succession. Thus, over large tracts of tropical rain forest the relative abundance of ground-nesting ant species may also remain fairly constant.

INTRODUCTION

Predators and physical disturbances have been shown to mediate the coexistence of space-limited sessile organisms in a number of temperate and boreal communities (Darwin 1859; Tansley & Adamson 1925; Summerhayes 1941; Paine 1966; Harper 1969; Dayton 1971; Grime 1973; Vance 1979; Fox 1981; Smedes & Hurd 1981; Paine & Levin 1981). However, relatively few studies have examined the role of disturbances in tropical rain forests where they could maintain the exceptional diversity of such space sequestering sedentary organisms as canopy trees and ground nesting ant colonies (Janzen 1970; Connell 1970, 1978, 1979; Hartshorn 1978; Whitmore 1978; Huston 1979; Acevedo 1981; Levings & Franks 1982). Nevertheless, the characteristic mosaic form of these tropical communities, which could be a result of localized perturbations, has long been recognized (Aubréville 1938; Richards 1952; Wilson 1958).

* Present address: School of Biological Sciences, University of Bath, Bath BA2 7AY, U.K.

In this paper we examine the contribution of foraging by *Eciton burchelli* (Westwood) to patchiness and coexistence in the ant fauna of Barro Colorado Island (BCI), Panama. There are approximately fifty-five colonies of these army ants on BCI, and in total their massive raid swarms sweep over an area of 10 million m^2 each year; equivalent to two-thirds of the area of BCI (Franks 1980, 1982a). *Eciton burchelli* hunts a wide variety of leaf litter arthropods, though the majority of its prey items are from a relatively small number of the 100 or more ant species (Levings 1981) that forage or nest on the forest floor (Rettenmeyer 1963; Franks 1980, 1982c). Most of the non-social arthropod prey of *E. burchelli* recover their normal densities within a few days by migrating back into raided areas: their ant prey, however, take several months to recover (Franks 1980). In the absence of army ant raids, competition for nesting sites and foraging space limits the abundance of some of these prey species and many other ground-nesting ants (Franks 1980; Levings & Franks 1982). *E. burchelli*, by cropping some of these competing species may provide space in which others can flourish.

In such a situation the frequency at which areas are raided and re-raided will be one of the factors that determine community composition. Indeed a number of studies, in other communities, have shown that the temporal and spatial pattern of disturbance can determine whether perturbations increase or decrease species diversity (Milton 1940, 1947; Paine & Vadas 1969; Nicholson, Patterson & Currie 1970; Armstrong 1976; Lubchenco 1978; Paine 1979). Recently, Connell (1978, 1979) summarized such studies by suggesting that maximum diversity in substrate-limited communities is often maintained only in non-equilibrium states by intermediate levels of disturbance. This hypothesis contends that in the absence of disturbance some species are competitively displaced, with the result that fewer species are present if the community attains a state of competitive equilibrium. Disturbance may promote continuous gap-phase or micro-succession in parts of a community and thereby preserve species richness among patches (Fox 1981). Predictive theory, which can test the intermediate-disturbance hypothesis, has been developed by modelling population dynamics in habitats consisting of discrete cells (Skellam 1951; Armstrong 1976; Caswell 1978; Crowley 1981). Disturbance generates ephemeral free space, represented by empty cells, which some species are better at finding, while other species can competitively exclude these better dispersers from occupied cells. In such systems extinction can be postponed for considerable periods of time (Caswell 1978; Atkinson & Shorrocks 1981). If the factors which govern the birth rate and death rate of patches are known, community composition can be predicted (Levin & Paine 1974; Paine & Levin, 1981).

One unusual technique for investigating the effects of a predator's disturbance regime has been outlined by Caswell (1978) referring to the starfish–mollusc interaction described by Paine (1966, 1971) and Dayton (1971): he suggested that 'It would probably not occur to anyone to study this system within a single cell; this would involve following a starfish around and studying the patches he leaves behind him after feeding'. This approach is taken here, in an examination of both the foraging patterns of the army ant colonies and the changes in the ant community in the aftermath of swarm raids. This investigation is facilitated by the extremely stereotyped temporal and spatial patterns of foraging in these army ants.

ARMY ANTS' SEARCH PATTERN

On BCI all *Eciton burchelli* colonies alternate statary phases (bouts of central place foraging), with nomadic phases (periods of migration) (Fig. 1). These activity cycles follow a fixed endogenous rhythm governed by the production of discrete generations of workers (Schneirla 1971). The *Eciton* queen lays eggs in the middle of the statary phase from which larvae hatch at the end of the same phase. With its voracious larvae to feed the colony becomes nomadic. The larvae pupate at the end of the nomadic phase and the new workers eclose at the end of the subsequent statary phase. During a statary phase the adult ants have only themselves to feed and the colony remains at the same nest site for 20 days on average, raiding on only 13 days (Schneirla 1971; Willis 1967). In the subsequent nomadic phase raiding occurs on each of the next 15 days and usually at dusk, on 86% of nomadic days the entire colony emigrating to a new temporary nest site (Schneirla 1971; Willis 1967). On the 14% of nomadic days without emigrations the army ants remain at the same bivouac site and raid and emigrate in a new direction on the next day.

Raiding differs only in frequency and duration between phases. Foraging is also qualitatively similar in colonies of different size: all raid only during daylight with swarms that mostly remain on the ground. The average swarm is 6 m wide, though they sometimes contain up to 200 000 ants and exceed 14 m in width (Willis 1967). The average lengths of nomadic and statary raids are 116 m ($n = 38$, S.D. $= 48$) and 89 m ($n = 25$, S.D. $= 41$), respectively (Franks 1980; Franks & Fletcher 1983). Generally, only one swarm is produced per colony per day and the raiding ants are continuously linked to the nest by a principal trail of workers returning with prey and others moving out to join the swarm. When a colony emigrates the principal trail of that day's nomadic raid is followed exactly. Thus, the spatial pattern of migration is constrained and determined by the colony's foraging pattern (Schneirla 1940).

The spatial pattern of foraging and migration in colonies of *E. burchelli* has been recently analysed, by comparing it first with null hypotheses based on randomness and then with a series of alternative 'adaptive' hypotheses. In this way a precise description of the search pattern of these predators had been formulated (Franks 1980; Franks & Fletcher 1983). This description will be summarized here.

During a single day's raid the swarm front sweeps from side to side in tight oscillations, so that throughout the day overall progress tends to be in a straight line. A complete statary phase consists on average of fifteen raids radiating out from the hub of the central nest site. This includes the nomadic raids leading to and from the statary nest. Each successive raid is positioned on average 123° ($n = 41$, S.D. $= 40$) anti-clockwise from its predecessor. This closely approximates 126·4° which is the optimum angle to maximize the separation of both successively produced and actually neighbouring raids. Thus, successive raids are separated in both space and time. As some overlap in raid paths is inevitable close to the statary bivouac this temporal spacing of neighbouring raids will be advantageous because it provides time for some prey to regain their former abundance so that they can be cropped again. Similar designs, that minimize self-shading, occur in plants that exhibit spiral phyllotaxis (Leigh 1972).

Successive statary nests are separated by an average distance of 530 m (Willis 1967), which is significantly further than would be achieved by a random walk of the thirteen, 81 m emigrations that occur in an average nomadic phase. Three models have been devised *a priori*, each of which could explain this nomadic navigation. The first would involve the army ants choosing a direction for their entire nomadic phase, and compensating for deviations from this preferred compass bearing. The second would be for each raid and subsequent emigration to be constrained to follow roughly the same compass bearing as these activities on the previous day. The third would involve the army ants mostly doing a random walk, but sometimes being constrained to migrate in a single direction by, for example, topographical features.

Each model predicts a unique distribution of angles between successive nomadic emigrations. For example, the second model predicts that the angles between successive emigrations will be distributed normally with a mean of 0° and a standard deviation of 60°. The army ants actually distribute emigration angles normally about a mean of $+11 \cdot 75°$ with a S.D. of $60 \cdot 2°$ ($n = 65$); both of these parameters are not significantly different from those predicted by the second model and they are significantly different from the predictions of the other possible navigation models (Franks and Fletcher, 1983). Thus, the army ants navigate in the nomadic phase by each new raid being constrained to follow roughly the same compass bearing as taken on the previous day.

To test the fixity of these foraging patterns one *E. burchelli* colony was transferred to Orchid Island, a small *Eciton*-free neighbour of BCI. The foraging of this colony was analysed at intervals over the course of a year. Though its diet was significantly and predictably different from colonies on BCI in a manner consistent with raiding almost exclusively through previously unraided areas (Franks 1980, 1982b), the spatial and temporal pattern of its foraging was almost identical to colonies on the larger island (Franks 1980; Franks & Fletcher 1983).

This experiment and the above analyses suggest that the spatial pattern of raiding is almost as preprogrammed as the temporal pattern of activity in these army ants, with future raid directions being determined almost solely by previous raid directions. These stereotyped search patterns facilitate the analysis of the disturbance regime created by the foraging of all the *E. burchelli* colonies on BCI.

ESTIMATING THE DISTURBANCE PATTERN

To calculate the frequency at which areas of the forest floor are raided and re-raided, the foraging pattern of the whole *E. burchelli* population on BCI must be estimated. This is logistically possible only through the use of a computer simulation model. The precise details of the model will be presented elsewhere; a short verbal description will suffice here.

The forest floor is represented as a lattice of squares, the width of each square is taken to be 10 m as an approximation of the average width of a raid, allowing for the side-to-side movements of the swarm. The foraging arena, which consists of 10 000 such squares representing 1 km², is rolled into a seamless surface so that colonies cannot leave the arena. The simulation colonies are governed by temporal and spatial rules of foraging and migration that cause them to mimic almost exactly the patterns exhibited by colonies on BCI (Fig. 1). All raid and emigration distances are precisely determined as are the angles between successive statary raids; but raids occur with a probability of 0·65 on any one statary day and nomadic emigrations occur with a probability of 0·86 on any one nomadic day. Furthermore, the angles between successive nomadic emigrations are distributed with a mean of $+12°$ and a standard deviation of $60°$. Thus, the movements of the model colonies are not entirely deterministic; rather they are as variable as those of real colonies.

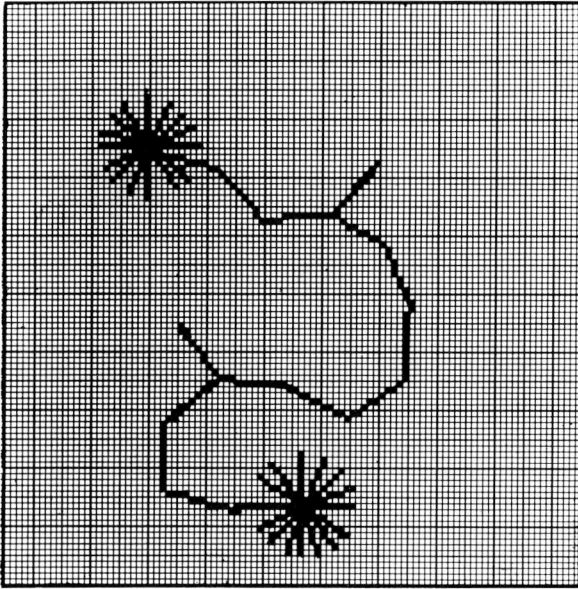

FIG. 1. A scale drawing of the foraging pattern of an individual *E. burchelli* colony showing two statary phases and the intervening nomadic phase. Each small square in the arena represents a square which is 10 m on a side.

One important finding from the simulation is that model colonies, when at a density similar to real colonies on BCI, collide with one another at a greater frequency than can be occuring in nature (Franks & Fletcher 1983). There are no recorded observations of any collisions between *E. burchelli* colonies, even though more than 1 000 nomadic raids have been observed on BCI (Rettenmeyer 1963; Willis 1967; Schneirla 1971). The model colonies were then programmed to stop raiding when they encountered squares raided by other army ants within the last 20 days. Furthermore, if a nomadic colony encounters such a square it fails to emigrate that day, and then raids and emigrates in a new direction on the next day. The new raid direction is selected to mimic the directions taken by real colonies when they also failed to emigrate in the nomadic phase. With this refined behaviour, which is based entirely on reasonable assumptions concerning the colony specificity and longevity of trail pheromones (Franks & Fletcher 1983), the model colonies collide at a greatly reduced frequency and miss emigrations on approximately 14% of nomadic days. Intriguingly, their foraging efficiency, in terms of the ages of squares they visit, differs insignificantly from model colonies that were programmed to fail to emigrate at random on 14% of nomadic days.

During the simulation, the age of each square in the arena is recorded and it increases by one at the end of each 'day', unless the square has been raided that day whereupon its age returns to zero. In addition, a record is kept of the ages of all the patches raided by each colony. For each experimental density of colonies we ran the model until the patch ages were at equilibrium which occurred, on average, in 15 colony-years. Only after this time were the following statistics recorded: (i) the frequency distribution of all patch ages in the foraging arena, and (ii) the frequency distribution of all patch ages visited by the colonies. Histograms of the mean results of five replicates per colony density are depicted in Fig. 2.

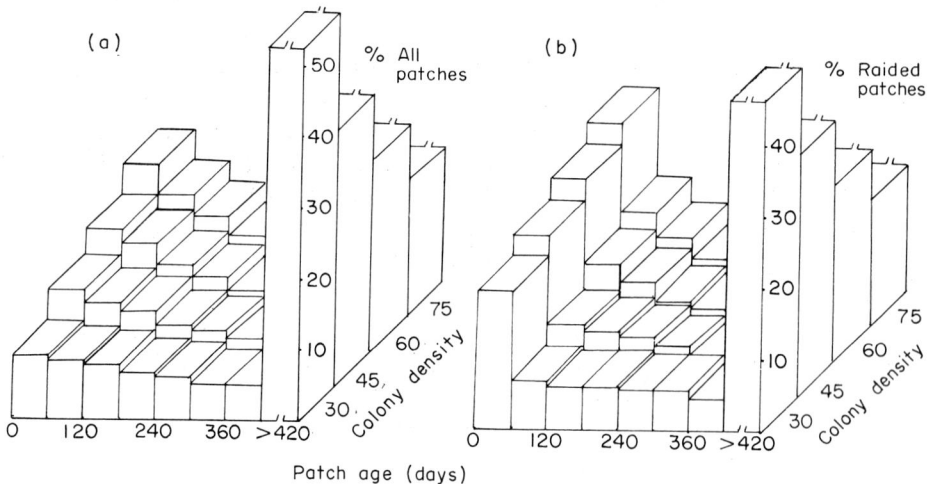

FIG. 2. Results of the simulation modelling for an area representing an average 1 km^2 of BCI. Histograms of frequency distributions of patch age as a function of army ant density. The latter is represented as the total number of colonies that would be on BCI at the given density. (a) The ages of all patches. (b) Patch ages raided by the army ants.

SUCCESSION IN THE AFTERMATH OF SWARM RAIDS

To compare the diversity of the forest floor ant fauna in areas raided by army ants and in not recently raided control areas, transects of sugar-baited pit-fall traps have been used. This non-disruptive technique was devised to sample small numbers of foraging worker ants from colonies present in the immediate vicinity of the traps. A transect consists of a line of twenty traps set at 2 m intervals. The traps were plastic-capped, 6×2.5 cm glass vials. Each vial could be entered by the foraging ants through a 0.5 cm hole in its cap. The traps were buried cap deep in the soil and each contained 10 ml of bait. The bait consisted of 200 g of sucrose dissolved in a solution of 50 ml of 96%

ethanol in 1·5 l of water. A roof-shaped leaf was placed over each vial to prevent the dilution of its contents by rain water. Worker ants entering the vial drown in the bait. A transect in a raid area was laid along the path taken by the principal trail; other transects were haphazardly placed straight lines. Each transect of vials was left in the forest for 48 hours. Transects were first placed in raid areas 1 day after the swarm, they were replaced 7, 14, 21, 35, 49 and 77 days later. Identical sampling regimes were maintained over the same periods of time in areas not recently raided by the army ants. All the traps were individually numbered and the ants they trapped were sorted and counted. The sampling was conducted in the dry season of 1979.

RESULTS

The simulation model estimates that with a density of fifty-five *Eciton burchelli* colonies on BCI, 14·5% of the island surface has been raided within 60 days; 48·5% has been raided within 240 days, and 51·5% has escaped the army ants for more than 240 days. This distribution of patch ages is maintained by the army ants foraging 23·5% of their time in patches less than 60 days old, 53% in patches less than 240 days old and 47% in areas that had not been previously raided for more than 240 days (Fig. 2). There is little variation between years. For example, at a density equivalent to sixty colonies on BCI, over 5 simulation years, on average 52·5% of the island has been foraged within 240 days with a standard deviation around this mean of only 1·56%. Moreover, in all replicates of the simulation this is the highest variance recorded both for all patch ages and the ages of raided patches.

In the aftermath of swarm raids there are more species of ants of the genus *Pheidole* than in other areas. Furthermore, there is a greater turn-over of these species in raided areas than in not recently foraged areas (Table 1).

The abundance of one species of *Paratrechina* increased significantly in raided areas, as described by $p = 2·49 \exp^{0·01D}$ ($r = 0·84$ $P < 0·02$), where p is the mean number of traps per transect with *Paratrechina*, and D is the number of days counted from the first run of the transect. There was no significant increase in the abundance of *Paratrechina* in not recently raided areas.

TABLE 1. The number of species of *Pheidole* in four recently raided and four not recently raided areas. Succession species are those which have clearly left or entered the censused area during the sampling period. They are defined as those species which occurred in the first two and not in the last two transects per area, or vice versa. The significance of the differences between the two types of areas are determined by one-tailed *t*-tests

		Recently raided areas	Not recently raided areas		
Pheidole spp. collected in first 48 hr sample of each transect.	$\bar{X}$	11·75	8·00	$t = 3·0$	$P < 0·05$
	S.D.	1.26	2·16		
Total number of *Pheidole* spp. in all samples of each transect.	$\bar{X}$	15·75	10·25	$t = 3·63$	$P < 0·01$
	S.D.	2·06	2·22		
Succession Species	$\bar{X}$	7·25	3·50	$t = 2.38$	$P < 0·05$
	S.D.	2·63	1·73		

DISCUSSION

There is a higher diversity of ant species in areas recently raided by *Eciton burchelli*, and as these patches age the ant community undergoes succession. Furthermore, at any one time a large fraction of the area of Barro Colorado Island is exhibiting such a turn-over of ant species. The simulation model estimates that the fifty-five *Eciton burchelli* colonies on BCI maintain the leaf litter fauna in a mosaic of patches approximately half of which have been raided within 240 days.

This present study supplements one that utilized an exclosure/enclosure experiment to make a more traditional investigation of the role of predators in patch dynamics (see Dayton 1971; Connell 1975). The earlier study (Franks 1980) utilized the long-term exclosure provided by Orchid Island, a small *Eciton*-free neighbour of BCI, and also involved the experimental introduction of an army ant colony to the smaller island. The results of this experiment will be briefly considered here, so that the process of succession reported in this paper can be placed in a larger context.

Before an *Eciton burchelli* colony was transferred from BCI to Orchid Island, the leaf litter ant communities of the two islands were compared. This was accomplished by mapping the dispersion patterns of nests of forest floor ants (Franks 1980; Levings & Franks 1982). On both islands there was a significant overdispersion of ant nests in all mapped quadrats. However, on Orchid Island the hexagonal packing of nests was more highly significant in each quadrat than in any of the quadrats on BCI. Furthermore, the prey species of *E. burchelli* were more than twice as abundant on the smaller island. These findings suggest that competition for space is ubiquitous but most intense in the absence of army ant predation, because their prey are amongst the competitively dominant species. The transferred army ant colony responded to this greater abundance of prey by changing its diet significantly: 86% of its prey items were social insects compared with 55% for colonies on BCI (Franks 1980, 1982b).

The major ant prey species of *Eciton burchelli* are members of the two subfamilies Ponerinae and Formicinae. The leaf litter ant fauna is dominated by species belonging to these two subfamilies, and also such myrmicines as species of *Pheidole*. However, these army ants have never been seen to attack *Pheidole* nests, whose workers commonly weigh less than one-tenth as much as workers of prey species (Levings & Franks 1982). Notwithstanding the difference in the size of individuals in these subfamilies, the spacing patterns of nests show that many ponerine, formicine and myrmicine species have similar abilities to sequester space from one another.

This suggests that prey colonies can deny space to, and limit the distribution and abundance of many *Pheidole* colonies. One process which might be responsible for the spacing of all nests is the predation or ejection of colony-founding queens by workers of established nests. A number of myrmicine workers, or a single formicine or ponerine, could kill or chase off a queen of any of the other species (Franks 1980; Levings & Franks 1982). However, it seems that such predation of queens by workers is preferentially intraspecific because the most significant patterns of nest overdispersion were within species.

Predation of incipient colonies by established ones may be an extremely important process which may act together with army ant predation to generate available space and maintain the diversity of the leaf litter fauna. If new colonies are preferentially denied space by established nests of the same species, such space will tend to be more available to other species. This process is analogous to that postulated by Janzen (1970) and Connell (1971) to explain the coexistence of tropical rain forest trees. Seedlings near the parent plant are exposed to their parents' population of species-specific herbivores. The only seedlings to survive are those at some distance from their parent and other established conspecifics. Each tree-specific guild by herbivores thus creates space in which other tree species can become established. Although such a scheme may not operate for some canopy trees (Hubbell 1979, 1980; Hubbell & Foster 1983) many of the prerequisites seem to occur in the ant community considered here (Levings & Franks 1982).

The results of an experiment with artificial nest-sites demonstrates one of the interactions between predation of queens by established colonies and predation of established colonies by army ants. Incipient colonies, specifically of *E. burchelli* prey species, occur in greater abundance in artificial nest sites placed in recently raided areas than in similar nests in control areas (Franks 1982b). The simplest explanation is that in the aftermath of swarms when prey colonies have been killed or cropped to smaller size, intraspecific predation of queens of prey species may be reduced, with the result that incipient nests of these species can be founded in greater numbers.

It thus appears that both the predation of queens and the predation of canopy-tree seeds and seedlings affect species-specific replacement probabilities and create pattern diversity which may maintain species diversity. Furthermore, swarm raids can be considered to give rise to a process similar to that created by tree-fall gaps because both initiate a process of succession involving many species in the community.

The gaps created both by falling trees and raid swarms cause local changes in their respective communities that persist for considerable periods of time (Brokaw 1982; Franks 1980). Notwithstanding the influx of incipient colonies of prey species into the gaps created by swarm raids, it takes these populations about 200 days to increase to the abundance found in non-raided areas. Their increase in abundance can be described by a logistic curve, estimated from the frequency at which workers of prey species are captured in the baited pit-fall traps (Franks 1980).

The first stage in the succession in the aftermath of a raid is characterized by the rapid increase in the abundance of one species of *Paratrechina*. Members of this genus are classic opportunists. They occupy new areas not just through the formation of new colonies but by the growth of existing ones; colony emigrations are frequent and they typically use flimsy, unstable nest sites. These habits are facilitated by their unicolonial social organization with no aggressive interactions or boundaries between colonies (Holldobler & Wilson 1977). The rapid influx of *Paratrechina* may in part cause the greater turnover of *Pheidole* species in raided areas. Indeed, the process of succession in the ant community is most likely driven by changes in the competitive environment which affect colony growth and replacement probabilities rather than changes in the abiotic environment (see Horn 1975; Connell & Slatyer 1977).

That such ant genera as *Pheidole* and *Paratrechina* were more successful at quickly exploiting the ephemeral opportunities provided by army ant raids than the prey species of *E. burchelli* was to be expected. The workers of these opportunists are only a fraction of the size of the workers of prey species. Colonies with smaller workers should be able to produce them faster at a given rate of energy availability, and such colonies are likely to grow faster and in the short term out-compete those of large bodied ants (Wilson 1971).

The reduction in competition that occurs in the foraging paths of *E. burchelli* may be important not only for those species of *Pheidole* that newly enter raided areas but also those species that were originally present. Recently, Brian (1979) has presented data that suggest that the output of sexuals by ant colonies, albeit in a much simpler community, is affected both in quantity and sex ratio by their competitive environment. Hence, just as with canopy tree species which depend at one or all stages in their life histories on growth in a gap to reach maturity (Richards 1952; Garwood 1982; Brokaw 1982), many ant species may depend on army ant gaps for their eventual output of sexuals.

However, the disturbance caused by raids differs in two important ways from the disturbances caused by tree falls: Firstly, swarms selectively crop competitive dominants and secondly, there will be a coupled interaction between the frequency of raids and community composition. That prey species are among the competitive dominants was shown by their greater abundance on the pre-introduction Orchid Island. Thus, the army ants' maintenance of diversity is similar to the best documented cases of so called key-stone predators mediating the coexistence of competitors (Paine 1966; Harper 1969). The interaction between the rate of disturbance and community composition is extremely important because species abundances will remain relatively constant only if there exists a dynamic equilibrium between gap recovery and gap formation. This might not be the case where physical perturbations cause the disturbance. It is more likely where the disturbance is created by a predator in search of its prey, as in the case reported here.

Indeed, there have been approximately fifty colonies of *E. burchelli* on BCI throughout the extensive period that this population has been censused (Schneirla 1949, 1956; Willis 1967; Franks 1982a). The constancy in the size of this army ant population is probably due in part to their ant prey populations being limited by competition, to the high handling costs that *E. burchelli* colonies suffer when they attack large prey colonies, and to the army ants foraging more often in already denuded areas as their own population density increases (Franks 1980, 1982c).

In addition to the number of *Eciton burchelli* colonies on BCI being fairly constant over a considerable period, the simulation model further suggests that the patch age distribution on BCI is likely to be near an equilibrium with little variation between years. Thus, the army ants will not only preserve the diversity of the ant community but will also maintain a fairly constant relative abundance of species.

This study emphasizes the necessity of sampling tropical populations over large areas through many years if their dynamics are to be understood. If one was to sample only a small area of the leaf litter fauna for a short time, the world would indeed appear stochastic, with army ant raids apparently occurring at random. The scale of sampling is a crucial factor in the assessment of the stability of other insect populations in the tropics (Wolda 1978). Only when large tracts of tropical rain forest are sampled over a number of years will predictable patterns and processes unfold.

ACKNOWLEDGMENTS

This paper stems from field work that benefitted greatly from the support and encouragement of many people on Barro Colorado Island. Facilities and help were generously provided by the staff of the Smithsonian Tropical Research Institute. Particularly stimulating discussions with S. H. Bartz, E. Broadhead, B. Hölldobler, T. J. Givnish and E. O. Wilson, helped to shape this paper. This research was supported by a studentship from the Natural Environment Research Council and a fellowship from the Royal Commission for the Exhibition of 1851 both to NRF. Computing facilities were supported by a grant from the Maurice Pechet Foundation.

REFERENCES ·

Acevedo, M.F.L. (1981). On Horn's Markovian model of forest dynamics with particular reference to tropical forests. *Theoretical Population Biology*, **19**, 230–250.

Armstrong, R.A. (1976). Fugitive species: experiments with fungi and some theoretical considerations. *Ecology*, **57**, 953–963.

Atkinson, W.D. & Shorrocks, B. (1981). Competition on a divided and ephemeral resource: a simulation model. *Journal of Animal Ecology*, **50**, 461–471.

Aubréville, A. (1938). La fôret coloniale: les fôrets de l'Afrique occidentale française. *Annales Academic des Sciences Coloniales, Paris*, **9**, 1–245.

Brian, M.V. (1979). Habitat differences in sexual production by two co-existent ants. *Journal of Animal Ecology*, **48**, 943–953.

Brokaw, N.L. (1982). Treefalls: frequency, timing and consequences. *The Ecology of a Tropical Forest* (Ed. by E. G. Leigh, Jr., A. S. Rand & D. W. Windsor), pp. 101–108. Smithsonian Institute Press, Washington D.C.

Caswell, H. (1978). Predator-mediated co-existence: a nonequilibrium model. *American Naturalist*, **112**, 127–154.

Connell, J.H. (1970). On the role of natural enemies in preventing competitive exclusion in some marine animals and in rain forest trees. *Dynamics of Populations* (Ed. by P. J. den Boer & G. R. Gradwell), pp. 298–312. PUDOC, Wageningen.

Connell, J.H. (1975). Some mechanisms producing structure in natural communities: a model and evidence from field experiments. *Ecology and Evolution of Communities* (Ed. by M. L. Cody & J. M. Diamond), pp. 460–490. Harvard Press, Cambridge, Massachusetts.

Connell, J.H. (1978). Diversity in tropical rain forests and coral reefs. *Science*, **199**, 1302–1310.

Connell, J.H. (1979). Tropical rain forests and coral reefs as open nonequilibrium systems. *Population Dynamics* (Ed. by R. M. Anderson, L. R. Taylor & B. Turner), pp. 141–163. Symposium of the British Ecological Society, London. Blackwell Scientific Publications, Oxford.

Connell, J.H. & Slatyer, R.O. (1977). Mechanisms of succession in natural communities and their role in community stability and organization. *American Naturalist*, **111**, 1119–1144.

Crowley, P.H. (1981). Dispersal and the stability of predator–prey interactions. *American Naturalist*, **118**, 673–701.

Darwin, C. (1859). *On the Origin of Species*. Reprinted 1964. Harvard University Press, Cambridge, Massachusetts.

Dayton, P.K. (1971). Competition, disturbance and community organization: the provision and subsequent utilization of space in a rocky intertidal community. *Ecological Monographs*, **41**, 351–389.

Fox, J.F. (1981). Intermediate levels of soil disturbance maximize alpine plant diversity. *Nature,* **293,** 564–565.

Franks, N.R. (1980). *The evolutionary ecology of the army ant* Eciton burchelli *on Barro Colorado Island, Panama.* PhD thesis, University of Leeds.

Franks, N.R. (1982a). A new method for censusing animal populations: the number of *Eciton burchelli* army ant colonies on Barro Colorado Island, Panama. *Oecologia,* **52,** 266–268.

Franks, N.R. (1982b). Social insects in the aftermath of the swarm raids of the army ant, *Eciton burchelli. The Biology of Social Insects.* Proceedings of the 9th International Congress of the International Union for the Study of Social Insects. (Ed. by M. D. Breed, C. D. Michener & H. E. Evans), pp. 275–279. Westview Press, Boulder, Colorado.

Franks, N.R. (1982c). Ecology and population regulation in the army ants, *Eciton burchelli. The Ecology of a Tropical Forest* (Ed. by E. G. Leigh, Jr., A. S. Rand & D. W. Windsor), pp. 389–395. Smithsonian Institute Press, Washington D.C.

Franks, N.R. & Fletcher, C.R. (1983). Spatial patterns in army ant foraging migration: *Eciton burchelli* on Barro Colorado Island, Panama. *Behavioural Ecology & Sociobiology* (in press).

Garwood, N.C. (1982). Seasonal rhythms of seed germination in a semi-deciduous tropical forest. *The Ecology of a Tropical Forest* (Ed. by E. G. Leigh, Jr., A. S. Rand & D. W. Windsor), pp. 173–185. Smithsonian Institute Press, Washington D.C.

Grime, J.P. (1973). Control of species density in herbaceous vegetation. *Journal of Environmental Management,* **1,** 151–167.

Harper, J.L. (1969). The role of predation in vegetational diversity. *Brookhaven Symposium in Biology,* **22,** 48–62.

Hartshorn, G.S. (1978). Tree falls and tropical forest dynamics. *Trees as Living Systems* (Ed. by P. B. Tomlinson & M. H. Zimmerman), pp. 617–683. Cambridge University Press, Cambridge.

Holldobler, B. & Wilson, E.O. (1977). The number of queens: An important trait in ant evolution. *Naturwissenschaften,* **64,** 8–15.

Horn, H.S. (1975). Markovian processes of forest succession. *Ecology and Evolution of Communities* (Ed. by M. L. Cody & J. M. Diamond), pp. 196–211. Harvard Press, Cambridge, Massachusetts.

Hubbell, S.P. (1979). Tree dispersion, abundance, and diversity in a tropical dry forest. *Science,* **213,** 1299–1309.

Hubbell, S.P. (1980). Seed predation and the coexistence of tree species in tropical forests. *Oikos,* **35,** 214–229.

Hubbell, S.P & Foster, R.B. (1983). Diversity of canopy trees in a neotropical forest and implications for conservation. *Tropical Rain Forest: Ecology and Management* (Ed. by S. L. Sutton, T. C. Whitmore & A. C. Chadwick), pp. 25–41. Blackwell Scientific Publications, Oxford.

Huston, M. (1979). A general hypothesis of species diversity. *American Naturalist,* **113,** 81–101.

Janzen, D.H. (1970). Herbivores and the number of tree species in tropical forests. *American Naturalist,* **104,** 501–528.

Leigh, E.G. (1972). The golden section and spiral leaf arrangement. *Growth by Intussusception* (Ed. by E. S. Deevy), pp. 163–176. Transactions of the Connecticut Academy of Arts, 44.

Levin, S. & Paine, R.T. (1974). Disturbance, patch formation and community structure. *Proceedings of the National Academy of Sciences, U.S.A.,* **71,** 2744–2747.

Levings, S.C. (1981). *Some aspects of tropical community structure.* PhD thesis. Harvard University, Cambridge, Massachusetts.

Levings, S.C. & Franks, N.R. (1982). Patterns of nest dispersion in a tropical ground ant community. *Ecology,* **63,** 338–344.

Lubchenco, J. (1978). Plant species diversity in a marine intertidal community: importance of herbivore food preference and algal competitive abilities. *American Naturalist,* **112,** 23–39.

Milton, W.E.J. (1940). The effect of manuring, grazing and cutting on the yield, botanical, and chemical composition of natural hill pastures. *Journal of Ecology,* **28,** 326–356.

Milton, W.E.J. (1947). The yield, botanical and chemical composition of natural hill herbage under manuring controlled grazing and hay conditions. 1. Yield and Botanical. *Journal of Ecology,* **35,** 65–89.

Nicholson, I.A., Patterson, I.S. & Currie, A. (1970). A study of vegetational dynamics: selection by sheep and cattle in *Nardus* pasture. Animal populations in relation to their food resources (Ed. by A. D. Watson), pp. 129–143. Blackwell Scientific Publications, Oxford.

Paine, R.T. (1966). Food web complexity and species diversity. *American Naturalist*, **100**, 65–75.

Paine, R.T. (1971). A short-term experimental investigation of resource partitioning in a New Zealand rocky intertidal habitat. *Ecology*, **52**, 1096–1106.

Paine, R.T. (1979). Disaster, catastrophe and local persistence of the sea palm *Postelsia palmaeformis*. *Science*, **205**, 685–687.

Paine, R.T. & Levin, S.A. (1981). Intertidal landscapes:disturbance and the dynamics of pattern. *Ecological Monographs*, **51**, 145–178.

Paine, R.T. & Vadas, R.L. (1969). The effects of grazing by sea urchins, *Strongylocentrotus* spp., on benthic algal populations. *Limnology and Oceanography*, **14**, 710–719.

Rettenmeyer, C.W. (1963). Behavioural studies of army ants. *University of Kansas Science Bulletin*, **44**, 281–465.

Richards, P.W. (1952). *The Tropical Rain Forest*. Cambridge University Press, Cambridge.

Schneirla, T.C. (1940). Further studies of the army-ant behaviour pattern. Mass organization in the swarm raiders. *Journal of Comparative Psychology*, **29**, 401–450.

Schneirla, T.C. (1949). Army-ant life and behaviour under dry-season conditions. 3. The course of reproduction and colony behaviour. *Bulletin of the American Museum of Natural History*, **94**, 7–81.

Schneirla, T.C. (1956). The army ants. *Smithsonian Institute Annual Report, 1955*, 379–406.

Schneirla, T.C. (1971). *Army Ants: A Study in Social Organization* (Ed. by H. R. Topoff) W. H. Freeman, San Francisco.

Skellam, J.G. (1951). Random dispersal in theoretical populations. *Biometrika*, **38**, 196–218.

Smedes, G.W. & Hurd, L.E. (1981). An empirical test of community stability: resistance of a fouling community to a biological patch-forming disturbance. *Ecology*, **62**, 1561–1572.

Summerhayes, V.S. (1941). The effect of voles (*Microtus agrestis*) on vegetation. *Journal of Ecology*, **29**, 14–48.

Tansley, A.G. & Adamson, R.S. (1925). Studies of the vegetation of the English chalk. III. The chalk grasslands of the Hampshire-Sussex border. *Journal of Ecology*, **13**, 177–223.

Vance, R.R. (1979). Effects of grazing by the sea urchin, *Cetrostephanus coronatus*, on prey community composition. *Ecology*, **60**, 537–546.

Whitmore, T.C. (1978). Gaps in the forest canopy. *Tropical Trees as Living Systems* (Ed. by P. B. Tomlinson & M. H. Zimmerman), pp. 639–655. Cambridge University Press, Cambridge.

Willis, E.O. (1967). The behaviour of bicolored antbirds. *University of California Publications in Zoology* (Berkley), **79**, 1–127.

Wilson, E.O. (1958). Patchy distributions of ant species in New Guinea rain forests. *Psyche*, **65**, 26–38.

Wilson, E.O. (1971). *The Insect Societies*. Belknap Press of Harvard University Press, Cambridge, Massachusetts.

Wolda, H. (1978). Fluctuations in the abundance of tropical insects. *American Naturalist*, **112**, 1017–1045.

PART II
PLANT–ANIMAL INTERACTIONS

Distribution of secondary metabolites in rain forest plants: toward an understanding of cause and effect

P. G. WATERMAN

Phytochemistry Research Laboratory, Department of Pharmaceutical Chemistry,
University of Strathclyde, Glasgow G1 1XW, Scotland, U.K.

SUMMARY

1 Available information on the distribution of secondary metabolites in and between rain forest plants is reviewed and related to existing hypotheses on the allelochemic role of these compounds.

2 It has been proposed that tannins and lignins (fibre) act as digestibility-reducers and community surveys of forests do indicate that they occur in highest levels in apparent plants and plant parts suited to this type of protection. Studies on food selection by herbivores confirm that fibre content, particularly in relation to nutrient levels, does exert a major influence on observed preferences.

3 A considerable number of investigations of food selection by both insects and mammalian herbivores have failed to demonstrate a comparable role for tannins. While it remains probable that tannins are able to influence food choice it is considered that this has been over-emphasized in the development of allelochemic hypotheses. Other possible functions for tannins are noted; particularly a role for foliar tannins in N-conservation by suppression of the activity of nitrifying bacteria.

4 Some secondary metabolites do clearly act as toxin type allelochemics but there is still insufficient data to permit a general examination of the distribution of these compounds. A number of studies do suggest that the structural diversity among toxin type compounds is maximized among sympatric species, possibly to limit the gain of an herbivore breaching any specific toxin defence.

INTRODUCTION

The secondary metabolites produced by plants occur in great numbers and enormous structural diversity. Their biogenesis is clearly under genetic control and this is reflected in the association of various structural classes of metabolites with groups of related taxa (Hegnauer 1963–1974). Although their adaptive significance is unclear in most cases it is now widely held that they are functional (some perhaps anachronistic) and should not be dismissed as waste products. In recent years there has been growing interest in the potential of many compounds to act as defensive agents (allelochemics) by inhibiting or deterring the activity of pathogens, herbivores, and competing plants. The circumstantial evidence in support of the allelochemic role is strong. The biomedical literature is full of reports that confirm that many secondary metabolites possess properties that render them toxic to at least some of the potential predators of their producer (see the reviews of Levin 1976; Swain 1977; contributors to Rosenthal & Janzen 1979).

Since the recognition of the allelochemic role for some secondary metabolites there have been a number of attempts to construct hypotheses to rationalize the structural diversity and distribution of these compounds, both within and between plants, in terms of their defence capability. Rhoades & Cates (1976) have proposed that allelochemics with antiherbivore properties can be broadly divided into digestibility-reducers and toxins, the properties of which are listed in Table 1. Both Feeny (1976)

TABLE 1. Comparison of the characteristics of toxins and digestibility-reducers, the two major classes of allelochemics found in plants

Toxins	Digestibility-reducers
(1) 'Qualitative'—active in small amounts, cheap to produce.	'Quantitative'—usually the effect is proportional to the amount produced.
(2) Usually small lipophilic molecules that are able to cross animal membranes to reach site of action.	Act in the gut and do not need to cross membranes. Usually large, often highly polar, molecules.
(3) Act at a specific target site within the target organism.	Interfere with some aspect(s) of the digestive processes, either actively (tannins) or passively (lignins).
(4) Exposed to the predators' system for detoxification. Toxic effects can be completely nullified in adapted predators.	Do not come into contact with normal enzymatic detoxification processes but the degree of activity may be influenced by physical factors and pH.
(5) Selection for maximum diversity to overcome detoxification processes.	Tannins and lignins are structurally conservative. Some less common groups are structurally more like toxins.

and Rhoades & Cates (1976) have suggested that the toxin type of allelochemic will be most suited to the protection of plants or plant parts of low predictability (unapparent), while digestibility-reducing compounds, which should be more generally effective but which need to be present in much higher concentrations, will be more appropriate to the defence of those that are more predictable (apparent). These hypotheses have more recently been refined (Rhoades 1979), and McKey (1979) has reviewed the distribution of allelochemics within plants in relation to them. Janzen (1974), on the other hand, has attempted to relate investment in secondary metabolites as allelochemics to nutrient stress; arguing that investment will be greatest on nutrient-poor sites, since the metabolic cost to the plant in replacing lost photosynthate will be greater than it would be on nutrient-rich sites. As pointed out by Gartlan *et al.* (1980) the concept of apparency and the nutrient stress hypothesis need not be alternatives as species-poor stands and long-lived (apparent) leaves are both liable to result from poor nutrient availability in an ecosystem.

These hypotheses have largely been developed on the basis of widespread but fragmentary data on the distribution and toxicity of secondary metabolites. Their evaluation requires information from detailed studies of the chemistry of plant communities gathered in parallel with data on the ecology of that community and its interaction with herbivores and other deleterious agents. In this paper I will review the results, so far, of our own studies on the community chemistry of a number of sites in rain forest in Africa, India, South East Asia and Central America and its relation to folivory by primates. Other recent work relevant to an analysis of these hypotheses on the distribution of secondary metabolites in rain forest plants will be included.

DISCUSSION

Digestibility-reducing compounds

The two major classes of digestibility-reducers, in terms of distribution and quantities produced are the polyphenols, known collectively as tannins, and lignin, which with its associated cell wall polysaccharides forms fibre. There is a very considerable literature that confirms the ability of tannins to inhibit digestive processes by being able to complex with proteins, both dietary proteins and digestive enzymes (Swain 1979). The role of lignin is more passive, although not entirely so, being related to its resistance to the digestive enzymes of most herbivores and its ability to 'protect' associated polysaccharides from digestion and slow food passsage rates. Other classes of secondary metabolites that can reduce digestion include proteinase-inhibitors (Rosenthal & Janzen 1979) and some simple phenolics, mono- and sesquiterpenes, and alkaloids (Waterman et al. 1980).

Distribution of tannins and fibre between plant parts

Information on the distribution of allelochemics between different parts of the same plant is scattered through the literature (McKey 1979). Probably the most comprehensive set of data available for rain forest plants is that for species from the Douala-Edea Forest Reserve in Cameroun (Gartlan et al. 1980). Table 2 gives the results of pair-wise comparisons of the levels of condensed tannins in mature leaves, young (not full-sized) leaves, barks and seeds from the same species.

Inspection of Table 2 reveals one striking and very consistent result: seeds depart radically from the vegetative tissues of the same plant in their condensed tannin content in two ways. Firstly, seeds contain significantly lower concentrations than do the vegetative parts. In the unusual cases of differences in the opposite direction the magnitude is usually small, only some Diospyros spp. (Ebenaceae) and two Ouratea spp. (Ochnaceae) run strongly counter to the dominant trend and even here the vegetative parts remain quite tannin-rich. By contrast, species with tannin-rich vegetative parts often have seeds that are tannin-poor or devoid of tannin. The second point is that there appears to be little correspondence between tannin content rank of a species based upon seeds and its rank based on any part of the vegetative parts.

Condensed tannin levels in the parts of fruit external to the seed are often considerable, even where the seed itself is tannin-free. An extreme example of this is the fruit of a *Hippocratea* vine from Douala-Edea in which the testa analyses for over 50% tannin while the embryo analyses for less than 2%. High tannin levels in the seed coat are probably able to combat fungal infestation (Sanders & Mixon 1978) and reduce the overall digestibility of the seed (Waterman *et al* 1980). Seed coats are also often very fibrous. A tannin-based defence system has been considered to be particularly appropriate to fleshy fruits (McKey 1979) and it has been demonstrated that some immature commercial fleshy fruits are highly astringent due to the presence of tannin and that astringency and apparent tannin content decreases as the fruit matures and

TABLE 2. Pair-wise comparison of condensed tannin content between different parts of the same species, using Wilcoxon sign test, paired *t*-test performed on log-transformed data, and Spearman rank correlation (r_s). Data taken from Gartlan *et al.* (1980), using Douala-Edea species only. ML = mature leaves, YL = young leaves, SD = mature seeds, BK = bark

Comparison	n	$\bar{x}$	Sign test	Paired *t*-test	r_s
ML/YL	28	7·49/9·41	11 NS	1·63 NS	0·70 $P < 0·001$
ML/SD	37	7·75/4·02	10 $P < 0·05$	4·21 $P < 0·001$	0·26 NS
ML/BK	42	6·50/4·48	12 $P < 0·05$	2·18 $P < 0·05$	0·70 $P < 0·001$
YL/SD	16	12·18/3·42	2 $P < 0·01$	4·39 $P < 0·001$	−0·12 NS
YL/BK	18	9·76/6·67	4 $P < 0·01$	2·12 $P < 0·05$	0·85 $P < 0·001$
SD/BK	39	3·32/5·60	15 NS	3·25 $P < 0·01$	0·08 NS
BK/WOOD	19	4·09/1·24	1 $P < 0·01$	3·25 $P < 0·01$	0·50 NS

becomes palatable (Goldstein & Swain 1963). There is still very little information on tannin levels in wild, fleshy fruits but that which is available suggests that similar processes are in operation, in that fruits of this type are more likely to contain tannins than are other types and tannin levels do appear to decrease as fruits ripen (Wrangham & Waterman 1984).

Differences between the major vegetative parts are less obvious (Table 2). There are consistent and significant differences among mean values for Douala-Edea materials that suggest the sequence: young leaves > mature leaves ≃ barks. However, the magnitude of these differences are much lower than those between each of them and seeds and there is a strong tendency for levels to vary in concert between species. The apparently higher levels in young leaves requires some comment. We have found this to be a consistent feature for rain forest flora from a number of different sites (Gartlan *et al.* 1980; Oates, Waterman & Choo 1980; P. G. Waterman, unpublished) and this is supported by other studies of rain forest foliage (Milton 1979; Coley 1980a). The higher mean values for condensed tannins in young leaves may, in part, be due to greater ease of extractability. However, it does seem probable that condensed tannins often make up a greater percentage of the dry weight of young leaves than they do of mature. This is not meant to imply a loss of these compounds from the mature leaf but a dilution of the material already present as the leaf expands. By contrast, fibre content of leaves nearly always increases as the leaf matures (Choo 1981; Choo *et al.* 1981). Rhoades (1979) regards young leaves as unapparent and mature leaves as apparent for most woody perennials. In as much as fibre/lignin usually increases as leaves mature it can be said that digestibility-reducing compounds are found in greater amounts in the more apparent resource. The evidence available for foliage of rain forest climax species now strongly suggests that this is not true of tannins.

Both barks and the woods underneath them are very fibrous and often highly lignified. Gartlan *et al.* (1980) compared the tannin contents of barks and woods of fourteen rain forest trees from Douala-Edea, all but one belonging to either the Guttiferae or Ebenaceae. The pattern observed, which is consistent in these two chemically very different families, is for significantly higher levels of both total phenolics and condensed tannins in the bark (Table 2). This is consistent with published information, and may reflect highly polymerized and poorly extractable tannins in the wood (McKey 1979).

Distribution of tannins and fibre between species

Rhoades & Cates (1976) found that about 80% of the deciduous and evergreen woody perennials for which information was available contained tannins but this was true for less than 20% of annuals and herbaceous perennials. From our own investigations of rain forest communities in Cameroun (Douala-Edea), Uganda (Kibale Forest), south India (Kakachi) and Costa Rica (Santa Rosa National Park) we can confirm that a large proportion of rain forest tree species, certainly greater than 70%, do yield significant quantities of either hydrolysable or condensed tannins, or both (Gartlan *et al.* 1980; Oates *et al.* 1980; Choo 1981; Janzen & Waterman 1983). Our data indicates that some plant families common in tropical forests produce tannins in all species (Ebenaceae, Combretaceae, Rhizophoraceae) and many others do so in a majority of species (Annonaceae, Guttiferae, Euphorbiaceae, Leguminosae—Mimosoideae and Caesalpinioideae). By contrast a few families, such as the Icacinaceae and Logania-ceae, rarely, if ever, yield tannins in significant amounts.

There is still little information to hand on levels of digestibility-reducing compounds in the herb layer of forests, but what is available does tend to indicate a low investment in both tannins and fibre, as anticipated by Rhoades and Cates (1976). This is supported by Choo (1981) who, in an investigation of the herb layer of montane forest on Mount Visoke, Rwanda, has found the foliage to be less fibre-rich and less likely to contain tannins than any of the forest tree communities analysed.

Within the tree community we have so far been unable to find any chemical differentiation that relates to stratification in the forest. For example, the foliage of *Diospyros obliquifolia* White (Ebenaceae) and *D. hoyleana* White, which are shrub and understorey species at Douala-Edea, contains more tannin than does that of many of the canopy species of *Diospyros* at the same site. From what scant data are at present available it does not appear possible to differentiate between liane and tree foliage but that of epiphytes and vines of the forest edge may be less rich in both fibre and tannins.

Coley (1980a, b) has studied the chemistry of foliage from fast-growing shade-intolerant (colonizing) and slow-growing, shade-tolerant (climax) species on Barro Colorado Island in central America. Her analyses have demonstrated that colonizers, as a group, produce less tannin-rich and less fibrous foliage than do climax species. The greater investment in digestibility-reducing compounds, coupled with lower rates of observed insect grazing on those species, is taken to support the hypothesis that the most predictable (apparent) food resource will have the highest defence investment. By contrast, many of the species that colonize the sporadically occurring light gaps would be expected to use toxins as allelochemics rather than digestibility-reducers. At present there is no data available to confirm or deny that colonizers invest more heavily in toxins than do climax species, but it is clear that some colonizing species are tannin-rich. One interesting example in Cameroun is the small tree *Barteria fistulosa* Mast. (Passifloraceae). Analysis of the foliage of fifteen individuals growing in light gaps at Douala-Edea has revealed an average of 19·10% condensed tannin (S.D. 5·89%) (Waterman, Ross & McKey 1983). The foliage of eleven individuals found existing within the closed canopy forest averaged only 11·96% (S.D. 6·42%), significantly less than the light gap individuals ($P < 0.01$). There was no comparable difference in fibre levels. The greater emphasis on tannin production by individuals in the light gaps may appear paradoxical but could simply reflect the realization of full metabolic potential, whereas those growing in the shade of the closed canopy are unable to sustain the same level of activity.

A comparison of condensed tannin concentrations in the leaves of deciduous and evergreen trees has so far failed to show persistent trends. However, it is noticeable that at Douala-Edea the deciduous *Cleistopholis staudtii* Engl. *et* Diels (Annonaceae) and *Discoglypremna caloneura* Prain and *Maprounea membranacea* Pax. *et* Hoffm. (both Euphorbiaceae) are tannin-poor, whereas almost all of the considerable numbers of sympatric evergreen species of these families are tannin-rich (Gartlan *et al.* 1980). Foliage of deciduous and evergreen species in the predominantly deciduous lowland forest of Costa Rica (Janzen & Waterman 1983) shows absolutely no differences in condensed tannin levels in young leaves, but as leaves age evergreen species become, on average, more tannin-rich although differences never attain significance. On the other hand, the fibre content of evergreen species does appear to be significantly greater than in deciduous species at all stages of leaf development analysed. Thus, total investment in digestibility-reducing compounds is probably greater in evergreen species at the Costa Rican site.

Distribution of tannins and fibre between different forests

The most detailed comparison for which data are at present available is between lowland rain forest at Douala-Edea and Compartment 30 of the Kibale Forest (McKey *et al.* 1978; Gartlan *et al.* 1980). Mean concentrations of all phenolics and of condensed tannins in particular are significantly greater in foliage from Douala-Edea, the differences being very marked (Table 3). Where analysis is restricted to common tree species differences in tannin levels are further enlarged (Table 3). Smaller data sets for fibre content (Choo *et al.* 1981) and for protein content (Waterman *et al.* 1980) show that the former is also to be found in greater amounts in Douala-Edea foliage but the latter occurs in greater amounts in Kibale foliage (Table 3).

There are a number of possible explanations for the extreme differences found in tannin levels in these forests. Douala-Edea is a coastal forest growing on extremely acidic, nutrient-deficient, sandy soils, whereas Kibale is growing on relatively rich soils (Gartlan *et al.* 1980). Thus, it is tempting to see this as a classic example of heavy investment in defence chemistry by species growing on a nutritionally-poor site, as predicted by Janzen (1974). However, the two sites are very different not only in their soils but also in altitude, rainfall, and species composition. The only species analysed from both sites is *Symphonia globulifera* L. *f.* (Guttiferae), in which phenolic levels are very similar whatever the source. Clearly the differences occur because successful

TABLE 3. Mean percentage values for total phenolics (TP), condensed tannins (CT), acid detergent fibre (ADF) and protein in mature leaves from five rain forests. DE = Douala-Edea, Cameroun, KI = Kibale, Uganda (Gartlan *et al.* 1980); KA = Kakachi, South India (Oates *et al.* 1980); SR = Santa Rosa, Costa Rica (Janzen & Waterman 1983); SE = Sepilok, Sabah (A. G. Davies & P. G. Waterman, unpublished)

Site	TP		CT		ADF		Protein	
	$\bar{x}$	n	$\bar{x}$	n	$\bar{x}$	n	$\bar{x}$	n
DE—all species	6·93	74	5·63	74	55·5	31	12·3	21
DE—twenty most common species	7·20	17	5·84	17	n.a.		n.a.	
KI—all species	3·88	19	3·31	19	39·2	16	17·7	14
KI—twenty most common species	3·41	15	2·36	15	n.a.		n.a.	
KA	6·28	15	5·91	15	42·2	15	11·7	14
SR—deciduous	5·69	53	4·88	53	38·1	53	n.a.	
SR—evergreen	7·21	15	6·65	15	49·2	15	n.a.	
SE—Dipterocarpaceae	6·52	9	4·54	9	60·9	9	n.a.	

n.a. = data not available.

species at Douala-Edea have foliage rich in digestibility-reducers while successful species from Kibale are often relatively deficient in these compounds. While variation in nutrient availability from the soil is a plausible cause for the differential investment in digestibility-reducers there do remain a number of confounding variables which can only be assessed by comparative analyses at other rain forest sites.

A number of relevant studies are in progress. The Kakachi site in south India is at about the same altitude as Kibale and has a somewhat higher rainfall (Oates *et al.* 1980). Levels of condensed tannins found among common species are comparable to those found at Douala-Edea but fibre levels are comparable to Kibale (Table 3). The Korup National Park lies to the north of Douala-Edea. Rainfall is higher than Douala-Edea and so is species diversity, with considerable overlap between the two sites. Soils at Korup are certainly less acidic and may be somewhat richer in N and P (J. S. Gartlan, unpublished). Tannin levels at Korup are comparable to those at Douala-Edea and no distinction appears possible regarding investment by the same species at the two sites. Unfortunately, there are as yet no figures for fibre levels in Korup foliage. For mature leaves from species at Santa Rosa National Park tannin levels are high but fibre levels generally low, probably because of the much greater proportion of deciduous species (Table 3). Analysis of a number of the common

Dipterocarpaceae of lowland rain forest in Sabah suggests tannin levels comparable to Douala-Edea and fibre levels greater than recorded at other sites (Table 3).

From the above series of comparisons a pattern does begin to emerge. In our earlier reports regarding the comparative allelochemistry of Douala-Edea and Kibale (McKey *et al.* 1978; Gartlan *et al.* 1980) we drew attention to the high tannin levels found at Douala-Edea and related this to the nutrient-deficiency hypothesis. With at least some data to hand from four other sites and from Coley (1980a) it seems likely that the emphasis was placed on the wrong forest. It is not Douala-Edea that is exceptional in foliar tannin production, as it is matched by all other sites studied since. It is Kibale that is exceptional in that mature foliage of dominant species appears to contain significantly less tannin than does any comparable set of material analysed.

By contrast, the levels of fibre found in mature foliage follows a more easily rationalized pattern. Highest levels are found among the foliage of lowland forests (Douala-Edea, the dipterocarps of Sabah, almost certainly Korup) while higher altitude sites and those that are predominantly deciduous have foliage with significantly less fibre.

Role of digestibility-reducing compounds in mediating food selection by herbivores

The digestibility of foliage is widely used to predict forage quality for domestic animals and its strong negative correlation with fibre content, both *in vivo* and *in vitro*, has been consistently demonstrated (Barnes & Marten 1979). This relationship has recently been confirmed for foliage from a wide range of rain forest trees (Choo *et al.* 1981). Among domestic herbivores voluntary intake is clearly established as a correlate of fibre content (Hendriksen, Poppi & Minson 1981) and the same is true for at least some of the east African savanna herbivores and for colobine and howler monkeys (Waterman 1983). The lower fibre content and hence greater digestibility of many young leaves is certainly a major factor in their preferential selection by many generalist folivores. The ratio between protein and fibre contents of leaves is a better predictor of selection than either measures alone for both howler monkeys (Milton 1979) and at least some colobine monkeys (Waterman & Choo 1981). Insects feeding on fibre-rich mature leaves have slower growth rates than those feeding on young leaves (Feeny 1976) and fibre and nutritional factors are considered to be the best overall predictors of grazing susceptibility (Coley 1980a). Thus, in most respects, fibre does appear to play the role of a digestibility-reducing factor, which is not to say that this is its *raison d'etre*, and to have a distribution pattern in general agreement with that predicted from defence chemistry hypotheses.

For tannins the situation is by no means as clear cut. Digestibility of rain forest foliage does show a negative correlation with tannin content but, compared to fibre, the relationship is weak (Waterman *et al.* 1980; Choo *et al.* 1981). The supposed non-specific reaction between tannins and proteins has recently been shown to be highly specific (Hagerman & Butler 1981), depending on the structure and properties of both participants and showing great variability in both strength of complexation and pH of maximum stability for the complex. While the potential toxicity of tannins is established from numerous feeding experiments, notably on the rat and chick, there is a growing body of data indicating their inability to deter feeding by insects (Coley 1980a; Bernays 1981; Becker & Martin 1982) and possible beneficial effects in ruminants (Jones & Mangan 1977). Our own studies on food selection by primates suggest that there is a clear preference for foliage devoid of tannins or with low tannin levels. Addition of tannins to the digestibility-reducer portion of nutrient/digestibility-reducer equations does tend to enhance correlation with selection, but only to a small extent (Waterman & Choo 1981; Waterman 1983). The larvae of saturniid moths appear more tolerant to tannins than do the larvae of sphingid moths (Janzen & Waterman, 1983). However, in neither primate food selection nor sphingid host selection is a high tannin concentration an absolute deterrent. Tannins may play a more definite role in the protection of fruits and seeds, perhaps primarily from fungal attack.

While not dismissing an allelochemic role for foliar tannins it does seem likely that their potential in this respect has been over-emphasized and that their contribution is secondary. What then of other roles? Rhoades (1977) has suggested that the atypical β-tannins of *Larrea* spp. (Zygophyllaceae) (the creosote bush of the deserts of S.W. U.S.A.) act as an anti-desiccant and as a u.v. screen. Is seems unlikely that the former of these roles is attributable to typical tannins but the latter warrants further investigation in the light of recent findings on tannin levels in leaves of *Barteria fistulosa* (see earlier). Many tannins are certainly anti-fungal and may also inhibit bacteria. Their greatest impact may well be seen in the leaf litter and soil where they have been reported to inhibit the activity of invertebrate reducers (Cameron & LaPoint 1978), fungi (Harrison 1971) and nitrifying bacteria (Rice & Pancholy 1973). If, to date, analyses of tannins in rain forest foliage support any hypothesis it is that of Jordan, Todd & Escalante (1979) who have proposed that low soil pH and high concentrations of tannins in the root mat of forests are valuable in N-conservation, by suppressing nitrifying bacteria and slowing litter decomposition.

Toxins

For most classes of toxins analysis at the community level is difficult because of the absence of general assay techniques of the type applicable to tannin and fibre quantification. Toxins are structurally very variable and there may often be no alternative to their isolation and characterization if their ecological role is to be analysed; this can be a time-consuming and complicated process. General detection tests, which tell you nothing about quantity, structure or toxicity, are available for alkaloids and have been used to screen the flora of Douala-Edea and Kibale. The most interesting result to have emerged is that alkaloid distribution is not independent of that of tannins, alkaloids being more likely to occur in tannin-poor species and *vice versa* (Gartlan *et al.* 1980). Tannins and alkaloids do interact chemically and tannins are known to diminish the toxic effects of alkaloids which, from an allelochemic viewpoint, makes their separation sensible. A similar dichotomy between alkaloids and tannins is seen in Santa Rosa National park (Janzen & Waterman 1983).

The absence of comprehensive data for any site makes it impossible to discuss relationships between toxin chemistry and herbivory at a community level in anything other than purely speculative terms. Their susceptibility to specific detoxification processes is well illustrated by the strong interrelationships between radiating groups of plants and insects, classic examples of which include papilionid butterflies and the alkaloid and coumarin containing Magnoliales, Rutales and Umbellales (Ehrlich & Raven 1964; Berenbaum 1981) and bruchid beetles and non-protein amino acid producing Leguminosae (Janzen 1973). Larger animals also often exhibit the ability to detoxify these compounds. Among the ruminant-like colobine monkeys the ability to eat a number of plant parts known to contain significant amounts of highly toxic alkaloids is attributed to the capacity of the rumen microflora to metabolize these compounds (Waterman 1983). To date, simple stomached primates do not appear to show the same capacity.

One area that has been the subject of some speculation concerns the optimum distribution of toxins within a plant and between closely-related sympatric species. Toxins occur in all plant parts, often in highest levels and greatest structural diversity in barks and to the least extent in woods. This subject has recently been reviewed in considerable detail by McKey (1979) and our own studies so far add nothing more. Janzen (1973) suggests that maximizing the diversity in toxin chemistry among sympatric species would minimize the deleterious impact of an herbivore breaching the toxin defence system. Cates & Rhoades (1977) pointed out a number of cases where groups of closely-related, sympatric, alkaloid-producing species did differ in their alkaloid composition to show unique patterns. Waterman *et al.* (1978) found that the Toddalioideae (Rutaceae) of the forest zone in Ghana had patterns of distribution that minimized overlap in chemistry between species growing under the ecologically most similar conditions. Our own investigations on the toxin chemistry of the flora of Douala-Edea have shown two further examples that appear to represent a maximizing of diversity within the biogenetic limitations of the species concerned. Among species of the genera *Mammea* and *Garcinia* (Guttiferae) the distribution of neoflavonoids, xanthones, biflavonoids and lactones in the bark lead to each class of compound being found in a significant proportion (but not all) of the guttiferous population (Table 4).

TABLE 4. Distribution of toxin type secondary metabolites in the barks of five sympatric Guttiferae from Douala-Edea: N = neoflavonoid, X = xanthone, Bz = benzophenone, Bf = biflavonoid, L = lactone. Data from Crichton (1980)

Species	Secondary metabolite				
	N	X	Bz	Bf	L
Mammea africana Sabine	+	−	−	−	−
Garcinia mannii Oliv.	−	−	(+)	+	(+)
G. conrauana Engl.	−	−	−	−	+
G. densivenia Engl.	−	+	−	+	−
G. ovalifolia Oliv.	−	+	+·	−	−

+ = major component; (+) = minor component; − = apparently absent.

Among three sympatric species of *Xylopia* (Annonaceae) there is a common theme in the biogenesis of diterpenes, in one species the trachylobane type is formed, in a second the kolavane type and in the third a unique dimer (Hasan 1981).

CONCLUSIONS

In the 7 years since the proposals of Feeny (1976) and Rhoades & Cates (1976) a considerable body of relevant data has accrued but this is still insufficient to test many aspects of their hypotheses. The role of fibre as a major mediator of food selection because of its digestibility-reducing properties is firmly established and its distribution follows many of the predicted patterns for this type of allelochemic. Tannin distribution similarly complies with these patterns but, unfortunately, evidence for the ability of tannins to influence food selection to the degree one would expect if this were its primary function, especially in foliage, is difficult to come by. While it is certainly true that tannins can and do influence food choice the present position suggests that their abilities in this respect may well have been over-emphasized.

With regard to the toxin type of allelochemic, general statements remain impossible. All compounds that look like toxins are not toxins; they may be allelopathic, or acting as attractants, or have some as yet undefined primary function. Furthermore, many of the compounds that are observed today may be anachronisms that no longer fulfil the role for which they were selected. In this respect it is not surprising that the isoquinoline alkaloids, the earliest type to be evolved by angiosperms, are today less toxic as a class than the more recently evolved indole alkaloids (Levin & York 1978). Notwithstanding these caveats it is firmly established that many secondary metabolites are capable of giving substantial protection from many potential predators by exerting anti-herbivore properties.

ACKNOWLEDGMENTS

Extensive comparisons of rain forest chemistry of the type discussed here will of necessity involve extensive collaboration. I particularly acknowledge the collaboration of A. G. Davies, J. S. Gartlan, D. H. Janzen, D. B. McKey, J. F. Oates, and T. T. Struhsaker in the collection of plant material and in making available the data from field studies in the relevant forests. The contributions of the following, whilst research students in my laboratory, made this work possible: G. M. Choo, E. G. Crichton, C. M. Hasan, R. A. Hussain, C. N. Mbi, and J. A. M. Ross. The investigations carried out at Strathclyde were financed by Grant No. 3/3455 from the Natural Environment Research Council.

REFERENCES

Barnes, R.F. & Marten, G.C. (1979). Recent developments in predicting forage quality. *Journal of Animal Science*, **48**, 1554–1561.

Becker, P. & Martin, J.S. (1982). Protein-precipitating capacity of tannins in *Shorea* (Dipterocarpaceae) seedling leaves. *Journal of Chemical Ecology*, **8**, 1353–1367.

Berenbaum, M. (1981). Effect of linear furanocoumarins on an adapted insect (*Papilio polyxenes*). *Ecological Entomology*, 6, 353–360.

Cameron, G.N. & LaPoint, T.W. (1978). Effects of tannins on the decomposition of chinese tallow leaves by terrestrial and aquatic invertebrates. *Oecologia (Berlin)*, 32, 349–366.

Cates, R.G. & Rhoades, D.F. (1977). Patterns in the production of antiherbivore chemical defences in plant communities. *Biochemical Systematics & Ecology*, 5, 185–193.

Choo, G.M. (1981). *Plant chemistry in relation to folivory by some colobine monkeys*. Ph.D. thesis, University of Strathclyde.

Choo, G.M., Waterman, P.G., McKey, D.B. & Gartlan, J.S. (1981). A simple enzyme assay for dry matter digestibility and its value in studying food selection by generalist herbivores. *Oecologia (Berlin)*, 49, 170–178.

Coley, P.D. (1980a). *Ecological and evolutionary responses of tropical trees to herbivory: a quantitative analysis of grazing damage, plant defenses and growth rates*. Ph.D. thesis, University of Chicago.

Coley, P.D. (1980b). Effect of leaf age and plant life history patterns on herbivory. *Nature, London*, 284, 545–546.

Crichton, E.G. (1980). *Phytochemical studies on some west African Guttiferae*. Ph.D. thesis, University of Strathclyde.

Ehrlich, P.R. & Raven, P.H. (1964). Butterflies and plants: a study of coevolution. *Evolution*, 18, 586–608.

Feeny, P. (1976). Plant apparency and chemical defense. *Recent Advances in Phytochemistry*, Vol. 10 (Ed. by J. W. Wallace & R. L. Mansell), pp. 1–40, Plenum Press, New York.

Gartlan, J.S., McKey, D.B., Waterman, P.G., Mbi, C.N. & Struhsaker, T.T. (1980). A comparative study of the phytochemistry of two African rain forests. *Biochemical Systematics & Ecology*, 8, 401–422.

Goldstein, J.L. & Swain, T. (1963). Changes in tannins in ripening fruits. *Phytochemistry*, 2, 371–383.

Hagerman, A.E. & Butler, L.G. (1981). The specificity of proanthocyanidin–protein interactions. *Journal of Biological Chemistry*, 256, 4494–4497.

Harrison, A.F. (1971). The inhibitory effect of oak leaf litter tannins on the growth of fungi in relation to litter decomposition. *Soil Biology & Biochemistry*, 3, 167–172.

Hasan, C.M. (1981). *Phytochemical studies on some west African Annonaceae*. Ph.D. thesis, University of Strathclyde.

Hendricksen, R.E., Poppi, D.P. & Minson, D.J. (1981). The voluntary intake, digestibility and retention time by cattle and sheep of stem and leaf fractions of a tropical legume (*Lablab purpureus*). *Australian Journal of Agricultural Research*, 32, 389–398.

Hegnauer, R. (1963–1974). *Chemotaxonomie der Pflanzen*, Vol. 1–6. Birkhauser Verlag, Basel.

Janzen, D.H. (1973). Community structure of secondary compounds in plants. *Pure & Applied Chemistry*, 34, 529–538.

Janzen, D.H. (1974). Tropical blackwater rivers, animals, and mast fruiting by the Dipterocarpaceae. *Biotropica*, 6, 69–103.

Janzen, D. H. & Waterman, P. G. (1983). A seasonal census of phenolics, fibre and alkaloids in foliage of forest trees in Costa Rica: some factors influencing their distribution and relation to host selection by Sphingidae and Saturniidae. *Biological Journal of the Linnean Society* (in press).

Jones, W.T. & Mangan J.L. (1977). Complexes of the condensed tannins of sainfoin (*Onobrychis viciifolia* Scop.) with fraction-1 leaf protein and with submaxillary mucoprotein, and their reversal by polyethylene glycol and pH. *Journal of the Science of Food & Agriculture*, 28, 126–136.

Jordan, C.F., Todd, R.L. & Escalante, G. (1979). Nitrogen conservation in a tropical rain forest. *Oecologia (Berlin)*, 39, 123–128.

Levin, D.A. (1976). The chemical defenses of plants to pathogens and herbivores. *Annual Review of Ecology & Systematics*, 7, 121–159.

Levin, D.A. & York, B.M. (1978). The toxicity of plant alkaloids: an ecogeographic perspective. *Biochemical Systematics & Ecology*, 6, 61–76.

McKey, D.B. (1979). The distribution of secondary compounds within plants. *Herbivores, Their Interaction with Secondary Plant Metabolites* (Ed. by G. A. Rosenthal & D. H. Janzen), pp. 56–133. Academic Press, New York.

McKey, D.B., Waterman, P.G., Mbi, C.N., Gartlan, J.S. & Struhsaker, T.T. (1978). Phenolic content of vegetation in two African rain forests: ecological implications. *Science*, 202, 61–64.

Milton, K. (1979). Factors influencing leaf choice by howler monkeys: a test of some hypotheses of food selection by generalist herbivores. *American Naturalist*, **114**, 362–378.

Oates, J.F., Waterman, P.G. & Choo, G.M. (1980). Food selection by the South Indian leaf-monkey, *Presbytis johnii*, in relation to leaf chemistry. *Oecologia (Berlin)*, **45**, 45–56.

Rhoades, D.F. (1977). Integrated antiherbivore, antidesiccant and ultraviolet screening properties of creosotebush resin. *Biochemical Systematics & Ecology*, **5**, 281–290.

Rhoades, D.F. (1979). Evolution of plant chemical defense against herbivores. *Herbivores, Their Interaction with Secondary Plant Metabolites* (Ed. by G. A. Rosenthal & D. H. Janzen), pp. 3–54. Academic Press, New York.

Rhoades, D.F. & Cates, R.G. (1976). Toward a theory of plant antiherbivore chemistry. *Recent Advances in Phytochemistry*, Vol. 10 (Ed. by J. W. Wallace & R. L. Mansell), pp. 168–213. Plenum Press, New York.

Rice, E.L. & Pancholy, S.K. (1973). Inhibition of nitrification by climax ecosystems. II. Additional evidence and possible role of tannins. *American Journal of Botany*, **60**, 691–702.

Rosenthal, G.A. & Janzen, D.H. (1979). *Herbivores, Their Interaction with Secondary Plant Metabolites.* Academic Press, New York.

Sanders, T.M. & Mixon, A.C. (1978). Effect of peanut tannins on percent seed colonization and *in vitro* growth by *Aspergillus paraciticus*. *Mycopathologia*, **66**, 169–173.

Swain, T. (1977). Secondary compounds as protective agents. *Annual Review of Plant Physiology*, **28**, 479–501.

Swain, T. (1979). Tannins and lignins. *Herbivores, Their Interactions with Secondary Plant Metabolites* (Ed. by G. A. Rosenthal & D. H. Janzen), pp. 657–682, Academic Press, New York.

Waterman, P.G. (1983). Food acquisition and processing by primates as a function of plant chemistry. *Food Acquisition and Processing by Primates* (Ed. by D. J. Chivers), Plenum Press, New York (in press).

Waterman, P.G. & Choo, G.M. (1981). The effects of digestibility-reducing compounds in leaves on food selection by some Colobinae. *Malaysian applied Biology*, **10**, 147–162.

Waterman, P.G., Mbi, C.N., McKey, D.B. & Gartlan, J.S. (1980). African rainforest vegetation and rumen microbes: phenolic compounds and nutrients as correlates of digestibility. *Oecologia (Berlin)*, **47**, 22–33.

Waterman, P.G., Meshal, I.A., Hall, J.B. & Swaine, M.D. (1978). Biochemical systematics and ecology of the Toddalioideae in the central part of the west African forest zone. *Biochemical Systematics & Ecology*, **6**, 239–245.

Waterman, P.G., Ross, J.A.M. & McKey, D.B. (1983). Factors affecting levels of some phenolic compounds, digestibility and nitrogen content of the mature leaves of *Barteria fistulosa* (Passifloraceae). *Journal of Chemical Ecology* (in press).

Wrangham, R. W. & Waterman, P. G. (1984). Condensed tannins in fruits eaten by chimpanzees. *Biotropica* (in press).

Vertebrate responses to fruiting seasonality within a Bornean rain forest

M. LEIGHTON* AND D. R. LEIGHTON*

Department of Forestry, Oxford University

SUMMARY

1   Changes in diets and densities of frugivorous diurnal vertebrates were monitored, together with the availability of seed and fruit pulp resources, for 2 years in a Bornean lowland tropical rain forest. For virtually all vertebrates, preferred fruit types were highly seasonal, and much more abundant in the first year than in the second. The variable responses of vertebrates to periods of low fruit availability are examined to identify implications for forest conservation and management.

2   Birds with specialized diets of large-seeded fruits with lipid-rich flesh (*Rhyticeros undulatus, R. corrugatus, Ducula aenea, D. badia, Ptilinopus jambu, Gracula religiosa,* and *Calyptomena viridis*), psitticine seed predators (*Loriculus galgulus* and *Psittinus cyanurus*) and the bearded pig (*Sus barbatus*) left the study site when their fruit resources became scarce. Some orang-utan (*Pongo pygmaeus*) and rhinoceros hornbill (*Buceros rhinoceros*) individuals also emigrated. Although local densities of all these species vary directly with food abundance, their ranging systems may be different (huge, but fixed home ranges, migration, or nomadism). The spatial requirements of these species, especially as they relate to the spatial scale of phenological differences between forest formations and between localities within the same formation were not identified. Different formations may have fruiting peaks that complement one another or some may be relatively aseasonal. Different localities within a forest formation may differ stochastically in phenology.

3   Frugivores with fixed home ranges respond to periods of low fruit availability by increasing their dietary proportions of non-fruit foods and of aseasonal fruit types. Plant taxa that fruit outside community peaks in fruit production may be extraordinarily important in maintaining sedentary vertebrate populations, many of which provide service as seed dispersal agents. Temporally staggered fruiting by trees with large-seeded capsular fruits (especially species of Meliaceae and Myristicaceae) were exploited by territorial hornbills when fruit was scarce. Similar fruiting behaviour by woody climbers of the Annonaceae provided fruit for primates and smaller birds outside fruiting peaks. Intrapopulation fruiting asynchrony and frequent crop production by species of climbing and strangling *Ficus* guarantee relatively continuous availability of figs for many frugivorous species.

4   The host trees which fig climbers and stranglers rely upon for structural support are commonly large dipterocarps and *Eusideroxylon zwageri*, the principal commercial

*Present address: Department of Anthropology, Harvard University, Cambridge, MA 02138, U.S.A.

timber trees in Borneo. This association suggests that logging adversely affects densities of figs for vertebrates. In selectively logged forest adjacent to the study area, adult and juvenile figs were less common than in primary forest.

5 Long-term studies that characterize alterations in population biology and fruiting phenology of important fruit trees following forest disturbance are advised.

INTRODUCTION

The generalization that the species richness of vertebrate communities in tropical forests is due in part to the continuous availability of food resources (especially fruit and nectar) (Orians 1969) should not obscure the fact that phenological studies of evergreen tropical rain forests have, without exception, documented temporal unevenness in fruit production that is not compensated for by interspecific variation (Medway 1972; Frankie, Baker & Opler 1974; Whitmore 1975; Putz 1979; Foster 1980). This unevenness has a seasonal component in that fluctuations in phenological activity recur annually in association with seasonal climatic changes. Seasonality is sufficiently intense to influence the compositions of nectarivorous bird communities in Central America (Feinsinger 1979; Feinsinger & Colwell 1978; Stiles 1980). In addition to annual variation there is marked between-year variation in the numbers of trees fruiting, fruiting species, and fruit crop sizes (Medway 1972; Foster 1980). In the most dramatic case, Foster (1982) described widespread starvation of frugivores following climatically-induced fruit crop failures on Barro Colorado Island, Panama, in 1970.

Here we document the temporal patterns of ripe fruit availability for different birds and mammals during 2 years within a lowland dipterocarp rain forest in Borneo. Co-evolutionary analyses of fruit–vertebrate interactions will be dealt with in separate papers that dissect the phenological patterns of plants and the fruit and seed preferences of vertebrates in this forest. Emphasis is here placed on observations with implications for conservation and forestry practices in Malesian forests. First, we identify vertebrates that respond to periods of low fruit and seed availability through emigration to more favourable habitats. These frugivores seem especially vulnerable to local extinction because they require continuous access to a complete range of complementary habitats (Terborgh & Winter 1980). Secondly, we identify plant taxa that fruit during seasons or years of low resource supply, thereby permitting maintenance of populations of frugivores that have fixed home ranges and do not escape unfavourable periods through emigration. These plant groups have been appropriately called 'keystone mutualists' (Gilbert 1980), signifying that their loss will in turn deplete or eliminate populations of animals that are agents of seed dispersal for these and a diversity of other plants. One such taxon is a species-rich guild of fig (*Ficus*) species, used as primary or subsidiary fruit resources for many vertebrates. These *Ficus* are species of both climbing (subg. *Ficus* sections *Rhizocladus* and *Kalosyce*; see Corner 1965), and tree-like habit (subg. *Urostigma*) that share features of fruit morphology and phenology. We examined the associations of these figs with their host trees to assess the effects of timber extractions.

Study site

All data were collected between August 1977 and September 1979 within a 3 km² site (0°24′N, 117°16′E) along the Sengata River in the Kutai Nature Reserve (now National Park), East Kalimantan, Indonesia. The site partially overlaps an area used in previous primate studies (Rodman 1973, 1977, 1978). The forest is dipterocarp lowland evergreen rain forest (Whitmore 1975) on sandstone that has been uplifted. The major gradient of importance to local distributions of both plants and vertebrates is one of moisture and structure. The forest near the river is occasionally flooded (at greater than yearly intervals), and stands on relatively flat alluvial terrain at 40–60 m elevation. This riparian forest grows on wetter soils, is of lower stature and carries higher liana loads in comparison with the taller, more open forest on the well-drained ridges and ridge slopes. The dominant big trees of the study area are *Eusideroxylon zwageri*, especially in alluvial sites, and species of Dipterocarpaceae. Overall, these forests are extremely rich in species, *c.* 600 tree and 170 liana and strangler species fruited during the 2 years of the study.

Annual rainfall for the 2 years was 2245 mm and 2108 mm, respectively. The temporal patterns of rainfall in these and two other years indicate little seasonality except for lower rainfall during August to September. Only 2·4 mm of rain fell over 23 days in September 1977. General or gregarious flowering followed in the subsequent 2 months, in turn producing a broad fruiting peak from February to May 1978, which in particular included many infrequently-fruiting canopy and emergent trees (see Medway 1972).

METHODS

The availability of fruit and seed resources was monitored by censuses of plots and along a 27-km trail system. Monthly censuses of the randomly placed plots (thirty of 0·5 ha in the first year, reduced to twenty-five of 0·25 ha in the second year) were exhaustive, in that all individual lianas, epiphytes and trees ≥ 4 cm diameter at breast height (dbh) observed to fruit or flower were tagged, mapped, measured for dbh, identified to species or assigned a temporary species code, and incorporated into the phenological sample, which eventually exceeded 5000 individuals. States of fruiting and flowering were recorded and detailed data added on fruit abundance within patches (here defined as individual fruiting plants) of ripe fruit. Plants were provisionally identified in the field, but botanical collections were made of all distinct taxa. The phenology of species poorly represented in plots was determined by monitoring individuals along trails. A special study of fig phenology included monthly censuses of over 400 individuals of different fig species along a subset of the trails.

The frugivorous vertebrates (any species seen eating fruit flesh or seeds) we studied were mostly birds and diurnal mammals, although some information was gleaned for bearded pigs (*Sus barbatus*) and various civets (Viverridae). Measures of diets and inferences about preferred fruit and seed types were derived from observations of fruit and seed eating obtained during censuses along the trail system, and from following groups of foraging primates, hornbills and squirrels. Watches at fruit trees, totalling 4025 hours or 7413 man–tree hours, contributed to and substantiated these inferences about diets. These data on diets and tree visitation will be published separately. Six research assistants gathered data on the larger birds and mammals, but only M.L. collected data on small frugivorous birds.

Some closely studied primate and hornbill species were known with certainty to occur in groups with fixed ranges. Changes in the local abundances of other vertebrates were established from monthly rates of encounter along the trail system. Observations of small bulbuls (Pycnonotidae) and other birds were too few to examine fluctuations in their abundances, despite the likelihood that some are 'nomadic' (Medway & Wells 1976). Only distinct groups were tallied for each species on any given day, and frugivorous birds in transit over the forest were not counted. Censuses were conducted in the morning or late afternoon, when frugivores are most active. The opportunistic scheduling of research activities at any one time precluded equal coverage of the trail system and equal census effort per month. Any given census traversed both riparian and upland habitats, however, and few trails were walked twice on a given day. Differences between months in total sampling time were normalized by expressing animal abundances as rates of encounter. Although we realize that all possible biases in measures may not have been eliminated, only the dramatic changes in local abundances of species are discussed here.

In June 1979, ten 0·5 ha plots were randomly selected and established in forest approximately 0·5 km NW of the study site. This forest had been selectively logged in January 1977 for commercial (> 50 cm dbh) dipterocarps and *Eusideroxylon*, and was closely similar to the primary forest study area in soils, topography and original structure. All individuals of *Ficus* species (for the hemiepiphytic 'strangling' forms of subg. *Urostigma*, all individuals with root in the ground) were censused, assigned to species and separated into adult (i.e., fig-producing) and juvenile classes, based on M.L.'s accumulated experience with the size-structures of different fig species in this forest.

RESULTS

Fruit and seed selection within the frugivorous community

With few exceptions, frugivores exploited a given fruit species at a particular stage of ripeness, digesting either the ripe flesh (aril, mesocarp, sarcotesta, etc.) or eating (= preying upon) the unripe seed (the embryo and its attendant endosperm or cotyledons). This is an important distinction because primates and the squirrel *Callosciurus prevostii* exploited some fruit taxa for ripe pulp but others for nearly mature seeds.

The frugivorous birds in this study were almost exclusively fruit swallowers that digested the flesh and passed or regurgitated the seed(s). Since these birds could not swallow fruits wider than their gapes, the primary fruit character structuring avian diets in this frugivorous community is the widest diameter of the cross-section of the pulp-seed unit. Most fig fruits, however, are sufficiently soft for even small birds to feed on large figs by tearing off chunks and swallowing them. A second important distinction is between fruits with a thin pericarp or rind (many drupes and berries) and those with a thick inedible husk that splits as the fruit ripens (viz. capsules). Some birds (the black magpie, *Platysmurus leucopterus*, and the six species of hornbills with laterally flattened bills) force open capsules along the suture lines, while other birds must wait until the fruits fully dehisce, exposing the flesh + seed unit. A final distinction is between fruits with watery pulp, rich in soluble sugars and fruits with oily, lipid-rich and often drier pulp (Snow 1971, 1981). In this study, all birds seemed to prefer lipid-rich fruits, but since most such fruits have large seeds and since most capsular fruits have lipid-rich pulp (M. Leighton & D. R. Leighton, unpublished), many smaller-gaped birds ingested predominantly sugar-rich (viz. small) fruit. Large-gaped birds generally ignored sugar-rich fruits.

Important taxa with lipid-rich capsular fruits are Myristicaceae (especially *Myristica* and *Horsfieldia*), Meliaceae (*Chisocheton, Dysoxylum* and many *Aglaia*) Euphorbiaceae (many *Macaranga* and *Baccaurea*) and *Durio* (Bombacaceae). The drupaceous, lipid-rich fruits without husks include many species of Lauraceae, Burseraceae and Annonaceae (*Polyalthia, Cananga*). Sugar-rich bird fruit (often berries with many tiny seeds) are produced by the diverse treelets, trees, lianas and epiphytes of *Ficus*, Melastomaceae and Rubiaceae in this forest.

The major avian consumers of lipid-rich fruits, in order of decreasing body mass, were six hornbills (Bucerotidae), three pigeons (*Ducula aenea, D. badia* and *Ptilinopus jambu*), hill mynah (*Gracula religiosa*), black magpie, five barbets (four *Megalaima* spp. and *Calorhamphus fuliginosus*) and green broadbill (*Calyptomena viridis*). The smaller-bodied birds that more frequently consumed sugar-rich fruits were fairy bluebird (*Irena puella*), eleven bulbuls (Pycnonotidae) and *Dicaeum* and *Prionochilus* flowerpeckers.

Three species of *Treron* (green pigeons) and two small parrots, *Loriculus galgulus* and *Psittinus cyanurus*, were seed predators. It was noted that green pigeons fed principally on seeds and flesh from ripe figs. The parrots were seen to chew small 3–6 mm diameter seeds from diversely-structured fruits (*Dillenia*, several Euphorbiaceae).

The major group of diurnal, pulp-eating mammals comprised four primates: two macaques (*Macaca fascicularis* and *M. nemestrina*), the gibbon (*Hylobates muelleri*) and the orang-utan (*Pongo pygmaeus*). These primates preferred a fruit type characterized by an inedible, but indehiscent rind or husk, yellow to orange or brown, that was peeled or bitten off before the sugar-rich flesh and its enclosed seed(s) were swallowed. Such 'primate-fruits' are produced by genera of Anacardiaceae (*Dracontomelon, Koordersiodendron*), Euphorbiaceae (many indehiscent *Baccaurea*), Guttiferae (*Garcinia*), Sapindaceae (*Dimocarpus, Nephelium*), Tiliaceae (*Microcos*) and many woody climbers, particularly Annonaceae. These four primates were more generalized feeders than birds, exploiting the green flesh of many typical 'bat-fruits' (see van der Pijl 1972) and those sugar-rich bird berries that occurred in large trees and lianas. There were differences between the primates in their use of these fruit types and in the extent of seed predation. Macaques and orang-utans preyed upon seeds of Fagaceae

(*Castanopsis, Lithocarpus*) and *Xylopia* (Annonaceae). Orang-utans preyed upon seeds of *Durio* and many Euphorbiaceae. All primates ate unripe seeds of Leguminosae. The leaf monkey *Presbytis hosei* was not seen to consume fleshy fruit parts, but was an important seed predator. It showed a broader seed diet than the other primates, including seeds of Lauraceae and Sapotaceae, for example.

One squirrel, *Callosciurus prevostii*, mostly consumed fleshy fruit parts of both lipid-rich and primate-fruits, but also ate some seeds. Four other squirrels were almost exclusively seed predators. *Ratufa affinis* and *Callosciurus notatus* ate seeds from a great diversity of taxa, while *Sundasciurus hippurus* and especially *Rheithrosciurus macrotis* apparently specialized on relatively large seeds with hard testas.

Limited observations of civets suggested that they eat ripe fruits similar in morphology to primate-fruit, and that some civets, e.g. *Arctictis binturong*, fed predominantly on figs. Bearded pigs consumed whole fruits, primarily for their seeds. The diverse seeds that pigs ate (Burseraceae, *Dillenia, Irvingia, Lithocarpus*, Sapotaceae, etc.) seem to be similar in their occurrence in large patches on the ground, in keeping with the large body mass and grouping tendencies of pigs. Other mammals not studied but possibly frugivorous include deer and nocturnal bats, flying squirrels, porcupines and rats. The similarity between these feeding observations from Borneo and those reported for primates and squirrels from Malaya (Chivers 1981) suggest that these frugivore–fruit associations may be common within Sundaland.

Seasonal changes in fruit and seed availability

Temporal variability in the availability of ripe fruit patches is displayed for three fruit morphological classes (lipid-rich, sugar-rich bird and sugar-rich primate) in Fig. 1. These classes were chosen because they most simply partition fruits according to vertebrate diets. Each distinct fruit crop produced by an individual plant within a plot has been tallied only for the month in which the crop peaked in ripe fruit production. Two understorey treelets, *Pternandra sp.* (Melastomaceae) and *Urophyllum sp.* (Rubiaceae), however, fruited almost continuously. We have estimated that two-thirds of the individuals of these two species were producing ripe fruit each month; the resulting density of patches due to these common treelets is given by the dashed line in the curve for sugar-rich bird fruits (Fig. 1). Since larger lianas and trees were utilized more frequently by frugivores, fruit patch densities for these plants are plotted separately in Fig. 1 to reflect more closely fruit and seed availability.

Fruiting was heaviest from February to May during the first year, 1978. An annual pattern is discernible for all three fruit classes (Fig. 1), but the second year's peak is less intense. The major cause of this difference was synchronized fruit production in the first year, especially by many canopy species that fruited only this one time. Annual variation was least marked within the sugar-rich bird fruits, which are mostly lianas, epiphytes and understorey treelets. Densities shown in Fig. 1 within any class include fruit patches of all fruit diameters and plant sizes, but even if the classes are subdivided by using these two variables, the general temporal patterns remain the same. Classes of fruit not plotted in Fig. 1, comprising 'bat-fruits' and various non-fleshy nuts and wind-dispersed fruits, showed the same within- and between-year patterns of availability. Since the relatively large seeds preferred by vertebrate seed predators occurred disproportionally on large plants, the availability of seed resources generally followed the uneven pattern shown among the lipid-rich and primate fruits, and not that of the smaller-seeded, sugar-rich bird fruit.

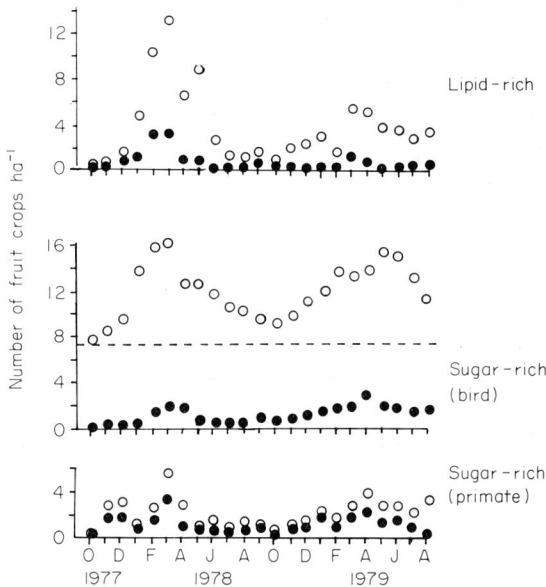

Fig. 1. Monthly changes in the densities of ripe fruit patches over 2 years. Patches are the fruit crops of individual plants and are tallied for their month of maximum ripe fruit production. Totals are summed over vegetation plots: (O) all patches of the specific fruit morphological type; (●) large patches only (large trees ≥ 25 cm dbh for lipid-rich; large trees and lianas for primate; large trees and fig stranglers and climbers for sugar-rich bird).

In sum, resource availability for all birds and mammals, whether they are flesh or seed eaters, was highly variable in time, marked by a single large peak in supply followed by a prolonged period of resource scarcity. Only *Treron* pigeons, which specialized on an aseasonal subset of these resources, did not face this variation.

Emigration in response to low fruit availability

Breeding in frugivorous rodents has been correlated elsewhere with fruit availability (Medway 1972), and seasonal breeding has been documented for Sarawak birds (Fogden 1972). In this study, breeding in frugivorous birds was evident only during the fruiting peak. Six hornbill species nested and successfully fledged offspring from January to May 1978; there were no breeding attempts outside this period (Leighton 1982). Perhaps more profound from a conservation viewpoint, however, are patterns of emigration and diet shift during periods of low fruit availability. Survival during these periods is probably the critical determinant of frugivorous vertebrate densities here, as in Malaya (Medway & Wells 1976).

Monthly changes in rates of sightings of several frugivores (Fig. 2), were positively correlated with changes in fruit availability (compare with Fig. 1). Some or most of the individuals of these populations apparently emigrate in response to local food shortages. Especially common among the emigrants are birds that are specialized

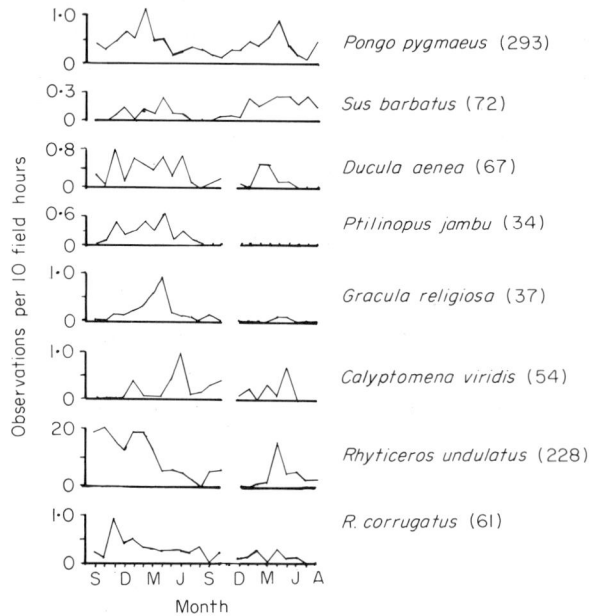

FIG. 2. Monthly changes in abundance of frugivores are correlated with changes in the availability of their preferred fruit and seed types (Fig. 1). Observations are of independent groups seen. Breaks in curves are unsampled months. Total sample sizes in parentheses. Other emigrating species with smaller sample sizes are not plotted.

feeders on lipid-rich fruit. These birds were rarely or never seen hunting animal prey and were uncommon visitors to fig patches. This guild of emigrants included hornbills, (*Rhyticeros*), pigeons (*Ducula, Ptilinopus*), the hill mynah (*Gracula*), and the green broadbill (*Calyptomena*) (Fig. 2). In addition, the few observations of a second *Ducula* species (*D. badia*) and of the two small psitticine seed predators suggested that they also emigrated in response to lowered food availability. These species were never totally absent from the study site; they showed up at the rare fruit trees available at times of low fruit supply, which implies a monitoring of resources that could underlie the coordination of frugivore and resource densities. Coordination can be fine-tuned; for example, fruiting in the second year by the particularly fecund individuals of *Maranthes corymbosa* was perhaps entirely responsible for the reappearance of large numbers of *Rhyticeros* hornbills and *Ducula* pigeons (Fig. 2). The commonness of these birds in the first year was in contrast due to staggered fruiting by a diverse mixture of large trees.

Evidence for the population-wide movements of mammals was obtained only for bearded pigs. Their local abundance was directly related to changes in the supply of large patches of fruits or seeds on the ground. Sightings of the horsetailed squirrel *Sundasciurus hippurus* were also seasonal and correlated with the abundance of its preferred seeds, but this squirrel was observed to scatter-hoard seeds and is likely to be undersampled during fruit lows because it presumably switches its behaviour from arboreal seed predation to recovering seeds it has buried in the ground.

In some frugivores, ranging patterns differ between age classes. Juveniles and subadult rhinoceros hornbill (*Buceros rhinoceros*) travel in loosely coordinated flocks of eight to twenty birds through the contiguously aligned territories of adult pairs. The infrequent appearance of these flocks in our site suggests that they range over huge areas, perhaps adjusted to local resource levels. The scanty data collected for helmeted hornbills (*Rhinoplax vigil*) indicated that they may behave similarly (Leighton 1982).

The correlation between peaks in local densities of orang-utans (Fig. 2) and large patches of primate fruits (Fig. 1 and unpublished) was due to movement through our area by non-residents, particularly subadults. These often travelled in pairs or trios in contrast to the more solitary ranging of resident adult males and females (Rodman 1973). Similar differences in ranging among orang-utan age classes have been noted in Sumatra (Rijksen 1978) and in other parts of Borneo (MacKinnon 1974; Galdikas 1978), and may be patterned, at least in part, on changes in resource availability.

Diet shifts, and plant taxa that act as keystone mutualists

All vertebrates that maintain fixed ranges or territories year-round shift diets to some extent during times of fruit scarcity, consuming more of their less preferred fruit species and food types. Vertebrates with high energetic demands per unit body mass (all birds, from bulbuls to hornbills, and the two squirrels, *Callosciuris notatus* and *C. prevostii*) supplement frugivory with hunting animal prey. Larger animals that are primarily seed predators (the giant squirrel *Ratufa affinis* and the leaf monkey *Presbytis hosei*) eat more foliage. Primates that eat primarily fleshy fruit parts shift to eating more animal prey and/or foliage (*Macaca fascicularis* and *Hylobates muelleri*), or more bark (*Pongo pygmaeus*, see Rodman 1977). Nevertheless, daily energy demands are most efficiently met by fruit consumption.

Although in seasons with low fruit availability there is still a diversity of fruit species available, plant groups of particular importance in ameliorating fruit scarcity can be singled out. One such group, the treelets that produce small, but frequent and relatively aseasonal, crops of sugar-rich fruits utilized by bulbuls and other small omnivorous birds, is indicated in Fig. 1. Within this group is a set of plant species typical of the primary forest understorey (many Melastomaceae and Rubiaceae) and a set typical of the successional habitat on the wet soils that occur along rivers or in unstable sites on steep slopes where water seeps from the bases of cliffs (e.g. *Ficus* sect.

Sycocarpus, Leea). Three other plant groups that act as keystone mutualists by maintaining vertebrates during fruit lows are discussed below.

Birds, primates and woody climbers of the Annonaceae

Ten canopy species of big woody climbers of the Annonaceae have 1–2 seeded, bird-type fruit, and eleven species have multi-seeded, primate-type fruit. The species of each set in aggregate provide a relatively constant variety of fruit species and density of patches (Fig. 3a, b). Densities of fruiting individuals of both classes were higher in the

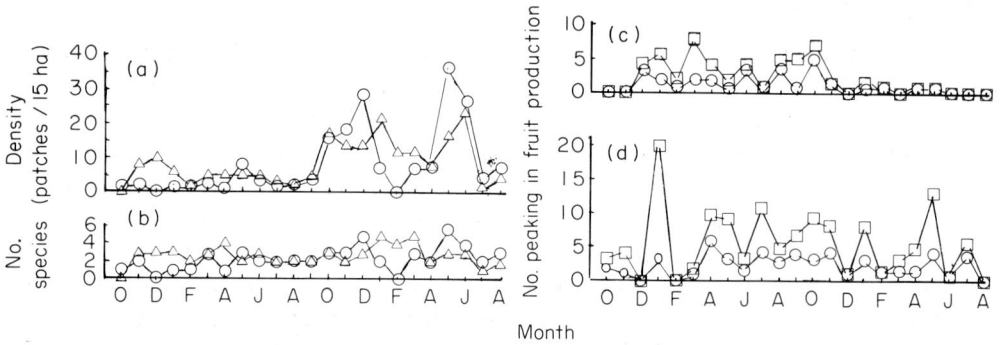

FIG. 3. Two sets of plant taxa that in aggregate produce fruit relatively aseasonally. (a) and (b): (○) ten Annonaceae climbers that produce bird-fruit; (△) eight Annonaceae climbers that produce primate-fruits. These samples are from plot samples only. (c) and (d): fifteen species of Myristicaceae and twenty species of Meliaceae, respectively; (○) numbers of species with ripe patches; (□) total numbers of patches of all species. Samples are combined from plot and trail samples, totalling 1·2 km².

second year than in the first, partly from phenological differences and partly from our chance selection of plots with higher average densities of these lianas in our second year's sampling. Eight of the bird-type species have fruit diameters of 6–10 mm; consequently, they are available to virtually all frugivorous birds, although large-bodied birds infrequently use these generally small-sized patches. In addition, the fleshy parts of these bird-type fruits are somewhat lipid-rich, but unlike most lipid-rich fruits, they are eaten by frugivorous primates (especially by gibbons).

Hornbills, green broadbills and capsular fruits

Four hornbills that maintain year-round territories (*Anorrhinus galeritus, Anthracoceros malayanus, Buceros rhinoceros* and *Berenicornis comatus*) exploit a succession of crops produced by a diverse set of trees with large-seeded fruits that have thick, dehiscent husks (particularly of the Meliaceae and Myristicaceae). These trees ripen small numbers of fruit each day for 3–12 weeks, but even a few of the large, lipid-rich arils can contribute significantly to a hornbill's daily energy needs (Leighton 1982). In Fig. 3c, d are plotted the numbers of species and individual trees of Meliaceae and Myristicaceae that were at their peak fruit production each month. Only the large trees

($\geqslant 25$ cm dbh) of importance to hornbills that were within the trail or plot samples ($1 \cdot 2$ km^2) are tallied. Trees from this set whose fruits are < 21 mm in diameter were also exploited by large flocks of *Calyptomena viridis* and were the major resource patches for these birds. Note the extreme diversity of this set of plants and the rarity of each species (Fig. 3c, d). Myristicaceae are represented by fifteen species (one *Gymnacranthera*, four *Horsfieldia*, five *Knema*, five *Myristica*). Meliaceae are represented by nineteen species (five *Aglaia*, three *Chisocheton* and twelve *Dysoxylum*). The reliance by hornbills on this mixture of rare species is critically important for the conservation of these birds.

Vertebrate frugivores and figs

The reproductive biology of figs (reviewed by Janzen 1979) makes them uniquely suited to play roles as keystone mutualists for many vertebrates. The species of importance to diurnal birds and mammals were the *Ficus* of either liana habit (*F. ruginervia*, subg. *Kalosyce* and seven species of section *Rhizocladus*, subg. *Ficus*) or of tree-like or strangling form (twenty-two species of subg. *Urostigma*). All of these species have brightly coloured, relatively soft fruits that can be eaten piecemeal and thus can be exploited by the full range of frugivorous birds. Individual fig plants ripened crops synchronously, in 1–3 weeks in *Urostigma* and somewhat longer in the climbers, but individuals of a population were seen to produce crops asynchronously and aseasonally. The result is a continual, but stochastically fluctuating local availability of these ephemeral fig patches (Fig. 4a, b).

Three species of green pigeons (*Treron capellei*, *T. curvirostra* and *T. olax*) were observed to specialize on figs, digesting both ripe flesh and seeds. Five species of barbets (four *Megalaima* species and *Calorhamphus fuliginosus*) relied primarily on figs, though they all consumed lipid-rich fruits when these were available. Barbets and green pigeons apparently have huge ranges, as they were sometimes noted travelling for several kilometers when leaving figs. Changes in their population densities could not be shown, however; it was always possible to find barbets and green pigeons at fruiting figs. Large numbers of all age and sex classes of the *Treron* pigeons have been netted at night in Malaya (Medway & Wells 1976). There, these birds make nocturnal dispersal flights, presumably adjusting their local densities relative to densities of fruiting figs.

Many vertebrates other than the fig specialists consume more figs when preferred fruits become scarce. This behaviour is illustrated for three primates, three hornbills and the squirrel *C. prevostii* in Fig. 4 (compare with Fig. 1). It is probably characteristic of other frugivorous birds and of civets. Vertebrates vary in their use of figs, but even those that neglect figs in favour of alternative fruits (e.g. the hornbills *A. galeritus* and *B. comatus* compared with the other hornbill species) turn to figs when other fruits are uncommon (Leighton 1982). There are other fig species not illustrated Fig. 4, e.g. those associated with bat exploitation (van der Pijl 1972; Bonaccorso 1979) and geocarpic species. Geocarpic species produce aseasonal crops of on- or underground figs which are exploited by terrestrial mammals, presumably deer and pigs (M. Leighton, pers. obs.).

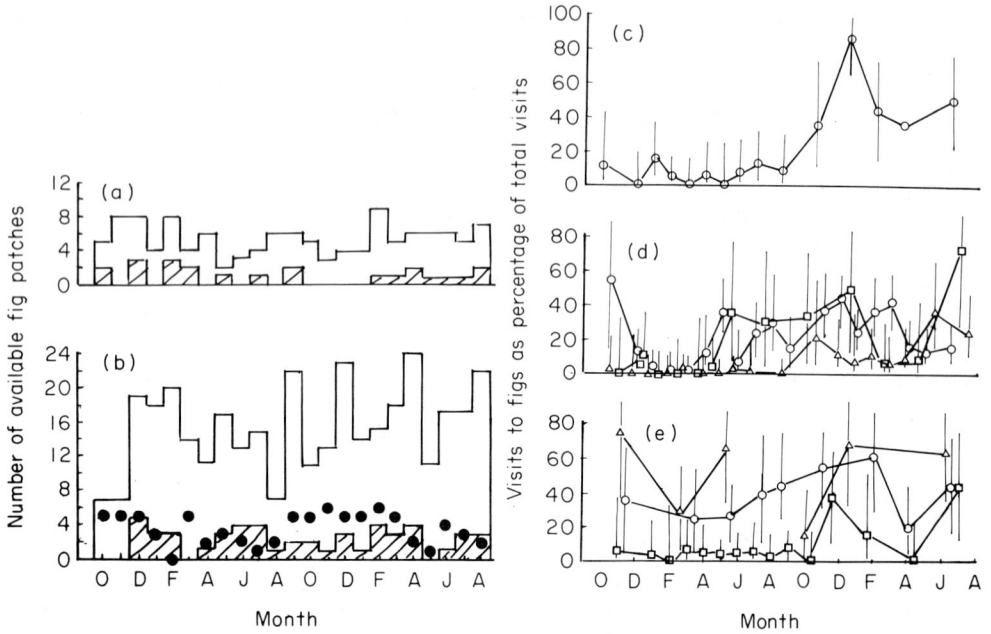

FIG. 4. Aseasonal availability of figs and diet switching by frugivores to higher fig patch visitation when preferred fruits are scarce (Fig. 1). (a) fig climbers of either *Kalosyce* (▨) or *Rhizocladus* (□). (b) *Urostigma* fig plants of species with figs ≤ 11 mm diameter (▨) and of species with larger figs (□). (●) numbers of patches each month in the vegetation plots. Histograms are total frequencies of crops of ripe figs produced in combined trail and plot samples. Changes in relative fig visitation are for (c), the squirrel *Callosciurus prevostii*; for (d) the primates *Macaca fascicularis* (△), *Pongo* pymaeus (□), and *Hylobates meulleri* (○), and for (e) the hornbills *Buceros rhinoceros* (△), *Anthracoceros malayanus* (○), and *Anorrhinus galeritus* (□). Verticle bars are 95% confidence intervals based on the binomial.

DISCUSSION

Forest disturbance and the conservation of keystone mutualists

The large trees of Meliaceae and Myristicaceae whose seeds are dispersed by hornbills, and which in turn provide them with major resource patches during poor fruiting periods are, in our area, primary forest trees that occur at very low densities. The sizes of hornbill groups are influenced by the densities of these fruit patches (Leighton 1982), as probably are hornbill population densities through selection on territory sizes. It follows that destruction of primary forest would lower the densities of these trees in rough proportion to the intensity of disturbance, thereby adversely affecting hornbill densities.

Commercial timber trees as hosts for Ficus

To examine the potential impact of forest alteration on fig densities, we contrasted the distribution of the 362 mature (i.e. fruit-producing) *Ficus* individuals of the thirty climbing and strangling species (those summed in Fig. 4) from the plot and trail samples among host trees of different sizes. The relative availability of host trees of different size classes were compiled from counts of trees $\geqslant 20$ cm dbh within ten of the 0·5 ha phenological plots, randomly selected. These plots averaged $81·7 \pm 9·1$ trees $\geqslant 20$ cm dbh. Counts of stems in dbh class 11–20 cm were made in one quarter of each of the ten plots.

Comparison of the two frequency distributions showed that mature figs occurred disproportionally in large trees. For instance, 64% of the figs had host trees > 60 cm dbh, whereas these comprised only 17% of the trees > 20 cm dbh. Secondly, figs were particularly prevalent in Dipterocarpaceae (30·9% of all 362 mature figs) and in *Eusideroxylon zwageri* (27·7%), the major commercial timber trees. Figs were overrepresented in *Eusideroxylon* in comparison with its availability in different size classes. In five equal-sized classes of trees from 21–120 cm dbh, *Eusideroxylon* contained 23·3%, 40·4%, 43·5%, 32·1% and 28·3% of all figs, respectively, yet this host tree made up only 6·5%, 10·4%, 9·7%, 23·2% and 13·3% ($P < 0·01$ for three classes), respectively, of the available trees. When this associaton between figs and *Eusideroxylon* has been allowed for, the distribution of figs among dipterocarps is not significantly disproportionate to their availability. However, 45% of all figs were in trees of > 80 cm dbh and 64% of such large trees sampled within the plot were dipterocarps.

It is commonly maintained that selective logging does not decrease fig fruit availability because foresters do not cut timber trees if they are entwined by the anastomosing roots of large strangling figs (i.e. the species of subg. *Urostigma*). This may be true, but overemphasis on the giant fig stranglers of the tropics has engendered a misconception about the more usual sizes and aspect of the mature individuals of these so-called strangling figs. Of the 285 mature *Urostigma* individuals (from twenty-six species) in the combined trail and plot sample, a mere twelve of them had killed their host tree. Although comparative quantitative data from other forests are unavailable, this relatively low proportion of 'giant stranglers' within a local fig flora is probably not anomalous. Species such as *F. benjamina*, *F. crassiramea*, *F. kerkhovenii* and *F. sumatrana* typically encircle the host and grow to large sizes (Corner 1965; pers. obs.), but these species are few and relatively rare compared to the more common species that send down a pillar root near the host trunk and do not encircle the host. Such figs offer no impediment to cutting and harvesting the clear bole, nor do the important, but overlooked, climbing figs.

The association between figs and commercial timber trees suggests that low-intensity selective logging, even if only of trees > 50 cm dbh as prescribed in Indonesia, will drastically alter the densities of fig trees, at least in the short term. This was indeed the case in the selectively-logged forest near the study site (see Methods). The density of figs judged to be adults in ten plots, $1·4 \pm 1·4$ per 0·5 ha, was lower than the $3·3 \pm 2·4$ adult figs in the 29 phenological plots in primary forest ($P < 0·005$, Wilcoxon sum of ranks). Juvenile figs (i.e. those that were non-reproductive, but with a root reaching the ground) were also less common in the selectively logged plots ($P < 0·001$). Controlled, long-term studies are badly needed to examine species-specific changes in fig population biology and fruiting phenology in logged forest.

'Nomadic' species and the phenological mosaic

Variation in fruit resource availability at local forest sites permits wide-ranging species to persist in the community along with species with fixed ranges. Although these species are referred to as 'nomadic' or 'migratory', correlations between fruit abundance and local animal abundance such as we have documented in this study could result if such animals are philopatric when resources are abundant, but then wander to or search for more favourable habitats as resources decline, thus becoming distributed among habitats so that they appear to track local resource flushes. At least three distinct ranging systems would be indistinguishable from our simple correlative data. First, our 3 km² site could simply be a portion of a much larger, continuously used home range for a group or flock of animals. If *Ducula* and *Rhyticeros* have monospecific communal roosts as their flocking behaviour suggests (and see Medway & Wells 1976), then roost membership may be relatively constant and the long daily flights by subgroups of the flocks, would traverse a large (i.e. 100 km in diameter?) home range. Secondly, these populations may be truly migratory, in the sense of a cyclical use of alternative habitats; there is no evidence for this, at least up altitudinal gradients (Medway & Wells 1976). That individually-recognized orang-utans desert an established home range, then reappear up to 2 years later (Galdikas 1978), suggests either migratory behaviour or very large home ranges for these individuals. Thirdly, some species, especially the frugivorous birds, may be nomadic in that they do not switch habitats recurrently within a given area, but move away from resource-poor areas without strong tendencies to retrace their pathways. Low rates of recoveries of banded birds, particularly smaller frugivores (e.g. bulbuls), have encouraged Medway & Wells (1976) to infer that these species are nomadic in Malaya.

We might expect that the patterns of synchrony or asynchrony in fruiting between forest localities have selected for particular kinds of ranging behaviour. The nature of this phenological mosaic is not yet known. Consider three possibilities. First, habitats may have complementary fruiting phenologies, being regularly out of phase with one another. It is easiest to imagine this connected to some gradient, say an elevational one, in which climatic cues for flowering are staggered in time, as may be the case for Costa Rica (Stiles 1980); this possibility has not been examined in Southeast Asia. Secondly, some habitats may be relatively aseasonal in fruit production compared to lowland dipterocarp forest, thereby providing a refuge from fruit scarcity in lowland forest. Frugivores may range into the lowlands to take advantage of fruit flushes, then retreat to such refuges during harsh periods. Possible aseasonal habitats within the daily range of frugivorous birds include peat swamp, mangrove, montane and freshwater swamp forest (see Whitmore 1975; Foster 1980). In this study, flocks of *Ducula aenea* were observed to follow the river while travelling through the study site. During resource-poor periods, they stop at riparian fruit trees of *Cananga odorata* (Annonaceae), a tree species that was observed to fruit frequently and over long periods. In Malaya, *Ducula badia* roost in montane forest, but make daily flights to the lowlands to forage (Medway & Wells 1976). Orang-utans may take refuge in areas with high densities of the palm *Borassodendron borneensis*. Exploitation of the leaf base of this palm increased during fruiting lows and stands of this species are very patchy within East Kalimantan (Dransfield 1972).

Finally, 'nomads' may search for and track fruit flushes that occur stochastically within the same or between different forest formations. We can imagine two distinct sources of such stochasticity in fruit production. First, local variation in tree species composition within a formation (Whitmore 1975), may lead to sites being out of phase with one another. Species fruiting during fruit lows in our study site, unimportant because of their rarity, could provide a fruit-rich habitat at these times if they were common. This suggestion is not so far-fetched, since the peak in immigrant *Ducula* pigeons and *Rhyticeros* hornbills during the second year was tied to fruiting by a single species, *Maranthes corymbosa* (Chrysobalanaceae). This plant was unrepresented in the 9 ha of vegetation plots (!), but eleven trees were fruiting at this time in the trail sample of 110 ha. That this fruiting phenomena, of critical importance to four large-bodied species, was completely missed by a sample of over 1700 canopy trees under surveillance in vegetation plots, indicates that large samples are necessary to understand the impact of fruiting phenology on vertebrates.

While it is recognized that conservationists need to understand the ranging patterns of these wide-ranging frugivorous species (Foster 1980; Terborgh & Winter 1980), the pay-offs from studies of tagged birds are likely to be poor (see Medway & Wells 1976). More feasible, and of great interest for understanding the community organization and evolution of tropical forests, would be simultaneous studies monitoring the phenologies of different forest types over a broad region.

ACKNOWLEDGMENTS

We are grateful to the Indonesian Government and to our sponsors, the Indonesian Institute of Sciences, for permission to conduct research in Indonesia. Fieldwork was supported by an NSF grant to Peter S. Rodman. DRL thanks the New York Zoological Society for financial assistance. Preparation of this manuscript was completed while ML held an NSF NATO Postdoctoral Fellowship.

REFERENCES

Bonaccorso, F.J. (1979). Foraging and reproductive ecology in a Panamanian bat community. *Bulletin of the Florida State Museum Biological Sciences*, **24**, 360–408.

Chivers, D.J. (1981). *Malayan Forest Primates*. Plenum Press, New York.

Corner, E.J.H. (1965). Check-list of Ficus in Asia and Australia with keys to identification. *Garden's Bulletin, Singapore*, **21**, 1–186.

Dransfield, J. (1972). The genus *Borassodendron* (Palmae) in Malesia. *Reinwardtia*, **8**, 351–363.

Feinsinger, P. (1979). Asynchronous migration patterns and the coexistence of tropical hummingbirds. *Migrant Birds in the New World Tropics* (Ed. by E. S. Norton & A. Keast), pp. 411–419. Smithsonian Institution Press, Washington, D.C.

Feinsinger, P. & Colwell, R.K. (1978). Community organization among neotropical nectar-feeding birds. *American Zoologist*, **18**, 779–795.

Fogden, M.P. (1972). The seasonality and population dynamics of tropical forest birds in Sarawak. *Ibis*, **114**, 307–343.

Foster, R.B. (1980). Heterogeneity and disturbance in tropical vegetation. *Conservation Biology* (Ed. by M. E. Soulé & B. A. Wilcox), pp. 75–92. Sinauer, Sunderland, Mass.

Foster, R.B. (1983). Famine on Barro Colorado Island. *The Ecology of a Tropical Forest: Seasonal Rhythms and Long-term Changes* (Ed. by E. Leigh, Jr., A. S. Rand & D. Windsor), pp. 201–212. Smithsonian Institution Press, Washington, D.C.

Frankie, G.W., Baker, H.G. & Opler, P.A. (1974). Comparative phenological studies of trees in tropical wet and dry forests in the lowlands of Costa Rica. *Journal of Ecology*, **62**, 881–919.

Galdikas, B.R.F. (1978). *Orangutan adaptation at Tanjung Puting Reserve, Central Borneo.* Ph.D. thesis. University of California, Los Angeles.

Gilbert, L.E. (1980). Food web organization and conservation of neotropical diversity. *Conservation Biology* (Ed. by M. E. Soulé & B. A. Wilcox), pp. 11–34. Sinauer, Sunderland, Mass.

Janzen, D.H. (1979). How to be a fig. *Annual Review of Ecology and Systematics*, **10**, 13–51.

Leighton, M. (1982). *Fruit resources and patterns of feeding, spacing and grouping among sympatric Bornean hornbills (Bucerotidae).* Ph.D. thesis, University of California, Davis.

MacKinnon, J. (1974). The behaviour and ecology of wild orangutans (*Pongo pygmaeus*). *Animal Behaviour*, **22**, 3–74.

Medway, Lord (1972). Phenology of a tropical rainforest in Malaya. *Biological Journal of the Linnaean Society*, **4**, 117–146.

Medway, L. & Wells, D.R. (1976). *The Birds of the Malay Peninsula*, **5**, Broadwater Press, Welwyn Garden City, Herts.

Orians, G.H. (1969). The number of bird species in some tropical forests. *Ecology*, **50**, 783–801.

Pijl, L. van der (1972). *Principles of Dispersal in Higher Plants.* Springer-Verlag, New York.

Putz, F.E. (1979). Aseasonality in Malaysian tree phenology. *The Malaysian Forester*, **42**, 1–24.

Rijksen, H.D. (1978). *A Field Study on Sumatran Orangutans (Pongo pygmaeus Abelii Lesson 1827).* H. Veenman and B. V. Zonen, Wageningen, Netherlands.

Rodman, P.S. (1973). Population composition and adaptive organisation of orang-utans of the Kutai Nature Reserve. *Comparative Ecology and Behaviour of Primates* (Ed. by R. O. Michael & J. H. Crook), pp. 171–209. Academic Press, London.

Rodman, P.S. (1977). Feeding behaviour of orang-utans of the Kutai Nature Reserve. *Feeding and Ranging Behaviour of Lemurs, Monkeys and Apes* (Ed. by T. H. Clutton-Brock). Academic Press, London.

Rodman, P.S. (1978). Diets, densities, and distributions of Bornean primates. *Ecology of Arboreal Folivores* (Ed. by G. G. Montgomery), pp. 465–478. Smithsonian Institution Press, Washington.

Snow, D.W. (1971). Evolutionary aspects of fruit-eating by birds. *Ibis*, **113**, 194–202.

Snow, D.W. (1981). Tropical frugivorous birds and their food plants: a world survey. *Biotropica*, **13**, 1–14.

Stiles, F.G. (1980). The annual cycle in tropical wet forest hummingbird community. *Ibis*, **122**, 322–343.

Terborgh, J. & Winter, B. (1980). Some causes of extinction. *Conservation Biology*, (Ed. by M. E. Soulé & B. A. Wilcox). pp. 119–134. Sinauer, Sunderland, Mass.

Whitmore, T.C. (1975). *Tropical Rain Forests of the Far East.* Clarendon Press, Oxford.

Fruit and seed biology of the neotropical species of *Parkia*

H. C. HOPKINS* AND M. J. G. HOPKINS*

Botany School, and AERG, Department of Zoology,
Oxford University, South Parks Road, Oxford

SUMMARY

1 The pantropical legume genus *Parkia* (Leguminosae: Mimosoideae) has about sixteen species in the Neotropics, most of which are large forest trees. Ten species were studied during a year of field work in Amazonian Brazil.

2 The fruit is a two-valved pod, sometimes dehiscent, with coriaceous, ligneous or fleshy valves, containing up to about thirty seeds and sometimes sticky gum. The farinaceous endocarp found in some palaeotropical species is absent.

3 The relatively large, hard seeds have various insect predators of which bruchid beetles are the most important.

4 Minor differences in the morphology and behaviour of the fruits reflect different dispersal mechanisms. Different pod types are adapted for dispersal by agoutis, water, large (extinct?) herbivores, and arboreal animals. In some other species the mechanism of dispersal is unclear.

5 Fruit and seed biology are influenced by other aspects of reproductive biology, especially adaptations to bat-pollination. Some of the possible quantitative, positional and temporal relationships between flowering and fruiting are considered. In general, seed dispersal in *Parkia* seems to be a less precise process than pollination.

INTRODUCTION

The importance and multiplicity of plant–animal interactions in tropical rain forest ecology has frequently been stressed. In this paper we explore some of the relationships between a genus of trees, their vertebrate dispersal agents and seed predators, and insect seed predators in neotropical forests. Many recent studies of fruit biology in the Neotropics have dealt with complex feeding assemblages associated with single tree species (e.g. Howe & De Steven 1979; Howe & Vande Kerkhove 1979; Bonaccorso, Glanz & Sandford, 1980) or with single classes of dispersal agent (e.g. Gottsberger 1978; Smythe 1978; Fleming & Heithaus 1981) or with seed predators (e.g. Janzen 1980; Johnson 1981). Here we concentrate on one plant genus in order to show how minor differences in fruit morphology and behaviour reflect differences in dispersal mechanisms, and how the agents involved in reproductive biology, i.e. pollinators, dispersers and seed predators, interact in a variety of complex ways. We believe that the value of such studies lies not in investigating specific ecological theories, but in the

* Present address: New York Botanical Garden, Bronx, New York 10458, U.S.A.

insight they give into relationships between different stages of a plant's life cycle, and the patterns of evolution within groups of related species. This knowledge will be of fundamental importance in our understanding of tropical rain forests and their conservation.

MATERIALS AND FIELD SITES

Parkia (Leguminosae: Mimosoideae) is a pantropical genus with centres of distribution in South America, Africa and South East Asia. Most species are large forest trees. The majority of neotropical species are pollinated by bats (Carvalho 1960; Vogel 1968; H. C. Hopkins 1984a), though a few are apparently entomophilous (H. C. Hopkins 1984a).

Observations were made on the fruits and seeds of ten of the sixteen neotropical species of *Parkia* in Brazil in 1979. Our main field site was at the Estação Experimental de Silvicultura Tropical of the Instituto Nacional de Pesquisas da Amazônia (INPA), 60 km north of Manaus, Amazonas, where four species grow in Terra firme forest (*P. nitida* Miq., *P. decussata* Ducke, *P. pendula* (Willd.) Benth. ex Walp. and *P. multijuga* Benth.) and two in forest around white sand campinas (*P. panurensis* Benth.; ex H. C. Hopkins and *P. igneiflora* Ducke). At Belém, Pará, further observations were made on *P. multijuga* in Terra firme forest and várzea (forest seasonally flooded by white water) in biological reserves of EMBRAPA, and *P. ulei* (Harms) Kuhlm., a Terra firme species was observed in cultivation. In addition, we observed *P. discolor* Spruce ex Benth., which grows in forest on white sand seasonally flooded by black water (igapó), on the lower Rio Negro, Amazonas, and *P. cachimboensis* H. C. Hopkins, a dwarf campina species, was studied near the Força Aérea Brasileira airbase on the Serra do Cachimbo, Pará. The only one not studied in a forest habitat was *P. platycephala* Benth., which we observed in cerrado (savanna-like vegetation) in central Piauí.

The tree climbing methods of Perry (1978) were used where appropriate to gain access to tree crowns. Voucher specimens are listed in Hopkins (1981, pp. 360–363) and more detailed notes on habitats and distributions will be given elsewhere (H. C. Hopkins 1984b). Quantitative data on seed crop sizes and the proportions of seeds damaged by insect predators will also be presented elsewhere.

STRUCTURE OF THE INFRUCTESCENCE
AND FRUIT

The unit of pollination is the capitulum, composed of many tiny flowers on a receptacle with a swollen apex. Each hermaphrodite flower is potentially capable of producing a single pod, but for spatial and mechanical reasons only a few develop. After pollination most flowers drop and the receptacle hardens and swells. Up to twenty flowers may produce pods on large receptacles, or only one in species with small receptacles (*P. ulei* and *P. multijuga*). The receptacle is borne on a peduncle which in turn is borne on an axis of a compound inflorescence. In bat-pollinated species the peduncles are usually long and pendent so that the pods hang at the edge or beneath the crown or within it, but in two the capitula and infructescences are erect. The insect-pollinated species have very short peduncles. Usually one to three capitula per compound inflorescence branch produce fruit.

The young pods are usually green and start to develop immediately after pollination, growing about 1 cm per day until they are full sized when the seeds start to enlarge. When almost mature, 8–10 weeks after flowering, the seeds shrink slightly and the testa hardens and darkens.

In all the neotropical species of *Parkia* the fruit is a two-valved pod with a short stipe (Fig. 1). It is typically leathery, sometimes woody or fleshy, and may contain or produce sticky gum. The pod may be indehiscent or dehiscent along one or both sutures, and contain fifteen to thirty-four seeds, in one or two series. There are sometimes septa between the seeds. In contrast to many of the Old World species, there is no dry, yellow, farinaceous endocarp.

Variations in shape, texture and behaviour of the fruits of those species studied in the field allow the recognition of the following six categories.

(i) In *P. panurensis* (Fig. 1a), *P. nitida* and *P. igneiflora* the pods are dark brown, coriaceous and indehiscent. The seeds are in a single series and the mature pod contains gum. Within this group there are minor variations in the toughness of the pod walls and the distance that they hang from the foliage. The pods of *P. gigantocarpa* Ducke are much longer (up to 60 cm) and they hang within the crown. In *P. decussata* (Fig. 1d) they are velutinous and are held above the crown on erect peduncles.

(ii) The pods of *P. discolor* (Fig. 1b) are similar in general structure but the immature pods are red and the inner part of the pod wall is white and pithy. At maturity the pod walls have several fibrous layers and sometimes contain small amounts of gum. The pods are indehiscent and are held around the edge of the crown, but they drop at maturity.

(iii) In *P. cachimboensis* (Fig. 1c) the pods dehisce down one, or sometimes both sutures. The valves are red-brown, velutinous, and there is no gum. On dehiscence the seeds may either remain in the pod, hang around the edge of it suspended by their funicles, or drop to the ground. The pods of *P. ulei* are rather similar, and those of *P. velutina* Benoist have thicker, more woody valves.

(iv) The pods of *P. multijuga* (Fig. 1g) are unique in the genus. The black valves are hard, woody and indehiscent, and there is no gum. Usually only one pod forms per receptacle. At maturity the pods fall to the ground.

(v) In *P. pendula* (Fig. 1f) the pods dehisce down the blunt adaxial suture only. They are subligneous with a blue-black bloom and hang below the flattened or umbrella-shaped crown. There is no gum within the pod, but at dehiscence large quantities are produced along the thickened adaxial sutures and the seeds are released into this. This very sticky gum is water soluble and the pods, often still attached to the peduncle and receptacle, fall to the ground, usually after the seeds are gone. The seeds are arranged in a single to partially double series. The pods of *P. paraensis* Ducke are identical except that the seeds are always in two rows with alternate seeds close to the adaxial and abaxial sutures, respectively.

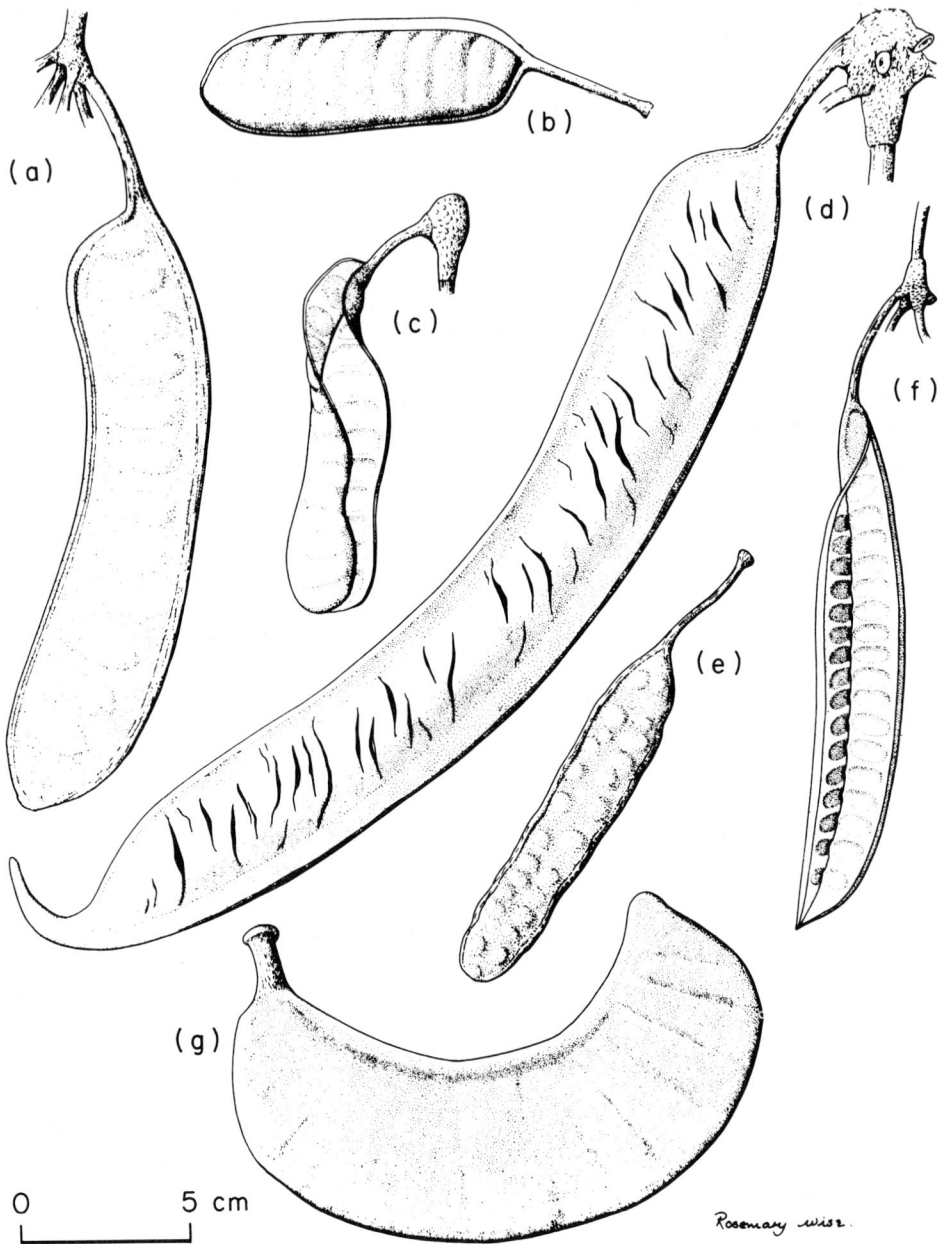

FIG. 1. Morphology of some neotropical *Parkia* pods. (a) *P. panurensis* (b) *P. discolor* (c) *P. cachimboensis* (d) *P. decussata* (e) *P. platycephala* (f) *P. pendula* (g) *P. multijuga*. Drawn from specimens collected by H. C. Hopkins & M. J. G. Hopkins, deposited at the Instituto Nacional de Pesquisas da Amazônia and the Forest Herbarium, Oxford.

(vi) The pods of *P. platycephala* (Fig. 1e) are yellow-brown to purplish-black, indehiscent and often curled. The pod wall is tough and fleshy, often pitted and sticky. The seeds are in two rows, each seed within a smooth-walled cavity. Mature pods fall to the ground.

SEED STRUCTURE AND GERMINATION

The seeds are typically ellipsoid or discoid with a thick, hard testa which closely envelops the fleshy cotyledons. The testa is usually dark brown or black, though medium brown in *P. platycephala* and marbled in *P. pendula*, and there is an almost completely closed pleurogram (a horseshoe-shaped line on both faces of the seed). The majority of species have medium sized seeds, $12–22 \times 5–13 \times 4–9$ mm and weigh 0·25–0·83 g. In *P. pendula* and *P. platycephala* they are smaller, $6·5–11·0 \times 4·0–6·5 \times 2·5–3·5$ mm, and weigh 0·06–0·13 g. The larger cuneate seeds of *P. multijuga*, $35–60 \times 10–17 \times 11·0–16·5$ mm, weigh 3·3–7·5 g. Bravato (1974) describes the morphology of seeds of *P. pendula, P. discolor, P. nitida* and *P. igneiflora* in detail.

In several species there is a thin membraneous layer of 'papery' material around the seeds which is readily detached except at the pleurogram. On contact with water it becomes gelatinous. Its origin is uncertain but it may either be the outer layer of the testa or the inner layer of the endocarp. It is present in all the species previously mentioned except *P. pendula, P. platycephala* and *P. cachimboensis* although seeds of the last do become slippery when wetted, as do those of some palaeotropical species (Corner 1951). Duarte (1978) suggested that the mucilage around *P. multijuga* seeds retains water for the germinating embryo, but this function is largely discounted by Grubert (1974), who states that the most widespread function of mucilage is atelechory, or the limitation of dispersal by anchoring seeds to their substrate. Alternatively, mucilage (and gum or resin) may be important in protecting seeds against predation by insects (Janzen 1975; Prance & Mori 1978).

In some palaeotropical species the seeds are soft and germinate quickly, thereby avoiding desiccation (e.g. *P. bicolor*, Mensbruge 1966). In other Old World species and in all the New World ones studied, the testa is hard and under artificial conditions it must be scarified mechanically or chemically before germination (Coutinho & Struffaldi 1971; Masson, Ricse & Tuchia, 1979). However, Rizzini (1977) found scarification of *P. pendula* seeds was insufficient to cause germination. Duarte (1978) found that brief soaking in water promoted germination of *P. multijuga* and *P. gigantocarpa*, although Coutinho & Stuffaldi (1971) found this ineffective for *P. discolor* ('*P. auriculata*').

OBSERVATIONS ON DISPERSAL AND
SEED PREDATION

We observed or deduced that a wide variety of biotic and physical agents interact with *Parkia* fruits. It is not always possible to differentiate between dispersal and predation, especially as these processes are not mutually exclusive, and an agent could in fact be the principal dispersal agent despite accounting for substantial seed loss. Our observations of dispersal and predation of seeds are described for each agent.

(i) *Parrots.* Damage attributable to parrots was commonly seen on pods of several species where the pod wall had been torn away in short pieces exposing the seeds for removal (Fig. 2a, b). Other methods of attack are seen in herbarium material (Fig. 2c, d). Large proportions of the seed crops of most of our study trees of *P. igneiflora, P. panurensis, P. decussata* and *P. nitida* were removed by parrots and few seeds were taken by other agents; pods which were not attacked hung in the tree for up to several months. Similar damage was occasionally seen on immature *P. multijuga* pods, *P. pendula* before dehiscence (Fig. 2e) and *P. ulei* (British Guiana Forest Department 2493).

We saw parrots feeding on indehiscent *Parkia* pods on only one occasion. A flock of five dusky parrots, *Pionus fuscus* (Müller), were disturbed while feeding in a *Parkia panurensis* tree. They flew to a nearby *P. igneiflora* and continued feeding. Each parrot perched on a receptacle and bent down to attack the pods, ripping off and dropping sections of pod wall, in order to reach the seeds. We could not tell exactly how the seeds were handled, but one bird flew away with a *P. panurensis* seed in its beak. However, parrots are wasteful feeders and under one *P. igneiflora* tree, 137 of the 215 seeds missing from the pods were found on the ground.

Willis (1977) implies that macaws (*Ara ararauna* and *A. macao*) are attracted to fruiting *P. pendula* trees near Manaus, and J. M. Ayres (pers. comm.) has seen large flocks of red macaws at *P. pendula*. We observed a flock of five red fan parrots, *Deropytus acciptrinus* (L.), feeding at the dehisced pods of *P. pendula* and as in the preceding case the parrots clung to the receptacles and reached down to take the seeds and/or gum.

The vernacular names of several *Parkia* species imply a relationship with parrots, for example '*faveira arara tucupi*' (macaw-sauce bean tree).

(ii) *Monkeys.* Some pods from study trees of *P. panurensis, P. nitida* and *P. decussata* showed another type of damage. Holes had been made in the pod wall but not reaching as far as either suture, and exposing one or two seeds (Fig. 2f) or a row of seeds (Fig. 2g). Usually the seeds were removed, but some were left entire (Fig. 2f) or only the testa remained. J. M. Ayres (pers. comm.) confirmed that such damage is typical of monkeys, especially *Chiropotes satanus* (Hoffmannsegg), which was one of several species seen in the area, and which feeds largely on fruits. The remains of seeds showed that they had been bitten into, so they are unlikely to be passed whole in faeces. Spider monkeys, *Ateles paniscus* (L.), were present in our main study area (J. M. Ayres & J. M. Rankin, pers. comms), but we did not see any. Van Roosmalen (1980) records them eating the fruit of *P. nitida* in Surinam. Izawa (1975) records three other species of monkey (*Lagothrix lagothricha, Alouatta seniculus* and *Pithecia monachus*) eating the seeds of *P. nitida* ('*P. oppositifolia*') in Colombia. Their behaviour was at least partially destructive but whether they might have been acting as dispersal agents is unclear.

A. J. Rylands (pers. comm.) has observed a small tamarind monkey feeding on the gum of *Parkia pendula* pods.

(iii) *Rodents.* Though very few pods of *P. multijuga* were produced in 1979, much of

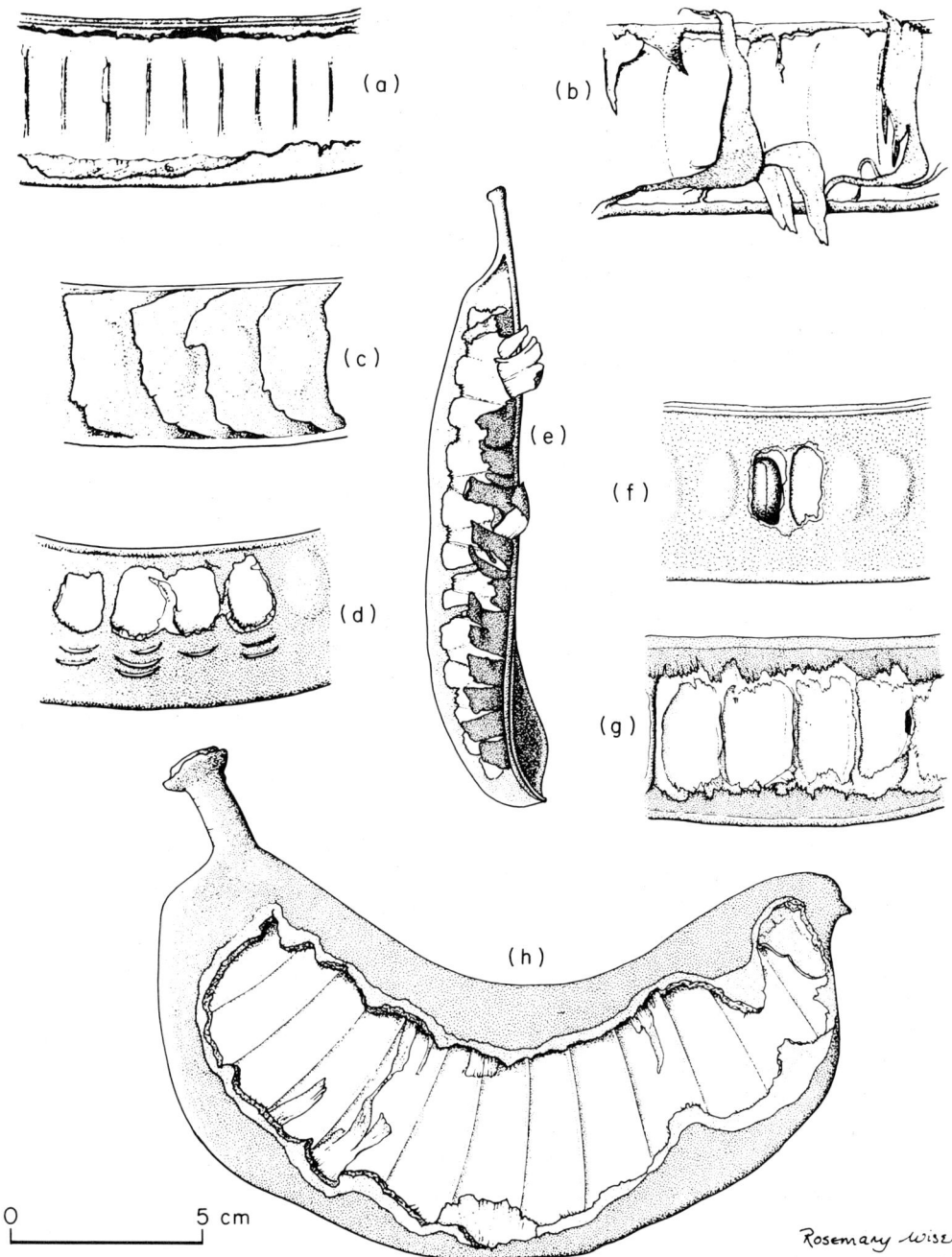

FIG. 2. Damage to *Parkia* pods by seed dispersal agents and predators: (a)–(e) parrot damage (f)–(g) monkey damage (h) agouti damage (a) & (f) *P. panurensis* (b) & (g) *P. decussata* (c) & (d) *P. nitida* (e) *P. pendula* (h) *P. multijuga*.

the heavy crop of the previous year showed damage as seen in Fig. 2h. When the tough pods were given whole to captive agoutis (*Dasyprocta* sp.) they showed identical damage. When we gave seeds to an agouti in a large enclosure at Museu Goeldi, Belém, it nibbled one end off the first seed and then buried it, covering the disturbed ground with a leaf, and subsequent seeds were buried without being tasted. This scatter-hoarding behaviour is identical to that described for agoutis in Panama by Smythe (1978) who estimated primary dispersal distances as up to 150 m. However, we never saw agoutis feeding on *P. multijuga* in the wild and none was caught in seed-baited traps near adult trees. Two seed grids of thirty-six seeds each laid out in different areas in the forest near parent trees produced contrasting results. All the seeds were removed from one within 7 days, presumably by rodents, while none was removed from the other after 30 days, and eight remained after 160 days, though none germinated. Six piles of ten seeds each were also removed very quickly.

In a few cases damage attributable to rodents was found on pods of *Parkia panurensis* and *P. igneiflora* which had dropped in high winds. Traps baited with pods failed to catch anything, however.

(iv) *Large terrestrial animals.* We observed cattle, donkeys and goats eating the fleshy pods below *P. platycephala* trees, and farmers collect the pods to feed to stock. The small seeds can probably pass through a herbivore's gut but we did not examine faeces. One of the vernacular names for this tree is '*fava de boi*' (ox-bean).

The white-lipped peccary, *Tayassu peccari* (Link) has been recorded feeding on *Parkia multijuga* (J. M. Ayres, pers. comm.), trampling the pods, eating the seeds and almost certainly destroying them.

(v) *Water.* Ducke (1948) noted that the corky indehiscent pods of *Parkia discolor* trees growing at the heads of lakes and by slow rivers, are adapted to floating. On the lower Rio Negro the fruits mature as the river rises and floods, drop at maturity and float away. When the river level falls many of the previous season's pods are found on the high water mark of the floods, often disintegrating but with some seeds still inside. Prolonged soaking in water for 17 months improved the germination rate of scarified seeds compared with ones kept dry (from 63% to 82%, sixty seeds per treatment).

(vi) *Insects.* Many groups of insects were found to feed on the pods and seeds. These include seed and pod borers of the beetle families Bruchidae, Cerambycidae, Scolytidae, Anobiidae, and Anthribidae, as well as Hymenoptera and Lepidoptera. Various other beetles of the families Colydiidae, Curculionidae, Cucujidae, and Sylvanidae were also found, but these did no significant damage. By far the most important seed predators for all the *Parkia* species studied were the Bruchidae. Seed loss to bruchids was usually in the range of 5–30% and reached 80%. A total of ten taxa of bruchids were found, and their pattern of occurrence on their hosts was unusual in that up to six were found on the same host, and most had relatively wide host ranges (M. J. G. Hopkins 1983).

Three distinct strategies of attack were observed (M. J. G. Hopkins 1984); eggs were laid on immature pods, mature pods, or on mature seeds exposed by dehiscence or by frugivores. In all cases the bruchid larva develops within a single seed, pupates and emerges, killing or at least severely weakening the seed.

DISCUSSION

Pod characters and dispersal agents

The pod characters and dispersal agents of nine neotropical species of *Parkia* are summarized in Table 1.

For two species the structure and behaviour of the fruit is clearly adapted for dispersal by specific agents; *P. multijuga* by scatter-hoarding rodents and *P. discolor* by water. Dispersal by fish is well documented in Amazonia (Goulding 1981) but we have no evidence that pods of *P. discolor* are taken by fish, and therefore upstream dispersal is probably effected by backflows or surface winds.

Parkia platycephala is evidently adapted for dispersal by large terrestrial animals, but it is not clear which are involved. Tapirs and peccaries are possible as both are known to disperse the seeds of some plants (Janzen 1981a; Everitt & Gonzalez 1981). However, this may be a case where the plant evolved its dispersal syndrome in the

TABLE 1. Summary of pod characters of nine neotropical *Parkia* species and their dispersal agents

| *Parkia* species | Texture | Pod characters | | | Dispersal agents |
		Dehiscence	Gum	Fall at maturity	
P. panurensis (and *P. nitida*, *P. igneiflora* & *P. decussata*)	coriaceous-subligneous	−	+	−	arboreal animals
P. discolor	'corky'	−	+	+	water
P. cachimboensis	subcoriaceous	+	−	−	?
P. multijuga	woody	−	−	+	rodents
P. pendula	subligneous	+	+	−	arboreal animals
P. platycephala	fleshy	−	−	+	large terrestrial animals

presence of the now extinct Pleistocene megafauna, and is an anachronism in the sense of Janzen & Martin (1982). Paul S. Martin (*in litt.*) has suggested that gomphotheres (e.g. *Haplomastodon*) or horses (*Equus*) might have been likely dispersal agents, although the pods have been reported as toxic to modern horses.

Parrots are frequently recorded as destructive seed predators (Higgins 1981; Howe 1980). Clearly, where they attack immature *Parkia* pods they must be purely destructive. However, for four species, *P. panurensis*, *P. igneiflora*, *P. nitida* and *P. decussata*, they are the principal removers of seeds from pods, and are probably the main agents responsible for dispersal, at least in our study area. Although they certainly destroy a proportion of the seeds, this does not preclude them from being instrumental in dispersal. Seeds dropped by parrots are perhaps more likely to germinate because of scarification than if the pod had simply dehisced (Corner 1976, 1:164), or they may be made available to scatter-hoarding rodents. In addition, seeds on the ground will be less readily detected and attacked by bruchids than those in the crown. The presence of a tough indehiscent pod wall, lack of pulp, arils or other fleshy structures to attract other frugivorous birds, as well as the fact that unattacked pods remain hanging in the trees for months, indicate the lack of other arboreal dispersal agents. It is possible that in other areas spider monkeys are the principal dispersers. However, in our study area we observed seedlings of these four species well away from the parent trees, indicating that dispersal and regeneration are occurring.

The function of the gum is unclear, but its presence within the pod probably has some significance in dispersal. It could cause the seeds to be more difficult to handle, or it may be a reward for the dispersal agent, which might drop, regurgitate, or excrete the seed after removing the gum. Intact seeds of other species of plant have been recorded in the stomachs of neotropical parrots (Haverschmidt 1954; Moojen, Carvalho & Lopes 1941; Schubart, Aguirre & Sick 1965), though whether such seeds are actually viable is questioned by Janzen (1981b).

The small-seeded *Parkia pendula* is more problematical. We consider that this species may also be dispersed by arboreal animals (birds or monkeys), though Janzen & Martin (1982) have suggested that it may have been dispersed by some element of the Pleistocene megafauna. This species and *P. paraensis* are particularly worthy of further study.

All the monkey damage we observed was apparently destructive, and this contrasts with the palaeotropical species for which there are many references to primates, amongst other animals, eating the pulpy endocarp (references in Hopkins, 1981, pp. 149–152).

We were unable to identify specific dispersal agents for *P. cachimboensis*. Johnson (1981) lists several other legumes with similar pods which he considers to be dispersed by gravity and water and probably scatter-hoarding rodents. Where we observed this species it grew on ground subject to flash floods, and the seeds may be dispersed by surface run-off as in some desert plants (Friedman & Stein 1980).

Duarte (1978) suggested that the pods of *P. gigantocarpa* are water dispersed, but their structure is very similar to those of *P. nitida*, so they are probably dispersed primarily by arboreal animals. We made no observations of dispersal of *P. ulei*, but M. G. M. van Roosmalen (pers. comm.) considers spider monkeys to be its principal dispersal agents in Surinam.

Relationships between flowering and fruiting

When fruit and seed biology are viewed in the broader context of reproductive biology, many relationships between pollination, dispersal and seed predation become apparent.

There are several quantitative relationships between flowering and fruiting. For instance, the chiropterophilous species produce more pods per infructescence than the entomophilous ones (*P. ulei* and *P. multijuga*), and this also results in differences in the spatial arrangement of the pods. The high proportion of female-sterile capitula in some species is probably related to the production of a larger floral display attractive to pollinators when resources available for fruit production are limited (H. C. Hopkins 1984a) as suggested in other cases by Lloyd (1979) and Arroyo (1981). Although only a few flowers per capitulum produce mature pods, sometimes more pods are initiated and later aborted. This may be an adaptation against seed predation by those bruchids which lay eggs on very young pods. Young aborted pods from *P. panurensis* had many eggs on them, and the tree might be able to selectively abort the most heavily attacked pods. Early pod and seed abortion can also act as a predator satiation strategy (Janzen 1969). Other possible reasons for this phenomenon are discussed by Stephenson (1981).

In all cases, pollination and hence fruit production occur in the canopy, and where dispersal occurs on the ground the pods simply drop at maturity. Other relationships between the positions of flowers and fruits are more complex. Factors influencing capitulum position may be related not only to accessibility to pollinators but also to inaccessibility of fruits to seed predators. Four neotropical species which are all pollinated by the bat *Phyllostomus discolor* (Wagner) have capitula held free of the foliage but at different distances from the crown. The pods are morphologically similar but there is an inverse correlation between the toughness of the pod wall and the distance they are held from the foliage. The tough pods of *P. nitida* and *P. decussata* are held no more than 1 m from the crown, while those of *P. igneiflora*, which are somewhat thinner-walled, are held up to 3 m from the foliage. Those of *P. panurensis* are intermediate in both respects.

The timing of flowering and fruiting will be influenced by competition for pollinators and dispersal agents, amongst other factors. Competition for pollinators is more likely to be crucial because each capitulum opens for only a single night or day whereas the pods may hang in the tree or remain of the ground for weeks after maturity until dispersed. At our study site north of Manaus, five of the species were chiropterophilous (*P. panurensis*, *P. igneiflora*, *P. nitida*, *P. decussata* and *P. pendula*) and apparently largely shared the same pollinator, *Phyllostomus discolor* (H. C. Hopkins 1984a). In this situation sequential flowering to reduce competition for bats and pollen wastage might be predicted, and this is largely the case (H. C. Hopkins 1984a). However, since fruit formation follows immediately after flowering, it is also more or less sequential, and some of the bruchids with wide host ranges are thus able to attack the seed crops sequentially.

CONCLUSIONS

Wheelright & Orians (1982) have pointed out the contrast between pollination and seed dispersal. Whereas pollination tends to be a very precise process, with specific, often coevolved vectors, dispersal is much less exact and there are few instances of obligate relationships. This contrast is certainly true for *Parkia*, in which most species are clearly adapted for either bat- or insect-pollination, but for which identification of seed dispersal agents is much more problematic. Indeed, *P. platycephala* is thriving despite the extinction of the dispersal agents with which it probably evolved its dispersal syndrome.

ACKNOWLEDGMENTS

Our field work in Brazil was done in collaboration with the Instituto Nacional de Pesquisas da Amazônia at Manaus. We are grateful to the former directors, Dr W. E. Kerr and Dr E. Salati, and to the former director of the Museu Paraense 'Emílio Goeldi', Dr L. Scaff, for their cooperation and help. We also thank Dr E. Lleras and Mr F. White for their advice and encouragement, the Força Aérea Brasileira for transport to the Serra do Cachimbo, Dr J. M. Rankin for feeding *P. multijuga* pods to her agoutis and for the loan of animal traps, Mrs R. Wise for the illustrations, all those who have readily told us of their observations on *Parkia*, and Drs C. Lumer, S. A. Mori and G. T. Prance, and an anonymous reviewer for their comments on the manuscript. This work was supported by the Druce Bequest, a Royal Society Leverhulme Studentship and an SERC NATO fellowship to HCH and by a fellowship from the Royal Commission for the Exhibition of 1851 to MJGH.

REFERENCES

Arroyo, M.T.K. (1981). Breeding systems and pollination biology in Leguminosae. *Advances in Legume Systematics* (Ed. by R. M. Polhill & P. H. Raven), pp. 723–769. Royal Botanic Gardens, Kew.

Bonaccorso, F.J., Glanz, W.E. & Sandford, C.M. (1980). Feeding assemblages of mammals at fruiting *Dipteryx panamensis* (Papilionaceae) trees in Panama: seed predation, dispersal, and parasitism. *Revista de biología tropical*, **28**, 61–72.

Bravato, M. (1974). Estudio morphologico de frutos y semillas de las Mimosoideae (Leguminosae) de Venezuela. *Acta botánica Venezuélica*, **9**, 317–361.

Carvalho, C. T. de (1960). Das visitas de morcegos às flôres (Mammalia, Chiroptera). *Analis da Academia Brasileira de Ciências*, **32**, 359–377.

Corner, E.J.H. (1951). The leguminous seed. *Phytomorphology*, **1**, 117–150.

Corner, E.J.H. (1976). *The seeds of Dicotyledons.* Cambridge University Press, Cambridge.

Coutinho, L.M. & Struffaldi, Y. (1971). Observações sobre a germinação das sementes e o crescimento das plântulas de uma leguminosa da mata amazônica de igapó (*Parkia auriculata* Spruce Mss.). *Phyton, Buenos Aires*, **28**, 149–159.

Duarte, A.P. (1978). Contribução ao conhecimento da germinação de algumas essências florestais. *Rodriguésia*, **30**, 439–446.

Ducke, A. (1948). Árvores amazônicas e sua propagação. *Boletim do Museu paraense 'Emilio Goeldi'*, **10**, 81–92.

Everitt, J.H. & Gonzalez, C.L. (1981). Germination of Honey Mesquite (*Prosopis glandulosa*) seeds after passage through the digestive tracts of peccaries. *The Southwestern Naturalist*, **26**, 432.

Fleming, T.H. & Heithaus, E.R. (1981). Frugivorous bats, seed shadows, and the structure of tropical forests. *Biotropica*, **13** (Suppl.), 45–53.

Friedman, J. & Stein, Z. (1980). The influence of seed-dispersal mechanisms on the dispersion of *Anastatica hierochuntica* (Cruciferae) in the Negev Desert, Israel. *Journal of Ecology*, **68**, 43–50.

Gottsberger, G. (1978). Seed dispersal by fish in the inundated regions of Humaitá, Amazonia. *Biotropica*, **10**, 170–183.

Goulding, M. (1981). *The Fishes and the Forest.* University of California Press, Berkley.

Grubert, M. (1974). Studies on the distribution of myxospermy among seeds and fruits of Angiospermae and its ecological significance. *Acta biologica Venezuélica*, **8**, 315–551.

Haverschmidt, F. (1954). Evening flights of the southern everglade kite and the blue and yellow macaw in Surinam. *Wilson Bulletin*, **66**, 264–265.

Higgins, M.L. (1981). Intensity of seed predation on *Brosimum utile* by Mealy Parrots (*Amazona farinosa*). *Biotropica*, **11**, 80.

Hopkins, H.C. (1981). *Taxonomy and reproductive biology of, and evolution in the bat-pollinated genus* Parkia. D. Phil. thesis, University of Oxford.

Hopkins, H.C. (1984a). Floral biology and pollination ecology of the neotropical species of *Parkia. Journal of Ecology,* **72,** (in press).

Hopkins, H.C. (1984b). The New World species of Parkia (Leguminosae: Mimosoideae). *Flora Neotropica* (in press).

Hopkins, M.J.G. (1983). Unusual diversities of seed beetles (Coleoptera: Bruchidae) on *Parkia* (Leguminosae: Mimosoideae) in Brazil. *Biological Journal of the Linnean Society,* **19,** (in press).

Hopkins, M.J.G. (1984). The seed beetles (Bruchidae) of *Parkia* (Leguminosae: Mimosoideae) in Brazil: Strategies of attack. Proceedings of the Leeds Philosophical and Literary Society (Scientific Section) (in press).

Howe, H.F. (1980). Monkey dispersal and waste of a neotropical fruit. *Ecology,* **61,** 944–959.

Howe, H.F. & De Steven, D. (1979). Fruit production, migrant bird visitation, and seed dispersal of *Guarea glabra* in Panama. *Oecologia (Berlin),* **39,** 185–196.

Howe, H.F. & Vande Kerckhove, G.A. (1979). Fecundity and seed dispersal of a tropical tree. *Ecology,* **60,** 180–189.

Izawa, K. (1975). Foods and feeding behavior of monkeys in the upper Amazon Basin. *Primates,* **16,** 295–316.

Janzen, D.H. (1969). Seed-eaters versus seed size, number, toxicity and dispersal. *Evolution,* **23,** 1–27.

Janzen, D.H. (1975). Behavior of *Hymenaea courbaril* when its predispersal seed predator is absent. *Science,* **189,** 145–147.

Janzen, D.H. (1980). Specificity of seed-attacking beetles in a Costa Rican deciduous forest. *Journal of Ecology,* **68,** 929–952.

Janzen, D.H. (1981a). Digestive seed predation by a Costa Rican Baird's Tapir. *Biotropic,* **13** (Suppl.), 59–63.

Janzen, D.H. (1981b). *Ficus ovalis* seed predation by an orange-chinned parakeet (*Brotogeris jugularis*) in Costa Rica. *Auk,* **98,** 841–844.

Janzen, D.H. & Martin, P.S. (1982). Neotropical anachronisms: the fruits the gomphotheres ate. *Science,* **215,** 19–27.

Johnson, C.D. (1981). Interactions between bruchid (Coleoptera) feeding guilds and behavioral patterns of pods of the Leguminosae. *Environmental Entomology,* **10,** 249–253.

Lloyd, D.G. (1979). Parental strategies of angiosperms. *New Zealand Journal of Botany,* **17,** 595–606.

Masson, J.L., Ricse, T. & Tuchia, O.E. (1979). Pruebas de tratamiento pre-germinativo de algunas semillas nativas. *Revista Forestal del Peru,* **9,** 81–90.

Mensbruge, G. de la (1966). La germination et les plantules des essence arborées de la forêt dense de la Côte d'Ivoire. *Centre de Technologie des Forets Tropical, Nogent sur Marne,* **26,** 132–145.

Moojen, J., Carvalho, J.C. de & Lopes, H. de S. (1941). Observações sobre o conteúdo gastrico das aves brasileiras. *Memórias do Instituto Ozwaldo Cruz,* **36,** 405–444.

Perry, D.R. (1978). A method of access into crowns of emergent and canopy trees. *Biotropica,* **10,** 155–157.

Prance, G.T. & Mori, S.A. (1978). Observations on the fruits and seeds of neotropical Lecythidaceae. *Brittonia,* **30,** 21–33.

Rizzini, C.T. (1977). Nota sobre um embrião dormente em leguminosa esclerodermica. *Rodriguésia,* **29** (42), 33–39.

Roosmalen, M.G.M. van (1980). Habitat preferences, diet, feeding strategy and social organization of the black spider monkey (*Ateles paniscus paniscus* Linnaeus 1758) in Surinam. *RIN-rapport 80/13,* Rijksinstituut voor Natuurbeheer, Arnhem, Leersum en Texel.

Schubart, O., Aguirre, A.C. & Sick, H. (1965). Contribução para o conhecimento da alimentação das aves brasileiras. *Archivos de zoologia do Estado de São Paulo,* **12,** 95–249.

Smythe, N. (1978). The natural history of the Central American agouti (*Dasyprocta punctata*). *Smithsonian Contributions to Zoology,* **257.**

Stephenson, A.G. (1981). Flower and fruit abortion: proximate causes and ultimate functions. *Annual Review of Ecology and Systematics,* **12,** 253–279.

Vogel, S. (1968). Chiropterophilie in der neotropischen Flora. 1. *Flora,* Abt. B, **157,** 562–602.

Wheelwright, N.T. & Orians, G.T. (1982). Seed dispersal by animals: contrasts with pollen dispersal, problems of terminology, and constraints on coevolution. *American Naturalist,* **119,** 402–413.

Willis, E.O. (1977). Lista preliminar das aves da parte noroeste e áreas vizinhas da Reserva Ducke, Amazonas, Brasil. *Revista Brasileira de biologia,* **37,** 585–601.

Annual variation in a neotropical seed-dispersal system

HENRY F. HOWE

Program in Evolutionary Ecology and Behavior,
Department of Zoology, University of Iowa,
Iowa City, Iowa 52242, U.S.A.

SUMMARY

1   A 3-year study shows that Panamanian *Virola surinamensis* (Myristicaceae) fruits are dispersed by six highly frugivorous birds and one monkey in a forest inhabited by seventy-eight species of fruit-eating birds and mammals.

2   The integrity of the disperser assemblage is evidenced by constancy in the face of four-fold variation in median crop size from one year to another and dramatic changes in community phenologies brought about by aberrant rains.

3   Neither crop size, kurtosis of individual fruiting schedules, nor nutritional composition of arils influence the proportion of fruits taken from individual trees.

4   The ratio of aril to seed weight consistently influences the proportion of fruits taken from individual trees, the effect being most pronounced during seasons or shorter periods of *Virola* fruit scarcity.

5   Conspecific fruit produced within the immediate vicinity of individual trees significantly depressed individual dispersal during 2 years; heavy use by birds which had apparently been denied other sources of food and destructive and wasteful use by monkeys obscured any effect during a season of aberrant rains.

6   Potential selection on fruit characters is apparently periodic; selection on fecundity *per se* is evidently continual.

INTRODUCTION

Tropical fruits differ enormously in size, abundance, and nutritional properties, implying both distinct phylogenetic trends and a variety of means of attracting and sustaining dispersal agents. On one level, it is important to know what features of a 'dispersal system,' or a fruiting plant and its associated animals, distinguish it from others. Comparative natural histories of different plant species permit association of features of the fruit and crop with attributes of an enormous variety of fruit-eating animals that might serve as dispersal agents (Snow 1971; van der Pijl 1972; McKey 1975). Of interest on a second level are sources of variation in dispersal of seeds of individuals within a population of plants. Direct assessment of properties of the crop, fruit, population, or community that promote or depress fruit removal allows an inference of possible sources of natural selection on plants and their dispersal agents, without the confounding phylogenetic distinctness endemic to comparative studies

211

(Howe & Estabrook 1977). The objective here is to pose and test hypotheses on each level using the model system of a neotropical nutmeg, *Virola surinamensis* (Rol.) Warb. (Myristicaceae) in the seasonal rain forest of Central Panama.

Virola surinamensis offers a good test of morphological dispersal syndromes. The tree produces a distinctive fruit obviously adapted for animal consumption (Fig. 1). Brilliant red coloration, a scentless and easily detached aril, and dehiscence early in the day foretell dispersal by birds (Van der Pijl 1972). The oily texture of the aril and the large (2 cm long) seed suggest high investment in individual fruits, and consequently predict low fecundity (McKey 1975). Together, these attributes lead to the expectation of a limited assemblage of birds that rely upon such fruits for a major portion of their diets (McKey 1975; Howe & Estabrook 1977). Systematic observations over three seasons should indicate whether such general predictions of natural history have foundation.

Factors that influence fruit removal are poorly understood. Dispersal agents are in limited supply if seed removal is less than complete (McKey 1975), and if differential reproduction *vis à vis* dispersal leads to varying lifetime probabilities of seed removal for different plants within a population (Howe & Estabrook 1977). At a first approximation, it is useful to determine sources of variation in dispersal within populations. Characteristics of either a tree or its surroundings may influence the proportion of seeds taken during any given year. A plant might, for instance, regulate production of fruits so as to make best use of a limited assemblage of dispersal agents. Observable consequences should include relatively high fruit removal from trees of intermediate fecundity, and a positive relation between the proportion of fruits taken and the degree of platykurtosis, or flattening, of the individual fruiting curves. Dispersal agents may also choose trees on the basis of fruit quality. Birds might, for instance, prefer trees with particularly nutritious arils, or they might favour plants which offer a large edible reward for the indigestible seed that must be consumed with the pulp. The surroundings may additionally play a role. If feeding assemblages are truly limited from the perspective of the plant, close proximity of fruiting neighbours should depress removal from an individual tree, thereby giving an advantage to isolated plants or those fruiting out of synchrony with others in the population. The relative importance of factors intrinsic to the plant or imposed by the environment may be expected to vary from season to season, depending upon the abundance and distribution of fruits of the same or other species and the shifting preferences of the frugivore guild.

MATERIALS AND METHODS

Study site and tree

Frugivory and fruit removal at *Virola surinamensis* were studied from April to early September of 1979–1981 at the Smithsonian Tropical Research Institute field station on Barro Colorado Island, Panama. The general features of the island are described by Croat (1978). In 1979 the *Virola* study site included 23 ha in and adjacent to Lutz

Watershed; the following 2 years 10 ha were added in the same area, in addition to 7 ha at the head of Shannon Ravine. Trees were in remnants of 'old forest' thought to be over 460 years of age, surrounded by advanced second growth more than 70 years old (Foster & Brokaw 1982). Although insular since the building of the Panama Canal 70 years ago, the Barro Colorado forest appears representative of seasonal moist forests in the area, harbouring approximately 365 species of trees (Croat 1978). Some insectivorous birds have become extinct since the building of the canal (Willis 1974), but seventy-eight fruit-eating birds and mammals still inhabit the forest (see Enders 1935; Willis & Eisenmann 1979). None of the large frugivores likely to disperse wild nutmegs are extinct; indeed they are well-represented on the island (see Willis 1980). Annual rainfall from 1962 to 1982 averaged 2530 ± 615 mm. Precipitation during 1979 (2664 mm) and 1980 (2105 mm) was unexceptional. A record rainfall during 1981 (4633 mm) was 3·4 standard deviations above the 20 year mean. Similarly, fruit production of other species was unexceptional during the first two seasons, but approached failure for many species during 1981 (R. Foster, pers. comm.; see Foster 1982a, b). In short, the study period encompassed both 'normal' and highly unusual seasons in a typical seasonal moist forest.

Virola surinamensis occurs from Costa Rica and Panama to the Guianas and Brazil, with disjunct populations in the Lesser Antilles (Croat 1978). On Barro Colorado Island this species, known as *V. nobilis* in the older literature, is a canopy or emergent tree of mature forest. Fruits consist of a single grey seed 2 cm long and 1·5 cm wide, surrounded by an easily detached laciniate red aril 1 mm thick, all enclosed in a dehiscent fibrous orange capsule (Fig. 1). The entire dry weight is approximately 5 gm, with the aril weighing approximately 1 gm and the capsule and seed averaging 2 gm each (Howe & Vande Kerckhove 1981). The fruit closely resembles the commercial nutmeg of Asia (*Myristica fragrans*), and is in fact known locally as 'wild nutmeg.' *V. surinamensis* is a dioecious species that flowers during the dry season from January to April. Individual plants may be found fruiting during any month of the year (Croat 1978), but the vast majority bear ripe fruit between April and early September, with a wet-season peak in July or August (Fig. 2). Maximum fruit production precedes the wettest months of the year, probably ensuring seedling establishment well before the onset of severe drought. In the greenhouse, seeds with arils attached were killed by mould, while those with arils removed by animals or me germinated in 2–4 weeks (Howe & Vande Kerckhove 1981). Assuming approximately one mature reproductive per ha in suitable old forest on Barro Colorado Island, the entire breeding population of both sexes probably numbers 700–800 individuals.

General procedures

This outline summarizes general procedures and defines the samples used. More detail is given by Howe & Vande Kerckhove (1981). Between late May and early September 1979, I studied fruit and frugivores at twenty-two *Virola* trees, of which seventeen yielded complete data for the season as well as suitable samples of preserved fruits. From April to early September in 1980 and 1981, I studied fruit and visitors at twenty-eight trees in the same site and in Shannon Ravine. Fifteen trees were alive and in fruit all 3 years; this is a 'subsample' of use in comparing means from one year to the next. Twenty-five trees were alive and in fruit during 1980 and 1981, permitting a wider sample for a lesser period of time. These 'complete' samples of twenty-five are particularly useful for analyses of correlation and regression in which sample size is critical.

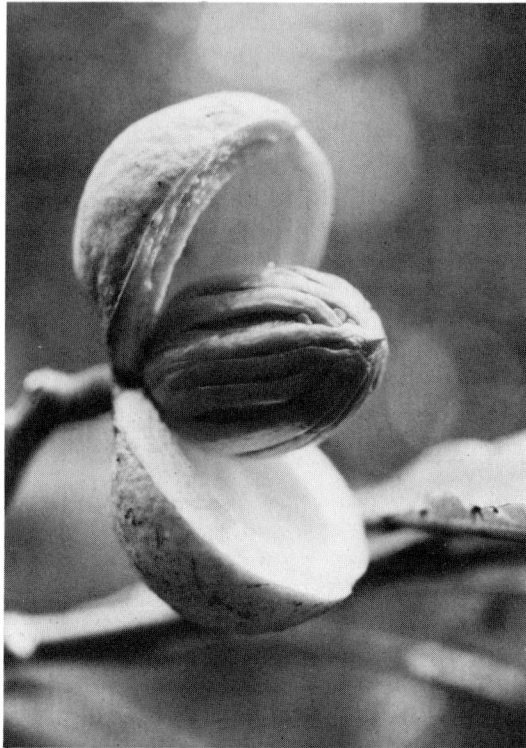

FIG. 1. *Virola surinamensis* fruit, as displayed to fruit-eating animals. The fruit consists of a fibrous capsule that dehisces in early or mid morning to expose a large (2-cm long) grey seed almost completely surrounded by a laciniate, brilliant red aril.

Trees

Fruit traps allow estimation of the quantity of fruit debris falling under tree crowns. Traps covering approximately 10% of the area under the canopies were placed at random. Traps consist of 1 m² plastic frames covered by 1·5 mm plastic mesh. Each horizontal frame is elevated 0·2–1·7 m above the ground, depending on topography. Traps catch all debris, including capsules which permit an estimate of the total crop size and undispersed seeds which permit estimates of the number and proportion of fruits left at the trees. Each set of crop estimates is unique because it is derived by dividing the number of parts (e.g. seeds, capsules) caught by a known area under the crown into the total area sampled. Coatis (*Nasua narica*) that forage for arils (not seeds) under the canopies are discouraged from tampering with traps by regular sprayings of counted fruits with insect repellent. During fruit scarcity, when animals nonetheless raid traps, weekly counts of trap contents are replaced by daily counts and intensified spraying. Such extreme methods are effective because fruit fall is concentrated during morning hours when traps can be efficiently tended.

Fruits for nutritional analyses and dry weight determinations were picked at random from the ground, frozen, and freeze-dried to constant weight (8–10 days) on

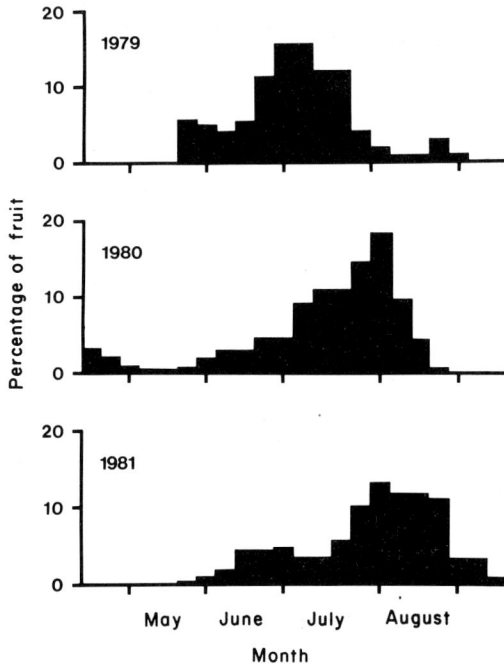

FIG. 2. Weekly fruit production of 15 *Virola surinamensis* trees, expressed as a percentage of the total production during the season.

Barro Colorado Island. Composite samples of 8–15 arils were secured from seventeen trees in 1979. In 1980, samples of twenty arils were obtained from each of twenty-eight trees. Samples of 8–20 arils were taken from twenty-eight trees in 1981, when low production and heavy animal use precluded wider sampling. These samples are unbiased with respect to bird use, as evidenced by equivalence in aril and seed weight of fruits taken from the trees and found underneath (Howe & Vande Kerckhove 1981). Protein, lipid, soluble carbohydrate, and phenolic extractions were accomplished commercially in 1979. Parallel analyses and a fibre analysis were done in my laboratory with 1980 and 1981 samples (Manasse 1982; unpubl.).

In 1979, censuses consisted of four randomly timed rounds of twenty-four trees on 3 days per week, from late May through late August. In 1980 and 1981, five randomly timed rounds of the same trees were accomplished on 2 days per week. For purposes of comparison, the number of 'tree scans' for all years was standardized at 3400 by randomly eliminating some rounds throughout the 1979 season. In all cases a 'round' consisted of a 2-km walk, accomplished during an hour, to the same trees. Each tree is scanned for presence of dispersal agents, permitting a gross evaluation of visitation throughout the day and season at a large sample of trees. Howe (1980) and Howe & Vande Kerckhove (1981) discuss biases elsewhere. Diurnal censuses were supplemented each year with night censuses of twenty trees between 19.30 and 21.30 hours, at the peak of nocturnal frugivore activity. These night-time censuses during June and July, amounting to 308 tree scans with an electric lamp and binoculars each season, document presence or absence of nocturnal animal activity.

Statistics

Computations were accomplished with the SAS package at the University of Iowa. Parametric analyses are used where assumptions are met; non-parametric analyses are used when normality is in question. Parametric means are accompanied by standard deviations, non-parametric medians by 25–75% quartiles. Parametric statistics on proportions extreme enough (i.e. below 0.25 or above 0.75) to be influenced by a binomial distortion are checked with computations of data transformed with the angular transformation (Sokal & Rohlf 1969). In no case is interpretation altered. Proportions or percentages are therefore given to facilitate interpretation.

RESULTS

Natural history

This tree, according to the existing theoretical framework, should be playing to a small gallery of connoisseurs. The fruit should possess a rich aril capable of ensuring the efficient dispersal of small crops of large seeds. Effective dispersal agents of *Virola* are likely to be birds, attracted by red displays and morning dehiscence. The large size of the seed and relative rarity of such rich fruits should result in facultative specialization by members of a limited assemblage of large frugivores primarily dependent on fruit for food.

First, *V. surinamensis* does produce a rich fruit in relatively limited supply. Howe & Vande Kerckhove (1981) show that the arils are 1.59 ± 0.19 g, surrounding a seed averaging 3.18 ± 0.32 g fresh weight ($n = 20$). Composite samples of arils from seventeen trees average $63.1 \pm 14.0\%$ lipid and $2.5 \pm 0.7\%$ protein, leading to an overall mean energetic content of 27.9 ± 0.8 kJ/g. Manasse (1982) replicates these results for two subsequent seasons. Moreover, crop sizes are small by standards of the rain forest. The sub-sample of fifteen trees monitored from 1979 to 1981 indicates a median production per tree well under 10 000 fruits in the year of heaviest production, and medians well under half of that for the other 2 years (Table 1). Wider samples of 17, 25, and 25 trees give virtually identical results, despite inclusion of a greater range of fecundities. The prediction of small crops of rich fruits holds.

TABLE 1. Annual variation in fruit production at *V. surinamensis* trees

Year	N	Range	Median (25–75% quartiles)
		Subsample**	
1979	15	384–10 412	2218 (1699–4066)
1980	15	820–17 922	8579 (3939–12880)
1981	15	927–26 163	3931 (2651–6605)
		Entire sample***	
1979	17	214–10 412	2082 (1326–3584)
1980	25	428–31 006	8579 (4161–12493)
1981	25	638–26 163	3990 (2687–6687)

Kruskal-Wallis statistic: **$P < 0.01$; ***$P < 0.001$.

Secondly, few of the seventy-eight fruit-eating birds and mammals in the Barro Colorado forest actually eat *V. surinamensis* fruits. Extended watches that document both visitation and feeding rates show that toucans (*Ramphastos swainsonii*) are by far the most important single dispersal agents, although five other birds and one monkey remove some fruits in viable condition (Table 2). An important point is that some common visitors are ineffectual dispersal agents. At least as many *Ramphastos sulfuratus* toucans visit this tree as their larger congeners, but are far less important because they eat fewer fruits (also see Howe 1981). *Ateles geoffroyi*, a frugivorous monkey, discards more fruits than it eats, and kills some in the gut (Howe & Vande Kerckhove 1981). One common visitor, a small cotinga (*Tityra semifasciata*), is not a dispersal agent; it strips arils from fruits and drops the seeds under the tree crown (but note Howe 1981). *Cebus capuchinus*, a monkey frequently seen during 1980 and 1981, either nips the base of the aril and drops the rest of the aril and seed, or peels and discards the aril and eats the seed. Its destructive effect is obvious. Significantly, censuses over 3 years show the core of the feeding assemblage to be stable, although relative abundances vary (Table 3). The most notable variations are heavy use of *Virola*

TABLE 2. Contributions of different visitors to the removal and waste (seeds dropped) of *V. surinamensis* fruits (modified from Howe & Vande Kerckhove 1981)*

Binomial	Total handled	
	Wasted (%)	Removed (%)
Penelope purpurascens	0	9
Trogon massena	0	10
Baryphthengus martii	2	14
Pteroglossus torquatus	0	1
Ramphastos swainsonii	2	35
Ramphastos sulfuratus	2	8
Tityra semifasciata	5	0
Ateles geoffroyi	9	3

* Derived from sightings and feeding rates recorded during eight 5-hour watches at each of eight trees.

TABLE 3. Annual differences in census counts at twenty-three *V. surinamensis* trees (standardized to 3400 tree checks each)*

Binomial	Number of sightings		
	1979	1980	1981**
Penelope purpurascens	7	6	14
Trogon massena	7	12	11
Baryphthengus martii	13	4	6
Pteroglossus torquatus	7	8	16
Ramphastos swainsonii	31	38	40
Ramphastos sulfuratus	52	52	39
*Tityra semifasciata****	18	48	20
Ateles geoffroyi	50	57	91
*Cebus capuchinus****	0	8	31
Total	185	233	267

* During 1980 and 1981, four trees were added to the nineteen censused in 1979.
** Annual distributions differ, $\chi^2 = 91\cdot2$, $P \ll 0\cdot001$.
*** Not dispersal agents.

fruits by inefficient foragers such as *Ateles* and *Cebus* in 1981, a year of massive fruit failure in the forest. Night censuses indicate heavy use of *Virola* by nocturnal frugivores only during fruit superabundance in 1980, when many fruits remained on the trees until dark (Table 4). No bats were seen eating these fruits in this or other extensive studies on Barro Colorado (Morrison 1978; Bonaccorso 1979). The number of visitors of all species reflected crop size during each season ($r = 0\cdot81$, $0\cdot59$, and $0\cdot83$; all $P < 0\cdot01$), but the number of species eating *Virola* only increased with crop size in 1980 ($r = 0\cdot52$; $P < 0\cdot05$). Notably, the addition was the seed-eating *Cebus* rather than a dispersal agent. The prediction seems secure that *V. surinamensis* relies upon a limited, albeit taxonomically heterogeneous, feeding assemblage.

Thirdly, a high proportion of fruits is taken each year. The fifteen trees in fruit each year of the study indicate a depression of fruit removal during the season of plenty in 1980 ($\bar{x} = 46\%$), but averages close to 60% during the other years (Table 5). Considerable variation exists, but the evidence at hand shows a rather efficient

TABLE 4. Annual differences at night census counts at twenty-two *V. surinamensis* trees (standardized at 308 tree checks)

Binomial	Number of sightings		
	1979	1980	1981
*Didelphis marsupialis**	0	1	0
Aotus trivirgatus	0	4	0
*Nasua narica**	0	1	0
Potos flavus	0	18	3

* Not dispersal agents.

TABLE 5. Annual variation in the percentage of fruits taken from fifteen *V. surinamensis* trees

Year	Range	Mean ($\pm$ S.D.)*
1979	13–91	60 ± 20
1980	24–73	46 ± 15
1981	40–77	59 ± 10

* $F = 4.08$, $P < 0.025$.

dispersal system as compared with others evaluated in like manner (e.g. Howe & De Steven 1979; Howe 1980).

Differential dispersal

In any size category, trees with large crops virtually always disperse more seeds than those with small ones, indicating an ultimate numerical advantage in high fecundity within a tree population (Howe & Vande Kerckhove 1981). But small trees grow into large ones; the lifetime dispersal of a tree is the sum of the proportion taken each season times the number of fruits produced each season. To determine likely sources of natural selection, one must evaluate sources of variance in dispersal, including those under the control of the parent and those over which the parent can exert no influence. The most likely variables in the first category are crop size and phenology, aril composition, and the amount of edible pulp that accompanies an indigestible seed. Ecological circumstance may also account for considerable variance; the most apparent measure available is the number of competing fruits of the same species in the immediate vicinity of an individual tree.

Firstly, crop size does not influence the proportion of fruits removed from individual *V. surinamensis* trees. If birds had difficulty finding small trees and were satiated at large ones, the highest proportion of fruits taken should be from plants of intermediate fecundity. A second order polynomial regression of the proportion taken against crop size shows that neither first nor second order terms explain any variance in dispersal success (Table 6). At a second level of analysis, trees with relatively platykurtotic (flattened) fruiting phenologies should make best use of a limited disperser assemblage, while those with leptokurtic (peaked) displays are likely to satiate the visitor assemblage. Three seasons of weekly phenology data show first that

TABLE 6. Significance of first and second order terms of a polynomial regression of percentage of the crop removed and crop size at *V. surinamensis*

Year	N	$P(\chi)$	$P(\chi^2)$
1979	17	> 0.58	> 0.67
1980	25	> 0.72	> 0.97
1981	25	> 0.15	> 0.26

the population as a whole has a sharply peaked fruiting season (Fig. 2), and more importantly that kurtosis values for individual trees average well above 2, indicating strong leptokurtosis (Table 7; see Zar 1974). Furthermore, the expected negative correlation between the proportion dispersed and the degree of leptokurtosis does not materialize; correlation coefficients for analyses for twelve trees with good phenology data in 1979 and twenty-four trees with comparable data in 1980 and 1981 are 0·08, 0·13, and −0·21, respectively. None approach significance. There is no evidence that either the amount of fruit on a tree or its schedule of production explain any variance in the proportion of fruits taken by animals. Fruiting phenology may be controlled by quite different factors, such as flowering phenology and weather.

TABLE 7. Kurtosis values for crops of *V.
surinamensis*

Year	N	Range	Mean (±S.D.)
1979	12	1·6–4·0	2·8±1·5
1980	24	1·4–4·3	2·8±0·6
1981	24	1·5–3·6	2·3±0·5

Secondly, the nutrient content of the arils does not influence dispersal. Howe & Vande Kerckhove (1981) show up to four-fold differences in the presence of ash (0·9–1·3%), protein (1·6–3·6%), lipid (46·0–86·2%), and nonstructural carbohydrate (6·6–12·6%) in aril samples from seventeen trees; these results are replicated with larger samples by Manasse (1982). Yet none of the differences in absolute or proportional contents of arils account for significant variance in the fraction of fruits removed (Table 8).

Thirdly, the mean ratio of edible aril to seed ballast explains some variance in relative dispersal success (Table 9, 10). By far the strongest association, accounting for 52% of the variation in the proportion of seeds dispersed, occurred in 1979 during a season of relative scarcity of *Virola* fruits. Some variance can be explained by the same ratio during the subsequent 2 years. Such results are consistent with the observation that seeds regurgitated by birds in the forest are significantly smaller than those available on *Virola* trees (see Howe & Vande Kerckhove 1981; p. 1101). As an independent test of the enhanced effect of the aril/seed ratio during scarcity, I divided

TABLE 8. Correlation of the proportion of fruits removed with components of *V. surinamensis* arils*

Component (g/aril)	1979 (r)	1980 (r)	1981 (r)
Protein	0·30	−0·03	0·23
Lipid	0·26	0·01	0·02
Fibre	—	0·00	0·03
Available carbohydrate	−0·22	−0·17	−0·13
Ash	−0·35	0·02	0·25

* For 1979, $N = 17$ trees; for 1980, $N = 28$; for 1981, $N = 17$–25.

TABLE 9. Results of the regression of proportion of seeds removed against the ratio of aril to seed weight in *V. surinamensis*

Year	r^2	Significance
1979	0·52	0·001
1980	0·14	0·06
1981	0·14	0·06

the 1980 and 1981 seasons into an 'early' half when fruits were relatively scarce, and a 'late' half when fruits were by comparison superabundant (see Fig. 2). During 1980, sixteen trees bore at least 5% of their crops in each half; during 1981, twenty-three trees did the same. Notably, the ratio of aril to seed was positively correlated with the fraction of fruits taken early in the season, but no correlation could be detected at the peak of the season (Table 10). Even when the overall influence of the aril/seed relation is weak, a retrospective analysis shows that times of scarcity within a season promote selectivity among dispersal agents.

Lastly, the proximity of neighbours plays a role during some seasons. These trees are clumped. Many areas of forest have no adult *Virola* trees, but 0–5 neighbours occur within a 50 m radius of any given tree ($\bar{x} = 3$). Here I define the proximate neighbourhood as the number of fruits within a 50 m radius of an individual, corresponding to a guess of what a toucan might easily see from a tree crown. Over the course of a season, the median number of fruits with which a tree must compete for dispersers ranges from 7000 to 18 000 (Table 11). Interestingly, the strongest depression of individual dispersal due to the proximity of neighbouring fruits occurred during the year of scarcity, with some depression during the year of plenty (Table 12). No effect could be detected in 1981, when widespread crop failure in other plants evidently led to wholesale exploitation of *Virola* by efficient and inefficient visitors alike.

TABLE 10. Seasonal shift in the influence of the aril/seed ratio on removal of *V. surinamensis* fruits

Year	N	Early (r)	N	Late (r)
1980	16	0·58*	16	0·38
1981	23	0·58**	23	0·40

* $P < 0.05$; ** $P < 0.01$.

TABLE 11. Estimates of *V. surinamensis* fruits within 50 m of each of fifteen conspecific individuals during the season

Year	Median	25–75% quartiles
1979	7054	2930–9019
1980	17 939	4758–39096
1981	8267	2924–20625

TABLE 12. Results of the regression of the proportion of
fruits taken on the number of *V. surinamensis* fruits within
50 m of seventeen to twenty-five individual trees

Year	N	R	r^2	Significance
1979	17	−0·53	0·28	0·05
1980	25	−0·38	0·14	0·06
1981	25	−0·25	0·06	NS

In sum, the relative contributions of parental and population attributes to
individual dispersal vary annually. The systematic exclusion of variables used here
reflects the manner in which hypotheses were conceived and tested, but overestimates
the total variance explicable in the study. One is tempted to add the variance explained
by fruit attributes directly to that explained by neighbourhood effects. During 1979,
this would suggest an explained variance of 80%; in subsequent years the totals would
be 28% and 14%, respectively. But correlations among variables reduce the totals. A
retrospective multiple regression shows the same general trends, but reduces the
partitioned and total variances explained (Table 13). However, the primary message
remains: attributes of the fruit are far more influential in securing removal during
scarcity than superabundance.

TABLE 13. Variance explained by a stepwise multiple
regression of the proportion of *V. surinamensis* fruits
taken against the aril/seed ratios and number of
conspecific fruits within a 50 m radius

	Variation explained (%)		
Year	Aril wt/seed wt	Competing fruits	Total
1979	52	8	60
1980	8	6	14
1981	8	0	8

DISCUSSION

These results have broad implications, both at the level of comparative natural history
and at the more problematic level of identifying features that frugivores use to select
among trees. This examination supersedes others in the important respect that it
documents a stable disperser assemblage from one year to another, despite broad
swings in weather and associated phenomena. It also suggests that selection on fruit
attributes is most likely during times of stress. At other times, neighbourhood
influences obscure effects of differences among the fruit characteristics of parental
trees, perhaps by default leading to selection for high fecundity, *per se*.

In general, results reported here are an overall confirmation of the expectation that
Virola surinamensis should produce a rich fruit in limited supply, and be dispersed by a
restricted subset of birds that vie for a particularly favoured resource (McKey 1975;
Howe & Estabrook 1977). That the aril is rich is beyond question: few approach its

energetic reward (see Snow 1962; White 1974). The four-fold range of median crop size measured, from 2000 to 8700 per tree, suggests an ample resource. But many wind-dispersed species are one to two orders of magnitude more fecund in this forest (C. Augspurger, Pers. comm.), while animal-dispersed figs produce millions of seeds in a year (Morrison 1978). Even *Tetragastris panamensis*, which possesses a sugary fruit eaten by monkeys and other frugivores, bears as many as 100 000 arillate seeds in a season (Howe 1980). By comparison, *Virola* produces a small crop. That the feeding assemblage is limited is clear from the replicated observation that only seven to eight animals of the eighty or so fruit-eating animals in the forest regularly eat *Virola* fruits. No comparable data from other communities are available to support the assertion that feeding specialization is facultative (cf. Howe & Vande Kerckhove 1979), but the assertion gains strength from the observation that key members of the feeding assemblage do not co-occur with this tree in South America (Ridgely 1976; de Schauensee & Phelps 1978). Overall, the framework conceived by Snow (1971) and McKey (1975) has stood one of its first major tests.

Perhaps the more important general result is that the 'dispersal system,' defined as *Virola surinamensis* and its associated animals, maintains a remarkable integrity in the face of considerable annual variation in both the properties of the tree population and the community at large. Despite a four-fold variation in median crop size from one year to the next, fruit superabundance only adds one seed predator (*Cebus*) and one common nocturnal visitor (*Potos*) to the assemblage. The influence of the first is obvious; that of the second might be guessed by the anecdotal observation of more than 450 insect-riddled *Virola surinamensis* seeds under a hollow occupied by a kinkajou (H.F. Howe, pers. obs.; see Janzen *et al.* 1976). Still remarkable is the fact, more fully discussed elsewhere, that several common and well-studied frugivores co-exist with *Virola surinamensis* and its small-seeded congener *V. sebifera* and simply do not eat the fruits (Morrison 1978; Bonaccorso 1979; Milton 1977, Howe 1981; Howe & Vande Kerckhove 1981). The integrity of the assemblage even weathered a season of fruit scarcity in the forest, brought on by a record annual rainfall more than three standard deviations above the norm. Under such circumstances one might expect a wholesale scramble for whatever fruit is available, as was observed at some tree species in 1969 (Foster 1982a; see Leck 1972; Foster 1977). But the assemblage remained stable in composition, albeit with heavy and destructive use by monkeys (see below). Given that seed size is not the limiting feature of *Virola* visitation (Howe 1981), I can only speculate that chemical deterrents exclude wasteful frugivory by mammals under all but extreme conditions (Howe & Vande Kerckhove 1981).

The attempt to partition variance in dispersal success has produced several important lessons. First, the observation that some variables thought to be important fail to influence the proportion of fruits taken demands a re-organization of existing theoretical frameworks. Secondly, I do identify a variable (i.e. aril/seed ratio) of obvious interest to dispersal agents, as reflected in the differential dispersal of individual trees. Lastly, the most far-reaching result is the documentation of annual variation in the influence of parental attributes as compared with emergent qualities of the population. The potential for selection is periodic, not constant.

Initial attempts to infer dispersal strategies of tropical trees relied upon comparisons of the size and quality of fruit crops of different species (Snow 1971; McKey 1975), leading to analogous predictions for intraspecific competition for dispersal agents (Howe & Estabrook 1977). Failure of aril quality to influence dispersal success may simply reflect coarse techniques which rely upon composite samples rather than statistical treatments of data derived from single arils. But the results are so overwhelmingly negative that it is reasonable to suppose that frugivores simply do not discriminate minor differences in aril composition. Sorensen (1981) reports comparable negative results in use of berries by English birds. Interspecific choice may involve categorical detection of particularly important nutrients, or a gross assessment of the amount of pulp that can be acquired for the amount of indigestible seed consumed (Herrera 1981a). Perhaps the only active discrimination of *Virola* arils is the rejection of more than half of the fresh fruits handled by *Ateles* monkeys, suggesting a possible chemical defence against inefficient use by monkeys which habitually knock down more fruits than they eat (Howe 1980; Howe & Vande Kerckhove 1981).

Failure of crop size and phenology to influence proportional dispersal is more important, because it pinpoints deficient assumptions in earlier models. Howe & Estabrook (1977) assume, as do others (e.g. Heinrich & Raven 1972), that forager activity is under the control of individual plants. But this carries the implicit assumption that the interaction between animal and plant is independent of other plants. Such would be unlikely unless distributions were uniform or random. I suspect that crop size fails to influence relative dispersal in stands of *Virola* because one or more neighbouring trees strongly influences the amount and quality of visitation at any particular individual. Assuming that tropical trees are generally clumped rather than spaced (Ashton 1969; Hubbell 1979, 1980), the general case must be that each individual plant faces a unique constellation of competitive interactions from neighbours of the same and different species (Howe & Smallwood 1982; see Mack & Harper 1977). This uniqueness is in part a consequence of the enormous diversity of potential neighbours in a tropical community, in part a reflection of the wide range of crop sizes borne by trees of different age and exposure to light. Use by birds of *Virola* stands of varying collective fecundity 'spreads the assemblage thin,' and in so doing blunts the force of interaction between a particular tree and the animals that might visit it.

The influence of aril and seed ratio on individual dispersal is not surprising in light of previous insights from comparative studies. Snow (1971) and McKey (1975) comment that birds are likely to weigh the advantage of selecting one species over another on the basis of the reward obtained for the seed bulk and ballast that must be consumed; this is the concept of foraging 'profitability' applied to frugivory (Herrera 1981b). But the fact that birds use the aril/seed ratio to discriminate among trees within a population presents a paradox, because it suggests directional selection for dispersibility associated with small seed size. Trees with large seeds obviously occur. Howe & Vande Kerckhove (1980) suggest that extremes of the 'reward/bulk continuum' reflect two potent sources of selection in a forest in which frugivores may be either common or scarce (see Foster 1982a). Selection might favour small-seeded trees with dispersible fruits when fruit-eating animals are common, and large-seeded plants that produce highly competitive seedlings when fruit-eating animals are absent (Howe & Richter 1982). Most trees have fruits of intermediate character, representing a 'trade-off' between sources of selection detectable only at the extremes of the continuum. This view must be altered slightly in view of the observation that the absence of frugivores is not a pre-requisite for an advantage to large seeds and seedlings; large seeds are dispersed as well as small ones when fruits are common. What we apparently witness is a periodic advantage for a high ratio of aril to seed, and frequent advantage to the numerical superiority of large crop size.

At first sight, it seems anomalous that fruit abundance overrides selectivity. Within the framework of predation theory, one expects selectivity to increase as the overall abundance of resources increases (MacArthur 1972). Predators eat prey of unknown distributions as they become available. The prey are independent of one another, and of course attempt to avoid capture. A forager in a 'patch' simply eats more of the best prey, the more easily they are caught. But this study suggests that the rules change when scattered trees of known location produce particularly palatable fruits; the early birds get the best fruits. During scarcity at *Virola*, birds must often travel considerable distances to find trees at which they can efficiently eat their fill. Birds either visit the preferred plants at or close to dawn, or take the documented risk that competitors will deplete the best fruits (Howe 1981; Howe & Vande Kerckhove 1981). During plenty, there is little work involved in finding *Virola* crops, and birds do not compete for fruits. Extreme scarcity might lead to a breakdown of selectivity or force use of alternative foods, but the general message here is that selection on fruit characters occurs only during times of relative dearth. At other times, the trees with the highest fecundity are favoured regardless of fruit character.

Finally, population and community effects need discussion. Neighbourhood effects are well-documented in populations of small herbs (Mack & Harper 1977; Harper 1977). Positive (Silander 1978; Augspurger 1981) and negative (Carpenter 1976; see Lloyd 1980) density-dependence occurs in the effect of flower number on seed set. Depression of dispersal by competing neighbours both shows that the *Virola* assemblage is limited and that neighbour influence occurs in the dispersal of large trees. The absence of such an effect in 1981 is probably attributable to both increased fruit use by proper dispersal agents and opportunistic adjustments by clumsy foragers during a spectacularly aberrant year. The result is bedlam in the data. Record rains caused massive crop failures in other species (R. Foster, pers. comm.; see Foster 1982a, 1982b), offering a rare insight into community effects. *Virola* crops were intermediate between those of other years, indicating unusual stability in fruit production in the face of climatic variation that affected many other species. Paradoxically, these intermediate crops were dispersed with high efficiency without selectivity among trees. Apparent causes were unusually heavy use by birds denied other sources of food, and heavy and destructive use by *Ateles* and *Cebus* monkeys. Part of the commotion in the data is due to the fact that trees favoured by proper dispersal agents were often heavily visited by monkeys as well; in 1981 a negative correlation existed between the fraction of seeds taken and the number of monkeys recorded in censuses ($r = -0.45$, $P < 0.05$), at those trees actually visited by primates. The scramble for food in general, and the chaotic waste by monkeys in particular, obliterated measurable effects among the trees. What we see is a remarkably stable assemblage exploiting a remarkably predictable food resource, in the face of variation in the fortunes of other animals and plants as extreme as any likely to occur in a diverse tropical rain forest.

ACKNOWLEDGMENTS

This project was made possible with the facilities of the Smithsonian Tropical Research Institute. R. Manasse, E. Schupp, and G. Vande Kerckhove each worked in the field for one season; L. Brophy, A. Herre, W. Richter, and C. Taft assisted for lesser, but critical, periods of time. Analyses on arils collected in 1979 were performed at Colorado State University; R. Manasse replicated the analyses in 1980 and 1981. P. Davidar, K. Grove, J. Hayes, S. Hendrix, S. Koptur, J. Wright, and a reviewer offered helpful comments on the manuscript. Work was supported by the National Institute of Health (BSRG PS07035-13), the National Science Foundation (DEB 7922237), and the University of Iowa.

REFERENCES

Ashton, P.S. (1969). Speciation among tropical forest trees: some deductions in light of recent evidence. *Biological Journal of the Linnean Society*, **1**, 155–196.

Augspurger, C.K. (1981). Reproductive synchrony of a tropical shrub: experimental studies on effects of pollinators and seed predators on *Hybanthus prunifolius* (Violaceae). *Ecology*, **62**, 775–788.

Bonaccorso, F.J. (1979). Foraging and reproductive ecology in a Panamanian bat community. *Bulletin of the Florida State Museum Biological Sciences*, **24**, 360–408.

Carpenter, F.L. (1976). Plant–pollinator interactions in Hawaii: pollination energetics of *Metrosideros collina* (Myrtaceae). *Ecology*, **57**, 1125–1144.

Croat, T.B. (1978). *The Flora of Barro Colorado Island*. Stanford University Press, Palo Alto.

Enders, R.K. (1935). Mammalian life histories from Barro Colorado Island, Panama. *Bulletin of the Museum of Comparative Zoology, Harvard University*, **78**, 385–502.

Foster, M.S. (1977). Ecological and nutritional effects of food scarcity on a tropical frugivorous bird and its fruit source. *Ecology*, **58**, 73–85.

Foster, R.B. (1982a). Famine on Barro Colorado Island. *The Ecology of a Tropical Forest: Seasonal Rhythms and Long-term Changes* (Ed. by E. G. Leigh, Jr., A. S. Rand & D. S. Windsor), pp. 201–212. Smithsonian Press, Washington.

Foster, R.B. (1982b). The seasonal rhythm of fruit fall on Barro Colorado Island. *The Ecology of a Tropical Forest: Seasonal Rhythms and Long-term Changes* (Ed. by E. G. Leigh, Jr., A. S. Rand & D. S. Windsor), pp. 151–172. Smithsonian Press, Washington.

Foster, R.B. & N. Brokaw (1982). General character of the vegetation. *The Ecology of a Tropical Forest: Seasonal Rhythms and Long-term Changes* (Ed. by E. G. Leigh, Jr., A. S. Rand & D. S. Windsor), pp. 67–82. Smithsonian Press, Washington.

Harper, J.L. (1977). *Population Biology of Plants*. Academic Press, New York.

Heinrich, B. & Raven, P. (1972). Energetics of pollination. *Science*, **176**, 597–602.

Herrera, C.M. (1981a). Fruit variation and competition for dispersers in natural populations of *Smilax aspera*. *Oikos*, **36**, 51–58.

Herrera, C.M. (1981b). Are tropical fruits more rewarding to dispersers than temperate ones? *American Naturalist*, **118**, 132–144.

Howe, H.F. (1980). Monkey dispersal and waste of a neotropical fruit. *Ecology*, **61**, 944–959.

Howe, H.F. (1981). Dispersal of a neotropical nutmeg (*Virola sebifera*) by birds. *Auk*, **98**, 88–98.

Howe, H.F. & De Steven, D. (1979). Fruit production, migrant bird visitation, and seed dispersal of *Guarea glabra* in Panama. *Oecologia*, **39**, 185–196.

Howe, H.F. & Estabrook, G.F. (1977). On intraspecific competition for avian dispersers in tropical trees. *American Naturalist*, **111**, 817–832.

Howe, H.F. & Richter, W. (1982). Effects of seed size on seedling size in *Virola surinamensis*: a within and between tree analysis. *Oecologia*, **53**, 347–351.

Howe, H.F. & Smallwood, J. (1982). Ecology of seed dispersal. *Annual Review of Ecology and Systematics*, **13**, 201–218.

Howe, H.F. & Vande Kerckhove, G.A. (1979). Fecundity and seed dispersal of a tropical tree. *Ecology*, **60**, 180–189.

Howe, H.F. & Vande Kerckhove, G.A. (1980). Nutmeg dispersal by tropical birds. *Science*, **210**, 925–927.

Howe, H.F. & Vande Kerckhove, G.A. (1981). Removal of wild nutmeg (*Virola surinamensis*) crops by birds. *Ecology*, **62**, 1093–1106.

Hubbell, S.P. (1979). Tree dispersion, abundance, and diversity in a tropical dry forest. *Science*, **203**, 1299–1309.

Hubbell, S.P. (1980). Seed predation and the coexistence of tree species in tropical forests. *Oikos*, **35**, 214–229.

Janzen, D.H., Miller, G.A., Hackforth-Jones, J., Pond, C.M., Hooper, K. & Janos, D.P. (1976). Two Costa Rican bat-generated seed shadows of *Andira inermis* (Leguminosae). *Ecology*, **57**, 1068–1075.

Leck, C.F. (1972). Seasonal changes in feeding pressures of fruit and nectar eating birds in the Neotropics. *Condor*, **74**, 54–60.

Lloyd, D.G. (1980). Demographic factors and mating patterns in angiosperms. *Demography and Evolution in Plant Populations* (Ed. by O. Solbrig), pp. 67–88. Blackwell, Oxford.

MacArthur, R. (1972). *Geographical Ecology*. Harper & Row, New York.

Mack, R. & Harper, J. (1977). Interference in dune annuals: spatial pattern and neighborhood effects. *Journal of Ecology*, **65**, 345–363.

Manasse, R.S. (1982). *The impact of neighborhood effects on the dispersal success of wild nutmeg.* M. S. Thesis, University of Iowa.

McKey, D. (1975). The ecology of coevolved seed dispersal system. *Coevolution of Animals and Plants* (Ed. by L. E. Gilbert & P. Raven), pp. 159–191, University of Texas Press, Austin.

Milton, K. (1977). *The foraging strategy of the howler monkey in the tropical forest of Barro Colorado Island, Panama.* Ph.D. thesis, New York, University. New York, New York.

Morrison, D.W. (1978). Foraging ecology and energetics of the frugivorous bat *Artibeus jamaicensis*. *Ecology*, **59**, 716–723.

van der Pijl, L. (1972). *Principles of Dispersal in Higher Plants*. 2nd edn. Springer-Verlag, Berlin.

Ridgely, R.S. (1976). *A Guide to the Birds of Panama*. Princeton University Press, Princeton.

de Schauensee, R.M. & Phelps, W.H., Jr. (1978). *A Guide to the Birds of Venezuela*. Princeton University Press, Princeton.

Silander, J.A., Jr. (1978). Density-dependent control of reproductive success in *Cassia biflora*. *Biotropica*, **10**, 292–296.

Snow, D. (1962). The natural history of the Oilbrid, *Steatornis caripensis*, in Trinidad, W. I. II. Population, breeding ecology, and food. *Zoologica*, **47**, 199–221.

Snow, D. (1971). Evolutionary aspects of fruit-eating in birds. *Ibis*, **113**, 194–202.

Sokal, R.R. & Rohlf, F.J. (1969). *Biometry*. Freeman, San Francisco.

Sorensen, A. (1981). Interaction between birds and fruit in a temperate woodland. *Oecologia*, **50**, 242–249.

White, S.C. (1974). *Ecological aspects of growth and nutrition in tropical fruit-eating birds.* PhD. thesis, University of Pennsylvania, Philadelphia.

Willis, E.O. (1974). Populations and local extinctions of birds of Barro Colorado Island, Panama. *Ecological Monographs*, **44**, 153–169.

Willis, E.O. (1980). Ecological roles of migratory and resident birds on Barro Colorado Island, Panama. *Migrant Birds in the Neotropics* (Ed. by A. Keast & E. S. Morton), pp. 205–225. Smithsonian Press, Washington.

Willis, E.O. & Eisenmann, E. (1979). A revised list of birds of Barro Colorado Island, Panama. *Smithsonian Contributions to Zoology*, **291**, 1–31.

Zar, J.H. (1974). *Biostatistical Analysis*. Prentice-Hall, Englewood Cliffs, New Jersey.

Leaf damage in tropical rain forest canopies

G. R. W. WINT

Zoology Department, South Parks Road, Oxford OX1 3PS

SUMMARY

1 Leaf damage levels of three comparable tropical rain forest canopies were examined in relation to three questions: what is the level of herbivore damage in a tropical rain forest canopy, does it vary between sites or between plant categories, and when does the damage occur?

2 Between-site variation in leaf damage levels and damage type was very low despite major contrasts in plant species composition, plant diversity, herbivore species and herbivore type.

3 Levels of damage to leaves from vines were lower than those from trees.

4 Apparent damage levels (excluding those leaves which have abscissed) were higher than previously reported, and actual damage levels (taking abscission levels into account) may be considerably higher.

5 Most apparent and actual leaf damage occurs when the leaves are young.

6 The similarities in leaf damage levels between sites and the differences in leaf damage levels between plant categories are discussed.

INTRODUCTION

Insects are probably the most important arboreal herbivores; the larger herbivores (e.g. apes, iguanas, etc.) seem to consume relatively little of the available foliage (Leigh & Smythe 1978; Nagy & Milton 1979). Published evidence suggests that chewing insects take about 7–10% of the leaf area (J. Procter, pers. comm.; Bray 1964; Nielsen 1978; Leigh & Smythe 1978), though much less—perhaps 1%—in terms of primary production. However, indirect effects of phytophagous insects are widespread both on the scale of the habitat (e.g. Chew 1974; Owen & Wiegert 1976; Golley 1977) and of a single plant, branch or leaf (Haukioja 1980; Varley 1967; McGregor 1968; Rhoades 1979).

Many of these effects are likely to be general ones caused by all herbivores rather than due to the action of particular herbivore species, so it is necessary to have some idea of the overall levels of insect grazing in order to assess the importance of herbivore impact on their food plants. This is particularly true of tropical rain forests (TRF) about which there is little information on herbivore impact. Further, the facts which are available are largely based on litter or understorey samples, and it is in the TRF canopy that the majority of herbivore–plant interactions are thought to occur.

The present paper describes a preliminary attempt to fill some of these gaps by looking at herbivore impact as represented by leaf damage in the canopies of three comparable rain forest sites. Three questions are examined:

(i) What is the level of insect herbivore damage in a tropical rain forest canopy?

(ii) Does herbivore damage vary between sites and/or between broad categories of plant such as trees and epiphytes?

(iii) When does the damage occur?

Study sites

Samples were taken from three sites: one in the San Blas region of coastal Panama (8° 48'N, 77° 40'W); and two neighbouring areas on the Eastern coast of Papua New Guinea, south of Lae (7° 25'S, 147° 16'E). All three sites consisted of seasonal lowland evergreen rain forest, with similar climatic regimes, and were sampled during their respective dry seasons. The three sites were structurally similar—each with fairly distinct understorey (particularly rich in palms in Panama), a more or less continuous leaf layer at 25–30 m and emergent species reaching 40–50 m.

Despite this overall similarity between sites, there were several important differences, beyond the obvious contrast in species composition, between the Panama and Papua New Guinea (PNG) sites (summarized in Table 1). The most outstanding of

TABLE 1. Some differences between study sites

	Panama	PNG North	PNG South
Terrain	Flat	Flat	Sloping
Drainage	Good	Poor	Good
Dominant emergents	Many spp.	*Anisoptera thurifera*	*Anisoptera thurifera* and others
Mean tree density $\bar{x}$	4·24	5·46	6·92
100 m² S.E.	0·11	0·45	0·15
Transect length (m)	90	50	40
Number of samples			
trees	33	34	26
vines	—	23	27
Number of spp. sampled			
trees	23	7	23
vines	—	11	20

these were soil and drainage, plant species diversity and mean tree density. The Panama site had a lower mean tree density/100 m² than PNGS (South) or PNGN (North) ($d = 2·75$, 55 d.f., $p < 0·01$ and $d = 2·39$, 55 d.f., $P < 0·05$, respectively), due largely to a higher number of small trees which were more clumped. This was reflected in the number of canopy samples collected per meter of transect. Furthermore, tree diversity was high in PNGS and Panama sites and the drainage good, while in the PNGN site, tree diversity was considerably lower and the drainage poor.

METHODS

Sample collection

Leaf samples were collected from each site along transect lines at the level of the continuous leaf layer (CLL), some 25–30 m above ground level, using a series of specially built aerial walkways. These are catwalk bridges suspended from emergent trees so as to rest at canopy level (Sugden *et al.*, in press). The resultant transect lengths were *c.* 90 m in Panama, 50 m in PNG North and 40 m in PNG South. Leaves were collected by means of telescopic pruners which gave a reach of 8 m either side of the walkways as well as above and below them.

The samples consisted of at least 100 sun leaves from the outer layers of the tree crowns. Samples of both CLL and emergent trees were taken from the same height range (20–30 m), the actual choice of branches being determined by accessibility. In PNG, samples were taken from vine species as well as tree species.

Immediately after collection, the branches were examined for insect herbivores, scored for frequency of damage types and % leaf damage levels, then oven dried and pressed.

Scoring for damage level

One hundred randomly selected mature leaves from each branch sample were scored for % leaf damage on a scale of 0–5, with an additional class for undamaged ('perfect') leaves in the PNG samples. The score classes corresponded to: $0 = 0–5\%$, $1 = 6–30\%$, $2 = 31–50\%$, $3 = 51–70\%$, $4 = 71–90\%$ and $5 = 91–100\%$ leaf area removed. In addition to this scoring, the types of damage other than leaf area removal were recorded—selectively eaten or skeletonized, mined, rolled, galled, and diseased—as were the scars left by leaves which had abscissed. Young (not fully expanded) and semi-mature leaves (fully expanded but different in colour or texture to mature leaves) were also examined and scored separately.

The mean damage level of each branch sample was calculated by multiplying the number of leaves within each damage score class by the mean of that score class ($P = 0$, $0 = 2\cdot5\%$, $1 = 15\%$, $2 = 40\%$, $3 = 60\%$, $4 = 80\%$ and $5 = 95\%$ leaf area removed). This provided a % leaf damage for each sample based on visual scoring. The accuracy of these estimates was assessed by comparing the visual estimates of twenty branch samples (10 from PNG and ten from Panama) with 'mechanical' estimates obtained using a leaf area meter. A leaf area meter is unable to measure % damage caused by, e.g. miners and skeletonizers which were included, though not separately, in the visual estimates. It also relies on the reconstruction of the original shapes of heavily damaged leaves—those within score classes 4 and 5—which is likely to be very inaccurate. To compensate for these errors, the leaf area meter was used on leaves in score classes P–3, and the damage due to miners etc. and heavily damaged leaves added on. Thus, a full statistical comparison between visual and 'mechanical' estimates is not possible as the two sets of data are not fully independent. However, a plot of the two estimates (Fig. 1) suggests that the visual scores give rise to overestimates of % leaf area removal, and that the data from each country is biased differently. To compensate for this, the % leaf damage figures quoted in the results section have been corrected from the visual estimates using the relationships given (Fig. 1) for the samples from each country.

Throughout, the number of missing leaves—as indicated by leaf scars—has been excluded from the calculations of % leaf damage, as the cause of leaf abscission was not known. Their inclusion as herbivore damaged leaves is therefore uncertain. The % leaf damage levels used are therefore apparent damage levels, rather than actual leaf damage levels, the latter being applicable only if the levels of herbivore induced abscission are known and included in the damage estimates.

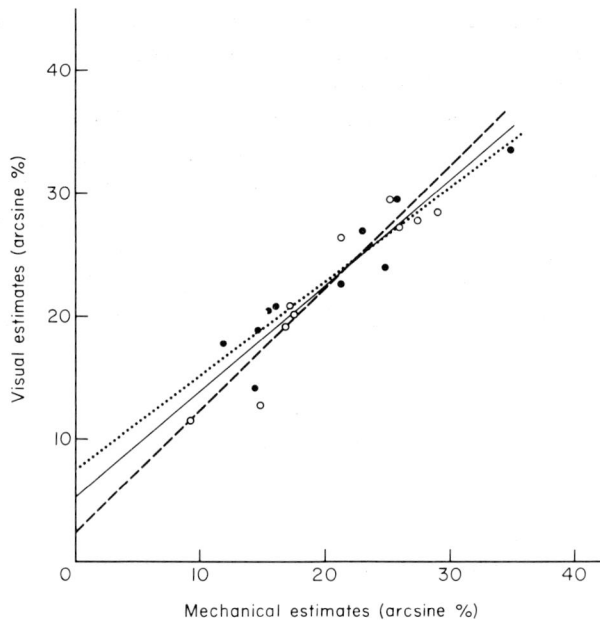

FIG. 1. Calibration curve for leave damage estimates (●) PNG, $N = 10$: (○) Panama, $N = 10$: (– – –) Panama, $y = 2·44 + 0·98x$, $r = 0·89$, $P < 0·01$; (·····) PNG, $y = 7·5 + 0·76x$, $r = 0·87$, $P < 0·01$; (——) Both, $y = 4·10 + 0·98x$, $r = 0·87$, $P < 0·01$.

Damage development

Selected branches of four tree species were tagged and the leaves mapped so that each leaf was individually identifiable. Every week for up to 9 weeks thereafter the leaves were scored for presence/absence, and if present then for damage level and type and leaf length. New leaves were included in the study as they appeared on the tagged branches. These new leaves were used to establish a relationship between leaf age and leaf length for each species, which was then used to age those growing leaves of which the emergence time was not known. Samples of untagged leaves, adjacent to the tagged foliage, and of known age, were examined when possible for leaf toughness using a penetrometer (Wint 1979). Leaf toughness, like leaf length, increases rapidly when the leaves are young and stabilizes at maximum levels when the leaves are mature (Wint 1979). These maxima were used as a further indicator of leaf maturity.

RESULTS

Herbivore types

Panama and PNG rain forests support markedly different types of herbivore. In Panama, casual observation suggested that as much as 80% of the Apparent leaf damage may be due to leaf-cutter ants (*Atta* sp.). Mammalian and reptilian herbivores were also seen, though in small numbers. In PNG there are neither leaf-cutter ants nor large vertebrate herbivores, and the majority of leaf damage was probably caused by Lepidoptera, Coleoptera and Orthoptera.

In all three sites, the largest component (approx. 95%) of the Apparent leaf damage was caused by animals which left gaps or in holes in the leaves ('chewers'). Of the other damage categories (Fig. 2), skeletonizing ('selective eating') was most frequently recorded, the mean site frequencies ranging from *c.* 2–8%, while of the remaining four damage types only miners were recorded on more than an average of 2% of the leaves counted at any site. Statistically significant differences in the proportions of these secondary damage types can be found between habitats (e.g. between miners in

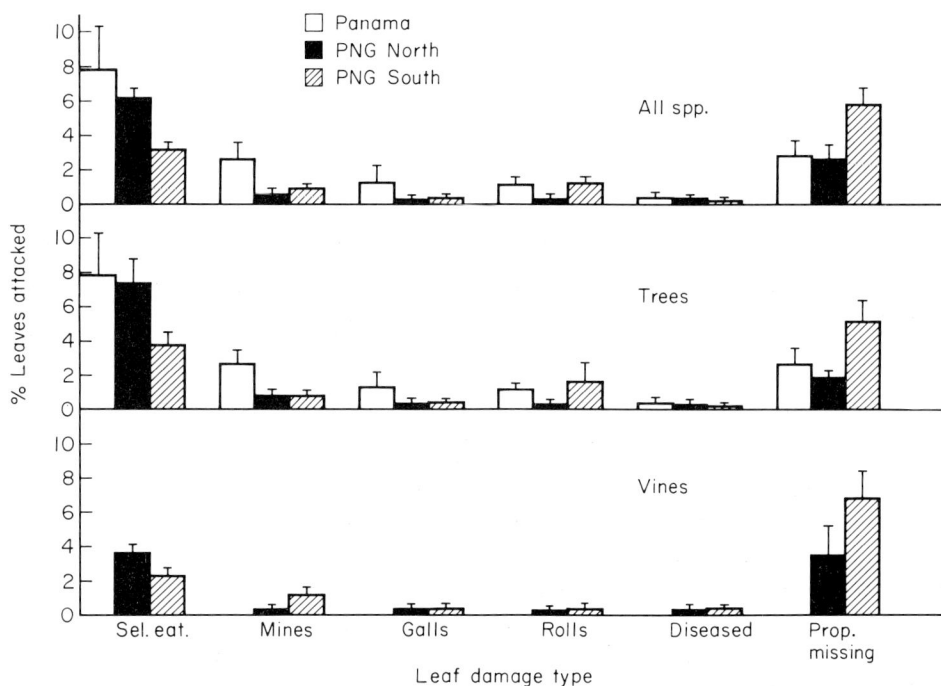

FIG. 2. Frequencies of leaf damage types (excluding 'chewed') in three rain-forest canopies (Sel. eat = skeletonized; prop. missing = proportion missing; others as stated).

Panama and PNG trees) but such a small area of the leaves was damaged that relative
to the 'chewers' they are of little importance.

Branch samples, each containing at least 100 leaves, were collected from 133 canopy
plants: thirty-three from Panama, forty-seven from PNG North and fifty-three from
PNG South. Of these twenty-three samples from PNG North and twenty-seven from
PNG South were vine species, and the rest were trees. No vines were collected from
Panama. The mean Apparent damage levels for the individual branch samples ranged
from 2·02% to 76·8% in Panama, 1·4 to 31·5% in PNG North and 0 to 35·4% in PNG
South.

The majority of samples were taken from separate species though several species
replicates were obtained, particularly from the PNG North site. The Apparent damage
levels of these species replicates (Fig. 3) suggest that each species suffers a characteristic
level of Apparent leaf damage with relatively little variation within species, so that it is
possible to demonstrate significant separation between species damage levels that
differ by as little as 8%. This also lends support to the validity of point sampling for
apparent herbivore impact.

A third measure of leaf damage levels is the mean Apparent damage level for each
site. When all species examined within each site are considered together, the habitat
means range from *c.* 9% to *c.* 12·5% (Fig. 4), and do not differ significantly from each

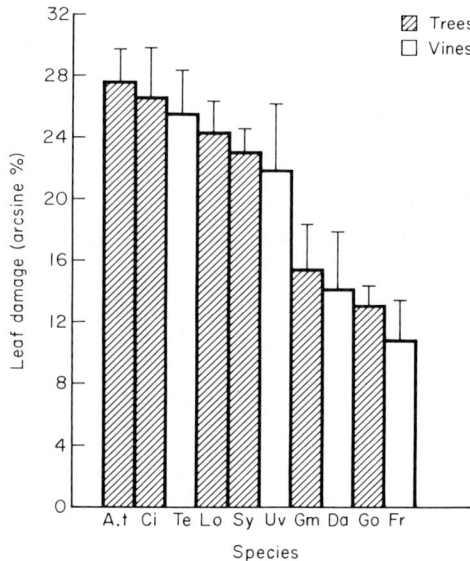

FIG. 3. Mean (and standard error) apparent leaf damage levels of some canopy species. (A.t. = *Anisoptera
thurifera*, *n* = 5; Ci = *Cinnamomum* sp., *n* = 4; Te = *Tetracera* sp., *n* = 4; Lo = *Lophopetalum* sp., *n* = 6;
Sy = *Syzygium* sp1, *n* = 4; Uv = *Unidentified* vine, *n* = 5; Gm = *Gmelina* sp., *n* = 4; Da = *Dahlbergia* sp., *n* = 4;
Go = ? *Gonostylus* sp., *n* = 3; Fr = *Freycinetia* sp., *n* = 3.)

other, $(d < 1.89, P > 0.1)$, though this may be due to high within-sample variation. However, these figures are surprisingly similar in view of the major differences in site characteristics and herbivore type described earlier. The figures are somewhat higher than have been found by other workers (e.g. Leigh & Smythe 1978; Bray 1964), and illustrate the value of collecting leaf samples directly from the canopy rather than using litter samples which may overlook the more heavily damaged or more rapidly decomposed leaves.

If the tree and vine samples are considered separately, the similarity between sites becomes more striking. The site means for the tree samples from Panama, PNG North and PNG South are 12·7%, 12·5% and 13·7%, respectively. The equivalent figures for the vines from PNG North and PNG South (no vines were sampled in Panama) are

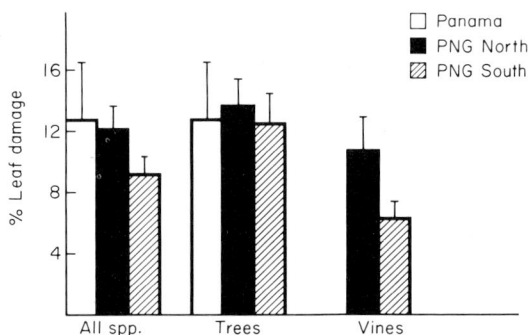

FIG. 4. Apparent mean (+95% c. level) leaf damage levels (% leaf area) in three rain forest canopies.

10·7% and 6·2%, respectively (Fig. 4). The tree figures are all statistically indistinguishable $(d < 0.49$, NS) but are all significantly greater than those from the vine samples of PNG South $(d > 2.99, P < 0.01)$, but not from the PNG North vine samples $(d < 1.17,$ NS).

It is likely that these figures are underestimates of the % leaf area removed by herbivores. The habitat means for the % of missing leaves range from approximately 3% to 6%, of which a proportion are likely to be due to herbivore activity. Further, the damage caused by sucking insects may reduce photosynthetic area. The figures are, however, likely to be accurate estimates of the % area removed in those leaves examined as it is thought that holes expand at the same rate as the lamina during leaf growth (Coley 1979; Reichle et al. 1973). Therefore, the % leaf area removed remains constant irrespective of when the damage occurred. The timing of the damage must have a major effect on the biomass of leaf material removed and thus the point sampling used in this study reveals little about herbivore load.

Damage development

The timing of herbivore damage was examined in two ways: by point sampling of the young foliage collected with the branch samples, and by continuously monitoring the damage levels of the growing leaves of selected species.

The young leaves collected on the branch samples of mature leaves were generally less damaged than was the mature foliage. The habitat mean Apparent damage levels for the immature foliage were 5·8%, 4·3% and 3·6% for the Panama, PNG North and PNG South sites, respectively. These are from approximately 30–50% of the levels found in old leaves. As leaves mature in a relatively short period relative to leaf life, this suggests that the rate of herbivory on young leaves much exceeds that on old leaves.

Damage levels were monitored in the growing leaves of four species, two from Panama (*Eschweilera* sp. and *Swartzia panamensis* Benth) and two from PNG (*Anisoptera thurifera* BL. subsp. *polyandra* (Bl.) Ashton and *Syzygium* sp.).

In three of the species (*Eschweilera*, *Swartzia* and *Anisoptera*) the Apparent damage levels (i.e. with the missing or abscissed leaves ignored) stabilize when the leaves become mature. Leaf maturity was indicated by maximum leaf length or maximum leaf toughness (Fig. 5). This is unlikely to be a hole expansion phenomenon for the

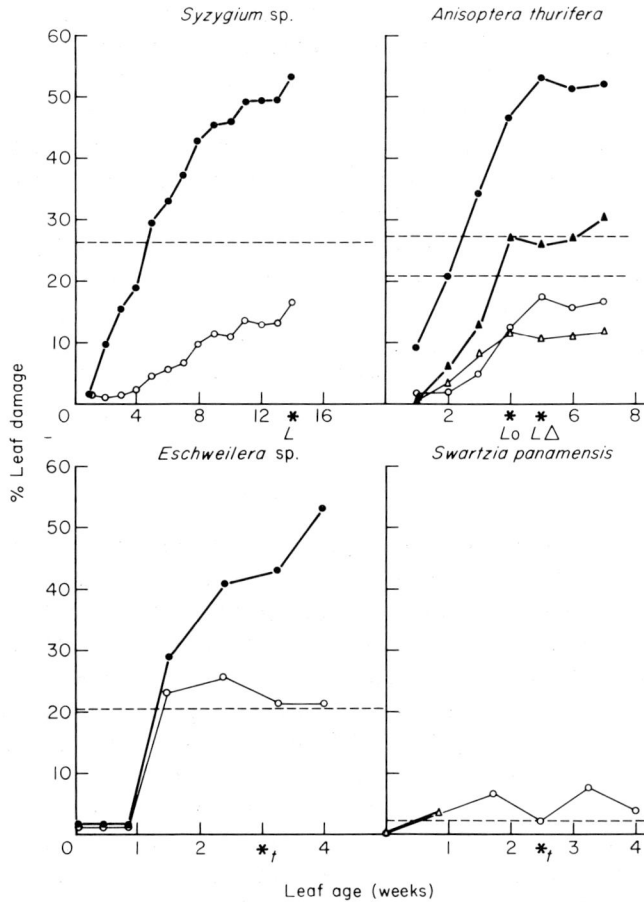

FIG. 5. Development of leaf damage levels with leaf age: closed symbols (●, ▲) % damage including missing leaves; open symbols (○, △) % damage excluding missing leaves (each symbol refers to a specific individual); * maximum length (*L*) or toughness (*t*); (– – –) apparent damage level of mature leaves.

reasons mentioned earlier, which suggests that the majority of herbivore damage occurs in these species when the leaves are young. In the fourth species—*Syzygium*, which in contrast to the other three, is a continuously flushing species—Apparent leaf damage appears to increase linearly with time. However, extrapolation of the data shown suggests that even in this species, the Apparent damage levels of the younger leaves would reach that of the surrounding mature foliage (which shows a fairly constant damage level) within about 20 weeks of leaf flush. Published information concerning leaf longevity is very sparse, though it is likely that, as an evergreen species, *Syzygium* retains its leaves for a year or more (M. Swaine, pers. comm.). Here again the majority of herbivore damage occurs in the young leaves.

During this monitoring programme limited observations revealed that those leaves which abscissed during the study period were those which were heavily damaged. This suggests that much of the abscission was herbivore-induced. If these missing leaves are incorporated into the damage level figures (Fig. 5) to give 'Actual' damage levels, the results from three species (all except *Eschweilera*) suggest substantially similar conclusions to those reached above, in that the rate of herbivore damage is lower in mature than young leaves. However, though in *Swartzia*, Actual and Apparent % leaf damage was identical (as there were no missing leaves recorded from this species), in *Syzygium* and *Anisoptera* Actual damage levels are approximately three times the Apparent damage levels. Thus, Apparent leaf damage estimates may be considerable underestimates of the actual damage levels.

The data from *Eschweilera* also indicates that Actual leaf damage may markedly exceed Apparent damage but, in contrast, suggests that Actual damage levels may continue to increase after Apparent levels have stabilized. This in turn suggests that abscission (which may be herbivore-induced) continues after the leaves have become mature, and that the stable Apparent leaf damage levels may reflect a damage level at which the leaf abscission occurs.

CONCLUSIONS

The results of this preliminary study suggest that, in comparable tropical rain forest canopies during the dry season, the Apparent herbivore pressure on vines is less than that on trees; there is little variation in the Apparent damage levels or damage type between trees in widely separated sites despite major contrasts in plant species composition, plant diversity, herbivore species and in herbivore type; the Apparent damage levels are somewhat higher than previously reported, and the Actual damage levels may be considerably higher; and finally that the majority of Apparent and Actual leaf damage occurs when the leaves are young.

The reasons for the striking quantitative similarities between habitats remain unclear, especially as Apparent herbivore damage levels were measured in a way that says little about herbivore load in absolute terms, and ignores the effects of sucking insects completely. The similarities may be coincidental given the low number of sites examined, but this would not be consistent with relatively constant and species-specific Apparent damage levels between sites, nor with the significant differences that were found between trees and vines. Both these factors suggest deterministic rather than stochastic processes are operating to produce the observed levels of leaf damage.

Should the quantitative similarity between sites be real rather than coincidental, then it may be due to similarities in either herbivore load or in the plants' response to herbivore damage. Information of the type presented here can contribute little definite to estimates of herbivore load unless the proportion of missing leaves is constant across species so that Apparent leaf damage bears a fixed relationship to Actual leaf damage. Also, it would be necessary to know when the damage occurred. However, if the thresholds for herbivore-induced abscission of the type found in *Eschweilera* are widespread, then such a process might contribute to quantitative similarities in Apparent leaf damage between sites, especially if it operates via physiologically determined thresholds.

However, as the mean proportion of missing leaves in each site is similar, it seems that the Actual damage levels within the different areas are closely comparable. This argues that herbivores utilize a constant proportion of the foliage in a tropical rain forest.

The differences in Apparent damage levels between tree and vine species in PNGS may also reflect differences in herbivore load or plant response to damage. Perhaps the herbivore load on vines is lower in association with their reduced apparency (*sensu* Feeny 1976); or perhaps photosynthetic area is at less of a premium in vines than trees so that the vines' response to herbivore damage occurs at a lower Apparent damage level than that of the canopy trees.

Such speculations are well beyond the scope of this paper, and answers can only be provided by more and repeated sampling of different sites to provide accurate estimates of herbivore load, damage they cause and the plants' response.

ACKNOWLEDGMENTS

My thanks are due to Professor G. C. Varley, The Poulton Fund, Unilever, the British Army, The Royal Air Force and many members of Operation Drake for financial material and logistic support. In particular, I am grateful to Col. J. Blashford-Snell, Sgt M. Christie, Sgt L. Gallagher, Cpl D. Watret, Andrew Mitchell, Stephen Sutton and Andrew Sugden for their help and advice. Drs Henty of Lae Herbarium, PNG, and Forman of Kew Gardens, London, gave me considerable help with the inevitable taxonomic problems. I also would like to thank Dr R. Johns of Lae Polytechnic, PNG, who made it possible to use the Bulolo Forestry College Field Plots in PNG, and provided a great deal of vital botanical information. Andrew Sugden, Cathy Kennedy, Dot Jackson, Chris West, Charlie Gibson and an anonymous referee provided much-needed criticism of various drafts of the manuscript.

REFERENCES

Bray, J.R. (1964). Primary consumption in three forest canopies. *Ecology*, **45**, 165–167.
Chew, R.M. (1974). Consumers as regulators of ecosystems: an alternative to energetics. *Ohio Journal of Science*, **74**(6), 359–369.

Coley, P.D. (1979). Effects of leaf age and plant life history patterns on herbivory. *Nature (London)*, **284**, 545–546.

Feeny, P.P. (1976). Plant apparency and chemical defence. *Biochemical Interactions Between Plants and Insects* (Ed. by J. Wallace & R. Mansell), pp. 1–40. Recent Advances in Phytochemistry, 10.

Golley, F.B. (1977). Insects as regulators of forest nutrient cycling. *Tropical Ecology*, **18**(2), 116–123.

Haukioja, E. (1980). On the role of plant defences in the fluctuation of herbivore populations. *Oikos*, **35**, 202–213.

Leigh, E.G. Jr & Smythe, N. (1978). Leaf production, leaf consumption and the regulation of folivory on Barro, Colorado Island. *The Ecology of Arboreal Folivores* (Ed. by G. G. Montgomery), pp. 33–50. Smithsonian Institute Press, Washington.

McGregor, K. (1968). *Productivity relations between insects and oak leaves.* D.Phil. thesis, Oxford University.

Nagy, K.A. & Milton, K. (1979). Energy metabolism and food consumption by Wild Howler monkeys (*Alouatta palliata*). *Ecology*, **60**(3), 475–480.

Nielsen, B.O. (1978). Above-ground food resources and herbivory in a beech forest ecosystem. *Oikos*, **31**, 273–279.

Owen, D.F. & Weigert, R.G. (1976). Do consumers maximize plant fitness? *Oikos*, **27**, 488–492.

Reichle, D.E., Goldstein, R.A., van Hook, R.I. & Dodson, G.J. (1973). Analysis of insect consumption in a forest canopy. *Ecology*, **54**, 1076–1084.

Rhoades, D.F. (1979). The evolution of plant chemical defence against herbivores. *Herbivores; their interaction with Secondary Plant* (Ed. by G. A. Rosenthal & D. H. Janzen), pp. 331–350. Academic Press, London.

Sugden, A.M., Mitchell, A.W., Sutton, S.L. & Wint, G.R.W. (In press). Aerial walkways in rain-forest canopies. Construction and use in Panama, Papua New Guinea and Sulawesi. *Symposium on the Natural History of Panama* (Ed. by A. Gentry), Annals of the Missouri Botanical Gardens.

Varley, G.C. (1967). The effects of grazing by animals on plant productivity. *Secondary Productivity of Terrestrial Ecosystems* (Ed. by K. Petrusewicz), pp. 773–777. Państwowe Wyndawnictwo Naukowe, Warsaw.

Wint, G.R.W. (1979). *The effect of the seasonal accumulation of tannins upon the growth of Lepidopteran larvae.* D.Phil. thesis, Oxford University.

Effects of insect herbivory and artificial defoliation on survival of *Shorea* seedlings

PETER BECKER*

Forest Research Institute, Kepong, Selangor, Malaysia

SUMMARY

1 Beginning 21 months after fruitfall, seedling survival in five understorey cohorts each of the dipterocarps *Shorea leprosula* and *S. maxwelliana* was measured for 2 years in a Peninsular Malaysian lowland rain forest. Leaf damage, due in large part to insect herbivores, was quantified by measuring percentage of surface area lost. Artificial defoliation experiments, comprising 25% and 100% leaf area removal and apical bud removal, were performed.

2 Mean height of 2-year old, untreated seedlings was significantly greater for *Shorea leprosula* compared with *S. maxwelliana*, 142 v. 90 mm.

3 Mortality of untreated *Shorea leprosula* seedlings was significantly higher than that of untreated *S. maxwelliana* seedlings, 27·3 v. 15·6% year^{-1}, calculated over the entire study period. In some cohorts of both species the mortality rate was constant with time, while in other cohorts it increased sharply midway in the study and then declined.

4 Thirteen per cent of the surface area of extant mature leaves of *Shorea leprosula* seedlings was damaged, compared with only 5% for *S. maxwelliana,* and relatively more of the latter species' mature leaves were damage-free. Fourteen species of chewing insects were found feeding on *S. leprosula* seedling leaves, but just four species fed on *S. maxwelliana*.

5 Only 100% defoliation significantly increased the mortality rates of *Shorea leprosula* and *S. maxwelliana* seedlings; 25% defoliation and apical bud removal did not affect mortality in either species. Therefore, natural herbivory, which usually causes less leaf-area loss than 25% defoliation, probably does not generally affect survival of 2-years old *S. leprosula* and *S. maxwelliana* seedlings.

6 *Shorea maxwelliana* seedlings died more slowly than *S. leprosula* seedlings after 100% defoliation. Relatively more *S. leprosula* than *S. maxwelliana* seedlings began refoliating within 2 months of this treatment, so *S. maxwelliana*'s longer survival was probably not due to greater supplementation of its energy reserves with photosynthate from new leaves. Since untreated seedlings of both species had similar starch reserves, defoliated *S. maxwelliana* seedlings may have survived longer by utilizing their energy reserves more slowly than *S. leprosula* seedlings did. In natural circumstances a lower respiratory rate may enable *S. maxwelliana* to persist longer in understorey than *S. leprosula* by helping to maintain a positive energy balance when assimilation rates are low.

---

* Present address: Division of Biological Sciences, University of Michigan, Ann Arbor, Michigan 48109, U.S.A.

INTRODUCTION

Dipterocarp trees in Malaysia produce large synchronous fruit crops at irregular intervals of several years (Burgess 1972; Janzen 1974). When individual trees fruit sporadically during intervening years, few of their seeds survive severe pre- and post-dispersal predation by insects (Chan 1980). In contrast, mast seed crops of dipterocarps produce dense carpets of seedlings. Because the fruits are usually weakly dispersed by wind and gravity, seedlings are concentrated near parent trees (Whitmore 1975). Dipterocarp seedlings in understorey either do not grow or increase in height by only a few centimetres per year once their first few leaves expand (Fox 1972; Liew & Wong 1973). Whitmore (1975) speculated that interspecific differences in survival of dipterocarp seedlings in understorey reflect differences in their photosynthetic rates or photosynthesis/respiration ratios.

A mast fruiting of dipterocarps in Peninsular Malaysia occurred in 1976. Two years later at Pasoh Forest Reserve, seedlings of *Shorea maxwelliana** still occurred at high densities, sometimes nearly 100 m^{-2}. They were often mixed with dense stands of conspecific seedlings and saplings from previous fruit crops. *S. leprosula* seedlings occurred at much lower densities and their leaves showed more extensive damage by insects. I studied the seedling demography of both species to determine whether they had different abilities to persist in understorey. Artificial defoliation at several intensities assessed whether natural herbivory was likely to affect seedling survival.

METHODS

The study was conducted in unlogged lowland rain forest in Pasoh Forest Reserve, Negri Sembilan, Peninsular Malaysia, about 140 km south-east of Kuala Lumpur. Soepadmo (1978) has briefly described Pasoh's vegetation, soils, and meteorology.

Demography

Four or eight 1-m wide transects extending 10–20 m from the bases of five adult trees each of *Shorea leprosula* and *S. maxwelliana* were laid out in the cardinal directions ($\pm 30°$). During May–July 1978 all surviving seedlings of these two species from the August 1976 fruit crop (Chan 1980) within the transects were tagged with numbered plastic loops and counted. These seedlings were recensused five times during the next 2 years with 1·5–4 months elapsing between the earlier censuses and 8 months between the later ones (Fig. 1). The final census of *S. maxwelliana* seedlings at one site was omitted due to insufficient time. The time elapsed during a particular census interval varied by as much as 33 days among conspecific populations.

Sites were selected for the presence of several hundred or more seedlings and the absence of large (> 5 m) openings in the canopy. Initial study population sizes were 254–458 seedlings for *Shorea leprosula* and 345–1824 for *S. maxwelliana*. All sites

---

* Nomenclature follows that of Symington (1943).

occurred on level ground, and those for a particular species were several hundred metres apart.

A seedling was considered dead when its stem lost flexibility and was easily broken. Doubtful mortalities were confirmed by the absence of green inner bark. When only the tag, but no seedling remnant was found, the seedling was counted as dead. If a seedling's tag was not found after careful searching in two consecutive censuses, the seedling was considered dead at the first census in which its tag was missing.

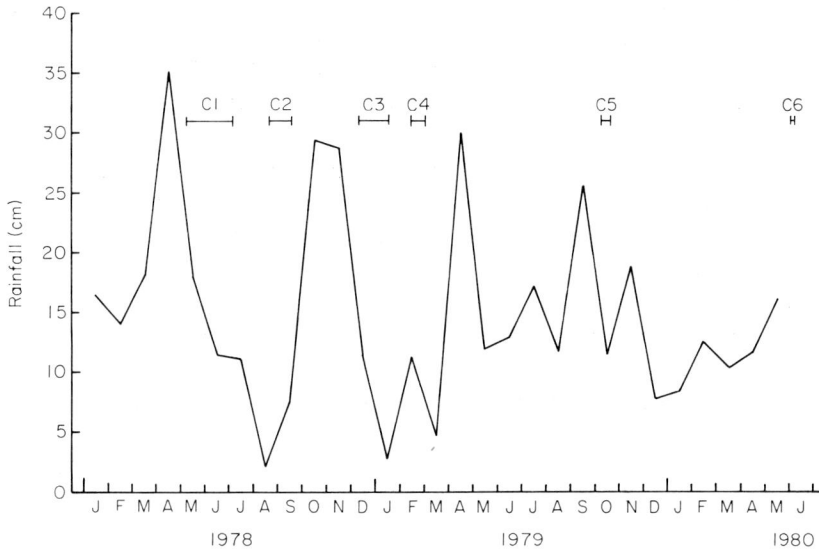

FIG. 1. Monthly rainfall and seedling census (C) periods (horizontal lines) throughout the study. Rainfall data are from Pasoh Forest Research Centre records (unpubl.) for the large clearing near the station buildings. Experimental defoliations were performed on selected seedlings during the third and fourth census periods.

Artificial defoliation

Seedlings from the ten study populations were artificially defoliated in three ways, using scissors. For '25% defoliation' each unfolded leaf was cut parallel to the midrib to remove c. 60% of the lamina's right-half width at its broadest point (estimated if the leaf was previously damaged). From outlines of different sized leaves of both species on graph paper, I had determined that this procedure would remove 25% of an undamaged lamina's surface area. For the experiments I ignored previous natural damage to a leaf. For '100% defoliation' all immature and mature leaves were severed where the petiole joined lamina. For 'apical bud removal' the stem was severed immediately below all apical buds on a seedling (sometimes multiple leaders occurred). Seedlings were artificially defoliated once only. Moribund seedlings lacking unfolded leaves were excluded from all of the above treatments and also from the untreated control groups. All three treatments were performed during the third census (experiment 1), but only the last two treatments were made during the fourth census (experiment 2) due to insufficient numbers of seedlings (Fig. 1).

During the first census every nth seedling in the transects was selected for observations on phenology, growth, and insect damage, with n chosen to obtain c. 100 seedlings at each site. The non-moribund seedlings of these groups were used as the controls in the artificial defoliation experiments. The control groups in experiment 2 are a subset of the corresponding control groups in experiment 1, excluding seedlings that died or became moribund during the interim. Control groups were so selected to avoid perturbing the seedlings designated for phenological study and to obtain seedlings that were distributed throughout the transects similarly to the experimental seedlings.

At all of the *Shorea leprosula* sites and two of the *S. maxwelliana* sites, treatments for both experiments were assigned sequentially to all non-moribund seedlings not in the control group during the third census so that approximately equal numbers of seedlings would eventually receive the three types of treatment. At the remaining *S. maxwelliana* sites, treatments for experiment 1 were assigned sequentially to every nth eligible seedling during the third census and for experiment 2 during the fourth census with n chosen to obtain, as nearly possible, 100 seedlings for each treatment. At the different sites seedlings numbered 45–86 in control groups and 17–139 in treatment groups.

Analysis of results

Mortality rates, M (% year^{-1}), were calculated as:

$$M = 100[D/(A - E)](365/T) \qquad (1)$$

Where D = number of seedlings that died during census interval (excluding E); A = number of seedlings alive at beginning of census interval; E = number of seedlings that died due to large limb- or tree-falls, burial under termite mud, or trampling or uprooting by animals during census interval; T = number of days elapsed during census interval.

For calculations involving the final census, the middle term of eqn (1) was replaced by $[D/(A - E - U)]$, where U = number of seedlings whose tags were first missing at the final census. Seedling deaths listed for E were excluded from all mortality rate calculations because their occurrence was unrelated to seedling vigour. They affected 0·4–5·1% (usually < 3%) of A in the ten untreated *Shorea leprosula* and *S. maxwelliana* populations during the interval between the first and third censuses. For treatment and control groups of these species, E was 0–8·3% ($\leq$ 3% in the majority of cases) of A for the durations of experiments 1 and 2.

All analyses of variance for mortality data were made with the computer program BMDP2V (Dixon 1981). Mortality rates of untreated seedlings of *Shorea leprosula* and *S. maxwelliana* were compared by analysis of variance with species as the grouping factor and census as a repeated measures factor. Data were ln-transformed as suggested by the Box–Cox algorithm, which resulted in compliance with the symmetry assumptions of the repeated measures model (Dixon 1981).

Analyses of the effects of the artificial defoliation treatments on seedling survival were performed separately for each species and experiment to minimize the combination of heterogeneous sources of variance. For the analysis of treatment effects over the entire experimental period, I used Dunnett's t-test (Winer 1971), which is designed for the comparison of several treatments with a single control. Because mortality rates of seedlings with different treatments were (erratically) correlated within sites, treatments were analysed as a repeated measures factor in the analysis of variance used to generate the error variance for these tests. The untransformed data had homogeneous variances (F_{max}-test) and they complied with the symmetry assumptions of the repeated measures model.

Analysing the effects of the defoliation treatments during successive census intervals was not straightforward. There is no completely satisfactory multiple comparisons test for a design with two repeated measures (census and treatment), and numerous approximations were necessary in the approach used here. In most instances the data exhibited significant heterogeneity of variances and did not meet the symmetry assumptions of the repeated measures model. These problems were not alleviated by transformation of the data, so the untransformed observations were used. The error variance for the treatment–control comparisons was a weighted combination of the treatment and treatment $\times$ census error variances, with degrees of freedom adjusted according to the Satterthwaite approximation (Winer 1971). The least significant difference was calculated according to the usual formula for planned comparisons with probabilities adjusted by the Dunn-Šidák method for an experiment-wise error rate of $\alpha = 0.05$ (Sokal & Rohlf 1981). Because the actual significance levels differ in an unknown way from the stated value due to heterogeneous variances, the results of these tests are presented here merely as guidelines.

Seedling heights were analysed by a nested analysis of variance with species as a fixed factor and populations as a random factor. Satterthwaite's approximation was used for the test of significance between species because sample sizes were unequal (Sokal & Rohlf 1981). The ln-transformed data had homogeneous variances (Levene's test, computer program BMDP7D; Dixon 1981).

RESULTS

Seedling height

At the third census untreated seedlings of *Shorea leprosula* were significantly taller than *S. maxwelliana* (F [1, 8] = 104.6, $P < 0.001$ for ln-transformed data), and there were significant differences in height among populations within species (F [8, 787] = 3.92, $P < 0.001$). Measured from the cotyledonary node to the highest living node, *S. leprosula* seedlings were 142 (138–147) mm tall, compared with 90 (87–93) mm for *S. maxwelliana* (geometric $\bar{X}$ (95% confidence interval), $n = 360$ and 437, respectively).

TABLE I. Total and leaf litterfall (t ha^{-1} year^{-1}) compared for forest types from four climatic zones

| | Bray & Gorham (1964) | | IBP Woodlands data set O'Neill & DeAngelis (1980) | |
| | Total | Leaf | Total | Leaf |
Climatic zone	litterfall	litterfall	litterfall	litterfall
Arctic	1·0	0·7	3·3	2·2
Cold temperate	3·5	2·5	4·6	3·0
Warm temperate	5·5	3·6	4·7	3·5
Equatorial	10·9	6·8	9·3	6·6

PROBLEMS OF COMPARING LITTERFALL DATA

Definition of litterfall fractions

A large number of studies have failed to adequately define the fractions of litterfall. A common and important omission is that of the size limits of woody litterfall. Where the wood size limits have been defined they range from < 1 cm to < 10 cm diameter and thus comparisons of litterfall measurements which include wood fall must be made with caution.

The leaf fraction is usually the best defined, but even this is not straightforward and the following are examples of the difficulties which occur. Some workers, e.g. Golley *et al.* (1975) have used 'leaf litterfall' for leaves and other fractions including small wood. Other workers have not included all parts of the leaves in the leaf fraction. For example, Haines & Foster (1977) regarded the 'numerous rachises of compound leaves' as small wood. Further problems arise from large palm leaves which fall infrequently. In one Colombian forest investigated by Fölster & de las Salas (1976) there was 'leaf litterfall' (6·5 t ha^{-1} year^{-1}) and a separate category for 'large palm leaves' (2·1 t ha^{-1} year^{-1}). The two values have been combined in the literature to produce a new value for leaf litterfall of 8·6 t ha^{-1} year^{-1} which is not really comparable with leaf-fall results which do not include large palm leaves. Finally, the difficulties must be considered which result from the different treatments of the smaller leaf fragments. For example, Edwards (1977) found that 96% of 'non-woody material' fall in a montane forest in New Guinea was leaves and that 34% of it passed through a 5 mm sieve (Edwards 1982). By contrast the four lowland forests investigated by Proctor *et al.* (1983b) had a trash fraction (< *c.* 2·5 mm), of 11–18% of the litterfall which was not investigated in detail and not included in the leaf-fall estimate.

Most workers have made no mention of a trash fraction yet clearly this can be an important proportion of small litterfall. The trash fraction will be greatly influenced by levels of herbivory since it includes comminuted plant parts and animal detritus. Few workers have considered the influence of herbivory on litterfall, although grazing is known to vary greatly between forests.

Replication of litter traps and reliability of means

Newbould (1967) recommended that at least twenty litter traps should be used in a sample area and the intensity of sampling should aim at a standard error of the mean of $\pm 5\%$ (equivalent to about $\pm 10\%$ for 95% confidence limits). Many studies have used less than twenty traps; problems of expressing non-normally distributed litterfall results have been largely ignored; often no indication of the reliability of the mean has been given; and frequently the random or subjective placing of the traps has prevented any statistical calculations. The problems of adequate reliability of the mean are compounded with those of the definition of litterfall fractions. Thus, the 'large palm leaves' of Fölster & de la Salas (1976) would have much wider confidence limits than the main leaf fraction. Wood-fall becomes increasingly difficult to determine as its size increases. Even the fall of wood $\leqslant 2$ cm diameter may be difficult to estimate precisely. In four lowland forests investigated by Proctor et al. (1983), thirty-five replicate 0·25 m^2 traps gave results, for wood litterfall ($\leqslant 2$ cm diameter), which had 95% confidence limits of 25–38% of the means.

Length of study period

Newbould (1967) recommended that litterfall studies should go on for at least 3 and preferably 5 years. Few studies have been carried out for 3 years and apparently only two for 5 years or more. There are, however, a number of instances of a substantial litterfall difference between years: the most extreme is that reported by Blasco & Tassy (1975) in the montane forest in India which in one year had a litterfall which was 38% less than the 3-year average. Other studies have produced much smaller differences between years and there seems to be no way of predicting how a particular forest will vary in this respect.

All tropical forests show a substantial seasonal variation in litterfall (the least appears to be the c. 20% difference between the highest and least monthly values for a montane forest in Venzuela investigated by Medina & Zelwer 1972) and hence studies which have been made for much less than a year must be treated with caution. Some very high litterfall values have resulted from extrapolations from measurements made for a relatively short period during heavy litterfall (Kira et al. 1964; Stark 1971). Shorter measurement periods may be acceptable for leaf-fall measurements in forests which are almost completely deciduous.

Regeneration structure of the forest

Edwards & Grubb (1977) have discussed the problems of forest sampling in relation to forest growth phases: pioneer, building, mature or degenerate. However little is known about the scale of growth phase patterns and, since it differs between forests, it is difficult to assess the importance of the forest growth phase in comparing litterfall results. A wide range of sample areas have been used (Proctor 1983). Edwards (1977) attempted to sample within areas of 20×10 m which appeared to approximate to the size of a natural regeneration unit. His study included three areas of this size in mature or late building phases and one in a gap. In the event there was surprisingly little difference between the gap site with 7·9 t ha^{-1} year^{-1} litterfall and the other sites which had litterfalls from 7·2 to 7·7 t ha^{-1} year^{-1}. Greater differences between 'gap' and 'forest' would be expected in forests with a coarser mosaic of phases.

A further consideration is the extent of canopy retention of litter for varying periods in forests of different structural complexity. It would not be surprising for example if, as they fell, upper canopy leaves lodged on branches or other leaves. The extent of this effect is unknown but it could smooth out differences between growth phases in measured litterfall.

Differences in methodology

The summary tables in Proctor (1984) reveal important differences in methodology. Litter traps have varied in size and shape from circular collectors of less than 0·1 m^2 surface to an oblong polythene sheet of 10·8 m^2. Trap size and shape could greatly influence the results. A number of studies have made litterfall collections from cleared areas of the forest floor. These must prevent the collection of a trash fraction since it will be inseparable from the soil. The collection intervals between sampling have varied greatly, and this means that weight losses will have occurred to varying extents within the traps. A few workers have corrected for this effect. The temperatures at which litterfall is dried can influence litterfall dry weights by several per cent. Methods have varied from drying in air to using ovens with temperatures up to 105 °C.

Chemical analysis of litterfall

Most of the sample problems just discussed also affect the results of chemical analyses. In particular, the length of time that the litter is left in the traps will be very important for some elements such as potassium which are readily leached. The chemical composition of litterfall collections made from the ground may well be influenced by the soil. Moreover, litterfall has been chemically analysed by a wide range of methods which may not give comparable results.

The percentage ash (inorganic material) in litterfall has been measured occasionally and that of leaf litterfall is known to range from 2·4 to 10% of the oven dry weight (M. Gautam-Basak & J. Proctor, unpubl.). This may be an important consideration when precise estimates of organic matter production are required.

CONCLUSIONS

The reasons for measuring small litterfall were mentioned in the Introduction but it is now clear that most estimates of litterfall are in some way inadequate. Interpretations of litterfall data must therefore be made with caution, and the summary tables in Proctor (1984) include information that enables individual studies to be evaluated.

There have been a number of attempts to produce predictive models of litterfall using environmental variables, but I have been dissuaded from doing a similar exercise because of the following considerations. First, there are the problems which I have discussed in this paper of the comparability of litterfall results. Since so many litterfall studies are unsatisfactory there is the difficulty of knowing which data to leave out of the model. Secondly, there are difficulties in obtaining comparable and relevant climatic and soil and plant nutrient data. Finally, we know so little of the control of the proportions of production which fall as litter. Litterfall undoubtedly varies with the climatic zone (Table 1) but it is doubtful if useful predictive models within the tropics can be made at present.

ACKNOWLEDGMENTS

Full acknowledgments are given in Proctor (1984).

REFERENCES

Blasco, F. & Tassy, B. (1975). Étude d'un écosystème forestier montagnard du Sud de l'Inde. *Bulletin d'Ecologie*, 6, 525–539.

Bray, J.R. & Gorham, E. (1964). Litter production in forests of the world. *Advances in Ecological Research*, 2, 101–157.

Edwards, P.J. (1977). Studies of mineral cycling in a montane rain forest in New Guinea II. The production and disappearance of litter. *Journal of Ecology*, 65, 971–992.

Edwards, P.J. (1982). Studies of mineral cycling in a montane rain forest in New Guinea V. Rates of cycling in throughfall and litter fall. *Journal of Ecology*, 70, 807–827.

Edwards, P.J. & Grubb, P.J. (1977). Studies of mineral cycling in a montane rain forest in New Guinea I. The distribution of organic matter in the vegetation and soil. *Journal of Ecology*, 65, 943–970.

Fölster, H. & de las Salas, G. (1976). Litter fall and mineralization in three tropical evergreen forest stands, Colombia. *Acta Cientifica Venezolana*, 27, 196–202.

Golley, F.B., McGinnis, J.T., Clements, R.G., Child, G.I. & Duever, M.J. (1975). *Mineral Cycling in a Tropical Moist Forest Ecosystem*. University of Georgia Press, Athens, Georgia, U.S.A.

Haines, B. & Foster, R.B. (1977). Energy flow through litter in a Panamanian forest. *Journal of Ecology*, 65, 147–155.

Kira, T., Ogawa, H., Yoda, K. & Ogino, K. (1964). Primary production by a tropical rainforest of southern Thailand. *Botanical Magazine Tokyo*, 77, 428–429.

Medina, E. & Zelwer, M. (1972). Soil respiration in tropical plant communities. *Tropical Ecology with an Emphasis on Organic Production* (Ed. by P. M. Golley & F. B. Golley), pp. 245–269. University of Georgia, Athens, Georgia, U.S.A.

Newbould, P.J. (1967). *Methods of Estimating the Primary Production of Forests*. IBP Handbook No. 2. Blackwell Scientific Publications, Oxford.

O'Neill, R.V. & DeAngelis, D.L. (1980). Comparative productivity and biomass relations of forest ecosystems. *Dynamic Properties of Forest Ecosystems* (Ed. by D. Reichle), pp. 411–449. Cambridge University Press, Cambridge.

Proctor, J. (1984). Tropical forest litterfall II. The data set. *Tropical Rain Forest: Ecology and Management, Supplementary Volume* (Ed. by A. C. Chadwick & S. L. Sutton). Proceedings of the Leeds Philosophical and Literary Society (Science Section) (in press).

Proctor, J., Anderson, J.M., Fogden, S.C.L. & Vallack, H.W. (1983). Ecological studies in four contrasting lowland rain forests in Gunung Mulu National Park, Sarawak II. Litterfall, litter standing crop and preliminary observation on herbivory. *Journal of Ecology*, 71, 261–283.

Stark, N. (1971). Nutrient cycling II: nutrient distribution in Amazonian vegetation. *Tropical Ecology*, 12, 177–201.

Vitousek, P. (1982). Nutrient cycling and nutrient use efficiency. *The American Naturalist*, 119, 553–572.

APPENDIX I

Litterfall measurement techniques

In April 1982 several workers were asked about the possibility of standardizing measurements of small litterfall. Their replies stressed that some of the methods must differ with the specific object of the study and that there will be special considerations at each site. Nevertheless, there was sufficient agreement to enable the following suggestions to be made.

(i) As far as possible the forest study site should be described floristically and structurally and details should be given on its climate (monthly values), precise location and situation, and its soils. There can be no general recommendations on site dimensions but consideration should be given to the growth phase (pioneer, building, mature, senescent) of the samples. In some cases (e.g. phenological studies in connection with work on large arboreal herbivores) sampling is probably best done along transects of several hundred metres.

(ii) Litterfall should be collected in traps which are made of fine material but which are well drained. There were many views on trap shape and size but areas between 0·25 and 1·0 m^2 were preferred.

(iii) Usually a quantity estimate is the major requirement and then a restricted random method of sampling (giving an even coverage of the site or transect and producing results that are amenable to statistical analysis) will be best. It should involve at least two traps placed randomly within each subdivision of the site or transect. This will enable a fully valid estimate of residual variance and sampling error to be made. The traps should be permanently in place and not re-randomized. Ideally, the intensity of sampling should aim to give 95% confidence limits which are less than 10% of the means for all fractions and total litterfall. This is likely to involve the use of twenty or more traps. Several workers have commented that such small confidence limits may be unrealistic, particularly for fruit fall, and it must be accepted that few studies will achieve this precision.

Where the main aim of the litterfall sampling is the detection of phenomena (e.g. phenological patterns or the mapping of litterfall production) then systematic sampling is required and no confidence limits can be applied to the results.

(iv) The study should go on for at least 1 year and preferably 3 years or longer. The traps should be emptied at intervals not greater than 2 weeks and often weekly litterfall collections will be necessary for fleshy fruits, and during very wet periods, particularly when chemical analysis of the litterfall is intended. The possibility should be checked of animals disturbing the traps or stealing fruits from them between collections.

(v) After collection, the litterfall should be air-dried or oven-dried as soon as possible and then sorted into carefully defined fractions. The following are suggested but the number of fractions will depend on the purposes of the study:
  (a) *Leaves* with their petioles and foliar rachises. Large leaves (e.g. those of palms) which fall infrequently should be treated separately.
  (b) *Reproductive parts.* It may sometimes be useful to separate flowers from fruits.

If studies of decomposition are to be undertaken then a separation of woody, fleshy and leafy reproductive parts may be desirable.

(c) *Small branches and bark*. There was wide agreement that 2·0 cm diameter was a reasonable upper limit for the woody litterfall fraction collected in small traps ($\leqslant 1$ m^2). The fraction might then be comprised of: twigs and branches $\leqslant 2·0$ cm diameter (tapered twigs should be broken at the 2·0 cm diameter point) and bark fragments ($\leqslant 2·0$ cm along the longest axis or judged to have come from branches $\leqslant 2·0$ diameter). It can be argued that a category of twigs $< 1·0$ cm diameter is useful since this (at least in deciduous forests) accounts for a year's growth and its fall can be more precisely estimated. If time permits, therefore, perhaps woody litterfall $< 1·0$ cm diameter could be quantified also.

(d) *Trash fraction* which includes frass, unrecognizable remains and fine particles. Light brushing is necessary to remove fine particles adhering to large fragments. This fraction might simply be described as passing through a sieve of 2 mm or 5 mm mesh. (The larger size means less labour in categorizing litter particles between 2 and 5 mm diameter.) If time permits, quantification of the frass fraction might be used to give information on herbivory.

(vi) All results should be expressed on an oven-dry (105 °C to constant weight) basis and this will usually involve redrying, in the laboratory, samples or subsamples of litterfall. The results should be given (for all the fractions defined above) in g m^{-2} year^{-1} or t ha^{-1} year^{-1} with 95% confidence limits.

Litter production and decomposition in a coastal hill dipterocarp forest

GONG WOOI-KHOON AND ONG JIN-EONG

School of Biological Sciences, Universiti Sains Malaysia,
Penang, Malaysia

SUMMARY

1   Small litter (leaf and total) production was studied in a ridge forest within a coastal hill dipterocarp forest over a 2-year period. The total litter productivity was estimated at 7.45 t ha^{-1} year^{-1} of which 72% was leaf-litter productivity. Litter production was affected by rainfall, more litter falling during the dry season.

2   The rate of decomposition of litter was found to be relatively slow, possibly due to the coriaceous texture of the leaves studied. After 14 months, strings of leaves left on the forest floor had lost only 61% (*Anisoptera curtisii*), 76% (*Calophyllum curtisii*) and 73% (*Shorea curtisii*) of their material.

3   The mean standing crop of leaf litter and total litter estimated during the dry and wet seasons were found to be 3.11 t ha^{-1} (leaf) and 4.89 t ha^{-1} (total).

4   The turnover rate of this standing crop of litter was estimated as 172% per year for leaf litter and 153% per year for total litter.

5   The relationship between the standing biomass of this forest and its litter dynamics is discussed and compared with that of the lowland dipterocarp forest.

INTRODUCTION

Most of the work on litter dynamics in the tropics has been done in Africa (e.g. Laudelout & Meyer 1954; Greenland & Kowal 1960; Nye 1961; Madge 1965; Bernhard-Reversat 1972) and in South/Central America (e.g. Jenny, Gessel & Bingham 1949; Klinge & Rodrigues 1968; Ewel 1976; Tanner 1980, 1981).

In South East Asia, some work has been done in Thailand (Kira *et al.* 1967), in New Guinea (Edwards 1977; Edwards & Grubb 1977), in Australia (Brasell, Unwin & Stocker 1980); in a lowland dipterocarp forest in Peninsular Malaysia (Gong 1972; Lim 1978; Ogawa 1978; Yoda 1978), and in four contrasting lowland rain forests in East Malaysia (Proctor *et al.* 1983). As the structure and species composition of hill dipterocarp forests is quite different from that of lowland dipterocarp forests (see Wyatt-Smith 1963), this study was conducted to look into the rate of litterfall and decomposition in a coastal hill dipterocarp forest and to compare the litter dynamics of this forest with that of the lowland dipterocarp forest.

STUDY SITE

The study site is the Pantai Acheh Forest Reserve in the north-west corner of Penang Island. This is largely a coastal hill forest, for most of it occurs on hilly terrain and only about 10% on slopes of less than 18°. The soil on granitic rock is generally poor and shallow (Ong & Dhanarajan 1976). The forest was selectively logged for timber between the late 1910s and the late 1930s so large parts of it have been disturbed.

The study site is along a ridge from 70 m to 300 m above sea level. The forest here has been very little disturbed (or has recovered from disturbance) as indicated by the presence of several large trees of *Shorea curtisii* Dyer ex King (Dipterocarpaceae), *Gluta elegans* Kurz (Anacardiaceae), and *Anisoptera curtisii* Dyer (Dipterocarpaceae). This forest fits the category of 'seraya-ridge forests' as described by Wyatt-Smith (1963).

METHODS OF STUDY

Litterfall

Traps and dry weights

At the start of this study (November 1979) ten litter traps consisting of plastic coated fibreglass mesh material (1 mm mesh size) sewn onto a stiff wire frame of 1×1 m and depth 0·1 m were set out along a line at 10 m intervals ascending the ridge. In January 1980, the number of traps was increased to twenty, in March to forty, and in November to eighty (with traps 1–60 ascending the ridge from 70 to 300 m, and traps 61–80 parallel to the first row but 10 m distant at 220–300 m). The traps were suspended from trees at about 30 cm above ground.

Litter was collected from all of these traps at approximately monthly intervals, taken back to the laboratory, oven-dried at 105 °C, sorted into leaf and other components (twigs of 2·5 cm diameter or below, reproductive parts, and a fine fraction of insect frass, dead insects, debris etc.) and weighed. The mean leaf and total fine litterfall for every collection period was calculated.

Climatic factors

Monthly meteorological records for the Bayan Lepas Station, Penang (the nearest meteorological station with complete records) were examined for the period of the study (November 1979–November 1981) for the following factors:
  (i) Rainfall—total monthly;
  (ii) Temperature—mean daily, mean daily maximum, mean daily minimum;
  (iii) Relative humidity—mean daily, mean daily maximum, mean daily minimum;
  (iv) Sunshine—mean total hours;
  (v) Wind—speed.
As rainfall appeared to be the only factor that varied to any extent, it was decided to concentrate on how this factor affected litterfall. The rainfall data for the Teluk Bahang Catchment Area were used, as the study area was very close to this catchment area.

Pearson's correlation coefficient, r, and r^2 were calculated for leaf and total litter against various rainfall data.

Litter decomposition

Leaf decomposition study

Three species with leaves commonly found on the forest floor were studied: *Anisoptera curtisii, Calophyllum curtisii* King and *Shorea curtisii*.

Freshly fallen leaves (as judged by appearance) of these species were collected from the forest floor and sorted into sets comprising leaves of various sizes such that all sets were similar. The number of leaves used for each set was: *Anisoptera*, seven; *Calophyllum*, six, and *Shorea*, eight, and random sets of leaves were then sewn onto nylon strings (via the lamina adjoining the mid-rib) such that the leaves did not overlap, while other sets were taken back to the laboratory for oven-drying so as to obtain wet to dry weight conversions.

The strings of leaves were left on the forest floor (with one end attached to a plastic baseline tied between two trees). At every collection time, three strings of leaves for all species were collected randomly, wiped clean carefully, oven-dried and weighed. The mean loss in weight was then calculated for every species.

Turnover rate of standing crop of litter

The amount of litter accumulated on the forest floor was estimated during four collection periods through the study period, two in January (during the dry season) and two in November (at the end of the wet season).

During all collection periods, between four and twenty 1×1 m quadrats were randomly selected and all fine litter (including twigs of 2·5 cm diameter and below) within every quadrat collected for oven-drying before sorting into leaf, twig, fruit and flower, and miscellaneous (insects, insect frass, debris etc.) components and weighed.

The mean floor litter accumulation over the 2 year period was then calculated and used to estimate the rate of turnover of litterfall in the forest.

RESULTS

Litterfall

Traps and dry weights

The mean leaf and total fine litterfalls for twenty collection periods over the 2-year study are presented in Table 1 and Figure 1. It can be seen that in general leaf-fall pattern was very closely related to total litterfall.

The annual leaf litterfall was calculated to be 5·36 t ha^{-1} year^{-1} and the total litter, 7·45 t ha^{-1} year^{-1}. Thus, leaf litter constituted 72% of the total litterfall.

Mean daily values for leaf and total litterfalls for the first year (collection periods 1–10) were 1·46 g m^{-2}day^{-1} and 2·16 g m^{-2}day^{-1}, respectively, and those for the second year (collection periods 11–20) were 1·49 g m^{-2}day^{-1} and 1·92 g m^{-2}day^{-1}, respectively.

TABLE 1. Leaf and total litterfall during different collection periods over 2 years in a coastal hill dipterocarp forest (values presented as means $\pm$ S.E.)

No.	Collection period Time	No. of traps	Dry weight ($g\,m^{-2}day^{-1}$) Leaf litter	Total litter
(1)	11.11.79–15.12.79	10	$1\cdot63\pm0\cdot52$	$2\cdot32\pm0\cdot41$
(2)	15.12.79–23.1.80	10	$2\cdot77\pm0\cdot29$	$5\cdot01\pm0\cdot45$
(3)	3.1.80–7.2.80	20	$2\cdot43\pm0\cdot15$	$3\cdot12\pm0\cdot28$
(4)	17.2.80–17.3.80	30	$1\cdot12\pm0\cdot12$	$2\cdot60\pm0\cdot15$
(5)	17.3.80–22.4.80	40	$1\cdot52\pm0\cdot18$	$2\cdot19\pm0\cdot23$
(6)	22.4.80–12.6.80	40	$1\cdot48\pm0\cdot10$	$1\cdot83\pm0\cdot12$
(7)	12.6.80–30.7.80	40	$0\cdot54\pm0\cdot03$	$0\cdot87\pm0\cdot08$
(8)	30.7.80–30.8.80	40	$0\cdot78\pm0\cdot05$	$1\cdot52\pm0\cdot12$
(9)	30.8.80–29.9.80	40	$0\cdot63\pm0\cdot04$	$1\cdot40\pm0\cdot18$
(10)	29.9.80–31.10.80	40	$0\cdot54\pm0\cdot03$	$0\cdot74\pm0\cdot05$
(11)	31.10.80–29.11.80	40	$0\cdot64\pm0\cdot07$	$1\cdot03\pm0\cdot13$
(12)	29.11.80–29.12.80	76	$1\cdot03\pm0\cdot08$	$1\cdot36\pm0\cdot11$
(13)	29.12.80–17.2.81	77	$1\cdot96\pm0\cdot07$	$2\cdot16\pm0\cdot08$
(14)	17.2.81–26.3.81	67	$2\cdot83\pm0\cdot19$	$3\cdot27\pm0\cdot21$
(15)	26.3.81–4.5.81	72	$1\cdot77\pm0\cdot09$	$2\cdot30\pm0\cdot12$
(16)	4.5.81–27.5.81	64	$2\cdot17\pm0\cdot16$	$2\cdot57\pm0\cdot17$
(17)	27.5.81–29.6.81	79	$1\cdot93\pm0\cdot14$	$2\cdot57\pm0\cdot16$
(18)	29.6.81–20.8.81	78	$0\cdot99\pm0\cdot05$	$1\cdot43\pm0\cdot08$
(19)	20.8.81–6.10.81	80	$0\cdot89\pm0\cdot04$	$1\cdot36\pm0\cdot06$
(20)	6.10.81–7.11.81	78	$0\cdot65\pm0\cdot04$	$1\cdot19\pm0\cdot09$
Mean			$1\cdot47$	$2\cdot04$
Annual fall ($t\,ha^{-1}year^{-1}$)			$5\cdot36$	$7\cdot45$

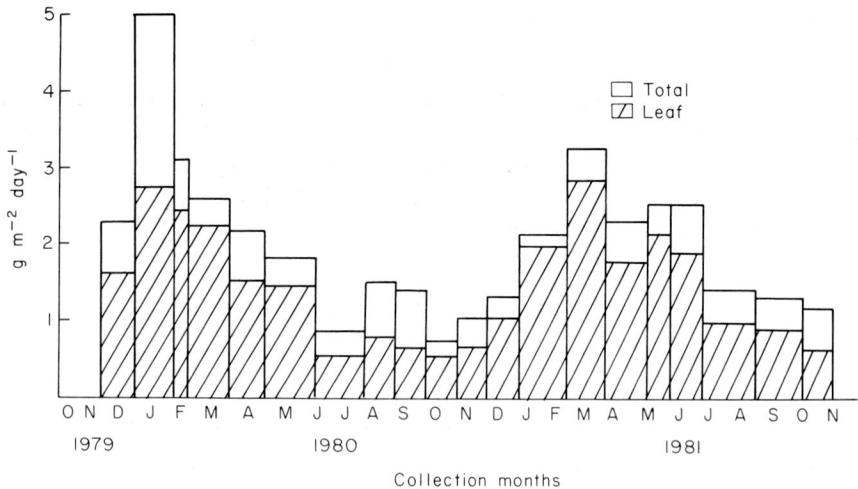

FIG. 1. Mean leaf (▨) and total (□) litterfall during different collection periods over 2 years in a coastal hill dipterocarp forest.

Climatic factors

Figure 2 shows the meteorological conditions prevailing in the study region. It is obvious that rainfall is the only factor that shows some seasonality. The Teluk Bahang rainfall data follow a similar trend to that of the Bayan Lepas data but differ in absolute quantities. The rainfall received during the various litter collection periods are presented in Table 2. Pearson's correlation coefficient, r, for leaf litterfall with rainfall is -0.76 which is significant at $P < 0.05$. Pearson's correlation coefficient, r, for total litterfall with rainfall is -0.68, which is significant at $P < 0.05$.

Thus, it can be seen that litterfall is negatively related to rainfall, with more litterfall during the dry months compared with the wet months.

Litter decomposition

Leaf decomposition study

Table 3 summarizes the percentage loss of leaf material after varying periods of time in *Anisoptera, Calophyllum* and *Shorea*. The variation between replicates ($n = 3$) was extremely high as shown by the high standard errors. As such, three replicates for a species at every collection time is too few to allow meaningful statistical comparison between species and between collection times.

However, the general trend in the three species is similar, the mean percentage loss being 28% after 3 months, 47% after 11 months and 70% after 14 months. It appears that loss became more rapid after 11 months.

Turnover rate of standing crop of litter

Table 4 summarizes the amount of accumulated floor litter present at the four different sample times during the study period. The mean leaf litter that accumulated on the forest floor was 3.11 t ha^{-1}, 64% of the mean total litter that accumulated (4.89 t ha^{-1}). Comparing these figures with those obtained for the annual production of litter, it was calculated that the rate of turnover of leaf litter was 1.72 times a year (172%) and that of total litter 1.53 times a year (153%).

DISCUSSION

Litterfall

Nye (1961) obtained values of 10.5 and 6.9 t ha^{-1}year^{-1} for total fine litter and leaf litter productivity respectively for a 40 year old secondary forest in Ghana; Golley *et al.* (1975) obtained the value of 11.3 t ha^{-1}year^{-1} for total litter in a tropical moist forest in Panama and Lim (1978) obtained values of 8.9 and 6.4 t ha^{-1}year^{-1} for total and leaf litter respectively for Pasoh, a lowland dipterocarp forest in Peninsular Malaysia. For the same forest, Ogawa (1978) obtained values of 10.6 and 6.3 t ha^{-1}year^{-1} for

Litter dynamics in dipterocarp forest

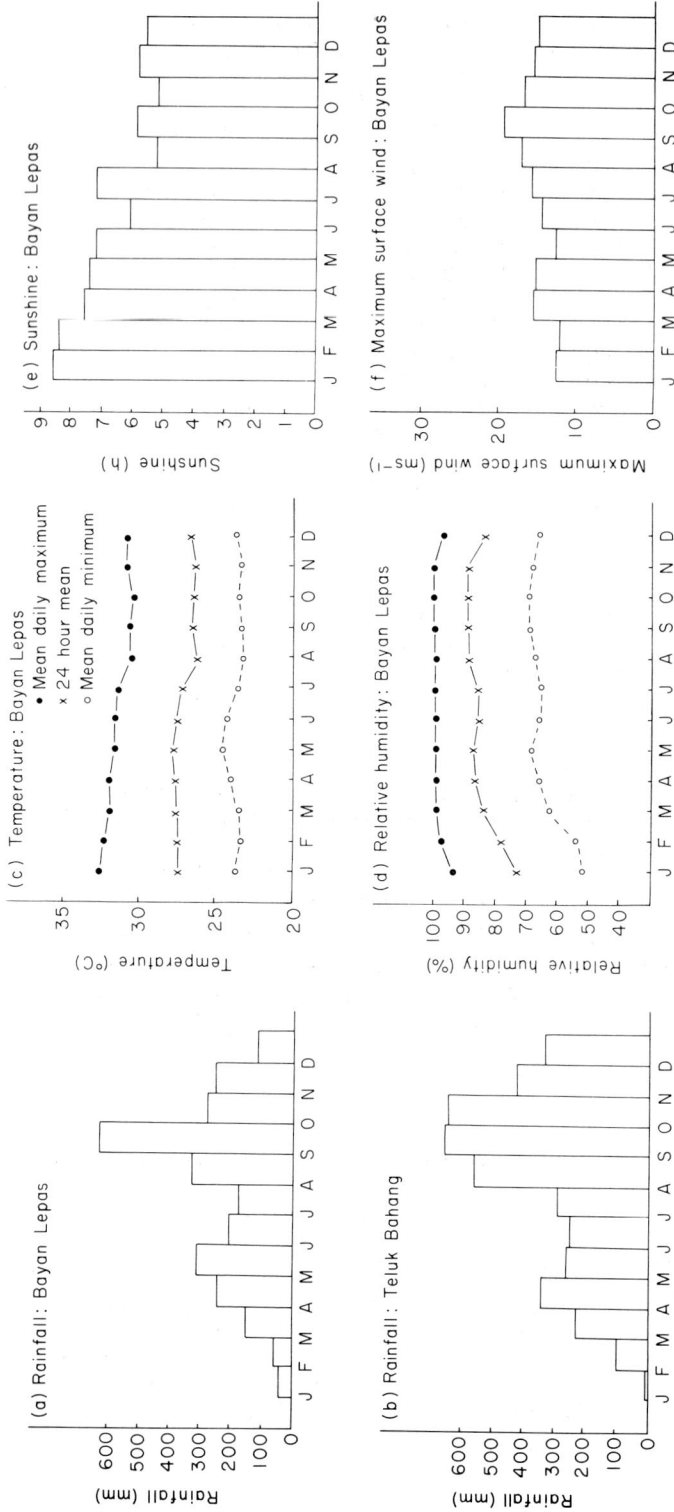

FIG. 2. The meteorological conditions prevailing in the study region for 1980: (a) rainfall, Bayan Lepas Station; (b) rainfall, Teluk Bahang Station; (c) temperature, Bayan Lepas Station (●) mean daily maximum, (×) 24 hour mean, (○) mean daily minimum); (d) relative humidity, Bayan Lepas Station (●) mean daily maximum, (×) 24 hour mean, (○) mean daily minimum); (e) sunshine, Bayan Lepas Station; (f) maximum surface wind, Bayan Lepas Station.

TABLE 2. The rainfall received during the various
litter collection periods, Teluk Bahang Station

No.	Collection period Time	Rainfall (mm)
(1)	11.11.79–15.12.79	193·9
(2)	15.12.79–23.1.80	1·8
(3)	23.1.80–7.2.80	49·2
(4)	17.2.80–17.3.80	163·4
(5)	17.3.80–22.4.80	333·5
(6)	22.4.80–12.6.80	256·3
(7)	12.6.80–30.7.80	262·1
(8)	30.7.80–30.8.80	554·5
(9)	30.8.80–29.9.80	649·5
(10)	29.9.80–31.10.80	637·3
(11)	31.10.80–29.11.80	414·5
(12)	29.11.80–29.12.80	322·3
(13)	29.12.80–17.2.81	43·2
(14)	17.2.81–26.3.81	45·5
(15)	26.3.81–4.5.81	531·6
(16)	4.5.81–27.5.81	299·0
(17)	27.5.81–29.6.81	155·4
(18)	29.6.81–20.8.81	220·2
(19)	20.8.81–6.10.81	289·0
(20)	6.10.81–7.11.81	515.4

TABLE 3. The percentage loss of leaf material left on the forest floor after
different times (values are means $\pm$ S.E.; $n = 3$)

Species	3 months	% Loss of leaf material after 5 months	11 months	14 months
Anisoptera curtisii	31·4 $\pm$ 5·5	27·2 $\pm$ 0·6	39·0 $\pm$ 8·5	60·7 $\pm$ 5·4
Calophyllum curtisii	28·5 $\pm$ 4·5	36·5 $\pm$ 10·8	68·5 $\pm$ 17·4	76·3 $\pm$ 4·6
Shorea curtisii	25·2 $\pm$ 1·2	36·8 $\pm$ 4·8	33·7 $\pm$ 11·9	72·5 $\pm$ 15·8
Mean	28·4	33·5	47·1	69·8

TABLE 4. Accumulated litterfall in 1×1 m quadrats at different collection times (values in table are means $\pm$ S.E.)

Date	No. of quadrats	Leaf	Twig	Litter standing crop (g m^{-2}) Fruit/ Flower/Bud	Miscellaneous	Total
January 1980	20	237·1 $\pm$ 15·4	188·8 $\pm$ 23·6	0	34·4 $\pm$ 5·0	460·3 $\pm$ 30·4
November 1980	20	472·8 $\pm$ 42·5	150·8 $\pm$ 19·4	3·2 $\pm$ 3·1	21·3 $\pm$ 6·6	648·2 $\pm$ 50·2
January 1981	14	153·9 $\pm$ 18·1	84·4 $\pm$ 20·7	0	49·0 $\pm$ 16·4	287·4 $\pm$ 45·9
November 1981	4	381·0 $\pm$ 44·0		179·3 $\pm$ 46·3		560·5 $\pm$ 59·5
Mean		311·2				489·1

total (including branches up to 10 cm diameter) and leaf litter. Bray & Gorham (1964) cited Mitchell's values of 6·3 t ha^{-1}year^{-1} for a lowland dipterocarp forest in Malaysia. Proctor *et al.* (1983) obtained values of 8·8 and 5·4 t ha^{-1}year^{-1} for total fine and leaf litter respectively for a lowland dipterocarp forest in Sarawak.

The productivity of fine litter in the coastal hill dipterocarp forest here in Penang, was estimated as 7·5 and 5·4 t ha^{-1}year^{-1} for total and leaf litter respectively. These values are lower than those obtained by Lim (1978) and Ogawa (1978) in Pasoh but are comparable to those reported by Mitchell (cited in Bray & Gorham 1964) for both lowland dipterocarp and hill forests. The total is lower than, but the leaf litter is the same as, the values obtained by Proctor *et al.* for a lowland dipterocarp forest in Sarawak. Comparing with an upper montane rain forest in Jamaica where Tanner (1980) obtained values of 5·5 and 5·3 t ha^{-1} year^{-1} for total and leaf litter respectively in a mull ridge forest, it can be seen that the total is higher but the leaf litter is similar in amount.

Peak leaf litterfall in this forest was obtained during the dry months. This agrees well with Madge (1965) who found highest levels of leaf-fall during the dry season. Lim (1978) did not find any significant correlation between litterfall and rainfall in Pasoh while Ogawa (1978) suggested that higher leaf-fall occured during the wet months. Proctor *et al.* (1983) also found that the leaf litterfall peaked in a lowland dipterocarp forest in Sarawak at a time of a peak of rainfall.

Litter decomposition

The rate of loss of material was slow in all three species studied (Table 3), the highest loss after 11 months being 69% in *Calophyllum* and only 34% in *Shorea*. In the lowland dipterocarp forest at Pasoh, the rate of loss of leaf material was extremely rapid, the loss being as much as 99% in the case of *Shorea maxwelliana* after only 5 weeks (Gong 1972). Bullock & Khoo (1969) found that the leaves of *Croton laevifolius* showed 75% to 80% losses in 5 weeks, while *Saurauia tristyla* showed only 13% loss in the same time under the same conditions at Gombak, a hill dipterocarp forest in Peninsular Malaysia.

Tanner (1981) has suggested that the lower rate of decomposition in upper montane as compared to lowland rain forests may be the result of lower temperature, different leaf characteristics and differences in water relations.

In the present study, the differences in the rate of decomposition could well be due to the differences in leaf texture (*Anisoptera curtisii*, *Calophyllum curtisii* and *Shorea curtisii* have thick, coriaceous leaves, whilst the leaves of *Shorea maxwelliana* and *Croton laevifolium* are thinner) as well as site differences.

It should be noted here that the decomposition rates obtained in this study should not be taken as representative but should be considered to be nearer the lower limits. The turnover rates obtained are more representative of the forest. The turnover rate of leaf litter of 1·72 times per year (172%) lies within the range obtained in lowland rain forests. For example, Klinge & Rodrigues (1968) obtained a decomposition rate of 93% per year in Brazil, Cornforth (1970) obtained a value of 164% in Trinidad and

Hopkins (1966) obtained a value of 240% in Nigeria. The turnover rate of 172% is higher than those obtained by Wiegert (1970) and Edwards (1977) who obtained values of 94% and 120% for a montane forest in Puerto Rico and New Guinea respectively. The turnover rate of total fine litter was estimated at 153%, about half the rate obtained by Ogawa (1978) who cited values of 330% for total fine litter at Pasoh.

The coastal hill dipterocarp forest thus has a lower total fine litter productivity and a slower rate of turnover of this litter when compared with the lowland dipterocarp forest. If this results in a slower cycling of minerals, one could speculate that the coastal hill forest has a slow growth or is not able to support as high a standing biomass as the lowland dipterocarp forest, as the biological cycle of nutrients is one of the principal processes supporting the production of organic matter (Duvigneaud & Denaeyer De-Smet 1970). However, the standing biomass obtained in the study site in the coastal hill forest is estimated to be about 700 t ha^{-1} (unpubl.) whereas the standing biomass at Pasoh is estimated as 500–550 t ha^{-1} (Kato, Tadaki & Ogawa 1978). This suggests that the species found in the site of the present study are well adapted to the conditions prevailing, resulting in the site being able to support a high standing biomass despite the relatively low litter productivity and slow turnover of this litter. This is confirmed by the observation (unpubl.) that the big biomass here is due largely to the presence of a number of large *Shorea curtisii* trees—a species which may well be adapted to the ridge environment on hill dipterocarp forests (Burgess 1969).

In conclusion, we would like to reiterate that although the coastal hill dipterocarp forest has a lower litter productivity and a slower rate of turnover of this litter than the lowland dipterocarp forest, it is capable of supporting just as high or even a higher standing biomass. It appears that coastal hill dipterocarp forests may have evolved a mechanism of utilizing the slower rate of cycling of material by slow but sustained growth. The whole-scale logging of such forests could cause permanent damage to a unique ecosystem as well as drastic erosion. If logging is to be carried out, it has to be extremely selective, with care taken not to damage large areas. It is, however, best that these forests be kept as nature or wildlife reserves.

ACKNOWLEDGMENTS

We would like to thank our Vice-Chancellor, Y. B. Tan Sri Datuk Haji Hamdan Sheikh Tahir and our Dean, Professor Ishak T. Kechik for their support of this study. This study was partially funded by the Universiti Sains Malaysia short-term research grant and the Man and the Biosphere Programme, for which we are grateful. The meteorological data for the Bayan Lepas Station and the Teluk Bahang catchment area were provided by the Meteorological Department, Ministry of Transport and the Penang Water Authority respectively.

Thanks are also due to Mr Bakar Othman, Mr Mohd Hussain Yahya and Mr Mohd Zamri Othman for their valuable field assistance. Mr Bakar and Mr Hussain also helped with the laboratory analysis. We are especially grateful to Dr T. C. Whitmore for reading the draft and his most helpful comments.

REFERENCES

Bernhard-Reversat, F. (1972). Décomposition de la litière de feuilles en forêt ombrophile de basse Côte-d'Ivoire. *Oecologia Plantarum*, **7**, 279–300.

Brasell, H.M., Unwin, G.L. & Stocker, G.C. (1980). The quantity, temporal distribution and mineral-element content of litterfall in two forest types at two sites in tropical Australia. *Journal of Ecology*, **68**, 123–139.

Bray, J.R. & Gorham, E. (1964). Litter production in forests of the world. *Advances in Ecological Research*, **2**, 101–157.

Bullock, J.A. & Khoo, B.K. (1969). The litter layer. *Malayan Nature Journal*, **22**, 136–143.

Burgess, P.F. (1969). Ecological factors in hill and mountain forests of the states of Malaya. *Malayan Nature Journal*, **22**, 119–128.

Cornforth, I.S. (1970). Leaf fall in a tropical rain forest. *Journal of Applied Ecology*, **7**, 603–608.

Duvigneaud, P. & Denaeyer-De Smet, S. (1970). Biological cycling of minerals in temperate deciduous forests. *Analysis of Temperate Forest Ecosystems* (Ed. by D. E. Reichle), pp. 199–225. Chapman and Hall, London.

Edwards, P.J. (1977). Studies on mineral cycling in a montane rain forest in New Guinea II. The production and disappearance of litter. *Journal of Ecology*, **65**, 971–992.

Edwards, P.J. & Grubb, P.J. (1977). Studies of mineral cycling in a montane forest in New Guinea I. The distribution of organic matter in the vegetation and soil. *Journal of Ecology*, **65**, 943–969.

Ewel, J.J. (1976). Litter fall and leaf decomposition in a tropical forest succession in eastern Guatemala. *Journal of Ecology*, **64**, 293–308.

Golley, F.B., McGinnis, J., Clements, R.G., Childs, G.I. & Duever, M.J. (1975). *Mineral Cycling in a Tropical Moist Forest Ecosystem*. University of Georgia Press, Athens, Georgia, 248 pp.

Gong, W.K. (1972). *Studies on the rates of fall, decomposition and nutrient element release of leaf litter of representative species in a lowland dipterocarp forest*. B.Sc. (Hons.) thesis, University of Malaya.

Greenland, D.J. & Kowal, J.M.L. (1960). Nutrient content of the moist tropical forest of Ghana. *Plant and Soil*, **12**, 154–174.

Hopkins, B. (1966). Vegetation of the Olokemeji Forest Reserve, Nigeria IV. The litter and soil with special reference to their seasonal changes. *Journal of Ecology*, **54**, 687–703.

Jenny, H., Gessel, S.P. & Bingham, F.T. (1949). Comparative study of decomposition rates of organic nutrients in temperate and tropical regions. *Soil Science*, **68**, 419–432.

Kato, R., Tadaki, Y. & Ogawa, H. (1978). Plant biomass and growth increment studies in Pasoh Forest. *Malayan Nature Journal*, **30**, 211–224.

Kira, T., Ogawa, H., Yoda, K. & Ogino, K. (1967). Comparative ecological studies on three main types of vegetation in Thailand IV. Dry matter production with special reference to the Khao Chong Rain Forest. *Nature and Life in South East Asia*, **5**, 149–194.

Klinge, H. & Rodrigues, W. (1968). Litter production in an area of Amazonia Terra Firma Forest I. Litter fall, organic carbon and total nitrogen contents of litter. *Amazonia*, **1**, 287–302.

Laudelout, H. & Meyer, J. (1954). Les cycles d'elements mineraux et de matiere en forest equatoriala Congolaize. *Transactions of the Fifth International Congress of Soil Science, Leopoldville 1954*, Volume 2, pp. 267–272.

Lim, M.S. (1978). Litter fall and mineral nutrient content of litter in Pasoh Forest Reserve. *Malayan Nature Journal*, **30**, 275–280.

Madge, D.S. (1965). Leaf fall and litter disappearance in a tropical forest. *Pedobiologia*, **5**, 273–288.

Nye, P.H. (1961). Organic matter and nutrient cycles under moist tropical forest. *Plant and Soil*, **13**, 333–346.

Ogawa, H. (1978). Litter production and carbon cycling in Pasoh Forest. *Malayan Nature Journal*, **30**, 367–373.

Ong, J.E. & Dhanarajan G. (1976). On a National Park for Pulau Pinang. *Malayan Nature Journal*, **29**, 277–281.

Proctor, J., Anderson, J.M., Fogden, S.C. & Vallack, H.W. (1983). Ecological studies in four contrasting lowland rain forests in Gunung Mulu National Park, Sarawak II. Litterfall, litter standing crop and preliminary observations on herbivory. *Journal of Ecology*, **71**, 261–283.

Tanner E.V.J. (1980). Litter fall in montane rain forests of Jamaica and its relation to climate. *Journal of Ecology*, **68**, 833–848.

Tanner, E.J. (1981). The decomposition of leaf litter in Jamaican montane rain forest. *Journal of Ecology*, **69**, 263–275.

Wiegert, R.G. (1970). Effects of ionizing radiation on leaf fall, decomposition and litter microarthropods of a montane rain forest. *A Tropical Rain Forest* (Ed. by H. T. Odum & R. F. Pigeon), pp. H89–100. United States Atomic Energy Commission, Oak Ridge, Tennessee.

Wyatt-Smith, J. (1963). Manual of Malayan Silviculture for inland forests Volume II. *Malayan Forest Records* No. 23.

Yoda, K. (1978). Organic carbon, nitrogen and mineral nutrients stock in the soils of Pasoh Forest. *Malayan Nature Journal*, **30**, 229–251.

Decomposition in tropical forests

J. M. ANDERSON

Department of Biological Sciences, Wolfson Ecology Laboratory,
University of Exeter, Exeter EX4 4PS

M. J. SWIFT

Department of Botany, University of Zimbabwe, P.O. Box M.P.167,
Mount Pleasant, Harare, Zimbabwe

INTRODUCTION

It is a widely held belief that plant litter decomposes rapidly in the humid tropics, hence tropical rain forest soils have a low organic matter content and a major proportion of the ecosystem nutrient capital is located in plant biomass. The origins of these assumptions are obscure (Whitmore 1975) but are simply refuted by the widespread occurrence of podsols in tropical rain forests (Klinge 1966) in which more than 60% of the nitrogen and phosphorus capital may be located in the deep, organic humus-horizons of these soils (Klinge & Rodrigues 1968a, b). Nonetheless, the underlying dogma persists. Sanchez (1976), for example, presents extensive analytical data which show that temperate and tropical soils have similar organic matter contents, but he still concludes that 'in tropical rain forests neither temperature nor moisture limits decomposition at any time. These forests produce about five times as much biomass and soil organic matter as comparable temperate forests but the rate of organic matter decomposition is also about five times higher. Thus equilibrium organic matter contents are similar'.

It is the purpose of this paper to investigate the validity of generalizations regarding decomposition rates in tropical rain forests. We consider firstly the basis for comparisons of litter decomposition rates in different ecosystems and then attempt to interpret variations in decomposition rates at regional and local scales in terms of the regulatory variables of decomposition processes. We conclude by considering the importance of investigating decomposition processes for an understanding of forest dynamics, particularly when forests are cleared for agriculture.

COMPARATIVE MEASUREMENTS OF LITTER DECAY

The three most widely used measures of litter decomposition in terrestrial ecosystems are soil respiration, litterfall/standing crop quotients (*k*-values) and direct measurements of weight losses from litter bags. While these may continue to be the most convenient methods for comparative studies, each of them represents an over-simplification of the processes of decomposition and none of them provide true measurements of decay rates. The uncritical use of these methods may therefore hinder rather than assist our understanding of tropical decomposition processes.

Soil respiration is derived from respiration of the whole heterotroph community, mainly fungi and bacteria, plus the respiration of living roots. Root respiration is a very variable and poorly quantified component of soil respiration and estimates for the contribution of roots to total soil CO_2 efflux range between 21% at Pasoh in Malaysia (Ogawa 1978) and 67–82% for the root mat in an Amazonian forest at Manaus (Medina *et al.* 1980); a similar range of values has been recorded for temperate forests (Anderson 1973a). Thus, while soil respiration may be an indication of total carbon fluxes through the soil system (Schlesinger 1977) it is not a measure of carbon turnover by heterotrophic organisms or litter production. A comparison of soil respiration rates in tropical rain forests will not therefore be made (see Schlesinger 1977 and Medina *et al.* 1980 for reviews of the literature). Measurements of soil respiration, including root-free controls or methods such as those employed by Medina *et al.* (1980), can provide data on temporal and seasonal effects of temperature and moisture variation on heterotroph activity at different depths of the soil and litter profile. The importance of such measurements for an understanding of soil processes will become evident.

The relationship between litterfall and litter standing crops on the forest floor is widely used to compare litter decay rates or turnover times of forest floor materials. The use of these decay constants dates back to the classical studies by Jenny and co-workers in the 1940s, notably Jenny, Gessel & Bingham (1949), Greenland & Nye (1959) and the review by Olson (1963). Olson (1963) criticizes these earlier studies for their confusing differences in approach and proposes the use of the decomposition rate parameter 'k' which is calculated as the litterfall divided by the soil organic matter standing crop under 'steady-state' conditions. Thus, tropical rain forests have k-values greater than 1, suggesting that the turnover of soil organic matter occurs in a year or less, while values of k for temperature forests are less than 1, and may be below 0·1 for coniferous forests, indicating turnover times ranging from a few years to several decades. Olson (1963) has, however, contributed further confusion by relating measured litter inputs to the soil system with total soil organic matter standing crops. It is rarely possible to calculate k values for total litter in terrestrial ecosystems, and not with the data set used by Olson, for three principal reasons. Firstly, living and dead roots are difficult to measure and differentiate and therefore have to be arbitrarily assigned to contribute to either input or organic matter standing crop. Secondly, large wood falls, particularly tree boles, are highly variable in space and time (at scales of hectares and decades) but make a significant contribution to soil organic matter standing crops. (For example, Yoda (1978) notes that deep humus layers were only observed at Pasoh where large fallen trunks had nearly decomposed.) Finally, the measured litterfall fractions are rarely divided into comparable fractions to the litter standing crop; in particular, the smaller particle sizes collected as 'leaf litter' are not generally defined.

Nevertheless, provided that the same litter components are represented in both inputs and standing crops the quotient, referred to below as the litter turnover coefficient k_L, represents the only basis on which geographical patterns of litter decay can be compared throughout the humid tropics with currently available data of very variable quality.

Finally, another widely used, short-term comparative measurement of litter decay is the loss of weight from material enclosed in mesh bags. Often different mesh sizes are used to exclude animals, or different size groups of animals, so that losses can be partitioned into the component processes of decomposition: microbial catabolism, the leaching of water-soluble materials and comminution through the feeding activities of animals. However, the separation of these processes and the measurement of weight or chemical composition of the residual material introduces a number of artefacts which make the results difficult to relate to other site measurements. These include different moisture regimes in the enclosed material to ambient conditions, the mesh size may exclude key faunal groups, animal/microbial interactions in decomposition cycling processes are altered or eliminated and the fate of material lost from the bags cannot be followed. This last point is of particular importance since fragmented or faecal material may be subject to totally different biotic and abiotic conditions to the parent material. The significance of this effect is considered below.

VARIATION IN LITTER DECOMPOSITION RATES

Data for litterfalls and litter standing crops in lowland rain forests and a few seasonal forests are given in Table 1 together with calculations of k_L for each site. Studies from lower montane rain forests and temperate deciduous forests are also given for comparison. The distribution of the data in Fig. 1 supports the proposition of Olson (1963) that litter turnover in tropical forests takes less than a year (i.e. $k > 1$). However, it is also clear that there is a substantial range in the rate of decomposition of both leaves and other components of small litter. Total small litter, which includes around 30–40% of woody materials, has a slower turnover rate than leaf litter but the relative differences between sites are generally consistent for these two types of litter resources of rather different composition. However, the extent of variation in lowland tropical forest decomposition rates (k_L values from 1·1 to 3·3 for small litter) is such that a number of sites are within the range exhibited by temperate deciduous forests (k_L from 0·4 to 1·4). Data for small litter turnover in montane forests show a closer similarity to k_L values for temperate forests than tropical lowland forests. Thus, the assumption that decomposition rates in tropical rain forests are always higher than in temperate zones is not borne out.

Comparisons of weight loss rates from leaves in litter bags can only be made in general terms since supporting data on decay rate determinants, particularly fauna populations, are generally lacking. This last parameter is important since mesh size influences access to different size groups of animals and the abundance of certain groups will determine rates of comminution.

Litter bag studies reported in the literature have been carried out over different time periods ranging from a few months to more than a year. For comparative purposes loss rates may be expressed as per cent per year, or per cent per day, assuming a linear pattern of weight losses although this is an over-simplification of the time-course of decomposition (Swift, Heal & Anderson 1979).

The results for litter-bag studies (Table 2) show that while the highest rates of

TABLE 1. Litterfalls, litter standing crops and turnover coefficients (k_L) for a range of tropical forests and temperate deciduous forests. Values are for total small litter* except where leaves are specified

Study no.	Forest type and locality	Altitude (m)		Litterfall (t ha^{-1} year^{-1})	Litter standing crop (t ha^{-1})	Turnover coefficient (k_L) leaves	Turnover coefficient (k_L) small litter	Source
	Tropical lowland moist forests							
(1)	Malaya, Pasoh Dipterocarp forest	10		10·6	3·2		3·3	Ogawa (1978), Yoda (1978)
			leaves	6·3	1·7	3·6		
(2)	Ivory Coast	50–100	leaves					Bernhard (1970)
	Banco, plateau valley			8·1	2·5	3·3		
	valley			7·8	2·1	3·8		
	Yapo, plateau			6·6	2·4	2·8		
	valley			5·7	2·0	2·9		
(3)	Zaire	300		12·3	3·9		3·2	Laudelout & Meyer (1954)
(4)	Nigeria							Hopkins (1966)
	Evergreen forest		leaves	7·2	3·0	2·4		
	Seasonal forest		leaves	4·7	1·0 (wet season) 2·4 (dry season)	2·8		
(5)	Nigeria	250		5·6	1·7 (wet season) 2·5 (dry season)		2·2	Madge (1965)
(6)	Ghana, Kade	150	leaves	9·7	4·9		2·0	John (1973)
				7·4	3·0	2·5		
(7)	Columbia	30		8·5	5·0		1·7	Jenny, Gessel & Bingham (1949)
(8)	Trinidad: *Mora* forest							Cornforth (1970)
	Vallencia	40		6·8	4·2		1·6	
	Matura	200		7·0	3·9		1·8	
(9)	Nigeria: bush fallow three sites			7·0–9·7	6·9–11·7		0·6–1·3	Swift *et al.* (1981)
			leaves	4·6–6·6	3·8–4·9	0·9–1·7		
(10)	Sarawak, Mulu							Anderson, Proctor & Vallack (1983)
	Alluvial forest	50		9·4	5·5		1·7	
			leaves	6·6	3·8	1·8		
	Dipterocarp forest	225		7·7	5·9		1·3	
			leaves	5·4	3·2	1·7		

TABLE 1. (cont.)

Study no.	Forest type and locality	Altitude (m)		Litterfall (t ha^{-1} year^{-1})	Litter standing crop (t ha^{-1})	Turnover coefficient (k_L) leaves	small litter	Source
	Heath forest	170		8·1	6·1		1·3	Anderson, Proctor & Vallack (1983)
			leaves	5·6	3·9	1·4		
	Forest over limestone	300		10·4	7·1		1·5	
			leaves	7·3	4·2	1·7		
(11)	New Guinea	100		9·8	8·2		1·2	M. J. Swift (unpubl.)
			leaves	7·3	5·0	1·5		
(12)	Panama, Barro Colorado	150		13·3	11·2		1·2	I. N. Healey & M. J. Swift (unpub.)
			leaves	7·0	2·8	2·6		
(13)	Brazil, Manaus	45		7·6	7·2		1·1	Klinge (1973)
			leaves	6·1	4·0	1·5		
(14)	Malaya, Penang Dipterocarp forest			7·5	7·7		1·0	Gong & Ong (1983)
			leaves	5·4	5·1	1·1		
	Tropical montane rain forests							
(15)	Colombia	1630		10·1	16·5		0·6	Jenny, Gessel & Bingham (1949)
(16)	Puerto Rica	460	leaves	4·8	5·1	0·9		Wiegert (1970)
(17)	Jamaica	1550	leaves	4·9–5·5	8·1–11·7	0·5–0·7		Tanner (1981)
(18)	New Guinea	2450		6·8–7·6	6·1–7·7		1·0–1·4	Edwards (1977)
	Temperate deciduous forests							
(19)	Holland			3·1	3·6		0·9	Witkamp & van der Drift (1961)
(20)	Belgium, Virelles			5·6, 5·3	5·6, 4·8		1·0, 1·1	Duvigneaud & Denaeyer De Smet (1970)
(21)	U.K., Meathop			5·4	7·1		0·8	J. Satchell in Swift et al. (1979)
			leaves	3·2	2·0	1·6		
(22)	U.S.A., Florida			10·7	8·2		1·3	Lugo, Gamble & Ewel (1978)
(23)	New Jersey			6·2	7·6		0·8	Lang & Forman (1978)
(24)	Missouri			3·5	6·1		0·6	Rochow (1975)
(25)	Tennessee: three sites			4·0–4·5	8·4–10·5		0·4–0·5	Harris, Goldstein & Henderson (1973)
(26)	Minnesota			4·6	12·6		0·4	Reiners & Reiners (1970)

* Leaves, fruit, twigs and small branches (generally less than 2·5–5 cm diameter but unspecified in many studies).

weight losses (more than 200% year^{-1}) are greater than the fastest rates in temperate forests (less than 200% year^{-1}) there is considerable overlap between litter decomposition rates for the slowest tropical species and the fastest temperate species. Furthermore, although the rates of litter disappearance from coarse-mesh bags are generally higher than from fine-mesh bags this is not a particularly dominant feature of these results, suggesting that the impact of the macrofauna may not be as great as has previously been postulated (Swift *et al.* 1979).

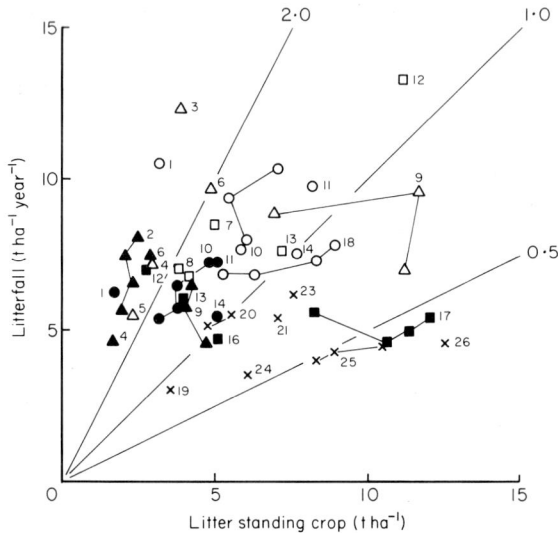

FIG. 1. Relationships between litterfall and litter standing crops in tropical rain forests of Africa ($\triangle$), S.E. Asia and New Guinea ($\bigcirc$), and the Neotropics ($\square$). Total small litter is shown as open symbols and leaf litter as solid symbols. Data for small litter in temperate deciduous forests ($\times$) are shown for comparison. The numbers beside the symbols refer to the data sets in Table 1. Lines have been drawn delimiting portions of the figure with litterfall/standing crop (k_L) quotients ranging from less than 0.5 to greater than 2.0. Studies carried out within a locality during a comparative programme of research are linked by lines.

The overall conclusion from this analysis of such limited data is that it is probably more important to seek the causes of variation in decomposition rates within the tropical forest biome than to seek for major differences between tropical and temperate forests.

DETERMINANTS OF LITTER DECAY RATES

Swift *et al.* (1979) suggested that decomposition processes are regulated by three groups of variables: the nature of the decomposer community (the animals and the micro-organisms, O), the characteristics of the organic matter which determine its degradability (resource quality, Q) and the physicochemical environment (P) which operates at macroclimatic and edaphic or micro scales. The decomposition rates of all materials are governed by these variables though their relative importance can vary from site to site and resource to resource (leaves, wood, fruits, etc.). These variables interact but may be considered to have a hierarchial structure in the way that they influence one another in the decreasing rank order: macroclimate > microclimate > resource quality > organisms. Supporting information on these parameters is not

TABLE 2. Percentage weight losses from leaves in litter-bag studies carried out in tropical and temperate deciduous forests. Studies were carried out over widely differing periods of time and therefore results are expressed as % year^{-1} for comparative purposes; thus, weight losses from rapidly decomposing leaves may exceed 100% over 1 year

Site	Coarse mesh*	Medium and fine mesh†
Tropical lowland rain forests		
Nigeria (Madge 1965)	219–548	
(Swift *et al.* 1981) bush fallow	244–352	174
Ivory Coast (Bernhard-Reversat 1972)		153–212
Panama (Healey & Swift, unpubl.)	150–352	120–183
Sarawak (Anderson *et al.* 1983)	52–61	53–65
Amazon (Irmler & Furch 1980)	35–80	
Tropical montane rain forests		
New Guinea 2500 m (Edwards 1977)	26–95	
Jamaica 1400 m (Tanner 1981)		26–95
Temperate deciduous forests		
Belgium (Mommaerts-Billiet 1971)	20–200	
United Kingdom (Bocock & Gilbert 1957)	34–186	
(Bocock *et al.* 1960)	37–96	
(Anderson 1973b)	26–58 (7 mm)	27–50
Canada, Quebec (Maldague 1967)	66–77	
Hungary (Toth, Papp & Lenkey 1975)		36–68
U.S.A., New Hampshire (Gosz, Likens & Bormann 1973)		32–58 (3 mm)
Tennessee (Shanks & Olson 1961)		25–75
New York (Woodwell & Marples 1968)		59
Virginia (Orndoff & Lang 1981)		31–43
New Brunswick (Strojan 1978)		37–39
Minnesota (McBreyer & Cromack 1980)		29 (3 mm)

* 10 mm or greater, unless stated.
† 2 mm or less, unless stated.

available for the majority of decomposition studies in temperate regions, let alone the tropics, and therefore we consider examples where a single factor appears to predominate in order to demonstrate its effects. In each section we attempt to explain how these factors may relate to the variations in decomposition rates demonstrated in the previous section.

Organisms

The decomposition of plant litter is brought about by a complex community of fungi, bacteria and invertebrate animals. The interactions within and between these groups

Tropical decomposition processes

make the detailed processes of decomposition extremely difficult to investigate. At a gross level, however, the disappearance of intact litter from the forest floor is mainly a function of the nature and intensity of animal feeding activities; though this litter comminution is only a component process of decomposition (which also includes catabolism and leaching) and therefore cannot be equated with total litter decomposition (Swift *et al.* (1979). The macrofauna and some elements of the mesofauna (particularly termites) show some discrete patterns of distribution which can be related to rates of litter disappearance from the forest floor (Table 3) but for most of the

TABLE 3. Population densities (no. m^{-2}) of saprotrophic macrofauna in rain forest sites, illustrating possible regional and local differences in the contribution of animals to litter comminution. Data are presented for four sites in Mulu National Park for comparison with the results of litter-bag studies given in Table 5. For details see text

| | Sarawak (Mulu)* | | | | | |
	Alluvial forest	Dipterocarp forest	Heath forest	Forest over limestone	Nigeria (Ibadan)†	Brazil (Manaus)‡
Annelida						
'earthworms'	42	26	24	6	34	n.d.
Mollusca						
Pulmonata	<1	<1	0	6	n.d.	n.d.
Crustacea						
Isopoda	26	17	20	40	415	27
Decapoda	<1	0	0	0	—	—
Myriapoda						
Diplopoda	17	3	21	71	1210	20
Insecta						
Blattodea	9	8	10	8	n.d.	8
Orthoptera	6	4	8	17	n.d.	<1
Coleoptera	46	63	35	15	260	279
Isoptera	254	1148	1408	50	30	1087
Total						
excluding Isoptera	148	122	118	163	1919	335

Source: * Anderson *et al.* (1983);
† Madge (1965);
‡ Fittkau & Klinge (1973).

mesofauna, and most notably the microfauna (protozoa and nematodes), no such patterns have been shown. General considerations lead to the conclusion that, although varying in species composition, a microflora (fungi and bacteria) of comparable 'functional capacity' is probably resident at all sites and would not be a factor contributing to variation in litter decay rates. Thus, it is variation in the fauna and in P and Q acting on the microflora which determines variation in decay rates.

In temperate deciduous forests the role of earthworms in surface litter comminution, mainly associated with *Lumbricus terrestris* L., and pedogenesis is very variable and tends to be over-emphasized. There also appears to be an a priori expectation by temperate ecologists that tropical earthworms have equivalent roles in litter comminution, but there is little evidence that this is so. Firstly, none of the tropical earthworm families are known to contain species which draw leaves down into the soil, as is a feature of temperate mull forest soils, and secondly the biomass of tropical earthworms is generally smaller than in temperate forests though their activity may be higher. The relatively low density and biomass of earthworms at Mulu (Sarawak) is similar to the populations ($0–44$ m^{-2}) and biomass ($0–0\cdot2$ g m^{-2}) at Pasoh (Abe & Matsumoto 1979). These results may be compared to 250 m^{-2} ($4\cdot5$ g m^{-2}) in a Nigerian forest (Madge 1965), $4\cdot4$ g m^{-2} in bush fallow and $2\cdot5$ g m^{-2} in cultivated Nigerian soil (Cook et al. 1980), $7–102$ m^{-2} ($0\cdot2–3\cdot6$ g m^{-2}) in natural and cultivated soils in Uganda (Block & Banage 1968), and $100–400$ m^{-2} ($3–6$ g m^{-2}) in humid Ivory Coast savanna (Lavelle 1975). Temperate deciduous forest on high base status soils frequently exceed 100 g m^{-2} biomass of earthworms but this is reduced to less than 10 g m^{-2} in acid forest soils (Edwards & Lofty 1977). The high surface casting rates of tropical earthworms (Madge (1965) records over 36 t ha^{-1} year^{-1}) may result in the burial of litter and a change in the environment in which decomposition takes place. There is, however, no current evidence of a central role for earthworms in surface litter decomposition in tropical rain forests although casts are known to be higher in carbon and mineral nutrients (Cook et al. 1980) than parent material. It is therefore probable that they are indirectly involved in enhancing microbial activity and nutrient fluxes.

The soil macrofauna of Mulu (Collins, Anderson & Vallack 1983) and Manaus (Fittkau & Klinge 1973) are similar in the low abundance and biomass of litter-feeding groups and again contrast markedly with temperate deciduous forests. The termite populations, however, are high in these two forests compared with other fauna but these figures mask the trophic roles of the groups involved. A major proportion of the Mulu populations are humus-feeding termites, which may have key roles in determining levels of available phosphorus in soils (Anderson & Wood, 1983), but do not attack intact litter resources. The litter-feeding Macrotermitinae are poorly represented in Mulu and are absent from the Neotropics. However, the abundance of Macrotermitinae is a notable difference between the Mulu and Pasoh forests.

Total termite populations at Pasoh were estimated at $3000–4000$ m^{-2} ($2\cdot2–2\cdot6$ g m^{-2}) of which 60% were wood feeders, 25% soil feeders and 15% litter feeders. Wood and litter feeding *Macrotermes* species made up over 70% of the biomass and 32% of the daily litterfall was consumed by *Macrotermes carbonarius* (Matsumoto & Abe 1979). Lower litter standing crops were recorded in the vicinity of *M. carbonarius* mounds than elsewhere on the forest floor. The seasonal forests of Africa also have comparatively high populations of Macrotermitinae, while the evergreen forests contain more humus-feeders. Nye (1961) in Ghana and Hopkins (1966) in Nigeria both attributed a major role to termites in the disappearance of litter from the forest floor but neither the groups involved nor population densities were determined in these studies. The distribution and abundance of the Macrotermitinae thus appears to be an important determinant of decomposition pathways, particularly for wood. Collins (1981) describes an extreme situation where almost all the dead wood in Nigerian Guinea savanna was removed by these termites and little microbial decomposition took place *in situ*.

The low abundance of litter-feeding macrofauna in the Mulu sites has been noted and weight losses showed no relationship to fauna populations: the highest litter weight loss rates from coarse-mesh bags were recorded in the heath forest, which has the lowest macrofauna populations, while the comparatively large populations of millipedes, woodlice and snails in the forest on limestone are not reflected by litter comminution rates. In fact, higher weight losses were recorded from fine-mesh than coarse-mesh bags on this site, possibily as a consequence of moister microclimatic conditions. It is probable that the absence of a general correlation between macrofaunal distribution and decomposition rates is due to the highly opportunistic and flexible nature of the decomposer food web. Whilst a particular group of animals, such as termites, may strongly and predominantly influence the pattern of decomposition processes, in their absence other groups of organisms, including the microflora, may show 'compensatory activity' so that the overall pattern of decomposition processes is not markedly affected. Consequently the current predictive value of faunal studies in relation to decomposition rates appears to be very low. This is emphasized by the paradox that rain forests generally appear to have lower soil fauna populations and biomass than temperate deciduous forests although tropical forest litterfalls, and nutrient inputs to the decomposer system, are several times higher than those of temperate forests.

Resource quality

The plant litter input to the decomposer community may be regarded as presenting a diverse range of resources of varying 'decomposability'. The resistance of a particular resource to decay may be related to one or more of a variety of intrinsic factors ('hardness', lignin content, nutrient content, plant secondary compounds, mass and particle size) which are embraced by the term resource quality (Swift *et al.* 1979). Thus, leaves in general are of higher resource quality and are decomposed more quickly than twigs and other woody materials. The components of resource quality act by regulating the activity of decomposer organisms and, as with environmental factors, variations in Q interact from site to site with variations in the organisms. For instance, wood which is a relatively intractable resource in one site may decay rapidly in another because of termite activities.

Resource quality therefore loosely accounts for variations in decomposition rate between different resources within the same or adjacent sites. For instance, I. N. Healey & M. J. Swift (unpubl. data) showed that for different leaf species in the forest at Barro Colorado Island, Panama, decomposition rates ranged between 150% and 352% year^{-1} from coarse-mesh litter bags and 120% to 183% year^{-1} from fine-mesh bags in the same site.

Resource quality attributes of mixed (freshly fallen) leaf litters in the four Mulu forests are shown in Table 4. Nitrogen, phosphorus, potassium and calcium show a general pattern of decreasing concentrations in the order: forest on limestone (LF) > alluvial forest (AF) > dipterocarp forest (DF) > heath forest (HF); though leaves from the limestone site have lower concentrations of potassium relative to the site rank order for other nutrients. Lignin and polyphenol concentrations show the opposite

TABLE 4. Leaf litter resource quality and disappearance rates of surface litter in four rain forest sites in Mulu National Park, Sarawak. Litter decomposition was estimated from weight losses of leaves in coarse- and fine-mesh litter bags and the turnover coefficient k_L was derived from litterfall/standing crop quotients. Soil organic matter standing crops (SOM) in the four sites are also shown. Data from Anderson, Proctor & Vallack (1983)

Site	Mineral elements (%)				Lignin (% dry wt)	Polyphenols (% tannin eq)	Litter bag wt loss at 1 year (%)		Turnover coefficient (k_L)		SOM* (t ha^{-1})
	N	P	K	Ca			Fine	Coarse	leaves	total	
Lowland evergreen forest											
valley (alluvial)	0·8	0·03	0·4	2·0	31·1	1·7	52·8	60·4	1·8	1·7	230
ridge (dipterocarp)	0·8	0·01	0·4	0·4	37·9	1·9	48·9	55·5	1·7	1·3	198
Heath forest (kerangas)	0·4	0·01	0·1	0·5	39·6	2·3	59·1	61·3	1·4	1·2	318
Forest over limestone	1·1	0·04	0·1	3·5	39·3	1·5	65·2	52·0	1·7	1·5	164

* 0–30 cm in AF, DF and HF; 0–11 cm in LF.

rank order to mineral nutrients for the three main sites, in common with resource quality attributes of most temperate forest litters, and the heath forest litter therefore has the lowest overall Q for saprotrophs. The leaves from the forest on limestone, however, have a high Q in all respects except the lignin concentrations which are similar to the heath forest. This unusual combination of high nutrient and high lignin concentrations makes it difficult to assess, a priori, the initial resource quality attributes of the limestone forest litter and emphasizes the need for basic research in this field.

In most respects the chemical composition of temperate and tropical forest leaves are very similar except for the high lignin concentrations recorded for the Mulu leaves (Anderson *et al.* 1983). There are few comparable data for tropical leaf litter but Singh (1969) reported lignin concentrations of 20–30% in a number of tree species from deciduous forests in India. High lignin concentrations may be a characteristic feature of long-lived leaves and, if so, it is likely that there are basic differences in litter resource quality between seasonal and evergreen forests.

There is no correlation between litter bag weight losses and resource quality for the four Mulu forest sites; in particular, the highest weight losses were recorded for the heath forest leaves which have the lowest Q. There is better agreement between Q and leaf litter k-values (which effectively integrate decay rates to the depth of the litter layer) but, while the highest soil organic matter standing crops occur in the heath forest, there is no correlation between Q and soil organic matter in the other sites.

Comprehensive data are available for mineral nutrient concentrations in tropical rain forest litter, particularly in leaves, but not for other resource quality attributes in the majority of decomposition studies. Reviews by Brasell, Unwin & Stocker (1980) and Proctor (1983) show that leaf litter nutrient concentrations range from 0·6 to 1·8% N, 0·02 to 0·44% P, 0·04 to 0·91% K, 0·2 to 3·0% Ca and 0·13 to 0·48% Mg. The leaf litters from Manaus, Mulu and Pasoh are towards the lower end of this range. In particular, the phosphorus concentrations in the Mulu leaf litters (0·01–0·04%) include much lower values than those at Manaus (0·03%) which were considered to be exceptionally low by Klinge & Rodrigues (1968a). The African forest litters appear to have higher nutrient concentrations, e.g. leaf litter from Kade, Ghana (Nye 1961) contained 1·9% N, 0·09% P and 1·0% K and showed higher rates of litter turnover than Mulu and Manaus. If percentage nitrogen is taken as an indication of litter resource quality there is a weak but significant overall correlation ($r = 0·49$, $P = 0·02$) between litter k-values and nitrogen concentrations in lowland forest litters from the main geographic regions (Africa: Laudelout & Meyer 1954; Nye 1961; Bernhard 1970. S.E. Asia: Proctor *et al.* 1983; Lim 1978. Neotropics: Klinge & Rodrigues 1968a; Cornforth 1970). Insufficient data are available for a more detailed analysis of relationships between Q and decomposition at this scale.

Climatic factors

The regulatory roles of physical environmental factors (mainly temperature and moisture) can be considered at climatic, edaphic (soil) or micro scales. In the latter case the major effects are to induce local variations in the activities of decomposer organisms. This will not therefore greatly influence the major between-site differences show in Fig. 1 but may account for some of the within-site or locality variation. It is therefore to the macro-scale, that of climate, that we address our discussion.

Meentemeyer (1978) has derived a function relating litter decomposition in temperate and tropical forests to actual evaporation (AE) and predicts that at an AE greater than 1500 mm year^{-1} annual litter decay rates will be five times annual litter input to the forest floor. However, his data for the tropics are based on West African studies with particularly high litter decay rates and the function overestimates decay rates in most other tropical rain forests, other than Pasoh, by a factor of at least 2 or 3. In addition, Meentemeyer's values for AE, calculated by the Thornthwaite method, are closer to potential evapotranspiration (PE) or annual precipitation for the African sites than the values given by the M. I. Budyko complex equation in the UNESCO (1977) world maps of global water balances. We have attempted to relate litter k_L-values for rain forests to AE, PE and annual precipitation given in UNESCO (1977) but obtained no meaningful relationships let alone statistically significant correlations.

The particular problem with this approach is illustrated by the data for Manaus, Mulu, Penang and Pasoh (Table 1). Manaus and Mulu have similar k_L-values for leaves and small litter which are less than half those for Pasoh. However, Manaus and Pasoh have similar mildly seasonal climates with the mean annual rainfall around 2000 mm, while Mulu shows comparatively little seasonality with a mean annual rainfall exceeding 5000 mm. Finally, Penang has a similar climate to Pasoh but k_L-values which are less than a third of those for the other site. Clearly, at this scale, decomposition rates are not simply related to gross climatic variables and other factors are contributing to between-site variation.

However, the temporal effects of macroclimate on decomposition processes within forest sites are well documented for markedly seasonal forests where litter may accumulate during the dry season and decay rapidly during the wet season (Fig. 2). Some seasonality of litterfall and decomposition is a feature of most tropical forests but more information is needed about the balance of these processes at different times of the year. In many tropical forests peak litterfall occurs during the dry season but in Mulu maximum small litterfalls were associated with months of maximum rainfall (Proctor *et al.* 1983). The relationship between the onset of rain and the accumulation and decomposition of litter is a sensitive mechanism linking climate and the availability of plant nutrients. In Nigeria, Swift, Russel-Smith & Perfect (1981) found that during the dry season substantial amounts of P, N and other nutrients accumulated on the forest floor in the undecomposed leaf litter. Within 4 weeks of the onset of the rains all the accumulated P and half of the N was released through decomposition of the litter. By contrast, in the Mulu forests, these nutrients were immobilized in leaf litter and in most sites showed small losses of initial concentrations from litter bags after a year in the field (Anderson, Proctor & Vallack 1983). Wetting and drying events, both seasonal and temporal, are known to be important processes for carbon and nutrient mineralization (Swift *et al.* 1979). The flushing of savanna soils

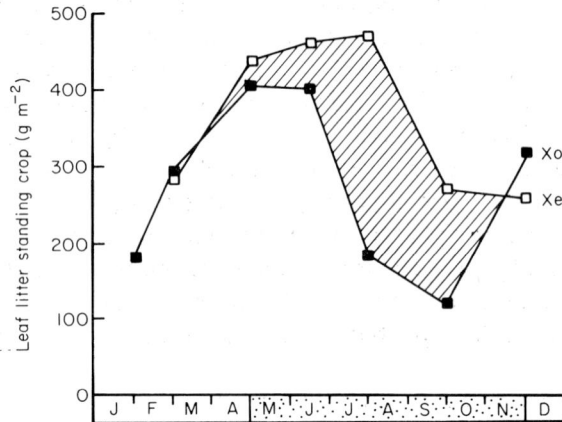

FIG. 2. The relationship of decomposition to climate. The observed change in standing crop of the leaf litter in the Panamanian forest during the year (Xo) is shown together with the theoretical line for the standing crop (Xe) if there was no decomposition, i.e. by addition of the monthly observed leaf litterfall to the initial standing crop for the month. The shaded area thus shows the estimated amount of leaf litter decomposed during each period between observations. Months with rainfall greater than 100 mm are shown stippled.
Healey & Swift (unpubl.) in Swift *et al.* (1979).

was demonstrated several decades ago by Birch & Friend (1956), but we know of no detailed studies in rain forests.

PATTERNS AND PROCESSES OF DECOMPOSITION IN RAIN FORESTS

In general terms there is some evidence of regionality in litter turnover coefficients (k_L), with values greater than 2 for most African forests and between 1 and 2 for forests in S.E. Asia and the Neotropics, and the results of litter bag studies generally support this pattern. Both resource quality and particular groups of soil fauna appear to be contributory factors but gross climatic characteristics of the regions do not show the expected operation as the primary variable. Given the observed effects of seasonal climates on decomposition it is likely that an insufficiently sensitive expression of climate as a regulatory variable has been used, particularly in view of possible interactions with the variables of O and Q. We hypothesize that these interactive effects will include:

(i) climatic determination of qualitative and quantitative characteristics of the decomposer fauna community;

(ii) effects of seasonality on mineral and lignin concentrations in litter standing crop through variations in the timing of leaf-fall and the longevity of leaves;

(iii) variations in the resource quality, quantity and location of root inputs under different climatic regimes;

(iv) wetting and drying effects on carbon and nutrient mobilization and mineralization, particularly at the interchange between wet and dry seasons.

Meentemeyer (1978) has formulated a potentially useful approach to the interaction of these variables in a model linking decay rates to AE and lignin concentrations. His equation appears to have a good predictive value for temperate deciduous forests and for gradients in litter decomposition rates within the U.S.A., but underestimates leaf litter decomposition rates in Mulu by at least a factor of 2. We conclude that insufficient information is available at the present time to formulate realistic global models of decomposition. In particular, information is lacking on edaphic factors since both the litter bag studies and the litter turnover coefficients k_L bias interpretation of litter decomposition in tropical forests towards processes operating in the surface litter layers when the soil environment may be totally different at depth. Furthermore, the contribution of roots to soil organic matter must be taken into account.

A postulated effect of varying decomposition rates, implicit in the quotation from Sanchez (1976) cited above, is that there will be accompanying variations in the accumulation of soil organic matter. Thus, we may expect that if there is a high variation in decomposition rate then there will be reciprocal variations in the soil organic matter standing crops.

This relationship is explored in Fig. 3 where surface litter and soil organic matter standing crops have been plotted for forests located from the Equator to near the Arctic Circle. Surface litter standing crops show a wide range of values in most regions but there is evidence of a gradient in litter decomposition rates when it is considered that mean annual litter production varies from about $9\cdot3$ t ha^{-1} to $3\cdot3$ t ha^{-1} over the same latitudes (O'Neill & De Angelis 1981). Soil organic matter standing crops,

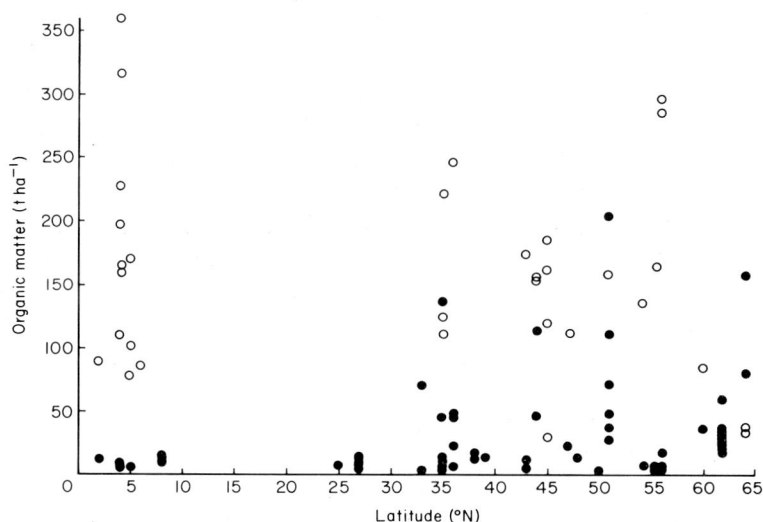

FIG. 3. Surface litter (●) and soil organic matter standing crops (○) in lowland forests ranging from equatorial regions to near the Arctic Circle. For comparative purposes tropical rain forest sites within 10° south of the Equator have been plotted at the same number of degrees north. Data from De Angelis, Gardner & Shugart (1981) and Proctor et al. (1983).

however, show no evidence of such a gradient and a wider range of values is shown for tropical rain forests than between tropical rain forests and the forests of temperate and boreal regions. Waterlogging can lead to the development of organic soils in the tropics (Mohr & van Baren 1954), particularly in montane forest (Whitmore & Burnham 1969; Grubb 1977; Tanner 1981), and the extensive lowland peat forests of west Malaysia are an extreme example of this phenomenon (Whitmore 1975). Other contributory factors to soil organic matter accumulation in tropical regions are the toxicity of aluminium ions to micro-organisms in acid soils and the complexing of humus materials with clays, particularly in volcanic soils containing allophane (Sanchez 1976). Edwards & Grubb (1977) noted high organic matter contents to considerable depths in the profiles of montane forest soils in New Guinea and suggested that stabilization by clay mineral complexing may be responsible.

The high organic matter contents of the four Mulu sites cannot be explained from available data, though Anderson *et al* (1983) suggest that waterlogging is a major factor in the heath forest podsol, and this serves to illustrate the necessity of integrated measurements of O, P and Q at different levels in the soil and litter profile in such studies. Interpretation of differences in the rates of nutrient fluxes through organic and mineral soil types, particularly in relation to the effects of disturbances, clearly depend upon a knowledge of the processes governing the accumulation of soil organic matter. Furthermore, decomposition studies are rarely carried out for sufficient periods of time for the effects of intractable fractions of the resources to be expressed. The experiments of Jenkinson & Ayanaba (1977) on litter decomposition rates in a cultivated Nigerian soil, using ^{14}C-labelled grass, are a good illustration of this effect. Decay rates showed a good fit to a double exponential model in which about 70% of the litter material decomposes with a half-life of 0·25 years and the remainder with a half-life of 8 years. In order to balance soil organic matter content, around 1% in the top 15 cm, with inputs it was necessary to postulate the existence of intractable fractions with a vastly greater half-life than those dominating losses over 2 years. In sites where comminution is a major component of weight losses on the soil surface the decomposition rate of faeces and litter fragments which settle into the humus layers may manifest this slow component of the decomposition time series and not the rapidly disintegrating experimental material in the litter layers.

EFFECTS OF DISTURBANCE ON DECOMPOSITION AND MINERAL CYCLING

The effects of disturbance on forest soil processes are manifested in changes in the regulatory variables operating at different scales ranging from very local events, such as tree-falls, the meso-scale of windthrow or patch cultivation to the large scale perturbation of clear felling for timber or modern agriculture.

Tree-falls

Tree falls are recognized as important local events for maintaining the mosaic structure of forest tree species but the regrowth of seedlings in these gaps has been often interpreted in terms of the direct effects of changed light and moisture regimes. There are, however, also important indirect effects of the altered environment on plant growth through changes in decomposition and mineralization rates (Whitmore 1975). The opening of the canopy involves soil temperature changes as well as changes in the distribution and composition of precipitation compared with throughfall. Tree-falls also involve a large pulsed input of green leaves with high nutrient content and rapid decay potential. The effects of nutrients released under this combination of events can be related to the demonstration by Janos (1983), that the differential growth of seedlings is affected by the nature of mycorrhiza infections, to provide a testable hypothesis for a mechanism of forest tree replacement in gaps.

A tree-fall also deposits on the forest floor a massive bulk of nutrient-poor, highly lignified material in the form of stem and branch debris. The stumps and major roots of the tree also form a localized centre of low quality resources. The rate of decomposition of these materials may be very slow and, although Lang & Knight (1979) have claimed that tree boles may disappear within 10 years, the implication from studies of large woody litter turnover rates is that wood above about 3 cm diameter takes at least 15 years to decompose in tropical forests. Particular hardwood species may take much longer to decompose.

The significance of this is broad. The wood provides a source of energy for a wide range of micro-organisms and animals which may influence the general biology of the forest, and a physical habitat for many more. The resource is initially nutrient-poor but studies in temperate forests have shown that as decomposition proceeds it may become enriched by uptake of nutrients from ground and rainwater, and by import in colonizing animals (Swift, 1977; Ausmus 1977; Janzen 1976; Heal, Swift & Anderson 1982). Consequently, there may be a period in which the soil surrounding the fallen tree or stump becomes starved of nutrients as a result of immobilization by the wood decomposer community. Ultimately this package of nutrients will be released to enrich the surroundings. It is thus interesting to speculate whether the growth of seedlings and saplings within a tree gap is regulated by the nutrient uptake and release pattern of wood deposited in the area.

Cultivation

Clearance of forest and the preparation of land for cultivation involves more extreme environmental modifications. A study of field and fallow cultivation in Nigeria (Swift *et al.* 1981) showed that the temperature range at the surface of the soil was 18 °C in cultivated plots, compared with a diurnal variation of 3 °C within fallow forest plots, and the surface soil had a greater tendency to desiccate. The process of ploughing or hoeing alters the soil structure and the burial of litter results in extreme modifications of the material, physicochemical environment and the biota involved in decay. These changes result in an enhancement of litter decomposition in cleared areas of forest (Cunningham 1963; Swift *et al.* 1981) and accelerated nutrient release. However, Jenkinson & Ayanaba (1977) were unable to detect differences in carbon mineralization rates from ^{14}C-labelled rye grass (*Lolium multiflorum* Lam. cv Westerwolth) between open-field and forest-shade sites at I.I.T.A. in Nigeria. It is difficult to interpret the results of these experiments because soil temperatures were not measured in the sites and moisture conditions in the incubation tubes were also not determined. However, the overall decay rates in Nigeria, at mean annual soil temperatures of approximately 26 °C, were four times higher than in agricultural plots at Rothamsted (U.K.) at 9·2 °C.

Information on the effects of agriculture on soil organisms is generally lacking but the importance of such studies for tropical systems is shown by the Nigerian project of Perfect, Cook & Swift (1980). The conversion of fallow rain forest to cow-pea (*Vigna unguiculata* L.) cultivation resulted initially in a dramatic decline in the abundance and diversity of all soil animal groups. After 2 years the numbers recovered but the community was considerably altered and with lower diversity. Similarly, whilst earthworm casting activity returned to levels comparable to those of the fallow, the dominant species was different. Maize was cultivated with and without DDT as an additional agricultural treatment before the plots were allowed to return to bush fallow. Crop production was lower in the pesticide treated plots and although soil nutrients were depleted by continuous cultivation there were no differences in the depletion from plots with higher yields. It was suggested that the more rapid decline in the fertility of the plots with a history of DDT treatment may be associated with pesticide effects on the soil biota (Perfect *et al.* 1979).

Termites are profoundly affected by forest clearance and cultivation. In Sarawak, Collins (1983) showed that in cleared forest there were six species compared with twenty-five in virgin forest and that the Macrotermitinae were less affected than other groups. In Nigeria four out of the original twenty-four species surviving after 14 years of cultivation were *Microtermes* (Macrotermitinae) which increased to over five times those in bush sites; most of the species lost were soil-feeding termites (Wood, Johnson & Ohiagu 1977). The role of soil-feeders in forest soils is unknown but their potential involvement in nutrient fluxes is indicated by the increased exchangeable cations and other nutrients after passage of soil through the termite gut. Concentrations of available phosphorus in mounds, constructed from faecal material, were up to seventy times those of the surrounding soil in a Nigerian forest (Anderson & Wood 1983).

One of the greatest changes in cleared and cultivated forest systems is in the qualitative and quantitative characteristics of litter inputs and has been recognized for some time as one potential feature leading to loss of soil fertility under cultivation (Nye & Greenland 1960). Factors other than the quantity of litter may profoundly affect the efficiency of nutrient return to the plant; but these are less well understood. In particular, the decrease in heterogeneity of litter constituents and the loss of synchrony between decomposition and plant growth should be emphasized since these factors can be manipulated by agricultural management.

The litter input from most arable crops lacks the lower resource quality components (woody resources in particular) that tend to stabilize nutrient cycling in forest ecosystems. The overall quality of agricultural litter may also be higher than the equivalent from natural ecosystems, because premature cutting of the crop may be carried out before nutrient withdrawal occurs. Thus, the major part of the litter will decompose in a relatively short time with very little 'buffering' from slow release components. This tendency for nutrient release to be confined to a relatively short period of time is enhanced by the altered environmental conditions discussed earlier.

The timing of litter input to the decomposers in agricultural systems is commonly dictated by management practices, particularly the cutting and ploughing-in of standing trash. The initiation of decomposition will commonly occur before seed planting and it is possible to predict that maximum nutrient release may occur *before* the crop is sufficiently established to benefit from the availability of nutrients (Fig. 4).

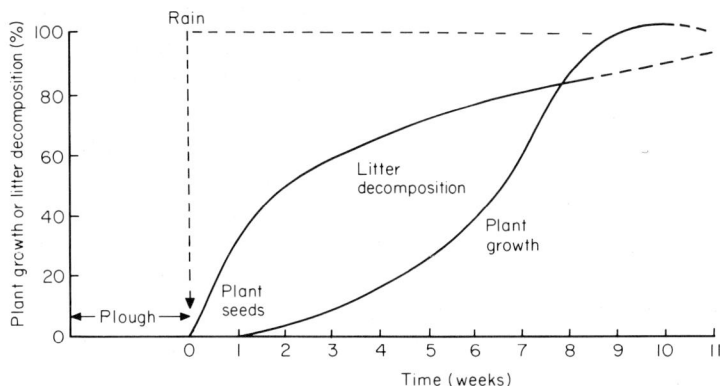

FIG. 4. The lack of integration between nutrient release from decomposing litter and nutrient demand by the plant in a tropical crop ecosystem. The curves for litter decomposition and plant growth are given as closest approximations to the availability of nutrients from decomposition and the demand of nutrients for growth respectively. After Swift (1982).

Under leaching conditions this could result in the loss from the system of a significant component of the nutrient return. This lack of integration between the release of nutrients by decomposition and their uptake by annual crops contrasts strongly with the 'tight cycling' described for forest ecosystems. It may well be one of the major features leading to nutrient loss and it is one that could be avoided by the correct timing of litter inputs, e.g. by mulching practices. More research is urgently needed in this area.

CONCLUSIONS

Decomposition processes can be investigated at many different scales of space, time and resources but at all levels the variables, O, P and Q, as defined, can be identified. The interaction of these variables in a mosaic of micro-sites determine the gross characteristics of decomposition for a particular forest site but a particular factor may locally dominate surface litter decay rates or soil organic matter accumulation. Thus, resource quality or the characteristics of the litter-feeding macrofauna can result in higher decay rates in temperate forests than tropical rain forests, or vice versa, which conflict with the general assumptions about latitudinal gradients of decomposition rates.

Changes in the decay rate determinants, through tree-falls, or shifting cultivation or large-scale perturbations to the forest disrupt the integration between the plant and decomposition subsystems. At the small scale these disturbances are accommodated by ecosystem homeostatic processes, though there are implications for seedling regrowth in tree gaps, but the disruption of natural processes on larger scales requires urgent study. On one hand information is needed for soil conservation and forest management and on the other the decline in soil nutrient status and productivity one or two seasons after forest clearance is a feature of low intensity tropical agricultural systems. Temperate agriculture has bypassed the problem by using fertilizers or mixed farming. Alternative solutions are required for areas of the tropics employing planned manipulation of decomposition and nutrient release such as mulching, mixed cropping and other litter resource management techniques and these are being actively investigated in a number of research centres. The most urgent requirement is long-term studies into the effects of disturbance on soil biological processes in natural systems as a baseline for management.

ACKNOWLEDGMENTS

We are grateful to Drs Ian Bailie and Tim Whitmore for helpful discussion and comments on the manuscript.

REFERENCES

Abe, T. & Matsumoto, T. (1979). Studies on the distribution and ecological role of termites in lowland rainforest of West Malaysia. 3. Distribution and abundance of termites in Pasoh Forest Reserve. *Japanese Journal of Ecology*, **29**, 337–351.

Anderson, J.M. (1973a). Carbon dioxide evolution from two temperate deciduous woodland soils. *Journal of Applied Ecology*, **10**, 361–378.

Anderson, J.M. (1973b). The breakdown and decomposition of sweet chestnut (*Castanea sativa* Mill.) and beech (*Fagus sylvatica* L.) leaf litter in two deciduous woodland soils. I. Breakdown, leaching and decomposition. *Oecologia*, **12**, 251–274.

Anderson, J.M., Proctor, J. & Vallack, H.W. (1983). Ecological studies in four contrasting areas of lowland rain forests in Gunung Mulu National Park. III. Decomposition processes and nutrient losses from leaf litter. *Journal of Ecology*, **71**, 503–528.

Anderson, J.M. & Wood, T.G. (1983). Mound composition and soil modification by soil-feeding termite species (Termitinae, Termitidae) in a Nigerian riparian forest. *Pedobiologia* (in press).

Ausmus, B. (1977). Regulation of wood decomposition rates by arthropod and annelid populations. *Soil Organisms as Components of Ecosystems* (Ed. by U. Lohm & T. Persson), pp. 180–192. Ecological Bulletins (Stockholm) 25. Swedish Natural Science Research Council, Stockholm.

Bernhard, F. (1970). Étude de la litière et de sa contribution au cycle des éléments mineraux en forêt ombrophile de Côte d'Ivoire. *Oecologia Plantarum*, **5**, 247–266.

Bernhard-Reversat, F. (1972). Decomposition de la litière de feuilles en forêt ombrophile de basse Côte d'Ivoire. *Oecologia Plantarum*, **7**, 279–300.

Birch, H.F. & Friend, M.T. (1956). Humus decomposition in East African soils. *Nature*, **178**, 500–501.

Block, W. & Banage, W.B. (1968). Population density and biomass of earthworms in some Uganda soils. *Revue d'Ecologie et Biologie du Sol*, **5**, 515–521.

Bocock, K.L. & Gilbert, O.J.W. (1957). The disappearance of leaf litter under different woodland conditions. *Plant and Soil*, **2**, 179–185.

Bocock, K.L., Gilbert, O., Capstick, C.K., Twinn, D.C., Waid, J.S. & Woodman, M.J. (1960). Changes in leaf litter when placed on the surface of soils with contrasting humus types. *Journal of Soil Science*, 11, 1–9.

Brasell, H.M., Unwin, G.L. & Stocker, G.C. (1980). The quantity, temporal distribution and mineral-element content of litter fall in two forest types at two sites in tropical Australia. *Journal of Ecology*, 68, 123–139.

Collins, N.M. (1981). The role of termites in the decomposition of wood and leaf litter in the Southern Guinea savanna of Nigeria. *Oecologia*, 51, 389–399.

Collins, N.M. (1983). The effect of logging on termite (Isoptera) diversity and decomposition processes in lowland dipterocarp forests. *Tropical Ecology and Development* (Ed. by J. I. Furtado), pp. 113–121. International Society of Tropical Ecology, Kuala Lumpur.

Collins, N.M., Anderson, J.M. & Vallack, H. (1983). Studies on the soil invertebrates of lowland and montane rain forests in Gunung Mulu National Park. *Gunung Mulu National Park. Sarawak: an Account of Its Environment and Biota* (Ed. by A. C. Jermy & K. P. Kavanagh), *Sarawak Museum Journal*, Suppl. 2 (in press).

Cook, A.G., Critchley, B.R., Critchley, U., Perfect, T.J. & Yeadon, R. (1980). Effects of cultivation and DDT on earthworm activity in a forest soil in the sub-humid tropics. *Journal of Applied Ecology*, 17, 21–29.

Cornforth, I.S. (1970). Leaf fall in a tropical fall forest. *Journal of Applied Ecology*, 7, 603–608.

Cunningham, R.K. (1963). The effect of clearing a tropical rain forest soil. *Journal of Soil Science*, 14, 334–345.

De Angelis, D.L., Gardner, R.H. & Shugart, H.H. (1981). Productivity of forest ecosystems studied during the IBP: the woodlands data set. *Dynamic Properties of Forest Ecosystems* (Ed. by D. E. Reichle), pp. 567–672. Cambridge University Press, Cambridge.

Duvigneaud, P. & Denaeyer De Smet (1970). Biological cycling of minerals in temperate deciduous forests. *Analysis of Temperate Forest Ecosystems* (Ed. by D. E. Reichle), pp. 199–225. Chapman & Hall, London.

Edwards, C.A. & Lofty, J.R. (1977). *Biology of Earthworms*, 2nd edn. Chapman & Hall, London.

Edwards, P.J. (1977). Studies of mineral cycling in a montane rain forest in New Guinea. II. The production and disappearance of litter. *Journal of Ecology*, 65, 971–992.

Edwards, P.J. & Grubb, P.J. (1977). Studies of mineral cycling in a montane rain forest in New Guinea. I. The distribution of organic matter in vegetation and soil. *Journal of Ecology*, 65, 943–969.

Fittkau, E.J. & Klinge, H. (1973). On biomass and trophic structure of the Central Amazon rain forest ecosystem. *Biotropica*, 5, 2–14.

Gong, W.-K. & Ong, J.-E. (1983). Litter production and decomposition in a coastal hill dipterocarp forest. *Tropical Rain Forest: Ecology and Management* (Ed. by S. L. Sutton, T. C. Whitmore & A. C. Chadwick), pp. 275–285. Blackwell Scientific Publications, Oxford.

Gosz, J.R., Likens, G.E. & Bormann, F.H. (1973). Nutrient release from decomposing leaf and branch litter in the Hubbard Brook Forest, New Hampshire. *Ecological Monographs*, 43, 173–191.

Greenland, D.J. & Nye, P.H. (1959). Increases in carbon and nitrogen contents of tropical soils under natural fallows. *Journal of Soil Science*, 9, 284–299.

Grubb, P.J. (1977). Control of forest growth and distribution on wet tropical mountains: with special reference to mineral nutrition. *Annual Review of Ecology and Systematics*, 8, 83–107.

Harris, W.E., Goldstein, R.A. & Henderson, G.S. (1973). Analysis of forest biomass pools, annual primary production and turnover of biomass for mixed deciduous forest watershed. *Proceedings of the Working Party on Forest Biomass of IUFRO* (Ed. by H. Young), pp. 41–64. University of Maine Press, Orono.

Heal, O.W., Swift, M.J. & Anderson, J.M. (1982). Nitrogen cycling in United Kingdom forests: The relevance of basic ecological research. *Philosophical Transactions of the Royal Society of London*, Series B, 296, 427–444.

Hopkins, B. (1966). Vegetation of the Olokemeji forest reserve, Nigeria. IV. The litter and soil with special reference to their seasonal changes. *Journal of Ecology*, 54, 687–703.

Irmler, U. & Furch, K. (1980). Weight energy and nutrient changes during the decomposition of leaves in the emersion phase of Central Amazonian inundation forests. *Pedobiologia*, 20, 118–130.

Janzen, D.H. (1976). Why tropical trees have rotten cores. *Biotropica*, 8, 110.

Jenkinson, D.S. & Ayanaba, A. (1977). Decomposition of Carbon-14 labelled plant material under tropical conditions. *Journal of Soil Science*, 41, 912–915.

Jenny, N., Gessel, S.P. & Bingham, F.T. (1949). Comparative studies of decomposition rates of organic matter in temperate and tropical regions. *Soil Science*, **68**, 419–432.

John, D.M. (1973). Accumulation and decay of litter and net production of forest in tropical West Africa. *Oikos*, **24**, 430–435.

Klinge, H. (1966). Verbreitung tropischer Tieflandspodsole. *Naturwissenschaften*, **17**, 442–443.

Klinge, H. (1973). Biomasa y materia orgánica del suelo en el ecosistema de la pluviselva centro-amazónica. *Acta Ciencia Venezolana*, **24**, 174–181.

Janos, D.P. (1983). Tropical mycorrhizas, nutrient cycles and plant growth. *Tropical Rain Forest: Ecology and Management* (Ed. by S. L. Sutton, T. C. Whitmore & A. C. Chadwick), pp. 327–345. Blackwell Scientific Publications, Oxford.

Klinge, H. & Rodrigues, W.A. (1968a). Litter production in an area of Amazonian terra firme forest. Part I. Litter-fall, organic carbon and total nitrogen contents of litter. *Amazoniana*, **1**, 287–302.

Klinge, H. & Rodriques, W.A. (1968b). Litter production in an area of Amazonian terra firme forest. Part II. Mineral nutrient content of the litter. *Amazoniana*, **1**, 303–310.

Lang, G.E. & Forman, R.T.T. (1978). Detrital dynamics in a mature oak forest: Hutchinson Memorial Forest, New Jersey. *Ecology*, **59**, 580–595.

Lang, G.E. & Knight, D.H. (1979). Decay rate for boles of tropical trees in Panama. *Biotropica*, **11**, 316–317.

Laudelout, H. & Meyer, J. (1954). Les cycles d'élémentes mineraux et de matière organique en forêt equitoriale congolaise. *Transactions of the Fifth International Congress of Soil Science*, **2**, 267–272.

Lavelle, P. (1975). Consummation annuelle de terre par une population naturelle de verse de terre (*Millsonia anomala* Omodeo, Acanthodrilidae-Oligochaetes) dans la savane de Lamto (Côte d'Ivoire). *Revue d'Écologie et Biologie du Sol*, **12**, 11–24.

Lim, M.T. (1978). Litter fall and mineral nutrient content of litter in Pasoh Forest Reserve. *Malayan Nature Journal*, **30**, 375–380.

Lugo, A.E., Gamble, J.F. & Ewel, K.C. (1978). Organic matter budget in a mixed-hardwood forest in North Central Florida. *Environmental Chemistry and Cycling Processes* (Ed. by D. C. Adriano & I. L. Brisbin), pp. 790–800. D.O.E. Symposium. Series 45 (CONF-760429). Technical Information Centre, U.S.D.O.E., Washington.

Madge, D.S. (1965). Litter fall and litter disappearance in a tropical forest. *Pedobiologia*, **5**, 273–288.

Maldague, M.E. (1967). Vitesse de décomposition de différents types de litières forestières. *Progress in Soil Biology* (Ed. by O. Graff & J. Satchell), pp. 409–419. North Holland, Amsterdam.

Matsumoto, T. & Abe, T. (1979). The role of termites in a equatorial rain forest ecosystem of West Malaysia. II. Leaf litter consumption on the forest floor. *Oecologia*, **38**, 261–274.

McBreyer, J.F. & Cromack, K. (1980). Effect of snow-pack on oak-litter breakdown and nutrient release in a Minnesota forest. *Pedobiologia*, **20**, 47–54.

Medina, E., Klinge, H., Jordan, C. & Herrera, R. (1980). Soil respiration in Amazonian rain forests in the Rio Negro basin. *Flora*, **170**, 240–250.

Meentemeyer, V. (1978). An approach to the biometeorology of decomposer organisms. *International Journal of Biometeorology*, **22**, 94–102.

Mohr, E.C.J. & van Baren, F.A. (1954). *Tropical Soils*. van Hoeve, Hague.

Mommaert-Billiet, F. (1971). Aspects dynamics de la partition de la litière de feuilles. *Bulletin of the Royal Botanical Society of Belgium*, **104**, 181–195.

Nye, P.H. (1961). Organic matter and nutrient cycles under moist tropical forest. *Plant and Soil*, **13**, 333–346.

Nye, P.H. & Greenland, D.J. (1960). The soil under shifting cultivation. Commonwealth Agricultural Bureau, Farnham Royal.

Ogawa, H. (1978). Litter production and carbon cycling in Pasoh forest. *Malayan Nature Journal*, **30**, 367–373.

Olson, J.S. (1963). Energy storage and the balance of producers and decomposers in ecological systems. *Ecology*, **44**, 322–331.

O'Neill, R.V. & De Angelis, D.C. (1981). Comparative productivity and biomass relations of forest ecosystems. *Dynamic Properties of Forest Ecosystems* (Ed. by D. E. Reichle), pp. 411–449. Cambridge University Press, Cambridge.

Orndoff, K.A. & Lang, G.E. (1981). Leaf litter redistribution in a West Virginia hardwood forest. *Journal of Ecology*, **69**, 225–235.

Perfect, J.T., Cook, A.G., Critchley, B.R., Critchley, U., Davies, A.L., Swift, M.J., Russel-Smith, A. & Yeadon, R. (1979). The effect of DDT contamination of the productivity of a cultivated forest soil in the sub-humid tropics. *Journal of Applied Ecology*, **16**, 705–719.

Perfect, T.J., Cook, A.C. & Swift, M.J. (1980). The effects of changing agricultural practice on the biology of a forest soil in the sub-humid tropics. I. The soil fauna. *Tropical Ecology and Development* (Ed. by J. I. Furtado), pp. 531–540. International Society of Tropical Ecology, Kuala Lumpur.

Proctor, J. (1983). Tropical forest litterfall. *Tropical Rain Forest: Ecology and Management* (Ed. by S. L. Sutton, T. C. Whitmore & A. C. Chadwick), pp. 267–273. Blackwell Scientific Publications, Oxford.

Proctor, J., Anderson, J.M. Fogden, S.C. & Vallack, H.W. (1983). Ecological studies in four contrasting lowland rain forests in Gunung Mulu National Park, Sarawak. II. Litterfall, litter standing crop and preliminary observations on herbivory. *Journal of Ecology*, **71**, 261–284.

Reiners, W.A. & Reiners, N.M. (1970). Energy and nutrient dynamics of forest floors in three Minnesota forests. *Journal of Ecology*, **58**, 497–519.

Rochow, J.J. (1975). Mineral nutrient pool and cycling in a Missouri forest. *Journal of Ecology*, **63**, 985–994.

Sanchez, P.A. (1976). *Properties and Management of Soils in the Tropics*. Wiley, London.

Schlesinger, W.H. (1977). Carbon balance in terrestrial detritus. *Annual Review of Ecology and Systematics*, **8**, 51–81.

Shanks, R.E. & Olson, J.S. (1961). First-year breakdown of leaf litter in Southern Appalachian Forests. *Science*, **134**, 194–195.

Singh, K.P. (1969). Studies in decomposition of leaf litter of important trees of tropical deciduous forest at Varanasi. *Tropical Ecology*, **10**, 292–311.

Strojan, C.L. (1978). Forest leaf litter decomposition in the vicinity of a zinc smelter. *Oecologia*, **32**, 203–212.

Swift, M.J. (1977). The roles of fungi and animals in the immobilization and release of nutrient elements from decomposing branch-wood. *Soil Organisms as Components of Ecosystems* (Ed. by U. Lohm & T. Persson), pp. 193–202. Ecological Bulletins (Stockholm), 25. Swedish National Science Research Council, Stockholm.

Swift, M.J. (1983). The importance of detrital resources in natural and managed terrestrial ecosystems. *Proceedings of the Silver Jubilee Symposium, International Society for Tropical Ecology* (Ed. by K. C. Misra) Bhopal, India (in press).

Swift, M.J., Heal, O.W. & Anderson, J.M. (1979). *Decomposition in Terrestrial Ecosystems*. Blackwell Scientific Publications, Oxford.

Swift, M.J., Russel-Smith, A. & Perfect, T.J. (1981). Decomposition and mineral nutrient dynamics of plant litter in a regenerating bush-fallow in the sub-humid tropics. *Journal of Ecology*, **69**, 981–995.

Tanner, E.V.J. (1981). The decomposition of leaf litter in Jamaican montaine rain forests. *Journal of Ecology*, **69**, 263–273.

Toth, J.A., Papp, L.B. & Lenkey, B. (1975). *Litter decomposition in an oak-forest ecosystem* (Quercetum petreae Cerris) *in Northern Hungary studied in the framework of 'Sikfokut Project' Biodegredation et Humification* (Ed. by G. Kilbertus, O. Reisinger, A. Mourey & J. A. Cancela da Fonseca), pp. 41–58, Piersance Editeur, Sarraguemines.

UNESCO (1977). *Atlas of World Water Balance*. UNESCO, Paris.

Whitmore, T.C. (1975). *Tropical Rain Forests of the Far East*. Clarendon Press, Oxford.

Whitmore, T.C. & Burnham, C.P. (1969). The altitudinal sequence of forests and soils on granite near Kuala Lumpur. *Malayan Nature Journal*, **22**, 99–118.

Wiegert, R.G. (1970). Effects of ionising radiation on leaf fall, decomposition and litter macroarthropods of a montane rain forest. *A Tropical Rain Forest* (Ed. by H. T. Odum & R. F. Pigeon), pp. H 89–100. United States Atomic Energy Authority, Oak Ridge, Tennessee.

Witkamp, M. & van der Drift. J. (1961). Breakdown of forest litter in relation to environmental factors. *Plant and Soil*, **15**, 295–311.

Wood, T.G., Johnson, R.A. & Ohiagu, C.E. (1977). Populations of termites (Isoptera) in natural and agricultural ecosystems in Southern Guinea Savanna near Mokwa, Nigeria. *Geo-Eco-Trop*, **1**, 139–148.

Woodwell, G.M. & Marples, T.G. (1968). The influence of chronic gamma irradiation on production and decay of litter in an oak-pine forest. *Ecology*, **49**, 456–465.

Yoda, K. (1978). Organic carbon, nitrogen and mineral nutrients stock in the soils of Pasoh Forest. *Malayan Nature Journal*, **30**, 229–251.

Termite populations and their role in litter removal in Malaysian rain forests

N. M. COLLINS*

*Centre for Overseas Pest Research, Termite Research Group,
c/o British Museum (Natural History), Cromwell Road, London SW7*

SUMMARY

1 Estimates are given of the density and type of termites in soil, dead wood, and epigeal or arboreal nests in Dipterocarp, Kerangas and Alluvial rain forests at Gunung Mulu, Sarawak, East Malaysia.

2 Consumption of organic matter by termites in Mulu forests is calculated to range from 7 to 36 g(d.w.) m^{-2} $year^{-1}$ (0·9–3·4% of litter production) much lower than a calculated 155–174 g(d.w.) m^{-2} $year^{-1}$ (14·7–16·3% of litter production) at Pasoh forest, Peninsular Malaysia.

3 At Pasoh, the fungus-growing subfamily Macrotermitinae consumes a calculated 129–139 g(d.w.) m^{-2} $year^{-1}$, over 75% of the total taken by termites. The fungus-growers are absent or rare in the forests at Mulu, hence the lower impact of termites there.

4 The variation in impact of the Macrotermitinae may be a result of lower rainfall at Pasoh (2000 mm $year^{-1}$) than at Mulu (5000 mm $year^{-1}$). With their symbiotic fungi, the Macrotermitinae are well adapted to feeding on litter in the drier surroundings of Pasoh. This advantage is lost in the wetter surroundings of Mulu where decomposition processes are dominated by free-living micro-organisms. In addition to consuming litter, termites may accelerate the nutrient cycle by comminuting soft litter and building galleries through dead wood.

INTRODUCTION

The majority of termite species are found within tropical latitudes (24°N–24°S), although some species reach 45°. Termites are common in all rain forests except in Queensland, Australia, where species diversity is low. Species numbers from localities in Africa, Asia and the Americas north of the Equator (Fig. 1), indicate that termites are not a very diverse group of insects, reaching a maximum of only about sixty species in equatorial rain forests.

Termite populations and diversity decrease rapidly with increasing altitude as well as latitude (Collins 1980a). Collections from Gunung Mulu (2376 m) in Sarawak (4°03 N, 114°56 E) revealed fifty-eight species in lowland Dipterocarp forest, but only ten species in montane forests above 1000 m, and none above 1860 m (Collins 1980a; 1983).

* Present address: IUCN Conservation Monitoring Centre, 219(c) Huntingdon Road, Cambridge CB3 0DL.

The termites of rain forests are predominantly of the family Termitidae (higher termites); the lower termite family Rhinotermitidae is also significant, particularly wood-feeding genera in the Heterotermitinae (*Heterotermes*), Coptotermitinae (*Coptotermes*) and Rhinotermitinae (*Schedorhinotermes, Parrhinotermes, Prorhinotermes,*

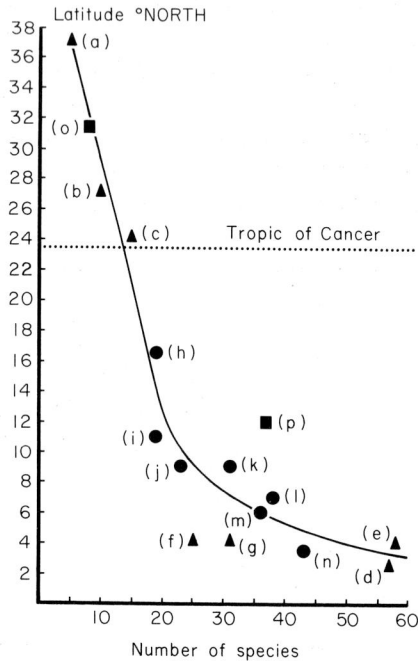

FIG. 1. The number of termite species at world-wide latitudes north of the Equator. Datum points refer to collections from individual ecosystems and vegetation types except for the four most northerly collections, which are complete for the regions indicated. Data from South East Asia: (a) Japanese Islands; (b) Ryukyu Islands; (c) Formosa (in Abe 1979); (d) Dipterocarp forest, West Malaysia (Abe 1978); (e) Dipterocarp forest, Sarawak; (f) Kerangas forest, Sarawak; (g) Alluvial forest, Sarawak (Collins 1983). Data from Africa: (h) Sahel savanna, Senegal (Lepage 1972); (i) Northern Guinea savanna, Nigeria (Sands 1965); (j) Southern Guinea savanna, Nigeria (Wood, Johnson & Ohiagu 1977); (k) Riparian forest, Nigeria; (l) Semi-deciduous forest, Nigeria (Wood *et al.* 1982); (m) Derived savanna, Ivory Coast (Josens 1972); (n) Rain forest, Cameroun (Collins 1977). Data from the Americas (o) Arizona desert, U.S.A. (W. L. Nutting in Wood & Sands 1978); (p) Riparian forest, Brazil (Mathews 1977, Wood *et al.* 1982).

and *Rhinotermes*). The other four families of lower termites (Mastotermitidae, Kalotermitidae, Hodotermitidae, Serritermitidae) are of little or no significance in rain forests. Quantitative studies on termite populations and communities in rain forests are limited to Pasoh forest, Peninsular Malaysia, and the Gunung Mulu National Park, Sarawak, East Malaysia. In this paper the termite community in the forests at Mulu will be described, and compared with data from Pasoh.

TERMITE POPULATIONS IN MULU RAIN FORESTS

Study sites

One hectare plots were set up in three lowland forest types, Alluvial (AF), Dipterocarp (DF) and Kerangas or Heath (KF). AF is found on undulating river plains subject to intermittent flooding, DF on free-draining lowland ridges and slopes, and KF on humus podzols on free-draining sandstone terraces. Further details of the sites, their vegetation and their soils may be found in Collins (1979a), Anderson, Jermy & Cranbrook (1982), Proctor et al. (1983a) and Tie et al. (1979).

In designing a sampling programme, one 5×10 m plot was closely investigated in each forest type. Soil was turned over to a depth of 10–15 cm, all dead wood was split open, and epigeal or arboreal nests noted. Figure 2 shows the results for KF and DF

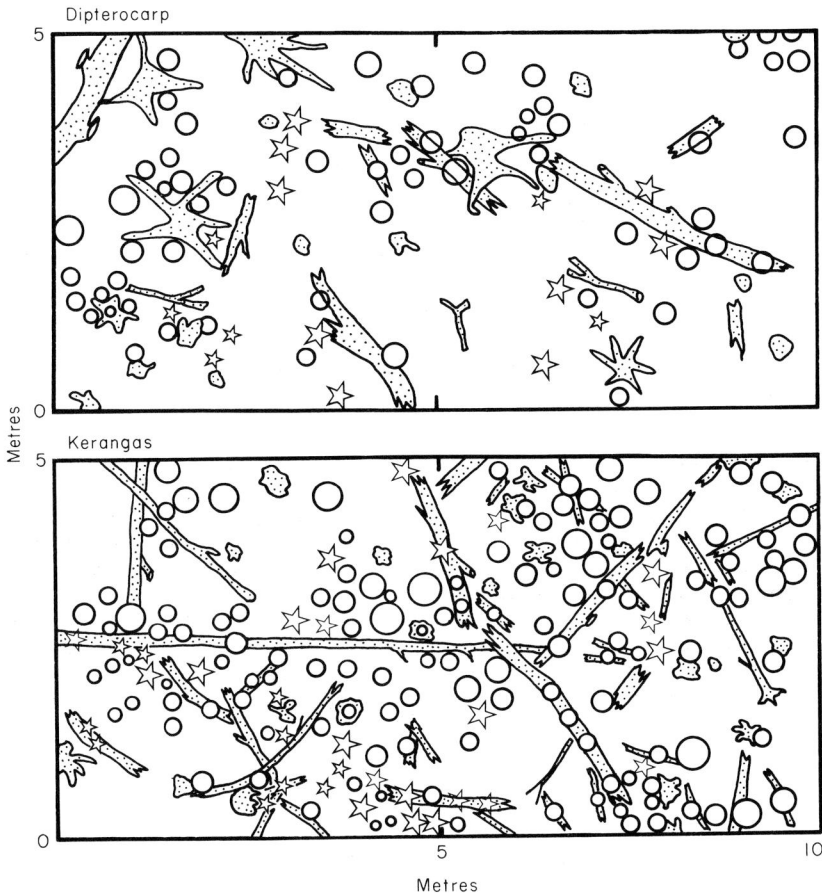

FIG. 2. Ground plans of 10×5 m plots in Dipterocarp and Kerangas forest searched for termite accumulations and nests to a soil depth of 15 cm. Standing trees and dead wood are indicated by stippled areas; accumulations and nests of termites are represented by circles and stars, respectively, of approximately proportional sizes.

only. In the heterogeneous AF, frequently-flooded soils contained few termites while in freely-drained areas termites were distributed in a similar way to those in DF. The KF contained more termite nests and concentrated groups, more dead wood with termites, more pole-like trees and fewer large buttressed trees than the DF. In all cases the termites' distribution obviously required separate sampling procedures for colonies in soil, wood, and epigeal or arboreal nests.

Termites in soil

Sampling programmes for soil macrofauna were fully described in an earlier publication (Collins 1979a). Mean abundance figures for five bimonthly sets of soil core samples (Table 1) showed no significant differences or seasonal trends. Termites represented 38–60% of the total numbers of soil macrofauna, and 22–53% of total biomass. The lower limits of these values are from AF. As expected, most termites were soil feeders from the Termitinae and Nasutitermitinae, but wood feeders from the Rhinotermitidae, Termitinae and Nasutitermitinae also occurred regularly. Macrotermitinae were absent or rare.

Termites in wood

The populations of termites in dead wood have never been estimated on a field scale. Unsuccessful attempts were made to extract and count the termites in the wood from a number of random 1-m^2 quadrats, and a semi-quantitative system of ranking, which estimated orders of magnitude, was finally developed. Ten 5×5 m stratified random plots in each of the three forests were cleared of woody litter, and each item examined for termites. Item size (2–5 cm, 6–10 cm, > 10 cm diameter), species, and density of termites present were recorded. Density was estimated visually on a scale of 10^2, 10^3 or 10^4 and above. The estimates will certainly tend to be low. Some *Coptotermes* species have populations at feeding sites in excess of 10^5 (Spragg & Paton 1980), and this may also be true for *Schedorhinotermes*. The number of woody items examined, and the proportions attacked by the various termite groups are shown in Table 2. The proportion of woody items attacked was low in AF (18%), but higher in KF (31%) and DF (50%). There are no data on the turnover rate of wood litter, but with 30–50% of the standing crop attacked (in KF and DF) at any one time, virtually all wood litter is probably attacked by termites at some stage.

In Table 3 the records of termites in wood are divided between the three population ranks and four taxonomic groupings. For each taxon the total population estimate is divided by the area surveyed to give density. Hence, for Rhinotermitidae in KF the population density is derived from:

$$[(8 \times 10^2) + (21 \times 10^3) + (8 \times 10^4)] \times 1/250 = 407 \text{ termites m}^{-2}$$

The estimated density of termites in wood is lowest in AF, and over three times higher in KF than DF, despite a higher estimated biomass of dead wood in DF than in KF (Proctor *et al.* 1983b). Rhinotermitidae are dominant in the wood litter of all three forests, with Macrotermitinae absent or rare.

TABLE 1. Abundance and biomass of subterranean termites in three lowland forest sites

	Rhinotermitidae	Termitinae	Nasutitermitinae	Macrotermitinae	Population total (no. m^{-2})	% of soil macrofauna	Total biomass (g)	% of soil macrofauna
Kerangas	193	1013	199	—	1405	57	3·573	53
Alluvial	48	89	97	20	245	38	0·522	22
Dipterocarp	226	564	330	5	1125	60	1·779	42
Dipterocarp, Pasoh*						65		75

* Data from Abe (1979, 1982) and Kondoh *et al.* (1980).

TABLE 2. The percentages of woody items in diameter size classes showing signs of termite attack (ten 5 × 5 m plots sampled). Some items were attacked by more than one type of termite

	Rhinotermitidae	Termitinae	Nasutitermitinae	Macrotermitinae	Total % attack	No. items examined
Kerangas						
2–5 cm	15	4	3	—	21	112
6–10	26	18	—	—	44	72
> 10	36	6	—	—	41	17
All items					31	201
Alluvial						
2–5 cm	6	1	6	1	13	154
6–10	16	—	10	—	25	53
> 10	20	—	—	4	24	25
All items					18	232
Dipterocarp						
2–5 cm	36	7	4	—	45	110
6–10	40	14	2	—	55	47
> 10	36	30	6	—	57	30
All items					50	187

TABLE 3. The number of woody items in ten 5 × 5 m plots in each of three forest types containing an estimated 10^2, 10^3, or 10^4 termites, with conversions to estimated density m^{-2} of termites in wood

	Kerangas				Alluvial				Dipterocarp			
	10^2	10^3	10^4	No. m^{-2}	10^2	10^3	10^4	No. m^{-2}	10^2	10^3	10^4	No. m^{-2}
Rhinotermitidae	8	21	8	407	10	11	—	48	48	12	—	67
Termitidae												
Termitinae	5	8	2	114	1	—	—	<1	13	7	—	33
Nasutitermitinae	—	3	—	12	8	6	—	27	2	3	1	53
Macrotermitinae	—	—	—	—	3	—	—	1	—	—	—	—
Totals	13	32	10	533	22	17	—	76	63	22	1	153

Termites in epigeal and arboreal nests

Termite density in epigeal and arboreal nests was estimated from nest censuses extrapolated to total populations from data in the literature. Table 4 shows comparatively low densities of epigeal and arboreal nest at Mulu. Small nasute and termitine nests such as these may reach densities of 60 to > 800 nests ha^{-1} in Africa and Australia (Collins 1980b; Lee & Wood 1971). No Macrotermitinae nests were found in the Mulu surveys.

In Table 5, data from soils, wood and above-ground nests are amalgamated to give estimates of total termite populations in Mulu. Comparison of the three forest types shows that the AF has an impoverished termite fauna (390 m^{-2}), presumably as a result of flooding. KF (2271 m^{-2}) and DF (1572 m^{-2}) densities are considerably higher but still only within the middle range for forests given by Wood *et al.* (1982).

TABLE 4. The estimated populations of termites in nests above ground in three types of lowland rain forest

	Population per nest	Kerangas		Alluvial		Dipterocarp	
		Nest density (ha^{-1})	Population density (no. m^{-2})	Nest density (ha^{-1})	Population density (no. m^{-2})	Nest density (ha^{-1})	Population density (no. m^{-2})
Termitinae							
*Termes**	3×10^4	—	—	—	—	1	3
*Procapritermes**	3×10^4	—	—	—	—	1	3
Dicuspiditermes†	46×10^3	—	—	3	14	2	9
Subtotals		—	—	3	14	4	15
Nasutitermitinae							
Bulbitermes†	$42{\cdot}4 \times 10^3$	8	34	9	38	7	30
Hospitalitermes‡	6×10^5	5	300	—	—	3	180
Longipeditermes†	$78{\cdot}7 \times 10^3$	—	—	1	8	3	24
Subtotals		13	334	10	46	13	234
Grand totals		13	334	13	60	17	249

* These genera are probably secondary inhabitants of *Dicuspiditermes* nests. Populations of 30 000 per nest is a conservative estimate.

Figures for populations per nest from † Abe & Matsumoto (1979) or ‡ Collins (1979b).

CONSUMPTION BY TERMITES

Ranges of published termite consumption rates

In Table 6, rates of consumption by termites in field and laboratory trials are listed. For Rhinotermitidae and Nasutitermitinae the data are fairly consistent, with standard deviations of less than 40% of the mean. In calculations of population consumption rates, well-supported figures of 20 mg g^{-1} day^{-1} for Rhinotermidae and 10 mg g^{-1} day^{-1} for Nasutitermitinae will be used. In contrast, research on Termitinae gives no indication of a general level. The primitive pantropical wood-feeding genera (*Amitermes, Microcerotermes*) have received little attention, and for the soil-feeding genera it is difficult to distinguish between soil processed and actual amounts of organic matter and humus consumed. Consumption of soil by *Cubitermes* sp. has been estimated at 0·72–0·91 mg termite^{-1} day^{-1} and consumption of organic matter at 0·65–0·84 mg termite^{-1} day^{-1} (Okwakol 1976, 1980). Individual termite biomass was not given, but using data on nest population (17 646) and biomass (55·2 g) a mean individual biomass of 3·13 mg may be calculated (Okwakol 1976, Tables 11, 13). This indicates consumption rates of 230–291 mg g^{-1} day^{-1} of soil, and 208–268 mg g^{-1} day^{-1} of organic matter. These are likely to be overestimates, and the impact of *Cubitermes* on soil organic matter may be less deleterious than Okwakol (1980) indicates; but the experiments are the only quantitative assessment of the impact of soil-feeding termites. Maldague's (1964) estimate for *Cubitermes fungifaber* was re-calculated by Lee & Wood (1971) from data on oxygen consumption and is artificially lowered by an excessive biomass estimate (11 g m^{-2} for a population of only 1000 m^{-2}). Hébrant's (1970) figure of 4110 mg g^{-1} day^{-1}, calculated by Wood (1978) extrapolation by Wood & Sands (1978). Two data points have been omitted from the Macrotermitinae in Table 6. Josens (1972) and Josens & Corveaule (1973) report 565 mg g^{-1} day^{-1} for four species of fungus-growers, but they used a baiting method which may have unnaturally attracted termites to the area (Wood 1978). Abe (1982) reports an estimated consumption rate of 199 mg^{-1} day^{-1} for *Macrotermes carbonarius* (Hagen), a high level discussed below.

Estimates of consumption by termites in Mulu and Pasoh

No estimates of the overall consumption by termites have been made in any rain forest and quantitative estimates have been achieved for only three species, *Macrotermes carbonarius, Longipeditermes longipes* (Haviland) (Matsumoto & Abe 1979) and *Hospitalitermes umbrinus* (Collins 1979b).

Use of generalized consumption rates to extrapolate from termite populations to their overall role in litter removal can only be approximate, but may give valuable insight into rain forest dynamics. Table 7 is an attempt to calculate total consumption

TABLE 7. Consumption calculations for termites in four lowland rain forests in Malaysia

	Kerangus Mulu	Alluvial Mulu	Dipterocarp Mulu	Dipterocarp Pasoh§
Rhinotermitidae				
Population (m^{-2})	600	96	293	No estimates
Biomass* (g m^{-2})	1·800	0·288	0·879	
Consumption‡ (g m^{-2} year^{-1})	13·14	2·10	6·42	
Termitinae				
Population (m^{-2})	1127	103	612	1280–1730
Biomass† (g m^{-2})	1·887	0·172	1·024	2·17–2·86
Consumption‡ (g m^{-2} year^{-1})	20·66	1·88	11·21	23·76–31·32
Nasutitermitinae				
Population (m^{-2})	544	170	616	943–1093
Biomass† (g m^{-2})	0·412	0·129	0·467	0·61–0·95
Consumption‡ (g m^{-2} year^{-1})	1·50	0·47	1·70	2·23–3·47
Macrotermitinae				
Population (m^{-2})	—	21	5	934–984
Biomass† (g m^{-2})	—	0·134	0·032	5·91–6·32
Consumption‡ (g m^{-2} year^{-1})	—	2·93	0·70	129·43–138·41
All termites				
Population (m^{-2})	2271	390	1526	3160–3810
Biomass (g m^{-2})	4·10	0·72	2·40	8·69–10·13
Consumption (g m^{-2} year^{-1})	35·30	7·38	20·03	155·42–173·20

* Biomass of Rhinotermitidae estimated at 3 mg (w.w.) per individual.

† Individual biomass of Termitinae (1·674 mg), Nasutitermitinae (0·758 mg), and Macrotermitinae (6·376 mg) estimated from the mean value of data from Pasoh (Abe 1979, Table 4).

‡ Consumption (in g (d.w.) m^{-2} year^{-1}) estimated using consumption rates (in mg (d.w.) g^{-1} day^{-1}) of 20 (Rhinotermitidae), 30 (Termitinae), 10 (Nasutitermitinae) and 60 (Macrotermitinae).

§ Populations and biomass taken from Abe (1979), Table 4.

TABLE 4. The estimated populations of termites in nests above ground in three types of lowland rain forest

	Population per nest	Kerangas		Alluvial		Dipterocarp	
		Nest density (ha^{-1})	Population density (no. m^{-2})	Nest density (ha^{-1})	Population density (no. m^{-2})	Nest density (ha^{-1})	Population density (no. m^{-2})
Termitinae							
*Termes**	3×10^4	—	—	—	—	1	3
*Procapritermes**	3×10^4	—	—	—	—	1	3
Dicuspiditermes†	46×10^3	—	—	3	14	2	9
Subtotals		—	—	3	14	4	15
Nasutitermitinae							
Bulbitermes†	$42 \cdot 4 \times 10^3$	8	34	9	38	7	30
Hospitalitermes‡	6×10^5	5	300	—	—	3	180
Longipeditermes†	$78 \cdot 7 \times 10^3$	—	—	1	8	3	24
Subtotals		13	334	10	46	13	234
Grand totals		13	334	13	60	17	249

* These genera are probably secondary inhabitants of *Dicuspiditermes* nests. Populations of 30 000 per nest is a conservative estimate.

Figures for populations per nest from † Abe & Matsumoto (1979) or ‡ Collins (1979b).

CONSUMPTION BY TERMITES

Ranges of published termite consumption rates

In Table 6, rates of consumption by termites in field and laboratory trials are listed. For Rhinotermitidae and Nasutitermitinae the data are fairly consistent, with standard deviations of less than 40% of the mean. In calculations of population consumption rates, well-supported figures of 20 mg g^{-1} day^{-1} for Rhinotermidae and 10 mg g^{-1} day^{-1} for Nasutitermitinae will be used. In contrast, research on Termitinae gives no indication of a general level. The primitive pantropical wood-feeding genera (*Amitermes*, *Microcerotermes*) have received little attention, and for the soil-feeding genera it is difficult to distinguish between soil processed and actual amounts of organic matter and humus consumed. Consumption of soil by *Cubitermes* sp. has been estimated at 0·72–0·91 mg termite^{-1} day^{-1} and consumption of organic matter at 0·65–0·84 mg termite^{-1} day^{-1} (Okwakol 1976, 1980). Individual termite biomass was not given, but using data on nest population (17 646) and biomass (55·2 g) a mean individual biomass of 3·13 mg may be calculated (Okwakol 1976, Tables 11, 13). This indicates consumption rates of 230–291 mg g^{-1} day^{-1} of soil, and 208–268 mg g^{-1} day^{-1} of organic matter. These are likely to be overestimates, and the impact of *Cubitermes* on soil organic matter may be less deleterious than Okwakol (1980) indicates; but the experiments are the only quantitative assessment of the impact of soil-feeding termites. Maldague's (1964) estimate for *Cubitermes fungifaber* was re-calculated by Lee & Wood (1971) from data on oxygen consumption and is artificially lowered by an excessive biomass estimate (11 g m^{-2} for a population of only 1000 m^{-2}). Hébrant's (1970) figure of 4110 mg g^{-1} day^{-1}, calculated by Wood (1978)

TABLE 5. Estimates of total termite densities (number m^{-2}) in three lowland rain forest types, Sarawak

	Kerangas				Alluvial				Dipterocarp			
	Soil	Mound	Wood	Total	Soil	Mound	Wood	Total	Soil	Mound	Wood	Total
Rhinotermitidae	193	—	407	600	48	—	48	96	226	—	67	293
Termitidae												
Termitinae	1013	—	114	1127	89	14	<1	103	564	15	33	612
Nasutitermitinae	198	334	12	544	97	46	27	170	330	234	53	617
Macrotermitinae	—	—	—	—	20	—	1	21	5	—	—	5
Total populations (m^{-2})	1404	334	533	2271	254	60	76	390	1125	249	153	1527

is disproportionate to other figures and the estimate by Josens & Corveaule (1973) is not based on empirical data. No consumption figure for Termitinae is well-supported experimentally and in later calculations a working figure of 30 mg g^{-1} day^{-1} will be used.

The Macrotermitinae have a wide range of consumption rates with a standard deviation of 65% of the mean (Table 6). However, their nests range from simple

TABLE 6. Recorded rates of consumption by various termites in *field and laboratory trials

	Consumption rates (mg (d.w.) g^{-1} termites (w.w.) day^{-1})	Source
Rhinotermitidae		
Coptotermes acinaciformis (Froggatt)	17·8	Gay et al. 1955
Coptotermes amanii (Sjöstedt)	26·8	Becker 1967
Coptotermes lacteus (Froggatt)	12·2	Gay et al. 1955
Heterotermes aureus (Snyder)	19·0	Haverty & Nutting 1974
Reticulitermes lucifugus (Rossi)	19·3	Becker 1967
Psammotermes hybostoma Desneux*	13·7	Lepage 1974
Prorhinotermes simplex (Hagen)	8·0	Hrdý & Zelaný 1967
Mean ± s.d.	16·7 ± 6·1	
Termitinae		
Cubitermes sp.*	208–268	Okwakol 1976, 1980
Cubitermes fungifaber (Sjöstedt)	42·1	Maldague 1964, Lee & Wood 1971 p. 134
Cubitermes exiguus Mathot	4110·0	Hébrant 1970, Wood 1978
Various humivores	ca. 8·2	Josens & Corveaule 1973
Nasutitermitinae		
Nasutitermes exitiosus (Hill)*	10·6	Lee & Wood 1971
Nasutitermes exitiosus	12·2	Gay et al. 1955
Nasutitermes costalis (Holmgren)	2·0	Hrdý & Zelaný 1967
Nasutitermes rippertii (Rambur)	9·0	Hrdý & Zelaný 1967
Trinervitermes geminatus Wasmann*	7·2	Ohiagu 1979
Hospitalitermes umbrinus (Haviland)*	8·3	Collins 1979b
Mean ± s.d.	8·6 ± 3·3	
Macrotermitinae		
Ancistrotermes cavithorax (Sjöstedt)*	27·1	Collins 1981a, Wood & Sands 1978
Macrotermes bellicosus (Smeathman)*	132·0	Collins 1981b
Macrotermes subhyalinus (Rambur)*	32·9	Lepage 1974
Microtermes spp.*	80·6	Collins 1981b, Wood & Sands 1978
Odontotermes spp.*	44·3	Collins 1981b, Wood & Sands 1978
Odontotermes smeathmani (Fuller)*	48·0	Lepage 1974
Mean ± s.d.	60·8 ± 39·5	

subterranean cavities to complex epigeal mounds, and their feeding may be seasonally restricted or spread across the whole year (Collins 1981a). Measured variability in consumption rates may therefore by a true reflection of variation in nature. Consumption by Macrotermitinae is generally higher than by other groups because a large proportion of digestion occurs on the fungus combs rather than in the termite guts (Collins 1981a, b). The mean value of 60 mg g^{-1} day^{-1} has also been used in extrapolation by Wood & Sands (1978). Two data points have been omitted from the Macrotermitinae in Table 6. Josens (1972) and Josens & Corveaule (1973) report 565 mg g^{-1} day^{-1} for four species of fungus-growers, but they used a baiting method which may have unnaturally attracted termites to the area (Wood 1978). Abe (1982) reports an estimated consumption rate of 199 mg^{-1} day^{-1} for *Macrotermes carbonarius* (Hagen), a high level discussed below.

Estimates of consumption by termites in Mulu and Pasoh

No estimates of the overall consumption by termites have been made in any rain forest and quantitative estimates have been achieved for only three species, *Macrotermes carbonarius*, *Longipeditermes longipes* (Haviland) (Matsumoto & Abe 1979) and *Hospitalitermes umbrinus* (Collins 1979b).

Use of generalized consumption rates to extrapolate from termite populations to their overall role in litter removal can only be approximate, but may give valuable insight into rain forest dynamics. Table 7 is an attempt to calculate total consumption

TABLE 7. Consumption calculations for termites in four lowland rain forests in Malaysia

	Kerangus Mulu	Alluvial Mulu	Dipterocarp Mulu	Dipterocarp Pasoh§
Rhinotermitidae				
Population (m^{-2})	600	96	293	No estimates
Biomass* (g m^{-2})	1·800	0·288	0·879	
Consumption‡ (g m^{-2} year^{-1})	13·14	2·10	6·42	
Termitinae				
Population (m^{-2})	1127	103	612	1280–1730
Biomass† (g m^{-2})	1·887	0·172	1·024	2·17–2·86
Consumption‡ (g m^{-2} year^{-1})	20·66	1·88	11·21	23·76–31·32
Nasutitermitinae				
Population (m^{-2})	544	170	616	943–1093
Biomass† (g m^{-2})	0·412	0·129	0·467	0·61–0·95
Consumption‡ (g m^{-2} year^{-1})	1·50	0·47	1·70	2·23–3·47
Macrotermitinae				
Population (m^{-2})	—	21	5	934–984
Biomass† (g m^{-2})	—	0·134	0·032	5·91–6·32
Consumption‡ (g m^{-2} year^{-1})	—	2·93	0·70	129·43–138·41
All termites				
Population (m^{-2})	2271	390	1526	3160–3810
Biomass (g m^{-2})	4·10	0·72	2·40	8·69–10·13
Consumption (g m^{-2} year^{-1})	35·30	7·38	20·03	155·42–173·20

* Biomass of Rhinotermitidae estimated at 3 mg (w.w.) per individual.

† Individual biomass of Termitinae (1·674 mg), Nasutitermitinae (0·758 mg), and Macrotermitinae (6·376 mg) estimated from the mean value of data from Pasoh (Abe 1979, Table 4).

‡ Consumption (in g (d.w.) m^{-2} year^{-1}) estimated using consumption rates (in mg (d.w.) g^{-1} day^{-1}) of 20 (Rhinotermitidae), 30 (Termitinae), 10 (Nasutitermitinae) and 60 (Macrotermitinae).

§ Populations and biomass taken from Abe (1979), Table 4.

by termites in forests at Mulu and Pasoh. The Mulu studies approach completeness in terms of the termite communities examined, but the Pasoh data lack studies on the wood-feeding Rhinotermitidae. Both studies may underestimate the importance of termites nesting and feeding entirely in tree trunks or canopies, even though their faunas have been described (Abe 1978; Collins 1983). Although the biomasses of Mulu termite populations were estimated, they were not divided between taxonomic groups (Collins 1979a; Collins, Anderson & Vallack 1983). For comparability between the Mulu and Pasoh data, individual biomass estimates for each taxon except Rhinotermitidae have been calculated (Table 7) from population and biomass data given by Abe (1979, Table 4). No data are available for Rhinotermitidae and an estimate of 3 mg per individual has been assumed. Using these figures the population biomasses have been calculated, and population consumption estimated using the rates given above. In Table 7, the populations and consumption of all estimated taxa are higher in Pasoh Dipterocarp than in any Mulu forest. The most striking difference is in the Macrotermitinae, which are virtually absent in Mulu, but dominant at Pasoh. The Pasoh biomass and faunal composition are similar to data from southern Guinea savanna in Nigeria, where the highly seasonal rainfall is 1175 mm year^{-1} (Collins 1981a). There the termite biomass (10·6 g (w.w.) m^{-2}, Wood & Sands 1978) is dominated by fungus-growing termites, which take 23% of annual wood and leaf production and 95% of the litter consumed by all termites (Collins 1981a). The Macrotermitinae have evolved an ability to utilize fresh litter to an extent unparalleled by other termites or invertebrates. The fungus combs operate as external digestive organs, maintained in ideal metabolic conditions inside the nests. The symbiosis permits the Macrotermitinae to feed in relatively dry areas, where other termites and invertebrates are curtailed by lack of the fungal and microbial activity needed to bring the litter to a threshold level of palatability (Collins 1981a). Pasoh is one of the driest forest areas in Malaysia (rainfall 2000 mm year^{-1}, Abe 1982) while Mulu is one of the wettest (rainfall 5000–7000 mm year^{-1}, Walsh & Proctor 1982). Although the vegetation on the lower slopes of Mulu and at Pasoh are both classified as DF, they are at extreme ends of a climatic spectrum. No botanical differences caused by climate have been documented, but the termites indicate fundamental differences in the decomposition processes. At Pasoh, where relative dryness may slow down fungal and microbial activity, the fungus-growers are at an advantage over other types of termite and other decomposers. In Mulu, however, constant wetness encourages bacterial, fungal and other forms of decay while the Macrotermitinae, their main ecological advantage being lost, are reduced to a minor role.

ECOLOGICAL IMPACT OF LITTER REMOVAL BY TERMITES

In Table 8 termite consumption is shown to be a far lower proportion of annual litter production at Mulu than at Pasoh. The small role of termites in leaf litter removal in Mulu has also been demonstrated by litter-bag studies, where loss rates from large and small mesh bags were not significantly different (Anderson, Proctor & Vallack 1983).

Decomposition processes at Mulu were comparatively slow and were not dominated by animal feeding activites (Collins *et al.* 1983). This is fundamentally different to the rapid decomposition rates at Pasoh, where animals, particularly termites, play a substantial part. Experimental estimates of respective leaf litter removal by *Macrotermes carbonarius*, *Longipeditermes longipes* and other soil animals at Pasoh were 142, 7 and 0·3 g m^{-2} year^{-1}, 24% of annual leaf litter production (Abe 1982; Matsumoto & Abe 1979). Data for these two leaf-feeding species alone accounts for 149 g m^{-2} year^{-1}, over 85% of the total termite consumption of organic matter calculated here (Table 7). This unlikely result highlights the important difference between consumption and

TABLE 8. Estimated consumption by termites calculated as a proportion of total litterfall at various Malaysian localities

Locality	Rainfall (mm year^{-1})	Litter production (kg ha^{-1} year^{-1})	Consumption by termites (kg ha^{-1} year^{-1})	Percentage of litter production consumed by termites
Kerangas, Mulu	5698*	10 500‡	353	3·4
Alluvial, Mulu	5087*	12 800‡	110	0·9
Dipterocarp, Mulu	5107*	9600‡	200	2·1
Dipterocarp, Pasoh	2000†	10 600§	1554–1732	14·7–16·3

* Walsh & Proctor (1982).
† Abe (1982).
‡ Proctor et al (1983b).
§ Ogawa (1974), and Matsumoto & Abe (1979).

comminution of litter. Matsumoto & Abe (1979) estimated consumption by *M. carbonarius* and *L. longipes* by following the weekly loss of surface area from marked leaves and extrapolating to the total standing crop. One end of the experimental leaves was marked with vinyl tape and any piece of leaf which was removed between weekly checks was assumed to have been consumed by termites, provided that the leaf showed termite mandible marks. Pieces of leaf cut off and dropped could not be distinguished, and consumption was perhaps thus overestimated. Comminution is an important decomposition process which speeds fungal and bacterial decay by increasing surface area. One interpretation of these important experiments at Pasoh is that the biomass processed by termites may be up to two or three times greater than the actual amount of litter consumed. Comminution by termites has not been adequately studied, although Sands (1969) and Abe (1980) have noted that termites transport bacteria and fungi into dead wood. Termite galleries in tree stumps accelerate decomposition and nutrient cycling (Kitchell *et al.* 1979), and it would be short-sighted to consider the impact of termites simply in terms of litter consumption. Table 8 shows that in the varied rainfall conditions in Malaysian forests, the role of termites in consumption of litter ranges from 1% to 16%. The level depends partly on drainage (levels reduced in flooded areas), and partly on the abundance of Macrotermitinae in the termite fauna. In terms of the materials processed by termites, these figures may be greatly exceeded, but quantification is difficult. A *Coptotermes* nest in the base of a moribund emergent tree such as *Shorea* may consume or comminute only a few kg of wood, but if the tree is felled as a result, then up to 20 t (w.w.) of timber and its nutrient content will be made available for translocation into the decomposition subsystem of the forest floor. The termites will also have played a part in the natural removal of old trees, and their replacement with new growth. To confirm these ideas, further detailed research on termites is needed in a range of rain forests.

ACKNOWLEDGMENTS

I thank the Royal Geographical Society, the Sarawak Forest Department, the British Ecological Society and ICIPE, Nairobi, for support in various ways. M. M. Stephens kindly helped with the diagrams.

REFERENCES

Abe, T. (1978). Studies on the distribution and ecological role of termites in a lowland rain forest of West Malaysia 1. Faunal composition, size, colouration and nest of termites in Pasoh Forest Reserve. *Kontyu*, **46**, 273–290.

Abe, T. (1979). Studies on the distribution and ecological role of termites in a lowland rain forest of West Malaysia 2. Food and feeding habits of termites in Pasoh Forest Reserve. *Japanese Journal of Ecology*, **29**, 121–135.

Abe, T. (1980). Studies on the distribution and ecological role of termites in a lowland rain forest of West Malaysia 4. The role of termites in the process of wood decomposition in Pasoh Forest Reserve. *Revue d'Ecologie et de Biologie du Sol*. **17**, 23–40.

Abe, T. (1982). Ecological role of termites in a tropical rain forest. *The Biology of Social Insects* (Ed. by M. D. Breed, C. D. Michener & H. E. Evans), pp. 71–75. Westview Press, Boulder.

Abe, T. & Matsumoto, T. (1979). Studies on the distribution and ecological role of termites in a lowland rain forest of West Malaysia 3. Distribution and abundance of termites in Pasoh Forest Reserve. *Japanese Journal of Ecology*, **29**, 337–351.

Anderson, J.A.R., Jermy, A.C. & Cranbrook, Earl of (1982). *Gunung Mulu National Park: A Management and Development Plan*. Royal Geographical Society, London.

Anderson, J.M., Proctor, J. & Vallack, H.W. (1983). Ecological studies in four contrasting lowland rain forests in Gunung Mulu National Park, Sarawak III. Decomposition processes and nutrient losses from leaf litter. *Journal of Ecology*, **71**, 503–528.

Becker, G. (1967). Die Temperature-Abhängigkeit der Frasstatigkeit einiger Termitenarten. *Zeitschrift für angewandte entomologie*, **60**, 97–123.

Collins, N.M. (1977). Oxford expedition to the Edea-Marienberg Forest Reserve, United Republic of Cameroon, 1973. *Bulletin of the Oxford University Exploration Club, New Series*, **3**, 5–15.

Collins, N.M. (1979a). A comparison of the soil macrofauna of three lowland forest types in Sarawak. *Sarawak Museum Journal*, **27**, 267–281.

Collins, N.M. (1979b). Observations on the foraging activity of *Hospitalitermes umbrinus* (Haviland), (Isoptera:Termitidae) in the Gunong Mulu National Park, Sarawak. *Ecological Entomology*, **4**, 231–238.

Collins, N.M. (1980a). The distribution of soil macrofauna on the West Ridge of Gunung (Mount) Mulu, Sarawak. *Oecologia*, **44**, 263–275.

Collins, N.M. (1980b). Inhabitation of epigeal termite (Isoptera) nests by secondary termites in Cameroun rain forest. *Sociobiology*, **5**, 47–54.

Collins, N.M. (1981a). The role of termites in the decomposition of wood and leaf litter in the Southern Guinea savanna of Nigeria. *Oecologia*, **51**, 389–399.

Collins, N.M. (1981b). Consumption of wood by artifically isolated colonies of the fungus-growing termite *Macrotermes bellicosus*. *Entomologia Experimentalis et Applicata*, **29**, 313–320.

Collins, N.M. (1983). The termites (Isoptera) of the Gunung Mulu National Park, with a key to the genera

INTRODUCTION

In his comprehensive account of tropical rain forest, Richards (1952) noted that mycorrhizas might predominate among rain forest plants, but that little could be said with certainty about their ecological significance. Since that statement, sufficient data have accumulated to conclude that mycorrhizas are ubiquitous and important for the mineral nutrition, growth, and survival of lowland tropical plants, although knowledge of the role of mycorrhizas in tropical ecosystems is far from complete. In this paper I review the occurrence of mycorrhizas in the lowland humid tropics, their potential role in nutrient cycling, effects on plant growth, and possible influence on species composition of lowland humid tropical plant communities.

TYPES OF MYCORRHIZAS

Most tree species that are mycorrhizal have vesicular-arbuscular mycorrhizas, although some have ectomycorrhizas. This paper is mainly concerned with woody species and these two types of mycorrhizas. Orchid mycorrhizas (Lewis 1975) are abundant in the lowland tropics, but are considered here only with respect to nutrient cycles. Mycorrhizal types are distinguished on the bases of the taxonomic position of host and fungus, morphology, and anatomy; clear distinction between types is critical to understanding their different ecological roles.

Vesicular-arbuscular mycorrhizas

Almost all plants are capable of forming vesicular-arbuscular mycorrhizas (VAM) with fungi in a single zygomycetous family, the Endogonaceae (Gerdemann 1968). The submerged roots of aquatics usually are not infected, but some tropical freshwater (Bagyaraj, Manjunath & Patil, 1979), temperate swamp (Keeley 1980) and salt-marsh (see Gerdemann 1968) species can be mycorrhizal. I know of no published examinations of tropical swamp or mangrove species for mycorrhizas.

At present, over sixty species of VAM fungi have been described (see Hall & Fish 1979) in four genera (Gerdemann & Trappe 1974). Many are cosmopolitan, but some may be strictly tropical, e.g. *Acaulospora foveata* and *A. tuberculata* (Janos & Trappe 1982). The spores produced by VAM fungi are large and not wind-dispersed, although they may be moved with soil transported by wind or water. Earthworms, ants, wasps, and birds (McIlveen & Cole 1976) can transport spores with soil, but because of the low numbers of spores in tropical soils, (Janos 1980a), and the small amounts of soil carried, these are insignificant vectors. Rodents may be the principal long-distance vectors of VAM fungi (Maser, Trappe & Nussbaum 1978): spores have been found in faecal samples from Peru (L. H. Emmons 1982), and as stomach contents in the Galapagos (D. A. Clark, pers. comm.).

Most VAM infection in tropical rain forest is transmitted from root to root. This is possible in species-rich forests because VAM fungi have virtually unrestricted host ranges (Janos 1980b). The fungi cannot grow if unassociated with host roots

Tropical mycorrhizas, nutrient cycles and plant growth

DAVID P. JANOS

Department of Biology, University of Miami, P.O. Box 249118,
Coral Gables, FL 33124, U.S.A.

SUMMARY

1 Most rain forest tree species form vesicular-arbuscular mycorrhizas (VAM). Only a few species from several unrelated plant families form ectomycorrhizas (EM) in the tropics, although those that do are often locally abundant as colonizing species or forest dominants.

2 Both VAM and EM improve the uptake of mineral nutrients, especially immobile ones such as phosphorus, with their extensive, well-distributed mycelia. In addition, the mycorrhizal fungi of orchids and some EM fungi may directly recycle nutrients from litter by decomposing it. VAM fungi are unlikely to do so.

3 Mycorrhizal fungi almost completely close tropical mineral cycles by their efficient uptake of mineral nutrients from the soil, their advantageous position for scavenging mineral nutrients from dying roots, and their possible interspecific transfer of mineral nutrients.

4 VAM have been shown to improve the growth and survival of several tropical plants; only two indigenous rain forest tree species have been tested for response to EM, both of which showed improved growth. Species are facultatively or obligately dependent on VAM or EM for mineral nutrient uptake and growth, or are non-mycorrhizal.

5 Different dependencies on VAM or EM are adaptations to different soil fertilities and probabilities of mycorrhizal infection: EM species are favoured by seasonal dryness, inhibited nitrification, and extremely low mineral retention by soils such as white sands; facultatively mycotrophic species are favoured by high soil fertility; non-mycorrhizal species are favoured by slow rates of mycorrhiza formation by competing dependent species. Most mature-forest tree species are obligately mycotrophic.

6 Changes in soil fertility or in the probability of mycorrhizal infection can influence succession by favouring species with different dependencies on mycorrhizas. The probability of infection in rain forest soil can change markedly because these soils do not contain large numbers of spores.

7 EM species often dominate low-diversity tropical forests on poor soils because they have specific, highly-beneficial fungal associates. VAM hosts predominate in forests with moderate turnover rates on soils of intermediate fertility; their dependence on the same few mycorrhizal fungus species for mineral nutrient uptake limits their ability to competitively exclude one another, and thereby contributes to high within-habitat species diversity.

INTRODUCTION

In his comprehensive account of tropical rain forest, Richards (1952) noted that mycorrhizas might predominate among rain forest plants, but that little could be said with certainty about their ecological significance. Since that statement, sufficient data have accumulated to conclude that mycorrhizas are ubiquitous and important for the mineral nutrition, growth, and survival of lowland tropical plants, although knowledge of the role of mycorrhizas in tropical ecosystems is far from complete. In this paper I review the occurrence of mycorrhizas in the lowland humid tropics, their potential role in nutrient cycling, effects on plant growth, and possible influence on species composition of lowland humid tropical plant communities.

TYPES OF MYCORRHIZAS

Most tree species that are mycorrhizal have vesicular-arbuscular mycorrhizas, although some have ectomycorrhizas. This paper is mainly concerned with woody species and these two types of mycorrhizas. Orchid mycorrhizas (Lewis 1975) are abundant in the lowland tropics, but are considered here only with respect to nutrient cycles. Mycorrhizal types are distinguished on the bases of the taxonomic position of host and fungus, morphology, and anatomy; clear distinction between types is critical to understanding their different ecological roles.

Vesicular-arbuscular mycorrhizas

Almost all plants are capable of forming vesicular-arbuscular mycorrhizas (VAM) with fungi in a single zygomycetous family, the Endogonaceae (Gerdemann 1968). The submerged roots of aquatics usually are not infected, but some tropical freshwater (Bagyaraj, Manjunath & Patil, 1979), temperate swamp (Keeley 1980) and salt-marsh (see Gerdemann 1968) species can be mycorrhizal. I know of no published examinations of tropical swamp or mangrove species for mycorrhizas.

At present, over sixty species of VAM fungi have been described (see Hall & Fish 1979) in four genera (Gerdemann & Trappe 1974). Many are cosmopolitan, but some may be strictly tropical, e.g. *Acaulospora foveata* and *A. tuberculata* (Janos & Trappe 1982). The spores produced by VAM fungi are large and not wind-dispersed, although they may be moved with soil transported by wind or water. Earthworms, ants, wasps, and birds (McIlveen & Cole 1976) can transport spores with soil, but because of the low numbers of spores in tropical soils, (Janos 1980a), and the small amounts of soil carried, these are insignificant vectors. Rodents may be the principal long-distance vectors of VAM fungi (Maser, Trappe & Nussbaum 1978): spores have been found in faecal samples from Peru (L. H. Emmons 1982), and as stomach contents in the Galapagos (D. A. Clark, pers. comm.).

Most VAM infection in tropical rain forest is transmitted from root to root. This is possible in species-rich forests because VAM fungi have virtually unrestricted host ranges (Janos 1980b). The fungi cannot grow if unassociated with host roots

(Gerdemann 1968); broad host ranges compensate for poor dispersal. VAM fungal species differ in effectiveness—the extent to which they stimulate host growth (Mosse 1973)—because of different abilities to grow in different soils (Lambert, Cole and Baker 1980). Fungal species in the VAM genus *Acaulospora*, for example, seem adapted to acid soils (Nicolson & Schenck 1979).

Although VAM are morphologically similar to uninfected roots, the characteristic anatomical structures responsible for their name (see Mosse 1959; Nicolson 1959; Gerdemann 1968) are revealed by decolourizing and staining whole, young, unsuberized, corticated roots (Phillips & Hayman 1970). Vesicles or the more ephemeral arbuscules must be observed to document VAM occurrence, even though typical dimorphic VAM fungus hyphae may be seen by microscopic examination of root surfaces. Much external mycelium is lost when roots are extracted from the soil.

Bowen (1980) recently reviewed how mycorrhizas function. Both VAM and ectomycorrhizal fungi enhance the supply of several mineral nutrients to their host; carbon compounds pass from host to fungus. Enhanced nutrient uptake, especially of poorly mobile ions such as phosphate, is attributable to the extensive, well-distributed absorbing surface provided by mycelium external to the root. VAM fungi take up phosphorus from the same pool of soluble phosphate that is utilized by uninfected plants (Mosse 1973), but exploit a larger volume of soil than do roots (Owusu-Bennoah & Wild 1980). This seems to be the basis for uptake of slowly exchangable soil phosphate (Owusu-Bennoah & Wild 1980) and sparingly soluble fertilizers (Mosse & Hayman 1980), although data of Höweler, Edwards & Asher (1981) suggest that hyphae are able to absorb phosphorus from lower concentrations than can uninfected roots. VAM fungi produce phosphatases (Macdonald & Lewis 1978) that allow utilization of organic phosphorus, especially under humid tropical conditions where hyphae can be in close contact with finely divided litter, and where acid soil reaction reduces the sorption of organic phosphates on soil surfaces (see Tinker 1975). Enhancement of nitrogen uptake by VAM is unlikely because nitrogen is highly mobile in soil solution and can freely diffuse to roots. VAM can have other effects on hosts, such as improved wilt-resistance (Safir, Boyer & Gerdemann 1972) or disease resistance (Daft & Okusanya 1973), but these may result secondarily from improved host mineral nutrition.

Ectomycorrhizas

In the lowland humid tropics, ectomycorrhizas (EM) are a regular feature of Dipterocarpaceae, Fagaceae and Pinaceae, and have been reported for species of several genera of Caesalpinioideae (Janos 1980a; Redhead 1980). In addition, EM have been observed by at least two investigators at different sites on species of Euphorbiaceae (*Uapaca*: Horak 1977; Redhead 1980), Gnetaceae (*Gnetum*: Horak 1977; St John 1980a), Myrtaceae (*Campomanesia*: Thomazini 1974; *Eucalyptus*: Horak 1977; *Eugenia*: Shamsuddin 1979; *Melaleuca*: Horak 1977), Nyctaginaceae (*Neea*: Janos 1980a; St John 1980a; *Pisonia*: Pegler & Fiard 1979), Papilionoideae (*Ormosia*: Edmisten 1970; St John & Uhl 1983), Polygonaceae (*Coccoloba*: Kreisel 1971; Janos 1980a) and Sapindaceae (*Allophylus*: Singer & Morello 1960; *Nephelium*: Alexander

1981). The EM habit seems to have evolved several times, often with species of groups noted for the production of resins or polyphenols that might control the spread of fungal associates within the root (see Marks & Foster 1973).

Native lowland tropical EM fungi are predominantly Basidiomycetes (Singh 1966; Horak 1977; Singer & Araujo 1979; Ivory 1980), although Ascomycetes are also involved (*Cenococcum* sp.: de Alwis & Abeynayake 1980). On a worldwide basis, EM fungal species number in the thousands (Trappe & Fogel 1977), but because of the paucity of EM hosts and investigations of them, few tropical species have been reported. Some tropical EM fungal species, such as the rough-spored boletes reported to associate with dipterocarps (Malloch, Pirozynski & Raven 1980), are holarctic; others are strictly tropical (Horak 1977). Most Basidiomycetes produce numerous small, wind-dispersed, spores which are broadly distributed. Restriction of species to the tropics probably resulted from adaptation to specific site factors such as high soil temperatures or high moisture regimes (see Bowen & Theodorou 1973), or from host specificity. Many species of EM fungi associate with a single genus or subgenus of host (Trappe & Fogel 1977); others such as *Cenococcum* spp. and *Pisolithus tinctorious* (Pers.) Coker & Couch (Marx 1977) have broad host ranges. Redhead (1980) found that the indigenous EM fungi of two Nigerian caesalpinioid legumes would not form mycorrhizas with an introduced pine, nor would an EM fungus of pine produce mycorrhizas on the legumes.

The distinguishing features of an EM are a fungal mantle of septate hyphae ensheathing the root, and a Hartig net composed of hyphae which penetrate between and surround the cortical cells. Intracellular penetration of cortical cells is uncommon, but can develop as roots age (Alexander & Hardy 1981) or in association with 'virulent' fungi (Norkrans 1950). Hyphae, and/or mycelial strands or rhizomorphs extend from the EM. In addition, the absorptive surface of EM roots *per se* is increased by their large diameter, many branches and the mantle.

EM, like VAM, improve the uptake of immobile mineral nutrients principally by extensive exploitation of the soil (Bowen 1980). Moreover, the EM mantle can buffer hosts against fluctuations in phosphorus supply by storing phosphorus when it is readily available and later releasing it to the host when exogenous availability is low (Harley & Lewis 1969). EM fungi produce phosphatase (Alexander & Hardy 1981), and can utilize organic phosphorus subject to the same constraints as VAM fungi. Some EM fungi excrete oxalate which is thought to increase the availability of organic phosphorus and nitrogen by releasing organic material from aggregation with minerals (Graustein, Cromack & Sollins 1977). Simple organic nitrogen compounds such as amino acids are utilized by EM fungi, although ammonium is probably their primary nitrogen source in nature (Alexander 1983). EM supply water to hosts (Duddridge, Malibari & Read 1980), and protect feeder roots from disease (Marx 1972).

OCCURRENCE OF MYCORRHIZAS

Surveys of tropical forest indicate that the absence of mycorrhizas is exceptional. Janse (1896) sampled plants at the periphery of a mid-elevation forest in Java, and found that all forty-six arborescent species examined had VAM. Of a total of seventy-five species from fifty-six families, he found only six herbaceous species lacked mycorrhizas. Johnston (1949) observed VAM in all thirteen forest tree species he surveyed in Trinidad, including some of the most common species on the island. Of his total of ninety-three species from several different habitats only thirteen were uninfected. Redhead (1968) looked at sixty-six species from twenty-five families in Nigeria; of these, fifty-one species were indigenous to lowland rain forest, and of the indigenous species, three had EM, and forty-four had VAM (Redhead 1980). Only very young plants or those from newly cleared and burnt nurseries lacked mycorrhizas. Shamsuddin (1979) reported that of about 200 species of Malaysian forest trees, only one lacked mycorrhizas. All forty species of Dipterocarpaceae examined, and some Pinaceae, Fagaceae and Myrtaceae had EM. In Sri Lanka, de Alwis & Abeynayake (1980) observed mycorrhizas on fifty-nine of sixty-three species belonging to twenty-six families. The five dipterocarp species examined had EM. St John & Uhl (1983) found all twelve forest and ten early-successional species that they examined from seventeen families to be mycorrhizal; three leguminous species had EM. An extensive survey conducted by St John (1980a) near Manaus, Brazil, however, stands in opposition to these other studies. He found three tree species out of eighty-six from thirty-seven families with EM, which agrees with the low numbers of EM species usually encountered, but did not observe mycorrhizas on twenty-five species.

Other data are either not from collections made in forest or are difficult to interpret, but accord with the prevalence of VAM on lowland tropical trees. Janos (1980b) inoculated seedlings of twenty-three tree species from fourteen families in Costa Rica with VAM fungi, and noted that all formed mycorrhizas. St John (1980b) listed sixty-four VAM species, including many of economic importance, from several habitats in Brazil other than the primary forest in his aforementioned study (St John 1980a). Thomazini (1974) observed that all sixty species she collected from Brazilian *cerrado* had mycorrhizas, but listed the majority of species as having 'endotrophic mycorrhizae with septate mycelia'. Her description implies mycorrhizas with ericaceous or orchidaceous affinities (see Lewis 1975), although VAM mycelia may become irregularly septate with age and many of the genera she lists are known to form VAM. She found two species had EM. Edmisten (1970) failed to find mycorrhizas in nine of thirty-two principal forest species in Puerto Rico; however, his results probably reflect the difficulty of observing VAM in sectioned roots. He listed six species as EM, but three of these are unusual records requiring independent confirmation.

Reports of EM from the lowland humid tropics are seldom well-documented, and some may be unreliable. Descriptions and photomicrographs of sectioned EM roots of native tropical species have rarely been published. Sections are needed because non-mutualistic fungi can form mantle-like structures giving the superficial appearance of EM (Levisohn 1954a). Some authors (e.g. Pegler & Fiard 1979) have listed plant species as EM apparently without root examination, because of proximity to a fungus fruiting-body in a genus thought to be obligately EM. Nevertheless, the families previously listed can be considered to contain EM species because of multiple, independent records.

Where EM species do occur in rain forest they are often locally abundant or clumped, either as (i) pioneer or gap-colonizing species (*Allophylus*: Singer & Morello 1960; *Neea*: Janos 1980a), or (ii) dominants of mature communities (*Coccoloba*: Kreisel 1971; *Aldinia*: Singer & Araujo 1979; *Eugenia*: Shamsuddin 1979; *Brachystegia*: Redhead 1980; Caesalpinioideae, Dipterocarpoideae, Fagaceae: Malloch, Pirozynski & Raven 1980; Janos 1980a). Janos (1980a) suggested that EM species are effective colonizers because their wind-dispersed fungus associates may invade disturbed areas more quickly than VAM fungi. Baylis (1975) speculated that a specific EM association might favour the competitive ability of a host species and promote its abundance.

Some tropical species can form both EM and VAM (*Hopea*: Shamsuddin 1979; *Glycoxylon inophyllum* (Mart. ex Miq.) Ducke: reported to have VAM by St John 1980b, and EM by Singer & Araujo 1979; *Casuarina*: National Research Council 1982a; *Eperua purpurea* Benth.: St John & Uhl 1983), an ability reported for only five genera of temperate zone trees (Levisohn 1954b; Vozzo & Hacskaylo 1974; Baylis 1975). Study of such species could reveal the relative ecological costs and benefits of VAM and EM. Vozzo & Hacskaylo (1974) noted a *Populus* species that normally formed EM had only VAM when growing in fertile flood-plain soil. Baylis (1975) observed a normally VAM myrtaceous species that had EM when growing in pure stands. Simultaneous VAM and EM infections of the same root tip have been observed (*Leptospermum*: Baylis 1962), but it is not known if either infection is mutualistic in such cases. Little is known of the physical or chemical constraints that result in the usual fidelity of host species to one mycorrhiza type.

ARE TROPICAL MINERAL NUTRIENT CYCLES DIRECT?

Richards (1952) predicted that rain forest nutrient cycles should be almost completely closed, minimizing mineral losses, because nutrient influx to these ecosystems is limited. The idea that mycorrhizal fungi might effect such closure by decomposing litter and transporting the mineral nutrients thereby released to their hosts is attractive; Went & Stark (1968a, b) proposed this idea as a 'direct mineral cycling' hypothesis. Although not conclusively demonstrated, direct nutrient cycling is presented as a property of tropical rain forests by several general texts (e.g. Farnworth & Golley 1973; Walter 1973; Smith 1980; National Research Council 1982b).

Demonstration of direct nutrient cycling has been confounded by imprecise definition, and especially by failure to properly distinguish between the potential involvement of VAM and EM. Closure of tropical mineral nutrient cycles can result from retention of mineral nutrients by superficial mats of roots and humus (Herrera *et al.* 1978a), and this phenomenon may be confused with direct nutrient cycling in the strict sense. Stark & Jordan (1978) demonstrated that such a root mat retained virtually all of the radioactive calcium and phosphorus solution they applied, but retention was attributed to rapid surface adsorption by organic material rather than to absorption by roots (Herrera *et al.* 1978a).

Direct nutrient cycling requires that mycorrhizal fungi decompose organic material. Orchid mycorrhizal fungi acquire carbon as decomposers (Lewis 1975), and transfer it to heterotrophic orchid protocorms. Hutchison (1981) demonstrated that orchid mycorrhizas supply other elements to mature orchids. Thus, orchids probably cycle minerals directly, but orchid mycorrhizas are distinct from other mycorrhiza types. Potential involvement of tree mycorrhizas in direct nutrient cycling is suggested by data of Herrera *et al.* (1978b) who showed that radioactive phosphorus was present in a mycorrhizal fungus hypha and the living root that it connected to a dead leaf labelled with the isotope. One cannot be sure, however, that the isotope was transported to the root through the hypha, or if the mycorrhizal fungus itself was responsible for release of the isotope from cells of the dead leaf. The directness of terrestrial mineral nutrient cycles can only be resolved by demonstration of enzymatic capability of VAM or EM fungi to mineralize litter.

Decomposition by mycorrhizal fungi

The ability of VAM and EM fungi to digest cellulose and lignin in the soil when associated with a host is unknown, but available data suggest that some EM fungi break down these compounds. There is little unequivocal evidence for either the ability or inability of VAM fungi to degrade these substances, although they seem less likely than EM fungi to have decomposing capability.

An EM was almost certainly involved in the observations of Herrera *et al.* (1978b) that hint at direct mineral cycling (Singer & Araujo 1979). Evidence is scant, however, for decomposition of organic materials by EM fungi associated with a host. Todd (1979) reported that five common temperate zone EM fungi in axenic culture with a host could break down hemicellulose, cellulose, litter and a model humic polymer labelled with radioactive carbon, as evidenced by the evolution of labelled carbon dioxide. Unfortunately, he published only an abstract, making evaluation of his observations difficult. In contrast, Thomas *et al.* (1982) found that seedlings with another EM fungus did not utilize more non-labile phosphorus than uninfected control seedlings.

Data on the ability of EM fungi to produce cellulolytic or lignin-degrading enzymes are conflicting. Most studies have involved pure cultures of fungi, and the mutualistic nature of those isolates that could grow on cellulose or degrade complex phenolics has been questioned. If the source of an isolate was a fruit-body and not a mycorrhizal root, the isolate might be a non-mycorrhizal strain. Moreover, simple soluble sugars contaminating media might cause apparent growth on complex substrates, leading to erroneous inference of decomposing ability. Despite such reservations, Hacskaylo (1973) and Trappe & Fogel (1977) concluded that although the majority of EM fungi seem to have little or no ability to break down complex carbon compounds, some species do. Recently, Giltrap & Lewis, (1981) suggested that some of the earlier reports of failure of EM fungi to grow on complex carbohydrates reflected growth inhibition by phosphate, rather than inability to degrade a complex substrate. Production of lignin-degrading polyphenol oxidases by some EM fungi has been confirmed (Giltrap 1982). The only report of successfully cultured indigenous tropical EM fungi did not include tests of cellulase or polyphenol oxidase production (de Alwis & Abeynayake 1980).

Some EM fungal species can exist as saprophytes in nature (Lewis 1975). Singer (1971) and Hacskaylo & Bruchet (1972) have observed two EM fungal species fruiting in the absence of hosts, suggesting that these strains are saprophytic. Norkrans (1950) showed that a fungus producing cellulase and growing on cellulose in culture, could form EM and ectendomycorrhizas. She hypothesized that glucose supplied to the fungus by a host could suppress cellulase production resulting in a stable mutualism. Giltrap & Lewis (1982) confirmed that synthesis of pectin-degrading enzymes by an EM fungus in pure culture could be repressed by large amounts of glucose. Small amounts of 'starter' glucose, however, can greatly facilitate the induction of pectin-degrading enzymes and utilization of cellulose as a carbon source by some EM fungi in pure culture (Giltrap & Lewis 1982; Norkrans 1950). Mycorrhizal fungi with such inducible enzymes, although ineffective competitors with other soil micro-organisms as saprophytes, and unable to live apart from their hosts, might be able to decompose litter when associated with a host. All evidence considered, it seems likely that there are EM fungus species with some saprophytic ability.

VAM fungi are less likely than EM fungi to decompose litter, although some authors imply that VAM fungi have this ability. Ultrastructural studies suggest that penetration of host roots by VAM fungi is not completely physical. The fungi seem to produce enzymes that loosen the fibrillar structure of the host cell wall, at least locally at hyphal tips (Holley & Peterson 1979). Mosse (1959) anecdotally remarked that VAM fungi appeared to accelerate the breakdown of organic matter. Nevertheless, she acceded that accelerated breakdown of organic matter could be an indirect effect of the presence of VAM fungi, for example, by stimulation of other micro-organisms (e.g. Barea, Azcon & Hayman 1975). Warner & Mosse (1980) felt that their data on spread of VAM fungi through soil in the absence of a host indicated saprophytic ability, but the fungi produced numerous, small secondarily-formed, 'vegetative spores' which could have caused the observed spread if infective.

The anatomy, phosphorus utilization pattern, and ubiquity of VAM imply that VAM fungi lack decomposing ability. No points of hyphal egress from living roots suggestive of exploitation of external carbon sources have been observed; infection spreads within roots away from penetration points (Mosse 1959; Nicolson 1959). Moreover, in several soils mixed with 25% peat, the one VAM fungal species tested utilized the same pool of soluble phosphorus as uninfected roots (Hayman & Mosse 1972). Similar results, however, were obtained with the sole EM fungal species tested in a comparable manner (Thomas *et al.* 1982). VAM fungi associate with a tremendous range of host-plants including most herbs; EM are formed by relatively few taxa of which very few are herbs (e.g. Fontana 1977). VAM fungi probably would not be so ubiquitous if they produced significant amounts of cellulase and were thereby more expensive of energy for hosts to control.

Closure of mineral nutrient cycles

Direct nutrient cycling is probably neither a general tropical phenomenon, nor an ecosystem-wide phenomenon. Rather, it is likely to be a property of orchid species and some EM trees. EM tree species can be locally abundant on extremely poor sites in the lowland tropics, such as those with Spodosols (Singer & Araujo 1979), for which direct nutrient cycling was originally hypothesized. Spodosols, however, constitute only 1% of the world's lowland humid tropical soils (National Research Council 1982b).

Closed mineral nutrient cycles that do not require decomposing ability of mycorrhizal fungi can be widespread. Root mats characterize some ecosystems (Herrera *et al.* 1978a) and single species (e.g. *Oenocarpus panamanus* Bailey: pers. observation). Whittingham & Read (1982) demonstrated that VAM fungi connecting individuals of different species could transport phosphorus from one to another. Reid & Woods (1969) inferred that EM fungi could similarly transport substances between conspecific individuals. If significant quantities of mineral nutrients become available to mycorrhizal fungi as host roots senesce, then such interconnections close mineral cycles.

There is little doubt that mycorrhizas are important for achieving almost complete closure of tropical mineral nutrient cycles for some elements such as phosphorus. Mycorrhizas are efficient at uptake from the soil solution to which mineral nutrients are added by precipitation (Kellman, Hudson & Sanmugadas 1982), throughfall, and stemflow (McColl 1970). Root turnover can be rapid in tropical forests (Jordan & Escalante 1980), and although production of above-ground biomass much exceeds root production per annum, root death may contribute a significant portion of the annual organic matter input to the soil (see Alexander 1983). By virtue of their position, mycorrhizal fungi associated with dying roots could be effective in scavenging nutrients from them in competition with other soil micro-organisms (Heap & Newman 1980), even though dependent on the exoenzymes of other micro-organisms for mineralization.

EFFECTS ON PLANT GROWTH

Because mycorrhizas increase mineral nutrient uptake from infertile or nutritionally imbalanced soils, VAM have often been observed to improve the growth of annual crops, and EM to benefit seedlings of temperate zone timber tree species. Improvements in growth of lowland tropical species have been obtained primarily with VAM on economically important species: *Citrus* varieties (Marx, Bryan & Campbell 1971), pasture legumes (*Centrosema, Lotus, Stylosanthes*: Crush 1974; *Leucaena*: Yost & Fox 1979; *Calopogon, Desmodium, Pueraria*: Waidyanatha 1980), pasture grasses (*Paspalum*: Mosse 1972; *Brachearia*: Mosse 1975; *Agrostis*: Pichot & Truong 1980), field crops (*Arachis*: Daft & El-Giahmi 1976; *Oryza*: Sanni 1976a; *Vigna*: Sanni 1976b; *Manihot*: Yost & Fox 1979; *Eupatorium, Guizotia, Tagetes*: Moawad 1980), fruits (*Carica*: Ramirez, Mitchell & Schenck 1975; *Litchi*: Pandey & Misra 1975; *Bactris*: Janos 1977; *Persea*: Menge *et al.* 1978; *Piper*: Krikun & Bar Joseph 1979; *Psidium, Solanum*: Janos 1980b), and ornamental or timber trees (*Acacia*: Johnson & Michelini 1975; *Khaya*: Redhead 1975; *Vitex*: Janos 1975a; *Pentaclethra, Terminalia, Virola*: Janos 1980b; *Enterolobium*: McHargue 1981). Formation of VAM is a prerequisite for nodulation of many legumes by nitrogen-fixing bacteria (Mosse 1977; Janos 1980b; McHargue 1981). Indigenous tropical EM fungi improved the growth of *Brachystegia eurycoma*

Harms, a common mature-forest tree in Nigeria (Redhead 1980), and *Neea laetevirens* Standl., a small tree of second-growth vegetation in Costa Rica (D. P. Janos, unpubl. data) Additional data on the growth effects of indigenous tropical EM fungi are lacking, however, which is surprising in view of the economic importance of the Dipterocarpaceae.

Experiments to demonstrate effects of mycorrhizas on growth usually are conducted in pots of sterilized soil, but field (see Mosse & Hayman 1980) and nursery (see Mikola 1973) studies have shown similar effects. Cautious qualitative extrapolation from plant responses in limited volumes of soil to anticipated responses in the field is justified. VAM inoculation can improve plant growth in unsterilized fields (Mosse & Hayman 1980) by accelerating mycorrhiza formation or by introducing strains that are more effective than indigenous fungi. Pines cannot be grown where they are not native unless inoculated with EM fungi (Mikola 1973). VAM inoculation has improved seed yields of annual crops (see Khan 1975; Sanni 1976a), and VAM and EM have improved fruit and timber tree seedling survival (e.g. Janos 1977, 1980b; Menge *et al.* 1978; Trappe & Strand 1969). Thus, mycorrhizas may have the ability to influence the ecological fitness of plant species in natural vegetation.

Degrees of dependence on mycorrhizas

In a series of pot experiments with seedlings of thirty-two species of lowland tropical plants, Janos (1975a, 1977, 1980b) found that VAM improved the growth of twenty-eight species, including all of the mature-forest tree species, but that the species differed in their degree of dependence on VAM. Some were able to grow without mycorrhizas, although mycorrhizas improved their growth, while other species could neither grow nor survive without mycorrhizas. The former are facultatively mycotrophic; the latter, if unable to grow without mycorrhizas in the most fertile of their natural habitats, are ecologically obligately mycotrophic. EM species may be ranked along this same continuum. *Neea laetevirens* is facultatively dependent on EM; seedlings grew best when fertilized with ashes at a rate equivalent to that produced by land clearing, although the number of mycorrhizas per seedling decreased with fertilization (D. P. Janos, unpubl. data). Uninoculated *Pinus caribaea* Morelet did not respond to fertilizer applications (Vozzo & Hacskaylo 1971), suggesting obligate dependence on mycorrhizas.

Facultative mycotrophs probably are superior competitors to other species on fertile soils; obligately mycotrophic species are likely to be the best competitors under infertile conditions provided that mycorrhizas form (Janos 1980a). In fertile soil, facultatively mycotrophic species reject mycorrhizas which are of no benefit for mineral nutrient uptake and would exact a potentially detrimental energy cost (Bowen 1980). Their independence of mycorrhizas is correlated with fine roots and profuse root hairs (Baylis 1975; St John 1980c). Obligate mycotrophs have coarse, hairless roots, and are less subject than facultative mycotrophs to wounding and pathogenic infection, and to the potential disadvantages in infertile soil of greatly-overlapping mineral depletion zones (Tinker 1975) and rapid root-system turnover.

Several additional factors are correlated with independence of mycorrhizas.

Facultative mycotrophs may root more deeply (St John 1980a), produce greater root biomass, have higher root/shoot ratios (Azcón & Ocampo 1981), or have lower total mineral requirements (see Janos 1980b) than obligate mycotrophs. Growth rate (Janos 1975b) and tissue mineral concentration (Azcón & Ocampo 1981), however, need not be correlated with independence of mycorrhizas.

Tropical tree species that are strongly dependent on mycorrhizas often have large seeds (Janos 1980b) which favour the persistence of uninfected seedlings and the formation of large pre-infection root systems, maximizing the probability of infection. Obligate mycotrophs are often light-demanding, in part because of the energy requirements of mycorrhizal association. Of two co-occurring *Shorea* species (Dipterocarpaceae) in Malaysia, the species with the higher proportion of infected seedlings and the greater number of EM per infected seedling had the lower rate of seedling survival in forest understorey (P. Becker, pers. comm.). Mycorrhizas—a liability in shade—may have been sustained because of their importance to immediate, rapid seedling growth when canopy gaps open. Mature forest canopy and sub-canopy tree species tend to be obligately mycotrophic; many pioneer and early successional species are facultatively mycotrophic or non-mycorrhizal (Janos 1980b).

Species of Aizoaceae, Amaranthaceae, Brassicaceae, Caryophyllaceae, Chenopodiaceae, Commelinaceae, Cyperaceae, Fumariaceae, Juncaceae, Nyctaginaceae, Phytolaccaceae, Polygonaceae, Portulaccaceae, and Urticaceae usually do not form mycorrhizas (Gerdemann 1968), although VAM stimulated the growth of a chenopod (Williams, Wollum & Aldon 1974), and EM benefited the nyctaginaceous *Neea laetevirens*. Many species of Proteaceae in the genera *Hakea* (Lamont 1972), *Banksia* and *Personia* (Khan 1978) also are non-mycorrhizal, but species of other proteaceous genera have VAM (*Grevillea*: Bakshi 1974; *Helicia*: Janse 1896; *Roupala*: Thomazini 1974). In addition, some species of other families such as the Lecythidaceae (St John 1980a) and Sapotaceae (St John 1980a; de Alwis & Abeynayake 1980) may be non-mycorrhizal. *Ananas comosus* (L.) Merr. (Maeda 1954), *Areca catechu* L. (de Alwis & Abeynayake 1980), and *Durio zibethinus* Murr. (Shamsuddin 1979) are economically important tropical species that have been examined for mycorrhizas and found to lack them, although other members of the families of the latter two species are known to have VAM. Non-dependence on mycorrhizas needs to be confirmed by growth experiments.

Non-mycorrhizal species are not dependent on mycorrhizas even under infertile conditions because, like facultative mycotrophs, they have fine, highly-branched roots, numerous root hairs, or low tissue mineral requirements. *Hakea*, *Banksia* and *Personia* species produce dense clusters of rootlets on what are known as 'proteoid' roots. In addition, non-mycorrhizal species may liberate bound organic phosphorus by secreting organic acids (see Tinker 1975 and Graustein, Cromack & Sollins 1977), or have slow growth rates or durable tissues that compensate for limited nutrient supply. Non-mycorrhizal species actively reject mycorrhizal association because it is incompatible with their physiology, or in order to favour their persistence in competition with mycotrophic species (Janos 1980b). They are the only species that are effective competitors on infertile soils in the absence of mycorrhizal fungi.

Mineral nutrient availability (especially that of phosphorus), and the probability of mycorrhizal infection in different habitats (Janos 1980a) are probably the primary selective factors that produced different dependencies on mycorrhizas. In addition to the probability of infection, the factors most likely to influence the type of mycorrhiza upon which a host depends are seasonal dryness, periodic mineral nutrient availability, the form in which nitrogen is available, and suppression of decomposition by toxic compounds in litter or by low C/N ratio (see Janos 1980a).

Dependence on mycorrhizas influences, and is probably influenced by the dispersion characteristics and demography of plant species. For example, clumped or locally abundant non-mycorrhizal and EM species are likely to create conditions that favour their continued success: non-mycorrhizal species lower soil infectiveness; EM species increase infectiveness with respect to specific fungus associates (Janos 1980a). Non-mycorrhizal species and some EM species can have the demographic character-istics of pioneer or fugitive species because non-mycorrhizal plants can quickly establish without awaiting infection, and EM inoculum can build up very rapidly. Obligate mycotrophs probably are the best competitors under mature forest conditions; those with large seeds maximize the probability of seedling infection, and the continuance of mycorrhizal association is thereby favoured.

COMMUNITY COMPOSITION

Dependence of plant species on different types of mycorrhizas to different extents can influence the composition of both seral and mature plant communities. Janos (1980a) described how obligate mycotrophs could replace non-mycorrhizal and facultatively mycotrophic seral species during tropical succession. Replacement is caused by declining fertility as soils age, or by increasing probability of mycorrhizal infection subsequent to a succession-initiating event that reduced or eliminated mycorrhizal fungus populations. Direct effects of mycorrhizas on succession depend upon changes in probability of infection that can occur when persistent, large populations of spores are not present. Humid-tropical soils under native vegetation (Redhead 1977; Herrera & Ferrer 1980; Janos 1980a; St John & Uhl 1983), a tree nursery (Redhead 1977) and some tree plantations (Nadarajah 1980) usually contain few spores, although Waidyanatha (1980) found very many spores in rubber plantations. Spore numbers may decline rapidly if sporulation is infrequent, because spores germinate in the absence of hosts (Koske 1981) and are subject to predation and parasitism (Redhead 1977; Janos 1980a; Nadarajah 1980).

Mycorrhizal fungus population sizes are likely to be affected by plant community composition (Janos 1980a; Kormanik, Bryan & Schultz 1980), and, in turn, to influence it (Reeves *et al.* 1979; Shamsuddin 1980). Rapid mycorrhizal infection in a moderately fertile soil, for example, can allow an obligately mycotrophic seedling to outcompete a facultatively mycotrophic one which would otherwise outgrow it. VAM increased seedling survival of three strongly mycorrhiza-dependent tropical tree species in mixed plots of nine competing species that included non-mycorrhizal and facultatively mycotrophic ones (D. P. Janos, unpubl. data). These experiments also suggested that VAM reduce differences in competitive ability among all species at typical tropical soil fertilities, and thereby contribute to the high within-habitat species diversity characteristic of most tropical forests.

Species diversity in mature tropical forests is correlated with the presence of different types of mycorrhizas. Several of the genera that contain species occurring in monospecific stands in the tropics (Connell 1978) are known to include EM members. Perhaps, as Baylis (1975) suggested, optimal EM associations assist a species to dominance. Monospecific stands are frequently found on infertile white sands (Richards 1952) where decomposing ability of EM fungi would be highly advantageous. Hosts associated with EM fungi with decomposing ability are unlikely to be abundant on fertile soils, however, because of carbohydrate and defensive costs associated with controlling the fungi. On relatively fertile soils VAM species are abundant; their diversity is high in part because of the inability of host species to rapidly outcompete one another when depending on the same fungus species for mineral nutrient uptake. The hosts of EM fungi without decomposing ability are effective competitors with VAM species on fertile soils where nitrification is inhibited or water and phosphorus availability is seasonal (Janos 1980a). Niche differentiation between EM and VAM species probably contributes to very high diversity in mixed dipterocarp forest.

Forest composition with respect to mycorrhiza types and dependencies may be strongly influenced by forest turnover rates (Janos 1980a). Frequent or extensive disturbance can favour non-mycorrhizal or EM species that are effective colonizers. The presence of such species might, in turn, lower diversity by reducing VAM fungus populations and impeding the establishment of obligately mycotrophic VAM hosts. Because of differences in forest composition, productivity need not be highly correlated with fertility. Mycorrhizas, especially EM with decomposing ability, compensate for low soil nutrient availability; at high fertility, dominance by facultative mycotrophs might lead to incomplete resource exploitation and lower production than achieved by a mixed community at lower fertility. Mycorrhizas influence nutrient cycling, plant growth and productivity in tropical rain forest; they may influence species diversity as well. Species diversity is highest in rain forests with moderate turnover rates on soils intermediate in fertility between very nutrient-poor tropical white sands and rich, recent volcanics (see Huston 1980) perhaps because these conditions allow species of all degrees of dependence on both VAM and EM to coexist.

ACKNOWLEDGMENTS

I thank I. Alexander, P. Becker, G. Hartshorn, E. Leigh, L. McHargue, J. Proctor, P. Regal, H. Teas and K. Waddington for criticism of these ideas. My attendance of the Rain Forest Symposium was partially supported by National Science Foundation grant DEB-8117529 to Duke University on behalf of the Organization for Tropical Studies. This paper is contribution No. 87 from the Program in Tropical Biology, Ecology and Behaviour of the Department of Biology, University of Miami.

REFERENCES

Alexander, I.J. (1981). Mycorrhizas in the Sapindaceae. *Program and Abstracts*, p. 60. Fifth North American Conference on Mycorrhizae. Université Laval, Québec.

Alexander, I.J. (1983). The significance of ectomycorrhizas in the nitrogen cycle. *Nitrogen as an Ecological Factor* (Ed. by J. A. Lee, S. McNeill & I. H. Rorison). Blackwell Scientific Publications, Oxford (in press).

Alexander, I.J. & Hardy, K. (1981). Surface phosphatase activity of sitka spruce mycorrhizas from a serpentine site. *Soil Biology and Biochemistry*, **13**, 301–305.

de Alwis, D. P. & Abeynayake, K. (1980). A survey of mycorrhizae in some forest trees of Sri Lanka. *Tropical Mycorrhiza Research* (Ed. by P. Mikola), pp. 146–153. Clarendon Press, Oxford.

Azcón, R. & Ocampo, J.A. (1981). Factors affecting the vesicular-arbuscular infection and mycorrhizal dependency of thirteen wheat cultivars. *New Phytologist*, **87**, 677–685.

Bagyaraj, D.J., Manjunath, A. & Patil, R.B. (1979). Occurrence of vesicular-arbuscular mycorrhizas in some tropical aquatic plants. *Transactions of the British Mycological Society*, **72**, 164–167.

Bakshi, B.K. (1974). *Mycorrhiza and Its Role in Forestry*. PL 480 Project Report. Dehra Dun.

Barea, J.M., Azcon, R. & Hayman, D.S. (1975). Possible synergistic interactions between *Endogone* and phosphate-solubilizing bacteria in low-phosphate soils. *Endomycorrhizas* (Ed. by F. E. Sanders, B. Mosse & P. B. Tinker), pp. 409–417. Academic Press, London.

Baylis, G.T.S. (1962). *Rhizophagus*. The catholic symbiont. *The Australian Journal of Science*, **25**, 195–209.

Baylis, G.T.S. (1975). The magnolioid mycorrhiza and mycotrophy in root systems derived from it. *Endomycorrhizas* (Ed. by F. E. Sanders, B. Mosse & P. B. Tinker), pp. 373–390. Academic Press, London.

Bowen, G.D. (1980). Mycorrhizal roles in tropical plants and ecosystems. *Tropical Mycorrhiza Research* (Ed. by P. Mikola), pp. 165–190. Clarendon Press, Oxford.

Bowen, G.D. & Theodorou, C. (1973). Growth of ectomycorrhizal fungi around seeds and roots. *Ectomycorrhizae* (Ed. by G. C. Marks & T. T. Kozlowski), pp. 107–150. Academic Press, New York.

Connell, J.H. (1978). Diversity in tropical rainforests and coral reefs. *Science*, **199**, 1302–1310.

Crush, J.R. (1974). Plant growth responses to vesicular-arbuscular mycorrhiza. VII. Growth and nodulation of some herbage legumes. *New Phytologist*, **73**, 743–752.

Daft, M.J. & El-Giahmi, A.A. (1976). Studies on nodulated and mycorrhizal peanuts. *Annals of Applied Biology*, **83**, 273–276.

Daft, M.J. & Okusanya, B.O. (1973). Effect of *Endogone* mycorrhiza on plant growth. V. Influence of infection on the multiplication of viruses in tomato, petunia, and strawberry. *New Phytologist*, **72**, 975–983.

Duddridge, J.A., Malibari, A. & Read, D.J. (1980). Structure and function of mycorrhizal rhizomorphs with special reference to their role in water transport. *Nature*, **287**, 834–836.

Edmisten, J. (1970). Survey of mycorrhiza and root nodules in the El Verde forest. *A Tropical Rain Forest* (Ed. by H. T. Odum & R. F. Pigeon), pp. F15–F20. U.S. Atomic Energy Commission, Oak Ridge.

Emmons, L.H. (1982). Ecology of *Proechimys* (Rodential, Echimyidae) in Southeastern Peru. *Tropical Ecology*. **3**, 280–290.

Farnworth, E.G. & Golley, F.B. (Eds.) **(1973).** *Fragile Ecosystems*. Springer, New York.

Fontana, A. (1977). Ectomycorrhizae in *Polygonum viviparum* L. *Abstracts*, p. 53. Third North American Conference on Mycorrhizae. Athens, Georgia.

Gerdemann, J.W. (1968). Vesicular-arbuscular mycorrhiza and plant growth. *Annual Review of Phytopathology*, **6**, 397–418.

Gerdemann, J.W. & Trappe, J.M. (1974). *The Endogonaceae in the Pacific Northwest*. Mycologia Memoir, 5.

Giltrap, N.J. (1982). Production of polyphenol oxidases by ectomycorrhizal fungi with special reference to *Lactarius* spp. *Transactions of the British Mycological Society*, **78**, 75–81.

Giltrap, N.J. & Lewis, D.H. (1981). Inhibition of growth of ectomycorrhizal fungi in culture by phosphate. *New Phytologist*, **87**, 669–675.

Giltrap, N.J. & Lewis, D.H. (1982). Catabolite repression of the synthesis of pectin-degrading enzymes by *Suillus luteus* (L. ex Fr.) S. F. Gray and *Hebeloma oculatum* Bruchet. *New Phytologist*, **90**, 485–493.

Graustein, W.C., Cromack, K. & Sollins, P. (1977). Calcium oxalate: its occurrence in soils and effect on nutrient and geochemical cycles. *Science*, **198**, 1252–1254.

Hacskaylo, E. (1973). Carbohydrate physiology of ectomycorrhizae. *Ectomycorrhizae* (Ed. by G. C. Marks & T. T. Kozlowski), pp. 207–230. Academic Press, New York.

Hacskaylo, E. & Bruchet, G. (1972). Hebelomas as mycorrhizal fungi. *Bulletin of the Torrey Botanical Club*, 99, 17–20.

Hall, I.R. & Fish, B.J. (1979). A key to the Endogonaceae. *Transactions of the British Mycological Society*, 73, 261–270.

Harley, J.L. & Lewis, D.H. (1969). The physiology of ectotrophic mycorrhizas. *Advances in Microbiol Physiology*, 3, 53–81.

Hayman, D.S. & Mosse, B. (1972). Plant growth responses to vesicular-arbuscular mycorrhiza. III. Increased uptake of labile P from soil. *New Phytologist*, 71, 41–47.

Heap, A.J. & Newman, E.I. (1980). The influence of vesicular-arbuscular mycorrhizas on phosphorus transfer between plants. *New Phytologist*, 85, 173–179.

Herrera, R., Jordan, C.F., Klinge, H. & Medina, E. (1978a). Amazon ecosystems. Their structure and functioning with particular emphasis on nutrients. *Interciencia*, 3, 223–231.

Herrera, R., Merida, T., Stark, N. & Jordan, C.F. (1978b). Direct phosphorus transfer from leaf litter to roots. *Naturwissenschaften*, 65, 208–209.

Herrera, R.A. & Ferrer, R.L. (1980). Vesicular-arbuscular mycorrhiza in Cuba. *Tropical Mycorrhiza Research* (Ed. by P. Mikola), pp. 156–162. Clarendon Press, Oxford.

Holley, J.D. & Peterson, R.L. (1979). Development of a vesicular-arbuscular mycorrhiza in bean roots. *Canadian Journal of Botany*, 57, 1960–1978.

Horak, E. (1977). Biogeography of native ectomycorrhizal Agarics in the Southern Hemisphere. *Second International Mycological Conference Abstracts*, p. 305. University of South Florida, Tampa.

Höweler, R.H., Edwards, D.G. & Asher, C.J. (1981). Application of the flowing solution culture techniques to studies involving mycorrhizas. *Plant and Soil*, 59, 179–183.

Huston, M. (1980). Soil nutrients and tree species richness in Costa Rican forests. *Journal of Biogeography*, 7, 147–157.

Hutchison, C. (1981). The nutritional role of the endophyte in adult plants of *Goodyera repens*. *Program and Abstracts*, p. 43. Fifth North American Conference on Mycorrhizae. Université Laval, Québec.

Ivory, M.H. (1980). Ectomycorrhizal fungi of lowland tropical pines in natural forests and exotic plantations. *Tropical Mycorrhiza Research* (Ed. by P. Mikola), pp. 110–117. Clarendon Press, Oxford.

Janos, D.P. (1975a) Effects of vesicular-arbuscular mycorrhizae on lowland tropical rainforest trees. *Endomycorrhizas* (Ed. by F. E. Sanders, B. Mosse & P. B. Tinker), pp. 437–446. Academic Press, London.

Janos, D.P. (1975b). *Vesicular-arbuscular mycorrhizal fungi and plant growth in a Costa Rican lowland rainforest*. Doctoral dissertation, University of Michigan, Ann Arbor.

Janos, D.P. (1977). Vesicular-arbuscular mycorrhizae affect the growth of *Bactris gasipaes*. *Principes*, 21, 12–18.

Janos, D.P. (1980a). Mycorrhizae influence tropical succession. *Biotropica*, 12 (Suppl.), 56–64.

Janos, D.P. (1980b). Vesicular-arbuscular mycorrhizae affect lowland tropical rain forest plant growth. *Ecology*, 61, 151–162.

Janos, D.P. & Trappe, J.M. (1982). Two new *Acaulospora* species from tropical America. *Mycotaxon*, 15, 515–522.

Janse, J.M. (1896). Les endophytes radicaux de quelques plantes Javanaises. *Annales de Jardin Botanique Buitenzorg*, 14, 53–212.

Johnson, C.R. & Michelini, S. (1975). Effect of mycorrhizae on container grown *Acacia*. *Proceedings of the Florida State Horticultural Society*, 87, 520–522.

Johnston, A. (1949). Vesicular-arbuscular mycorrhiza in Sea Island cotton and other tropical plants. *Tropical Agriculture, Trinidad*, 26, 118–121.

Jordan, C.F. & Escalante, G. (1980). Root productivity in an amazonian rain forest. *Ecology*, 61, 14–18.

Keeley, J.E. (1980). Endomycorrhizae influence growth of blackgum seedlings in flooded soils. *American Journal of Botany*, 67, 6–9.

Kellman, M., Hudson, J. & Sanmugadas, K. (1982). Temporal variability in atmospheric nutrient influx to a tropical ecosystem. *Biotropica*, 14, 1–9.

Khan, A.G. (1975). Growth effects of vesicular-arbuscular mycorrhiza on crops in the field. *Endomycorrhizas* (Ed. by F. E. Sanders, B. Mosse & P. B. Tinker), pp. 419–436. Academic Press, London.

Khan, A.G. (1978). Vesicular-arbuscular mycorrhizas in plants colonizing black wastes from bituminous coal mining in the Illawarra region of New South Wales. *New Phytologist,* **81,** 53–63.

Kormanik, P.P., Bryan, W.C. & Schultz, R.C. (1980). Increasing endomycorrhizal fungus inoculum in forest nursery soil with cover crops. *Southern Journal of Applied Forestry,* **4,** 151–153.

Koske, R.E. (1981). *Gigaspora gigantea:* observations on spore germination of a VA-mycorrhizal fungus. *Mycologia,* **73,** 288–300.

Kreisel, H. (1971). Ektotrophe Mykorrhiza bei *Coccoloba uvifera* in Kuba. *Biologische Rundschau,* **9,** 97–98.

Krikun, J. & Bar Joseph, B. (1979). Pepper and mycorrhizae: a field study. *Program and Abstracts.* Fourth North American Conference on Mycorrhiza. Colorado State University, Fort Collins.

Lambert, D.H., Cole, H. Jr. & Baker, D.E. (1980). Adaptation of vesicular-arbuscular mycorrhizae to edaphic factors. *New Phytologist,* **85,** 513–520.

Lamont, B. (1972). The morphology and anatomy of proteoid roots in the genus *Hakea. Australian Journal of Botany,* **20,** 155–174.

Levisohn, I. (1954a). Aberrant root infections of pine and spruce seedlings. *New Phytologist,* **53,** 284–290.

Levisohn, I. (1954b). Occurrence of ectotrophic and endotrophic mycorrhizas in forest trees. *Forestry,* **27,** 145–146.

Lewis, D.H. (1975). Comparative aspects of the carbon nutrition of mycorrhizas. *Endomycorrhizas* (Ed. by F. E. Sanders, B. Mosse & P. B. Tinker), pp. 119–148. Academic Press, London.

Macdonald, R.M. & Lewis, M. (1978). The occurrence of some acid phosphatases and dehydrogenases in the vesicular-arbuscular mycorrhizal fungus *Glomus mosseae. New Phytologist,* **80,** 135–141.

Maeda, M. (1954). The meaning of mycorrhiza in regard to sytematic botany. *Kumamoto Journal of Science,* Series B, **3,** 57–84.

Malloch, D.W., Pirozynski, K.A. & Raven, P.H. (1980). Ecological and evolutionary significance of mycorrhizal symbioses in vascular plants (a review). *Proceedings of the National Academy of Sciences,* U.S.A., **77,** 2113–2118.

Marks, G.C. & Foster, R.C. (1973). Structure, morphogenesis, and ultrastructure of ectomycorrhizae. *Ectomycorrhizae* (Ed. by G. C. Marks & T. T. Kozlowski), pp. 2–42. Academic Press, New York.

Marx, D.H. (1972). Ectomycorrhizae as biological deterrents to pathogenic root infections. *Annual Review of Phytopathology,* **10,** 429–454.

Marx, D.H. (1977). Tree host range and world distribution of the ectomycorrhizal fungus *Pisolithus tinctorius. Canadian Journal of Microbiology,* **23,** 217–223.

Marx, D.H., Bryan, W.C. & Campbell, W.A. (1971). Effect of endomycorrhizae formed by *Endogone mosseae* on the growth of citrus. *Mycologia,* **63,** 1222–1225.

Maser, C., Trappe, J.M. & Nussbaum, R.A. (1978). Fungal–small mammal interrelationships with emphasis on Oregon coniferous forests. *Ecology,* **59,** 799–809.

McColl, J.G. (1970). Properties of some natural waters in a tropical wet forest of Costa Rica. *BioScience,* **20,** 1096–1100.

McHargue, L.A. (1981). V-A mycorrhizae improve growth and nodulation of two tropical leguminous trees. *Program and Abstracts,* p. 52. Fifth North American Conference on Mycorrhizae. Université Laval, Québec.

McIlveen, W.D. & Cole, H. Jr. (1976). Spore dispersal of Endogonaceae by worms, ants, wasps, and birds. *Canadian Journal of Botany,* **54,** 1486–1489.

Menge, J.A., Davis, R.M., Johnson, E.L.V. & Zentmyer, G.A. (1978). Mycorrhizal fungi increase growth and reduce transplant injury in avocado. *California Agriculture,* **32,** 6–7.

Mikola, P. (1973). Application of mycorrhizal symbiosis in forestry practice. *Ectomycorrhizae* (Ed. by G. C. Marks & T. T. Kozlowski), pp. 383–411. Academic Press, New York.

Moawad, M. (1980). Ecophysiology of vesicular-arbuscular mycorrhiza. *Tropical Mycorrhiza Research* (Ed. by P. Mikola), pp. 203–205. Clarendon Press, Oxford.

Mosse, B. (1959). Observations on the extra-matrical mycelium of a vesicular-arbuscular endophyte. *Transactions of the British Mycological Society,* **42,** 439–448.

Mosse, B. (1972). Effects of different *Endogone* strains on the growth of *Paspalum notatum. Nature,* **239,** 221–223.

Mosse, B. (1973). Advances in the study of vesicular-arbuscular mycorrhiza. *Annual Review of Phytopathology,* **11,** 171–196.

Son
Mi

1 Site and so
Mixed Diptero
and associated
2 These data
analysis. The si
by single and c
3 The excha
correlated and
reserve nutrien
than those wit
have soil parer
4 The associa
the floristic va
5 These resul
the nutrient c
suggests that p
tropical rain fc

Apart from th
research into tl
Borneo. Ecolo
zation of thes
relation to the
been reportec
Greig-Smith &
not yet been f
and implicatic

Mosse, B. (1975). Specificity of vesicular-arbuscular mycorrhizas. *Endomycorrhizas* (Ed. by F. E. Sanders, B. Mosse & P. B. Tinker), pp. 469–484. Academic Press, London.

Mosse, B. (1977). The role of mycorrhiza in legume nutrition on marginal soils. *Exploiting the legume*–Rhizobium *symbiosis in tropical agriculture* (Ed. by J. M. Vincent, A. S. Whitney & J. Bose), pp. 275–292. College of Tropical Agriculture, University of Hawaii, Miscellaneous Publication 145.

Mosse, B. & Hayman, D.S. (1980). Mycorrhiza in agricultural plants. *Tropical Mycorrhiza Research* (Ed. by P. Mikola), pp. 213–230. Clarendon Press, Oxford.

Nadarajah, P. (1980). Species of Endogonaceae and mycorrhizal association of *Elaeis guineensis* and *Theobroma cacao*. *Tropical Mycorrhiza Research* (Ed. by P. Mikola), pp. 232–237. Clarendon Press, Oxford.

National Research Council (1982a). *Innovations in Tropical Reforestation VI: Casuarinas*. National Academy Press, Washington, D.C.

National Research Council (1982b). *Ecological Aspects of Development in the Humid Tropics*. National Academy Press, Washington, D.C.

Nicolson, T.H. (1959). Mycorrhiza in the gramineae I. Vesicular-arbuscular endophytes, with special reference to the external phase. *Transactions of the British Mycological Society*, 42, 421–438.

Nicolson, T.H. & Schenck, N.C. (1979). Endogonaceous mycorrhizal endophytes in Florida. *Mycologia*, 71, 178–198.

Norkrans, B. (1950). Studies in growth and cellulolytic enzymes of *Tricholoma*. *Symbolae Botanicae Upsalienses*, 11, 1–126.

Owusu-Bennoah, E. & Wild, A. (1980). Effects of vesicular-arbuscular mycorrhiza on the size of the labile pool of soil phosphate. *Plant and Soil*, 54, 233–242.

Pandey, S.P. & Misra, A.P. (1975). Mycorrhizas in relation to growth and fruiting of *Litchi chinensis* Sonn. *Journal of the Indian Botanical Society*, 54, 280–293.

Pegler, D.N. & Fiard, J.P. (1979). Taxonomy and ecology of *Lactarius* (Agaricales) in the Lesser Antilles (West Indies). *Kew Bulletin*, 33, 601–628.

Phillips, J.M. & Hayman, D.S. (1970). Improved procedures for clearing roots and staining parasitic and vesicular-arbuscular mycorrhizal fungi for rapid assessment of infection. *Transactions of the British Mycological Society*, 55, 158–161.

Pichot, J. & Truong, B. (1980). Effect of endomycorrhizae on growth and phosphorus uptake of *Agrostis* in a pot experiment. *Tropical Mycorrhiza Research* (Ed. by P. Mikola), pp. 206–209. Clarendon Press, Oxford.

Ramirez, B.N., Mitchell, D.J. & Schenck, N.C. (1975). Establishment and growth effects of three vesicular-arbuscular mycorrhizal fungi on papaya. *Mycologia*, 67, 1039–1041.

Redhead, J.F. (1968). Mycorrhizal associations in some Nigerian forest trees. *Transactions of the British Mycological Society*, 51, 377–387.

Redhead, J. F. (1975). Endotrophic mycorrhizas in Nigeria: some aspects of the ecology of the endotrophic mycorrhizal association of *Khaya grandifoliola* C. DC. *Endomycorrhizas* (Ed. by F. E. Sanders, B. Mosse & P. B. Tinker), pp. 447–459. Academic Press, London.

Redhead, J.F. (1977). Endotrophic mycorrhizas in Nigeria: species of the Endogonaceae and their distribution. *Transactions of the British Mycological Society*, 69, 275–280.

Redhead, J.F. (1980). Mycorrhiza in natural tropical forests. *Tropical Mycorrhiza Research* (Ed. by P. Mikola), pp. 127–142. Clarendon Press, Oxford.

Reeves, F.B., Wagner, D., Moorman, T. & Kiel, J. (1979). The role of endomycorrhizae in revegetation practices in the semi-arid west. I. A comparison of incidence of mycorrhizae in severely disturbed vs. natural environments. *American Journal of Botany*, 66, 6–13.

Reid, C.P.P. & Woods, F.W. (1969). Translocation of C^{14}-labeled compounds in mycorrhizae and its implications in interplant nutrient cycling. *Ecology*, 50, 179–187.

Richards, P.W. (1952). *The Tropical Rain Forest*. University Press, Cambridge.

Safir, G.R., Boyer, J.S. & Gerdemann, J.W. (1972). Nutrient status and mycorrhizal enhancement of water transport in soybean. *Plant Physiology*, 49, 700–703.

Sanni, S.O. (1976a). Vesicular-arbuscular mycorrhiza in some Nigerian soils: the effects of *Gigaspora gigantea* on the growth of rice. *New Phytologist*, 77, 673–674.

Sanni, S.O. (1976b). Vesicular-arbuscular mycorrhiza in some Nigerian soils and their effect on the growth

    (c) Number of genera with $\geqslant 1$ tree species revised in the 82 families: 388

    (d) Total number of species in the 388 tree genera: 2397

    (e) Number of endemic species in the 388 tree genera: 653

The 653 endemic species constitute 27% of the tree flora, based on the eighty-two families so far revised. The remaining sixteen families are not expected to alter the percentage very much, hence 27% may be taken as a measure of the floristic difference separating the Peninsula from the surrounding regions.

On a one-to-one comparison, e.g. Peninsula versus Sumatra, Peninsula versus Borneo, or Peninsula versus Thailand, the floristic difference may be expected to rise to about 50%. Hence, the floristic differences are so great between the various land masses in Malesia that major conservation efforts have to be made separately on every land mass in order to adequately conserve the genetic components peculiar to each land mass.

On a family-by-family analysis, the largest numbers of endemic species are contributed by the two largest families: Euphorbiaceae (101 endemics of a total of 344 species or 29%) and Myrtaceae (80 endemics of a total of 209 species or 38%). However, the relationship between endemism and family size is rather complicated. Large families must by implication be those that have speciated (and may still be speciating) freely. If their evolutionary strategy is to evolve different species to fill different ecological niches, while expanding their range, then one can expect to find not only a large number of species but also a high proportion of endemics.

This expectation, while fulfilled in Euphorbiaceae (29%) Myrtaceae (38%) and also Annonaceae (41%) and Guttiferae (33%), is not quite fulfilled in Dipterocarpaceae (18%) and Leguminosae (24%). The most startling departure from expectation is Moraceae in which only six out of 134 species, or 4% are endemic. The genus *Ficus* alone contributes 101 species to Moraceae in the Peninsula but nearly all of them range widely beyond the Peninsula. This indicates that the mechanisms of speciation and dispersal in *Ficus* may be quite different from those operating in other large taxa.

The small families, represented by one to ten species each in the Peninsula, total forty-eight families. These contribute only 205 species to the tree flora of the Peninsula, of which only twenty-seven species (13%) are endemic. This is substantially below the average of 27% and suggest that these small families not only consist mainly of species extending into the Peninsula from their main centres elsewhere, but also that they have an inherently conservative genetic constitution that retards their rate of speciation in the Peninsula.

REGENERATION BIOLOGY

Assuming that seed production is not limiting, the ability of species to maintain their place in a forest community is dependent next on the interplay of factors controlling the fate of seeds and seedlings. Let us briefly examine some of these factors, beginning with the fate of seeds on the forest floor.

The soil seed bank

Seeds deposited on the forest floor lie there for varying lengths of time and germinate or die at varying rates depending on the nature of the species. The forest floor may be regarded as a seed bank from which withdrawals are made through germination and seed-death. The characteristics of this seed bank may be used to define the regenerative capacity of the community from its own stored seed reserve.

However, direct studies on the soil seed bank *in situ* are complicated by uncertainties over the age of the seeds already there, as well as the impossibility of arranging for a representative sample of species to seed in the same time and place. We can get around this problem by building up a model from accumulated *ex situ* experiments in which fresh seeds are planted in soil and kept under warm, shaded and regularly watered conditions. I have used germination data from such experiments, involving 335 species and representing roughly 10% of the Malaysian woody flora (Ng 1980b) to construct a histogram (Fig. 3) showing the rate of loss of species from the soil seed bank against time of deposition in the soil.

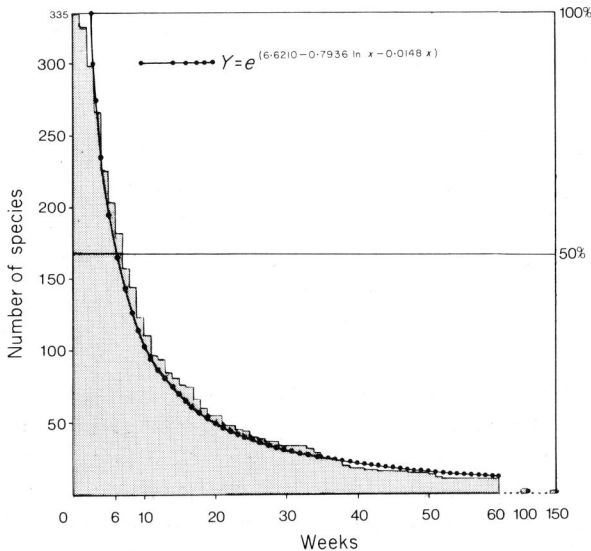

The equation shown on the figure:

$$Y = e^{(6\cdot6210 - 0\cdot7936 \ln x - 0\cdot0148 x)}$$

FIG. 3. Rate of loss of species from hypothetical soil seed bank under conditions normally suitable for germination (after Ng 1981a).

The result is a reversed 'J' distribution to which a smooth curve and mathematical formula can be fitted. I would suggest that this distribution represents the response of the tropical rain forest, *as a community* to two opposing selection forces. One force favours rapid germination and pulls the response curve towards zero on the time axis, while the opposite force favours delayed germination and pulls the response curve towards infinite time. The time-lapse at which 50% of the species are withdrawn from the seed bank is only 6 weeks! It is clear that the soil seed bank is virtually useless as a source of seeds for the establishment of the original composition of the forest after loss of the mature vegetation.

Effect of light on regeneration

Recent studies (Aminuddin & Ng 1982) have produced evidence to strengthen the hypothesis that forest soils act effectively as a seed bank mainly for pioneer species (Symington 1933; Liew 1973). The seeds of such species lie dormant under forest shade and are stimulated to germinate when the forest canopy is opened.

Seeds of primary forest species germinate both in light as well as in shade, as far as is known at present. However, the growth of their seedlings is heavily influenced by light quantity and quality, with each species performing optimally within a specific range of relative light intensity (Sasaki & Mori 1981).

Effect of humidity on regeneration

Whereas light intensity has long been identified as perhaps the most important single factor in seedling growth—so much so that most silvicultural operations revolve around canopy manipulation (Wyatt-Smith 1963)—the role of humidity has been neglected.

The tropical rain forest is a unique habitat not so much because of its light regime but because of its warmth and high humidity. It would be surprising if the species of the rain forest have not become humidity-dependent but what is the true extent and nature of humidity-dependence and how can it be demonstrated? From morphological observations, we know that most tropical rain forest trees have pulvini on their petioles, and the wrinkled nature of these pulvini suggest that they are active in adjusting the angle of the leaf blades. Such movements are rather more conspicuous in some families (e.g. Leguminosae, Euphorbiaceae and Oxalidaceae) than others but they probably occur to some extent in all trees.

In the giant forest legume *Intsia palembanica*, seedlings grown in chambers where humidity is kept high, do not droop their leaves as much as seedlings grown without shelter, and the sheltered seedlings appear to be healthier (Sasaki & Ng 1981). It is suggested, therefore, that humidity interacts with light intensity to control leaf angle, photosynthesis and growth. For *Intsia palembanica*, a combination of high light intensity and high humidity may be necessary for optimum growth. The example of *Intsia palembanica* may well be merely the tip of a widespread and hitherto unmeasured phenomenon.

Forests dry out gradually through alteration of the hydrological regime by agricultural and other disturbances at the periphery. As a result, the course of succession may be drastically changed through failure of humidity-dependent mechanisms operating at the regeneration level. A particularly striking humidity-dependent effect has been observed to operate during germination. In experiments with direct field planting of seeds of *Intsia palembanica* (Sasaki & Ng 1981), the (previously scarified) seeds germinate normally after imbibing soil water. Germination is epigeal, with the elongating hypocotyl carrying the cotyledons out of the soil. The testa is often not yet fully shed at this stage and may still surround the uplifted cotyledons. The air is a different environment from the soil and that can lead to trouble. Under open conditions, the uplifted testa dries and hardens to prevent the complete emergence of the cotyledons and hypocotyl.

Seedlings with cotyledons and epicotyl trapped in the testa, can rot from the top and die. Mortalities of up to 100% have been observed, e.g. in *Ryparosa* and *Scaphocalyx* in the Flacourtiaceae. The only way to save such seedlings is to remove the testa by hand as soon as the epicotyl is seen to be trapped.

This phenomenon was actually first described by Wright (1904) during studies on the germination of *Diospyros* in Ceylon (Sri Lanka). Wright termed such germination 'suicidal'. We now know that it is not a case of suicide but one of extreme specialization and dependence on high humidity during germination. Taxa that are vulnerable are those that happen to combine two separate characteristics: (i) germination involving the uplifting of the seed body with testa or albumen still surrounding it; (ii) a testa or albumen that softens in moisture and hardens when dry.

The species so far known to be highly vulnerable (in nursery experiments with twice-a-day watering) are in the Annonaceae (*Polyalthia cauliflora*, *P. cinnamomea*, *Xylopia caudata*), Ebenaceae (*Diospyros pendula*, *D. sumatrana*) and Flacourtiaceae (*Ryparosa kunstleri*, *Scaphocalyx spathacea*). The phenomenon may be more widespread in the field under uncertain rainfall conditions.

Effects of animals on regeneration

Animals have a negative effect through seed predation, defoliation, etc., but animal populations are subject to natural checks and balances. We have no evidence as yet in the Peninsula to implicate predation by animals as a possible factor in extinction of plants.

On the other hand, there are fruit-feeding animals which clean and disperse seed. Of special interest is the seed-cleaning aspect because various experiments have shown that some species are absolutely dependent on animals to render their seeds germinable. From my own observations, *Canarium* (Burseraceae), *Xanthophyllum* (Polygalaceae) and some species of *Calophyllum* (Guttiferae) require to have their fleshy fruit wall removed, while *Sloanea* (Elaeocarpaceae) requires its aril to be removed, before germination can take place. In *Calamus* (Palmae), Manokaran (1978) found the intact pericarp to be detrimental to germination. Even after the pericarp is removed, the sarcotesta of *Calamus* is detrimental and has to be removed (Mori *et al.* 1980). In *Xerospermum* (Sapindaceae) Yap (1976) found that fruits opened by monkeys germinated while fruits that had fallen on the ground without being opened, failed to germinate. In all these cases, germination is not merely inhibited; the seeds die. There is nothing to suggest, so far, that fleshy pericarp, sarcotesta or aril can induce dormancy.

It is perhaps significant that the two families of big trees in S.E. Asia which have the greatest number of large individuals per unit area are Dipterocarpaceae and Leguminosae, both of which do not require the seed cleaning services of animals. Some genera of Burseraceae (*Santiria*, *Dacryodes*) and the genus *Calophyllum* (Guttiferae) appear to be evolving away from drupes towards nuts, bypassing the need for seed cleaning. Nevertheless, many other genera with fleshy fruits may be so heavily dependent on birds and mammals that there could be crises in their regeneration because of changes in animal populations. One often sees nowadays, in the Peninsula, large crops of berries, drupes and tempting arillate seeds untouched on trees and eventually on the ground. Where are the animals that must surely have evolved to feed on them?

Seed sterility

Failure of seeds to germinate may be due to a variety of causes such as disease, predation, immaturity, deterioration, or even failure of embryogenesis. Most examples of sterility may be dismissed as sporadic accidents. When seed sterility becomes habitual in a species throughout its range it is a different matter worthy of close investigation.

The best known example of seed sterility is in *Dipterocarpus crinitus*, a common, widespread and large tree of lowland forest. I have never seen its seedlings, in spite of the fact that it fruits frequently and abundantly. I have made it a point, during the past 10 years to examine its fruits wherever I have encountered it in the forest and only once or twice have I found one with a healthy embryo. The rest are filled with undifferentiated non-germinating callus. Poore (1968) mapped the sizes and distribution of *D. crinitus* in a 26-ha plot of forest and concluded, from the low proportion of small trees in comparison with large ones, that the species was dying out in the sample area. However, seed sterility in this species has been documented for more than 50 years (Foxworthy 1932; Symington 1943), and attributed to insect attack, although in fact, no causal organism has ever been found. It looks as if the species is dying out everywhere in the Peninsula. It remains a mystery how such a species became common in the first place. Has some crucial factor in the environment changed in the past century to render the species sterile?

Other species with very high seed sterility include *Commersonia bartramia* (Sterculiaceae) and *Vernonia arborea* Buch.-Ham. (Compositae) both of which, paradoxically, are common pioneer species of forest edges. We simply do not understand at all what is happening to the reproduction of such species.

DISCUSSION

It is ironical that the climax equilibrium forests of the humid tropics should now prove to be far more fragile than all other vegetation types on earth. Seral vegetation, in adapting for life in landslips, forest gaps, fire-prone, drought-prone, or flood-prone habitats is, in a sense, pre-adapted to live with man, invade his fields, compete with his crops and mess up his backyard. Tropical rain forests are apparently devoid of all such pre-adaptation. Everything that rainforests do is 'wrong'; lack of colonizing ability, poor synchronization of reproduction, clumsy seeds, narrow tolerance of environmental change, and so on.

Through the actions of conservationists, national parks and nature reserves have been declared but their number and distribution are still far from adequate. Moreover, the conserved areas come in all shapes and sizes, with various histories of previous disturbance. Species pauperization can occur in them, through neglect and ignorance. In some reserves, e.g. Bukit Nanas in the centre of Kuala Lumpur, it is already obvious that the more weedy species are increasing at the expense of the less hardy primary forest species. The managers of parks and reserves will have to develop an awareness of the changes going on and attempt to remedy the situation. Actions that could be taken, include the rapid restoration of the canopy (to trap humidity and to recreate the proper understorey environment), restoration of height, prevention of hunting and cutting, and careful re-introduction of animals and plants previously known to exist there.

Nevertheless, many rare species will become extinct unless help can be quickly organized. This is because the forest has room for only a finite number of mature individuals. If we consider only big trees of 1·22 m (4 ft) girth and above, the number per hectare in the Peninsula ranges between fifty-five and ninety-five (Table 3). The

TABLE 3. Number of big trees (1·22 m or 4 ft girth and above) per hectare, in lowland and hill forests, Malaya

Reference	Plot size (ha)	Location and elevation	No. of big trees/ha
Cousens (1958)	62·7	Pangkor (up to 176 m)	68
Poore (1968)	23	Jengka (45–75 m)	68
Wyatt-Smith (1966)	1·0	Rengam (below 111 m)	55
Wyatt-Smith (1966)	1·6	Sg. Menyala (below 50 m)	67
Wyatt-Smith (1966)	1·6	Bt. Lagong (468–551 m)	95

chances of any given seedling growing to maturity are extremely poor, hence the collection of seeds of endangered species to be germinated and cared for in nurseries is greatly to be recommended.

Recently, I went to Sungei Menyala Forest Reserve, a small lowland area surrounded by rubber and oil palm plantations, to look for *Chrysophyllum lanceolatum* (Sapotaceae) an uncommon species which, according to herbarium records, was relatively more common here than elsewhere. After much searching I located one tree, which may well be the last of its species in the Peninsula. It was fruiting but the fruits were not quite mature. I returned 2 months later, hoping that animals would spare the fruits. It was no problem. The fruits were on the ground directly under the tree where they had probably lain for a couple of weeks. No animal had touched them. Even if they could germinate through the pericarp, (which I doubt) the seedlings could not have survived to maturity directly under the shade of the mother tree and the understorey vegetation. I now have the seedlings growing in Kepong. Perhaps out of these a new population will be built up in cultivation.

In 1971 Dr T. C. Whitmore brought to Kepong five seeds of *Maingaya malayana* (Hammamelidaceae) a rare endemic species (and genus) previously last seen in 1921. From these I successfully raised two trees which flowered profusely but fruited sparsely. Now we have two trees, three saplings and ten seedlings. Perhaps in ten more years, this species will grace the streets of Kuala Lumpur because of its profuse, attractive, and scented flowers.

I think the time has come to organize collecting drives to bring similarly threatened species into cultivation, first to be looked after, studied and displayed in arboreta, and eventually, if found hardy, to be planted as ornamental trees to bring variety to tropical towns and villages. From such *ex situ* plantings, materials can be obtained for restocking forests in which such species were previously known to exist.

For this to be done throughout the tropics, the numbers of local botanists must be increased everywhere. Local floristic studies should be encouraged; herbaria and arboreta should be multiplied. Local experts must be made available on the spot, to monitor the state of the forests, to advise local governments and to activate local conservation action. It is time for scientists in tropical countries to realise that the fate of a large part of the world's biotic resources now depends on their own ability and interest in planning, organization, research, education and conservation.

Tropical forests are doomed unless the people who live in the tropics can be motivated to act. Foreign expeditions and visiting scientists cannot save tropical forests, because the pressures on conserved areas are continuous, and require continuous local response and vigilance. Visiting scientists may be able to help in indirect ways, but they should first acquire some awareness of local sensitivities. Aspiring tropical scientists would do well to include Budowski (1974/75) in their compulsory reading.

In conclusion, I would like to state the obvious, that remedial management is not the best form of management, because it is dependent on continual human effort. The conservation of areas of forest large and intact enough to be self-sustaining must remain the paramount objective in nature conservation.

ACKNOWLEDGMENTS

I would like to acknowledge the financial contribution from the organizers of this symposium and from the British Council, which enabled me to present this paper. My assistant, Mr Low Chong Moi, prepared the necessary diagrams.

REFERENCES

Abdulhadi, R., Kartawinata, K. & Sukardjo, S. (1981). Effects of mechanised logging in the lowland dipterocarp forest at Lempake, East Kalimantan. *Malaysian Forester,* **44,** 407–418.
Aminuddin bin Mohammed & Ng, F.S.P. (1982). Influence of light on germination of *Pinus caribaea, Gmelina arborea, Sapium baccatum* and *Vitex pinnata. Malaysian Forester,* **45,** 62–68.
Ashton, P.S. (1976). Factors affecting the development and conservation of tree genetic resources in south-east Asia, *Tropical Trees: Variation, Breeding and Conservation* (Ed. by J. Burley & B. T. Styles), pp. 189–198. Academic Press, London, New York.
Budowski, G. (1974/75). Scientific imperialism. *Unasylva,* Winter 1974/75, pp. 24–30. FAO, Rome.
Corner, E.J.H. (1940). *Wayside Trees of Malaya.* Government Printer, Singapore.
Cousens, J.E. (1958). A study of 155 acres of tropical rain forest by complete enumeration of all large trees. *Malayan Forester,* **21,** 155–164.
Foxworthy, F.W. (1932). *Dipterocarpaceae of the Malay Peninsula.* Malayan Forest Record 10. Forest Department, Kuala Lumpur.

Hallé, F. & Ng, F.S.P. (1981). Crown construction in mature Dipterocarp trees. *Malaysian Forester*, **44**, 222–233.

Jacobs, M.R. (1955). *Growth Habits of the Eucalypts*. Government Printer, Canberra.

Keng, H. (1969). *Orders and Families of Malayan Seed Plants*. University of Malaya Press, Kuala Lumpur.

Lanly, J.-P. (1981). *Present situation and trends in tropical forests and plantations*. FORGEN-81/Misc. 4, FAO, Rome.

Liew, T.C. (1973). Occurrence of seeds in virgin forest top soil with particular reference to secondary species in Sabah. *Malaysian Forester*, **36**, 185–193.

Longman, K.A. & Jenik, J. (1974). *Tropical Forest and its Environment*. Longman, London.

Manokaran, N. (1978). Germination of fresh seeds of Malaysian rattans. *Malaysian Forester*, **41**, 319–324.

Mori, T., Zullfatah bin Haji Abd. Rahman & Tan, C.H. (1980). Germination and storage of Rotan manau (*Calamus manan*) seeds. *Malaysian Forester*, **43**, 44–55.

Ng, F.S.P. (1977). Shyness in trees. *Mature Malaysiana*, **2**, 20–23.

Ng, F.S.P. (1978). *Tree Flora of Malaya*, 3. Longman, Kuala Lumpur.

Ng, F.S.P. (1980a). The phenology of the yellow flame tree *Peltophorum pterocarpum*. *Malayan Nature Journal*, **33**, 201–208.

Ng, F.S.P. (1980b). Germination ecology of Malaysian woody plants. *Malaysian Forester*, **43**, 406–437.

Ng, F.S.P. (1981). Vegetative and reproductive phenology of dipterocarps. *Malaysian Forester*, **44**, 197–221.

Ng, F.S.P. & Low, C.M. (1982). *Check list of endemic trees of the Malay Peninsula*. Research Pamphlet 88. Forest Research Institute, Kepong.

Paijmans, K. (1973). Plant succession on Pago and Witori volcanoes, New Britain. *Pacific Science*, **27**, 260–8.

Poore, M.E.D. (1968). Studies in Malaysian rain forest. I. The forest on the Triassic sediments in Jengka Forest Reserve. *Journal of Ecology*, **56**, 143–196.

Purseglove, J.W. (1968). *Tropical Crops. Dicotyledons*. Vol. 2. Longman, London & Harlow.

Sasaki, S. & Mori, T. (1981). Growth responses of dipterocarp seedlings to light. *Malaysian Forester*, **44**, 319–345.

Sasaki, S. & Ng, F.S.P. (1981). Physiological studies on germination and seedling development in *Intsia palembanica* (Merbau). *Malaysian Forester*, **44**, 43–59.

Symington, C.F. (1933). The study of secondary growth on rain forest sites in Malaya. *Malaysian Forester*, **2**, 107–117.

Symington, C.F. (1943). *A Foresters' Manual of Dipterocarps*. Malayan Forest Record 16. Forest Department, Kuala Lumpur.

Whitmore, T.C. (1972). *Tree Flora of Malaya*. 1. Longman, Kuala Lumpur.

Whitmore, T.C. (1973). *Tree Flora of Malaya*. 2. Longman, Kuala Lumpur.

Wilcox, B.A. (1980). Insular ecology and conservation. *Conservation Biology* (Ed. by M. E. Soulé & B. A. Wilcox), pp. 95–117. Sinauer, Sunderland, Mass.

Wright, H. (1904). The genus *Diospyros* in Ceylon: its morphology, anatomy and taxonomy. *Annals of the Royal Botanic Garden Peradeniya*, **2**, 1–78.

Wyatt-Smith, J. (1963). *Manual of Malayan silviculture for inland forests*. Malayan Forest Record 23. Forest Department, Kuala Lumpur.

Wyatt-Smith, J. (1966). *Ecological Studies on Malayan Forests*. Research Pamphlet 52. Forest Research Institute, Kepong.

Yap, S.K. (1976). *Reproductive biology of some understorey fruit tree species*. Ph.D. thesis, University of Malaya, Kuala Lumpur.

Yap, S.K. (1982). The phenology of some fruit tree species in a lowland dipterocarp forest. *Malaysian Forester*, **45**, 21–35.

Yap, S.K. & Razali Husin (1980). The reproductive behaviour of Sesendok (*Endospermum malaccense*). *Malaysian Forester*, **43**, 37–43.

Ecological dynamics of tropical forest fragments

T. E. LOVEJOY AND R. O. BIERREGAARD
World Wildlife Fund U.S.A., Washington D.C., U.S.A.

J. M. RANKIN AND H. O. R. SCHUBART
Instituto Nacional de Pesquisas da Amazonia (INPA), Manaus, Brazil

INTRODUCTION

The rapid loss of forest in most parts of the tropics lends a particular urgency to conservation. One of the most important aspects of such efforts is to establish a series of protected representative ecosystems of these species-rich biological formations, and this inevitably involves questions of size, shape and the extent of connectability between the reserves and other forest areas.

A precise definition of the minimum critical size for an isolated remnant of tropical forest—namely, that area necessary to maintain a tropical forest community at close to its characteristic diversity (Lovejoy & Oren 1981)—is a somewhat elusive goal. Progress towards this goal will largely involve increased understanding of the forces which drive species to be lost from fragments after isolation, in a process which can be thought of as ecosystem decay.

Many of the initial insights and discussions of this topic have involved studies of tropical islands and remnant tropical forest patches (Diamond 1973, 1975, 1976; Leck 1979; Morton 1978; Odekoven 1980; Terborgh 1974, 1975; Willis 1974). Remnant forest patches obviously differ from islands in that the surrounding area can be a source of species whereas the sea itself cannot. However, in very few instances have the investigators had the advantage of the continuous history of the island, or forest patch, from the moment of isolation or, even more desirably, from sometime before isolation.

Once what is to be preserved—be it a community or a single species—is determined, information on ecosystem decay will be useful in making management and reserve design decisions. Does ecosystem decay take place in a predictable fashion? Are species lost in a predictable order? Does the decay process behave similarly in different taxonomic groups? Are the resultant assemblages a subset of the original assemblage or something very different?

THE MINIMUM CRITICAL SIZE OF ECOSYSTEMS PROJECT

The Minimum Critical Size of Ecosystems Study, a joint effort of INPA, (O Instituto Nacional de Pesquisas da Amazonia), and the World Wildlife Fund, in Central Amazonia is designed to provide just such information (Lovejoy 1980). The project takes advantage of Brazilian law which requires each Amazonian development project to

377

interactions of tropical rain forest trees with animal species, e.g. pollinators, herbivores, parasites, and dispersers or predators of fruits and seeds. These relationships are crucial in that they variously affect the tree's ability to reproduce, and also the ultimate success of that reproductive effort (cf. Ng 1983). Many of these relationships are in fact obligatory for successful reproduction and recruitment of new individuals into the population, e.g. the interdependency of frugivorous birds which during certain seasons feed almost exclusively upon the fruits of a single tree species which, in turn depends upon the bird species for successful seed dispersal (Howe 1977, 1983), or the Brazil nut tree (*Bertholletia excelsa*), which has a single cross pollinator (Lovejoy 1973).

Of these roles of tropical rain forest trees, those involving their ecological relationships with other species are the more ephemeral in the face of the effects of forest patch isolation through deforestation. Tropical rain forest trees are thus a classic example of organisms that become ecologically extinct long before the last remaining individual in the population dies, signifying the extinction of the species (Janzen 1973; Ng 1983). Unlike many animal species, trees will neither flee as felling takes place nor die soon afterwards due to problems related to changes in population densities and food resources. Only a small number of individuals, and fewer species, will be lost at the patch margin due to the burning of the surrounding deforested area which marks the completion of the isolation process. The short-term effects of isolation on the trees in the relict patch will not then be perceived through local extinctions at the species level (i.e. the removal of all individuals of that species in the patch), but rather through the changes in, or disappearance of, those ecological relationships critical to the maintenance of a successfully reproducing population. In the current study of ecosystem decay we must, in the case of trees, be able to identify and quantify ecological extinctions as early as possible in the reserve patches.

Ecological extinction due to unfavourable changes in habitat or to the loss or change in critical ecological relationships may be detected through changes in the demographic parameters of a population, as well as through observations of changes in growth rates or in the nature and frequency of species interactions before and after the isolation event. The present study has given special attention to the study of two groups of tree species.

(a) Tree species likely to be 'indicator' species, sensitive to the changes with isolation. This group includes those species with ability to rapidly colonize disturbed open sites at the reserve margins and in the surrounding felled area; shade-tolerant species with low dispersability requiring closed forest sites for germination and successful establishment; species for which relative abundance in the patch is high enough to permit statistical analysis and detection of very small changes in the population parameters.

(b) Tree species which are members of ecologically interdependent species constellations, such as animal-dispersed fruit-producing trees and obligate frugivores, which might be expected to change together with the effects of isolation.

Data collection for the study of tree species is focused on demography and reproductive biology; namely, phenology, reproductive effort, seedling establishment success, seedling survival and vegetative growth and mortality. Complete population surveys of all size classes of a species are conducted where seedling identifications have been confirmed, and all trees $\geqslant 10$ cm dbh are censused. All plants studied receive permanent numbered tags to facilitate future data collection. Species identifications are confirmed by botanical collections for all trees.

Emphasis has also been given to the study of tree-generated structural features (tree-falls, upright dead trees, etc.) which may change in parallel with population changes in both plants and animals. Trees are equally important as forest structural elements when dead as when alive. Dead trees further diversify the forest by forming larger or smaller gaps in the canopy and by upturning soil masses. Trees may fall over or may remain standing even long after death. They may kill other trees in falling or may die having caused no further immediate mechanical side effects. Thus, tree mortality affects both forest tree demographic structure and physical structure of the forest.

In the first 19 months after their isolation it was already possible to detect evidence of ecological change in forest structure, reproductive behaviour of some individual trees, and in plant–animal interactions in the reserves. The most striking changes have been in the number and distribution of wind-thrown, broken and upright dead trees in the 10 ha reserve. A greater than average concentration of wind-thrown and broken trees has accumulated on the windward margin (east) than in the core or in unisolated forest due to high winds off the open pasture. The importance of the prevailing winds is borne out by the observation that the leeward margin (with comparable topography) has no wind-thrown or broken trees recorded since isolation, and that the north and south margins have only a small number associated with steep slopes. The destruction of the windward forest margin will increase the proportion of tree-fall habitats in isolated reserves. These tree-falls will then serve as new colonization sites for burgeoning pasture populations of light-loving species, formerly present only in small numbers in original forest clearings. The isolated reserves will increase their populations of these species as new tree-falls form, coalesce and are invaded by propagules from the pasture populations (Lovejoy & Rankin 1979). This change on the forest margin can be seen in the vicinity of the experimental areas where a margin has been exposed for a longer time.

The mortality from sources other than wind has also increased in the isolated 10 ha reserve. Within the reserve core, the number of standing dead trees jumped dramatically from nine in 1981 to sixty-five in 1982. A slight bias in their distribution toward those corners of the reserve actually reached by the pasture fires at the time of isolation suggests that the effects of the burn are at least partially responsible for these deaths. Those trees not near the fires may have been affected by microclimate changes within the isolated reserve. While no quantitative data are yet available, many researchers have commented on the dry, hot winds which now blow through the understorey, and of the unusual dryness of the leaf litter in the dry season.

The most drastic changes in microclimate have occurred at the reserve margins where members of all size classes have been directly exposed to open conditions of the surrounding pasture. Sun-burned and withered leaves on many individuals attest to the stress to which these plants have been subjected.

384

Diamond,

Diamond,
   Conse

Diamond,
   preser
   Acad

Howe, H.F

Howe, H.F
   and N
   Scien

Janzen, D.

Leck, C.F.

Lovejoy, T

Lovejoy, T

Lovejoy, T

Lovejoy, T
   Sharp

Lovejoy, T
   design
   their
   1979.

Morton, E
   Birds:
   Unive

Ng, F.S.P.
   Ecolo
   Black

Oedekoven

Terborgh,
   24, 71

Terborgh,
   Trend
   New

Willis, E. C
   Mono

Editors' fo
Figures wi
subsequent
   This pap

Improving the monitoring of deforestation in the humid tropics

ALAN GRAINGER

Commonwealth Forestry Institute, University of Oxford, South Parks Road, Oxford

SUMMARY

1 FAO data are used to provide estimates of the total extent of the tropical moist forest biome (1081×10^6 ha) and its rate of deforestation (6×10^6 ha year^{-1}).

2 The accuracy of these estimates and the potential of remote-sensing techniques to give more accurate estimates of rates of deforestation are discussed.

3 A centralized, continuous monitoring system employing digital analysis of satellite imagery is recommended as the most feasible option.

INTRODUCTION

There is growing concern that deforestation in the humid tropics could lead to an irreversible loss of plant and animal genetic resources, a reduction in the potentially extractable volume of timber from primary forest species, environmental degradation, and even changes in global climate (Grainger 1980). Accurate information about the extent and rate of loss of the tropical moist forest biome is therefore required to enable judgement of the true scale of deforestation and to formulate appropriate corrective policies. The objects of this paper are to: (a) provide critical estimates of the total extent of the tropical moist forests and the rate of deforestation; (b) propose ways by which the monitoring of deforestation may be improved by using remote-sensing techniques. Initial estimates of deforestation rates have been made for a number of countries by comparing *surveys* of all or most of their forest areas based upon data collected at different times by aerial photography, side-looking airborne radar or satellite remote-sensing techniques. This paper suggests the need for a programme which frequently *monitors* changes in forest cover instead of producing detailed surveys of forest resources.

ESTIMATES OF THE AREA OF TROPICAL MOIST FORESTS

The tropical moist forests collectively cover an area of approximately 1×10^9 ha, more than one-third of all closed forests in the world. Forests in the humid tropics were defined as tropical moist forests by Sommer (1976). Included in this category were tropical ombrophilous, evergreen seasonal, semi-deciduous, evergreen needle-leaved, and drought-deciduous forest types in the UNESCO (1973) international system of vegetation classification, over the whole range from lowland to submontane and montane forest types. The definition essentially corresponds to the sum of the two forest types defined by Schimper (1903) as tropical rain forest and monsoon forest. A major reason for the use of such a wide definition as 'tropical moist forest' is that accurate data are not available on the areas of the distinct forest types which this term comprises. Sommer estimated a total area of 935×10^6 ha for the tropical moist forests in the early 1970s. This area was contained within the territories of sixty-five (present) countries or parts of countries, but comparison with later estimates was made difficult by the absence of a complete listing of national areas of tropical moist forest.

The recent report of the joint FAO/UNEP Tropical Forest Resources Assessment Project (Lanly 1981) enables an estimate of 1081×10^6 ha to be made for the total area of tropical moist forests in 1980 in sixty-two of the sixty-five countries listed by Sommer (1976) together with Puerto Rico (not listed by Sommer). Lanly (1981) is the most comprehensive and detailed assessment of tropical forests yet published, describing the situation in both humid and arid tropical regions, and extends to over 1500 pages in four volumes. The difference between this estimate of the area of tropical moist forests and the estimate by Sommer (1976) reflects the inclusion in the former of improved estimates of forest areas for many countries. Bearing in mind the comment made at the end of the previous paragraph, there are upward revisions of 29×10^6 ha for the African region (of which Zaire $= 16 \times 10^6$ ha) and of 107×10^6 ha for the Latin American region (of which Brazil $= 82 \times 10^6$ ha). Table 1 lists the areas of tropical moist forests for fifty-five countries included in Lanly (1981) in which, for most countries, they correspond to the total area of 'All Closed Broadleaved Forest'. Where a country (such as India) contains forest types other than tropical moist forests, the appropriate subtotal has been used when available. Areas of 'Coniferous Forest', listed by Lanly, have not been included in Table 1 owing to insufficient data. Haiti, listed by Sommer and by Lanly, has not been included because its forests have been defined by Lanly as mostly subtropical. Paraguay (listed by Sommer and by Lanly) and Argentina (listed by Sommer but not by Lanly) have not been included owing to insufficient data. Seven countries or parts of countries were listed by Sommer but not by Lanly. Best available estimates are given in Table 1 for Australia, Fiji, Hawaii, New Caledonia, Reunion, Solomon Islands and Vanuatu (New Hebrides), and for Puerto Rico (not listed by Sommer).

Lanly (1981) represents a major advance in the estimation of tropical forest areas. A uniform system of categorization is used to enumerate and classify all national forest areas. The results of remote-sensing surveys carried out in the 1970s are used to provide estimates of forest areas for 52% of the tropical moist forest biome (575×10^6 ha), including LANDSAT surveys of nineteen countries (of which eleven were undertaken by FAO itself), side-looking airborne-radar surveys of three countries (of which one had also been surveyed by LANDSAT), and aerial photographic surveys of five countries. Knowledge of the use of remote-sensing methods to provide source data (summarized in Table 1) is far more helpful than previous subjective impressions of accuracy. However, with relatively accurate data used as a basis for estimating only about half of the total area of the biome, this report does not provide a comprehensive base-line survey, even though one is badly needed.

MONITORING CHANGES IN FOREST COVER

Estimates of rates of deforestation

Deforestation is defined as the temporary or permanent removal of forest cover whether for agricultural or other purposes (Grainger 1980, 1983). Current estimates of the rate of deforestation in the humid tropics are of doubtful accuracy. The estimate of about 16×10^6 ha year^{-1} given by FAO at the Eighth World Forestry Congress (Anon. 1979) originated in an extrapolation by Sommer (1976) of 'reported' rates of deforestation (of varying accuracy and with no sources quoted) from thirteen countries: Bangladesh, Colombia, Costa Rica, Ghana, Ivory Coast, Laos, Madagascar, Malaysia, Papua New Guinea, the Philippines, Thailand, Venezuela, and North Vietnam (as it then was). Some 2×10^6 ha ($1 \cdot 2 \%$) of the total area of 163×10^6 ha of forest in these countries was reported as being cleared each year, although 'in most cases the character of the clearings is not known'. Extrapolating this percentage loss gave an annual rate of deforestation for the whole biome of at least 11×10^6 ha.

Lanly (1981) contains the first systematic approach to estimating deforestation. Estimated rates are listed for each country, with a total rate for the tropical moist forest biome of about 6×10^6 ha year^{-1} for fifty-five of the sixty-five countries listed by Sommer. This is substantially lower than the earlier estimate. Accuracy of the source data is still, however, a limiting factor. Local estimates of unverifiable accuracy have been used (as in Sommer (1976)) for seven countries, while for another six countries deforestation rates (totalling $2 \cdot 1 \times 10^6$ ha year^{-1}) have been based on comparisons of different remote-sensing surveys. The vast majority of national deforestation rates have been estimated by FAO itself, taking into account various rates reported to it by national bodies and/or using the best available estimates of the numbers of shifting cultivators and the average area of forest each cuts down every year together with statistics for the annual area of officially approved forest clearance.

Using remote-sensing to improve the monitoring of deforestation

Clearly, a major improvement is required in the way in which deforestation is monitored. This should preferably take the form of the development of techniques and operations specifically geared to monitoring deforestation at frequent intervals, instead of relying on the comparison of aerial photographic, satellite and side-looking airborne radar surveys undertaken at fairly long intervals as has happened previously. The high cost of aerial photographic and side-looking airborne-radar (Grainger 1983) survey methods would seem to preclude their use for frequent monitoring. Complete aerial photographic surveys have been quoted in Lanly (1981) as providing source data for only thirteen of the fifty-five listed countries and in only five of these (together with Sabah) were the surveys carried out wholly or partially since 1970.

Satellite remote-sensing, on the other hand, is relatively inexpensive. Images can be automatically and continuously gathered without the need for special flight missions. NASA's LANDSAT satellites scan an area of 34 225 km^2 in just 25 seconds, producing

TABLE 1. Areas of tropical moist forests in 1980 (a) and average annual rates of deforestation 1976–80 (b) (in ha × 10³)

	Total (a) hectares × 10³	Deforestation per annum (b) hectares × 10³	Major primary sources for Lanly (1981)
Africa	204622	1204	
Angola	2900	40	8
Benin	47	1·5	8, 15
Cameroon	17920	80	8
Central Afr. Rep.	3590	5	11
Congo	21340	5	11, 12
Equatl. Guinea	1295	15	
Gabon	20500	27	4, 11
Ghana	1718	15	
Guinea	2050	—	8
Guinea Bissau	660	15	2
Ivory Coast	4458	310	2, 10, 15
Kenya	690	11	14
Liberia	2000	41	9
Madagascar	10300	165	1
Nigeria	5950	285	5, 17
Reunion†	100	—	
Senegal	220	—	2, 6
Sierra Leone	740	5·8	2, 15
Tanzania	1440	10	
Togo	304	2	8
Uganda	750	10	10
Zaire	105650	165	
Asia and Pacific	263647	1608	
Australia*	600	—	
Bangladesh	927	8	7
Brunei	323	7	
Burma	31193	89	1, 8, 15, 16
Fiji*	800	—	
Hawaii‡	445	—	
India	16739	48	7
Indonesia	113575	550	2, 7
Kampuchea	7150	15	7, 9
Laos	7560	120	7
Asia and Pacific (cont.)			
Malaysia	20995	240	1, 4, 14
New Caledonia*	800	—	
Papua New Guinea	33710	21	1, 12
Philippines	9320	100	1, 11
Solomon Islands*	2300	—	
Sri Lanka	1659	25	1, 3
Thailand	8135	325	1, 6
Vanuatu†	16	—	
Vietnam	7400	60	8
Latin America	613103	3301	
Belize	1257	9	
Bolivia	44010	65	6, 14
Brazil	331750	1360	2, 5, 11, 16, 17
Colombia	46400	800	5
Costa Rica	1638	60	8
Cuba	1255	2	
Dominican Rep	444	2·1	8
Ecuador	14230	300	12
El Salvador	101	4	
Guatemala	3785	64	8
French Guiana	8900	1	
Guyana	18475	2·5	
Honduras	1855	53	8
Jamaica	67	1·5	
Mexico	14760	160	6, 10, 14
Nicaragua	4170	97	14
Panama	4165	31	
Peru	68778	160	5, 12, 14
Puerto Rico*	155	—	
Suriname	14830	2·5	
Trinidad & Tobago	208	1·2	13, 14
Venezuela	31870	125	12
Global total	1081372	6113	

All figures, except where indicated otherwise, correspond to totals in the category 'All Closed Broadleaved Forest' in Lanly (1981). For Brazil, India, Mexico and Peru appropriate subtotals have been used. National figures for total areas and regional figures for deforestation have been rounded to the nearest 1000 ha. In the absence of other references, estimates for national total areas have been made by FAO (in Lanly 1981) on the basis of available FAO and other data, and estimates of rates of deforestation have been made by FAO on the basis of available data. National total areas have been estimated for 1980 by extrapolation from most recent source data taking into account annual rates of deforestation. Further information on sources is given in Lanly (1981) and Grainger (1983).

Best available estimates have been included for eight countries, using data obtained from: * Myers (1980); † Persson (1974); and ‡ Nelson & Wheeler (1963).

Notes on major sources for estimates of National Total Areas in Lanly (1981)

(1) National aerial survey or survey of whole tropical moist forest area, pre-1970.
(2) As (1) but wholly or partially since 1970.
(3) Various aerial photographic surveys, pre-1970.
(4) As (3) but wholly or partially since 1970.
(5) National side-looking airborne-radar survey or survey of whole tropical moist forest area, wholly or partially since 1970.
(6) National LANDSAT survey or survey of whole tropical moist forest area.
(7) Partial LANDSAT survey.
(8) LANDSAT survey conducted by FAO.
(9) National forest inventory, pre-1970 or undated.
(10) National forest inventory, post-1970.
(11) Numerous inventories.
(12) National forest or vegetation map used as a major source.
(13) National estimates.

Notes on major sources for estimates of National Rates of Deforestation in Lanly (1981)

(14) National estimates.
(15) Aerial photographic surveys used in whole or in part.
(16) LANDSAT surveys used in whole or in part.
(17) Side-looking airborne-radar surveys used in whole or in part.

an image that is equivalent in coverage to over 5000 aerial photographs taken at a scale of 1:20 000. The two LANDSAT satellites normally in operation together have the capacity to scan the same area once every 9 days. Analysis of LANDSAT images can be accomplished in a fraction of the time required for that of aerial photographs of an equivalent area and for between a tenth and a third of the cost (Myers 1980; Barney, Johannsen & Barr 1977). Since the inception of the LANDSAT programme in 1972 a number of governments of tropical countries have, with the encouragement of FAO, USAID and other agencies, used LANDSAT imagery to improve their knowledge of national forest resources (see Table 1). The use of LANDSAT imagery to monitor tropical deforestation has been reviewed by Williams & Miller (1979), Talbot & Pettinger (1980), Green (1982, 1983) and Grainger (1983).

The desirability of a mainly satellite-based monitoring programme for tropical forests was recognized in Recommendation 25 of the UN Conference on the Human Environment held in Stockholm in 1972, and has since been reaffirmed by UNEP (1980) and a U.S. Government Task Force (U.S. Department of State 1980). FAO and UNEP agreed in 1973, in compliance with the Stockholm recommendation, to formulate such a monitoring programme. The subsequent Formulation Report (FAO 1975) envisaged a centralized programme carried out by a team of specialists who would, in the initial 5 year phase: obtain a global picture of the present state of tropical forest cover that would serve as a base-line for future monitoring activities; assess the changes in tropical forest cover over the preceding 10–20 years by studies of a number of test areas; prepare guidelines for future continuous monitoring activities (a 5-year frequency was considered adequate) and conduct applied research to adapt techniques for automated image analysis to the needs of the programme. Lanly (1981) is published as part of UNEP's Global Environmental Monitoring System (GEMS) and is presumably intended to fulfil the objectives of the initial phase of this programme, although only about half of the area of the biome has been surveyed by remote-sensing techniques. The Pilot Project in Benin, Togo and Cameroon (FAO 1980) ran into difficulties. Little progress was made in developing a methodology and techniques for the continuous monitoring system. Such experiences led FAO to recommend a change to a decentralized approach in which national forestry departments would be encouraged to establish their own LANDSAT image analysis facilities and report the results of their surveys to FAO. The manual analysis of photographic versions of LANDSAT images was also recommended in preference to automated analysis using computers.

The success of such a strategy in fulfilling the original aims of the programme is debatable. It could take between 10 and 20 years for the majority of countries to establish smoothly functioning image analysis centres. Given the magnitude of current estimates of tropical deforestation and the growing concern for both a greater understanding of the problem and the development of appropriate policies to control it, the wisdom of the proposal in the original Formulation Report (FAO 1975) for a centralized monitoring system therefore seems evident.

Before commenting on the relative merits of manual and automated satellite image analysis techniques it is useful to recall that the images collected by the LANDSAT

Multi-Spectral Scanner (MSS) are not equivalent to normal panchromatic photo-graphic images but are instead measurements of the intensity of radiation reflected from Earth in four discrete wavelength bands: green (Band 4), lower red (Band 5), upper red to near infra-red (Band 6), and near infra-red (Band 7). The image for each band is composed of 7.6×10^6 picture elements or pixels, each representing an area of 0·62 ha* on the ground. The intensity of radiation received as an analogue signal (averaged over the area of each pixel) is converted into digital form as one of 128 shades of grey on an ascending scale from white to black. The image is transmitted to a ground station as a sequence of more than 30×10^6 numbers (4 spectral observations for each of 7.6×10^6 pixels). An image may be purchased either as a digital tape containing these 30×10^6 numbers or as a photographic product, the most basic of which is a monochrome print or transparency which aims to replicate the image of one band in terms of the 128 shades of grey (Lillesand & Kiefer 1979).

While photographic image products are good approximations to the original array of numbers there are disadvantages in using them to detect change. Even with a large scale image (1:250 000) it is only possible to interpret and map areas of up to 2 or 3 mm square (FAO 1980) and these would be equivalent to areas of 25–60 ha on the ground. Thus, manual analysis of photographic products may well have acceptable accuracy for surveying large areas of forest for mapping purposes, but will be unable to detect many of the small clearings (just a few hectares in size) which are characteristic of much deforestation in the tropics. Visual comparison of photographic prints of Band 5 and Band 7 of images collected in 1972–73 and 1975–76 enabled the Royal Forest Department in Thailand to measure deforestation over that period using transparent overlays and a dot matrix estimation method (Morain & Klankamsorn 1978) but it is notable that the main type of deforestation detected was that which involved shrinkage of forest boundaries. Automated analysis of the digital tape of the image is able to work at the individual pixel level: correcting the image for scanning distortions which appear as stripes; mathematically transforming pixel values so that the image contains the maximum contrast between different vegetation and land-use types; superimposing two images of the same area to detect any change in forest cover which has taken place since the first image was collected, and in so doing correcting for differences in the alignment of the satellite on the two occasions so that each 0·62 ha area in one image is compared with its equivalent in the other.

Techniques have been developed to measure deforestation which do not require prior classification of different vegetation and land-use types. Wastenson *et al.* (1981) detected clear-cut areas in a forest in central Sweden by subtracting the spectral values in a Band 5 image collected in May 1978 from the corresponding values in an image collected in May 1979. They found that 98·6% of the pixels were correctly classified in the two classes 'clear-cut' and 'non-clear-cut' and that this method was applicable to detecting clear-cut areas larger than 2·5 ha in size. Detailed proposals to develop such techniques for use in monitoring system for the tropical forests have been made by C. Paul (1981, pers. comm.).

Essential to the success of such a monitoring system is the frequent availability of

* See footnote on p. 395.

images and, in principle, satellite remote-sensing is capable of fulfilling such a requirement. Remote-sensing of areas in the humid tropics by both satellite and aircraft in the visible and infra-red regions of the spectrum is, however, affected by the problem of extensive cloud cover. This problem can be at least partially overcome by maximizing the number of images that are collected, recorded and transmitted to Earth and by ensuring that images are collected, whenever possible, in periods known to have a high probability of little cloud. Previously, the availability of imagery of areas in the humid tropics has been constrained by the absence (except for South America and South Asia) of ground stations able to receive LANDSAT images of tropical moist forest areas in real time. The on-board recording of images for later transmission to a U.S. ground station has therefore depended upon NASA's scale of priorities for collecting images of particular areas. This situation should improve in the 1980s, with the opening of ground stations at Bangkok and Jakarta (serving South East Asia), and the start of new commercial operating procedures (including a better system for requesting the collection of images) for LANDSAT-4 (launched July 1982) and the French SPOT-1 satellite (to be launched in 1984) which could help to ensure that more images can be collected of areas of interest during periods of little cloud cover. Despite such advances, the tropical forest monitoring programme will require a high priority status so that the necessary image availability can be achieved.

CONCLUSIONS

The results of this study suggest the unreliability of current estimates of rates of deforestation in the humid tropics. A centralized continuous monitoring system, satellite-based and using a large component of automated image analysis as originally proposed in an FAO/UNEP study in 1975, is seen to be probably the only realistic way of achieving an estimate of acceptable accuracy of the actual rate of deforestation.

REFERENCES

Anon. (1979). Eighth World Forestry Congress, *Commonwealth Forestry Review*, **58**, 32–43.

Barney, T.W., Johannsen, C.J. & Barr, D. (1977). *Mapping Land Use From Satellite Images: A User's Guide.* University of Missouri.

FAO (1975). *Formulation of a tropical forest cover monitoring project.* FAO/UNEP, Rome.

FAO (1980). *Global Environment Monitoring System: Pilot project on tropical forest cover monitoring, Benin-Cameroon-Togo. Project implementation: Methodology, results and conclusions.* FAO/UNEP, Rome.

Grainger, A. (1980). The state of the world's tropical forests. *The Ecologist*, **10**, 6–54.

Grainger, A. (1983). Quantifying changes in forest cover in the humid tropics: overcoming current limitations. *Journal of World Forest Resource Management*, **1**, (in press).

Green, K.M. (1982). *LANDSAT in the Tropics: Guidelines for Habitat Evaluation and Monitoring.* Smithsonian Institution, Washington D.C.

Green, K.M. (1983). Using Landsat to monitor tropical forest ecosystems: realistic expectations of digital processing technology. *Tropical Rain Forest: Ecology and Management* (Ed. by S. L. Sutton, T. C. Whitmore & A. C. Chadwick), pp. 397–409. Blackwell Scientific Publications, Oxford.

Lanly, J.P. (Ed.) (1981). *Tropical forest resources assessment project (GEMS): Tropical Africa, Tropical Asia, Tropical America* (4 vols.). FAO/UNEP, Rome.

Lillesand, T.M. & Kiefer, R.W. (1979). *Remote Sensing and Image Interpretation.* Wiley, New York.

Morain, S.A. & Klankamsorn, B. (1978). *Forest mapping and inventory techniques through visual analysis of LANDSAT imagery: examples from Thailand.* Proceedings 12th International Symposium on Remote Sensing of the Environment, pp. 417–426. Manila.

Myers, N. (1980). *Conversion of Tropical Moist Forests.* U.S. National Research Council, Washington D.C.

Nelson, R.E. & Wheeler, P.R. (1963). *Forest resources of Hawaii—1961.* Division of Forestry, Department of Land and Natural Resources, Hawaii, in cooperation with U.S. Forest Service, Pacific SW Forest and Range Experimental Station, Honolulu.

Persson, R. (1974). *World forest resources.* Royal College of Forestry, Stockholm.

Schimper, A.F.W. (1903). *Plant-Geography upon a Physiological Basis* (transl. W. R. Fisher, G. Groom & I. B. Balfour). Oxford University Press, Oxford.

Sommer, A. (1976). Attempt at an assessment of the world's tropical forests. *Unasylva,* **28,** (112–113): 5–25.

Talbot, J.J. & Pettinger, L.R. (1980) Use of remote sensing for monitoring deforestation in tropical and sub-tropical latitudes. *Ciencia Interamericana* **21,** 63–71.

UNEP (1980), *Tropical woodlands and forest ecosystems.* UNEP Report (1980) 1, Nairobi.

UNESCO (1973). *International classification and mapping of vegetation.* UNESCO, Paris.

U.S. Department of State (1980). *The world's tropical forests: A policy, strategy and program for the United States.* Reports to the President by a U.S. Interagency Task Force on Tropical Forests, Washington D.C.

Wastenson L., Arnberg, W., Boresjo, L. & Ihse, M. (1981). Computer analysis of multi-temporal LANDSAT data for mapping of land-use, forest clear-cuts and mires: methodological studies. Proceedings 9th Annual Conference of the Remote Sensing Society, pp. 65–74. Reading, U.K.

Williams, D.L. & Miller, L.D. (1979). *Monitoring forest canopy alteration around the world with digital analysis of LANDSAT imagery.* NASA, Greenbelt, Maryland, U.S.A.

Author's footnote

Green (1983) gives an alternative estimate of pixel size, but the explanation for the difference is not simple. For a detailed treatment of this subject see:

Townshend, J.R.G. (1980). *The spatial resolving power of earth resources satellites: a review.* NASA Technical Memorandum 82020. Green Belt, Maryland, U.S.A.

Using Landsat to monitor tropical forest ecosystems: realistic expectations of digital processing technology

K. M. GREEN*

IMAGES, National Zoological Park, Smithsonian Institution, Washington, D.C. 20008, U.S.A.

SUMMARY

1 The need to monitor tropical forest ecosystems is discussed and a programme of remote sensing, in particular the Landsat satellite system, is described. The United States National Aeronautics and Space Administration (NASA) and the U.S. Department of the Interior operate, process, and distribute the data. Landsat orbit, sensors, and resolution are discussed.

2 The development of the Image Analysis and Graphic Facility for Ecological Studies (IMAGES), at the National Zoological Park, Smithsonian Institution, is outlined. This is a microcomputer turn-key facility that can digitally analyse a 10×10 km segment of the 185×185 km Landsat scene.

3 Different references provide varying estimates of forest cover in Bangladesh. In particular, the recent FAO–GEMS Report† indicates that between 6·4% and 8·6% of the country is covered by closed broadleaf forest.

4 Digital processing of Landsat data for the Madhupur Forest, Bangladesh, indicates that little forest actually remains, and intensive human use of this ecosystem has significantly degraded the once extensive forest region. The digital Landsat analysis for the Madhupur Forest indicates that only 91 km^2 of forest remain, of which only 28 km^2 can be considered undisturbed productive closed broadleaf forest. The results of this analysis demonstrate the need to use Landsat technology as a means of quantifying the status of tropical forests.

INTRODUCTION

The problem of loss of tropical forests has received considerable national and international attention during the past several years (Table 1). Although the reported rate of tropical forest conversion is variable, a unifying theme is the extremely serious problem with regards to the alteration and degradation of this extensive biomass.

The remote sensing techniques for itemizing and monitoring natural resources within tropical and subtropical countries have included aerial photographs and radar and satellite imagery. Recognition of the potential use of remote sensing from satellites for surveying natural tropical resources has been addressed by the Man and Biosphere

---

* Present address: Research Associate, Remote Sensing Systems Laboratory, Department of Civil Engineering, University of Maryland, College Park, MD 20742, U.S.A.

† Editors' note: referenced as Lanly (1981) by A. Grainger in this volume.

Program (Anon. 1979; UNESCO 1972, 1976, 1979), the U.S. Interagency Task Force on Tropical Deforestation (Department of State 1980), and Myers (1980) report to the National Academy of Sciences. The *Global 2000 Report to the President* (Council on Environmental Quality 1980) directed attention to the world's natural resources and environment, and stressed that the U.S. needed to improve long-term global analysis of emerging global problems such as tropical deforestation. Lastly, the National Academy of Sciences (NAS 1980) evaluated research priorities in tropical biology and strongly recommended improving the quantity, quality and focus of biological inventories in the tropics.

TABLE 1. The world's tropical forests

Title of publication	Date	Source
U.S. Strategy Conference on Tropical Deforestation	1978	Department of State (USAID) United States Agency for International Development
Tropical and Subtropical Forests Man and Biosphere	1972, 1974 1979	UNESCO
Global 2000 Report	1980	(CEQ) Council on Environmental Quality
Interagency Task Force on Tropical Deforestation	1980	Department of State Department of State
World Conservation Strategy	1980	IUCN/UNEP/WWF
Tropical Deforestation Hearings	1981	Committee on Foreign Affairs Subcommittee on International Organizations, U.S. Congress
Research Priorities in Tropical Biology	1980	(NAS) National Academy of Sciences
Conversion of Tropical Moist Forests	1980	MYERS Report to National Academy of Sciences
Tropical Forest Resources Assessment Project	1981	FAO/GEMS (Lanly 1981)
U.S. Strategy Conference on Biological Diversity	1982	Department of State, USAID

These documents clearly emphasize the need to monitor tropical forest ecosystems. Consequently, a program designed to meet such assessment needs should:
  (i) develop standardized procedures for evaluating the quantity and quality of tropical forests;
 (ii) develop a much needed source of baseline data for natural tropical forest cover;
(iii) monitor present cover with regard to ecological changes as a result of land use;
 (iv) promote a practical and technologically feasible methodology, available at relatively low cost, to accomplish this task;
  (v) be accessible to all tropical natural resource scientists.

As a natural resource scientist with considerable experience conducting field work in the tropics and utilizing satellite imagery for the inventory of tropical forests, I am convinced that the technology of remote sensing, in particular, Landsat, is very poorly understood by the tropical scientific community. In fact, application of Landsat technology for the inventory and monitoring of tropical forest biomass has been neglected or short-changed by many national and international agencies responsible for this technology transfer, primarily as a result of development and application of

Landsat technology for natural resource inventory without proper input from tropical resource scientists.

LANDSAT

Presently, the operation of Landsat by the United States National Aeronautics and Space Administration (NASA) and U.S. Department of the Interior, provides a technology capable of meeting the above requirements.

The first of a series of Earth Resources Technology Satellites (ERTS) was launched in July 1972. This first satellite operated until January 1978. Prior to the launch of ERTS-2 in January 1975, NASA officially renamed the ERTS program the 'Landsat' program and ERTS-1 was retroactively named Landsat 1 and ERTS-2 became Landsat 2.

Each satellite travels in a circular polar-to-polar orbit at an altitude of 900 km. Landsat circles the Earth once every 103 min, resulting in fourteen orbits per day. The sensors aboard the satellite image a 185 km swath, and successive orbits are about 2760 km apart at the Equator. As a result there are large gaps in coverage, particularly at the Equator between successive daily orbits. This fact is compensated for by a slightly westward shift in the next day's orbit. This satellite-orbit/earth-rotation relationship yields images that overlap a maximum of 85% in the polar latitudes and a minimum (about 14%) at the Equator. Landsats 1, 2 and 3 require 18 days of successive westward shifting to cover the globe. Thus, the satellite has the capability of passing over the same location once every 18 days or about twenty times a year. Landsat 4, launched in July 1982, completes this coverage in 16 days.

The Landsat satellite uses two remote sensing systems: a multispectral scanner system (MSS) and return beam vidicon (RBV). The MSS contains four sets of electronic optical sensors. Each sensor records light from a separate part of the electromagnetic spectrum. The RBV on Landsats 1 and 2 provided very little data and consequently MSS became the primary data source. Landsat 3 does provide the RBV data.

The ground resolution of the MSS is a ground resolution cell approximately 79×79 m but because of data format conversion, the resolution is referred to as a 56×79 m pixel (picture element) (0·44 ha). Each Landsat scene covers a 185×185 km area or scene. A nominal scene consists of 2340 scan lines with about 3240 pixels per scan line.

Processing and distribution

Data acquired by the Landsat satellite is transmitted to receiving stations operated not only by the United States, but by a number of foreign countries as well. The foreign ground stations operational or expected to be operational in the near future include two in Canada, one each in Brazil, Argentina, Sweden, Italy, South Africa, China, India, Thailand, Australia, and Japan. The U.S. operates three Landsat tracking and ground receiving stations located at NASA facilities in Greenbelt, Maryland; Goldstone, California; and Fairbanks, Alaska.

NASA has entered into formal agreements with a number of foreign countries by which NASA agrees to provide direct transmission of Landsat data to ground stations located in the participating countries. Foreign ground receiving stations have acquired a considerable amount of Landsat data and some data acquired outside the range of U.S. ground stations are available only from the specified foreign receiving stations. In accordance with NASA agreements, foreign stations are to provide data to interested users at a reasonable price. Furthermore, several countries containing tropical habitats have national Landsat programs.

The MSS data are converted onboard from analog to digital format. When a Landsat satellite is within receiving distance of the particular receiving station, RBV and MSS data are directly transmitted in real time and can be recorded on magnetic tape at the ground station. It should be noted that not all data is recorded regularly, resulting in serious gaps in Landsat coverage. When the satellite passes over areas without ground receiving stations, two onboard tape recorders are used to store data. These data are then transmitted to the ground when the satellite again over a receiving station.

Unfortunately, with regard to certain tropical areas, the tape recorders on board Landsat 3 have experienced malfunction seriously limiting the availability of data. The reader will note that because of the high degree of overlap between adjacent orbits in the northerly latitudes, the problem is inconsequental in this area, yet extremely important as the orbit nears the Equator and overlap diminishes. In addition, MSS cannot penetrate cloud cover, and if a particular region has frequent cloud cover, as is common in many tropical forest areas, one must acquire imagery at the time of year when cloud cover is minimal.

Two photo-like products of Landsat images are available for manual or hard copy interpretation: black and white prints of varying sizes, one for each individual MSS band (4, 5, 6, and 7), and colour-composite images produced by combining any three MSS bands.

Image interpretation

In the early 1970s attempts by this researcher to incorporate Landsat images into habitat evaluation procedures in Northern Colombia proved frustrating. Manual interpretation of separate bands, together with examination of colour composites, resulted in subjective estimates of forest cover. For many, the technology in those days did not provide much useful information.

The very recent and important development of techniques for the extraction of information by computers, as opposed to human operators, is still relatively new. This technology results in significant reduction of time and costs, and in improved accuracy and reproducibility. Digital processing with computers allows examination of each image data sample, can discriminate subtle intensity differences, and can perform sophisticated statistical tests on anything from individual samples to large aggregates of data.

Fortunately, I had the opportunity to return to Landsat technology in 1979 and work with computer Landsat data. The Resource Planning Unit of the World Bank has utilized Landsat to produce country mosaics for several developing countries. Working at the Environmental Research Institute of Michigan (ERIM), I interpreted a scene of Bangladesh that contained a forested region in which I had previously conducted field work. The opportunity to sit down and work with digital Landsat data on the ERIM computer system proved invaluable. Unlike manual interpretation of Landsat Photographs, machine processing produced spectral values and a flexible classification system, together with quantitative data. In fact, a significant result of the study was the documentation that little forest actually remained in the Madhupur Forest tract, and intensive human use of this ecosystem had significantly degraded the once extensive forest region (Green 1981).

Results of this study showed valuable potential for digitally processing Landsat data over information gleaned from manual interpretation of Landsat images. While manual interpretation would be useful for discriminating generalized locations of large expanses of forest types, only digital processing techniques could distinguish complex heterogeneous land cover.

Such information, when expanded and combined with further testing and evaluation, is extremely useful for ecologists, wildlife biologists and conservationists desiring up-to-date and extensive information on the changing forest ecosystems. It stands to reason that economists, agriculturalists and foresters involved in development projects, could also utilize this resource. Ultimately, once ground cover classification is established and verified, regular systematic monitoring of forest alteration and destruction could be accomplished.

Facility for ecological interpretation (IMAGES)

The purchase of an expensive computer facility like the 'General Electric Image 100' image processing system or the ERIM system, is impossible for biologists operating on already tight budgets. The author investigated the market and identified a low-cost computer program package. Funds were acquired from the Interagency Primate Steering Committee (IPSC) of the National Institutes of Health to purchase IMPAC (Image Analysis Package for Microcomputers), available through Egbert Scientific Software and established the Image Analysis and Graphic Facility for Ecological Studies (IMAGES). This facility operates within the Department of Zoological Research, National Zoological Park, Smithsonian Institution. IMAGES utilizes the Smithsonian Institution's Honeywell 6680 as a mainframe. IMPAC provides full digital computer analytic capabilities and is capable of creating and displaying full colour multi-spectral classification maps of Landsat data. The full statistical analysis capabilities include histogram generation and image ratioing. Interactive digital systems such as IMPAC are a cost-effective image transformation process. A complete IMPAC system with computer, terminal, printer, colour TV and disc memory sells for $15 000.

IMPAC programs are available on a single magnetic disc and ready to run on a microcomputer. The IMPAC system refers to the IMPAC program package together with the microcomputer and its accessories on which IMPAC runs. The most important component of the IMPAC system is the microcomputer. It is the development of these very low cost computer systems, based on microprocessors, that makes IMPAC possible. The microprocessor used for IMPAC is the Intel 8080.

Figure 1 illustrates the configuration of IMAGES including communication to the Honeywell mainframe at the Office of Computer Services (OCS). Because of the enormous amount of digital information contained in one Landsat scene, the microcomputer can only store a limited portion of that information. Thus, segments corresponding to a 10×8 km area are downloaded from the mainframe onto floppy discs in IMPAC, and consequent data analysis proceeds on these subscenes.

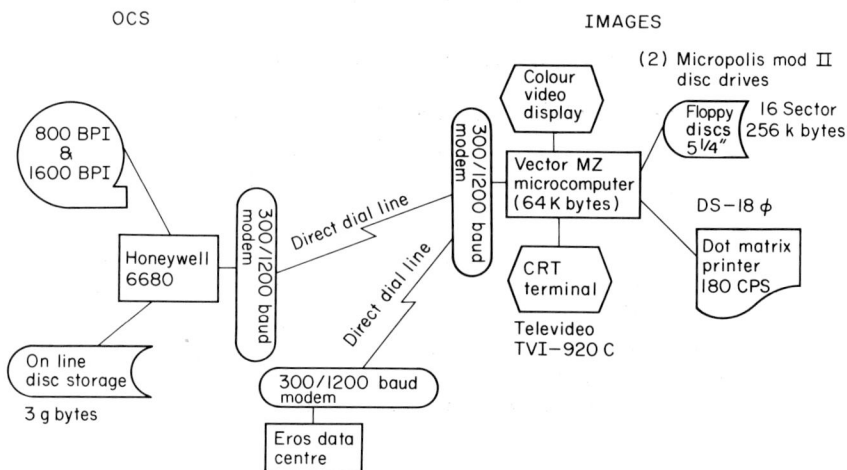

FIG. 1. An overview of IMAGES hardware system and interface with the Honeywell mainframe computer at the Office of Computer Service (OCS). BPI = bits per inch; CPS = characters per second; CRT = cathode ray display terminal.

Tropical field biologists often conduct long-term research. Although many projects focus on target organisms, usually ecological data is acquired that includes development of habitat classification. The objective of IMAGES is to use this knowledge, gathered by the researcher in the field, and provide land cover analysis. In particular, many primate populations, because of restricted habitat, are endangered or threatened. IMAGES can provide updated information on the status of these habitats. In addition, intensive studies in small areas can be used to generate population data by extrapolation to other similar habitats identified through digital processing of the Landsat images.

To aid the field worker, IMAGES has developed standardized procedures for gathering ground truth. Understanding that the field worker is not necessarily a trained botanist nor will understand the principles of remote sensing, guidelines have been refined so that these field workers can, with little extra time and energy, acquire the necessary information and forward this to IMAGES. IMAGES is presently providing technical support for field researchers in Nigeria, Cameroun, Uganda, Venezuela, and Mexico. This author has utilized Landsat data on IMAGES from Bangladesh and Brazil where field work had previously been conducted.

CASE STUDY: BANGLADESH

The problem with quantifying tropical forest cover is exemplified by a case study in Bangladesh. Available estimates of forest cover (Table 2) indicate that between 6·5% and 15% of the country is forested. The very considerable difference among these estimates is significant and warrants closer scrutiny. The first problem encountered is that these references do not necessarily employ the same categories, so that the

TABLE 2. Estimated forest area of Bangladesh

Amount forest area (km^2)	(% Land cover)	Source	
22052	15·4	Library of Congress	1980*
14344	10·0	Library of Congress	1980†
14344	10·0	UNESCO	1976
13440	9·3	Lanly/FAO	1981
13260	9·3	Myers NAS	1980‡
12420	8·6	Lanly/FAO	1981
9350	6·5	Lanly/FAO	1981

* Based on Bangladesh Monthly Statistical Bulletin of March 1978.
† From pp. 37 and 38.
‡ Based on Bangladesh Department Forestry data.

inventory of forest cover by forest type is difficult to interpret. The most detailed description of forest cover in Bangladesh is available in the recent extensive FAO (Lanly 1981) Asian Regional Tropical Forest Resources Assessment Project (part of the Global Environment Monitoring System—GEMS of FAO–UNEP). Applicable FAO forest categories are: (i) *closed broadleaf*, which encompasses tropical evergreen, semi-evergreen 'hill forests,' tropical moist deciduous and inland-sal forests; (ii) *open broadleaf*; (iii) *scrub broadleaf*; and (iv) *mangrove*. In contrast, the Library of Congress report uses the following categories: (i) semi-evergreen; (ii) low-grade deciduous; (iii) freshwater swamp; and (iv) mangrove or tidal. The lack of agreement between reports is further demonstrated by Myers' categories of: semi-evergreen, alluvial '*Shorea*,' and mangrove.

Table 3 summarizes the estimated area of natural woody vegetation in Bangladesh, as 9270 km^2 or 6·4% of the land surface. Note that this total forest cover is inclusive of both FAO's productive and unproductive closed broadleaf forest categories. This same FAO document indicates that there is another 3150 km^2 forest fallow that includes heavily logged or scrub vegetation. Therefore, if this forest category were added to the former, there is 12420 km^2 of forest in Bangladesh (8·6% of the surface area). However, the accuracy of these data are questionable since no quantitative data base exists for these estimates.

TABLE 3. Areas (km^2) of natural woody vegetation estimated end 1980* in Bangladesh

Closed broadleaf forest type	Productive	Unproductive	Total forest cover
Evergreen	4700	—	4700
Moist deciduous	—	520	520
Mangrove	3800	250	4050
Total	8500	770	9270
Total forest land cover of Bangladesh (%)			6·4

* FAO 1981, p. 120.

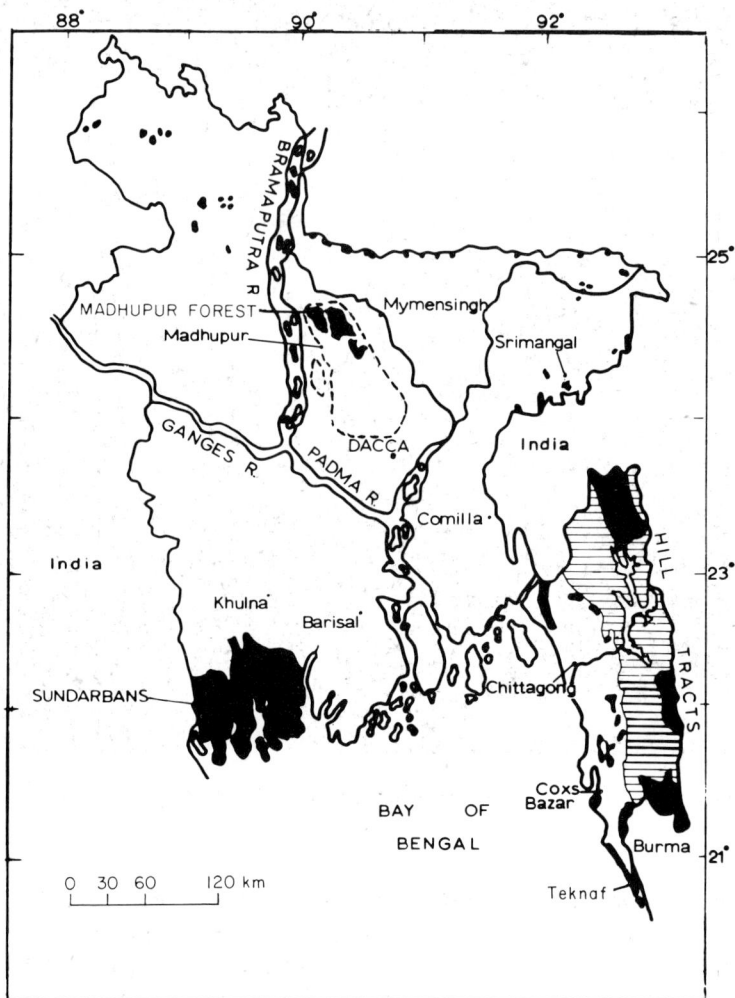

FIG. 2. Map of Bangladesh (modified from Ahmed 1968) showing forest regions: reserved forest (■); unclassified forest (▤); former extent of forest in Madhupur tract (- - - -).

It is possible, though, to examine a quantified data base for the Madhupur Forest Track of Bangladesh, as provided by digital Landsat analysis. Extensive survey work by this investigator on the status of forest habitat and wildlife populations in Bangladesh during 1976 (Green 1977, 1978) included prolonged research during

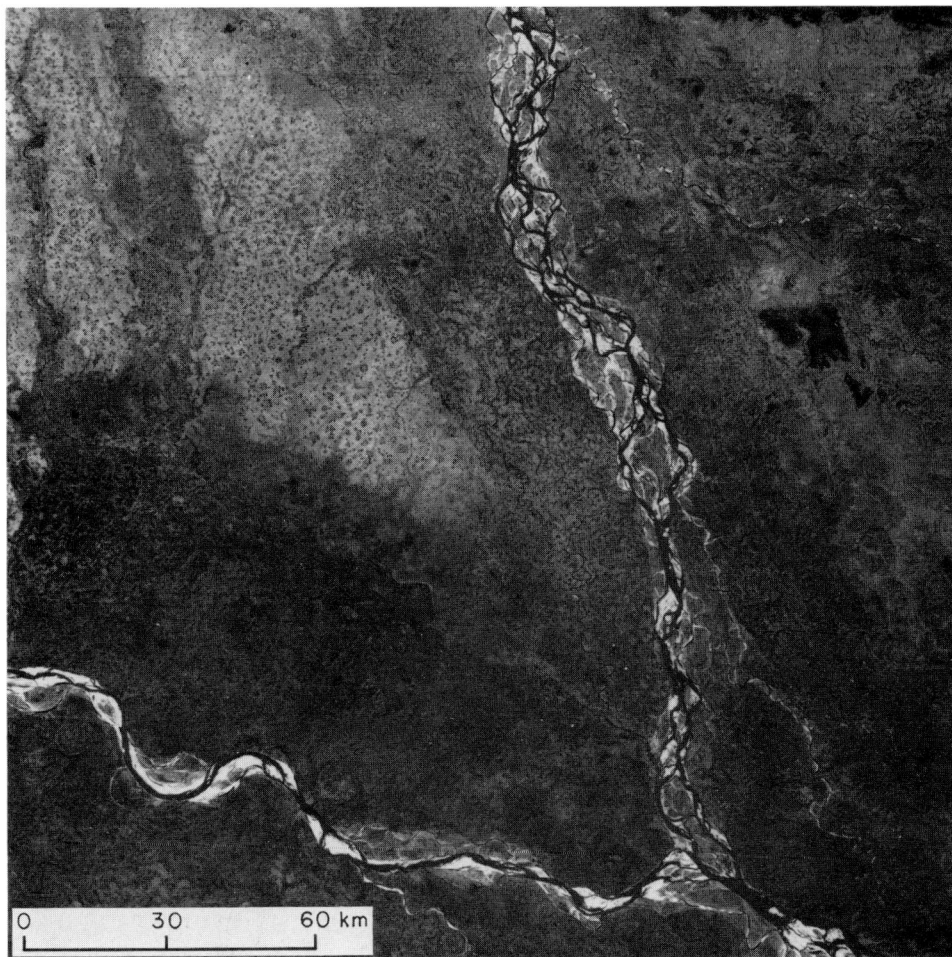

FIG. 3. Portion of Landsat Scene 2748-03294 (Band 5) showing the Madhupur Forest (dark area top right centre).

monthly visits to the Madhupur Forest from July to November 1976. The Madhupur Tract, a Pleistocene terrace, is located east of the Bramaputra River, south-west of Mymensingh, and is located north-west of Dacca in the Tangail and Mymensingh Districts. This terrace measures approximately 120 km long, north-west to south-east, and 8–21 km wide east to west (Fig. 2). Unlike most of the surrounding alluvial flood-plains, this region remains unflooded during the monsoon months. Today, the northern part of the Madhupur Tract contains a forested area, referred to as the Madhupur Forest, situated north and north-east of the town of Madhupur.

Digital processing of portions of the Landsat Image No. 2748-03294 (Figs 3 and 4) acquired on 8 February, 1977, provided classification of the Madhupur ground cover. Three large, but dissected, forested areas containing approximately 144 km² were

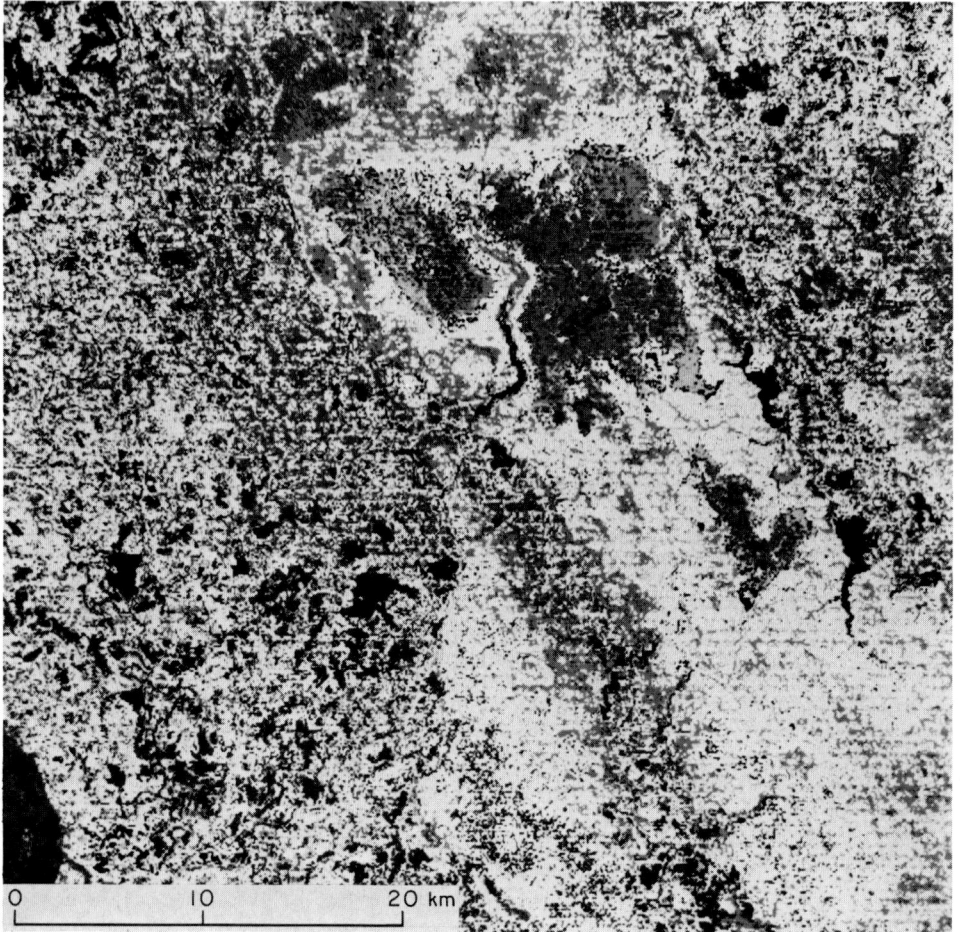

Fig. 4. Landsat monitoring of tropical forest cover for the Madhupur forest.

selected for classification based on the ground truth information and discernible ground features from the Landsat images. A total of fifteen land cover/land use categories were established, and aggregated into six major Level I categories (Table 4). In general, these six classes of forest cover account for 90·67 km² or 63% of the surface area in the Madhupur Forest. The final product of this study was the production of colour-coded positive transparencies and photographic products.

TABLE 4. Land cover/land use in the Madhupur Forest, Bangladesh*

Category		Total area (km^2)	% Land surface
Level I	Level II		
Water		2·8	1·8
	Lake water		
	Swamp/slough		
	Shallow/turbid		
	Turbid lake/vegetation		
Agriculture		32·4	22·5
	Paddy		
	Fallow 'baids'		
	Fallow jute		
Barren land		11·5	8·0
Wetlands		0·4	0·3
Forest		90·6	62·8
	Scrub		
	Mature mixed		
	Cutover mixed		
	Sal plantation		
	Regenerating		
Unclassified		6·7	4·6
Total		144·4	100

* Based on digital processing Landsat scene 2748-03294, acquired on 8 Feb.,
1977.

CONCLUSIONS

A significant result of this study concerns the present paucity of forest cover. Official, but outdated information, reports that the Dacca-Tangail District (also referred to as the Madhupur Tract) contained 699 km^2 of forest (Anon. 1976). A more conservative estimate of the forest in these regions, reported in the Forest Department's Madhupur working scheme, indicated only 337 km^2 of forest (Chowdhury 1973). However, based on intensive survey work primarily in the north-east sector of the main quadrant of the Madhupur forest, I indicated that the official Bangladesh Government statistics for forest cover could be reasonably reduced by 50% to 168 km^2 (Green 1978). The results of the computer analysis show that this too was an over-optimistic conclusion and that today this once extensive forest area has been reduced by 85% to forest cover of 91 km^2.

However, this Level I forest category is an aggregation of five Level II categories which, when considered in the context of the Tropical Forest Resources Assessment project (Lanly 1981), yield more useful information. This document uses the category of closed broadleaf forests for forests that have not been recently cleared by shifting agriculture and are not heavily exploited. Degradation to the tropical moist deciduous Madhupur forest includes deforestation from shifting cultivation and illicit cutting and lopping of trees. Land cover/land use categories of scrub, cutover, and regenerating forest cover account for 51 km^2. The amount of present undisturbed productive forest in the Madhupur Tract would then only be 28 km^2, or one-third of the 91 km^2 Level I forest cover quantity (Table 5).

TABLE 5. Amount of closed broadleaf forest in the Madhupur Tract, Bangladesh*

	Area (km²)	% of Madhupur Tract
Tropical moist deciduous	91	
Converted to plantation	12	0·13
Degraded	51	0·56
Scrub		
Cutover		
Regenerating		
Present undisturbed productive forest	28	0·30

* Based on digital processed Landsat data (Green 1981).

The results of this analysis overwhelmingly support the contentions of serious tropical forest degradation and demonstrates the utility and need for this type of tropical forest inventory data. The successful application of IMAGES in this context, as well as other applications of natural resource habitat evaluation in the tropics using Landsat data, provides strong evidence for further application of this technology as a means to generate much needed baseline data on tropical forests.

ACKNOWLEDGMENTS

I thank J. Grumm, V. Garber and L. Thomas for typing various parts of this manuscript. IMAGES is funded through the National Institutes of Health (NIH) Contract No. NO1-RS-0-2125 which also provided the travel support to attend the Symposium on Tropical Rain Forests. Friends of the National Zoo (FONZ), and the organizing committee of the meeting also provided financial assistance to help defray the costs of travel. Initial digital processing of the Madhupur forest was supported through the Resource Planning Unit of the World Bank at the Environmental Research Institute of Michigan (ERIM).

REFERENCES

Ahmed, N. (1968). *An Economic Geography of East Pakistan.* Oxford University Press, London.

Anonymous (1976). *Annual progress report of forests administration in Bangladesh for the year 1972–73.* Dacca, Bangladesh Government Press.

Anonymous (1979). Science and its implication to the assessment and management of natural resources. *Nature and Resources,* **15,** 2–6.

Chowdhury, A.M. (1973). *Working scheme for the Mymensingh Division, 1969–1970.* Dacca, Bangladesh Government Press.

Committee on Foreign Affairs (1981). Subcommittee on International Organizations, House of Representatives, U.S. Congress. *Tropical deforestation hearings.* U.S. Government Printing Office, Washington, D.C.

Council on Environmental Quality and the Department of State (1980). *The Global 2000 Report to the President.* Washington, D.C.

Department of State (1980). *The world's tropical forests: A policy, strategy, and program for the United States.* U.S. Agency Task Force on Tropical Forests.

Department of State (1982). U.S. Strategy Conference on Biological Diversity.

FAO (1981). *Tropical Forest Resources Assessment Project: Forest Resources of Tropical Asia.* Rome.

Green, K.M. (1977). Primate resources of Bangladesh. *Laboratory Primate Newsletter*, **16**, (4), 1–8.

Green, K.M. (1978). Primates of Bangladesh. A preliminary survey of population and habitat. *Biological Conservation*, **13**, 141–160.

Green, K.M. (1981). *Digital processing of tropical forest habitat in Bangladesh and the development of a low-cost processing facility at the National Zoo, Smithsonian Institution.* Proceedings of the Fifteenth International Symposium on Remote Sensing of Environment. Ann Arbor, Michigan.

IUCN-UNEP-WWF (1980. *World Conservation Strategy.* IUCN-UNEP-WWF, Switzerland.

Library of Congress (1980). Draft environmental profile of Bangladesh.

Myers, N. (1980). *Conversion of Tropical Moist Forests*, NAS, Washington, D.C.

NAS (1980). *Research Priorities in Tropical Biology.* Washington, D.C.

UNESCO (1972) MAB. Export Panel on Project 1: *Ecological effects of increasing human activities on tropical and subtropical forest ecosystems.* Paris, 16–18 May.

UNESCO (1976) MAB. *Regional meeting on integrated ecological research and training needs in tropical deciduous and semi-deciduous forest ecosystems of South Asia.* Varanasi, 5–11 October 1975.

UNESCO (1979) MAB-IUFRO. *International workshop on tropical rain forest ecosystems.* Hamburg-Reinber, 12–17 May.

PART IV

C · REGIONAL REPORTS

Tropical moist forest conservation in Brazil

IBSEN DE GUSMÃO CÂMARA

*Fundação Brasileira Para a Conservação da Natureza-FBCN, R. Miranda Valverde,
103-Botafogo-CEP 22281, Rio de Janeiro-RJ, Brasil*

SUMMARY

1   The rain forests of Brazil are situated in the south-western part of the country, along the Atlantic coast and on the Amazonian basin. Only the Amazonian forests still cover a large area today.

2   The south-western forest has been almost completely destroyed. Less than 2000 km^2 of it and a little more than 10 000 km^2 of the Atlantic forest are preserved as national parks and state reserves. Preservation of the remains of the Atlantic forest and its ecosystems are a great and urgent problem of conservation.

3   The Amazonian forests remain almost untouched in their greatest part. According to satellite data, up to 1979 only 1·11% of the dense tropical forest had been deeply altered by man.

4   The Brazilian Government has plans to keep at least 1 800 000 km^2 of the area covered by natural vegetation. There are 87 644 km^2 of natural parks, biological reserves and ecological stations already established. The main criterion for selection of protected areas has been the identification of Pleistocene refuges.

5   Intensive demographic increase, difficulties in enforcing the law and inadequate scientific knowledge of the region are causes of worry for the conservationists.

INTRODUCTION

In a very simplified way, the tropical moist forest of Brazil may be divided into three types (Fig. 1):

(i)   a narrow band of tropical rain forest along the coast, the so-called Atlantic forest;

(ii) a tropical seasonal forest covering the extensive plateau in the centre and southern parts of the country;

(iii) the huge Amazonian tropical rain forest.

Each one of these three types has intrinsic characteristics and shows considerable diversity of flora, according to the local geographical conditions, types of soil and amount of rainfall. In some areas, the tropical seasonal forest and Atlantic rain forest overlap each other making it difficult to distinguish the precise boundaries (Hueck 1972).

The southern part of the Atlantic forest covers mainly the seaward slope of the mountain chain that runs along the coast, from the State of Rio Grande do Sul to the South of Bahia. The northern part of that forest occupies a narrow strip of low level ground, near the sea.

The tropical seasonal forest originally extended from the watershed of the coastal

413

mountain chain to the interior, near the dividing line between the tropical and temperate zones, over a plateau with little relief and penetrating the territories of Argentina and Paraguay.

The biggest extension of rain forest in Brazil is occupied, of course, by the Amazonian forest that covers an area of approximately 2 800 000 km², about 90% of

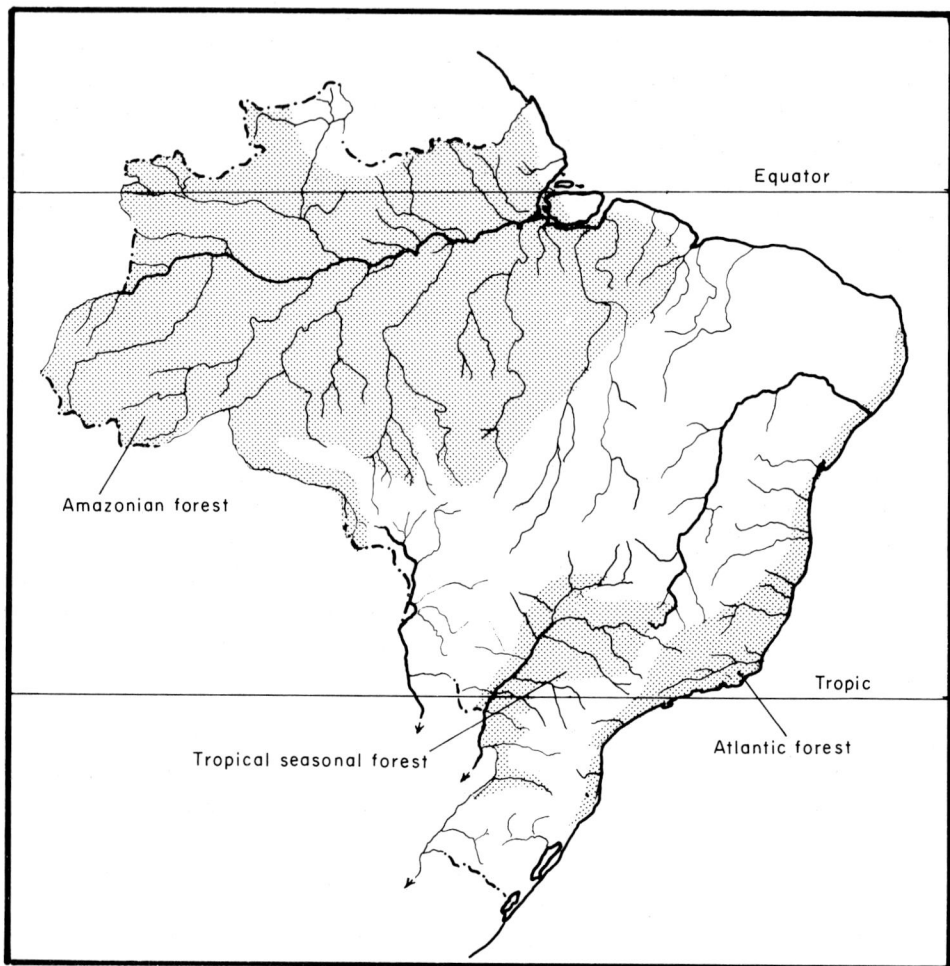

Equator

Amazonian forest

Tropic

Tropical seasonal forest

Atlantic forest

FIG. 1. Tropical moist forests of Brazil.

the Amazon Basin inside the boundaries of the country. The remaining 10% are covered by various quite different types of vegetation; solution of the problems related to conservation are difficult and complex, because of the variety of ecosystems needing preservation.

Before we analyse the situation of the rain forests in Brazil, it would be useful to indicate the legal types of conservation units existing in the country. The present legislation includes three categories of areas under governmental management for conservation purposes: parks, biological reserves and ecological stations. The main distinction between them is that the public may be admitted into the parks, under proper control, whereas the other two categories are only used for preservation and scientific research. Each one of the three categories may be created and managed by the Federal Government, the States and the municipalities.

We will begin the presentation of the Brazilian tropical moist forests by talking about the Atlantic rain and tropical seasonal ones. Both types are, or we should say, were located in the most densely populated areas of the country, where agricultural and traditional cattle-raising activities have been practiced for a long time. As a result the forested areas have suffered intensely from human actions.

The tropical seasonal rain forest has been almost completely destroyed during the last 100 years and only islands of vegetation remain, too small and scattered to be really significant for conservation purposes. Fortunately, samples of the former forest are preserved in the magnificent Iguaçu National Park (1560 km^2) and the Morro do Diabo State Reserve (371 km^2), besides a number of smaller reserves.

The situation of the Atlantic rain forest is very serious too, but a little better. In its southern part, access is difficult due to exceedingly steep mountainous areas, and extensive parts of the forest still exist as private and governmental property. Besides that, there is a reasonable number of parks, biological reserves and ecological stations. In the majority of cases, however, the areas of those reserves are not very large and a considerable proportion of them is still private property. The situation is worse on the northern part of the Atlantic forest, having been almost completely cleared by uncontrolled logging, agriculture and cattle raising. As in the case of the tropical forest, only a limited number of islands of forest remains there and the amount of governmental reserves is smaller than in the southern part. The main reserves in the Atlantic forest cover an area of 10 529 km^2 (Table 1).

Currently, the exorbitant price of land and the demographic pressure in that area of the country practically prevents the creation of new reserves. Even the problem of complete regularization of the decreed reserves has been difficult to solve. Illegal hunting, poaching, robbery of forest products and lack of proper control are permanent problems.

Preservation of the remains of the Atlantic forest is, probably, the greatest and most urgent problem of conservation in the country. Its extremely valuable ecosystems include a great number of endemic species, reduced to small and dispersed populations seriously threatened with extinction. Only to cite one example, fifteen of the seventeen species of south-eastern Brazilian primates are endangered or vulnerable. One of them is the extraordinarily interesting monkey called *muriqui* (*Brachyteles arachnoides*), the biggest and most ape-like Neotropical primate, which survives with very small and isolated populations. The same precarious conditions threaten many other species of plants and animals. The evaluation of their real status is uncertain and the knowledge of the overall situation is still quite unsatisfactory. The Atlantic forest is a prolific field for research and still holds many surprises. Even now species new to science are being discovered in the area.

TABLE 1. Parks and biological reserves of the Atlantic rain
forest

Name	Area (km^2)	State
Bocaina NP	700	Rio de Janeiro
Itatiaia NP	119	Rio de Janeiro
Tijuca NP	33	Rio de Janeiro
Serra dos Órgãos NP	100	Rio de Janeiro
Caparaó NP	104	Espírito Santo
Monte Pascoal NP	225	Bahia
Poço d'Anta NBR	50	Rio de Janeiro
Nova Lombárdia NBR	43	Espírito Santo
Córrego do Veado NBR	24	Espírito Santo
Sooretama NBR	240	Espírito Santo
Una NBR	100	Bahia
Serra do Taboleiro SP	900	Sta Catarina
Serra Furada SP	13	Sta Catarina
Murumbi I e II SP	732	Paraná
Iporanga SP	357	S. Paulo
Campos de Jordão SP	80	S. Paulo
Ilha Bela SP	270	S. Paulo
Ilha do Cardoso SP	236	S. Paulo
Jacupiranga SP	1500	S. Paulo
Serra do Mar SP	3150	S. Paulo
Rio Doce SP	1350	Minas Gerais
Desengano SP	225	Rio de Janeiro
Pedra Branca SP	125	Rio de Janeiro
Cantareira SBR	56	S. Paulo
Carlos Botelho SBR	376	S. Paulo
Itatins SBR	120	S. Paulo
Capão Bonito SBR	239	S. Paulo
Canela Preta SBR	18	Sta Catarina
Sassafrás SBR	87	Sta Catarina
Araras SBR	20	Rio de Janeiro
Total	10 592	

NP = National Park.
NBR = National Biological Reserve.
SP = State Park (or equivalent).
SBR = State Biological Reserve (or equivalent).
Reserves smaller than 10 km^2 were omitted.

We cannot foresee possibilities of amplifying significantly the reserves in the Atlantic forest, but it is possible and necessary to improve those already in existence, with better control and the purchase of lands still in private hands.

In the case of the Amazonian forests, we see the problems of conservation in a different way. The enormous size of the area, equivalent to approximately 28% of Europe, and the very low demographic density have been an effective natural protection not available in the southern forests. Even now, facing an intensive human occupation in some areas, the forest remains in its greatest part almost untouched. The large scale clearing of the Amazonian forest has been mentioned frequently and many people believe that its destruction is imminent. In reality, extensive clearing has happened but, in proportion to the total area, the damage is still relatively limited. The Government agency responsible for policy and management of forestry and forest control in Brazil has carried out a programme of forest monitoring, using the Landsat MSS satellite data (Green 1983). The conclusion was that, up to 1979, only 1·11% of the dense tropical forest had been deeply altered, corresponding to 31 000 km^2 out of 2 800 000 km^2 (Carneiro 1981a, b). At the present time the main reason for concern is not the extent of the clearing, but how fast it has taken place. From 1976 to 1978, the rate of deforestation was 9 km^2 per day, including all types of vegetation.

The Brazilian Government is quite conscious of the menace to the Amazonian forest and is now considering special legislation to protect it, based on deep and comprehensive studies carried on during 1979, aiming to establish a policy for the rational use of Amazonia. The main conclusion from those studies was the economic activities in the area should be subordinated to a careful ecological zoning of the region. At least 600 000 km^2 should be set aside for National Forests, to be developed under strict control by the Government, using non-destructive techniques. For new national parks and biological reserves, an additional 175 000 km^2 should be set aside. Since the Brazilian law already establishes that at least 50% of the natural vegetation cover has to be assigned for permanent preservation in every agricultural or cattle-raising project in the region, those measures would guarantee around 1 800 000 km^2 of natural and permanent vegetation. The above-mentioned conclusions are under consideration and a decision is expected soon.

Currently, there are already 87 644 km^2 of national parks, biological reserves and ecological stations in Amazonia (Padua 1981). New areas are being selected and in the future it is planned that 70 000 km^2 more are to be added. We believe that nowhere in the world is there such an ambitious project for conservation in a single country.

One of the major difficulties involved in the creation of reserves in Amazonia is how to choose a criterion for selection of areas to be preserved. Since the greatest part of the region remains as public land, the purchasing problem is not serious, but selection of the ecosystems to be preserved is exceedingly complex. Besides the rain forest, that covers about 90% of the area, many additional types of vegetation exist: swamp forests, bamboo forests, savannahs, periodic flood forests, open forests, floating meadows, mangroves and so on. The tropical rain forest itself is not homogeneous and it presents a considerable amount of endemic forms. An inventory of the vegetation cover of Amazonia by means of remote sensors has indicated an enormous variety of types (Veloso *et al.* 1974, 1975, 1976). In addition to these obstacles, the lack of knowledge about Amazonian ecology is an important factor to be considered.

The majority of reserves in the south of the country have been established mainly to preserve scenic landscapes. In many cases the only reason for their creation was the intent to save what could still be saved. In Amazonia, we plan to act in a more scientific manner. The Brazilian Institute for Forestry Development (IBDF), responsible for the creation of national parks and biological reserves, is using all available information for the selection of new areas of preservation, based mainly on the Pleistocene forest refuges theory.

During the last 25 years, several studies based on geomorphological, palynological and biological evidence have indicated the occurrence of marked alterations of climate and vegetation in Amazonia, during Plio-Pleistocene times (Brown & Ab'Saber 1979). A recent study published by the National Institute for Research on Amazonia (INPA) indicated that those fluctuations of climate, in a greater or lesser degree, continued during the Holocene, even into historical times (Absy 1979). Now, it seems irrefutable that several times, in the last millenia, dry and humid phases alternated and that, during dry phases, the rain forest was reduced to isolated areas, separated by bush or savannahs. Small remnants of them still exist within the forest, in some areas. It is presumed that inside these ancient islands of forest numerous endemic forms have been generated by genetic isolation, and we may suspect that the areas formerly occupied by those refuges still keep some of them.

Areas that possibly have been Pleistocene refuges were suggested by Haffer (1969, 1977), Vanzolini (1973), Vanzolini & Williams (1970), Prance (1973), Brown (1976, 1977), Brown & Ab'Saber (1979), besides other authors, based on studies of birds, lizards, plants, lepidoptera and geomorphology.

Meager as the evidence may be, short of better criterion, the Brazilian Institute for Forestry Development used the following priorities for the selection of areas for national parks and biological reserves (M. A. IBDF/FBCN 1979):
  (i) areas where two or more scientists indicated a probable existence of a Pleistocene refuge;
 (ii) areas where simultaneously a refuge and distinct vegetal formations may occur;
(iii) areas of ecological significance, not included in the former categories.

The acceptance of the above-mentioned criterion was submitted to several national and foreign scientists and conservationists. The majority approved it and no alternative proposals were suggested. As the delimitation of new reserves is urgent and considering the inadequacy of knowledge about the Amazonian ecology, the priorities were accepted as indicated. The first national park in Amazonia became effective during 1974. Since 1979, several reserves have been added, totalling 87 644 km^2 (Table 2). In the near future, the creation of eight new parks and other reserves is already scheduled, covering a total area of 59 800 km^2 (Fig. 2).

The measures to protect the Amazonian forest, mentioned above, are only the beginning, however. Even with the promulgation of adequate laws, the establishment of large reserves and the growing concern with the conservation of the area, many threats still exist. The Brazilian population is increasing by three million each year and the demographic pressure is considerable. The difficulties of enforcing the law in such extensive and remote areas and the inadequate scientific knowledge of the whole region are additional reasons of worry for the conservationists.

The simple management and control of almost 180 000 km^2 of strictly protected areas inside national parks and other biological reserves is a task of gigantic proportions. According to the present planning, at least 1 800 000 km^2 will require some kind of permanent control.

Today it is well known that the greatest part of the soils in Amazonia are acid and poor in nutrients, but they can be used for agricultural purposes with proper care (Schubart 1977). Only a very small percentage (about 6·6% or 320 000 km^2) is subject to

TABLE 2. Parks and Biological reserves of the Amazonian rain forest

Name	Area (km^2)	State or territory
(1) Amazônia (Tapajós) NP	10 000	Pará
(2) Pacaás Novos NP	7648	Rondônia
(3) Pico da Neblina NP	22 200	Amazonas
(4) Cabo Orange NP	6190	Amapá
(5) Jaú NP	23 210	Amazonas
(6) Jaru NBR	2681	Rondônia
(7) Rio Trombetas NBR	3850	Pará
(8) Lago Piratuba NBR	3950	Amapá
(9) Anavilhanas ES	3500	Amazonas
(10) Iquê ES	2000	Mato Grosso
(11) Maracá-Jipioca ES	720	Pará
(12) Maracá-Roraima ES	920	Roraima
(13) Rio Acre ES	775	Acre
Total	87 644	

NP = National Park.
NBR = National Biological Reserve.
ES = Ecological Station.

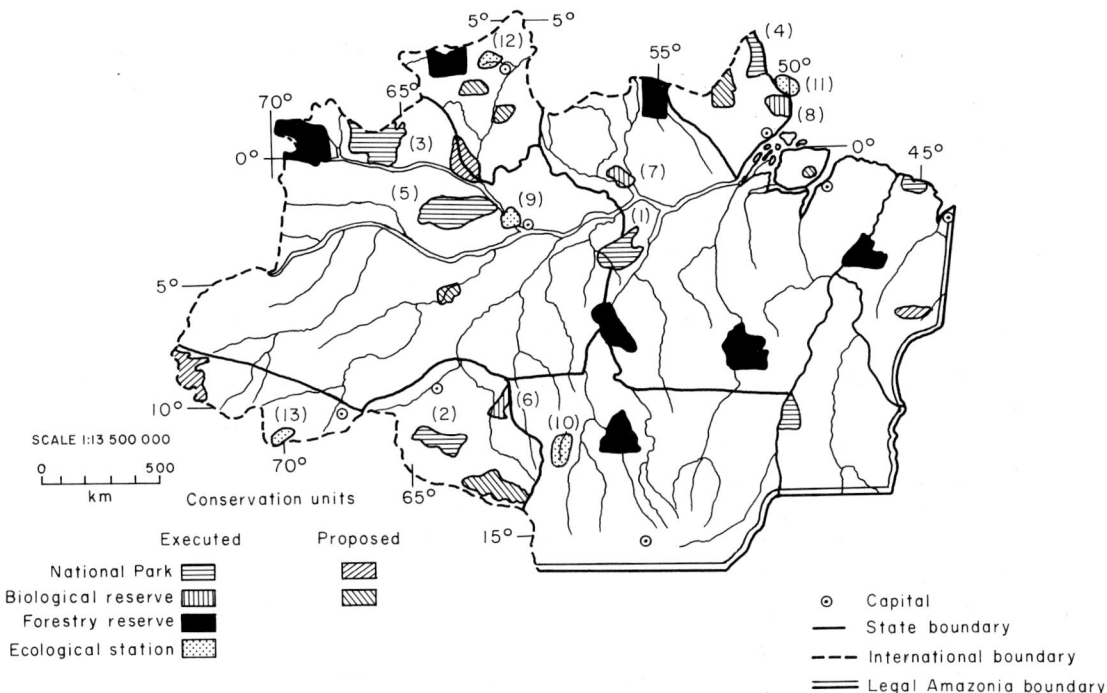

FIG. 2. Existing and planned conservation units in legal Brazilian Amazonia plus areas reserved for forestry (numbered as in Table 2). Note (cf. Fig. 1) that the Amazonian rain forest does not extend as far east as Legal Amazonia (source: RADAM/Brasil + working group (decree 83518, May 1979), new forestry policy for Brazilian Amazonia).

serious restrictions on fertility (Carvalho 1981). In the future, demographic and political pressures for the occupation of Amazonia may become difficult to overcome.

At this moment we cannot anticipate what would occur with a very extensive deforestation of the whole area. We already know that more than 50% of the rain that falls over the Amazon basin comes from evapotranspiration of the forest (Salati 1981). Large-scale destruction of it could change dramatically the amount of water in the drainage system of the basin and profoundly affect the ecosystems of all protected areas, indirectly. If such a situation arises, the aims of the creation of those areas may be frustrated by human action beyond their borders.

In spite of these difficulties and threats, it seems unlikely that the Amazonian forest will suffer the very extensive devastation that destroyed the rain forests of the south. We can expect that today the popular concern with ecology and the dissemination of scientific knowledge will compel the political leadership of the nation to deem essential a more rational and judicious use of the great forest.

REFERENCES

Absy, M.L. (1979). *A palynological study of Holocene sediments in the Amazon Basin.* Instituto Nacional de Pesquisas da Amazônia, Manaus.

Brown, K.S. Jr. (1976). Geographical patterns of evolution in neotropical Lepidoptera. *Journal of Entomology and Biology*, 44.

Brown, K.S. Jr. (1977). Centros de evolução, refúgios Quaternários e conservação do patrimônio genéticos na Região Neotropical. *Acta Amazônica*, **7**, (1), Manaus.

Brown, K.S. Jr. & Ab'Saber, A.N. (1979). Ice-age forest refuges and evolution in the Neotropics: correlation of paleoclimatological, geomorphological and pedological data with modern biological endemism. *Paleoclimas*, University of de São Paulo, São Paulo.

Carneiro, C.M.R. (1981a). *The national cover monitoring programme of Brazil.* Paper presented in XVII IUFRO World Congress, Sept. 1981. Brasília.

Carneiro, C.M.R. (1981b). *Monitoramento das modificações espaciais no ecossistema florestal da região amazônica brasileira.* E/CEPAL/PROJ.6/R.13. Restricted distribution. Brasília.

Carvalho, J.C.M. (1981). A conservação da natureza e recursos naturais na Amazônia Brasileira. *CVRD Revista*, Rio de Janeiro.

Green, K.M. (1983). Using Landsat to monitor tropical forest ecosystems: realistic expectations of digital processing technology. *Tropical Rain Forest: Ecology and Management* (Ed. by S. L. Sutton, T. C. Whitmore & A. C. Chadwick), pp. 397–409. Blackwell Scientific Publications, Oxford.

Haffer, J. (1969). Speciation in Amazonian forest birds. *Science*, 165.

Haffer, J. (1977). Pleistocene speciation in Amazonian birds. *Amazoniana*, 6(2).

Hueck, K. (1972). *As florestas da América do Sul—ecologia, composição e importância econômica.* Universtiy of Brasília, São Paulo.

M. A. IBDF/FBCN (1979). *Plano do Sistema de Unidades de Conservação do Brasil.* Brasília.

Padua, J.T.J. (1981). Situação atual do sistema de parques nacionais e reservas biológicas. *Boletim FBCN*, vol. 16, Rio de Janeiro.

Prance, G.T. (1973). Phytogeographic support for the theory of Pleistocene forest refugia in the Amazon Basin based on evidence from distribution patterns in Caryocaracea, Chrysobalanaceae, Dichapetalaceae and Lecythidaceae. *Acta Amazônica*, **3** (3), Manaus.

Salati, E. (1981). Floresta e clima da Amazônia. *Boletim FBCN*, vol. 16, Rio de Janeiro.

Schubart, H.O.R. (1977). *Critérios ecológicos para o desenvolvimento agrícola das terras firmes da Amazônia.* INPA, Manaus.

Vanzolini, P.E. (1973). Paleoclimates, relief and species multiplication in Equatorial forest. *Tropical Forest Ecosystem in Africa and South America* (Ed. by J.B. Meggers *et al.*). Smithsonian Press, Washington D.C., U.S.A.

Vanzolini, P.E. & Williams, E.E. (1970). South American Andes: the geographical differentiation and evolution of the *Anolis chrysolepsis* species group. *Arg. Zool. S. Paulo*, 19.

Veloso, H.P. *et al.* **(1974).** As regiões fitoecológicas, sua natureza e seus recursos econômicos. Estudo fitogeográfico. *Brasil, Departamento Nacional de Produção Mineral* (Levantamento de Recursos Naturais, 4). Rio de Janeiro.

Veloso, H.P. *et al.* **(1975).** As regiões fitoecológicas, sua natureza e seus recursos econômicos. Estudo fitogeográfico. *Brasil, Departamento Nacional de Produção Mineral* (Levantamento de Recursos Naturais, 8). Rio de Janeiro.

Veloso, H.P. *et al.* **(1976).** As regiões fitoecológicas, sua natureza e seus recursos econômicos. Estudo fitogeográfico. *Brasil, Departamento Nacional de Produção Mineral* (Levantamento de Recursos Naturais, 10). Rio de Janeiro.

Wildlands conservation in Central America

GARY S. HARTSHORN

Tropical Science Center, Apartado 8–3870, 1.000 San José, Costa Rica

SUMMARY

1   Conservation efforts in Belize have been oriented towards tiny wildlife sanctuaries for bird-watching on the mainland and protecting seabird rookeries on small mangrove islands. Half-Moon Caye National Monument protects one of the few true coral atolls in the Western Caribbean. Although representative forest ecosystems are not protected, the low population pressure and the emphasis on pine exploitation do not yet pose serious threats to the broad-leaved forests.

2   In 12 years, Costa Rica has developed a model system of twenty-two functional national parks and equivalent reserves. Though close to its goal of protecting 10% of the country, the Costa Rican National Park Service is having difficulty consolidating the national parks system due to numerous private land-holdings (23% of the parks area) and the very serious national economic problems. Costa Rica's part of the Friendship International Park (La Amistad) has recently been declared a biosphere reserve by UNESCO.

3   El Salvador's few conservation units have been seriously degraded by population pressures and the current civil war. Montecristo National Park contains the only significant forest remaining in the country, but the park suffered from uncontrolled logging and slash and burn agriculture long before this civil war.

4   Guatemala has established sixteen national parks since 1955, but only four meet the recommended international criteria. The Tikal World Heritage Site is the most significant conservation unit in Guatemala; most of the other conservation units are non-functional 'paper parks' (e.g. Río Dulce) or too small to effectively protect critical habitats or populations (e.g. Quetzal biotope). Terrorism and civil warfare have greatly reduced the government presence in conservation units. Guatemala's conservation efforts continue to suffer from the assassination of Mario Dary, the country's leading conservationist.

5   In the past few years Honduras has made impressive progress in conservation, highlighted by establishment of the Río Plátano Biosphere Reserve. Río Plátano is the most significant conservation unit in northern Central America, particularly because of its pristine nature and large size.

6   After the 1979 revolution, Nicaragua's new government created a National Park Service (SPN) to administer the two existing national parks. SPN is actively evaluating thirty-five wildlands for conservation potential and designation as conservation units.

7   Panama's national parks and equivalent reserves cover nearly 12% of the country; however, most of the conservation units are merely 'paper parks'. The remote Darién World Heritage Site remains intact because of its inaccessibility, but construction of the Pan-American Highway to the Colombian border would seriously threaten the integrity of an area that might be the most biologically rich in the world.

INTRODUCTION

Central America has served as a great mixing ground for the floras and faunas of North and South America. Tracks of puma and jaguar overlap in Honduras' Río Plátano biosphere reserve. Northern hemisphere conifers (pines, firs, spruces and cedars) extend as far south as Lake Nicaragua, but oaks dominate the high-elevation Talamanca forests of Costa Rica and Panama. Paramo—low, shrubby vegetation above tree-line that dominates the northern Andes—has its northernmost extension on Costa Rica's highest peak.

Central American forests are the habitats of a great diversity of tropical birds, mammals, herps and invertebrates (Moser 1975). Many so-called North American migratory birds spend more time in these tropical forests than in their brief northern summer habitat. Recent studies indicate that a surprising number of local bird species migrate altitudinally. Yet Central America's forests are being cut at a combined rate of not less than 300 000 ha year^{-1} (Table 1). Except for sparsely populated Belize, the other six countries have less than 45% of their land still in natural forests (MacFarland & Morales 1981). With human population growth averaging 3·0% for the region, Central America's population will nearly double by the year 2000. The inexorable advance of the agricultural frontier into the shrinking forests leaves little time—certainly no more than this decade—to establish protected conservation units. The current political strife in northern Central America and the severe economic problems buffeting the region make it difficult for government agencies responsible for national parks and equivalent reserves to protect the existing parks. How will they be able to add new conservation units and to consolidate the national conservation system?

This paper offers a country-by-country overview of the status of national parks and equivalent reserves. The latter include biological reserves, wildlife refugia, biosphere reserves, as well as those multiple-use areas, world heritage sites and natural

TABLE 1. Features of Central American countries

	Area*	Population 1977–78	Remaining wildlands*	1978 minimum rate of deforestation*	Protected area* (%)	Number of conservation units
Belize	22 975	140 000	19 500	50	0·36 (0·002)	2
Costa Rica	51 000	2 044 300	16 000	600	4327 (8·48)	22
El Salvador	21 156	4 310 000	200	—	30 (0·14)	2
Guatemala	108 889	6 531 000	32 000	750	988 (0·91)	6
Honduras	112 088	2 954 000	44 000	600	4410 (3·93)	5
Nicaragua	148 000	2 346 000	66 000	400	173 (0·12)	2
Panama	77 082	1 798 000	26 000	500	8609 (11·8)	7
Total	541 190	17 423 300	203 700		18 537 (3·43)	46

* Area in km^2.

monuments that protect significant natural ecosystems. Comments on biological and ecological aspects are kept to a bare minimum in this paper; however, pertinent literature references are included. The listing of national parks and equivalent reserves (Table 2 and Fig. 1) follows, where possible, the numeration of IUCN (1981).

REGIONAL SYNTHESIS

Central America's forty-six national parks and equivalent reserves cover 18 537 km^2, or about 3·5% of the region. About three-quarters of these conservation units have been established since 1970. Except in Belize, each country's early efforts focused on national parks. Only in the past few years have some countries established other types of conservation units, such as biological reserves, wildlife refugia and natural monuments. The early predilection for national parks is understandable and even justifiable, given the strong international recognition associated with national park status. If park consolidation and effective protection are achieved, a protected area can be reclassified to a more appropriate type of conservation unit.

In general terms, each country has an adequate legal base for conservation. Most conservation units have been established by presidential decree, thus they can be abrogated by another decree or simply ignored by the next president. Nevertheless, presidential interest in conservation can produce marvellous results, as shown by Costa Rica's impressive advances in conservation during the administrations of Daniel Oduber (1974–78) and Rodrigo Carazo (1978–82). Costa Rican law stipulates that a conservation unit established by presidential decree can only be changed by a two thirds vote of the Legislative Assembly.

Consolidation of conservation units is the most serious problem facing Central America's national parks and equivalent reserves. It is easy to promulgate a presidential decree, but it is much more difficult to implement the decree establishing a conservation unit. Consolidation means that boundaries must be established and maintained on the ground; privately-owned land should be expropriated; non-indigenous occupants need to be moved to new lands outside the unit; the biota must be protected from hunters and poachers; the area should be zoned for use; and a management plan developed. Failure to consolidate a conservation unit not only permits the destruction of biota and natural resources that were supposed to be protected, but it has the more insidious effect of inculcating disrespect for conservation. The all-too-common occurrence of 'paper parks' in Latin America, where a declared park is occupied by hundreds of squatters practising slash-and-burn agriculture, makes it nearly impossible to consolidate such parks. Ineffective government efforts to avoid 'paper parks' pose serious threats for other conservation units that may be still intact due to inaccessibility.

The inclusion of privately-owned lands within the boundaries of a conservation unit presents another obstacle to consolidation, largely because of government disinterest (e.g. El Salvador's Montecristo) or difficult economic conditions. The Costa Rican tradition of private land ownership is reflected in the estimate that 23% of the country's protected wildlands is still in private hands. As money became available, the

TABLE 2. National Parks and equivalent reserves in Central America

Conservation unit	Year of creation	Area (ha)	Elevations (m)	Biogeographic province	Ecological life zones*
Belize					
(1) Guanacaste Park Wildlife Sanctuary	1975	21	50	8.01.01	Sm
(2) Half-Moon Caye Natural Monument	1928/78	15	0–2	8.01.01	Sm
Costa Rica					
(1) Chirripó National Park	1975	43 700	1220–3819	8.16.04	TLMr,TMr,TSAr
(2) Corcovado National Park	1975	41 469	0–750	8.16.04	Tw, TPw, TPr
(3) Braulio Carrillo National Park	1978	32 000	500–2900	8.16.04	TPw,TPr,TLMr,TMr
(4) Tortuguero National Park	1970	18 947	0–299	8.16.04	Tw
(5) Rincón de la Vieja National Park	1974	11 700	640–1916	8.16.04	TPw,TPr,TLMr
(6) Santa Rosa National Park	1971/80	21 500	0–319	8.16.04	Td,Tm
(7) Hitoy-Cerere Biological Reserve	1978	9045	300–1025	8.16.04	Tm,TPw
(8) Carara Biological Reserve	1978	7600	10–638	8.16.04	Tm,Tw
(9) Volcán Poás National Park	1971	4000	1600–2708	8.16.04	TLMw,TLMr,TMw,TMr
(10) Isla de Coco National Park	1978	3200	0–634	8.43.13	TPr
(11) Monteverde Cloud Forest Reserve	1972	3100	1200–1870	8.16.04	TPw,TPr,TLMw,TLMr
(12) Volcán Irazú National Park	1955	2400	2900–3432	8.16.04	TMw,TMr
(13) Cahuita National Park	1974	1700	0–10	8.16.04	Tm
(14) Cabo Blanco Strict Nature Reserve	1963	1172	0–355	8.16.04	Tm
(15) Manuel Antonio National Park	1972	690	0–100	8.16.04	Tw
(16) La Selva Biological Station	1953	1362	35–200	8.16.04	Tw,TPw
(17) Islas de Guayabo, Negritos, Pájaros, Biological Reserves	1973	12	0–100	8.16.04	Td
(18) Barra Honda National Park	1974	2295	20–575	8.16.04	Td
(19) Rafael Lucas Rodríguez Wildlife Refuge (Palo Verde)	1978	7523	3–230	8.16.04	Td
(20) Palo Verde National Park	1980	2440	3–200	8.16.04	Td
(21) La Amistad International Park	1982	211 602	200–3549	8.16.04	Tw,TPw,TPr,TLMw,TLMr,TMr,TSAr
(22) Tapantí Wildlife Refuge	1982	5200	?	8.16.04	TPr
El Salvador					
(1) Montecristo National Park	1979	1990	1600–2418	8.16.04	SLMw
(2) Laguna Jocotal Wildlife Refuge	1978	1000	100	8.16.04	Sm

TABLE 2 (cont.)

Conservation unit	Year of creation	Area (ha)	Elevations (m)	Biogeographic province	Ecological life zones*
Guatemala					
(1) Tikal World Heritage Site	1955/79	57 600	200–250	8.01.01	Sm,Sw
(2) Río Dulce National Park	1955	24 200	0–1267	8.01.01	Sm,SLMw
(3) Lago Atitlán National Park	1955	13 000	1562	8.21.04	SLMm
(4) Volcán Pacaya Natural Monument	1963	2000	1300–2600	8.21.04	SLMw
(5) Quetzal Conservation Biotope	1977	1000	1580–2348	8.21.04	SLMw
(6) El Rosario National Park	1980	1030	?	8.01.01	?
Honduras					
(1) La Tigra National Park	1980	7571	1360–2290	8.21.04	Sm,SLMm
(2) Río Plátano Biosphere Reserve	1980	350 000	0–1326	8.16.04	Sm,Sw,SLMw
(3) Lago de Yojoa Multiple Use Area	1971	34 628	600–2744	8.21.04	Sw,SLMw,SMw
(4) Cusuco National Park	1959/80	15 000	0–2270	8.21.04	Sm,Sw,SLMw
(5) Bay Islands National Park	1960/80	33 800	0–413	8.16.04	Sm
Nicaragua					
(1) Volcán Masaya National Park	1979	5500	100–635	8.16.04	TPm
(2) Saslaya National Park	1971	11 800	200–1650	8.16.04	Sw,SLMw
Panama					
(1) Altos de Campana National Park	1977	4816	250–1034	8.02.01	Tm,TPw
(2) Volcán Barú National Park	1976	14 322	1544–3475	8.16.04	TLMw,TLMr,TMw,TMr
(3) Portobelo National Park	1976	17 364	0–979	8.02.01	Tw,TPr
(4) Darién World Heritage Site	1981	597 000	0–1500	8.02.01	Tm,Tw,TPw,TPr,TLMr
(5) Soberanía National Park	1979	22 000	20–200	8.02.01	Tm,Tw,TPw
(6) Barro Colorado Natural Monument	1923/79	5400	26–171	8.02.01	Tm
(7) La Amistad International Park	Proposed	200 000	200–3550	8.16.04	Tw,TPw,TPr,TLMr,TMr

* Ecological life zones: Td = Tropical dry, Tm = Tropical moist, Tw = Tropical wet; TPm = Tropical Premontane moist, TPw = Tropical Premontane wet, TPr = Tropical Premontane rain; TLMw = Tropical Lower Montane wet, TLMr = Tropical Lower Montane rain; TMw = Tropical Montane wet, TMr = Tropical Montane rain; TSAr = Tropical Subalpine rain; Sm = Subtropical moist, Sw = Subtropical wet; SLMm = Subtropical Lower Montane moist, SLMw = Subtropical Lower Montane wet; SMw = Subtropical Montane wet.

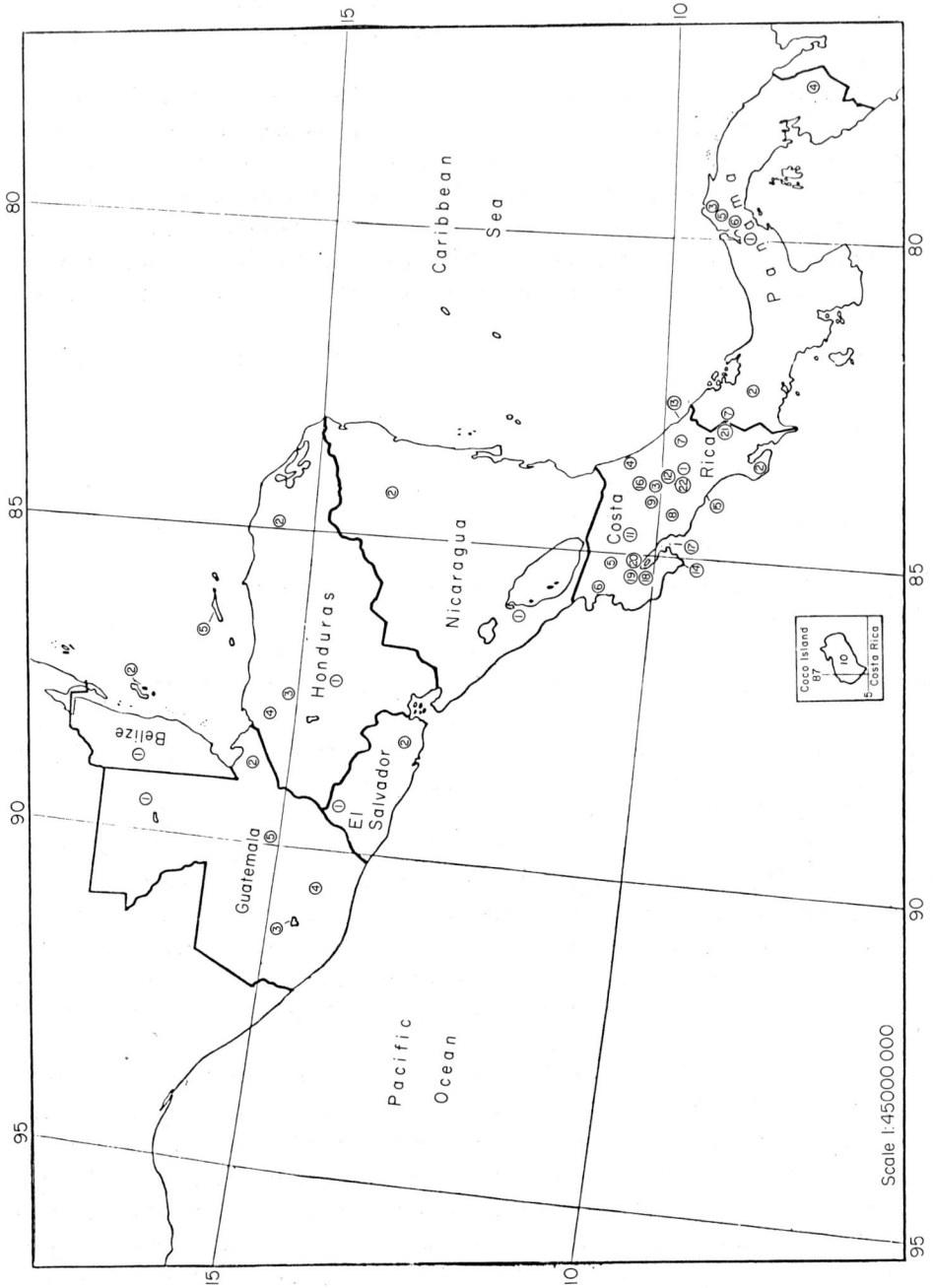

Fig. 1. National Parks and equivalent reserves in Central America (see Table 2 for information on each conservation unit).

SPN purchased key parcels, but the current economic debacle has seriously slowed the consolidation programme. In two recent cases, La Amistad and the Braulio Carrillo–La Selva corridor, the government has tried to avoid expropriation by segregating privately-held lands into a Protection Zone, where changes in current land use are prohibited.

The lack of ecological and cadaster surveys *prior* to legal establishment of a conservation unit has also hindered the consolidation process. Office-drawn boundaries often include operational farms, yet omit critical habitats or unique ecosystems. On an independent evaluation of Costa Rica's national parks and equivalent reserves, boundary modifications were recommended for two-thirds of the conservation units (CCT 1982). La Amistad International Park is the first case in Central America where ecological and cadaster field studies preceded legal establishment of a conservation unit.

Other than in Costa Rica, the sparse information available on established conservation units makes it difficult to assess their representativeness. The biogeographic provinces (see Table 2) used by IUCN are ecologically meaningless in Central America. For example, flora and fauna species overlap is probably less than 10% between Honduras' Río Plátano biosphere reserve and Costa Rica's Chirripó or Corcovado national parks, yet they occur in the same biogeographic province according to the IUCN classification system.

Estimates of major ecological life zones represented in each conservation unit (Table 2) suggest that subhumid and humid life zones are poorly represented in protected areas of Central America. This is not surprising since these humidity provinces are preferred for agriculture and human inhabitation, with a long history of natural resources degradation. The subhumid Pacific lowlands of Central America have very few conservation units due to the general absence of forests. Similarly, the dry highlands of northern Central America have few functional conservation units because of centuries of human use.

Private organizations have played critical roles in helping Central American countries establish and consolidate conservation units. Most obvious is the financial support of international or foreign conservation groups to government conservation agencies, as well as to private biological reserves. Although space does not permit the long listing of all the private donor organizations, they deserve much credit for donations that, more often than not, made the critical difference in the successful consolidation of several conservation units.

Worldwide concern about tropical deforestation has prompted a much more active participation of USAID in Central American conservation. AID's Central American portfolio includes grants to the Costa Rican Association for the Conservation of Nature (ASCONA), a loan to the Panama government to rehabilitate the Panama Canal watersheds, a loan to the Costa Rican government for conservation of natural resources, and country environmental profiles. The U.S. Nature Conservancy is helping the private Costa Rican National Parks Foundation raise funds for land acquisition (Barnard 1982). RARE (Rare Animal Relief Effort) is supporting a conservation education programme in eleven primary schools in Costa Rica, that complements ASCONA's public education efforts. CATIE's program in wildlands conservation is partially supported by the Rockefeller Brothers' Fund.

In the face of burgeoning populations and rampant deforestation, precious little time remains to add new conservation units or to consolidate existing national systems. Ecological evaluations of existing and potential units, such as has been completed in Costa Rica and is in progress in Nicaragua, are urgently needed in Panama, Honduras and Guatemala. The convulsive political situation and horrendous economic problems of most of the countries make it extremely difficult to maintain the conservation *status quo*. Even though responsible government institutions need strengthening and national conservation systems should be expanded and consolidated, the Central American governments simply lack the resources to accomplish their conservation goals. This is truly a critical decade for conservation in Central America. Yet in times of crises, the importance of education is often forgotten. Public education is crucial to the growth of environmental awareness and support for conservation. Without support of the general public, few national parks and equivalent reserves of Central America will survive into the twenty-first century.

STATUS OF CENTRAL AMERICAN NATIONAL PARKS AND EQUIVALENT RESERVES

Belize

The British administration created several small Crown Reserves and entrusted the administration of these bird sanctuaries to the Belize Audubon Society. The oldest, Half-Moon Caye Wildlife Sanctuary, was set aside in 1928. Seven Crown Reserves are tiny mangrove islands less than 2 ha in size and not described in the listing of national parks and equivalent reserves. The mangrove islands serve as rookeries for roseate spoonbills (*Ajaia ajaja*), wood storks (*Mycteria americana*), great egrets (*Egretta alba*), cormorants (*Phalacrocorax olivaceus*), boat-billed herons (*Cochlearius cochlearius*), anhingas (*Anhinga anhinga*), cattle egrets (*Bubulcus ibis*), white ibis (*Eudocimus albus*), reddish egret (*Dichromanassa rufescens*), tri-colored herons (*Hydranassa tricolor*), brown boobies (*Sula leucogaster*), white-crowned pigeons (*Columba leucocephala*) and magnificent frigatebirds (*Fregata magnificens*).

The colonial government created ten Forest Reserves totalling about 420 000 ha (18% of the country); however, they are considered reserves primarily for timber exploitation. Protection efforts focus on control and prevention of fires in the pine forests.

(1) *Guanacaste Park Wildlife Sanctuary*

The dominant feature of this park is a huge guanacaste tree (*Enterolobium cyclocarpum*). The 21 ha bird sanctuary was decreed in 1975 with tenure assigned by a conditional free grant to the Belize Audubon Society. The sanctuary is fenced and is used principally for bird watching.

(2) *Half-Moon Caye National Monument*

Half-Moon Caye bird sanctuary was converted to a National Monument in 1982 by the newly independent Belizean government. It is a 15 ha coral sand caye at the south-eastern end of Lighthouse Reef, one of the few true coral atolls in the Caribbean Sea. The western half of the island is a thriving rookery for the white phase of the red-footed booby (*Sula sula*) as well as for the magnificent frigatebird. Despite clear legal status as a wildlife sanctuary, Half-Moon Caye and the smaller island rookeries suffer from nest raiding by local fishermen for eggs and young birds. The Belize Fisheries Department is administratively responsible for Half-Moon Caye National Monument.

Costa Rica

Since the establishment of the National Park Service (SPN) in 1970, Costa Rica has made truly remarkable progress in conservation. Twenty-two national parks and equivalent reserves cover 8·47% of the country, one of the highest percentages of any country in the world. In contrast to many Latin American countries, Costa Rica's national parks and equivalent reserves are functional conservation units; each has on-site administrative and guard personnel. Management plans exist for most of the conservation units. SPN is responsible for all national parks and public biological reserves and through an intraministerial agreement with the Forest Service, the SPN administers two protection zones contiguous to national parks.

Two wildlife refuges, Palo Verde and Tapantí, are administered by the Wildlife Department (DVS). Two well-known private biological reserves are important components of the conservation system: Monteverde Cloud Forest Reserve is owned by the Tropical Science Center and the La Selva Biological Station is owned by the Organization for Tropical Studies.

Many of Costa Rica's conservation units are described and beautifully illustrated in the books by the first SPN director (Boza 1978; Boza & Mendoza 1981). Considerable ecological information on the biota of Santa Rosa, Palo Verde, Corcovado, La Selva and Monteverde also exists (Janzen 1983).

(1) *Chirripó National Park*

The highest peak in Costa Rica, several lakes of glacial origin and extensive paramo vegetation are the principal features of this national park in the central Cordillera de Talamanca. The Chirripó paramo is the northernmost occurrence of the high-altitude, shrubby vegetation that dominates the northern Andes. A fire set by visitors in March 1976, burned about 90% of the paramo. Post-fire recovery is being documented by a team of ecologists from the National University (UNA).

(2) *Corcovado National Park*

Many visitors consider Corcovado to be the gemstone of Costa Rica's system of national parks and equivalent reserves. Corcovado's lowland wet forests are the most spectacular I have seen in the tropics. The park includes entire watersheds of several rivers that flow onto the 10 000 ha Corcovado plain before interrupting the 19 km of pristine beach. Endangered large mammals such as white-lipped peccary, giant anteater, tapir and jaguar are well-represented in Corcovado. SPN is having considerable difficulty controlling the activities of independent gold miners in the rugged interior of the park.

(3) *Braulio Carrillo National Park*

This major national park is partly a consequence of a proposed highway through the rugged Cordillera Volcánica Central. Conservation opposition to construction of the San José-Guápiles highway played a major role in the establishment of Braulio Carrillo National Park. Extending from the peak of Volcán Barba (2900 m) down to 500 m on the Caribbean slope, Braulio Carrillo offers an exceptional altitudinal transect through three superhumid (potential evapotranspiration ratio < 0·25) ecological life zones.

Dr G. Stiles of the University of Costa Rica has found that a substantial proportion of the bird species in Braulio Carrillo are altitudinal migrants that spend part of the year in the Sarapiquí lowlands. To protect lowland habitat for altitudinal migratory species from Braulio Carrillo and to provide a forest corridor between the park and La Selva (see (16) below) the government decreed a 6000 ha protection zone to be administered by the SPN. The narrow protection zone (2–5 km wide) may be a minimum forest corridor between Braulio Carrillo and La Selva, but it is probably too small to support the numerous altitudinal migrants from Braulio Carrillo that require lowland forest for part of their yearly cycle.

With financial assistance from USAID, the SPN is actively preparing management plans and interpretative programs to capitalize on the considerable traffic expected on the San José-Guápiles highway. Uncontrolled construction of the highway right-of-way has devastated slope forests and dumped thousands of tons of sediments into two major rivers. But the most serious problem for Braulio Carrillo is a substantial number of private holdings within the park that the SPN lacks funds to purchase.

(4) *Tortuguero National Park*

Isolated low hills, extensive swamp forests, coastal lagoons and a long stretch of sandy beach comprise this extremely wet national park that is world-famous as the primary nesting area of the endangered green turtle (*Chelonia mydas*). Three decades of research by Dr Archie Carr and collaborators at Tortuguero have generated much greater understanding of sea turtle biology (see Carr 1976), as well as providing the impetus for establishment of Tortuguero National Park. In spite of legal protection and guards, turtle hunting, both on-shore and just off-shore, and egg-collecting are still problems in the park.

(5) *Rincón de la Vieja National Park*

The relatively low, isolated volcanic massif of Rincón de la Vieja in the Cordillera de

Guanacaste is the principal park feature. The park also has critical watershed functions, with thirty-two rivers and sixteen intermittent streams originating in the park. The Pacific slope drainages form the headwaters of the Río Tempisque, the principal river of the monsoonally dry Guanacaste lowlands.

(6) *Santa Rosa National Park*

Not only is Santa Rosa the most important historic site in the country, but it is the largest conservation unit in the seasonally dry lowlands of northwestern Costa Rica. Santa Rosa includes the recent 11 600 ha Murcielago addition; however, the two are separated by 13 000 ha of private land. These intervening lands have been recommended for inclusion in Santa Rose National Park (CCT 1982) and consolidation of all three blocks into one conservation unit is a top priority of the newly-formed National Parks Foundation.

Nancite beach is one of the principal nesting sites of the Pacific ridley sea turtle (*Lepidochelys olivacea*). Uncontrollable fires sweeping through dry, rank grasses are the major problem confronting Santa Rosa National Park.

(7) *Hitoy-Cerere Biological Reserve*

This little-known biological reserve is nestled in the rugged Caribbean foothills of the Cordillera de Talamanca. It is bordered on three sides by the Estrella, Talamanca and Telire Indian Reserves.

(8) *Carara Biological Reserve*

When the government expropriated the vast Hacienda Coyolar for agricultural colonization, the extensive forests were segregated to form the Carara Biological Reserve. It is the only large block of primary forest remaining on the lower slopes of the central Pacific region. The area is very rich biologically because it is in a transitional region between the southern perhumid life zones and northern subhumid life zones. Excellent accessibility from the Coastal Highway suggests reclassification to national park status (CCT 1982). Easy access to most of the reserve borders during the dry season facilitates illegal hunting, the principal problem affecting Carara wildlife.

(9) *Volcán Poás National Park*

This active volcano in the Cordillera Volcánica Central just north-west of the capital, San José, is the most visited of Costa Rica's national parks. A recent government loan from the Central American Bank for Economic Integration (BCIE) funded major improvements in tourist facilities, including visitors' centre, restaurant and a paved highway.

(10) *Isla de Coco National Park*

This oceanic island lies about 500 km south-west of the Costa Rican mainland. In contrast to the Galapagos Islands, Coco is extremely wet, with annual rainfall of about 7000 mm. The Coco Island finch (*Pinaroloxias inornata*) is closely related to the famed Darwin's finches of the Galapagos. Sizeable feral populations of domestic pigs and cats are the principal problem on Coco Island.

(11) *Monteverde Cloud Forest Reserve*

Straddling the low Cordillera de Tilarán in north-central Costa Rica, the Monteverde Reserve is an exceptional cloud forest laden with epiphytes and mosses. Monteverde has good populations of the resplendent quetzal and the endemic golden toad (*Bufo periglenes*); legitimately-identified feathers have been found of the oilbird (*Steatornis caripensis*). The private Monteverde Cloud Forest Reserve is owned and administered by the Tropical Science Center, a Costa Rican association involved in the conservation and rational use of natural resources in the tropics.

(12) *Volcán Irazú National Park*

The oldest of Costa Rica's national parks and equivalent reserves, Irazú functions exclusively as a tourist attraction. Volcanic eruptions in 1963–65 destroyed the vegetation near the summit and most of the rest of the park is used for agriculture or pasture. Because of the tourist attraction and the absence of significant natural ecosystems in the park, it has been proposed (CCT 1982) that Irazú National Park be joined with the nearby Ricardo Jiménez Oreamuno Recreational Area (Prusia) in a National Recreational Area.

(13) *Cahuita National Park*

This small park on the Caribbean coast includes 1100 ha of degraded terrestrial habitats and 600 ha of sea to protect Costa Rica's only coral reef that is about 6·5 km long and 300 m offshore. Unfortunately, the coral reef has deteriorated badly and shows considerable mortality, apparently caused by sedimentation. Because of its smallness and popularity with tourists, Cahuita should be re-classified to a National Recreation Area (CCT 1982).

(14) *Cabo Blanco Strict Nature Reserve*

The Cabo Blanco Reserve at the tip of the Nicoya peninsula was established in 1963 as a private reserve by Olof Wessberg. The nearby island of Cabo Blanco is a major rookery for frigatebirds and pelicans. Cabo Blanco is now administered by the SPN as a biological reserve.

(15) *Manuel Antonio National Park*

Manuel Antonio is the smallest of Costa Rica's national parks, but includes some of

the more beautiful Pacific beaches. It is very popular for recreation and tourism, hence
status as a National Recreation Area would be more appropriate (CCT 1982).
Pollution from nearby houses and the town of Quepos and sedimentation are affecting
the marine component of the park.

(16) *La Selva Biological Station*

La Selva was owned by Dr L. R. Holdridge from 1953 to 1968 when he sold it to the
Organization for Tropical Studies (OTS). Nearly three decades of research activities
have made La Selva a renowned site. The U.S. National Research Council
recommended La Selva as one of four tropical sites for long-term ecological research
(NRC 1980). The recent purchase by OTS of an adjoining property will permit
expansion of research activities into ecosystem processes and applied fields. The OTS is
actively collaborating with the National Parks Foundation to raise funds to
consolidate the Protection Zone corridor to Braulio Carrillo National Park (see (3)
above).

(17) *Isla de Guayabo, Negritos, Pajaros Biological Reserves*

Three small rocky islands in the Nicoya gulf serve as sea-bird rookeries, especially for
brown pelicans (*Pelecanus occidentalis*), magnificent frigatebirds, brown boobies (*Sula
leucogaster*) and anhingas. These islands would be more appropriate as a wildlife
refuge.

(18) *Barra Honda National Park*

Intricate and extensive limestone caverns are the primary feature of Barra Honda. All
the land is privately owned, with the consequence that terrestrial habitats are severely
degraded. Since the park does not contain important ecosystems or biota, Barra
Honda should be reclassified as a National Monument.

(19) *Rafael Lucas Rodríguez Wildlife Refuge (Palo Verde)*

Extensive seasonal lagoons on the Tempisque floodplain attract thousands of
migratory waterfowl in the dry season to the Palo Verde refuge. The Forest Service's
Wildlife Department (DVS) administers the Palo Verde refuge and has an active
research program on several waterfowl species. Palo Verde Wildlife Refuge also
includes one of the least disturbed blocks of dry forest remaining in north-western
Costa Rica.

(20) *Palo Verde National Park*

Bordering the Palo Verde Wildlife Refuge on the south, this national park was reduced
to about 25% of its original size due to the government's financial inability to

expropriate the large private holdings in the park. Seasonal lagoons remain in the park, but severe financial problems have hindered SPN consolidation of the park and protection of the waterfowl. The Palo Verde National Park should eventually be integrated into the Palo Verde Wildlife Refuge.

(21) *La Amistad International Park*

Friendship International Park extends along the Cordillera de Talamanca east from Chirripó National Park to the Panama border, where it is supposed to join Panama's component of this binational park. Costa Rica's Amistad Park covers about 192 000 ha, extending down to 900 m on the Pacific slope and 200 m on the Caribbean side. The 19 602 ha Las Tablas Protection Zone is considered part of Amistad, even though it was legally established as a separate unit because the lands are privately owned.

Amistad National Park includes seven of the twelve ecological life zones in Costa Rica and is estimated to contain at least two-thirds of the country's vertebrate fauna. The very large size of the park and its exceptional ecological diversity make Amistad potentially the most important conservation unit in Central America.

(22) *Tapantí Wildlife Refuge*

Practically no information is available on this new conservation unit administered by the DVS. It is near the Río Grande de Orosi at the northern end of the Cordillera de Talamanca, and it includes one of the major watersheds supplying the Río Macho and Cachí hydroelectric power plants.

El Salvador

The smallest country in Central America, El Salvador is the antithesis of Belize. El Salvador has the region's highest population density (Table 1) and is nearly completely deforested. No information is available for two national parks (Cerro Verde and Deininger) administered by the National Institute of Tourism (INSTU). Implementation of agrarian reform is purported to have tripled the number of protection units, but it is extremely doubtful that any unit can be protected during the current warfare.

(1) *Montecristo National Park*

El Salvador's last major remnant of primary forest is in this mid-elevation national park at the international border convergence with Guatemala and Honduras. The two principal forest types are oak-dominated cloud forest and oak–pine to 2100 m. Several threatened and endangered animal species are reported to occur in the park; however, the native wildlife has probably been seriously decimated by war and use of the Montecristo region by anti-government forces. Although managed and protected by the National Parks and Wildlife Service (DIGERENARE), Montecristo National Park has not been legally established and the majority of the land is privately owned.

Most of the lower slopes were deforested for subsistence agriculture prior to the creation of the park.

(2) *Laguna Jocotal Wildlife Refuge*

Laguna Jocotal is a eutrophic lake situated at the base of Volcán San Miguel. The refuge was established in 1978 to protect local and migratory waterfowl; however, it still lacks legal protection. The lake-shore vegetation is severely degraded and the lake tributaries carry pesticides used in the neighbouring cotton fields. About 300 families live along the lake margin, of whom 120 subsist on fishing in Laguna Jocotal.

Guatemala

Guatemala made an impressive start to conserve wildlands with the establishment of ten national parks in 1955. By 1973, sixteen national parks had been created, but only four meet international criteria for national parks (Godoy 1982): Tikal, Río Dulce, Atitlán and Pacaya. The auspicious start in 1955 is attributable primarily to the conservation of tourist attractions such as the Mayan ruins at Tikal. National parks and equivalent reserves are administered by various government agencies. Tikal is administered by the National Archaeology and History Institute (INAH), while Río Dulce is assigned to the Institute of Tourism (INGUAT). The National Forestry Institute's (INAFOR) Department of National Parks and Wildlife has legal responsibility for national parks and equivalent reserves, but has yet to develop protection and management programmes in any park. INAFOR's conservation priorities focus on recreational areas. Due to government disinterest in conservation, concerned biologists at the University of San Carlos formed a Center for Conservation Studies (CECON) in 1976, which led to the establishment of the University Biotope for the Conservation of the Quetzal. CECON has established three other biotopes and is considering five other possibilities (Godoy 1982).

The escalating violence between government and guerrilla forces has turned many wildlands into free-fire zones, relegating most conservation units to the status of 'paper parks'. Continued violence has drastically reduced tourism to Guatemala.

(1) *Tikal World Heritage Site*

The Tikal National Park, created by government decree in 1955, was reclassified in 1979 as a World Heritage Site in recognition of the Mayan temples, pyramids and stelae. The extensive forests have an abundance of mahogany (*Swietenia macrophylla*), chicle (*Manilkara achras*) and ramón (*Brosimum alicastrum*), possibly a consequence of Mayan silviculture to increase the abundance of these useful trees. The Tikal forests are reported to contain the following endangered or threatened animal species: giant anteater (*Myrmecophaga tridactyla*), ocelot (*Felis pardalis*), jaguar (*F. onca*), Baird's tapir (*Tapirus bairdii*) and crocodile (*Crocodylus moreletii*). Although some illegal hunting occurs within the protection areas, the principal problem is theft of archaeological items.

(2) *Río Dulce National Park*

Created in 1955 by presidential decree, Río Dulce National Park is a classic 'paper park'. It includes the Sierra de Mico, Lago Izabal and the Río Dulce, but most of the land is privately-owned and exact boundaries have never been fixed. In the absence of protection and management by INGUAT, deforestation and hunting are rampant. The same endangered or threatened animal species listed for Tikal are also reported for the Río Dulce National Park; however, it is unlikely that viable populations of large animals can survive in the park without complete protection from hunting and human encroachment. Several small settlements and the town of Livingston occur within the national park, and nickel mining is planned. Given the unlikelihood that the Río Dulce National Park can become a functional conservation unit, the area should be reclassified.

(3) *Lago Atitlán National Park*

The 1955 presidential decree that established Lago Atitlán National Park protects the 130 km^2 lake, but not the shoreline nor adjoining land. Rapid and uncontrolled development along the shore, particularly of summer homes, is causing serious erosion and pollution problems. The lake supports a small population of the endemic Atitlán grebe (*Podylimbus gigas*).

(4) *Volcán Pacaya Natural Monument*

The active Pacaya volcano was recognized as a natural monument by a 1963 presidential decree. Although a master plan for management and protection was prepared (Anon. 1974), it has not been implemented. The natural forests have been severely affected by volcanic activity (two major forest fires in the past 15 years) and subsistence agriculture. Many of the 100 families living near the volcano intensively cultivate corn on the upper slopes and use the highlands for pasture. Wildlife is scarce due to continuous hunting pressure. As in the case of Río Dulce National Park, the Volcán Pacaya Natural Monument is not a functional conservation unit.

(5) *Quetzal Conservation Biotope*

In 1977 the municipality of Salama, Baja Verapaz, donated about 900 ha of cloud forest to the University of San Carlos to establish a conservation unit for the resplendent quetzal (*Pharomachrus mocinno*), Guatemala's national bird. University of San Carlos' biologists have actively participated in biological inventories and research and development plans for the Quetzal Conservation Biotope (e.g. Dary & Ponciano 1980). Although hunting is common in the region, the biotope is now well protected. It is questionable if 900 ha of primary forest is sufficiently large to support a viable population of quetzals, hence the plans to enlarge the biotope to about 3000 ha should be strongly supported.

(6) *El Rosario National Park*

No information is available for this small (1030 ha) park in the Petén that was created by presidential decree in 1980.

Honduras

In the past 4 years Honduras has made great progress in conservation, with the creation of a national protected wildlands system, new national parks and Central America's first biosphere reserve. The General Directorate for Renewable Natural Resources (DIGERENARE) in the Ministry of Natural Resources is responsible for national parks and equivalent reserves. The Honduran Forest Development Corporation (COHDEFOR) has an active programme in watershed protection for Lake Yojoa and Cusuco. COHDEFOR controls the nationalized forest industry and forest reserves; however, since the latter are for timber exploitation they are not considered here as conservation units.

(1) *La Tigra National Park*

Created in 1980, this park includes the higher elevations of San Juancito mountains that are the source of potable water for the capital, Tegucigalpa. A master plan for protection and public use of the park is being implemented. Minor problems include lack of adequate patrolling and enforcement, as well as agricultural encroachment along the boundaries.

(2) *Río Plátano Biosphere Reserve*

A 1980 law changed the Ciudad Blanca Archaeological Reserve to the Río Plátano Biosphere Reserve, a vast area of approximately 350 000 ha in eastern Honduras. Major vegetation types include coastal mangroves, swamp forests fringing coastal lagoons, pine savannas, gallery forests and extensive mixed broad-leaved forests. In the absence of significant disturbance or hunting, this broad spectrum of habitats supports an impressive array of endangered species including manatee, jaguar, crocodile, giant anteater, harpy eagle, brocket deer and scarlet macaw. Two groups of Indians, the Paya and Miskito, also live in the reserve.

A management plan for the reserve has been prepared (Anon. 1980) and basic inventories of the natural and cultural resources have also been completed. DIGER-ENARE has received strong support from CATIE and WWF-UK helping to consolidate the Río Plátano Reserve. Not only is Río Plátano the first biosphere reserve in Central America, it is truly the most significant conservation unit in northern Central America. Except for the Tikal World Heritage Site all other conservation units in northern Central America are less than one-tenth the size of the Río Plátano Biosphere Reserve (see Table 1).

(3) *Lago de Yojoa Multiple Use Area*

The 79 km^2 Yojoa lake is the only large body of fresh water in Honduras, with the introduced largemouth bass supporting both commercial and sport fisheries. The Yojoa watersheds were declared as a forest reserve in 1971, but are now considered a multiple-use area (Betancourt & Dulin 1978) rather than a reserve for timber exploitation.

Despite full legal protection of the area, persistent problems include squatter invasions for subsistence agriculture, lake contamination from mining operations and fertilizer and pesticide runoff, and lack of control of the bass fishery.

(4) *Cusuco National Park*

The Cusuco Forest Reserve was decreed in 1959 and efforts are being made to convert the area to national park status. The Cusuco watersheds are the principal source of potable water for San Pedro Sula, Honduras' commercial centre. The municipality of San Pedro Sula maintains forest guards in the park and COHDEFOR has a fire control brigade stationed near the park. The surrounding area has been largely deforested for slash-and-burn agriculture and coffee growers are encroaching on the remaining mid-elevation forests.

(5) *Bay Islands National Park*

DIGERENARE has proposed converting the Guanaja Forest Reserve into the Bay Islands National Park, including the addition of about 10 000 ha of marine area and many beautiful coral reefs. The principal islands, Roatán, Guanaja and Utila, have been severely degraded and watershed destruction has reached a critical stage. Although the 1959 Fisheries Law declared coral reefs as protected areas, the Bay Islands' reefs have suffered considerable degradation. Numerous endemic wildlife races and species occur on the Bay Islands, but have greatly reduced populations due to habitat destruction. The Bay Islands lack effective enforcement of existing statutes protecting forests, wildlife and coral reefs.

Nicaragua

In 1980 the new government established the National Park Service (SPN) under the auspices of the Nicaraguan Institute of Natural Resources and the Environment (IRENA). Although only two conservation units existed prior to the 1979 revolution, the new government has initiated efforts towards a national system of protected wildlands. The SPN is evaluating thirty-five potential wildlands for classification as conservation units (Dilger & López 1982).

(1) *Volcán Masaya National Park*

This active volcanic complex lies only 20 km south-east of the capital, Managua.

Because of its attraction to local and foreign tourism, Nicaraguan dictator Anastasio Somoza was developing it as a showcase national park. Management and protection ceased during the recent civil war; after the revolution squatters invaded the national park that was closely identified with Somoza. These problems have been mostly solved by the new government; however, minor problems of firewood collecting and deer poaching persist. Detailed management and interpretative plans have now been implemented, so it appears that Nicaragua finally has a functional conservation unit.

(2) *Saslaya National Park*

This pristine park in the Zelaya hinterland has yet to be consolidated. Although protected so far by inaccessibility, the eastward expansion of the agricultural frontier will soon reach park boundaries. Protection and management will be necessary if Saslaya National Park is to be a viable conservation unit.

Panama

Panama has an impressive list of national parks and equivalent reserves, including the huge Darién World Heritage Site and part of the La Amistad International Park. Except for the Barro Colorado Natural Monument (BCNM) administered by the Smithsonian Tropical Research Institute, Panama's smaller parks have serious problems with squatter invasions, fire, hunting and general disrespect for conservation. The Renewable Natural Resources Directorate (RENARE) is the government agency responsible for administering Panama's national parks and equivalent reserves. RENARE's conservation efforts have been ineffective, in part due to weak leadership. Apart from BCNM, the best conservation effort in Panama is by the Cuna Indians in the autonomous Comarca de San Blas. But even their forests are coming under increasing pressure from non-Indian slash-and-burn agriculturalists and it is questionable that the Cuna can maintain their patrimony without more direct government help.

Panama has also declared eight forest reserves and two forest protectorates totalling some 300 000 ha; the former are primarily for timber exploitation, while the latter are supposed to be preserved as protection forests. Several key watersheds should be reclassified from forest reserves to hydrologic protection zones. Even though the critical Bayano watershed was classified as a forest protectorate, logging and slash-and-burn agriculture continue to destroy the native forests.

(1) *Altos de Campana National Park*

This park contains one of the watersheds contributing to Gatún lake and the Panama Canal. The xeric vegetation is caused by the shallow, porous soil and frequent fires set by local people. Forest cutting for agriculture, fire and hunting are serious problems that are increasing in the park.

(2) *Volcán Barú National Park*

The park extends from mid-elevation to the highest peak in the country. Although it is

Leigh, E.G., Jr, Rand, A.S. & Windsor, D.M. (Eds) **(1983).** *The Ecology of a Neotropical Forest: Seasonal Rhythms and Longer-Term Fluctuations.* Smithsonian Institution Press, Washington.

MacFarland, C. & Morales, R. (1981). *Planificación y manejo de los recursos silvestres en América Central: Estrategia para una década crítica.* CATIE, Turrialba, Costa Rica.

Moser, D. (1975). *Central American Jungles.* Time-Life, New York.

NRC (1980). *Research Priorities in Tropical Biology.* U.S. National Academy of Science, Washington.

Willis, E.O. (1974). Populations and local extinctions of birds on Barro Colorado Island, Panama. *Ecological Monographs,* **44,** 153–169.

in standing volume even between reserves occupying similar ecological zones. Outside forest reserves, estimated standing volume is 22 million m³ in the moist and Derived Savanna forest.

If it is assumed that mangrove and freshwater swamp forest outside the forest reserves represent an under-exploited source of timber occupying roughly 1·5 million ha and containing wood volume of about 25 million m³, the total standing volume in the Nigerian tropical forest zone is about 180 million m³. However, cumulative consumption of forest based products between 1975 and 2000 is estimated at 216 million m³. Thus, before the turn of the century, all existing standing timber above 60 cm diameter will have been consumed.

As if these statistics are not sufficiently daunting, the forest managers have to operate an unrealistic national forest policy which insists that the country must be self-sufficient in wood products. Additionaly, all the nation's wood requirements are supposed to be met from a forest estate whose size of 10% of total land area is acknowledged to fall short of international standards of 20–25%. Because of the critically low areas of the forest estate (Table 2), the area of productive high forest is only 2% of Nigeria's land area and there is persistent pressure from local communities and vested interests to de-restrict some of the richest high forests in the country. There is now very little chance of adding appreciably to the forest estate, notwithstanding recent efforts.

The small size of the forest estate in Nigeria and the possibility of timber shortage make necessary a re-appraisal of the objectives of forest management. Firstly, scope of management must be widened to include areas carrying productive high forests but which are at present outside the forest reserves. Secondly, there must be a renewed effort to obtain accurate data on the standing volume of areas inside and outside the forest reserves. In other words, the expense of a truly national forest inventory of all the Guinea and Derived Savanna, as well as moist tropical forests in the country must be borne if a realistic forest management policy is to emerge. Thirdly, the doctrine of national self-sufficiency in wood-based products must be sufficiently relaxed to allow the importation of unprocessed timber from neighbouring countries.

Timber-rich countries like Cameroun and Zaire must take good note of Nigerian experience and avoid its past mistakes. Indiscriminate exploitation and the ravages of shifting cultivation are the main causes of high forest destruction in Africa. At present, Central Africa has by far the most important forest resources on the continent while West Africa now has relatively limited forest resources in relation to the present rate of exploitation. For example, of 202 million ha of closed forests estimated for tropical Africa in 1975 (Lanly & Clement 1979), Central Africa accounted for 171 million ha. Unlogged forests made up approximately 90% (or 104 million ha) of the forests of Central Africa. The unlogged forests were distributed as shown in Table 3.

Lanly & Clement (1979) have pointed out that although these closed forests contain in volume generally more than 300 m³ per ha, the bole volume of the trees more than 60 cm diameter at breast height or above buttress (dbh) is only 60–120 m³ ha⁻¹, of which 6–10 m³ ha⁻¹ are at present being extracted as commercial logs. The majority of these forests are not under any form of management. It is imperative that these high forests

TABLE 3.

Country	Area of unlogged forests ($\times 10^6$ ha)
Zaire	65·0
Cameroun	14·2
Gabon	13·4
Congo	8·8

are managed in such a way that national and continental requirements for timber are met for as long as it is ecologically and economically feasible.

PATHWAYS OF SUCCESSION INDUCED BY HIGH FOREST UTILIZATION AND TREATMENT

Before options of management of the high forest are considered it is worth evaluating the pathways which can result from varying degrees of treatment in terms of the amount of soil exposure either by selective logging or through clearance of the original vegetation. The first dichotomy is whether the soil is in fact physically exposed and a monoculture of one or two species imposed on the site, contrasted with the situation in which large-scale removal of the woody species leads only to partial exposure of the soil, with the original ground vegetation and associated desirable saplings and poles intact (Kio & Ball 1982).

In the first major pathway two lines of development are possible. Firstly, the resulting plantation may modify the environment so that it becomes less suitable for subsequent recruitment of naturally-occurring woody species. The plantation grows into maturity creating a soil and physical environment which further inhibits recolonization of the site. At maturity the trees have to be clear-felled, replanted with the same species or regenerated by coppicing. Examples are forest sites cleared for teak and cocoa plantation. The route terminates in an essentially artificial system, unless the site is abandoned over a very long period. Secondly, species mixture may permit subsequent recruitment of early and late succession species (e.g. *Nauclea* and *Khaya* plantations). The trees and the early immigrants modify the site so that it becomes mainly suitable for recruitment of late succession species. As the plantation develops juveniles of late succession species continue to invade until the main tree components matures and is removed in thinnings and selective harvesting. This system terminates in an essentially natural system.

The second major pathway follows three successional routes. In the first, exploitation is intensive with the removal of all or most emergents or canopy trees. The resulting environment is suitable for establishment only of certain early succession species such as *Musanga* and *Trema*. As the time goes on and with further modification of the environment, late succession species are recruited and develop under the shelter of the early succession species. In time the earlier colonists are gradually eliminated.

The sequence continues until the resident species no longer facilitate the invasion and growth of other species. This model terminates in an essentially natural system.

The second and third successional routes of the second major pathway arise from an environment suitable for the establishment of any species soon after selective or moderately heavy exploitation. But certain early succession species may appear first due to peculiar life history, e.g. *Triplochiton*, *Ricinodendron* and *Combretodendron*. However, in the second route, early occupants further modify the site but with little or no effect on the recruitment of late succession species which grow side by side to maturity but with early succession species dying first. Over a long period the sequence continues until no species exists that can invade and grow while residents persist.

Early occupants associated with the third route further modify the environment so that neither early nor late succession species can be further recruited. As long as original individuals persist or continue to regenerate vegetatively they exclude or suppress subsequent invaders. The route terminates in an apparently artificial system unless remedial treatments are effected. Examples are *Oxystigma mannii* in swamp forests of Nigeria and *Cynometra* stands in Uganda.

In all these routes a crucial element is *time*, and the direction of development of a particular route can be changed radically from one to the other depending on the presence or absence of intermediate treatment/interference before maturity is attained.

PROBLEMS OF TROPICAL HIGH FOREST MANAGEMENT

It is often stated that although the tropical forest ecosystem is normally stable under constant environmental conditions, it is not well equipped to resist unexpected disturbances, most particularly human interventions. Selective removal of individuals or species, massive exploitation of part of the biomass and the exposure of the soil to light are occurrences that often have irreversible consequences. Thus, any interference must be carefully contemplated in terms of its intensity, nature and area covered, so as to avoid severe disturbance to the extent that the damage caused become irreparable.

The role of interspecific relations is only just being understood for simpler ecosystems, but it is now believed to be very important in tropical high forests. As an example, it is not quite clear whether some of the species in the forest are prevented from becoming more numerous because they actively exclude their own seedlings or because of chemical exclusion by other species. For an investigation in the Sapoba Forest Reserve in Nigeria, multivariate analyses of regeneration, parent tree feature and soil factors revealed that distribution of regeneration was closely associated with the distance to the parent trees, their number and their basal area. The strongest link was between regeneration and the sum of the reciprocals of the distances of the parent trees from the sample plots (Kio 1978).

The performance of *Terminalia ivorensis* in natural forest and under plantation condition is a case in point. In the unmanaged forests, it exists as healthy isolated trees. But in plantation it exhibits some startling features. It develops flat tops and dies back after 15–25 years of growth. Nitrogen mineralization in the litter is completely inhibited and a considerable amount of calcium accumulates in the rhytidoms (UNESCO 1978). In monoculture, *T. ivorensis* appears to poison itself.

Apart from the lack of understanding of the biological forces which have led to the evolution of a mature tropical forest in equilibrium with its environment, all attempts at forest management entail a certain amount of risk. It is possible to manage the tropical forest ecosystems as they are, or after only slight modification by silviculture and logging. Special agricultural techniques such as shifting cultivation may be used, or they may be completely transformed into simplified ecosystems, especially forest plantations or sown pasture.

Though foresters emphasize management based on modification of forest environment by exploitation and silvicultural treatments or complete transformation through plantation forestry, failure to recognize shifting cultivation as a management tool deserving of close study has prevented an early understanding of the ecological implications of forestry operations. These operations, unless they are on a very small scale, tend to have a long-term impact on the stands and their environment. They seem to affect species and genetic composition, general structure and growth, and increased exposure to radiation. The removal of tree biomass interferes with nutrient cycles, the microclimate is greatly affected by wind and rain, and water balance is similarly affected by changes in interception and evaporation.

Even the management systems favoured by foresters are full of unsolved and apparently insoluble problems. Measures taken to induce the regeneration of particular species appear only to aid the survival and growth of individuals already present (Kio 1978; UNESCO 1978). Felling and logging damage is inevitable during exploitation and its effects have discouraged the adoption of management regimes which should have maintained the ecosystem in its original condition, or which should have hastened the attainment of a structural equilibrium.

Selective felling is possible only in forests very rich in desirables. Ideally, the dynamics of stand structure after selective felling should change such that by the time of the next felling stand structure—in terms of commercial species and sizes—will be equivalent to that at the time of the previous felling, or should correspond to a superior structure desired in accordance with the objectives of management. However, success under selective felling depends on two conditions. The first is that a sufficiently large proportion of desirable species must pass from their size class at the time of first logging operation into commercial sizes at the time of the next. Residual trees after successive logging should be sufficiently healthy so that economic logging remains feasible. It seems true that selective felling is impracticable regardless of the structure, composition and dynamism of the original stands until minimum commercial sizes are appreciably reduced (Palmer 1975; UNESCO 1978).

Polycyclic exploitation is feasible wherever the forest is capable of producing a sustained volume and size yield from advance regeneration of saplings, poles and young trees. Under this condition logging damage is not critical since sufficient time is allowed between felling operations for full recovery of the majority of individuals in the stands. However, transition from pole to tree by economic species has to be rapid if the space created by heavy logging and poisoning treatments is not to be quickly occupied by fast-growing pioneer non-desirable species. Mervart (1972) has suggested that once past the small-pole stage, mortality of fast-growing trees is rather less than that of slower-growing trees, so that the desirables increase their proportional representation by volume.

Nevertheless, since polycyclic logging implies the regular return to an area for a harvest at intervals which may be less than the time taken by a desirable to grow from seedling to commercial size, successive yields may be so low that many foresters have advocated monocyclic exploitation. Other arguments used against polycyclic logging include the financial desirability of removing the whole commercially saleable stand in one operation; damage to the larger residual stems; lack of sufficient number of trees of desirable species in the middle size classes; the wiping out of advance regeneration by tractor tracks and during the construction of gantries. Particularly, in Nigeria, first logging has to be sufficiently intensive to discourage subsequent illegal felling. In a survey carried out by Ikumogunniyi (1980), estimated loss of revenue due to illegal logging was of the order of ₦26 million (₦1.00 = US$1.55) per year, involving 209 000 m³ of wood per annum. These figures were compiled only for the concession areas licensed to the six major wood processing factories in Nigeria. The actual scale of illegal felling may triple the figures given above.

The arguments for and against polycyclic system of forest management demonstrate the excruciating dilemma facing tropical silviculturists. Under Nigerian conditions neither a purely polycyclic nor monocyclic system seems adequate. Polycyclic harvesting was virtually indistinguishable from selective felling with all its faults. The scale of destruction and the enormous waste of resources inherent in a monocyclic system practised where only a small fraction of the standing volume is of immediate commercial value is considered unacceptable. It can only be justified if the intention is to convert the stand into a forest plantation.

TRENDS IN FOREST MANAGEMENT

Numerous studies have indicated that countries blessed with large areas of tropical high forest must assess the value of such forests in terms of wood and non-wood products. In some cases the non-wood products may be of great economic value to the community at large since the vegetable, wildlife, wild fruits, chewing sticks, ropes and rattans, wrapping leaves and other commodities which the natural forests contain cannot be artificially produced once these forests are wiped out (Kio & Bada 1981).

Hazards arising from large-scale removal of natural forests have been documented (Richards 1952, 1977; Kio 1976, 1978, 1980; Lundgren 1978; Dawkins 1980; Bamgbala 1981). The Nigerian experience is that silvicultural experiments concerning growth of individuals and stands were frequently assessed prematurely, leading to mistaken conclusions. Even experiments meant to test the effectiveness of treatments on regeneration continued to yield differences long after such experiments were abandoned. Re-assessment of old experiments have led to the conclusion that an economically and silviculturally attractive degree of regeneration can be obtained by natural regeneration methods and that the growth of residual stands after exploitation can be accelerated by appropriate silvicultural treatments (Kio 1979; Bamgbala 1981).

It is clear, however, that the big trees now creamed out of the tropical high forests will never again be produced, no matter what treatments are applied. Timber dealers will henceforth have to accept smaller tree dimensions. In Nigeria, a cursory visit to sawmills will at once show a complete change in exploitation patterns from the recent past. The highly selective logging which use to characterize forest exploitation in the colonial days is no longer in evidence. Assessment of timber royalty on area basis rather than on outturn volume is probably partially responsible for the phenomenal increase in timber output from forest reserves. Another reason is the proliferation of sawmills. The number of sawmills grew from 400 in 1975 to 1030 in 1981 (Kio & Ball 1982). Shortages of the popular desirables have led wood users to experiment with previously unknown species. The effect has been the general increase in the value of the standing volume per unit area compared to previous standards of utilization.

FAO has pioneered the classification of species according to appropriate end uses. The UNDP/FAO inventory project and the African Timber and Plywood Company (A.T. & P.) have both made a comparative classification of the usefulness of 122 tree species. Under the A.T. & P. system class 3 represented the limit of desirability, though large size trees in classes 4 and 5 might also be logged when encountered. For the FAO classification classes 6 and 7 are groups of species which are not at present utilized and which rarely exceed 60 cm diameter. About 57% of the species listed by A.T. & P. are seldom extracted in routine logging unless individuals are of exceptionally large size. Under the FAO system currently non-utilized species are less than half (45%) of the total number, representing a utilization efficiency of 12% over the A.T. & P. system. Even that, however, is a much greater utilization than in the 1950s when the extraction of up to fifty undividual species would have been considered revolutionary.

Ultimately, many more species will qualify for use as veneer and sawtimber as the knowledge of the properties of the lesser known species improves. For example, six species listed as least desirable by A.T. & P. have been classified by FAO as being suitable for decorative veneers and utility plywood! This trend is very likely to continue. There will probably also be a demand for species in the FAO utilization classes 6 and 7 for pulp or fuel. Momoh (1980) has reported that the wood requirement for the Nigerian Paper Mill Ltd would be partly met by clear-felling mixed hardwood stands of River Moshi Forest Reserve which is wholly in the Guinea Savanna belt. That forest reserve contains only a total of 22 m^3 ha^{-1} of useable wood.

The cost of harvesting currently non-economic species in the high forest will be relatively low since the more valuable species will absorb the cost of infrastructure, equipment and management. The valuable species producing veneer and sawlogs will in future continue to yield the highest returns. Examples from Scandinavian countries indicate that, notwithstanding the fact that more than half of the total harvest in these countries is accounted for by pulp wood, the stumpage from sawlog and veneer remains the backbone of the forest economy (Fries 1981). This is a warning that tropical counties in general and Nigeria in particular must not carelessly and recklessly destroy their valuable hardwood natural forests to replace them with vast areas of trees suitable mainly for pulpwood.

MANAGEMENT OPTIONS FOR THE TROPICAL HIGH FOREST

I have emphasized the need for foresters to look beyond the Forest Estate and assume some management control of wood resources outside forest reserves. The first step would be a nation-wide forest inventory as a major move towards a realistic land use classification. Silvicultural and management objectives have to be re-defined and research must continue to look for better utilization of the less desirable species. Large-scale afforestation should ideally be confined to degraded forests and the vast areas of Derived and guinea savanna that exist in most countries. The objective of agroforestry and communal forestry must be vigorously pursued and plans should be made well in advance for absorbing the large amount of wood that will be produced when private forestry becomes a reality, e.g., in Nigeria.

Inventory results will show areas of forests which must be conserved to protect watersheds, erosion channels, wildlife and samples of forest ecosystems. At the extreme are those stands which have been so highly degraded that it would be far cheaper to clear-fell and plant up such areas. The problem is how to manage the undisturbed and the logged-over forests which must be maintained under natural condition. The increment in exploited forests is usually low. The value usually quoted is 2–3 m^3 ha^{-1} $year^{-1}$ though recent experimental data suggest that if increment is calculated from all the growing stock, values up to 10 m^3 per ha^{-1} $year^{-1}$ may be obtained (Kio 1978). Nevertheless, increments are low when compared to plantations. But the advantage of basing the next harvest on the remaining understorey or regeneration is that establishment cost may be kept low compared to clear-felling and planting. The soil is also kept under constant shelter against erosion and subsequent harvest may yield more valuable wood.

Another possibility is to convert the mixed hardwood forest into more productive stands, still yielding sawtimber, by under-planting with fast-growing indigenous or exotic species. This approach retains the advantage of permanent ground cover. The more intensively managed stands that will yield more wood in shorter rotations, continue to yield other forest produce, and be easier to protect against encroachment. For the undisturbed, and partially disturbed high forest, Dawkins (1980) has advocated a modified 'girth-limit' system. Most reserves could be managed under a two-cycle felling system with a 40-year period. This will permit the fast-growing species induced or released by the fellings to grow to maturity within one cycle, while the slower-growing trees left standing because of their small size at the first cycle will be exploitable at the second cycle.

The girth-limit system would require greater control of logging to ensure that under-sized desirables are not felled illegally and to reduce logging damage. Dawkins also prescribed a set of silvicultural operations consisting of the elimination of all seriously defective trees over the minimum diameter, climber-cutting, repair of felling damage and the elimination of defective under-size (< 60 cm dbh) trees.

The success of the system advocated will rest on how effective the control is since, as an example, under the current area system of royalty assessment in Nigeria, short-sighted loggers feel they must harvest down to very small sizes to ensure adequate returns on their investment. Future modifications of this or any 'selection' type system must await the evaluation of results of past silvicultural experiments which are still being monitored.

CONCLUSION

In conclusion, it is necessary to re-state forestry policy as it relates to objectives of forest management. It emphasizes a sustainable increase in the economic production of timber, the conservation and improvement of the environment, and multiple-use management where feasible. Since a crisis situation might be reached in the supply and demand for timber towards the end of the century in some African countries new policy measures to increase wood production must be formulated. When deciding on these measures, expected direct return on investment should be only one of the considerations; others should include the possible environmental benefits of forestry and the contribution which increased wood production can make to national development and the living standards of rural populations.

In the existing forests, management prescriptions should be sufficiently flexible to allow the incorporation of new ideas as research results reveal better methods of treating the high forests. Ultimately, the success of any set of management measures will be determined by the number and skill of the forestry staff as well as the quality of forest research. The current situation is that most plantation schemes have limited chance of success due to extremely short supply of sub-professional and professional foresters. Training at every level must be accelerated.

Research should concentrate on simpler and well replicated experiments. Fries (1981) has suggested that the treatments to be tested have to be properly defined, clearly separated with respect to expected effects, and of real interest. He also suggested that the number of different treatments in one experiment should be reduced to a minimum, e.g. to a control plus two treatments. If the two treatments chosen represent degrees of basal area reduction, it would be possible to evaluate whether the relation is linear or curved. Similarly, Kio (1980) has indicated the value of 'archival research', i.e. re-assessment of abandoned experiments applying the most recent tools of statistical analyses, with emphasis on evaluation for multivariate relationships.

REFERENCES

Bamgbala, E.O. (1981). *Natural regeneration and afforestation in the high forest of Nigeria.* Presented at Department Seminar, Forestry Research Institute of Nigeria, Ibadan. 14 January 1981.
Dawkins, H.C. (1980). *The interpretation of inventory for management purposes in Nigeria moist lowland forest and proposals for long-term permanent monitoring plots.* Project Working Document No. 1. FAO, Ibadan.

FAO (1979a). *1977 Yearbook of Forest Products.* FAO, Rome, 1979.

FAO (1979b). *Forestry Development: Nigeria.* Project findings and recommendations. FO: DP/NIR/71/546 Terminal Report. FAO, Rome 1979.

Fries, J. (1981). *Report on meeting on IUFRO, S4.01.* Los Banos, Philippines, 20–30 January, 1981.

Ikumogunniyi, B.A. (1980). *Illegal felling activities and their harmful effects on Nigeria environment.* Presented at the Tenth Annual Conference of the Forestry Association of Nigeria, Sokoto, November 1980.

Kio, P.R.O. (1976). What future for natural regenerations of tropical high forest? An appraisal with examples from Nigeria and Uganda. *Commonwealth Forestry Review,* **55,** 309–318.

Kio, P.R.O. (1978). *Stand development in naturally regenerated forest in south-western Nigeria.* Ph.D thesis, Ibadan.

Kio, P.R.O. (1979). Management strategies in the natural tropical high forest. *Forest Ecology and Management,* **2,** 207–220.

Kio, P.R.O. (1980). *Problems of forest conservation in Africa.* Consultancy report to the United Nations Economic Commission for Africa, Addis Ababa, Ethiopia. Forest Resources Development and Conservation. No. RAF/78/025, August 1980.

Kio, P.R.O. & Bada, S.O. (1981). *Research in Agroforestry.* Third Annual Report presented to the International Development Research Centre, Ottawa, Canada, Department of Forest Resources Management, Ibadan. January, 1981.

Kio, P.R.O. & Ball, J.B. (1982). *Models for the sustained use of rain forest.* UNESCO–MAB/UNEP Regional Training Seminar on Impacts of Human Activities on the Rain Forest Ecosystem. University of Ibadan, Ibadan, 15–27 March 1982.

Lanly, J.P. & Clement, J. (1979). *Present and Future Forest and Plantation Areas in the Tropics.* F.A.O., FO:MSC/19/1, Rome.

Lundgren, B. (1978). Soil Conditions and Nutrient Cycling under Natural and Plantation Forests in Tanzanian Highlands. *Reports in Forest and Forest Soils* No. 31. Department of Forest Soils, Swedish University of Agricultural Sciences, Uppsala 1978.

Mervart, J. (1972). Growth and mortality rates in the natural high forest of Western Nigeria, *Nigeria Forestry Information Bulletin,* new series, No. 22.

Momoh, Z.O. (1980). *Meeting the wood requirements of pulp and paper mills in Nigeria.* Paper presented at Tenth Annual Conference of Forestry Association of Nigeria, Sokoto, November 1980.

Palmer, J.R. (1975): Towards more reasonable objectives in tropical high forest management for timber production. *Commonwealth Forestry Review,* **54,** no. 161–162, pp. 273–289.

Richards, P.W. (1952). *The Tropical Rainforest, an Ecological Study.* Cambridge University Press, Cambridge.

Richards, P.W. (1977). Tropical Forests and woodlands; an overview. *Agro-Ecosystems,* **3,** 225–238.

UNESCO (1978). *Tropical Forest Ecosystems.* UNESCO, Paris, 1978.

PART IV

D · THE GLOBAL CONCERN

The case for an Organization of Timber Exporting Countries (OTEC)

NICHOLAS GUPPY

The Pond, Haddenham, Cambridge, U.K.

At present rates of destruction (56 000–200 000 km^2 year^{-1}) all primary tropical rain forests (TRF) will have disappeared in 30 years time, and all TRFs of whatever description by 2060 A.D. This destruction, which is contrary to the long-term needs of mankind, is caused by a combination of economic and other factors which began to operate with accelerating force early in this century, and especially so within the last 10–15 years. As no international body exists solely concerned with the needs of tropical forests and forestry, I have proposed the formation of an Organization of Timber Exporting Countries (OTEC), the aim of which would be to achieve cooperation between TRF countries so as best to preserve and manage what is often their greatest single natural resource.

Discovering the causes of TRF destruction is like cutting into a multi-layered cake. At the top are obvious causes, such as population growth, increasing demand for forest products, and the 'raising of money'. In the first instance, already about 250 million shifting cultivators occupy some 300 million ha of TRF, and by the year 2000 A.D. there are expected to be 600 million on some 450 million ha. However, as agriculture already occupies virtually all suitable land, and only some 13 million ha of the forest lands which will be cleared by then are estimated to be suitable for permanent agriculture, the rest will rapidly degenerate into useless scrub and semi-desert accompanied by exacerbated erosion, ecological, economic and human problems. With regard to increasing demand, the World Bank estimates that 500–600 million m^3 year^{-1} of industrial and building wood additional to that used at present will be needed by 2000 A.D., plus an extra 200–900 million m^3 of fuel woods, while timber stocks will have fallen by 28 m^3 per caput in the developed world and 36 m^3 per caput in less developed countries. To meet this need FAO estimates that $50–60 \times 10^9$ year^{-1} must be invested over the next 20 years, $17–22 \times 10^9$ of this in the developing countries—a sum which no existing funding organization could provide, and on which the developing countries would have to pay interest, presumably by increased logging. As world demand outstrips supply, prices can be expected to rise steeply until eventually they reach the cost of replacement: by 1990 there should be strong incentives to invest in fast-growing tree species; and from 2010 even slow-growing hardwoods will be attractive.

Below the surface layers of the 'cake' are yet deeper layers of social, political, economic and ideological causes. Often much good agricultural land is, for social reasons, inaccessible to the poor and is not being used. In Brazil, 43% of farm land is owned by 1% of farmers, while 50% of the farmers own only 3% of the land. Outside of Amazonia there is enough farm land to give *c.* 1 ha to each individual Brazilian—more such land than is available in the U.S.A. Similarly, in Java 1% of farmers own 35% of agricultural land, and their large farms are less productive than small-holdings.

In both Brazil and Indonesia good agricultural soils are found on less than 2% of the remaining forested areas. Why then colonize these? The impetus stems from the political layer. To divert attention away from social causes, such as unused land holdings, or from agitation for taxation that would penalize inefficient land use or cause its redistribution—all unpalatable to the powerful—governments promote the idea of the 'new frontier' ready for colonization by the poor. This falls in very well with nationalism, concern about the loyalty of minority groups, and military considerations about defence and the routing out of dissidents. In the interests of national unity Brazil must settle Amazonia with good Brazilians, while 4 million Javanese are being 'transmigrated' to Kalimantan at a cost of over $1000 ha^{-1}.

The fuel for this destructiveness and its accompanying vast population movement is money. Over the past decade an enormous expansion of credit, operating within the framework of free trade provided by GATT, has led to unprecedented global economic expansion. In 1976 lending to developing countries totalled 75×10^9. Today, Brazil alone owes 90×10^9, and the world total is about 600×10^9.

The consequences of such 'aid' have been (a) an emphasis on imported technology and methods; (b) the strengthening of central governments through whom the funds flow; (c) the centralization of planning; (d) the creation of an elite bent on accumulating capital and land, often with accompanying corruption (when he died one official was said to have bank deposits of $80 millions, 11 000 times his salary); (e) emphasis on export crops (to achieve economic 'take-off') instead of self-sufficiency; (f) environmental destruction and (g) economic collapse when returns fail to materialize. In Amazonia, 7 million ha have been cleared, only 2% on soils suitable for permanent agriculture; 17·6% of this clearing has been done by peasants, 60% by highway developers and for cattle-ranching for export, the average productive life of each ranch being 2–7 years.

Can we discern below these biological, social, political, and economic layers an ultimate layer of motivation in the ideological conflict between the western and communist blocks which has led governments to encourage the making of such largely unsecured enormous loans?

Clearly, TRFs are considered disposable; they and their products are cashed in where possible, or destroyed and converted to other quick return uses.

Let us clarify some of the more important points in this situation.

(i) Figures of timber *production* from TRF countries as given by FAO and other sources are misleading, for there is almost no production in the strict sense, except from the few plantations that exist, and from the natural usable-timber increment of the forest (which in the case of mature forests is rather low, 10–15 t ha^{-1}, 32 according to some sources, up to 120 in young or secondary forest). Such figures in fact refer to harvesting the accumulated past production, and from a supply base that is rapidly diminishing as the area under forest is reduced.

(ii) There is no true market relationship between demand and supply for tropical timbers, because most rain forest trees take 80–150 years to grow, and the forests themselves take 400–600 years to reach maturity after felling. There is thus a very strong case, which even extreme monetarists must accept, for protecting TRFs from the action of purely market forces. This is doubly strong because of the important environmental and other benefits of TRFs. The existence, hitherto, of huge areas of natural TRF has meant that the available supply of tropical timbers and other forest products greatly exceeds the demand.

(iii) The cost of producing tropical timbers is unknown except in a very few cases such as plantation teak. Nor is there any guarantee that TRF can always be replaced once felled, because felling is often followed by rapid landscape and soil degradation. Farmers operating on short rotations, know their costs and can price accordingly. Forests have been 'grown by God' over huge periods of time and are largely government owned, while foresters are largely state employees, non-commercially-minded, operating a sort of charity to provide multi-billion dollar industries with their raw materials for high profit-making timber and forest products.

(iv) The price of tropical timbers has traditionally been negligible and based largely on demand plus extraction costs, with few constraints caused by shortages of supply. Where such constraints exist, as with some valuable furniture woods, prices have been consistently high and, as a result, individual trees are identified, sorted, extracted and processed with care. There are some 600 species of tropical timbers of known value, but 80% of world export trade is concentrated upon 15–20, and this export trade represents only between 1 and 2% of the total area of forest harvested. Some of the remainder reaches local markets; most is either burned or left, usually damaged.

The cheapness of tropical timbers can be shown by the size of reforestation loans from the World Bank and other institutions, which represent typically between 7% and 42% of the value of export trade in forest products; while exports of tropical forest products have risen proportionally much more than the living standards of the importer countries, who have used them preferentially because of their cheapness.

In consequence of these factors tropical timbers have been sold at far below their real value—which is their cost of replacement—and wastage is on a scale inconceivable in a world whose resources are finite and shrinking. Furthermore, this undervaluing of tropical timbers has led to the undervaluing of the forests in which they grow, so that their destruction—whether by logging, encroachment, planned settlement or agricultural and ranching—has been allowed to proceed apace. Only now are we beginning to realize the financially high as well as ecologically crucial value of the forests themselves: in ameliorating the climate and the atmosphere; in protecting the landscape by regulating run-off and retaining soils; in purifying water and providing the habitat for an immense variety of wildlife; in safeguarding genetic diversity (only twenty plants provide 90% of mankind's food, yet 80 000 edible plants are known, mostly in TRF); in supplying the raw materials for countless industries and crafts; and in providing houses, livelihoods and foods for millions of human beings, including tribal people who under internationally recognized legal codes have rights by virtue of long occupancy to many forests which are disposed of without their consent.

The destruction of TRF has thus become a 'licence to print money' for individuals, corporations and governments who adopt a simplistic, short-term, exploitative approach to the utilization of their potentially renewable resources, and it would be unrealistic to suppose that they would willingly give up this licence for long-term idealistic reasons. This will only happen if we can create an immediate short-term financial interest in the preservation of TRFs, so as to place them at least on economic parity with the alternative uses for their land. Nor is it entirely reasonable to suppose that a 'conservation' approach in which the aim is to preserve inviolate some 10% of the TRF has more than cosmetic value; indeed, it may well prove counter-productive, distracting attention away from the real issues by giving people the feeling that something is going to be saved. Certainly, valuable research is being done in pointing to the crucial areas and species, but as experience in the National Parks of eastern Africa is already showing on a small scale, there is no way in which even the best governments can preserve when all around is poverty, overcrowding, hunger and waste land. The basic economic needs of people and of the environment have to be solved together, and this is the aim of OTEC.

As conceived at present OTEC would be the secretariat of a series of agreements with individual governments, coordinating the efforts of the members in a forum which would eventually be epitomized in an OTEC Treaty which all members would sign.

Requirements of OTEC membership would include commitment to:

(i) reduce the felling of natural TRF by means of an annual harvesting quota (which could be auctioned in advance) down to sustained yield level or less;

(ii) regenerate natural TRF wherever possible on alienated rain forest lands unsuited to permanent agriculture, or alternatively to plant such lands with industrial or fuelwood species;

(iii) increase the price of forest products in step with the reduction in felling, in harmony with other OTEC members, up to replacement cost or beyond (such increases might be achieved by setting a reserve price to the auction mentioned in (i));

(iv) Utilize the revenues created, firstly as at (ii) and secondly to pay a proportion into a common fund whose functions would be to provide buffering finance when needed by members to help exert leverage on members not meeting their obligations, to repair damaged TRF and other ecosystems (even when outside membership territory), and to help solve the problems associated with TRF destruction including the needs of existing rain forest inhabitants;

(v) agree to a timetable for the above.

OTEC is intended to be self-financing through membership dues, but to make a start it would have to be funded. As it got under way price increases would generate revenue surpluses as follows. A 50% increase in prices would generate a surplus of $2·8 billion year^{-1} with an inflationary push (no multiplier effects included) of 0·17% in the world economy. A 300% increase would generate a surplus of $11·2 \times 10^9$ with an inflationary push of 0·68%; while if a 300% increase were accompanied by a 25% reduction in harvesting the surplus generated would drop to $8·4 \times 10^9$. These figures refer only to export prices and to the first steps in getting rain forest destruction under control: the selling of annual cutting quotas for local use as well as for exports would generate surpluses in local as well as external currencies. As prices go up we can expect a fuller utilization of the forests. Theoretically, areas logged could be reduced by

50–90% with no reduction in volume output if waste were eliminated. The inflationary push created would be a very small price to pay if the surplus revenues created abated the much more costly environmental and human catastrophes that today seem to be inexorably approaching.

As will be seen, the objects of OTEC are not quite the same as those of a typical cartel or an International Commodity Agreement such as is being striven for by UNCTAD. Although its revenues initially would derive from attempting to control and increase the market price of a product, its objectives would be much more: to manage or create a renewable natural resource in the interests, first, of all the producer nations and, secondly, of all mankind. Six countries—Indonesia, Malaysia, Singapore (as a re-exporter), Philippines, Brazil, Ivory Coast—export 85% by value of all tropical forest produce. These countries, together with a further five—Zaire, Peru, Papua New Guinea, Burma and Colombia—contain within their frontiers 75% of all TRF. To create an OTEC the decision makers of these eleven countries, and those of as many more rain forest countries as can be persuaded, must work determinedly together in the conviction that there is no alternative and that the benefits for all will be immense and certainly greater than produced by present-day destructiveness. No such benefit can be conceived as accruing unless a single organization speaks for the interests of all the TRF producer nations.

Since this idea was presented at the Leeds Symposium in 1982 there has been widespread discussion of it in a variety of tropical countries, in particular Brazil and Indonesia (whose Minister of the Environment, Dr Emil Salim, has referred to it in several speeches). A full account of the proposal is published elsewhere (Guppy 1983) and an article on the subject has been commissioned by Foreign Affairs, New York. The author has also been called upon to lecture upon the subject.

REFERENCE

Guppy, N. (1983). An organisation of timber exporting countries. *Malaysian Forester*, **46** (in press).

A strategy for preserving tropical forests

IRA RUBINOFF

Smithsonian Tropical Research Institute, Box 2072, Balboa, Republic of Panama

SUMMARY

1 The problems of deforestation of the tropics and solutions which have been suggested are described.

2 An international programme is proposed which will preserve a sample of the remaining forests in a system of large tropical forest reserves.

3 This system will include 1000 reserves of approximately 100 000 ha each, in forty-eight tropical nations.

4 To finance this system a fund is proposed based upon an assessment schedule for those developed nations with a per caput GNP in excess of $1500 year^{-1}.

5 Funding would exceed the cost of merely protecting each reserve. In most cases it would be sufficient to contribute to other economic needs, such as intensification of agriculture in other areas so as to ease the pressure on the remaining forests to provide new agricultural land.

INTRODUCTION

Tropical forests are assailed by a host of unrelenting and remorseless enemies. If unchecked, these forces will eliminate 50% of the world's remaining tropical forests by the end of this century. Associated with these forests, the greatest diversity of plants and animals found on earth will also become extinct, and mankind will lose, for ever, the opportunity of domesticating or harvesting these organisms for his own benefit. Many species will become extinct before their existence is recorded and their potential benefits and usefulness is assessed.

In this essay I propose a plan to preserve a sample of the world's remaining moist tropical forests through the establishment of an internationally financed system of Tropical Moist Forest Reserves. The preservation of large tracts of the world's remaining tropical moist forests would provide a proximate, albeit partial, solution to one of the most critical resource destruction problems that we will otherwise experience during the last two decades of this century. It is urgently needed because of the rapid rate at which the destruction is advancing and the irreversibility of its effects. The threatened resources cannot be replaced. No technological solutions will permit their recycling.

Forty-two percent of the tropics—some 1·9 billion ha, twice the land area of the United States—contain significant forest cover. Over 1 billion ha are closed moist forest; the remainder is relatively open, drier forest of the sort found in much of the southern parts of Africa or the Mato Grosso of Brazil. The world's remaining tropical moist forests are located in three regions: South and Central America, 42%; Asia,

465

Australia, Oceania, 21%; Africa, 37%. Already Latin America has lost 37%, Asia 42%, and Africa 52% of their original areas of tropical moist forest (Sommer 1976; Myers 1980). Eleven hectares of tropical forest are being cut world-wide each minute according to conservative estimates. An area of tropical forest greater than the United Kingdom or half the size of the state of California (245 000 km^2) is being lost each year (Council on Environmental Quality 1980). Not all of this cleared land is necessarily left entirely without forest. In some cases we witness a substitution of plantation or second growth depauperate forests for the original high diversity forests.

It is obvious that the tropical forests will become increasingly scarce and more valuable in years to come, because many of the developing nations which possess these forests are under heavy pressure to exploit them immediately for foreign exchange and to accommodate growing populations. It is unreasonable to expect developing nations to reverse, unaided, the conventional economics which stress immediate, short-term goals at the expense of long-term, less quantifiable benefits.

It is equally unrealistic to expect tropical nations, solely on the basis of small grants from private conservation organizations, to be effective custodians of parks and reserves called for in some of the elaborate global schemes. The great numbers of reserves enacted on paper and never supported on the ground bear grim testimony to the uselessness of conservation ethics without the concomitant financial resources to implement them.

A number of solutions have been suggested to solve or ameliorate the problems of tropical deforestation including: adoption of a new world-wide economic order; increased cooperation among nations to protect valuable resources; increasing the commodity price of timber through the formation of hardwood-exporting cartels (a solution which might turn out to be counter-productive by making it profitable to invest in the equipment necessary to extract timber from the most remote and inaccessible areas); the rental of tropical forests by developed nations; increased research and development on tropical forest resources; increased education and public awareness about tropical forests; development of alternate technologies to reduce demands for tropical forests products; and an attack on the cause of the pressures upon tropical forests including poverty, under-employment, food and energy deficiencies, and uncontrolled population growth (Myers 1979; Allen 1980; Goldsmith 1980; Nigh & Nations 1980; U.S. Interagency Task Force, 1980; IUCN 1980b).

UNESCO's World Heritage Convention (1972) establishes a system of natural and cultural sites of 'outstanding universal value' registered on a World Heritage List, and to be conserved, if necessary, with the assistance of the World Heritage Fund. It thus offers a combination of funding and an administrative framework that would promote the implementation of the Convention and ensure the quality of sites. However, in what pertains to the preservation of tropical forests the Convention has not produced a major impact. The List of World Heritage Sites in the 1982 *United Nations List of National Parks and Protected Areas* (IUCN 1982) does not include a single natural heritage site for Brazil, for example, nor for many other areas with extensive tropical forests. The World Heritage Convention appears to lack sufficient economic incentives to serve as an effective means for preserving the world's tropical forests.

Among the most promising of the various studies purporting to deal with the problems of future resources is *Global Future: Time to Act*, published in 1980 by the Council on Environmental Quality and the Department of State (U.S.A.). A series of refreshingly specific and comprehensive recommendations are made in order to counter the loss of biological diversity in certain ecosystems. Perhaps most significantly, this report recognizes the need for the richer countries 'to pay part or all of the costs of protection and management of critical areas that are unique to mankind.' However, the amount suggested of $1 billion over 10 years for establishing an international fund to assist developing nations manage reserves, is clearly insufficient to have a significant impact on the future of tropical forests.

Most of the recommendations in these studies embody admirable objectives and need to be urgently pursued. However, they are neither individually nor collectively capable of being pursued at a rate sufficient to prevent the elimination of 50% of the remaining tropical moist forest resource base by the end of this century. Nor will the nations possessing the tropical forests, for the most part fully aware of the rare and fragile resources which they possess, be able to defer the immediate economic exploitation of these resources.

INTERNATIONAL PROGRAMME

The strategy I propose requires establishment of a system of tropical moist forest reserves financed by all of the developed temperate zone nations. Payments for this system of reserves should not be regarded by the developed nations as altruistic but rather as self-serving expenditures; a vaccination now against potential future infection. In effect, we are already paying the oil-exporting nations more than the cost of finding, extracting, transporting and refining oil. Instead, we pay, and rather handsomely, into a trust for the social security of those nations when the oil runs out. It is therefore proposed that the developed nations pay now for their own future security, by investing in a trust whose aims would be to protect the diversity of life embodied in the tropical moist forests of the world.

The payments for a system of reserves must not be perceived to be an attempt on the part of the rich nations to meddle in the internal affairs of the developing countries. Participation in the programme must be voluntary and should not be viewed in any way as affecting these nations' sovereignty over their forest reserves.

According to the proposed plan, each host nation would receive an annual payment, the amount based on the area under protection, to act as custodian of reserve areas of tropical moist forests. Maintenance of the reserves would be monitored by annual inspections. If the area under protection has been reduced or there were more squatters than initially specified in the registration agreement, then the payments would be substantially reduced. Thus, there would be a direct economic incentive for rigorous protection of the reserves.

The capacities of forestry and park service institutions in many countries will be inadequate to absorb large amounts of external funds. In some cases it may prove necessary first to finance small technical assistance programmes to build up the infrastructure of the organizations charged with the custodianship and management of the reserve system within each country.

The funding which each participating nation receives should exceed the requirements of simply developing or enriching the infrastructure of national park or forestry conservation services in the participating countries. The proposed funding should cover the intensification and diversification of agriculture in other areas so as to ease the pressure on the reserves to provide new agricultural land. Funds could also be used to develop plantation forests in other areas in order to provide employment, firewood, and other needed forest products. They should also be sufficient for public education programmes in the participating nations so as to broaden acceptance of the concept of forest preservation and to develop respect for the reserve's borders, rules, and regulations. The payments should be made without any conditions on use other than the protection of the agreed-upon area at the time of registration.

Some nations participating in the programme may lack sufficient technical personnel to prepare the necessary surveys for registering their new reserves. In these cases, a programme of 'start-up' grants should be administered, which could employ consultants to prepare surveys, mapping, inventories, legal reviews of the relevant local and environmental laws, and the preparation of new legislative packages where these are a prerequisite for participation.

Clearly, detailed surveys and inventories will not be accomplished in the relatively short term allotted for preparing the registration documents— this would normally require a long-term activity of research and analysis of each reserve (Whitmore 1980). The preparation of the application would require approximately 1 year; less for reserves where much of the requisite data already exists. Registration should be left open for approximately 5 years after the programme is initiated or until the goal of 1000 tropical moist forest reserves of approximately 100 000 ha each is established. Some reserves will be considerably larger; as in Amazonia, for example, where the Brazilian government is already establishing reserves of which some are over 1 000 000 ha. Others may be considerably smaller.

It is, of course, recognized that many of the reserve boundaries will be a compromise based upon administrative and political constraints. Clearly, boundaries that include natural barriers such as mountain ranges or rivers are usually much easier to patrol than those which abut urban areas. Since selection of the areas to be included in the international reserve programme must be left up to the individual nations, areas can be selected for which there are a minimum of conflicting development plans. The hostility frequently associated with reserve establishment as being antidevelopment can at least be partially avoided (White & Bratten 1980).

What will this plan accomplish?

A goal of 100 million ha of the world's tropical moist forests established into a system of effective and carefully monitored reserves, and financed by contributions from the developed nations may seem ambitious. Actually, this represents only about 10% of the remaining tropical moist forests. The proposed plan for a system of tropical forest reserves will not stop the process of deforestation. What would be accomplished instead would be the establishment of a safety valve. Some diversity is preserved (Willis & Eisenmann 1979). Some options for the future are maintained. If we have erred, if 10% of the earth's remaining tropical moist forests is found to be insufficient to protect watersheds (Gentry & Lopez-Parodi 1980) or maintain climatic balance (Woodwell 1978), then at least there will be a reservoir of plants and animals adapted to life in the tropics to provide the source material with which to attempt to recolonize other areas. This process, should it prove necessary, would require vast scientific and technological developments. It is hoped that part of the revenues derived from the international reserve programme would encourage the more effective preservation of already existing parks and reserves, and thus indirectly contribute to the ultimate preservation of an area greater than the 10% of the tropical moist forests envisioned to be supported by this plan.

One criticism of the proposed scheme is that it could, by its existence, take pressure off extant national programmes, encouraging nations merely to register parks and reserves they had planned to declare anyway. This may not necessarily be bad. If any given nation is serious in its conservation commitment, and is prepared to allocate natural resources toward this end, then it would probably use the released funds to strengthen the infrastructure of extant parks, enlarge them, or establish new ones. If, as is too often the case, economic realities and/or lack of commitment only result in the establishment of new 'paper parks,' then the registration of a previously planned park in the new programme would at least ensure its protection. The revenue derived would help capitalize other immediate programmes and perhaps contribute to an ambiance in which conservation imperatives receive a greater priority and are more broadly appreciated within the nation.

There are about one thousand national parks, from the equator to the poles, listed in the *1980 United Nations List of National Parks and Equivalent Reserves* (IUCN 1980a). Unfortunately, in compiling this data, it was found that the information about the 'area of some of the parks varied by as much as 50% depending upon the source of information.' The compiler of the *1982 United Nations List of National Parks and Protected Areas*, unfortunately claims that the data available is still inadequate in order to judge the quality of management of many of the world's reserves (IUCN 1982). Parks and reserves presently make up less than 2% of the remaining tropical moist forest biome, and even that 2% is at risk.

Where will the funds come from and how much will it cost?

The strategy anticipates that the financing of the International Tropical Moist Forest Reserve System will be provided by those developed nations with per caput gross national products in excess of $1500 year^{-1} (World Bank 1980). For purposes of this plan, a system equivalent to a progressive income tax (beginning at $0·50 for GNP $1500, to $5·00 for GNP $10 000 and above) on all nations with a GNP over $1500, and not possessing tropical moist forests, would yield over $3 billion annually ($3 259 000 000). This system would require support from twenty-three of the nations in the OECD ($2613 000 000), seven nations with Centrally Planned Economies ($556 000 000), seven of the OPEC nations ($89 700 000), and six other developing or middle-income countries with GNP over 1500 dollars ($53 000 000) (Table 1). The international resource mobilization must become automatic, independent of the good will of the individual contributors, and flow through a multilateral institution such as the World Bank. This seems a great amount, yet it represents only a relatively small increase in the 1980 development assistance provided by the OECD nations. For some

Table 1. Sources of funds for the proposed international tropical forest reserve system

	Population (A) (million)	GNP/ caput (B)	Contribution/ year (C) (million)	Devel. Asst. (D) (million)	% Increase (E)
Organization for Economic Cooperation and Development					
Australia	14·2	7990	49·7	690	7
Austria	7·5	7030	26·3	174	15
Belgium	9·8	9090	44·1	714	6
Canada	23·5	9180	105·8	1151	9
Denmark	5·1	9920	23·0	448	5
Finland	4·8	6820	14·4	104	14
France	53·3	8260	213·2	3836	6
F.R. Germany	61·3	9580	275·9	3581	8
Greece	9·4	3250	14·1		
Iceland	0·2	8390	0·8		
Ireland	3·2	3470	4·8		
Italy	56·7	3850	85·1	320	27
Japan	114·9	7280	402·2	3070	13
Luxembourg	0·4	10 540	2·0		
Netherlands	13·9	8410	55·6	1547	4
New Zealand	3·2	4790	6·4	65	10
Norway	4·1	9510	18·5	491	4
Portugal	9·8	1990	4·9		
Spain	37·1	3470	55·7		
Sweden	8·3	10 210	41·5	1125	4
Switzerland	6·3	12 100	31·5	218	14
United Kingdom	55·8	5030	139·5	2453	6
United States	221·9	9590	998·6	4567	22
			Subtotal = $2613·6		
Organization of Petroleum Exporting Nations*					
Iran	35·8	2160	35·8	21	170
Iraq	12·2	1860	6·1	861	1
Kuwait	1·2	14 890	6·0	1099	1
Libya	2·7	6970	8·1	146	6
Qatar	0·2	12 740	1·0	251	1
Saudi Arabia	8·2	7690	28·7	1970	2
U. A. Emirates	0·8	14 230	4·0	207	2
			Subtotal = $89·0		

* Includes countries with a GNP in excess of $1500 per caput and excludes countries with a significant tropical moist forest habitat.

TABLE 1. (*cont.*)

	Population (A) (million)	GNP/ caput (B)	Contribution/ year (C) (million)	Devel. Asst. (D) (million)	% Increase (E)
Middle income countries					
Argentina	26·4	1910	13.2		
Hong Kong	4·6	3040	6·9		
Israel	3·7	3500	5·6		
Singapore	2·3	3290	3·5		
Uruguay	2·9	1610	1·5		
Yugoslavia	22·0	2380	22·0		
			Subtotal = $52·7		
Centrally planned economies					
Bulgaria	8·8	3320	13·2		
Czechoslovakia	15·1	4720	30·2		
German D.R.	16·7	5710	41·8		
Hungary	10·7	3450	16·1		
Poland	35·0	3670	52·5		
Romania	21·9	1750	11·0		
USSR	261·0	3700	391·5		
			Subtotal = $556·3		
			Total = $3259·0		

Data from *World Development Report*, (1980); The World Bank.

(A), (B) adapted from *World Development Report* (1980), The World Bank, Table 1, pp. 110, 111. (C) calculated on a scale of GNP.

$0–1500	= 0	$7–8000 = $3·5	
$1500–2000	= $0·5	$8–9000 = $4	
$2–3000	= $1	$9–10 000 = $4·5	
$3–4000	= $1·5	$10+ = $5	
$5–6000	= $2·5	C = A × B Scale	
$6–7000	= $3		

(D) adapted from *World Development Report*, (1980) Table 16; ibid.

(E)% increase in development assistance $E = \dfrac{C}{D} (100)$

countries, with the proposed additional contribution, this increase would still be below the 0·7% of GNP target for development assistance proposed by the United Nations.

In addition, the planned economy nations should not continue to shirk their responsibilities to contribute to this type of programme. Whatever their contemporary perception of the contribution of the West's former colonialistic or imperialistic policies to the economics of tropical nations, the problem of deforestation will affect all nations, and all should contribute to this plan, regardless of ideology.

Adjustments are possible to even out inequalities resulting from the formula used in deriving the amounts to be contributed annually by each participating nation. For example, a scale with smaller divisions than $1000 would be more equitable for some nations with GNPs just over the minimum, and special arrangements might have to be made in the case of countries with particularly awkward foreign exchange situations.

Several industrialized countries may wish to take additional measures to protect unilaterally the relatively small amounts of tropical moist forest under their custodianship. For example, Australia has about 6000 km² of moist forest remaining along the east coast of Queensland; and the United States could adopt a more aggressive policy towards protecting some of the remaining forested areas in the Hawaiian islands.

There is a possibility that some nations—which are middle income as classified by the World Bank and also possess tropical moist forests, e.g. Brazil—may wish to participate in the programme both as a contributor and as a receiver of support from the International Tropical Moist Forest Reserve System. (For purposes of this model, nations possessing substantial tropical moist forests are excluded from the calculations of income. However, if Brazil and Venezuela choose to contribute, as well as register reserves, an additional $74 000 000 would be available for the programme.)

Several possibilities have been suggested for the international organization necessary to administer such a plan. International Agencies such as the Consultative Group for International Agricultural Research (CGIAR) or the International Bureau of Plant Genetic Research (IBPGR) could serve as effective models for a new international organization to be formed with the specific mission of administering a programme for the establishment, inspection, and disbursement of payments for tropical moist forest reserves.

A new institution such as the World Development Fund proposed in the study, *North–South: A Programme for Survival* would be a better choice (Brandt Commission 1980). However, the machinery is not in place and once established would be concerned with all aspects of development. Thus, it could easily fail to provide immediately the priority necessary for preserving the rapidly diminishing tropical moist forests.

Of the traditional international agencies, the World Bank appears to be the best adapted to undertake the additional responsibility for establishing and financing a large network of protected areas. The World Bank has its purpose—the provision of funds and technical assistance for facilitating economic development in its poorer member countries. It has a global reach. The additional $3 billion year^{-1} would not swamp its administrative capabilities, although additional technical people would be needed, probably in a separate division devoted to giving rather than loaning money. The Bank would also be in an excellent position to provide technical advice and additional loans, where necessary, to combine with the revenues from reserve payments for other development projects in areas such as agriculture, reforestation, afforestation, restoration of eroded lands, colonization schemes, forestry training, land surveys and institution building. The Bank has already developed a philosophy towards forestry development, and it understands the role of human encroachment, principally from unplanned and poorly planned agriculture in the destruction of tropical forests (World Bank 1978).

Some of the management of the programme could be accomplished through the Bank's extant system of regional offices, many of which are located in countries with important areas of the world's remaining tropical moist forests, e.g. Cameroun,

Ghana, Ivory Coast, and Zaire in Africa; Indonesia and Thailand in Asia; and Bolivia and Colombia in South America. The Bank already conducts periodic reviews of borrower countries' economic situations and credit-worthiness. This process could be modified into an inspection procedure to ensure compliance with agreed-upon specifications for reserve management. When the inspection missions find that the safeguards are inadequate or that they have been ignored, then the Bank's leverage—the halting of disbursements—can be employed. However, supervision of compliance must be firm, not the delicate task that has sometimes been the case in loan projects.

An advisory committee of experts from organizations such as FAO, UNESCO, UNEP, IUCN, and WWF might be established to assist the World Bank with technical matters pertaining to the programme and to lend their weight to encouraging the developed nations to subscribe. With broad and immediate support from the interested nations, this is a plan that can be implemented almost immediately, with major components in place within 3 years, under ideal circumstances.

Initially, the programme will be applied only to natural, unmodified, tropical moist forest ecosystems. Later, as more subscriptions to the programme from developed and middle-income nations are forthcoming, auxiliary reserves may be added, including those involving varying degrees of management of the drier, open-canopy types of tropical forests. The International Tropical Moist Forest Reserve System would accept registration applications from the following nations (broadly defined).

South and Southeast Asia and Melanesia. Australia, Bangladesh, Brunei, Burma, Indonesia,* India, Kampuchea, Lao P.D.R., Malaysia,* Melanesia, Papua New Guinea, Philippines, Sri Lanka, Thailand, Vietnam.

Tropical Latin America. Belize, Bolivia,* Brazil,* Colombia,* Costa Rica, Cuba, Dominican Republic, El Salvador, Ecuador, French Guiana, Guatemala, Guyana, Honduras, Mexico, Nicaragua, Panama, Peru,* Puerto Rico, Suriname, Trinidad–Tobago, Venezuela.*

Tropical Africa. Cameroun, Congo, Gabon,* Ghana, Ivory Coast, Kenya, Liberia, Madagascar, Nigeria, Sierra Leone, Tanzania, Uganda, Zaire.*

An enormous area is contained within the political entitles just listed; unfortunately, in many cases, the remaining tropical forests have already been disturbed and grossly disrupted. There are remnant forests in all of these countries which should be preserved, but 80% of the world's tropical forests are found in the nine countries asterisked (*) above and they would form the core of the new programme.

DISCUSSION

There is precise enough information about the seriousness of the conversion of tropical forests to justify the common interest of all nations in the selection and establishment of the forest reserve system. What is now needed is a change in political perceptions, a political breakthrough in the North–South dialogue—one that will make a significant contribution to the world's stability in both economic and ecological terms.

Is this possible?

It is now 10 years since the authors of *The Limits to Growth* presented their World Model of the relationships between industrialization, population growth, malnutrition, depletion of non-renewable resources, and the deterioration of the environment, Meadows *et al* (1972). Their models generated much criticism and many world conferences, but very little in the way of new national or international policies designed to develop or even to question the need for viable alternatives to a global growth economy. Its publication did produce an increased awareness that some resources might indeed, by the end of the century, be reaching scarcity levels, and that the limited regeneration potential and carrying capacity of the world's ecosystems might negatively impair the quality of life the inhabitants of the developed nations of the world have come to expect. Many subsequent examinations of aspects of the global resource base have been published and, undoubtedly, more can be expected. In 1980, the Independent Commission on International Development Issues (The Brandt Commission) published its report that dealt with a variety of problems arising from the disparity between the nations of the developed North and the generally less-developed South. A good case was made for the participation of the developed world in a World Development Fund, which would be the mechanism for transfer of assistance funds designed to speed the development of Third World nations and to reduce the extent of world poverty. In spite of the advantage and long-range economic self-interest that would accrue to the developed world by stabilizing the Third World markets, with almost three-quarters of the world's population, there has not been a rush to adopt the Brandt Commission report. Nor, following the Charter of Algiers in 1967, has the plethora of international conferences succeeded in developing an operational system of compensating the developing nations for the costs of maintaining their environments at the expense of their trade and development (Nicholls 1973). However, action on the part of the developed nations to protect the world's environment is not entirely without precedent. The world-wide alarm which developed over radioactive fallout after the 1954 series of U.S. hydrogen bomb tests resulted in a Partial Test-Ban Treaty that prohibits detonations of nuclear weapons in the atmosphere, underwater and in outer space. In force since 1963, this treaty, at least for those nations possessing nuclear weapons, must be an expensive concession to the world's environmental quality and to their own future generations.

It seems clear that, in the short run, the developed world will not help the developing countries in any appreciable way until the threat for not doing so is immediate and personalized, to the extent that the quality of life of the developed world is immediately at risk or already seriously deteriorated. At present, the Organization for Economic Cooperation and Development–Development Assistance Committee nations are only contributing 0·34% of their GNP annually with the objective of promoting economic development in low income countries. Indeed, the contribution of the United States has been reduced from 0·32% to 0·18% of its GNP during the last 10 years, and there is even a threat by the present administration to reduce further its contribution toward multilateral organizations as the existing commitments expire.

Achieving the goal of enclosing some of the tropical forests will benefit everyone. The additional costs, while small in terms of the overall productivity of the developed nations, are nevertheless substantial. Three billion dollars annually will not easily be parted with, particularly at a time of high inflation and reduced government spending. To succeed, the plan will require the vigorous lobbying of non-governmental conservation groups for the subscription of their nations to an International Tropical Moist Forest Reserve System.

ACKNOWLEDGMENTS

This essay was begun while the author was a visiting Fellow at Wolfson College, Oxford and a visiting Scientist at the Department of Zoology, Oxford. I wish to thank A. W. Diamond, M. J. Eberhard, C. Elton, T. Lovejoy, M. Moynihan, N. Myers, P. Raven, M. H. Robinson, A. Rubinoff, D. White, T. C. Whitmore, M. Wright and F. Vollrath for their advice and comments.

REFERENCES

Allen, R. (1980). *How to Save the World.* Kogan Page. London.
Brandt, W. (1980). *North–South: A Program for Survival.* The Report of the Independent Commission on International Development Issues under the Chairmanship of Willy Brandt. Pan Books, London.
Council on Environmental Quality (1980). *The Global 2000 Report to the President: Entering the Twenty-First Century.* Prepared by the Council on Environmental Quality and the Department of State. Vol. 1, p. 47; Vol. 2, 766.
Council on Environmental Quality (1980). *Global Future: Time to Act.* Report to the President on Global Resources, Environment and Population. Council on Environmental Quality, Department of State. U.S. Government Printing Office. Washington, D.C.
Gentry, A.H. & Lopez-Parodi, J. (1980). Deforestation and increased flooding of the Upper Amazon. *Science,* **210,** 1354–1356.
Goldsmith, E. (1980). W.E.A.P. World Ecological Areas Programme: a proposal to save the world's tropical rain forests. *The Ecologist,* **1 & 2,** 1–4.
IUCN (1980a). *1980 United Nations List of National Parks and Equivalent Reserves.* International Union for Conservation of Nature and Natural Resources. Gland, Switzerland.
IUCN (1980b). *World Conservation Strategy.* International Union for the Conservation of Nature and Natural Resources. United Nations Environmental Program. World Wildlife Fund. Gland, Switzerland.
IUCN (1982). *1982 United Nations List of National Parks and Protected Areas.* International Union for the Conservation of Nature and Natural Resources. Gland, Switzerland.
Meadows, D.H., Meadows, D.L., Randers, J. & Behrens, Wm W. III (1972). *The Limits to Growth.* A Report for the Club of Rome's project on the predicament of mankind. Pan Books. London.
Myers, N. (1979). *The Sinking Ark.* Pergamon Press, Oxford.
Myers, N. (1980). *Conversion of Tropical Moist Forests.* National Academy of Science, Washington, D.C.
Nicholls, Y.I. (1973). *Source Book: Emergence of Proposals for Recompensing Developing Countries for Maintaining Environmental Quality.* International Union for Conservation of Nature and Natural Resources Environmental Policy and Law Paper, No. 5. Morges, Switzerland.
Nigh, R.B. & Nations, J. (1980). *Tropical Rain Forests.* The Bulletin of the Atomic Scientists, March, pp. 12–19.
Sommer, A. (1976). Attempt at an Assessment of the World's Tropical Moist Forests. *Unasylva,* **28,** (112+113), 5–24.
UNESCO (1972). *Convention concerning the protection of the world cultural and natural heritage.* General Conference, Seventeenth Session. Paris.

U.S. Interagency Task Force on Tropical Forests (1980). *The World's Tropical Forests.* A Policy, Strategy and Program for the United States. Report to the President. Department of State Publication 9117.

White, P.S. & Bratton, S.P. (1980). After preservation: philosophical and practical problems of change. *Biological Conservation*, **18**, 241–255.

Whitmore, T.C. (1980). The conservation of tropical rain forest. *Conservation Biology* (Ed. by M. E. Soule & B. A. Wilcox), pp. 303–318. Sinauer Associates, Massachusetts.

Willis, E.O. & Eisenmann, E. (1979). A Revised List of Birds of Barro Colorado Island, Panama. *Smithsonian Contributions to Zoology*, **291**, 31.

World Bank (1978). *Forestry, Sector Policy Paper.* The World Bank. Washington, D.C.

World Bank (1980). *World Development Report 1980.* Published for the World Bank. Oxford University Press. Oxford.

Woodwell, G. (1978). CO_2-deforestation relationships. *Proceedings of the U.S. Strategy Conference on Tropical Deforestation*, pp. 34–37. U.S. Department of State and U.S. Agency for International Development. Washington, D.C.

Rain forests and foreign policies: a look at Britain's impact

BRIAN JOHNSON

International Institute for Environment and Development,
10 Percy Street, London W1P 0DR

SUMMARY

1 Britain is not generally thought of as a country with a very significant impact on the world problem of depleting and diminishing tropical rain forests (TRF). Developing countries provide no more than a tenth of total timber imports, of which rather less than half are the hardwoods of natural tropical forests.

2 It is argued that Britain's potential influence on world use of tropical rain forests cannot be measured by her present or potential demand on TRF products.

3 With regard to some of the critical factors which could redirect present trends of depletion and destruction to TRFs, Britain has a substantial contribution to make. This is because Britain is a principal repository of knowledge on TRF, and a major centre for dissemination of information and influencing informed opinion with regard to international development policies.

4 British Government policy, though nowhere stated as such, leans to the view that public policy should be limited to trying to make the conditions for TRF exploitation more attractive to British private investment. As a result the British Government is running down the national capacity to provide important information relevant to other important aspects of TRF.

5 An outline is given for a strategy of dialogue within Britain. This would focus upon developing a new policy aimed to: promote sustained yield and good silviculture; increase capacity to provide assistance; seek to market expertise; help increase financial benefit from the remaining TRF; and to promote international discussion to increase comprehension of the wider values of TRF.

INTRODUCTION

In Britain, as elsewhere, recognition is growing that tropical deforestation is now a problem of global importance. At the same time, their dramatic nature, their fragility and their exploitability, and, above all, the flora and the fauna which they contain give the tropical forest regions of the world a singular appeal to public sensibility. Yet it seems true to say that the importance of the fate of tropical rain forests, and Britain's interest in their protection and better utilization, may be inadequately appreciated by policy makers in this country.

TROPICAL FORESTS' IMPORTANCE TO
FOREIGN POLICY

The remaining natural stands of tropical rain forest which still cover about a fourteenth part of the earth's surface, and nearly a fifth of that of developing countries (Spears 1979), have a stabilizing role which extends beyond the physical conditions of life. We have heard in this symposium about the loss of and threat to important and fascinating flora and fauna. We must also remember that tropical rain forest regions are the home and habitat of some three million indigenous forest people, many of whom are under direct threat of cultural and even physical extinction from the processes of deforestation. But the disappearance of tropical forests is also having a major impact on economic conditions and even political stability.

As far as Britain is concerned, policy makers in party offices and Whitehall alike are still conditioned to see these forests as sources of hardwood or, occasionally, as in the Environment Committee of the OECD recently, as reservoirs of biological diversity (OECD 1981). The fact that they also control local climates, and that their removal intensifies seasonal flooding with major loss of life and property, increases water shortages in dry seasons, accelerates erosion of agricultural land by both wind and water and increases siltation of rivers, irrigation channels and hydropower installations, is little considered when allocating resources to the forestry sector. These so-called 'downstream' effects tend instead to be the object of separate policies and projects and, in consequence, of much avoidable expenditure. Additional to such remedial expenditure are increasing calls for British disaster relief to help victims of flood and drought in places (e.g. India, Bangladesh) where such conditions are connected with the removal of forests. Such effects and expenditures are not yet, regrettably, a sufficiently central concern of overall economic development or foreign policy calculus. And yet, more urgently than the better advertised risks of reduced biological diversity, local and regional social and economic difficulties associated with deforestation appear today as causative factors in political instability and indeed military conflict. Political instability in Sudan, for example, arose from perpetual power cuts in Khartoum, the results of deforestation in Ethiopia causing silting at the Roseires Dam on the Blue Nile. Conflict in the Ogaden resulted from upland deforestation leading to migrations which fuelled the Ethiopian/Somali conflict. Other more or less direct contributions to conflict have occurred elsewhere, especially in Thailand and the Philippines.

On balance it appears probable that deforestation (or other major vegetation disturbance) has been an insignificant contributor to atmospheric carbon dioxide so far when compared with the burning of fossil fuels. However, a high rate of destruction of the remaining forests of the tropics could result in a major further release of carbon. Many estimates now consider that forest shrinkage and the attendant burning of wood represents 50–100% of the fossil fuel sources of CO_2, while other experts stress the disruption of climatic patterns through the albedo effect (as a consequence of the greater 'shinyness' of denuded parts of the earth's surface), also from greatly increased dust and particulate matter in the atmosphere, which stem from forest burning.

A wide range of actual and potential impacts arising from tropical deforestation has been touched upon here because, in a democratic mixed economy like Britain's, *all* should be considered in formulating both public policy and also private business judgments. Britain's impact should be considered, first in official policy towards trade, as it affects the tropical rain forest products, processed and unprocessed, including hardwoods, food and fibre, commodities and genetic materials; secondly, in public policy towards social development; thirdly, toward the ecosystem stabilizing function of forests; fourthly, in the contribution of the private sector whether in timber extraction, investment, supply of forestry equipment, silvicultural research and development and Britain's capacity to offer management and training facilities.

TROPICAL RAIN FORESTS IN BRITISH PUBLIC POLICY: A STORY OF RETREAT

Whether the focus is on public or private sector policy, Britain's present and potential role can only be understood in the light of her past relations with areas of the world where the tropical rain forests grow. In pre-World War II and Imperial days, this country directly managed the forest areas of twenty-one out of the thirty-seven nations which today have any significant area of tropical rain forest.

Tropical hardwoods were still much used in parquet floors and for structural and decorative joinery as well as furniture in the 1930s. And in those days, Britain imported on average rather more than three times the volume of tropical hardwood that she imported in 1979 (Empire Forestry Yearbook 1938 and U.K. Yearbook of Timber Statistics 1979). In fact, the total number of British experts working in tropical rain forest regions today, mostly for international agencies, is less than one-fifth of what it was in 1937.

At the end of the colonial period there was a reluctance on the part of many ex-colonies to continue their close ties with British colonial expertise. Instead diversification of advice was sought. At the same time, Britain without alternative employment for its cadres of trained foresters, also tended to resist investment in tropical forestry where expropriation and nationalization of British investments had not been uncommon. In 1979, only 12% of British wood and wood products by volume (994 200 m^3) came from tropical rain forest countries, and of these only 8% were tropical hardwoods, processed or unprocessed. Moreover these imports have varied erratically since the 1960s, showing a downward fluctuating volume from 1·5 million m^3 in 1961 to under 1 million m^3 in 1979, a fluctuation which has moved with fashions, such as for teak coffee tables in the 1960s and for rosewood in the 1970s.

So far as trade is concerned, there is no tariff on tropical hardwood imports into the United Kingdom, whether as logs, sawn wood or processed, except for certain categories of plywood. In 1979, 85% of hardwoods came from Malaysia, Brazil, the Ivory coast, Indonesia and the Philippines, while processed hardwoods in substantial quantities came from Singapore and South Korea. Britain today imports very little from a number of her traditional suppliers, such as Nigeria, Ghana, India and Burma.

Today, the heirs of the former Empire forest concessionaires are multinational companies or their subsidiaries, like Champion International, Westvaco, Georgia Pacific, United Paper, Mitsui, Toyomenka (the Weyerhauser Corporation, one of the largest of all lumbering companies, has now virtually ceased operations in tropical rain forest regions). Often their apparently short-sighted extractive behaviour results from the fact that the host country, desperate for foreign exchange to pay import bills, gives felling concessions sometimes of as little as 5 years in order to induce a rapid return of royalties and levies, without any guarantee that the land can be retained for clearing and investment in replantation. The forests are seen increasingly as an instant-withdrawal deposit account producing vital foreign exchange via hardwoods.

British Government expenditure directly on forestry in tropical rain forest countries is not easy to determine, as some of the significant aid for forestry is that given in the context of other rural development projects. In general, forestry projects supported by British bilateral aid fall into two main categories: afforestation as part of a rural development programme and 'pure' forestry which can be subdivided into Overseas Development Administration (ODA) projects and the commercial ventures of the Commonwealth Development Corporation. In general it can be said that British aid-supported forestry projects, whether woodlots or commercial forestry, are enhancing the environment in ways which are generally acknowledged in, e.g. ODA planning documents. British-supported forestry projects do have their drawbacks, however, which rarely attract official attention. Hydrological yields from catchments may be severely reduced. There may be competition between forestry and other land uses leading to greater pressure on marginal land. However, on balance, forestry projects are having essentially beneficial effects on the environment (International Institute for Environment & Development, unpubl.).

British bilateral expenditure on forestry projects had stayed static in recent years and even declined somewhat from a level in the late 1970s of about 2% of total bilateral flows. In fact, it is impossible to make any useful comparison between British bilateral and multilateral aid as regards forestry. However, it should be noted that the employment of British forestry experts in multilaterally financed projects under the aegis of the United Nations, its specialized agencies, the European Community, the World Bank or other regional development institutions greatly exceeds the number financed directly under British bilateral aid. In the face of recent cuts in Britain's overseas aid budget generally, forestry had little chance of holding its position. In the context of selecting priorities, Mr Neil Marten, when Minister for Overseas Development, stressed the great difficulties in cutting Britain's multilateral commitments. Moreover, as some 60% of British bilateral aid is in the form of large-scale long-term commitments to capital projects such as roads, harbours or dams, and is in future to be directed to projects which will directly benefit British industry, it is inevitable that cuts can only be made in that part of Britain's bilateral programme where benefits to Britain in the form of exports are least: in particular, low-technology, labour-intensive projects involving technical assistance in areas such as rural development. Hence, pleas to increase, or indeed even maintain funding for British centres of expertise in tropical forests—centres that represent the cumulative historical experience of many years of rain forestry management in all parts of the world—tend to fall on deaf ears in Whitehall.

The international politics of tropical forests, which inevitably also tend to influence the British Government's position, have not in recent times encouraged much change in priorities. Forests are not popular as foci for foreign aid because they are, almost by definition, sparsely populated with people, and aid funds inevitably tend to go to areas of high population density. This is reflected in the fact that the entire forestry department of the FAO receives only about 4% of FAO's overall budget, and also for example, the fact that the Commonwealth agricultural ministers have never once in two decades of annual meetings had forestry as a topic on their agenda.

This low priority occurs by mutual tacit agreement between donor and recipient of aid. Spears (1979) has stressed the positive view taken of deforestation by the government of many tropical forested countries; namely that, if successful, settlement programmes in the 130 million ha of forests that are likely to disappear before the year 2000, willy nilly, could provide living space, an assured food and fuel supply as well as a small income for at least 200 million poor people. Some at least of these very poor folk would be drawn from what the World Bank calls the 'poverty target group' of 600 million who will, according to McNamara (1978) still be living in conditions of absolute poverty at the end of the century. Such a view of the potential of tropical rain forests is not easy to counter with bald statements of their importance to the international community.

Moreover, foresters themselves, by focussing exclusively on the timber production aspect of forestry, have consistently tended to underestimate the other goods or services that tropical forests can generate, such as holding soils and providing agriculture with regular and dependable amounts of irrigation water. This problem is central to the limited effort made by Britain among other Western donor countries in promoting forest conservation.

THE PRIVATE SECTOR'S POSTURE

At present, British private sector investment is insignificant when compared with the activities of the multinationals referred to above. It consists principally of the operations of Unilever in Nigeria, Sarawak and the Solomon Islands, and a majority Unilever shareholding (along with Macmillan Bloedel) in a large Indonesian timber enterprise in East Kalimantan. Among other private investors, a few individuals have made speculative investments in forestry industries and concessions, e.g. Sir James Goldsmith who recently purchased a 25% stake in the Diamond Corporation, a forest industries conglomerate with Third World interests.

Other potential British investors in tropical rain forests include Shell and B.P. Though not interested in logging, at least under today's economic and political conditions, both are conducting research and development in areas like densified wood pellets as an oil substitute, and the breeding of much faster growing hardwoods which might revolutionize the economics of hardwood plantations, and, incidentally, could make a major contribution to saving standing natural rain forests in the process.

As regards other import and export interests, the firm of Price and Pearce is substantial as an importer and re-exporter of tropical hardwood products. British exports of equipment affecting the harvesting or processing of tropical hardwoods were of negligible significance at only £8·5 million in 1975 as against imports of £8·3 million.

So far as British forestry consulting expertise is concerned, again a lack of governmental commitment appears to have hampered British private sector successs in finding overseas work. Most U.K. forest expertise, which tends to concentrate on forestry management and landscaping, is channelled into the Commonwealth Forestry Institute in Oxford and into government bodies and entities such as the ODA and the Forestry Commission. Among the most enterprising of private forestry consulting organizations, the Economic Forestry Group recently undertook a small management contract for the Asian Development Bank in Burma, but the great bulk of their growing management operations remain in the U.K. and the southern United States. Generally speaking independent British consultancy organizations have not been successful in securing major forestry-related contracts.

Unhappily, no information was obtained in this brief survey of the importance of other tropical rain forest products apart from wood to the British economy and the importance of genetic material from these forests to British-based pharmaceutical and other companies.

One area of potential interest to the British private sector is the potential for capital investment in standing forest reserves for future use. A number of private schemes have been put forward here, and various approaches are at present being explored which might creatively combine several elements including: available natural standing forest as collateral for international borrowing (as was proposed by the Brazilian Government in 1979–80); the City of London's financial strength and flexibility as an organizer of consortium financing; the potential of research and development in quick growing hardwoods for plantations, and new technologies in rapid maturation of timber. Any collateral or plantation investment scheme involving British or other private finance in the Third World would, of course, have to have a governmental guarantee, perhaps along the lines of the U.S. Overseas Private Investors Corporation. It would then be important for the guarantor to attach certain environmental conservation requirements to the guarantee.

THE KNOWLEDGE SECTOR: THE BRITISH ACADEMIC AND INSTITUTIONAL CONTRIBUTION TO THE EXPLOITATION AND CONSERVATION OF TROPICAL RAIN FORESTS

Regarding the international standing of British knowledge and institutional capacity in tropical forestry, the 1980 Report to the President by a U.S. Inter-Agency Task Force on Tropical Forests concluded that: 'The U.K. has long been a world leader in tropical forestry'. (Anon. 1980).

Apart from the Commonwealth Forestry Institute, which includes a tropical silviculture unit and is a principal authority in tropical forest information, the

University of Aberdeen (with its particular experience in Malesian forestry biology) is acknowledged world-wide as a centre of expertise, whereas other focal points, such as at the Universities of Cambridge, Edinburgh, Hull, Leeds, Stirling and York are also significant. In addition, the ODA-supported Land Resources Development Centre* has appraised many tropical forest areas of the world and carried out land suitability studies. The Building Research Establishment (formerly the Forest Products Research Laboratory) is active in assessing tropical timbers, and the Tropical Products Institute* investigates other derivatives from tropical species.

The consensus received from a series of recent discussions with senior forestry experts in the ODA, the Commonwealth Development Corporation and three University centres with private-sector tropical forestry experts is that the tropical rain forest countries, to quote one official, are 'crying out' for British forestry expertise, a demand that cannot today be met.

One clear problem here is that the top British experts are all over-committed and younger people too rarely get a chance to gain experience working with counterparts overseas as countries naturally tend to demand the individual with strong experience. It is unfortunate in this respect that the British Government is not prepared to involve young potential British foresters in the World Bank Young Professionals' Scheme or subscribe to the FAO's Associated Expert Programme.

The need is not so much for a great expansion of existing facilities or institutions as it is to maintain the quality of accumulated knowledge, and not run down existing capacities. Oxford is the only centre of expertise in the world with a massive background of forest literature and records going back as much as 200 years. It also still has the finest tropical forestry library in the English-speaking world which should, it is thought, be linked with a network of research, and of the capabilities and records of others. The nature of tropical forestry makes the problem of access to knowledge quite different to the problems posed, say, by research on crops such as wheat or rice. With tropical forestry, a range of at least 150–250 species with widely different characteristics, regions of growth, etc. have to be handled. This makes attempts to achieve one central repository of knowledge problematic and probably mistaken. However, in developing and integrating a worldwide network of different aspects of forest studies, it seems that British expertise and data could play a vital role.

PRESENT PERFORMANCE VERSUS FUTURE POTENTIAL

In gathering the material for this brief review of the total impact and potential impact of British activity on tropical rain forests, one was struck by how *no one* had anything like an overall picture. Botanists agronomists, ecologists, meteorologists, soil scientists, sociologists, hydrologists, land-use planners and foresters all have a different viewpoint and all tend to parochialism. Spears (1979), himself a forest manager, summed up the problem well when he commented that 'the volume of specialist

* In late 1982 plans were afoot to reduce the size of these units as part of a general Government economy drive.

literature which has grown up around this subject would fill St Paul's Cathedral, whereas the number of papers which tackle this issue in a holistic way could probably fit into my briefcase.'

A valuable recent attempt to meet this problem of policy diffusion—or vacuum—was the official U.S. Government Inter-agency Task Force report already alluded to (Anon. 1980). Many of the facts that it presents, the questions which it asks and the suggestions that it makes should perhaps be collected, asked and made in some modest parallel exercise focussing upon the U.K. It would seem desirable, however, were such a parallel exercise to be undertaken, that it involve representatives of the business, financial, academic and conservation communities as well as representatives of government institutions and departments. Such an exercise could probably also be usefully conducted in at least half a dozen other Western member countries of the OECD who study, give aid to and invest in tropical forested countries. The combined results would represent a valuable base-line for a better informed dialogue within and between these countries, and particularly in their discussions with officials and experts of the host countries of the tropical forests.

It also seems to the author that diplomats and economists from both the 'developed' North and the 'underdeveloped' South could be educated in the process of such an examination as well as having a major contribution to make in terms of realism and practicability.

CONCLUSION

In conclusion, it seems possible to establish two facts regarding British policies towards forestry world-wide, and especially tropical forestry.

The first is that forestry has in the past—especially the last three decades of history—been a Cinderella in national, regional and international planning and policy formulation. The second is that, from the point of view of the national foreign policy interests of a developed country like Britain, the crisis in tropical rain forests is not only one of prospective shortfalls in satisfying demand for existing types of wood products in the next 20–30 years; it is a crisis likely to affect many aspects of the relations between nations. This is why it merits consideration as an important issue of policy, not only in the host countries of the tropical rain forests, but in Britain and in all other countries which consider themselves significant actors on the international stage.

ACKNOWLEDGMENTS

The author wishes to acknowledge the invaluable research help provided by Amanda Atha, and the support of the World Wildlife Fund (UK). Many other people gave of their valuable time, in particular Professor Duncan Poore, Dr John Spears, Mr Ronald Kemp and Dr Norman Myers. Finally, special thanks are due to Mrs Irene Hunter who so cheerfully typed successive drafts of the manuscript with her usual speed and precision.

REFERENCES

Anon. (1980). *The World's Tropical Forests: A Policy Strategy and Program for the United States.* Department of State publication 9117, International Organization and Conference Series 145. Washington.

McNamara, R.S. (1978). *Address to the Annual Meeting.* World Bank, Washington.

OECD (1981). Environment Committee. *ENV* (81) 20–1, December 1981.

Spears, J.S. (1979). Can the wet tropical forest survive? *Commonwealth Forestry Review*, **58**, 165–80.

Species index

See also the lists of species on pp. 29, 54–6, 319, 365.

Subject index